THE STRUCTURES OF EVERYDAY LIFE
The Limits of the Possible

Fernand Braudel

CIVILIZATION AND CAPITALISM
15th–18th Century

VOLUME I

THE STRUCTURES OF EVERYDAY LIFE

The Limits of the Possible

Translation from the French
Revised by Siân Reynolds

COLLINS
St James's Place, London
1981

William Collins Sons & Co Ltd
London · Glasgow · Sydney · Auckland
Toronto · Johannesburg

British Library CIP data
Braudel, Fernand
   Civilization and capitalism.
    Vol. I: The structures of everyday life. – Rev. ed.
   1. Social history – Modern, 1500–
   2. Social history – Medieval, 500–1500
   I. Title II. Civilisaton matérielle,
   économie et capitalisme, XVe–XVIIIe siècle.
English
909.08 HN13

First published in France under the title
Les Structures du Quotidien: Le Possible et L'Impossible, 1979
©Librairie Armand Colin Paris 1979

©English translation
William Collins Sons & Co Ltd London
and Harper & Row New York 1981

ISBN 0 00 216303 9

Photoset in Sabon
Made and Printed in Great Britain by
Butler & Tanner Ltd, Frome and London

*To Paule Braudel,
who has dedicated herself
to this book,
it is in turn dedicated.*

Translator's note

An early version of the first volume of this three-part work appeared in French in 1967, and was translated into English by Miriam Kochan in 1973, under the title *Capitalism and Material Life 1400-1800*. The French text has been so extensively revised by the author for the new French edition in three volumes that it was impossible to publish the original English edition as Volume I. It has therefore been reworked to incorporate new material and changes, but Miriam Kochan's translation was used as a basis for the present version, as I am happy to acknowledge, while taking full responsibility myself for the final text. Neither of the two other volumes has appeared in English before.

SIÂN REYNOLDS

ERRATA

On page 34, the penultimate paragraph should read:

The figures are few and not very reliable. They apply only to Europe and, as a consequence of some admirable research, to China. In these two cases, we have censuses and estimates that are almost valid. The ground may not be very solid, but it is reasonably safe to venture on to it.

Contents

	Introduction	page 23
	Preface	27
1	**WEIGHT OF NUMBERS**	31

Guessing the world population   31
Ebb and flow, 32 – The lack of statistics, 34 – How to calculate?, 38 – The equivalence of Europe and China, 39 – World population, 40 – Questionable figures, 41 – The relationship between the centuries, 46 – The old inadequate explanations, 47 – Climatic rhythms, 49.

A scale of reference   51
Towns, armies and navies, 51 – A France prematurely overpopulated, 54 – Density of population and level of civilization, 56 – Other points inferred from Gordon W. Hewes' map, 62 – Wild men and animals, 64.

The eighteenth century: watershed of biological régimes   70
Preserving the balance, 71 – Famine, 73 – Epidemics, 78 – The plague, 83 – The cycle of diseases, 88 – 1400-1800: a long-lasting biological *ancien régime*, 90.

The many against the few   92
Against the barbarians, 93 – The disappearance of the great nomads before the seventeenth century, 94 – The conquest of space, 98 – The resistance of cultures, 100 – Civilization against civilization, 102.

2   **DAILY BREAD**   104

Wheat   108
Wheat and other grains, 109 – Wheat and crop rotation, 114 – Low yields, compensations and disasters, 120 – Increased cultivation and higher yields, 122 – Local and international trade in grain, 124 – Grain and calories, 129 – The price of grain and the standard

of living, 133 – Bread of the rich, bread and gruel of the poor, 136 – To buy bread, or bake it at home?, 139 – Grain rules Europe, 143.

Rice 145
Rice cultivated dry and in paddy fields, 146 – The miracle of the paddy fields, 147 – The importance of rice, 152.

Maize 158
Well-ascertained origins, 158 – Maize and American civilizations, 159.

The dietary revolutions of the eighteenth century 163
Maize outside America, 164 – Potatoes: a great future, 167 – Eating other people's bread, 171.

The rest of the world 172
The people of the hoe, 174 – The primitive peoples, 178.

3 SUPERFLUITY AND SUFFICIENCY: FOOD AND DRINK 183

Eating habits: luxury and the foods of the masses 187
A belated luxury, 187 – Carnivorous Europe, 190 – The decline in meat consumption after 1550, 194 – Europe's privileged position, 199 – The extravagances of the table, 202 – Laying the table, 203 – The slow adoption of good manners, 206 – At the table of Christ, 207 – Everyday foods: salt, 209 – Everyday foods: dairy products, fats, eggs, 210 – Everyday seafoods, 214 – Cod fishing, 216 – The decline in the vogue for pepper after 1650, 220 – Sugar conquers the world, 224.

Drinks, stimulants and drugs 227
Water, 227 – Wine, 231 – Beer, 238 – Cider, 240 – The belated popularity of alcohol in Europe, 241 – Alcoholism outside Europe, 247 – Chocolate, tea, coffee, 249 – Stimulants: the glories of tobacco, 260.

4	**SUPERFLUITY AND SUFFICIENCY: HOUSES, CLOTHES AND FASHION**	266

Houses throughout the world 266
Rich building materials: stone and brick, 267 – Less favoured building materials: wood, earth, fabric, 272 – Rural dwellings in Europe, 274 – Urban houses and dwellings, 277 – The urbanized countryside, 281.

Interiors 283
The lack of possessions of the poor, 283 – Traditional civilizations and unchanging interiors, 285 – The double pattern of Chinese furniture, 288 – In Black Africa, 292 – The West and its many different types of furniture, 293 – Floors, walls, ceilings, doors and windows, 294 – Chimneys and fireplaces, 298 – Furnaces and stoves, 300 – Furniture makers and the vanities of buyers, 303 – The domestic interior seen whole, 306 – Luxury and comfort, 310.

Costume and fashion 311
When society stood still, 312 – If all the world were poor . . . , 313 – Europe and the craze for fashion, 315 – Is fashion frivolous?, 321 – The geography of textiles, 325 – Fashion in the broad sense: long-term change, 328 – Conclusions?, 333.

5	**THE SPREAD OF TECHNOLOGY: SOURCES OF ENERGY, METALLURGY**	334

The key problem: sources of energy 336
The human engine, 337 – Animal power, 341 – Wind engines and water engines, 353 – Sails: the European fleets, 362 – Wood, an everyday source of energy, 362 – Coal, 368 – Concluding remarks, 371.

Iron: a poor relation 373
The beginnings of metallurgy, 375 – Progress between the eleventh and fifteenth centuries in Styria and Dauphiné, 377 – Semi-concentrations, 380 – A few figures, 381 – Other metals, 382.

6 THE SPREAD OF TECHNOLOGY: REVOLUTION AND DELAYS — 385

Three great technological innovations — 385
The origins of gunpowder, 385 – Artillery becomes mobile, 387 – Artillery on board ship, 388 – Arquebuses, muskets, rifles, 392 – Production and costs, 393 – Artillery on a world scale, 396 – From paper to the printing press, 397 – The invention of moveable type, 399 – Printing and history, 401 – The triumph of the West: ocean navigation, 402 – The navies of the Old World, 402 – The water routes of the world, 406 – The simple problem of the Atlantic, 409.

Transport — 415
Fixed itineraries, 416 – On not exaggerating the importance of transport problems, 419 – Water transport, 421 – Antiquated means of transport, 422 – Europe, 423 – Low speeds and capacities, 424 – Carriage and carriers, 425 – Transport: a brake on the economy, 428.

Problems of the history of technology — 430
Technology and agriculture, 430 – Technology in itself, 431.

7 MONEY — 436

Imperfect currencies and economies — 441
Primitive currencies, 442 – Barter within monetary economies, 444.

Outside Europe: early economies and metallic money — 448
Japan and the Turkish Empire, 448 – India, 450 – China, 452.

Some rules of the currency game — 457
Competition between metals, 458 – Flight, saving and hoarding, 461 – Money of account, 464 – Stocks of metal and the velocity of monetary circulation, 466 – Outside the market economy, 468.

Paper money and instruments of credit — 470
Old practices, 471 – Cash and credit, 474 – Schumpeter's diagnosis: everything is money and everything is credit, 475 – Money and credit: a language, 477.

8 TOWNS AND CITIES 479

Towns: the problems of definition 479
Minimum size, combined weight, 481 – The ever-changing division of labour, 484 – The town and its newcomers: mainly the poor, 489 – The self-consciousness of towns, 491 – Towns, artillery and carriages in the West, 497 – Geography and urban communications, 498 – Urban hierarchies, 504 – Towns and civilizations: the case of Islam, 507.

The originality of Western towns 509
Free worlds, 510 – Towns as outposts of modernity, 512 – Urban patterns, 514 – Different types of development, 520.

The big cities 525
The states, 525 – The function of capital cities, 527 – Unbalanced worlds, 528 – Naples, from the Royal Palace to the Mercato, 532 – St Petersburg in 1790, 534 – Penultimate journey: Peking, 540 – London from Elizabeth I to George III, 547 – Urbanization, the sign of modern man, 556.

CONCLUSION 559
Notes 565
Index 605

Maps and Graphs

		page
1	In Mexico: man makes way for flocks	36
2	World population from the thirteenth to the nineteenth century	39
3	Internal migrations in China during the eighteenth century	45
4	The battle of Pavia	53
5	Overpopulated regions and zones from which there was emigration, France 1745	55
6	Civilizations, 'cultures' and primitive peoples, c. 1500 (after G.W. Hewes)	58–9
7	The Brazilian *bandeiras* (sixteenth to eighteenth centuries)	63
8	*Ancien régime* demography: baptisms and burials	72–3
9	French population trends before the Revolution	75
10	Eurasian migrations from the fourteenth to the eighteenth century	99
11	The price of wheat and oats according to the Paris market listings	112
12	Some diets of the past, reckoned in calories	131
13	Budget of a mason's family in Berlin about 1800	132
14	Wages and the price of rye in Göttingen, fifteenth to nineteenth century	134
15	Two examples of real wheat prices	135
16	Bread weights and grain prices in Venice at the end of the sixteenth century	142
17	Different names for maize in the Balkans	165
18	The hoe-cultivation belt	175
19	Melanesian and Polynesian migrations before the fourteenth century	179
20	The cattle trade in Northern and Eastern Europe in about 1600	193
21	A well-cistern in Venice: section and elevation	229

22	Apartments in sixteenth-century Paris	279
23	Horse-breeding areas in France in the eighteenth century	351
24	The great discoveries – the routes across the Atlantic	
25	The voyage of the *Saint-Antoine*	413
26	The speed at which news reached Venice	426-7
27	Paris at the time of the Revolution	496
28	Plan of St Petersburg in 1790	535
29	Peking in the eighteenth century	543

Illustrations

	page
Warsaw in 1795	32
The Plague of the Philistines	35
An idealized image of the Conquest of the New World (1564)	37
The Thames frozen over in 1814	50
A Bohemian village in 1675	60
A seal-hunt in Sweden in the seventeenth century	66
A boar-hunt in Bavaria	68
A Persian hunt in the seventeenth century	70
'Feeding the hungry' (sixteenth century)	76
Spanish soldiers, starving and in rags (1641)	77
San Diego feeding the poor (1645)	79
Treating syphilis by cauterization	82
A Chinese syphilis victim (eighteenth century)	83
A procession against the plague (fifteenth century)	86
Cattle plague in 1745	87
Street scene in Goa at the end of the sixteenth century	93
Mongol horsemen hunting (fifteenth century)	95
Caravan travelling to the desert	96
The Harvesters' Meal	106
Harvest-time in India (sixteenth century)	107
Gathering chestnuts (fourteenth century)	113
Ploughing (fourteenth century)	115
Seedtime (thirteenth century)	116
Van Gogh's *Harvester*	119
The harvester in the *Hours of Notre-Dame*	119
Transporting grain by mule in Italy	126
International grain trade on the Vistula	128
A meal of gruel, Holland (1653)	138
The market on the Perlachplatz, Augsburg (sixteenth century)	140–1

A bread-oven, Cracow (fifteenth century)	143
The density of mills	144
Rice seedlings, nineteenth-century China	148
Threshing rice by hand	153
Threshing rice with a flail in Japan	154
Two aspects of rice cultivation: ploughing and irrigating	156–7
Woman grinding maize	160
An Indian maize plantation	162
Incas planting and harvesting potatoes	168–9
Potatoes, the food of the humble	171
Harvesting wheat in America	173
Bartering goods in New Zealand	181
Luxury at a Venetian banquet (sixteenth century)	185
A feast in Paris (1707)	191
Butcher's stalls in Holland in the seventeenth century	194
A peasant meal (seventeenth century)	195
The sale of salt meat	198
The sophistication of Chinese cookery	200
The Wedding at Cana, with table laid	204
Ivory-handled cutlery (seventeenth century)	207
The Last Supper (tapestry, fifteenth century)	208
Old woman with eggs	213
Whale-fishing	217
Cod-fishing	219
The transport of spices	223
Sugar loaves and the manufacture of syrup	225
A seventeenth-century kitchen	231
'Drinking to get drunk'	233
A monastery meal	235
A tavern outside Paris (eighteenth century)	237
The brewery 'De Drye Lelyen' in Haarlem (1627)	240
Beer, wine and tobacco	242
The *kvass*-seller in Russia	245
Drinking chocolate in Spain	250
Drinking chocolate in Italy	251
Tea in China	252

Dutchmen sitting at table with the Chinese (eighteenth century)	253
Interior of a Turkish café in Istanbul	255
The Café Procope	259
'The solid enjoyment of bottle and friend'	263
The merry drinker	264
Vermeer's *Street in Delft*, c. 1659	269
A village near Nuremberg in 1600	270
The Pont de la Tournelle in Paris, 1620	271
Japanese house	274
Peasant houses in Germany (sixteenth century)	275
Dracy, a deserted village in Burgundy	277
The Villa Medici in Trebbio	281
'Russian soup' in the eighteenth century	284
Chinese bowl (eighteenth century)	287
The miniaturist (fifteenth century)	288
The writer (eighteenth century)	289
'Women of Hindustan', eating a meal	291
A stag-hunt at Aranjuez in 1665	292
A bourgeois interior in Germany (fifteenth centuy)	295
The Spanish *brasero*	298
Woman in front of the stove	301
Cooking without bending	302
Fifteenth-century dresser with gold vessels	305
A bourgeois interior in Holland (seventeenth century)	307
A Flemish interior (seventeenth century)	309
A Chinese mandarin (eighteenth century)	313
Peasants in Flanders in the sixteenth century	316
Black costume in the Spanish style	319
Zocoli, Venetian miniature stilts	320
Madeleine, Duchess of Bavaria	322
Turks in the fifteenth century	325
An English wool merchant	327
A fifteenth-century bathtub	329
Fashion and generation: Burgomaster Dirk Bas Jacobsz and his family	331

Harvesting with scythes in the Netherlands in the sixteenth century	336
Chinese hauliers on the tow-path	338
Detail of the silver mine of Kutna Hora, about 1490	340
A caravan of llamas in Peru	342
Egyptian water-wheel in the last years of the eighteenth century	345
Wild horses in eighteenth-century Manchuria	348
A horizontal water-wheel (fifteenth century)	353
Mechanism of a water-mill (1607)	354
A windmill	357
Wooden machines and gears	360
An English windmill (1652)	361
Woodcutters at work, about 1800	365
Seventeenth-century Lyons	368
A brass foundry in Thuringia	370
A French mine, about 1600	372
A seventeenth-century Japanese forge	374
The manufacture of sabres in Japan	375
Indian dagger with horse's head (seventeenth century)	379
A mechanized forge in the Tyrol	380
A fifteenth-century inn	382
The Croix-de-Lorraine silver mines in the Vosges (sixteenth century)	383
The first cannon	386
The first mobile artillery	389
Shipboard artillery	390
Seventeenth-century flagship	391
Arquebusiers in the sixteenth century	394
The Gutenberg Bible, known as the '36-line Bible'	398
Venice and the entrance of the lagoon (fifteenth century)	404
A boat with triangular sails	405
An early seventeenth-century merchantman	406
Chinese river boats	411
A seventeenth-century road	414
The roadside inn, nineteenth century	417

The workings of a lock (sketched in 1607)	420
Warsaw in the eighteenth century	429
The crane at Bruges, in the middle ages	432
Double crane in the port of Dunkirk (1787)	433
Two tax-collectors	438
'Herr Credit' is dead	441
Money struck in mulberry-tree bark	444
A bronze counter with the mark of the Peruzzi	446
A Massachusetts bank note (1690)	447
A fourteenth-century Chinese bank note and coins of the Ming period	453
Merchants in the streets of Peking	456
Minting money (1521)	461
The money-handler	462
Some thirteenth- and fourteenth-century gold coins	467
The pawnbroker	469
One of Law's bank notes	473
Aerial photograph of Brive	480
A market scene	485
Bilbao, supplied by boats and mule-trains	488
Sixteenth-century plan of Milan	493
Walls and gate of Peking (early eighteenth century)	494
Genoa in the fifteenth century	499
A market in Barcelona (eighteenth century)	502
The Port of Seville (sixteenth century)	505
The Grand Bazaar in Alexandria (late eighteenth century)	508
Nuremberg in the fifteenth century	513
The Notre-Dame bridge in Paris (eighteenth century)	516–7
The Old Square in Havana	521
Sixteenth-century Istanbul	523
St James's Square in the eighteenth century	529
Naples in the fifteenth century	530–1
A sedan chair	533
'Droshky of a citizen of St Petersburg' (eighteenth century)	539

22　*The Structures of Everyday Life*

A street in Peking (early eighteenth century)	541
The shops of Peking	545
The port of London at the end of the eighteenth century	550-1
Westminster in the time of the Stuarts	553

Introduction

WHEN, IN 1952, Lucien Febvre asked me to write this book for the collection *Destins du Monde* (*World Destinies*) which he had recently founded, I had no idea what an interminable venture I was embarking upon. The idea was that I should simply provide a summary of the work that had been done on the economic history of pre-industrial Europe. However, not only did I often feel the need to go back to the sources, but I confess that the more research I did, the more disconcerted I became by direct observation of so-called economic realities, between the fifteenth and the eighteenth centuries. Simply because they did not seem to fit, or even flatly contradicted the classical and traditional theories of what was supposed to have happened: whether the theories in question were Werner Sombart's (1902, and backed up by a wealth of evidence) or Josef Kulischer's (1928); or indeed those of economists themselves, who tend to see the economy as a homogenous reality which can legitimately be taken out of context and which can, indeed must, be measured on its own, since nothing is intelligible until it has been put into statistics. According to the textbooks, the development of pre-industrial Europe (which was studied quite exclusively of the rest of the world, as if that did not exist) consisted of its gradual progress towards the rational world of the market, the firm, and capitalist investment, until the coming of the Industrial Revolution, which neatly divides human history in two.

In fact, observable reality before the nineteenth century is much more complicated than this would suggest. It is of course quite possible to trace a pattern of evolution, or rather several kinds of evolution, which may rival, assist or at times contradict one another. This amounts to saying that there were not one but several economies. The one most frequently written about is the so-called market economy, in other words the mechanisms of production and exchange linked to rural activities, to small shops and workshops, to banks, exchanges, fairs and (of course) markets. It was on these 'transparent' visible realities, and on the easily observed processes that took place within them that the language of economic science was originally founded. And as a result it was from the start confined within this privileged arena, to the exclusion of any others.

But there is another, shadowy zone, often hard to see for lack of adequate historical documents, lying underneath the market economy: this is that elementary basic activity which went on everywhere and the volume of which is truly fantastic. This rich zone, like a layer covering the earth, I have called for want of a better expression *material life* or *material civilization*. These are obviously ambiguous expressions. But I imagine that if my view of what happened in the past is accepted, as it seems to be nowadays by certain economists for what is happening in the present, a proper term will one day be found to describe this infra-economy, the informal other half of economic activity, the world of self-sufficiency and barter of goods and services within a very small radius.

On the other hand, looking up instead of down from the vast plane of the market economy, one finds that active social hierarchies were constructed on top of it: they could manipulate exchange to their advantage and disturb the established order. In their desire to do so – which was not always consciously expressed – they created anomalies, 'zones of turbulence' and conducted their affairs in a very individual way. At this exalted level, a few wealthy merchants in eighteenth-century Amsterdam or sixteenth-century Genoa could throw whole sectors of the European or even world economy into confusion, from a distance. Certain groups of privileged actors were engaged in circuits and calculations that ordinary people knew nothing of. Foreign exchange for example, which was tied to distant trade movements and to the complicated arrangements for credit, was a sophisticated art, open only to a few initiates at most. To me, this second shadowy zone, hovering above the sunlit world of the market economy and constituting its upper limit so to speak, represents the favoured domain of capitalism, as we shall see. Without this zone, capitalism is unthinkable: this is where it takes up residence and prospers.

This triple division, which I gradually saw forming itself before my eyes, as the elements of observation fell into place almost of themselves, is probably what my readers will find the most controversial aspect of this book. Does it not amount to making too rigid a distinction – indeed a term by term contrast – between the market economy and capitalism? I did not myself take up this position hurriedly or without hesitation. But in the end I accepted that the market economy had, between the fifteenth and eighteenth centuries and indeed even earlier, been a restrictive order, and that like all restrictive orders, whether social, political or cultural, it had created an opposition, counter-forces, both above and below itself.

What I find most encouraging to my view of things is that the same schema can be used to show easily and clearly the articulations of present-day societies. The market economy still controls the great mass of transactions *that show up in the statistics*. But free competition, which is the distinctive characteristic of the market, is very far from ruling the present-day economy – as nobody would deny. Today as in the past, there is a world apart where an exceptional kind of capitalism goes on, to my mind the only *real* capitalism: today as in the past, it is multinational, a close relation of the capitalism operated by the great Indies Companies, and the monopolies of all sizes, official or unofficial, which existed then and which were exactly analogous in principle to the monopolies of today. Would we not call the Fugger or Welser firms *transnational* today, since they had interests all over Europe and had representatives both in India and Latin America? And Jacques Coeur's business empire in the fourteenth century was as big as the trading interests of the Netherlands in the Levant.

But the coincidences go further than this: in the wake of the economic depression following the 1973-4 crisis, we are beginning to see the development of a modern version of the non-market economy: hardly disguised forms of barter, the direct exchange of services, 'moonlighting' as it is called, plus all the various forms of homeworking and 'odd-jobs'. This layer of activity, lying below or alongside the market, has reached sufficient proportions to attract the attention of several economists: some have estimated that it may represent 30 or 40% of the gross national product, which thus lies outside all official accounting, even in industrialized countries.

So it was that a tripartite schema *became* the framework of a book which I had deliberately set out to write outside the world of theory, of all theories, and had intended to be guided by concrete observation and comparative history alone. Comparative both through time, using the language, which has never disappointed me, of the long term and the dialectic of past/present; and comparative through as wide a space as possible, since I wanted my study to cover the whole world if such a thing could be done. Well, concrete observation is still in the foreground. My purpose throughout has been to see and to let others see, by allowing what I show to speak for itself, in all the richness, complexity and heterogeneity of real life. If one could simply dissect reality and separate it into these three levels (which I regard as a useful basis for classification) history would be an exact science: which it obviously is not.

The three volumes that make up this book are entitled: *The Structures of Everyday Life: the limits of the possible*; *The Wheels of Commerce* and *The Perspective of the World*. The third is a chronological study of the forms and successive preponderant tendencies of the international economy. In a word, it is a *history*. The first two volumes are much less straightforward, and come under the heading of thematic research. The first volume (which has already been published in an earlier version) is a sort of 'weighing up of the world' as Pierre Chaunu has called it, an evaluation of the limits of what was possible in the pre-industrial world. One of these limits is the enormous place then occupied by 'material life'. The second volume, *The Wheels of Commerce*, compares the market economy and the higher activity of capitalism. It was essential to my purpose to distinguish between these two upper layers and explain them in relation to each other, both where they coincide and where they differ.

Will I be able to convince all my readers? Hardly. But at least I have found one unparalleled advantage in this dialectical approach: it has enabled me, by taking a new, and somewhat more peaceful route, to avoid and by-pass the passionate disputes which the explosive word *capitalism* always arouses. And in any case, the third volume has benefited from the explanations and discussions that have gone before: it should offend nobody.

So instead of one book, I ended up by writing three. And my determination to make this a book about the whole world gave me some work for which as a

Western historian I was unprepared, to say the least. Having lived and worked in an Islamic country (ten years in Algiers) and in America (four years in Brazil) was a great help. But for Japan, I have relied on the explanations and the private tuition of Serge Elisseff; for China I am grateful to Etienne Balazs, Jacques Gernet and Denys Lombard. Daniel Thorner, who could turn any well-motivated person into a budding specialist on India, took me in hand with his irresistible liveliness and generosity. He would turn up at my house early in the morning with bread and croissants for breakfast and books that I absolutely had to read. His name must come first in the list of people I have to thank: if I listed everyone, it would go on for ever. My pupils, lecture-audiences, colleagues and friends have all helped me. I cannot forget the filial assistance given me once again by Alberto and Branislava Tenenti; the co-operation of Michaël Keul and Jean-Jacques Hémardinquer. Marie-Thérèse Labignette assisted me in archive research and chasing bibliographical references, and Annie Duchesne in the endless labour of providing footnotes. Josiane Ochoa patiently typed various versions of the manuscript, up to ten times. Roselyne de Ayala, of Armand Colin Publishers, handled the problems of layout and publication with efficiency and punctuality. To all these immediate colleagues, I here express my more than grateful recognition. Lastly, if it had not been for Paule Braudel, who has been daily associated with my research, I should never have had the courage to rewrite the first volume and to finish the two massive tomes which complete it, or to check the logic and clarity needed for the summaries and explanations they contain. Once more we have worked side by side over a long project.

16 MARCH 1979

Preface

HERE I AM at the beginning of the first volume, and the most complicated of the three. Each chapter may not in itself seem difficult to the reader; but the complication is the insidious result of the large number of aims I have in mind, the painful uncovering of unusual themes which must all be incorporated into a coherent history, in short the difficult assembling of a number of *parahistoric* languages – demography, food, costume, lodging, technology, money, towns – which are usually kept separate from each other and which develop in the margin of traditional history. So why try to bring them together?

Essentially, in order to define the context in which pre-industrial economies operated, and to grasp it in all its richness. Can it not be said that there is a limit, a ceiling which restricts all human life, containing it within a frontier of varying outline, one which is hard to reach and harder still to cross? This is the border which in every age, even our own, separates the possible from the impossible, what can be done with a little effort from what cannot be done at all. In the past, the borderline was imposed by inadequate food supplies, a population that was too big or too small for its resources, low productivity of labour, and the as yet slow progress in controlling nature. Between the fifteenth and the eighteenth century, these constraints hardly changed at all. And men did not even explore the limits of what was possible.

It is worth insisting on this slow progress, this inertia. Overland transport, for example, very early possessed the elements which could have led to its being perfected. And indeed here and there, one finds faster speeds being reached because modern roads were built, or because vehicles carrying goods and passengers were improved, or new staging-posts established. But progress of this kind only became widespread by about 1830, that is just before the railway revolution. It was only then that overland transport by road became commonplace, regular, well-developed and finally available to the majority; so it was only then that the limits of the possible were actually reached. And this is not the only area in which backwardness persisted. In the end, the only real change, innovation and revolution along the borderline between possible and impossible came with the nineteenth century and the changed face of the world.

This gives the present book a certain unity: it is a long journey backwards from the facilities and habits of present-day life. Indeed it is a journey to another planet, another human universe. It is quite easy to imagine being transported to, say, Voltaire's house at Ferney, and talking to him for a long time without being too surprised. In the world of ideas, the men of the eighteenth century are our contemporaries: their habits of mind and their feelings are sufficiently close to ours for us not to feel we are in a foreign country. But if the patriarch of Ferney invited us to stay with him for a few days, the details of his everyday life, even the way he looked after himself, would greatly shock us. Between his world and ours, a great gulf would open up: lighting at night, heating, transport, food, illness, medicine. So we have to strip ourselves in imagination of all the surroundings of our own lives if we are to swim against the current of time and look for the rules which for so long locked the world into a stability which is quite hard to explain if one thinks of the fantastic change which was to follow.

In drawing up this inventory of the possible, we shall often meet what I called in the introduction 'material civilization'. For the possible does not only have an upper limit; it also has a lower limit set by the mass of that 'other half' of production which refuses to enter fully into the movement of exchange. Ever-present, all-pervasive, repetitive, material life is run according to routine: people go on sowing wheat as they always have done, planting maize as they always have done, terracing the paddy-fields as they always have done, sailing in the Red Sea as they always have done. The obstinate presence of the past greedily and steadily swallows up the fragile lifetime of men. And this layer of stagnant history is enormous: all rural life, that is 80 to 90% of the world's population, belongs to it for the most part. It would of course be very difficult to say where this leaves off and the sophisticated and agile market economy begins. There is certainly no clear demarcation line as between oil and water. It is not always possible to make a firm decision that a given actor, agent or action is on one side of the barrier or the other. And *material civilization* has to be portrayed, as I intend to portray it, alongside that *economic civilization*, if I may so call it, which co-exists with it, disturbs it and explains it *a contrario*. But that the barrier exists, and that there are enormous consequences, cannot be questioned.

This double register (economic and material) is in fact the product of a multisecular process of evolution. Material life, between the fifteenth and the eighteenth centuries, is the prolongation of an ancient society and economy, which are very slowly, imperceptibly being transformed; gradually and with all the success and failures such an enterprise entails, they are erecting above them a higher form of society, the full weight of which they are obliged to bear. Since the process began, there has been coexistence of the upper and lower levels, with endless variation in their respective volumes. In seventeenth-century Europe for instance, material life, the alternative economy, must have been swollen by the recession in the economy. It is certainly doing so in front of our own eyes, since the recession that began in 1973-4. So the boundary between the upper and lower storey is by nature uncertain: now one is ahead, now the other. I have known villages which were still living at the pace of the seventeenth or eighteenth century in 1929. Falling behind in this way may be deliberate or unintentional. The market economy was not strong enough before the eighteenth century to seize and mould according to its rules the great mass of the infra-economy, which was often protected by distance and isolation. Nowadays on the other hand, if there is a substantial sector outside the 'economy' or outside the market, it is more likely to reflect a refusal from below, than negligence or inadequacy of the exchange system organized by the State or society. The result, however, is bound to be analogous in more ways than one.

In any case, the co-existence of the upper and lower levels forces upon the historian an illuminating dialectic. How can one understand the towns without understanding the countryside, money without barter, the varieties of poverty without the varieties of luxury, the white bread of the rich without the black bread of the poor?

It remains for me to justify one last choice: that of introducing everyday life, no more no less, into the domain of history. Was this useful? Or necessary? Everyday life consists of the little things one hardly notices in time and space. The more we reduce the focus of vision, the more likely we are to find ourselves in the environment of material life: the broad sweep usually corresponds to History with a capital letter, to distant trade routes, and the networks of national or urban economies. If we reduce the length of the time observed, we either have the event or the everyday happening. The event is, or is taken to be, unique; the everyday happening is repeated, and the more often it is repeated the more likely it is to become a generality or rather a structure. It pervades society at all levels, and characterises ways of being and behaving which are perpetuated through endless ages. Sometimes a few anecdotes are enough to set up a signal which points to a way of life. There is a drawing which shows Maximilian of Austria at table, in about 1513: he is putting his hand into a dish. Two centuries or so later, the Princess Palatine tells how Louis XIV, when he allowed his children to sit up to table for the first time, forbade them to eat differently from him, and in particular to eat with a fork as an over-zealous tutor had taught them. So when did Europe invent table manners? I have seen a Japanese costume of the fifteenth century; and found it very like one of the eighteenth; and a Spanish traveller once described his conversation with a Japanese diplomat who was astonished and even shocked to see Europeans appear in such very different clothing at intervals of only a few years. Is the passion for fashion a peculiarly European thing? Is it insignificant? Through little details, travellers' notes, a society stands revealed. The ways people eat, dress, or lodge, at the different levels of that society, are never a matter of indifference. And these snapshots can also point out contrasts and disparities between one society and another which are not all superficial. It is fascinating, and I do not think pointless to try and reassemble these imageries.

So I have ventured in several directions: the possible and the impossible, the ground floor and the first storey: the images of daily life. This complicated the design of the book in advance. There are simply too many things to say. How shall I begin?*

---

* Notes to the text are all at the end of the volume.

I

Weight of Numbers

MATERIAL LIFE is made up of people and things. The study of things, of everything mankind makes or uses – food, housing, clothing, luxury, tools, coinage or its substitutes, framework of village and town – is not the only way of analysing daily life. The number of people who share the wealth of the world is also significant. The outward feature that immediately differentiates the present world from mankind before 1800 is the recent astonishing increase in the numbers of people. World population doubled during the four centuries covered by this book; nowadays it doubles every thirty or forty years. This is obviously the result of material progress. But the number of people is itself as much cause as consequence of this progress.

In any case number is a first-class pointer. It provides an index of success and failure. In itself it outlines a differential geography of the globe, with continents that are barely populated on the one hand and regions already overpopulated on the other, civilizations face to face with forms of life still primitive. It indicates the decisive relationships between the diverse human masses. Curiously enough, this differential geography is often what has changed least over the centuries.

What has changed entirely is the rhythm of the population increase. At present it registers a continuous rise, more or less rapid according to society and economy but always continuous. Previously it rose and then fell like a series of tides. This alternate demographic ebb and flow characterised life in former times, which was a succession of downward and upward movements, the first almost but not completely cancelling out the second. These basic facts make almost everything else seem secondary. Clearly, our starting point must be the people of the world. Only afterwards can we talk about things.

Guessing the world population

The difficulty is that if world population even today is only known within a 10% margin of error, our information concerning earlier populations is still

Warsaw in 1795. Soup being distributed to the poor near the column of King Sigismund III. (Photo Alexandra Skarżynska.)

more incomplete. Yet everything, both in the short and long term, and at the level of local events as well as on the grand scale of world affairs, is bound up with the numbers and fluctuations of the mass of people.

Ebb and flow

Between the fifteenth and the eighteenth century, if the population went up or down, everything else changed as well. When the number of people increased, production and trade also increased. Wasteland and woodland, swamp and hill came under cultivation; manufactures spread, villages and towns expanded, the number of men on the move multiplied; and there were many other positive reactions to the challenge set by the pressure of population-increase. Of course, wars and disputes, privateering and brigandage grew proportionately; armies or armed bands also flourished; societies created *nouveaux riches* or new privileged classes on an unusually large scale; states prospered – both an evil and a blessing; the frontier of possibility was more easily reached than in ordinary circumstances. These were the usual symptoms. But demographic growth is not an unmitigated blessing. It is sometimes beneficial and sometimes the reverse. When a population increases, its relationship to the space it occupies and the wealth at its disposal is altered. It crosses 'critical thresholds'[1] and at each one its entire structure is questioned afresh. The matter is never simple and unequivocal. A growing increase in the number of people often ends, and always ended in the past, by exceeding the capacity of the society concerned to feed them. This fact, commonplace before the eighteenth century and still true today in some backward countries, sets an insuperable limit to further improvement in conditions. For when they are extreme, demographic increases lead to a deterioration in the standard of living; they enlarge the always horrifying total of the underfed, poor and uprooted. A balance between mouths to be fed and the difficulties of feeding them, between manpower and jobs, is re-established by epidemics and famines (the second preceding or accompanying the first). These extremely crude adjustments were the predominant feature of the centuries of the *ancien régime*.

Looking more closely at Western Europe, one finds that there was a prolonged population rise between 1100 and 1350, another between 1450 and 1650, and a third after 1750; the last alone was not followed by a regression. Here we have three broad and comparable periods of biological expansion. The first two, which both fall within the period that interests us, were followed by recessions, one extremely sharp, between 1350 and 1450, the next rather less so, between 1650 and 1750 (better described as a slowdown than as a recession). Nowadays, any population growth in backward countries brings a fall in the standard of living, but fortunately not such a tragic drop in numbers (at least not since 1945).

Every recession solves a certain number of problems, removes pressures and benefits the survivors. It is pretty drastic, but none the less a remedy. Inherited property became concentrated in a few hands immediately after the Black Death in the middle of the fourteenth century and the epidemics which followed and aggravated its effects. Only good land continued to be cultivated (less work for greater yield). The standard of living and real earnings of the survivors rose. Thus in Languedoc between 1350 and 1450, the peasant and his patriarchal family were masters of an abandoned countryside. Trees and wild animals overran fields that once had flourished.[2] But soon the population again increased and had to win back the land taken over by animals and wild plants, clear the stones from the fields and pull up trees and shrubs. Man's increase itself became a burden and again brought about his poverty. From 1560 or 1580 onwards in France, Spain, Italy and probably the whole Western world, population again became too dense.[3] The monotonous story begins afresh and the process goes into reverse. Man only prospered for short intervals and did not realize it until it was already too late.

But these long fluctuations can also be found outside Europe. At approximately the same times, China and India probably advanced and regressed in the same rhythm as the West, as though all humanity were in the grip of a primordial cosmic destiny that would make the rest of man's history seem, in comparison,

34 *The Structures of Everyday Life*

of secondary importance. Ernst Wagemann, the economist and demographer, held this view. The synchronism is evident in the eighteenth century and more than probable in the sixteenth. It can be assumed that it also applied to the thirteenth and stretched from the France of St Louis to the remote China of the Mongols. If so, this would both shift and simplify the problem. The development of the population, Wagemann concluded, should be attributed to causes very different from those that led to economic, technical and medical progress.[4]

In any case, fluctuations like this, occurring more or less simultaneously from one end of the inhabited world to the other, make it easier to envisage the existence of numerical relationships between the different human masses which have remained relatively fixed over the centuries: one is equal to another, or double a third. When one is known, the other can be worked out; eventually, therefore, the total for the whole body of people can be assessed, though with all the errors inherent in such an estimate. The interest of this global figure is evident. However inaccurate and inevitably inexact, it helps to determine the biological evolution of humanity considered as a single entity, a single *stock* as statisticians would say.

The lack of statistics

Nobody knows the total population of the world between the fifteenth and eighteenth centuries. Statisticians working from the conflicting, sparse and uncertain figures offered by historians cannot agree. It would seem at first glance as if nothing could be constructed on such doubtful foundations. It is none the less worth trying.

The figures are few and not very reliable. They apply only to Europe and, as All these diseases, whether carried by whites or blacks, took on a new virulence. indigenous population, this time it was the newly arrived whites who were most that there are ratios between the various populations of the globe which if not

What about the rest of the world? There is nothing, or almost nothing, on India, which is not greatly concerned either with its history in general or with the statistics that might shed light on it. There is nothing in fact on non-Chinese Asia, outside Japan. There is nothing on Oceania, only skimmed by European travellers in the seventeenth and eighteenth centuries: Tasman reached New Zealand in May 1642 and Tasmania, the island to which he gave his name, in December of the same year; Cook reached Australia a century later, in 1769 and 1783; and Bougainville arrived at Tahiti, the New Cythera (which, by the way, he did not discover) in April 1768. In any case, is there really any need to discuss these thinly inhabited areas? Statisticians estimate two million for the whole of Oceania, whatever the period under consideration. Nor is there anything definite on Black Africa, south of the Sahara, except conflicting figures on the extent of the slave trade from the sixteenth century onwards – and it would be difficult to

The Plague of the Philistines by Nicolas Poussin. Until modern times, epidemics and famines regularly reduced any population increase. (Photo Giraudon.)

deduce all the rest from these, even if they were reliable. Lastly, there is nothing certain relating to America, or rather there are two sets of contradictory calculations.

Angel Rosenblat favours regressive estimation.[5] He starts from present-day figures and calculates backwards. For the whole of the Americas just after the Conquest, this approach produces a very low figure: between ten and fifteen million people. And this would have dropped still further to eight million in the seventeenth century, not increasing again until the beginning of the eighteenth century, and then only slowly. However, American historians at the University of California (Cook, Simpson, Borah – somewhat misleadingly known as 'The Berkeley School')[6] have made a series of calculations and extrapolations based on partial contemporary figures known for some regions of Mexico immediately after the European Conquest. The resulting totals are very inflated: eleven

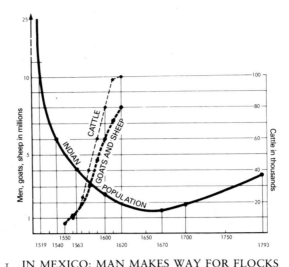

1 IN MEXICO: MAN MAKES WAY FOR FLOCKS
(From P. Chaunu, 'L'Amérique latine', in *Histoire Universelle*, 3, Encyclopédie de la Pléiade.)

million in 1519, according to the estimate put forward in 1948. In 1960, the addition of new documents or reappraisal of the old led its proponents to revise this already huge figure to 25 million inhabitants for Mexico alone. After that the population is reckoned to have decreased rapidly: 1532, 16,800,000; 1548, 6,300,000; 1568, 2,650,000; 1580, 1,900,000; 1595, 1,375,000; 1605, 1,000,000. A slow revival began after 1650 and became clearly defined after 1700.

These huge figures might tempt us to assume a total of some 80 to 100 million people for the whole of America in about 1500. No one is prepared to accept this blindly, despite the evidence of archaeologists and of so many of the chroniclers of the Conquest, including Father Bartolomé de Las Casas. What is quite certain is that the European Conquest brought a colossal biological slump to America, perhaps not in the ratio of ten to one but certainly enormous and quite incommensurate with the Black Death and its concomitant catastrophes in Europe in the disastrous fourteenth century. This was partly due to the hardships of a ruthless war and to the unparalleled burden of colonial labour. But the Indian population at the end of the fifteenth century suffered from a demographic weakness, particularly because of the absence of any substitute animal milk. Mothers had to nurse their children until they were three or four years old. This long period of breast-feeding severely reduced female fertility and made any demographic revival precarious.[7] Furthermore the Amerindian population, already barely holding its own, was overtaken by a series of terrible bacterial attacks similar to those dramatically spread by white men in the Pacific in the eighteenth and especially the nineteenth century.

An idealized image of the Conquest of the New World: the inhabitants of Florida greeting the French explorer R. de Londonnière in 1564. Engraving by Théodore de Bry after the painting by J. Lemoyne de Morgues. (Photo Bulloz.)

Disease – that is the viruses, bacteria and parasites imported from Europe or Africa – spread more rapidly than did the animals, plants and men that crossed the Atlantic. The Amerindian populations, who were adapted only to their own endemic microbes, were helpless in the face of these new perils. The Europeans had hardly set foot in the New World before smallpox broke out in Santo Domingo in 1493; it appeared in 1519 in besieged Mexico City, even before Cortez reached it, and in Peru in the 1530s, before the arrival of the Spanish soldiers. It spread to Brazil in 1560 and to Canada in 1635.[8] This disease, against which Europe had become partially immunised, made deep inroads into the native population. The same was true of measles, influenza, dysentery, leprosy, plague (the first rats are said to have reached America in 1544–6), venereal diseases (a large subject which will be dealt with later), typhoid and elephantiasis. All these diseases, whether carried by whites or blacks, took on a new virulence. There are of course still doubts about the exact nature of some diseases, but the virulent nature of the bacteriological invasion cannot be questioned: the Mexican population collapsed under the impact of several colossal epidemics – smallpox in 1521; and a form of 'plague' (perhaps typhus or influenza) in 1546, which made a second, devastating appearance in 1576-7, when it caused two million deaths.[9] Some of the West Indian islands were entirely depopulated. We must make a conscious effort to stop thinking of yellow fever as native to tropical America. It probably came from Africa. In any case, it appeared quite late on: in 1648 in Cuba, in 1685 in Brazil. From there it spread throughout the entire tropical zone of the New World. In the nineteenth century, it reached from Buenos Aires to the East Coast of North America and was even carried to the ports of Mediterranean Europe.[10] It is impossible to think of Rio de Janeiro in the nineteenth century without being haunted by this mortal spectre. A detail worth noting: whereas the large-scale epidemics had previously decimated the indigenous population, this time it was the newly arrived whites who were most vulnerable to a disease which had become endemic. In Porto Belo, in 1780, the crews of the galleons succumbed to the sickness and the great ships had to winter in the port.[11] So the New World suffered a series of terrible scourges. They were to reappear when the Europeans settled in the Pacific islands, another biologically separate world. Malaria, for example, arrived late in Indonesia and in Oceania; it took Batavia by surprise and destroyed it in 1732.[12]

The cautious calculations of Rosenblat and the romantic inventiveness of the Berkeley historians can thus be reconciled. Both sets of figures may be true or probable, depending on whether they refer to the period before or after the Conquest. We will therefore disregard the opinions of Woytinski and Embree. The latter once asserted that 'there were never more than ten million people between Alaska and Cape Horn at any time before Columbus'.[13] Today this is doubtful.

How to calculate?

The example of America shows how simple (even over-simple) methods can be applied to certain relatively reliable figures to arrive at others. Historians, accustomed to accept only things proved by irrefutable documentation, quite justifiably find these uncertain methods disturbing. Statisticians share neither their misgivings nor their timidity. 'We may be criticized for not dealing in minutiae,' says a sociological statistician, Paul A. Ladame; 'we would reply that details are not important: the order of magnitude alone is interesting.'[14] The order of magnitude: that is the probable upper and lower limits.

In this debate where both sides are right (or both wrong) we will take a look at the position from the calculators' point of view. Their method always assumes that there are ratios between the various populations of the globe which if not fixed are at least very slow to change. This was the opinion of Maurice Halbwachs.[15] In other words the population of the world has almost unvarying *structures* so that the numerical relationships between the different human groups are, roughly speaking, always the same. The Berkeley School deduced a total for the whole of America from partial Mexican statistics. Similarly, Karl Lamprecht and later Karl Julius Beloch calculated figures valid for Germania from approximate statistics for the population of the Trèves region in about 800.[16] The problem is always the same: starting from known figures and reckoning on a basis of probable proportions, to calculate probable, more comprehensive figures that will determine an *order of magnitude*. The range thus deduced will obviously never be entirely valueless as long as its limitations are recognized. Real figures would be better, but they do not exist.

The equivalence of Europe and China

For Europe, we can draw on the figures, calculations and arguments of several writers: K. Julius Beloch (1854-1929), the great forerunner of historical demography; Paul Mombert; J.C. Russell; and the latest edition of Marcel Reinhardt's book.[17] These figures are likely to agree, since each writer has scrupulously used those of his fellows. I have selected - or rather invented - the highest population levels, in order to extend Europe as far as the Urals, thus incorporating the 'uncharted' countries of Eastern Europe. The figures proposed for the Balkan peninsula, Poland, Muscovy and the Scandinavian countries are very dubious and scarcely more probable than those that statisticians suggest for Oceania or Africa. I think, however, that the extension is essential: it gives Europe the same area for any period that may be considered and achieves a better balance between an enlarged Europe on one hand and China on the other. This balance is confirmed as soon as reasonable - though not absolutely reliable - statistics appear in the nineteenth century.

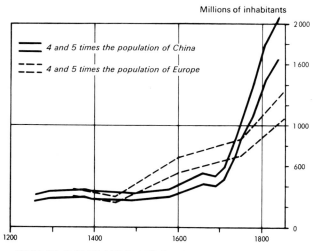

2 WORLD POPULATION FROM THE THIRTEENTH TO THE NINETEENTH CENTURY

The statistics for China are based on official censuses, but are not on that account, of course, unquestionably valid. They are derived from fiscal sources, which means they are very likely to involve fraud and deception. A.P. Usher[18] was right to think that the figures were, on the whole, too low; accordingly he increased them, with all the uncertainty an operation of this type involves. The latest historian[19] to venture into this field of hypothetical calculations has done the same thing. The original figures reveal flagrant impossibilities, increases and decreases abnormally large even for the Chinese. They probably often measure the level of 'order and authority in the Empire as much as the level of population'. Thus the overall figure fell by seven million in 1647 as compared with the preceding year, at the time of the vast Won San-Kwei peasant revolt. The absentees were not dead; they were avoiding central authority. When such rebels come to heel, the statistics register a sharp increase far exceeding even the maximum possible natural increase of the population.

In addition, the censuses were not always made on the same basis. Before 1735 they only counted the *jen-ting*, tax-payers, men aged between sixteen and sixty. Their number therefore has to be multiplied, assuming that they represented 28% of the total population. After 1741 on the other hand, the census counted the actual number of persons and gave the population as 143 million, while calculations based on the number of *jen-ting* produce a figure of 97 million for 1734. The two totals *can* be correlated, since calculation allows plenty of scope for juggling, but the exercise will satisfy no one.[20] However, specialists agree that these figures do have some value over the long term, and the oldest statistics – relating to the China of the Mings (1368-1644) – are by no means the most questionable.

We can thus see the sort of material we shall have to work with. These figures, represented on a graph, only establish an approximate balance between Europe (extended to the Urals) and China (limited to the main territory of its provinces). And today the balance inclines more and more in China's favour, because of its higher birth rate. But approximate as it is, this broad equivalence between Europe and China is probably one of the most visible structures in world history over the last five or six centuries. It offers a starting point for our approximate calculations of world population.

World population

According to the first valid statistics, which became available in the nineteenth century (the first real census – for England – was in 1801), China and Europe each represented roughly a quarter of all mankind. Obviously the validity of applying this proportion to the past is not automatically guaranteed. Europe and China, both then and now, are the most highly populated regions of the world. Since their rates of increase were higher than elsewhere, it might perhaps be appropriate to use a ratio of one to five for the period before the eighteenth century rather than of one to four, for either continent, in relation to the rest of the world. The precaution is just another indication of our uncertainty.

We will therefore apply the coefficients of four or five to the two curves for China and Europe to obtain four probable curves of world population, corresponding respectively to four (or five) Europes, or four (or five) Chinas. We shall have a complex curve which marks out a wide zone of possibilities (and errors) between the lowest and the highest figures on this graph. The line giving the development of the population of the world from the fourteenth to the eighteenth century would lie between these limits.

These calculations suggest that the world population increased, over the long term, between 1300 and 1800 (disregarding, that is, the violent but short-term regressions already mentioned). If we select the lowest estimate (250 million) for our starting point, 1300-50, and the highest (1380 million in 1780) for our point of arrival, a rise of over 400% would be registered (which may be a little hard to believe). When we fix the starting point at its maximum, 350, and the finishing point as 836 (the lowest figure given by Wilcox)[21] we would still have an increase of 138%. Taken over a period of half a millennium, it would correspond to a regular average growth (the regularity is obviously purely theoretical) of the order of 1·73 per 1000, a movement that would have been barely perceptible over the years if it had been constant. None the less, the population of the world probably doubled during this immense period of time. Neither economic crises, disasters nor massive mortality prevented the upward movement. This is indubitably the basic fact in world history from the fifteenth to the eighteenth century – and not merely in relation to the standard of living: everything had to adapt to the pressure of the whole.

Western historians will hardly find this surprising. They are aware of the numerous indirect signs (occupation of new territory, emigration, clearing of new land, agricultural improvements, urbanization) that corroborate the statistical data. On the other hand the conclusions and explanations they have deduced from them remain debatable. They thought the phenomenon was limited to Europe, but it is a fact – and the most important and disturbing fact that we will record in this book – that man surmounted the manifold obstacles to his numerical advance *in all the lands he occupied*. If this population-growth is not solely European but world-wide, several theories and explanations will have to be revised.

But before going that far, we must re-examine certain calculations.

Questionable figures

We have adopted the statisticians' method and have used the best-known figures – in this case, those for Europe and China – to estimate world population. Statisticians can hardly object to such a procedure; however, they themselves have tackled the same problem in a different way. They split up the operation

World population in millions from 1650 to 1950

	1650	1750	1800	1850	1900	1950
Oceania	2	2	2	2	6	13*
Africa	100	100	100	100	120	199**
Asia	257* 330** 250***	437* 479** 406***	602** 522***	656* 749** 671***	857* 937** 859***	1 272*
America	8* 13** 13***	11* 12,4** 12,4***	24,6** 24,6***	59 59 59	144 144 144	338*
Europe (European Russia included)	103* 100** 100***	144* 140** 140***	187** 187***	274* 266** 266***	423* 401*** 401***	594*
Totals 1 2 3	1 470 545 465	694 733.4 660.4	915.6 835.6	1 091 1 176 1 098	1 550 1 608 1 530	2 416

Sources: * United Nations Bulletin, December 1951. ** Carr Saunders. *** Kuczynski.
Figures without an asterisk are common to the three sources.
Carr Saunders' figures for Africa are given to the nearest 100.

and calculated the population of each of the five 'parts' of the world in turn (with a curious respect for 'the five continents' of the schoolbooks!) But what kind of result does this give?

It will be remembered that they attributed two million inhabitants to Oceania during the whole period. This is of little consequence, since the tiny figure is immediately absorbed in our margin of error. But their figure of 100 million for Africa over the whole period is worth questioning. This constant level of the population of Africa seems to us improbable, and the estimate made on this basis has obvious repercussions on the estimate for the whole.

We have summarized the experts' estimates in a table. Note that all their calculations begin late – in 1650 – and that they are all on the high side, even the recent research by United Nations services. On the whole I think these estimates are too high, at least in so far as they concern first Africa and then Asia.

It is rash at the starting point in 1650 to attribute the same figure (100 million) both to Europe, which was then dynamic, and to Africa, which was then backward (with the possible exception of its Mediterranean coast). It is no more reasonable to give Asia in 1650 both the lowest figure in the tables (250 or 257 million) and the very high figure of 330 rather hastily accepted by Carr Saunders.

Africa certainly had a hardy population in the middle of the seventeenth century. It withstood the increasing drain caused from the middle of the sixteenth century by the slave trade to America, while the earlier drain towards Islamic countries did not cease until the twentieth century. It can only have done so by virtue of some sort of biological strength. Its resistance to European penetration provides a further proof of health. The Black continent, unlike Brazil, did not open up to the Portuguese in the sixteenth century without defending itself. Travellers' tales afford glimpses of fairly close-knit peasant communities living in pleasant harmonious villages, later spoiled by the nineteenth-century European advance.[22]

The European might, however, have persisted in his attempts to seize lands in Black Africa if he had not been halted at the coasts by disease, the white man's burden. Intermittent or continuous fevers, 'dysentery, phthisis and dropsy', as well as numerous parasites, all took a very heavy toll[23] of Europeans. They were as great an obstacle to advance as the bravery of the warlike tribes. Furthermore the rivers were broken by rapids and bars: who would sail up the wild waters of the Congo? Again, the American adventure and trade with the Far East were mobilizing all available energy in Europe, whose interests in any case lay elsewhere. The Black continent supplied of its own accord gold dust, ivory and men, and cheaply too. Why ask more of it? As for the slave trade, it did not represent the vast numbers of people we too readily assume. It was limited in extent even towards America, if only by the capacity of the transport ships. By way of comparison, total Irish immigration between 1769 and 1774 only amounted to 44,000, or fewer than 8000 a year.[24] Likewise one or two thousand Spaniards on average left Seville for America annually in the sixteenth century.[25] But, even if we assume that the slave trade represented the completely unthinkable figure of 50,000 a year (it would in fact only have reached this level – if at all – in the nineteenth century, as the trade came to an end), such a total would only accord with an African population of 25 million at the most. In fact the population of 100 million attributed to Africa has no reliable basis. It probably relates to the first very dubious overall estimate suggested by Gregory King in 1696 (95 million). Thereafter, everybody has been content to repeat his figure. But where did he get it from himself?

However, some population estimates are available. For example J.C. Russell[26] estimates the population of North Africa in the sixteenth century at 3,500,000 (I had personally estimated it at about two million, but without any very sound arguments). There is still no data on sixteenth-century Egypt. Is two or three million a reasonable figure, given that the first solid estimates in 1798 refer to 2,400,000 inhabitants for Egypt, and that the present-day populations of Egypt and North Africa are roughly equivalent, each representing about a tenth of the entire African population? If we accept that the same proportions obtained in the sixteenth century, then the population of Africa might have been anywhere between 24 and 35 million, depending on which of the three figures mentioned above we adopt. The last refers to the end of the eighteenth century, the other two to the sixteenth. The suggested figure of 100 million is very far from these estimates. It is impossible to prove anything of course; but while I would be hesitant to fix any figure myself, I am fairly confident that we can dismiss the suggestion of 100 million.

The figures for Asia are also excessive, but it is not such a serious matter in this case. Carr Saunders[27] thinks that Wilcox's figure of 70 million for the population of China in about 1650 - six years after the Manchus had taken Peking - is wrong. He boldly proceeds to double it (150 million). Everything relating to this period of change in Chinese history is open to question (for example, the *jen-ting* could simply be, like the Western *households*, ordinary fiscal units). Wilcox, for his part, based his calculations on the *Tung Hua Lou* (translated by Cheng Hen Chen). Even if we assume that his figure is too low, we still need to take into account the terrible havoc wrought by the Manchu invasion. A.P. Usher calculated a figure of 75 million for 1575 and 101 for 1661.[28] The official figure for 1680 is 61; the estimated figure given by one author is 98, by another 120. But these are for 1680, when the Manchu régime had finally been established. A traveller in about 1639 spoke of some 60 million inhabitants and he was reckoning 10 people to a household, an unusually high coefficient even for China.

The extraordinary demographic increase in China did not begin until 1680, or more accurately until the reoccupation of Formosa in 1683. China was at first protected by the wide continental expansion that took her people to Siberia, Mongolia, Turkestan and Tibet. She was then obliged to engage in extremely intensive colonization within her own boundaries. All the low-lying lands and hills that could be irrigated were developed, followed by the mountainous areas where forest-clearing pioneers multiplied. New crops introduced by the Portuguese in the sixteenth century spread visibly at this period - ground nuts for example, sweet potatoes and, above all, maize, before the arrival from Europe of ordinary potatoes (which did not become significant in China until the nineteenth century). This colonization went relatively unchecked until about 1740. After that the portion of land reserved to each individual gradually diminished as the population indubitably increased more rapidly than cultivable space.[29]

These deep-seated changes help us to pinpoint a Chinese 'agricultural revolution' intensified by a powerful and overlapping demographic revolution. Probable figures are as follows: 1680, 120 million; 1700, 130; 1720, 144; 1740, 165; 1750, 186; 1760, 214; 1770, 246; 1790, 300; 1850, 430.[30] When in 1793 George Staunton, secretary to the English ambassador, asked the Chinese what the population of the Empire was, they answered proudly, if not truthfully: 353 million.[31]

But to return to the population of Asia, it is usually estimated at two to three

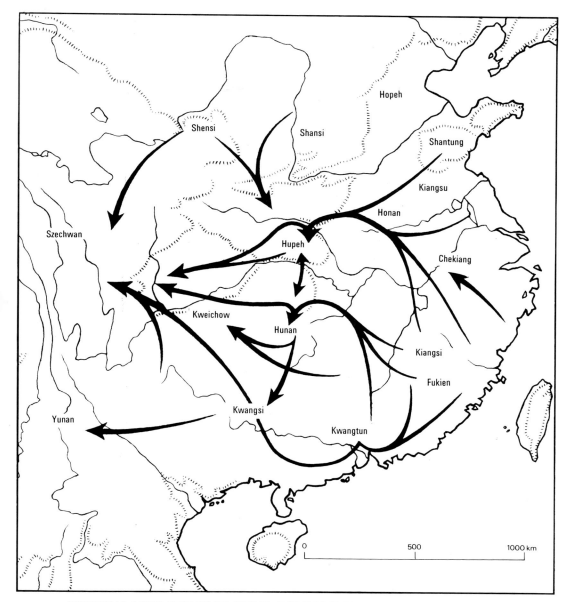

3 INTERNAL MIGRATIONS IN CHINA, DURING THE EIGHTEENTH CENTURY
The demographic explosion of the eighteenth century led to much migration from one province to another, summarized on this map. (From L. Dermigny, *Le Commerce à Canton au XVIIIe siècle*.)

times that of China. Two rather than three, because India does not really seem to be equal to the Chinese mass. An estimate (30 million) of the population of the Deccan in 1522, based on dubious documents, would give a figure of 100 million inhabitants for the whole of India.[32] This is higher than the contemporary official Chinese figure – but nobody is obliged to accept it. Moreover, in the course of the century, India suffered from famines which ravaged the northern provinces.[33] But recent studies by Indian historians have described the prosperity and the substantial demographic expansion of India in the seventeenth century.[34] However, an unpublished French estimate in 1797,[35] put the population of India at only 155 million, while China was already officially claiming 275 million in 1780. Kingsley Davis' statistical deductions do not back up this lower level for India.[36] But we cannot accept his figures blindly.

In any case, if we assume that Asia was demographically equal to two or three times China, its figures for 1680 would be 240 or 360 million; 600 or 900 in 1790. We must repeat that we prefer the lower figures, especially for the period around the middle of the seventeenth century. The total for the population of the world in about 1680 would be obtained by adding up the following: Africa 35 or 50 million; Asia 240 or 360; Europe 100; America 10 and Oceania 2. This gives us the same order of magnitude as our first calculation, with the same margin of doubt.

The relationship between the centuries

Spatial calculations, continent by continent, need not exclude the more difficult calculations on the time axis, century by century. Paul Mombert[37] provided the first model for this, relating to Europe in the period 1650-1850. He based his work on two principles: first, that the most recent figures are the least uncertain; second, that when working backwards from the most recent to the most ancient levels, *plausible* rates of increase between them must be assumed. This means accepting a figure of 266 million for Europe in 1850 and deducing (on the basis of a rise that is obviously not as steep as W.F. Wilcox assumes) the figure of 211 for 1800, 173 for 1750, and 136 and 100 for 1650 and 1600 respectively. The putative figure for the eighteenth century is higher than the usual estimates; part of the gains usually conceded to the nineteenth century have been given to the eighteenth. (I obviously cite these figures with due reservation.)

This method posits *reasonable* annual rates of growth, which are roughly corroborated by some partial investigations: from 1600 to 1650, 6·2 per 1,000; from 1650 to 1750, 2·4; from 1750 to 1800, 4; from 1800 to 1850, 4·6. We come back to K. Julius Beloch's figures for 1600 (nearly 100 million inhabitants for *all* Europe). But we have no valid index to follow the process further back from 1600 to 1300, an eventful period which saw a substantial recession between 1350 and 1450, followed by a sharp rise between 1450 and 1650.

We can probably, at our own risk, revert to Paul Mombert's ready solution. The least unreliable figure for 1600 is 100 million Europeans. This marked the peak of a long rise with three possible gradients: one of 6·2 per 1000, as indicated by the increase between 1600 and 1650; another of 2·4 per 1000 from 1650 to 1750; and the last of 4 per 1000 from 1750 to 1800. Logically we should assume a rate of increase at least equal to the last-mentioned, in order to take account of the intensity, suggested though not proved, of the rise in population between 1450 and 1600. This would produce a figure of approximately 55 million inhabitants for Europe in 1450. Now, if we concur with all other historians in thinking that the Black Death and its consequences robbed the continent of at least a fifth of its manpower, the figure for 1300-50 would be 69 million. I do not consider this figure improbable. The early devastation and poverty of Eastern Europe and the astonishing number of villages that disappeared throughout Europe during the 1350-1450 crisis all point to the possibility of this high level, in the region of Julius Beloch's reasonable estimate (66 million).

Some historians regard the sharp revival in an extended sixteenth century (1451-1650) as a 'recovery' after earlier recessions.[38] Our figures, if they are accurate, would represent a compensation and then a further addition. All this is obviously very debatable.

The old inadequate explanations

The question at issue mentioned at the beginning of the discussion remains: the *general* rise in world population. The old account must in any case be revised in the light of the demographic increase in China, which was as marked and as undeniable as in Europe. Historians may not like this: they have persisted in explaining Western demographic movements by the fall in urban mortality (which in any case remained very high),[39] the advance in hygiene and medicine, the decline in smallpox, improvements in the supply of drinking water, the decisive fall in infant mortality, plus a general fall in the mortality rate and a younger average age of marriage.

These factors are all very important in their own right. But they need to be corroborated by similar or equivalent explanations for countries outside Western Europe. In China, however, where marriages had always been 'early and fertile', one cannot point to any fall in the average age at marriage or leap in the birth rate. As for the hygienic condition of the towns, the huge city of Peking housed three million people in 1793, according to an English traveller,[40] and was probably smaller in area than London, which had nothing approaching this enormous figure. The congestion of families in the low-built houses is beyond imagining. Hygiene could make no progress here.

We have the same problem within Europe itself. How can we explain the rapid rise in the population of Russia (it doubled between 1722 and 1795: from

14 to 29 million) when doctors and surgeons were in short supply[41] and there was no sanitation in the towns?

Outside Europe, how can we explain the eighteenth-century rise in both the Anglo-Saxon and the Hispano-Portuguese populations of America, where neither doctors nor hygiene were particularly in evidence – certainly not in Rio de Janeiro (capital of Brazil since 1763) which had regular visitations of yellow fever and where syphilis raged in an endemic state (as in all Hispanic America) and putrefied its victims 'down to the bone'?[42] In short, therefore, every population could have grown in its own individual way. But why did all the increases occur at approximately the same time?

The space available to man would certainly have increased greatly everywhere – particularly with the general economic revival of the eighteenth century, although it would have started earlier than that. All the countries in the world colonized themselves at that time, settling their empty or half-empty land. Europe benefited from a surplus of living space and of food, thanks to her overseas territories and also to the European East which, according to the Abbé de Mably, was emerging from 'barbarism'. Southern Russia made as much progress in this direction as for example Hungary, which was covered in forest and swamps, and where the aggressive frontier of the Turkish empire had for so long been maintained; from that time on, the frontier was pushed far back southwards. There is no need to emphasize the increase in space and colonization in America. But it was also true in India, where colonization of the black earth lands of the *regur* in the Bombay region had begun.[43] It was even more the case in China, which was engaged in filling up so many spaces and deserts in or near its own lands. 'However paradoxical it may seem,' wrote René Grousset, 'if the history of China must be compared with that of any other great human collectivity, the history of Canada or the United States must be selected. In both cases what was involved essentially, over and above political vicissitudes, was the conquest of immense virgin country by a race of tillers who found only a poor semi-nomad population there before them.'[44] This expansion continued – or rather was resumed – with the eighteenth century.

However, if this resumption of expansion was general and world-wide, it meant that the number of people had increased. It was more consequence than cause. Space had, in fact, always been there for the taking, and within easy reach whenever men wanted or needed it. Even today, in our 'finite world' (as Valéry called it, using a term borrowed from mathematics) of which an economist has remarked that 'humanity no longer has a second Mississippi valley or a territory like Argentina at its disposal',[45] we are not short of empty space. The equatorial forests, the steppes, even the arctic regions and the true deserts where modern techniques may hold many surprises in store are still there to be exploited.[46]

Basically this is not the question. The real question is: why did these phenomena occur at the same time throughout the world when the space had always been available? The simultaneity is the problem. The international economy, effective but still so fragile, cannot assume sole responsibility for such a general and powerful movement. It too is as much consequence as cause.

Climatic rhythms

One can only imagine one single general answer to this almost complete coincidence: changes in climate. Today they are no longer dismissed by academics as a joke. Recent detailed research by historians and meteorologists shows constant fluctuations in temperature, pressure systems and rainfall. These variations affect trees, rivers, glaciers, the level of the seas, and the growth of rice and corn, olive trees and vines, men and animals.

Now the world between the fifteenth and eighteenth centuries consisted of one vast peasantry, where between 80% and 90% of people lived from the land and from nothing else. The rhythm, quality and deficiency of harvests ordered all material life. Sudden climatic catastrophes are reflected in the growth-rings of trees – and in the population figures of mankind. And some of these changes occur everywhere at the same time, although as yet we can only explain them by short-lived hypotheses (such as the now-abandoned theory of variations in the speed of the jet-stream). There was a general cooling down of the northern hemisphere, for example, in the fourteenth century. The glaciers advanced, ice-floes were more numerous and winters became more severe. The Vikings' route to America was cut off by dangerous icebergs: 'Now the ice has come ... no one can sail by the old route without risking death', writes a Norwegian priest in mid-fourteenth century. This climatic drama appears to have interrupted Scandinavian colonization in Greenland: the bodies of the last survivors, found in the frozen earth, are thought to be poignant testimony of this.[47]

Similarly the 'little ice age' (to use Dr Shove's expression)[48] during Louis XIV's reign was more of a tyrant than the Sun King. Everything moved to its rhythm: cereal-growing Europe and the rice fields and steppes of Asia; the olive groves of Provence and the Scandinavian countries where snow and ice lingered till late in the year and autumn returned so promptly that the corn no longer had time to ripen: this was the case in the terrible decade of the 1690s, the coldest for seven hundred years.[49] Natural disasters also multiplied in China in the middle of the seventeenth century – disastrous droughts, plagues of locusts – and a succession of peasant uprisings occurred in the interior provinces, as in France under Louis XIII. All this gives additional meaning to the fluctuations in material life and *may* explain their simultaneous appearance. The possibility of a physical coherence of the world and the generalization of a certain biological history common to all mankind suggests one way in which the globe could be said to be unified, long before the voyages of discovery, the industrial revolution or the interpenetration of economies.

If, as I am inclined to think, the climatic explanation has some truth in it, we must take care not to over-simplify it. Climate is a very complex system and its

The freezing over of rivers, streams and lakes is a valuable indicator of climatic change. In 1814 (as in 1683) the Thames froze over 'from London Bridge to Blackfriars Bridge' and was turned into a vast fairground. (Photo Snark.)

effect on the lives of plants, animals and people only comes about via very devious routes that vary according to place, crop and season. In temperate Western Europe, for example, there is 'a negative correlation between the quantity of rainfall from 10 June to 20 July' and 'a positive correlation between the percentage [of sunny days] in the period from 20 March to 10 May and the number of grains [on an ear] of corn'.[50] And if one seeks to argue that serious consequences resulted from a deterioration of the climate, one has to prove first that such deterioration occurred in the countries of the temperate zone, the most densely populated and in the past 'the most important for Western Europe's food supply'.[51] That may seem obvious. But the examples of direct influence of the climate on harvests so far put forward by historians too often relate to marginal regions or crops, such as corn in Sweden. In the present fragmentary state of research, it is impossible to generalize. But we should not prejudge too hastily the answers the future may provide. And we should bear in mind the congenital frailty of man compared to the colossal forces of nature. Whether it favours him or not, the calendar is man's master. Historians of the *ancien régime* are quite right to regard it as punctuated by the succession of good, not so good or bad harvests. These were the regular drumbeats which set in motion enormous fluctuations of prices on which so many other things depended. And who could fail to agree that this insistent background music was in part determined by the changing history of the climate? We know how vitally important the date of the monsoon still is today: a mere delay can cause irreparable harm in India. If the same thing happens two or three years running, it means famine. Here man has still not been able to free himself from these terrible shackles. But we would also do well not to forget the damage inflicted by the drought of 1976 in France and Western Europe, or the abnormal change in wind patterns which caused a catastrophic drought east of the Rocky Mountains, in the United States in 1964 and 1965.[52]

It is amusing to think that the men of former times would not have been put out by this climatic explanation, implicating as it does the heavens. They found it all too tempting to explain the course of everything terrestrial, including individual or collective destinies and disease, by the stars. In 1551 Oronce Finé, a mathematician and dabbler in the occult, made the following diagnosis in the name of astrology: 'If the Sun, Venus and the Moon are in conjunction in the sign of Gemini (the Twins), writers will earn little for that year and servants will rebel against their masters and lords. But there will be a great abundance of wheat on the land and roads will be unsafe because of the abundance of thieves.'[53]

A scale of reference

The present (1980) world population is about 4,000,000,000. Comparing this with the very approximate figures we have suggested for the past shows it to be five times the population of 1800, twelve times that of 1300.[54] These coefficients of 1 to 5 or 1 to 12, with all the values in between, are not magic numbers that explain everything - especially since they refer to realities which are not exactly the same. Mankind today cannot be described as mankind in 1300 or 1350 multiplied by twelve, even from a purely biological point of view, because the age pyramids are not the same - far from it. However, a comparison of the overall figures alone can open some perspectives for us.

Towns, armies and navies

By present-day standards then, the towns the historian discovers in his journeys back into pre-nineteenth-century times are small; and the armies miniature.

Cologne, at the intersection of two Rhine waterways - one up- and the other down-stream - and of important overland routes, was the largest town in Germany in the fifteenth century.[55] Yet it numbered only 20,000 inhabitants at a time when the rural and urban population in Germany was in a ratio of about ten to one and when a degree of urban congestion was already clearly apparent, however small the numbers may seem to us. A group of 20,000 was a significant concentration of people, energy, talents, and mouths to feed – much more so, proportionately speaking, than a community of 100,000 to 200,000 people today. Just think what the lively and original culture of Cologne must have represented in the fifteenth century. Similarly we can justifiably say that Istanbul in the sixteenth century, with at least 400,000 inhabitants (and probably 700,000),[56] was an urban monster, comparable in proportion to the largest agglomerations today. It needed every available flock of sheep from the Balkans to support it; rice, beans and corn from Egypt; corn and wood from the Black Sea; and oxen, camels and horses from Asia Minor. It also required every available man from the Empire to renew its population in addition to the slaves brought back from Russia after Tartar raids or from the Mediterranean coasts by Turkish fleets. All these slaves were offered for sale at the market of Besistan, in the heart of the enormous capital.

The armies of mercenaries who squabbled over Italy at the beginning of the sixteenth century also seem very small to us – between 10,000 and 20,000 men, ten to twenty pieces of cannon. These imperial soldiers with their remarkable leaders (Pescara, the *Connétable* de Bourbon, de Lannoy, Philibert de Chalon) who routed the other armies of mercenaries commanded by Francis I, Bonnivet or Lautrec, numbered no more than 10,000 old troopers, German *Landsknechte* and Spanish arquebusiers, all of them picked men, but worn out as rapidly as the Napoleonic army between the striking of the camp at Boulogne and the Spanish war (1803–8). They took the stage from La Bicoque (1522) to Lautrec's defeat at Naples (1528), reaching their zenith at Pavia (1525).[57] But these 10,000 mobile, furious and pitiless soldiers (they were responsible for the sack of Rome) represented a far greater force than 50,000 or 100,000 men would do today. Had there been more of them in earlier times there would have been no means of moving or feeding them, except in a country with infinitely rich land. The victory of Pavia was the triumph of the arquebusiers and even more of empty stomachs. Francis I's army was too well fed and protected from enemy cannon, between the walls of the town of Pavia which it was besieging and the ducal park, a game reserve surrounded by walls, where the battle unexpectedly took place on 24 February 1525.

Similarly, the terrible and decisive battle of Marston Moor (2 July 1644), the first defeat of the royalist army in the English Civil War, put in the field only a small number of troops: 15,000 royalists and 27,000 on Parliament's side. Cromwell's army 'could be accommodated on the *Queen Elizabeth* or the *Queen Mary*', as Peter Laslett put it in the first edition of his book, concluding that 'the tiny scale of life in the pre-industrial world' is a characteristic feature of 'the world we have lost'.[58]

In the light of this, certain feats, however inconsiderable they may seem by today's standards, regain their significance. The Spanish administration's ability to move galleys, fleets and *tercios* across the lands and seas of Europe from its

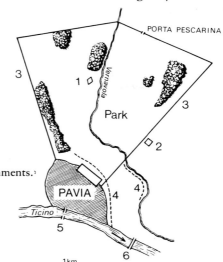

4 THE BATTLE OF PAVIA
1. Mirabello. 2. Casa de levrieri.
3. Brick walls round park. 4. French retrenchments.
5. San Antonio bridge, destroyed at beginning of seige. 6. Wooden bridge destroyed during the battle by the Duke of Alençon.

large supply points at Seville, Cadiz (later Lisbon), Malaga and Barcelona was really remarkable. Lepanto (7 October 1571), the scene of the confrontation between Islam and Christendom, was another striking achievement. The fleets of the two enemies between them carried a total of at least 100,000 men, either on the slender galleys or on the large round ships that accompanied them.[59] A hundred thousand men! Imagine any fleet today carrying 500,000 or a million men. Fifty years later, in about 1630, Wallenstein's record achievement in gathering 100,000 soldiers under his command[60] was an even greater feat, presupposing exceptional organization of food supplies. Villars' army, victorious at Denain (1712), numbered 70,000 men,[61] but this was the last-ditch effort of a country fighting for its life. The figure of 100,000 soldiers seems to have become normal in later years – at least in theory. Dupré d'Aulnay, Commissioner for War in 1744, explains that to provide for these numbers a massive delivery would have to leave the supply lines every four days carrying, at a rate of 120,000 rations a day (because some men received double rations), altogether 480,000 rations (800 per carriage). 'This would require only 600 carriages and 2400 horses, harnessed in fours,'[62] he concludes. Such organization seems to have been commonplace; there were even iron travelling-ovens to bake the bread ration. But a treatise on artillery at the beginning of the seventeenth century setting out the varied needs of any army equipped with cannon chooses the figure of 20,000 men.[63]

The proposition these examples illustrate can be repeated in innumerable other cases: the loss to Spain caused by the expulsion of the Moriscoes (1609-14) – a minimum of 300,000 according to quite reliable calculations;[64] to France by the repeal of the Edict of Nantes;[65] to Black Africa by the slave trade with the New World;[66] to Spain once more by the process of populating the New World with white men (departures in the sixteenth century at a possible average rate of 1000 annually; 100,000 in all). The relative smallness of all these figures represents a general problem: Europe, because of its political partition and the lack of flexibility in its economy, was not capable of dispensing with any more men. Without Africa it could not have developed the New World for many reasons, notably the climate, but also because it could not divert too much manpower from its own labour force. Contemporaries probably exaggerate easily, but the effects of emigration must have been felt on Sevillian life for Andrea Navagero to have said in 1526: 'So many people have left for the Indies that the town [Seville] is scarcely populated and almost in the hands of women.'[67]

K.J. Beloch followed a similar line of thought when he tried to make a fair assessment of seventeenth-century Europe divided between the three great powers who contested it; the Ottoman empire, the Spanish empire, and France under Louis XIII and Richelieu. He calculated that they each commanded a human mass of about 17 million in the Old World – and arrived at the conclusion that this was the minimum level that enabled a country to aspire to the role of a great power.[68] Times have changed.

A France prematurely overpopulated

As we go along, many other comparisons will suggest equally important explanations. Suppose that the world population in about 1600 was an eighth of its present total and that the population of France (calculated on its present-day political boundaries) was 20 million, which is probable but not absolutely certain. England then numbered at most 5 million.[69] If both countries had increased at the average world rate, England would number 40 million inhabitants today and France 160 million. This is a quick way of saying that France (or Italy, or even Germany in the sixteenth century) was probably already overpopulated; that France, in relation to its capacity at that period, was encumbered with too many people, too many beggars, useless mouths, undesirables. Brantôme was already saying that it was as 'full as an egg'.[70] Emigration, in the absence of any deliberate official policy, was organized as best it could be – to Spain in the sixteenth and seventeenth centuries in some volume, and later to the American 'islands'. Otherwise it was the haphazard consequence of religious exile, during 'that long blood-letting of France that began in 1540 with the first systematic persecutions [of the Protestants] and only ended in 1752–3, with the last great emigration movement following the bloody repressions of Languedoc'.[71]

Historical research has only recently shown the extent (hitherto unknown) of French emigration to the Iberian countries.[72] It is proved by statistical surveys as well as by continued emphasis in travellers' accounts.[73] Cardinal de Retz expressed extreme surprise in 1654 at hearing everyone in Saragossa (where there was a very great number of French artisans) speaking his language.[74] Ten years later, Antoine de Brunel wondered at the amazing number of *gavachos* (the

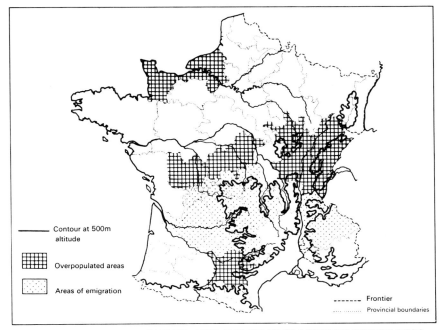

5 OVERPOPULATED REGIONS AND ZONES FROM WHICH THERE WAS EMIGRATION, FRANCE 1745
From F. de Dainville in *Population*, 1952, No. 1. For further comments, see Vol. III.

pejorative nickname given to the French) in Madrid; 40,000 he thought, who 'disguised themselves as Spaniards or claim that they are Walloons or from Lorraine or Franche-Comté to conceal the fact that they are French and to avoid being beaten up as such'.[75]

The French supplied the Spanish capital with artisans, odd-job men and retailers attracted by expectations of high salaries and profits. This was particularly true of masons and building workers. They also invaded the countryside: Spanish land would often have remained uncultivated without the peasant who came from France. These details indicate abundant, continuous and socially mixed emigration, an obvious sign of French overpopulation. Jean Hérauld, lord of Gourville, states in his memoirs that there were 200,000 French in Spain (1669) – an enormous but by no means improbable figure.[76]

Thus the deliberate birth control which appeared, or rather assumed prominence, with the eighteenth century, took place in a country that had suffered the scourge of numbers for centuries. 'The husbands themselves,' wrote Sébastien Mercier (1771), 'take care in their raptures to keep from adding a child to the household.'[77] After 1789, during the crucial years of the Revolution, a marked decrease in the birth rate clearly reveals the spread of contraceptive practices.[78]

Should not this phenomenon (which occurred earlier in France than elsewhere) be seen as a reaction to the long years of overpopulation?

Density of population and level of civilization

Given its dry-land area of 150 million square kilometres, the present average density of the world, with its 4 thousand million human beings, is 26·7 inhabitants to one square kilometre. The same calculation for the period between 1300 and 1800 would give the figure of 2·3 inhabitants to a square kilometre at the lowest estimate and 6·6 at the highest. Suppose we then calculate the actual area covered nowadays by the most populated regions (200 inhabitants or more per square kilometre). This would give us the main area of present-day *dense civilizations*, that is to say (and this calculation has been worked out over and over again), 11 million square kilometres. On this narrow belt, 70% of all human beings (almost three thousand million) are concentrated. The world of houses and wells is only a thin strip on the surface of the globe as Saint-Exupéry pointed out: as a pilot, he had only to make one mistake and his plane would be lost in the Paraguayan bush or the sands of the Sahara.[79] It is worth stressing how disproportionate, how ridiculously small the inhabited world really is. Man leaves nine-tenths of the globe empty, often through force of circumstance, but also out of neglect and because history, which is an unending series of efforts, has decided otherwise. 'Men did not spread evenly over the world like a layer of oil,' writes Vidal de La Blache, 'but originally clustered together like coral polyps': that is by piling up 'layer upon layer' at certain points 'to build reefs of human population'.[80] At first sight, the population density of the past seems so low that one is tempted to conclude that the really dense human settlement required to form a civilization was nowhere in existence between 1400 and 1800. In fact, the world at that time was already divided by the same partition and the same asymmetry into small, heavily populated areas and vast, empty, lightly peopled regions. Here again, the figures must be seen in perspective.

We know, almost exactly, the location of the civilizations, developed cultures and primitive cultures throughout the whole world in about 1500, on the eve of the impact of the European Conquest of America. Contemporary documents, later accounts, and research by past and present ethnographers have yielded a valid map, because we know that the cultural boundaries vary little in the course of the centuries. Man lives from choice in the framework of his own experience, trapped in his former achievements for generations on end. When we say man we mean the group to which he belongs: individuals leave it and others are incorporated but the group remains attached to a given space and to familiar land. It takes root there.

The map of the world in about 1500 (p. 58) drawn by the ethnographer Gordon W. Hewes is self-explanatory.[81] It distinguishes 76 civilizations and cultures, that is 76 areas of varied shape and size into which the 150 million square kilometres of dry land are divided. This map is very important and we will need to refer to it often. We will therefore examine it carefully from the outset. The 76 pieces of the jigsaw are classified, from area 1, Tasmania, to the 76th and last, Japan. There is no difficulty in reading the terms of classification, starting from the most elementary cultures: (1) 1 to 27 consist of primitive peoples, gatherers and fishermen; (2) 28 to 44, nomads and stockbreeders; (3) 45 to 63, peoples practising a still deficient form of agriculture, primarily peasants using hoes; they are oddly distributed in an almost continuous belt around the world; (4) finally, 64 to 76, civilizations; relatively dense populations possessing multiple assets and advantages: domestic animals, swing-ploughs, ploughs, carts, and above all towns. There is no need to emphasize that these last 13 pieces of the jigsaw are the developed countries, those parts of the world with the densest populations.

It must be added that the classification at the top levels is debatable on two scores. Do 61 and 62 – the Aztec or Mexican civilization and the Inca or Peruvian civilization – have full right to be placed at that level? The answer is yes as far as ability, brilliance, art and original turn of mind are concerned. It is equally so if we consider the ancient Mayas' wonderful science of calculation and the longevity of these civilizations: they survived the terrible impact of the European Conquest. On the other hand, the answer is no when we note that they used only hoes and digging sticks; that they had no large domestic animals (except llamas, alpacas and vicuñas); that they had no knowledge of the wheel, arch, cart or metallurgy in iron (known to the still modest cultures of Black Africa for centuries, even millennia). According to our criteria of material life, the answer is on the whole in the negative. We have the same misgivings and reservations about 63, the Finnish groups, which were then scarcely affected by the neighbouring civilizations.

The remaining 13 civilizations, seen on a world scale, form a long, thin ribbon round the whole of the Old World, a narrow belt of wells, tilled fields and dense populations, spaces that man held as securely as was then possible. Furthermore, as we have left the exceptional case of America on one side, we can say that the places where civilized man was to be found in 1500 were the places he had inhabited in 1400 and would inhabit in 1800, and even today. The list is not a long one: Japan, Korea, China, Indochina, the Indian Archipelago, India, Islam and the four different faces of Europe (the Mediterranean Latin, the richest; the Greek, the most unfortunate, submerged by the Turkish conquest; the northern, the hardiest; and the Russo-Lapp, the least sophisticated). Two odd cases need to be added to the list: 64, the robust Caucasian civilizations and 65, the ineradicable civilization of the Abyssinian tillers.

Here we have a total of perhaps 10 million square kilometres (almost twenty times the territory of present-day France), a tiny area, a belt of high densities very clearly specified and recognizable, *mutatis mutandis*, in the present-day geography of the world (where, we repeat, 70% of all human beings live on 11

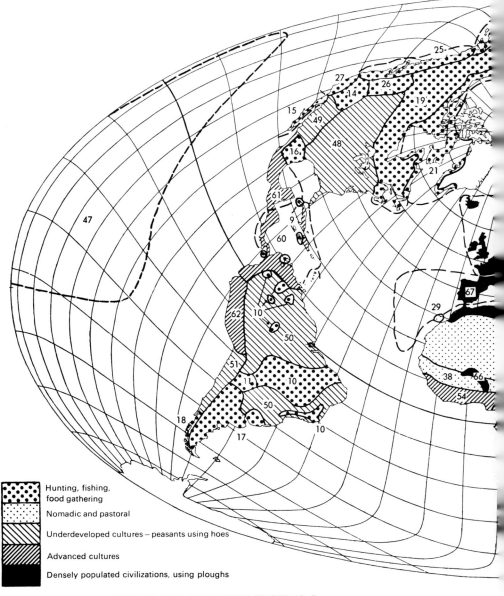

6 CIVILIZATIONS, 'CULTURES' AND PRIMITIVE PEOPLES C. 1500
(AFTER G.W. HEWES)

1. Tasmanians. 2. Congo Pygmies. 3. The Vedda (Ceylon). 4. Andamanese. 5. Sakai and Semang. 6. Kubu. 7. Punan (Borneo). 8. Negritos of the Philippines. 9. Ciboneys (Antilles). 10. Gê-Botocudos. 11. Gran Chaco Indians. 12. Bushmen. 13. Australians. 14. Great Basin. 15. Lower California. 16. Texas and north-eastern Mexico. 17. Patagonia. 18. Indians of the southern coast of Chile. 19. Athabascans and Algonkin (northern Canada). 20. Yukaghir. 21. Eastern and central Eskimos. 22. Western Eskimos. 23. Kamchadal, Koryak, Chukchi. 24. Ainu, Gilyak, Gol'dy. 25. North-west coast Indians (United States and Canada). 26. Columbia Plateau. 27. Central California. 28. Reindeer-herding peoples. 29. Canary Islands. 30. Sahara nomads. 31. Arabian nomads. 32. Pastoral mountain peoples in the Near East. 33. Pastoral peoples of the Pamir region and the Hindu Kush. 34. Kazakh-Kirghiz. 35. Mongols. 36. Pastoral Tibetans. 37. Settled Tibetans. 38. Western Sudanese. 39. Eastern Sudanese. 40. Somali and

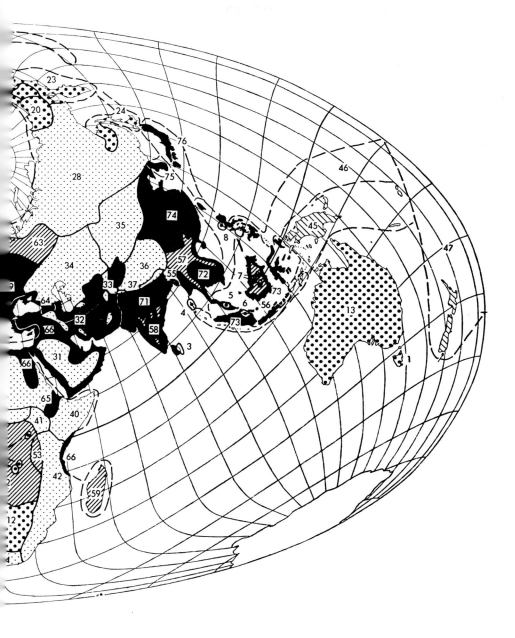

Galla of north-eastern Africa. 41. Nilotic tribes. 42. East-African stock-rearing peoples. 43. Western Bantu. 44. Hottentots. 45. Melanesian Papuans. 46. Micronesians. 47. Polynesians. 48. American Indians (Eastern United States). 49. American Indians (Western United States). 50. Brazilian Indians. 51. Chilean Indians. 52. Congolese peoples. 53. Lake-dwellers of East Africa. 54. Guinea coasts. 55. Tribes of the Assam and the Burmese highlands. 56. Tribes of the Indonesian highlands. 57. Highland people's of Indo-China. 58. Mountain and forest tribes of central India. 59. Malagasay. 60. Caribbean peoples. 61. Mexicans, Maya. 62. Peru and the Andes. 63. Finns. 64. Caucasians. 65. Ethiopia. 66. Settled Muslims. 67 South-western Europe. 68. Eastern Mediterranean. 69. Eastern Europe. 70. North-western Europe. 71. India (this map does not differentiate between Muslims and Hindus). 72. Lowlands of South-east Asia. 73. Indonesian lowlands. 74. Chinese. 75. Koreans. 76 Japanese.

A Bohemian village on the road to Prague, with its ploughed fields, forest and three fish ponds, in 1675: there are only about ten houses. Other villages drawn in the same series of plans are about the same size. Central Archives, Maps section, Orlik, A 14. (Photo courtesy of the Archives.)

million square kilometres). If we accept this present-day percentage of the population living in civilizations in relation to the population as a whole and take our extremes of reference into account, the kilometric density of the developed zones between 1300 and 1800 would lie between a minimum of 24·5 and a maximum of 63·6.[82] If we stop with K.J. Beloch at 1600, the average would lie between 28 and 35. This is an important threshold: if 17 million was the population required for a country to become a European power, on a world scale the level at which human settlement became sufficiently crowded, providing the density necessary to the life and prosperity of a civilization, was about 30 people to the square kilometre.

Continuing in 1600: Italy, which was well populated, had 44 inhabitants to the square kilometre; the Netherlands 40; France 34; Germany 28; the Iberian peninsula 17; Poland and Prussia 14; Sweden, Norway and Finland about 1·5 (but they were still imprisoned in a prolonged version of the primitive Middle

Ages and remained on the margins of Europe, with only small areas of territory participating in its life).[83] And China, with its seventeen provinces (the eighteenth, Kansu, came under Chinese Turkestan at that time), had a density scarcely over 20 (1578).[84]

Yet these levels, which seem so low to us, already pointed to obvious overpopulation. Wurttemberg, the most populous area of Germany (44 inhabitants per square kilometre)[85] at the beginning of the sixteenth century, was far and away the best place for the recruitment of *Landsknechte*; France, with a level of 34, was a vast reservoir of emigration and so was Spain, with only 17. However, the wealthy and already 'industrialized' countries of Italy and the Netherlands supported a heavier load of people and kept them in their own lands. For overpopulation is a function both of the number of men and the resources at their disposal.

A.P. Usher distinguishes three levels of population in historical demography. He places the population of the pioneer zones (thinking of the United States, he calls them 'frontier' zones) at the bottom of the scale. This is a population at its very beginning, in a space which has not, or hardly, been developed by man. In the second stage (China, India before the eighteenth century, Europe before the twelfth or thirteenth) the population ranges between 15 and 20 people to the square kilometre. Lastly comes the stage of 'high' density, over 20. The latter figure may seem too low. But it is clear that by traditional norms, the densities referred to above in Italy, the Netherlands and France (44, 40, 34) already correspond to demographic tension. Jean Fourastié has calculated that in France under the *ancien régime*, 1·5 hectares of cultivable land were required to support one man, allowing for crop rotation.[86] This is close to Daniel Defoe's estimate in 1709: 3 acres of good land or 4 of average land (1·2 to 1·6 hectares).[87] Any demographic tension, as we shall see, meant either being forced to choose between kinds of food (essentially between bread and meat); or radically transforming agriculture; or resorting to emigration.

These comments only take us to the threshold of the basic problems of a history of population. Among other things we still need to know the relationship between the urban and rural populations (this relationship is perhaps the basic indicator of growth in earlier history) and also the form the rural groups took, according to the norms of human geography. Near St Petersburg, at the end of the eighteenth century, the sordid farms of the Finnish peasants were scattered over the countryside fairly remote from each other; the houses of the German colonists were clustered together; and by comparison the Russian villages were large concentrations.[88] Central Europe north of the Alps had fairly small villages, as in Bavaria. I had the opportunity in Bohemia of looking at several surveys of the former estates of the Rosenbergs and Schwarzenbergs, near the Austrian frontier, a country of artificial lakes filled with carp, pike and perch. The central archives at Warsaw also contain many cadastral maps. I was struck by the very small size of the many villages in central Europe in the seventeenth and eighteenth centuries; very often they consisted of only a dozen or so houses. How far removed they are from the village-towns of Italy or the large market-towns between the Rhine, the Meuse and the Paris basin. Surely the small size of the village in so many eastern and central European countries was one of the basic causes of the fate of the peasantry? It was all the more vulnerable *vis-à-vis* the nobility because it lacked the solidity provided by large communities.[89]

Other points inferred from Gordon W. Hewes' map

At least three points emerge from the map:
(1) The permanence of the sites occupied by the 'cultures' (the first achievements) and the 'civilizations' (man's second achievement), for these sites have been reconstructed by a simple deductive method. Their boundaries have not changed. Their distribution therefore forms as marked a geographical feature as the Alps, the Gulf Stream or the course of the Rhine.
(2) The map also shows that man had already explored and exploited the whole world for centuries or millennia before the triumph of Europe. He was only stopped by major obstacles: vast expanses of sea, impenetrable mountains, dense forests (as in Amazonia, North America or Siberia) and immense deserts. Even so, closer inspection reveals that there was no expanse of sea able to escape man's spirit of adventure for very long and guard its secrets (the ancient Greeks knew about the monsoons in the Indian Ocean); no mountain mass that failed to reveal its access and passes; no forest man did not penetrate; no desert he did not cross. As for the 'habitable and navigable'[90] parts of the world, there is not the slightest doubt: the smallest patch already had an owner before 1500 (and before 1400 or 1300 as well). Even the forbidding deserts of the Old World harboured their share of humanity, in the form of the great nomadic peoples we shall mention later in this chapter. In short, the world 'our familiar home'[91] was 'discovered' a long time ago, well before the Great Discoveries. Even the inventory of vegetable wealth had been drawn up so precisely 'since the beginning of written history, that not one single nutritious plant of general usefulness has been added to the list of those previously known, so careful and complete was the exploration to which the primitive peoples subjected the plant world'.[92]

Europe therefore neither discovered America and Africa, nor first penetrated the mysterious continents. The nineteenth-century explorers of central Africa, so greatly admired in the past, travelled on the backs of black bearers. Their great mistake, Europe's mistake at that juncture, was to think they were discovering a sort of New World. Similarly the discoverers of the South American continent, even the *bandeirantes paulistas* who set off from the town of São Paulo (founded in 1554) were merely, for all their heroic adventures, rediscovering the old tracks and rivers the Indians already used with their canoes. And they were generally guided by the *Mamelucos* (Portuguese and Indian halfbreeds).[93] The same adventure was repeated, to the profit of the French, from

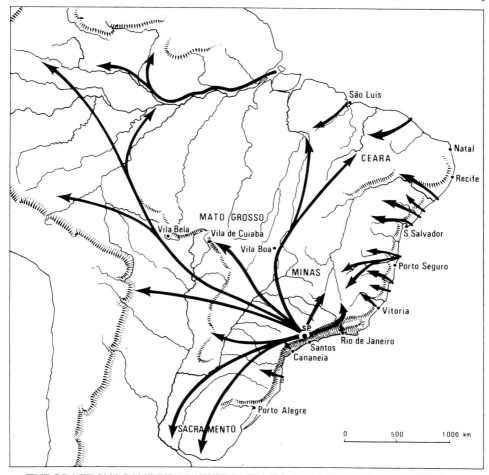

7 THE BRAZILIAN BANDEIRAS (SIXTEENTH TO EIGHTEENTH CENTURIES)
The *bandeiras* mostly set out from São Paulo (S.P. on the map). The *paulistas* went all over the Brazilian interior. (After A. d'Escragnolle-Taunay.)

the Great Lakes to the Mississippi in the seventeenth and eighteenth centuries, thanks to Canadian halfbreeds, the *bois brûlés* as they were called. Europeans very often rediscovered the world using other people's eyes, legs and brains.

Europe's own achievement was to discover the Atlantic and to master its difficult stretches, currents and winds. This late success opened up the doors and routes of the seven seas. From now on the maritime organization of the world was at the service of white men. Fleets, ships and still more ships ploughed the seas. Seafaring peoples, ports and shipbuilding yards – these were the glory of Europe, as Peter the Great was well aware on his first voyage to the West (1697): he went to work in Holland, in the shipbuilding yards of Saardam, near Amsterdam.

(3) One final comment: the small areas of dense population were not all of the same kind. The Indian Archipelago and Indochina really only had a scattering of populated regions, compared with the solidly occupied zones (Western Europe, Japan, Korea, China). India itself was not fully occupied by its mixed civilizations. Islam was a series of coasts – of *sahels* – on the margins of empty spaces, on the edges of deserts, rivers and seas, hugging the sides of Black Africa, on the coast of Slaves (Zanzibar) and the Niger loop, where it built and rebuilt its quarrelsome empires. Even Europe merged into emptiness towards the east, beyond the wild marches.

Wild men and animals

It is always very tempting to see only the civilizations. They are the main thing. Besides, they have expended a vast amount of skill on rediscovering their former selves, their tools, costumes, houses, practices, even their traditional songs. Their museums are there to be visited. Every culture has its own distinctive features: Chinese windmills turn horizontally; in Istanbul, the scissors have hollow blades, and the luxury spoons are made of wood from the pepper plant; Japanese and Chinese anvils are different from ours; not one nail was used to build the boats on the Red Sea and the Persian Gulf, and so on. And each has its own plants, domestic animals (or at any rate its own way of treating them), its characteristic houses, its own foods. The mere smell of cooking can evoke a whole civilization.

However, not all the beauty of the world nor all the salt of the earth was contained in the civilizations. Outside them, encircling their frontiers and sometimes even invading their territory, lurked primitive life, and the empty, echoing wastelands. Here was played out the saga of man and the animals, the golden legend of ancient peasant agriculture, a paradise in the eyes of the civilized who might wish to escape there from the constraints of urban life.

The Far East yields the most numerous examples of this wild humanity: the islands of the Indian Archipelago, the mountains of China, the north of the Japanese island of Yeso, Formosa or the heart of India. The European lands were free of these 'wild' tribes who burned up the high-ground forest and grew rice on the dry land they had cleared.[94] Europe domesticated its mountain people very early on, tamed them by not treating them as if they were pariahs. In the Far East, by contrast, no such communication or co-operation occurred. The innumerable clashes that took place there were unmercifully brutal. The Chinese waged an unceasing war against their wild mountain population, stock-raisers living in stinking houses. It was the same in India. In 1565, in the peninsula of the Deccan, the Hindu realm of Vijayanagar was annihilated on the battlefield of Talikota by the Muslim cavalry and artillery of the sultans of the north. The conqueror did not occupy the enormous capital immediately. It was left defenceless and without carts or beast of burden, which had all departed with the army. The wild people from the surrounding brush and jungle – Brindsharis, Lambadis and Kurumbas – then swooped down and pillaged it from end to end.⁹⁵

But these savages were already, as it were, confined and encircled by disapproving civilizations. The real savages lived elsewhere, on appalling land, but in a state of complete freedom, beyond the boundaries of the populated countries. They were what Frédéric Ratzel called the *Randvölker*, the marginal people known to German geographers and historians as the *geschichtlos* people – people without history (but is this true?). Once, 12,000 Chukchi lived on 800,000 square kilometres in the far north of Siberia; a thousand Samoyeds occupied 150,000 square kilometres of the frozen peninsula of Yamal.'⁹⁶ Because 'the poorest groups generally require the greatest space'⁹⁷ or, to put it the other way round, only an elementary life can be maintained by digging up roots and tubers and trapping wild animals in these vast and hostile spaces.

In any case, wherever human settlement is sparse, wild animals multiply, even if the land seems poor or useless. They are to be found wherever man is not. Travellers' tales are full of savage beasts. One seventeenth-century account describes tigers prowling round Asian villages and towns, and swimming out into the Ganges delta to surprise fisherman asleep in their boats. The ground around the mountain hamlets in the Far East is still cleared even today to keep the man-eaters at a distance.⁹⁸ No one feels safe after nightfall, not even inside a house. One man went out of his hut in a small town near Canton, where the Jesuit father de Las Cortes and his fellow sufferers were imprisoned (1626), and was carried off by a tiger.⁹⁹ A fourteenth-century Chinese painting represents an enormous tiger ocellated with pink, like some pet monster, amongst the flowering branches of fruit trees.¹⁰⁰ This was all too true throughout the Far East.

Siam consisted of the valley of the River Menam; its waters were alive with rows of houses on piles, bazaars, families crowded on to boats; on its banks stood two or three towns, including the capital. They were flanked by rice fields and then by great forests where the water penetrated vast expanses. The rare patches of forest that were permanently free from water harboured tigers and wild elephants (and, according to Kämpfer, even chamois).¹⁰¹ There were lions in Ethiopia, North Africa and Persia, near Basra and on the route from northwest India to Afghanistan. Crocodiles swarmed in the rivers of the Philippines,¹⁰² wild boar on the coastal plains of Sumatra, India and the Persian plateaux; wild horses were regularly hunted and lassoed, north of Peking.¹⁰³ Wild dogs howling in the mountains of Trebizond kept Gemelli Careri awake.¹⁰⁴ The wildlife of Guinea included small cows which were treated as game. However, both hunter and hunted took flight at the sight of bands of elephants and hippopotamuses, 'sea-horses' that ravaged 'the fields of rice, millet, and other vegetables' in the same regions. 'One sometimes sees troupes of three or four hundred at a time.'¹⁰⁵ And in the vast expanses of southern Africa, which stretched empty and unpopulated north of the Cape of Good Hope, there could be seen alongside the very few men 'who lived more like beasts than human beings', many 'savage' animals – lions and elephants said to be the biggest in the world.¹⁰⁶ And they in turn

A seal-hunt: this ex-voto of 1618 tells the tale of the Swedish hunters who were marooned on an ice-floe with their prey. They only reached land two weeks later. Stockholm, National Museum. (Photothèque A. Colin.)

bring to mind the elephants of North Africa, in the time of Hannibal of Carthage, many centuries earlier and the length of the continent away; or the elephant hunts, north again, but this time deep in Black Africa, which began to provide the Europeans with huge quantities of ivory from the sixteenth century on.[107]

The whole of Europe, from the Urals to the Straits of Gibraltar, was the domain of wolves, and bears roamed in all its mountains. The omnipresence of wolves and the attention they aroused make wolf-hunting an index of the health of the countryside, and even of the towns, and of the character of the year gone by. A lapse in vigilance, an economic setback, a rough winter, and they multiplied. In 1420, packs entered Paris through a breach in the ramparts or unguarded gates. They were there again in September 1438, attacking people this time outside the town, between Montmartre and the Saint-Antoine gate.[108] In 1640, wolves entered Besançon by crossing the Doubs near the mills of the town and 'ate children along the roads'.[109] Francis I created grand masters of the wolf-hunts in about 1520. They organized round-ups needing the participation of both lords and villagers. There was an example of this in 1765, again in the Gevaudan 'where the ravages of the wolves made people believe in the existence of an unnatural monster'.[110] 'It appears,' wrote a Frenchman in 1779, 'that they are trying to annihilate the species in France, as they did in England six hundred years ago, but it is not easy to round them up in a country as vast and as open on all sides as ours, although it might be practicable in an island like Great Britain.'[111] In fact the *Députés du Commerce* were discussing in 1783 a proposal made several years earlier, to 'introduce into England a sufficient number of wolves to destroy the greater part of the population'![112] Even for wolves France, whose territory was continuous with the continental land mass and the forests of Germany and Poland, was inevitably a geographical crossroads. The Vercors was still infested with wolves in 1851.[113]

A prettier sight would have been the hazel-grouse, pheasants, white hares and white partridges in the Alps, or the red-legged partridges roused by the horses of Thomas Münzer,[114] a Nuremberg doctor who with his friends travelled in the mountainous Valence hinterland in 1494. There was an abundance of game in the Rauhe Alb in Wurttemberg in the sixteenth century, but the peasants were forbidden to use large dogs on them; this right was reserved for the foresters.[115] Meanwhile in Persia, not only were there wild boar, stags, bucks, gazelles, lions, tigers, bears and hares, but also prodigious quantities of pigeons, wild geese, ducks, turtledoves, crows, herons and two types of partridge.[116]

Naturally, the more deserted the region, the more freely animal life multiplied. Father Verbiest (1682) when he travelled with the Emperor of China's enormous suite (100,000 horses) in Manchuria, was a reluctant and exhausted participant in some fantastic hunts: a thousand stags and sixty tigers were killed in one day.[117] Mauritius was still empty of people in 1639, but turtledoves and hares were so numerous and so unafraid that they were caught by hand.[118] In Florida in 1690 'quantities of wild pigeons, parrots and other birds were so numerous that boats often came away full of birds and birds' eggs'.[119]

Of course everything was magnified in the New World: there was a superabundance of uninhabited regions (*despoblados*) interspersed with a few tiny towns at enormous distances from each other. The twelve large wooden carrioles drawn by thirty pairs of oxen that accompanied the bishop of Santiago de Chile, Lizarraga, in 1600, took about twenty days to travel from Cordoba to Mendoza, in what later became Argentina.[120] Indigenous animals were few, with the exception of ostriches, llamas and seals in the south.[121] Instead, the empty countryside had been filled with animals (horses and cattle) brought from Europe, and these had multiplied. Enormous herds of wild oxen had worn regular paths across the plain; they remained at liberty until the nineteenth century. The silhouettes of the herds of wild horses huddled together sometimes looked like vague hillocks against the horizon. In the pampas where not the tiniest piece of wood could be found, 'not even as large as a little finger', a *chapeton*, a newcomer to America, caught a glimpse of one such small hillock in the distance and cried out in delight: 'Let's go and cut some wood!'[122]

We could end on that anecdote, but there are even more evocative images – in Siberia for instance, which was opened up to the Russians at about the same time that America was to the West Europeans. In the spring of 1776, a party of

A boar-hunt in Bavaria, with spears and firearms (1531). Bayerisches National-museum. (Photo by the Museum.)

Russian officers mistimed their departure from Omsk on their way to Tomsk: the ice on the rivers had begun to melt. They had to go down the Ob on a makeshift raft (hollowed-out tree-trunks roped together). The journey was perilous, but according to the Swiss military doctor who left us an account of it, there were moments of diversion: 'I counted at least fifty islands on which there were so many foxes, hares and beavers that we saw them coming down to the water's edge ... and we had the pleasure of seeing a she-bear with four cubs walking along the bank'. There were also 'an alarming quantity of swans, cranes, pelicans, wild geese and various kinds of duck, especially red ones ... The swamps are full of bitterns and woodcock, and the forests filled with grouse and other birds ... After sundown, these armies of winged creatures made such a terrifying clamour that we could not hear ourselves speak.'[123] At the farthest extremity of Siberia the vast and almost empty Kamchatka peninsula[124] gradually came to life with the beginning of the eighteenth century. Hunters and merchants were attracted to it by fur-bearing animals. The skins were brought up to Irkutsk by merchants and from there reached either China, via the neighbouring fair of Kiakhta, or Moscow and thence the West. The fashion for sea-otter dates from that period. Previously it was only used for clothing by hunters and natives. The hunt suddenly assumed gigantic proportions with the sharp rise in prices. By about 1770, it had developed into a large-scale operation. The ships, built and fitted at Okhotsk, had large crews, because the natives, who were often harshly treated, were hostile: they had been known to burn a ship and murder its crew. And the expedition had to carry supplies for four years, importing biscuit and meal from far away. The tremendous cost of provisions put the whole business in the hands of the merchants of Irkutsk, who divided up expenses and profits by a system of shares. The expedition would go as far as the Aleutians and might take four or five years. The kill took place at the mouths of rivers, where the otters came in large numbers. The trappers, the *promyschlennik*, either followed the animals in canoes and waited until they were forced to surface for breath, or held off until the first ice-floes formed, when hunters and dogs could reach the otters (clumsy out of the water) easily. They then ran from one otter to another stunning them as they passed, finishing them off later. Sometimes fragments of ice-floe broke off, carrying hunters, dogs and otter corpses out to the open sea. Ships might become frozen in, in these northern seas, with no wood or food: the crew had to live off raw fish. The hardships did not deter hunters from flocking to the area.[125] In 1786, English and American vessels appeared in the North Pacific. Kamchatka was quickly cleared of its beautiful animals as a result of this hunting. The trappers had to look farther afield, as far as the American coast, even as far as San Francisco, where Russians and Spaniards clashed at the beginning of the nineteenth century – without making any great impact on the mainstream of history.

Even at the end of the eighteenth century, vast areas of the earth were still a garden of Eden for animal life. Man's intrusion upon these paradises was a tragic innovation. The craze for furs explains why the sailing ship, *The Lion*, carrying the Ambassador Macartney to China, discovered five terribly dirty inhabitants (three French and two English) on Amsterdam Island in the Indian Ocean, around the fortieth degree of latitude south, on 1 February 1793. Boats from Boston, which sold at Canton either beaver skins from America or seal skins from the island itself, had set the five men ashore during an earlier trip. They had organized gigantic slaughter (25,000 animals during a summer season). Seals were not the only fauna on the islands. There were penguins, whales, sharks and dogfish, as well as innumerable other kinds of fish. 'Hooks and lines speedily procured enough fish to feed for a week the crew of *The Lion*.' Tench, perch, and particularly crayfish were found in profusion in fresh-water estuaries. 'The sailors ... let down into the sea baskets, in which were baits of sharks' flesh. In a few minutes the baskets being drawn up, were found half-filled with crayfish.' The birds were a fresh source of wonder: albatrosses with yellow beaks, great black petrels, 'silver birds' and blue petrels. Blue petrels were night birds hunted by birds of prey and also by the seal-hunters who attracted them with lighted torches – so successfully that they 'kill multitudes of them. They constitute indeed the principal food of these people who think it very good. This blue petrel is about the size of a pigeon.'[126]

In fact, until the eighteenth century, a Jungle Book could have been written about almost any part of the globe. We must resist the temptation to venture

A Persian hunt in the seventeenth century: with hawk, spear, sword, firearms and abundant game. Detail of miniature, Musée Guimet, Paris. (Photo Jean-Abel Lavand.)

further into the animal kingdom: but these glimpses tell us how small were the inroads made by human settlement.

The eighteenth century: watershed of biological regimes

What was shattered in both China and Europe with the eighteenth century was a biological *ancien régime*, a set of restrictions obstacles, structures, proportions and numerical relationships that had hitherto been the norm.

Preserving the balance

There is a constant tendency towards equilibrium between the patterns of birth and deaths. Under the *ancien régime* the two coefficients were both at around the same figure: 40 per 1000. What life added, death took away. The parish registers of the small commune of La Chapelle-Fougerets[127] (today part of the suburbs of Rennes) recorded 50 baptisms in 1609. Reckoning on the basis of 40 births per 1000 habitants and therefore multiplying the number of baptisms by 25, it is possible to suggest that the population of this large village was around 1250. The English economist William Petty reconstructed the population on the basis of deaths in his *Political Arithmetick* (1690), multiplying the figure by 30 (which was actually an under-estimate of the death rate).[128]

In the short term, credit and debit kept pace, so that when one side gained, the other reacted. In 1451 we are told that plague carried off 21,000 people in Cologne; over the next few years, 4000 marriages were celebrated.[129] Even if these figures are exaggerated, as everything would seem to indicate, the compensation is obvious. In 1581, 790 people – ten times more than in normal times – died at Salzewedel, a small place in the old Brandenburg Marches. Marriages fell from 30 to 10. But in the following year, despite the reduced population, 30 marriages were celebrated, followed by numerous compensatory births.[130] Immediately after a plague that was said to have halved the population of Verona in 1637 (but the chroniclers exaggerate freely), the soldiers of the garrison, almost all French – many of whom had escaped the plague – married the widows, and life gained the upper hand again.[131] Throughout Germany, which had suffered grievously from the disasters of the Thirty Years War, there was a demographic revival once the bad times were over. This was the phenomenon of compensation in a country quarter or half destroyed by the horrors of war. An Italian traveller visiting Germany shortly after 1648, at a time when the European population as a whole was stationary or in decline, remarked 'that there were few men of an age to bear arms, but an abnormally high number of children'.[132]

When the balance was not restored quickly enough the authorities intervened: Venice, normally so jealously closed, passed a liberal decree on 30 October 1348, just after the terrible Black Death, granting complete citizenship (*de intus et de extra*) to every individual who would come and settle there with his family and possessions within the period of a year. It must be added that the towns, as a general rule, only survived thanks to new blood from outside. But ordinarily people came of their own accord.

Increases and declines therefore alternated in the short term, regularly compensating each other. This is invariably demonstrated (until the eighteenth century) by the zigzag curves representing births and deaths anywhere in the West – whether in Venice or Beauvais. Those most vulnerable – young children, who were always at risk, or anyone with precarious means of support – would be carried off by epidemics if the balance required it. The poor were always the first to be affected. Innumerable 'social massacres' took place during these centuries. At Crépy, near Senlis, in 1483, 'a third of the town goes begging about the countryside, and old people are dying in squalor every day'.[133]

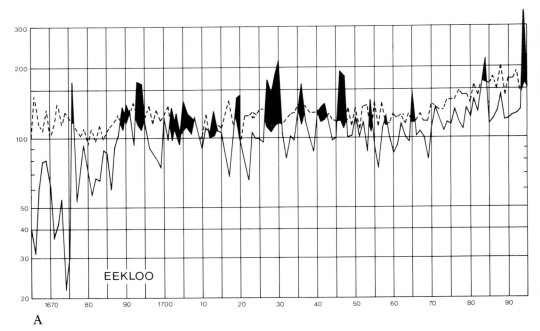

A

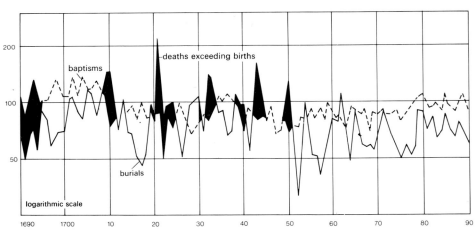

B

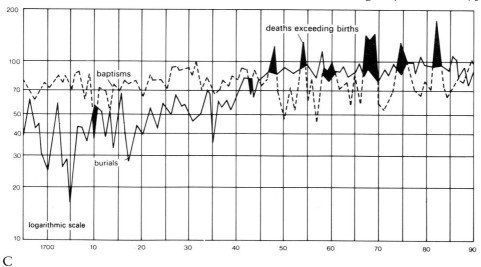

C

8 ANCIEN RÉGIME DEMOGRAPHY: BAPTISMS AND FUNERALS
Three examples: A. A Flemish town, Eekloo.
 B. A town in Provence.
 C. A town near Beauvais.
These case-studies, picked from hundreds of others, show the relationship between mortality and the birth rate. The areas shaded in black correspond to periods when there were more deaths than births. There are fewer such occasions as the eighteenth century advances, though there are exceptions, as the graph for Eyragues shows (B). Cf. also in Figure 9, the rise in mortality in France in 1779 and 1783. [After M. Morineau and A de Vos (A); R. Baehrel (B); and P. Goubert (C).]

Only with the eighteenth century did births gain over deaths, and this was to be the pattern regularly thereafter. But counter-attacks were still possible, as happened in France in 1772-3; and again in the population crisis that struck between 1779 and 1783 (see Figure 9). These alarms showed how precarious was an improvement of very recent origin and which was still subject to reverses, still at the mercy of the ever-hazardous balance between the demand for food and the possibilities of meeting it through production.

Famine

Famine recurred so insistently for centuries on end that it became incorporated into man's biological regime and built into his daily life. Dearth and penury were continual, and familiar even in Europe, despite its privileged position. A few overfed rich do not alter the rule. It could not have been otherwise. Cereal yields were poor; two consecutive bad harvests spelt disaster. These disasters were often absorbed in the Western world, possibly because of the climate. The same was true of China, where the early development of agricultural techniques, the construction of dykes and of a network of canals which could be used both for irrigation and for transport, and later the painstaking organization of the rice fields with their two harvests, made it possible for a certain balance to be maintained even after the demographic explosion of the eighteenth century. This was not the case in Muscovy, with its harsh, unreliable climate, nor in India where flooding and droughts could reach catastrophic proportions.

However, even in Europe, the 'miracle crops' – maize and potatoes, of which more later – took root quite late on, and modern intensive methods of agriculture were also slow to become established. For these and other reasons, famine constantly visited the continent laying it waste and destroying lives. A tragic forerunner of the Black Death was the devastation caused by food shortages between 1308 and 1318: beginning in northern Germany, then the centre and the east, they spread throughout Europe – to England, the Netherlands, France, southern Germany, the Rhineland – and even Livonia.[134]

Any national calculation shows a sad story. France, by any standards a privileged country, is reckoned to have experienced 10 *general* famines during the tenth century: 26 in the eleventh; 2 in the twelfth; 4 in the fourteenth; 7 in the fifteenth; 13 in the sixteenth; 11 in the seventeenth and 16 in the eighteenth.[135] While one cannot guarantee the accuracy of this eighteenth-century calculation, the only risk it runs is of over-optimism, because it omits the hundreds and hundreds of *local* famines (in Maine, in 1739, 1752, 1770 and 1785 for example),[136] and in the south-west in 1628, 1631, 1643, 1662, 1694, 1698, 1709 and 1713.[137] They did not always coincide with more widespread disasters.

The same could be said of any country in Europe. In Germany, famine was a persistent visitor to the towns and the flatlands. Even when the easier times came, in the eighteenth and nineteenth centuries, catastrophes could still happen: there were serious shortages in Silesia in 1730, in 1771-2 in Saxony and southern Germany;[138] and famine struck Bavaria, and moved beyond its frontiers in 1816-17: on 5 August 1817, the city of Ulm celebrated with thanksgiving the return to normal with the new harvest.

One could look for further statistics to Florence, which does not lie in a particularly poor region, but which experienced 111 years when people went hungry, and only sixteen 'very good' harvests between 1371 and 1791.[139] It is true that Tuscany, a hilly region concentrating on vines and olives, had been able thanks to its merchants, to count on Sicilian grain since the thirteenth century – and indeed could not have managed without it.

It would be rash to conclude that the towns, habitual grumblers, were the sole victims of these acts of God. They had warehouses, reserves, corn exchanges, purchases from abroad – in fact a whole policy directed towards future contingencies. Paradoxically the countryside sometimes experienced far greater suffering. The peasants lived in a state of dependence on merchants, towns and nobles,

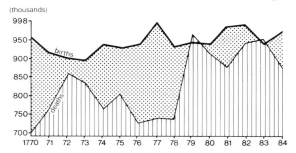

9 FRENCH POPULATION TRENDS BEFORE THE REVOLUTION
(From M. Reinhard and A. Armengaud, *Histoire générale de la population mondiale*.)

and had scarcely any reserves of their own. They had no solution in case of famine except to turn to the town where they crowded together, begging in the streets and often dying in public squares, as in Venice and Amiens in the sixteenth century.[140]

The towns soon had to protect themselves against these regular invasions, which were not purely by beggars from the surrounding areas but by positive armies of the poor, sometimes from very far afield. Beggars from distant provinces appeared in the fields and streets of the town of Troyes in 1573, starving, clothed in rags and covered with fleas and vermin. They were authorized to stay there for only 24 hours. But the rich citizens of the town soon began to fear that 'sedition' might be spread among the poor inside the town or in the surrounding countryside, and 'in order to make them leave, the rich men and the governors of the aforesaid town of Troye were assembled to find the expedient to remedy it. The resolution of this council was that they must be put outside the town … To do this, an ample amount of bread was baked, to be distributed amongst the aforesaid poor who would be assembled at one of the gates of the town, without being told why, and after the distribution to each one of his bread and a piece of silver, they would be made to leave the town by the aforesaid gate which would be closed on the last one and it would be indicated to them over the town walls that they go to God and find their livelihood elsewhere, and that they should not return to the aforesaid Troye before the new grain from the next harvest. This was done. After the gift the dismayed poor were driven from the town of Troye.'[141]

The attitude of the bourgeois hardened considerably towards the end of the sixteenth century, and even more in the seventeenth. The problem was to place the poor in a position where they could do no harm. In Paris the sick and invalid had always been directed to the hospitals, and the fit, chained together in pairs, were employed at the hard, exacting and interminable task of cleaning the drains of the town. In England the Poor Laws, which were in fact laws *against* the poor, appeared at the end of Elizabeth's reign. Houses for the poor and undesirable

'Feeding the hungry': one of the panels of an enamelled terracotta frieze by Giovanni della Robbia, representing various acts of charity. Sixteenth century, Pistoia, Hospital of the Ceppo. (Photothèque A. Colin.)

gradually appeared throughout the West, condemning their occupants to forced labour in workhouses, *Zuchthaüser* or *Maisons de force* for example, that body of semi-prisons, united under the administration of the *Grand Hôpital de Paris*, founded in 1656. This 'great enclosure' of the poor, mad and delinquent, as well as sons of good family placed under supervision by their parents, was one psychological aspect of seventeenth-century society, relentless in its rationality. But it was perhaps an almost inevitable reaction to the poverty and increase in numbers of the poor in that hard century. Significantly, in Dijon the municipal authorities went so far as to forbid the town's citizens to take in the poor or to exercise private charity. 'In the sixteenth century, the beggar or vagrant would be fed and cared for before he was sent away. In the early seventeenth century, he had his head shaved. Later on, he was whipped; and the end of the century saw the last word in repression – he was turned into a convict.'[142]

This was Europe. Things were far worse in Asia, China and India. Famines there seemed like the end of the world. In China everything depended on rice from the southern provinces; in India, on providential rice from Bengal, and on wheat and millet from the northern provinces, but vast distances had to be crossed and this contribution only covered a fraction of the requirements. Every crisis had wide repercussions. The famine of 1472, which hit the Deccan particularly harshly, caused large numbers who had escaped its consequences to emigrate to Gujerat and Malwa.[143] In 1555, and again in 1596, violent famine throughout north-west India, resulted in scenes of cannibalism, according to contemporary chroniclers.[144]

There was another terrible famine, almost everywhere in India, in 1630-31. A Dutch merchant has left us an appalling description of it: 'Men abandoned towns and villages and wandered helplessly. It was easy to recognize their condition: eyes sunk deep in the head, lips pale and covered with slime, the skin hard, with the bones showing through, the belly nothing but a pouch hanging down empty ... One would cry and howl for hunger, while another lay stretched on the ground dying in misery.' The familiar human dramas followed: wives and children abandoned, children sold by parents, who either abandoned them or sold themselves in order to survive, collective suicides.... Then came the stage when the starving split open the stomachs of the dead or dying and 'drew at the entrails to fill their own bellies'. 'Many hundred thousands of men died of hunger, so that the whole country was covered with corpses lying unburied, which caused such a stench that the whole air was filled and infected with it ... in the village of Susuntra ... human flesh was sold in open market.'[145]

Even when documents are not as detailed, one item is enough to convey the horror. In 1670 a Persian ambassador went to pay his respects to the Great Mogul, Aurangezeb. He returned home accompanied by 'innumerable slaves' (who were to be taken away from him at the frontier) whom 'he had had for almost nothing *because of the famine*'.[146]

We return hardened, consoled or resigned to privileged Europe as if from some nightmare journey. Western Europe only encountered similar horrors during the first dark centuries of the middle ages or else on its eastern borders, which were backward in so many respects. If one wants to measure 'the catastrophes of history by the proportion of victims claimed', writes one historian, 'the 1696-7 famine in Finland must be regarded as the most terrible event in European history'. A quarter or a third of the Finnish population disappeared at that time.[147] The East was the bad side of Europe. Famine raged there long

Spanish soldiers, starving and in rags, during the siege of Aire-sur-la-Lys. Behind them, the fortifications of the town. Detail from a painting by Pierre Snayers, 1641. (Photo Oronoz.)

after the eighteenth century, despite desperate recourse to 'famine foodstuffs' – wild herbs and fruit, formerly cultivated plants found amongst the weeds in fields, gardens, meadows, or the outskirts of forests.

However, this situation did sometimes recur in Western Europe, particularly in the seventeenth century, with the 'little ice age'. Near Blois in 1662 a witness reported that 'such poverty had not been seen for five hundred years'. The poor were on a diet of 'cabbage stumps with bran soaked in cod broth'.[148] The protest the Electors of Burgundy sent to the king in the same year recorded that 'famine this year has put an end to over ten thousand families in your province and forced a third of the inhabitants, even in the good towns, to eat wild plants'.[149] A chronicler adds that: 'Some people ate human flesh.'[150] Ten years earlier, in 1652, another chronicler, the *curé* Macheret indicated that 'the people of Lorraine and other surrounding lands are reduced to such extremities that, like animals, they eat the grass in the meadows, particularly those from the villages of Pouilly and Parnot in Bassigny ... and are black and as thin as skeletons'.[151] In 1693 a Burgundian noted 'the price of grain was so high throughout the realm that people were dying of hunger'; in 1694 near Meulan, wheat was harvested before it was ripe, 'large numbers of people lived on grass like animals'; the terrible winter of 1709 threw innumerable vagrants on to all the roads of France.[152]

All these gloomy examples should not of course be placed one after another. All the same let us not be too optimistic. Infallible signs of misery are the accounts of food deficiencies and the illnesses they caused: scurvy (which came into its own with the great sea voyages); pellagra, especially during the eighteenth century, as a result of an exclusive diet of maize; beri beri in Asia. The persistence of gruel and sops in the popular diet, and the bread made with inferior flours and only cooked once a month or every two months are equally revealing. The bread was almost always hard and mouldy. It was cut with an axe in some regions. In the Tyrol brown bread, made from pounded grain and very long-lasting, was baked two or three times a year.[153] The *Dictionnaire de Trévoux* (1771) says quite bluntly: 'The peasants are usually so stupid because they only live on coarse foods.'

Epidemics

One bad harvest was just about bearable; if there were two, prices went mad and famine set in. Famine was never an isolated event. Sooner or later it opened the door to epidemics,[154] which have their own individual cycles. Plague was the great, the terrible fear. 'A many-headed hydra', 'a strange chameleon', it assumed such varied forms that contemporaries unconsciously confused it with other diseases. Leader of the dance of Death, it was a fixture, a permanent structure in men's lives.

In fact it was only one disease among many others, intermingled in their

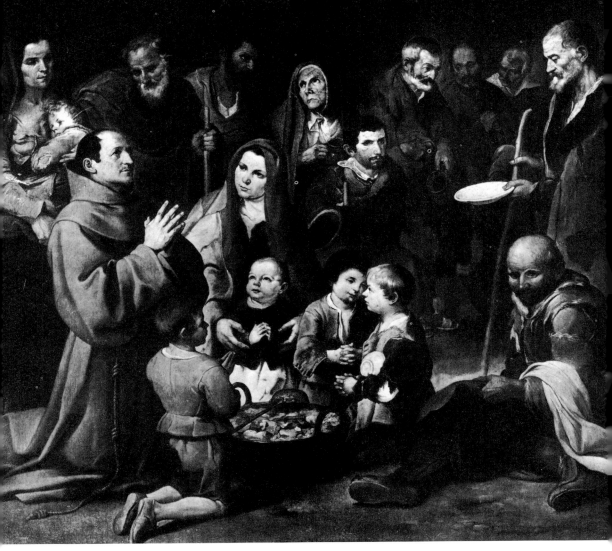

San Diego feeding the poor, a group of children and old people. A beggar holds out his begging-bowl. Painting by Murillo (1645). (Photo Anderson-Giraudon.)

frequent travels and contagious as a result of chaotic social mixing and the vast human reservoirs where disease could lie dormant until its next explosion. A whole book could be written on dense civilizations, epidemics and endemic diseases, and on the cycles according to which these determined travellers disappear and come back. To mention only smallpox: in 1775, when inoculation was beginning to be discussed, a medical book considered it 'the most general of all diseases'; ninety-five in every hundred people were affected; one in seven died.[155]

But a doctor today would at first glance scarcely know where he was among these diseases, obscured by their old names and the sometimes unusual descriptions of their symptoms. Furthermore there is no guarantee that they are always comparable to the diseases known today. Diseases change and have a history of their own, which depends on a possible modification of bacteria and viruses and of the human landscape in which they live.[156] Pure chance led Gaston Roupnel in 1922, with the help of a parasitologist friend, to discover that the 'purple fever' or purpura at Dijon and elsewhere in the seventeenth century referred to exanthematic typhus (transmitted by fleas).[157] 'Purple fever' was also used to describe the disease which in about 1780 'mowed down the poor Parisians of the Faubourg Saint-Marcel by the hundreds ... the gravediggers' arms were falling off'.[158] We still do not know exactly what it was.

What would the present-day doctor make of the plague in 1348 as described by Guy de Chauliac, whose *Grande Chirurgie* went into sixty-nine editions between 1478 and 1895? He gave two characteristic stages of the disease: first stage, quite long (two months), fever and spitting of blood; second stage, abscesses and pulmonary weakness. How would he diagnose the 1427 epidemic, inexplicably christened *ladendo* in Paris and described as a hitherto unknown malady? 'It begins in the back, as if one had a bad case of kidney stones, and is followed by the shivers; for eight to ten days one cannot drink, eat or sleep properly.' Then there was 'a cough which was so bad that when listening to a sermon people could not hear what the preacher was saying because of the great noise from the coughers'.[159] This was undoubtedly some sort of special influenza virus, like the 'Spanish flu' after the First World War or the 'Asian flu' that invaded Europe in 1956-8. Estoile described another variety:

> At the beginning of April (1595) the King (Henry IV) became very ill with a catarrh which distorted his whole face. Catarrhs like this were prevalent in Paris because it was very cold there for the time of year: they caused several strange and sudden deaths, *with the plague* [my italics] which spread in diverse places in the town; they were all scourges from God, which nonetheless produced as little visible improvement in conduct amongst the great as amongst the small.[160]

The sweating sickness on the other hand, *la suette anglaise* which ravaged England from 1486 to 1551, has today disappeared. It seems to have affected the heart and lungs and caused rheumatic pains; the victims had fits of shivering and sweated profusely and were often dead within hours. There were five major outbreaks – in 1486, 1507, 1518, 1529 and 1551 – which made many victims. Oddly enough, the disease which almost always struck first in London, never reached Wales or Scotland. And the epidemic of 1529, which was particularly violent, was the only one to cross the Channel, sparing France, but striking Holland and the Netherlands, Germany and even the Swiss cantons.[161]

And what was the disease that caused the epidemic in Madrid in August 1597 which, we are told, was 'non-contagious' and caused swelling of groin, armpit and throat? After the fever had broken out the sufferer was either cured in five or six days and recovered slowly; or died immediately. It must be added that these were poor people, who lived in damp houses and slept on the ground.[162]

There is another difficulty: different diseases break out simultaneously. 'They have scarcely anything in common except infection, such illnesses as diphtheria, *cholérine*, typhoid fever, *picotte*, smallpox, purple fever, the *bosse, dendo, tac* or *harion*, the *trousse galant* or *mal chaud*; or again whooping cough, scarlatina, grippe, influenza.'[163] This list was drawn up for France, but it applies elsewhere with variations. The current diseases in England were intermittent fevers, sweating sickness, chlorosis or 'green sickness', jaundice, consumption, falling sickness or epilepsy, vertigo, rheumatism, gravel, stones.[164]

The undernourished, unprotected population could offer little resistance to these massive attacks. I must admit that I was already more than half convinced by the Tuscan proverb I have often quoted: 'The best remedy against malaria is a well filled pot.' In confirmation, during the famine in Russia,[165] in 1921-3, an unimpeachable observer records that malaria broke out throughout the country and manifested the same symptoms as in tropical zones, even as far north as the Arctic circle. Undernourishment, on all the evidence, is a 'multiplying' factor in the spread of diseases.

There is another rule with no exceptions: epidemics jump from one human mass to another. Alonso Montecuccoli, sent to England by the Grand Duke of Tuscany, wrote (2 September 1603) that he would cross from Boulogne and not from Calais, where the English plague, following the trade route, had just arrived.[166] This is but a small example in comparison with the powerful waves that began in China and India and brought the plague to the West, via the ever-active relay points of Constantinople and Egypt. Tuberculosis was also an old scourge of Europe: Francis II (tubercular meningitis), Charles IX (pulmonary tuberculosis) and Louis XIII (intestinal tuberculosis) all fell victim to it (1560, 1574, 1643). But a form of tuberculosis more virulent than the established variety arrived, probably from India, in the eighteenth century. It was to become the leading disease of Romantic Europe and of the nineteenth century as a whole. Cholera also came from India, where it existed in an endemic state. It became general in the Peninsula in 1817 and then burst its bounds and swelled to a violent and terrible pandemic that soon reached Europe.

Another visitor, this time during the centuries actually covered by our study, was syphilis. Its origins are prehistoric, primitive skeletons having been found which bear its marks. There were known clinical cases before 1492. But syphilis reappeared after the discovery of pre-Columbian America: it was, people have said, the vengeance of the vanquished. Perhaps the most probable of the four or five theories supported by doctors today is the idea that the disease appeared – or rather reappeared – as a result of sexual relations between the two races (the influence of the *treponema pertenue* on the *treponema pallidum*).[167] In any case, the terrifying character of syphilis was revealed in Barcelona from the time of the celebrations of Columbus' return (1493), and it then spread rapidly. It was an epidemic, rapid and *mortal* illness. Within the space of four or five years

Treating syphilis by cauterization, from a woodcut dating from the late fifteenth century. Bibliothèque Nationale, Paris (Estampes).

Recepte en 'Pilules pour guerir le mal de Naples sans faire suër.

DROGVES.

Prenez.
{ *Miel blanc, ou de Narbonne, 2. onces.*
{ *Roses rouges seches pulverisées, 2. onces.*
{ *Precipité rouge,   demy once.*

PREPARATION.

Melez tout cela ensemble & incorporés le bien: Ensuite formés en de Pilules de la grosseur d'un Pois commun, pour l'usage suivant,
Donnés 4. ou 5. de ces Pilules aux plus foibles, pendant 3. matins de suite: Si le malade ne suë pas asses, vous augmenterez la dose,& il ne bougera pas du lit jusqu'à ce que le flux soit passé.

'Recipe for curing the Naples disease without making the patient sweat.' Mercury treatment in 1676.

it toured Europe, moving from one country to another under misleading names: Neopolitan disease, *mal français*, the French disease, or *lo mal francioso*; France, by virtue of its geographical position, had the doubtful honour of being most often named as its source. The barber-surgeons of the Hôtel-Dieu as early as 1503 were claiming that they could cure the disease by cauterization with red-hot irons. This virulent form of syphilis reached China in 1506-7.[168] Afterwards, and with the help of mercury, it assumed its classical attenuated form in Europe, evolving slowly with its cures and specialist hospitals (the Spittle in London).[169] Before that stage was reached it had probably attacked every level of society at the end of the sixteenth century, from beggars (male and female) to nobles and princes. Malherbe, known as the Père Luxure, 'boasted that he had sweated out the pox three times'.[170] Gregorio Marañon,[171] a famous historian and doctor, added a basis of hereditary syphilis to the customary diagnosis contemporary doctors made on Philip II. This can be retrospectively applied, without risk of error, to all princes of the past. Thomas Dekker (1572-1632), the dramatist, put into words what everyone in London was thinking when he said: 'As every throng is sure of a pick-pocket, as sure as a whoore is of the clyents all Michaelmas Tearme, and of the pox after the Tearme.'[172]

A Chinese syphilis victim. Illustration from 'Varieties of pox', painting on silk, eighteenth century. Bibliothèque Nationale, Paris, Cabinet des Estampes. (Photo by B.N.)

The plague

The enormous dossier of evidence on the plague is constantly growing. The disease was at least two-fold: pulmonary plague, a new form of illness that came to light with the pandemic of 1348 in Europe; and the older bubonic plague (buboes form in the groin and become gangrenous). These were the marks of God, 'God's tokens' or more usually simply 'tokens': in French, *tacs*, like the metal or leather counters tradesmen put into circulation. 'A single one can prove fatal...' The Black Death (pulmonary) was due to a virus transmitted by fleas from the *Mus Rattus*. It used to be said that these rats invaded Europe and its granaries immediately after the Crusades, avenging the East as the *treponema pallidum* avenged America in the early days of its discovery in 1492.

This over-simple and moralistic explanation should probably be abandoned. The *Mus Rattus*, the black rat, was noticed in Europe from the eighth century, even in the Carolingian period; the same applies to the brown rat (*Mus Decumanus*) which was not itself a carrier of plague germs and according to popular lore eliminated the *Mus Rattus*, the species responsible for the epidemics. Finally, the Black Death did not, as used to be thought, arrive in central Europe in the thirteenth century, but in the eleventh at the latest. Moreover the brown rats settled in the cellars of houses, while the domestic rat chose to live in attics close to food supplies. Their invasions overlapped before the process of exclusion began.

All this does not mean that rats, and fleas from rats, did not play a part in spreading disease. On the contrary, a very intensive study[173] (30,000 documents are involved) of the outbreaks of plague at Uelzen in Lower Saxony in 1560-1610 proves that they did. If the retreat of the disease in the eighteenth century is to be explained by external, or as economists would say, exogenous conditions, we can cite the substitution of stone for wooden houses after the great urban fires of the sixteenth, seventeenth and eighteenth centuries; increased personal and domestic cleanliness; and the removal of small domestic animals from dwellings – all steps which discouraged the breeding of fleas. But medical research in these fields is still continuing, and even since Yersin discovered the specific bacillus of the plague in 1894, discoveries that could modify present theories are still possible. For example, the bacillus itself is said to be preserved in the soil of certain areas of Iran and capable of infecting rodents. Were these danger zones therefore by-passed by the normal routes leading to Europe in the eighteenth century? One hesitates to ask this question, or to say that India and China, so frequently accused by historians, might plead extenuating circumstances.

Whatever the cause or causes, the scourge was subdued in the West in the eighteenth century. It made its last spectacular appearance in the famous plague of Marseilles in 1720. But it continued to be deadly in Eastern Europe: Moscow experienced a murderous plague in 1770. The Abbé de Mably wrote (in about 1775): 'The war, the plague or Pugachev have certainly carried off as many men as the partition of Poland.'[174] Kherson in 1783 and Odessa in 1814 received further terrible visitations. The last large-scale attacks known in Europe were not in Russia but in the Balkans, in 1828-9 and 1841. This was the Black Death, and once again wooden houses played a part in its spread.

Bubonic plague, for its part, remained endemic in hot and humid areas: southern China, India and at the very gates of Europe in North Africa. The plague of Oran (described by Albert Camus in *La Peste*) was in 1942.

The above account is extremely incomplete. But the over-plentiful documentation defeats the historian's good intentions by its very quantity. Preliminary research work would be required to construct annual charts of the localization of the disease. They would indicate its depth, extent and repeated violence: Besançon reported plague 40 times between 1439 and 1640; Dôle fell victim in 1565, 1586, 1629, 1632 and 1637; Savoy in 1530, 1545, 1551, 1564-5, 1570, 1580 and 1587; in the sixteenth century the whole of the Limousin was attacked 10 times, Orleans experienced it on 22 occasions; Seville, the heart of the world, was hit particularly hard in 1507-8, 1571, 1582, 1595-9, 1616 and 1648-9.[175] Losses were heavy every time, even if they fell short of the chroniclers' exaggerated figures, and even if there were 'little' plagues and some false alarms.

Detailed calculations for Bavaria from 1621 to 1635 produce appalling averages: for every 100 deaths in a normal year, Munich counted 155 in an abnormal year; Augsburg 195; Bayreuth 487; Landsburg 556 and Strauling 702. Children under a year old were primarily affected on each occasion, and women tended to be more susceptible than men.

Descriptions and examples must be compared – in the same way as all these figures have to be investigated and compared – because they often present the same drama, list the same more or less effective measures (quarantines, surveillance, inhalants, disinfection, roadblocks, close confinement, health certificates – *Gesundheitspässe* in Germany, *cartas de salud* in Spain), the same panic-stricken suspicions and the same social pattern.

At the first sign of the disease, the rich whenever possible took hurried flight to their country houses; no one thought of anything but himself: 'the plague making us cruel, as doggs, one to another' noted Samuel Pepys in August 1665.[176] And Montaigne tells how he wandered in search of a roof when the epidemic reached his estate, 'serving six months miserably as a guide' to his 'distracted family, frightening their friends and themselves and causing horror wherever they tried to settle'.[177] The poor remained alone, penned up in the contaminated town where the State fed them, isolated them, blockaded them and kept them under observation. Boccaccio's *Decameron* is a series of conversations and stories told in a villa near Florence at the time of the Black Death. Maître Nicolas Versoris, lawyer in the Paris Parlement, left his lodgings in August 1523. But three days after he reached his pupils' country house at the 'Grange Batelière', then outside Paris, his wife died of the disease – an exception that confirms the value of the customary precaution. The plague in Paris in that summer of 1523 once again struck at the poor. Versoris wrote in his *Livre de Raison*: 'death was principally directed towards the poor so that only a very few of the Paris porters, who used to run errands for a few pence and who had lived there in large numbers before the misfortune, were left.... As for the district of Petiz Champs, the whole area was cleared of poor people who previously lived there in large numbers.'[178] One bourgeois from Toulouse placidly wrote in 1561: 'the aforesaid contagious disease only attacks poor people ... let God in his mercy be satisfied with that.... The rich protect themselves against it.'[179] J.-P. Sartre was right when he wrote, 'The plague only exaggerates the relationship between the classes: it strikes at the poor and spares the rich.' In Savoy, when an epidemic was over, rich people, before returning to their carefully disinfected houses, would instal a poor woman inside for a few weeks, as a sort of guinea pig, to test at risk of her life whether the danger had really departed.[180]

Plague also multiplied what we would call dereliction of duty: municipal magistrates, officers and prelates forgot their responsibilities; in France whole parlements emigrated (Grenoble 1467, 1589, 1596; Bordeaux 1471, 1585; Besançon 1519; Rennes 1563, 1564). Cardinal d'Armagnac quite naturally forsook his town of Avignon, when it was affected by the disease in 1580, for Bedarrides and then Sorgues; he only returned after ten months' absence when all danger

A procession against the plague, led by the Pope. A monk has collapsed in the street. From the *Très Riches Heures* of the Duc de Berry, f° 71 v°, Condé Museum at Chantilly. (Photo Giraudon.)

had disappeared. 'He could say,' a bourgeois of Avignon noted in his journal, 'the opposite of the Gospel, *Ego sum pastor et non cognovi oves meas*.'[181] So who are we to blame Montaigne, mayor of Bordeaux, who did not resume his post at the time of the 1585 epidemic, or François Dragonet of Fogasses, rich Avignon citizen of Italian origin, whose leases provided for a time when he would be obliged to leave the town (which he did in 1588, during a fresh plague) and lodge with his farmers: 'In case of contagion (God forbid), they will give me a room at the house ... and I will be able to put my horses in the stable on my way there and back, and they will give me a bed for myself.'[182] When plague broke out in London in 1664 the Court left the town for Oxford and the richest members of the population hastened to follow suit with their hurriedly assembled families, servants and baggage. There was no litigation in the capital; 'the lawyers were all in the country'; ten thousand houses were abandoned, some with deal planks nailed over doors and windows; doomed houses were marked with a cross in red chalk.[183] It is remarkable how closely Daniel Defoe's retrospective (1720) account of the 1664 plague of London corresponds to the customary pattern, repeated thousands of times with the same actions (the dead thrown 'for the most part on to a cart like common dung'),[184] the same precautions, despair and social discrimination.[185]

No disease today, however great its ravages, gives rise to comparable acts of folly or collective dramas.

A careful observer who escaped the plague at Florence in 1637 (it was the great adventure of his life) describes the barricaded houses and empty streets, forbidden to all but food suppliers; the occasional priest might pass by, but more frequently it would be a patrol; sometimes the coach of a privileged individual granted rare permission to break the seals on his own house. Florence was dead: no business activities and no religious services – except for the odd mass which the officiant celebrated at the corner of the street and in which the people participated from behind closed windows.[186]

Father Maurice de Tolon, writing about the plague of Genoa in 1656,[187] in *Le Capucin charitable*, enumerated the precautions to be taken: do not talk to any suspect person from the town when the wind is blowing from him towards you; burn aromatics for disinfection; wash or better still burn clothes and linen belonging to suspected cases; above all pray; and help the guards. The extremely wealthy town of Genoa, the background to these comments, was subjected to clandestine looting because its rich palaces were abandoned. Meanwhile the dead piled up in the streets; the only way to rid the town of carcasses was to load them on to boats which were put out to sea and burned. As a sixteenth-century specialist, I must admit that the scenes presented by the plague-stricken towns in the following century, and their fatal losses, have long surprised me and continue to do so. The situation clearly deteriorated from one century to

Cattle plague in 1745. Dutch engraving by J. Erssen. (Rotterdam, Atlas Van Stolk.)

the next. Plague occurred in Amsterdam every year from 1622 to 1628 (the toll: 35,000 dead). It struck Paris in 1612, 1619, 1631, 1638, 1662, 1668 (the last).[188] It should be noted that after 1612 in Paris 'the sick were forcibly removed from their homes and transferred to the Hôpital Saint-Louis and to the maison de Santé in the faubourg Saint-Marcel'.[189] Plague struck London five times between 1593 and 1664-5, claiming, it is said, a total of 156,463 victims.

Everything improved in the eighteenth century. Yet the plague of 1720 in Toulon and Marseilles was extremely virulent. According to one historian, a good half of the population of Marseilles succumbed.[190] The streets were full of 'half-rotted bodies, gnawed by dogs'.[191]

The cycle of diseases

Diseases appear and alternately establish themselves or retreat. Some die out. This happened in the case of leprosy, which may well have been conquered in Europe in the fourteenth or fifteenth centuries by draconian isolation measures. (Today, strangely enough, lepers at large never spread infection.) It was also true of cholera, which disappeared from Europe during the nineteenth century; of smallpox, which seems to have been eliminated for good during recent years; and it may be true of tuberculosis and syphilis, which are now in retreat before the miracle of antibiotics. One cannot, however, make any definite claims for the future, because syphilis is said to be reappearing today with some virulence. This had also been true of plague: after a long absence between the eighth and the fourteenth century, it broke out violently as the Black Death in 1348, ushering in a new plague cycle which did not die out until the eighteenth century.[192]

In fact these virulent attacks and retreats might have originated from the fact that humanity had lived behind barriers for so long, dispersed, as it were, on different planets, so that the exchange of contagious germs between one group and another led to catastrophic surprise attacks, depending on the extent to which each had its own habits, resistance or weakness in relation to the pathogenic agent concerned. This is demonstrated with amazing clarity in a recent book by William H. MacNeill.[193] Ever since man escaped from his primitive brutishness and came to dominate all other living creatures, he has exerted over them the *macroparasitism* of the predator. But he is at the same time constantly attacked and besieged by minute organisms – germs, bacilli and viruses – and is thus a prey to *microparasitism*. Is this mighty struggle at some deep level the essential history of mankind? It is perpetuated by linked chains of living beings: the pathogen which may, under certain circumstances survive independently, usually passes from one living organism to another. Man, who is one, but not the only target of this continual bombardment, adapts himself, secretes antibodies and may arrive at an acceptable equilibrium with these foreign creatures that live with him. But the process of adaptation and immunity takes time. If some pathogen escapes from its 'biological niche' and is unleashed on a hitherto untouched population which has not acquired natural defences, the result is a catastrophic epidemic. MacNeill thinks, and he may well be right, that the pandemic of 1348 which we call the Black Death and which ravaged virtually the whole of Europe, was the result of Mongol expansion which reactivated the silk routes and made it easier for pathogens to travel across continental Asia. Similarly, when the Europeans at the end of the fifteenth century unified the trade routes of the world, pre-Columbian America was in turn struck a terrible blow by diseases previously unknown there, which the Europeans brought with them. In return, a new form of syphilis struck Europe and reached China in record time, by the early sixteenth century, whereas maize and sweet potatoes which were both 'American' in origin did not arrive in the Far East until the last years of the century.[194] Nearer home, a similar biological drama occurred in 1832, when cholera from India arrived in Europe.

But it is not only a question of man's greater or lesser vulnerability, or greater or lesser immunity to infection, in these cases of diseases which first attack then retreat. Historians of medicine have suggested, rightly in my view, that every pathogenic agent has its own history, which runs parallel to that of its victims, and that the evolution of diseases largely depends upon changes, and sometimes mutations, in the agents themselves. Here lies the cause of the complicated advances and retreats of disease, the surprise appearances or epidemic outbreaks, and the quiescence and sometimes complete disappearance of certain illnesses. One example, with which we are today familiar, of mutations in a microbe or virus, is that of the disease we call *grippe*, or influenza.

The word *grippe*, denoting a disease which 'seizes' or takes hold of its victims, may only date from the spring of 1743.[195] But the illness itself is known, or thought, to have existed in Europe since the twelfth century. It was one of the diseases unknown in the Americas, and it decimated the Indian population there when it arrived. In 1588, it laid low (but did not kill) the entire population of Venice, to the point where the Grand Council was empty – something that never happened during outbreaks of plague; and the epidemic did not stop there, but spread to Milan, France, Catalonia and the Americas.[196] Influenza or grippe was already the disease that spreads 'like wildfire', just as it is today. Voltaire, on 10 January 1768 wrote: 'The grippe, on its way round the world, has passed through our little Siberia (Ferney, near Geneva) and has attacked my old and sickly face a little.' But a multitude of symptoms are covered by the generic name: to mention only the most famous outbreaks, the so-called 'Spanish influenza' of 1918 – which caused more deaths than the First World War – was not at all the same disease as the 'Asian flu' of 1957. In fact, there are several different strains of influenza, and if vaccines against them are not entirely reliable, it is because the influenza virus is undergoing constant and rapid mutation. The vaccines are almost always one epidemic behind. Indeed in some laboratories, in order to get ahead in the race against time, efforts have been made to make current flu viruses mutate in test tubes, so as to combine in a single vaccine all the possible mutants which might correspond to future outbreaks. The flu virus is perhaps a particularly unstable one, but other pathogenic agents may well have been transformed with the passage of time. This might explain the variations in tuberculosis, which is by turns mild and virulent; or the waning in the strain of cholera originating in Bengal, which may be being replaced today by a strain from Indonesia; or the appearance of new and sometimes relatively short-lived diseases, like the 'sweating-sickness' in sixteenth-century England.

1400-1800: a long-lasting biological ancien régime

So the human battle for existence was waged on at least two fronts: against the scarcity and inadequacy of the food supply – this was 'macro-parasitism' – and against the many and insidious forms of disease that lay in wait. On both fronts, mankind was in a precarious situation throughout the *ancien régime*. Before the nineteenth century, wherever he lived, man could only count on a short expectation of life, with a few extra years in the case of the rich. 'Notwithstanding the baneful luxuries in which the European rich indulge, and the disorders of repletion, inactivity and vice to which they are subject,' according to one English traveller (1793), 'the mean duration of their lives exceeds about ten years that of their inferiors, whom excessive fatigue has contributed to wear out before their time; whom poverty has deprived of the means of proportional comfort and subsistence.'[197]

This separate demography for the rich is lost in the scale of our averages. In the Beauvaisis in the seventeenth century 25 to 33% of new-born children died within twelve months; only 50% reached their twentieth year.[198] Thousands of details demonstrate the precariousness and brevity of life in those far-off times. 'No one was surprised to see the young Dauphin, Charles (the future Charles v) govern France at the age of seventeen, in 1356, and disappear in 1380 at forty-two with the reputation of a wise old man.'[199] Anne de Montmorency, the *Connétable* who died on horseback at the battle of Porte Saint-Denis at the age of seventy-four (1567) was an exception. The emperor Charles v was an old man when he abdicated at Ghent in 1555 at the age of fifty-five. His son, Philip II, who died at seventy-one (1598), had aroused the liveliest hopes and fears amongst his contemporaries at each danger signal during his twenty-year period of failing health. Finally none of the royal families escaped the terrifying rate of infant mortality of the period. A 'guide' to Paris in 1722[200] lists the names of princes and princesses laid to rest since 1662 in the Val-de-Grâce founded by Anne of Austria: they are mainly children a few days, months or years old.

The poor endured an even harsher fate. In 1754 an 'English' author could still note: 'Far from being well-to-do, the peasants in France do not even have the necessary subsistence; they are a breed of men who begin to decline before they are forty for lack of a return proportionate to their efforts: humanity suffers by comparing them with other men and above all with our English peasants.

With the French labourers, their external appearance alone proves the deterioration of their bodies.'[201]

As for Europeans who lived outside their continent, and were unwilling 'to subject themselves to the habits and diet of the countries to which they have newly come and obstinately pursue their own fantasies and passions there ... [the result is that] they find their own graves'.[202] These reflexions of the Spaniard Coreal, apropos of Porto Belo, are echoed by the Frenchman Chardin, and by the German Niebuhr, who attributed the high mortality among Englishmen in India principally to their own misguidedness, their excessive consumption of meat and the 'violent wines of Portugal', which they drank during the heat of the day, and their exceedingly tight clothing, designed for European climates and very different from the 'loose and floating' garments of the natives.[203] But if Bombay was 'the graveyard of the English', the city's climate had something to do with it: it was so lethal that there was a proverb 'Two monsoons in Bombay are a man's lifetime'.[204] At both Goa, where the Portuguese lived in great style, and Batavia, another pleasure city for the European, the other side of an elegant and expensive existence was the frightful mortality rate.[205] Rough colonial America was no more charitable. Remarking upon the death of George Washington's father, Augustine, at the age of forty-nine, a historian wrote: 'But he died too soon. To succeed in Virginia, you had to survive your rivals, neighbours and wives.'[206]

The same applied to non-Europeans. At the end of the seventeenth century a traveller in Siam remarked: 'Despite the abstemiousness which prevails amongst the Siamese ... they do not appear to live any longer' than people in Europe.[207] A Frenchman wrote of the Turks in 1766: 'Although the Turkish physicians and surgeons do not have the knowledge that our Faculties of Medicine and surgery claim to have had for a hundred years, they live as old as we do, if they can escape the terrible scourge of the plague which continually devastates this Empire.'[208] Osman Aga, a Turkish interpreter who learnt German during a long period of captivity in 1688-99 and described his life in Christendom in a lively and sometimes picaresque fashion, was married twice. Only two children of the three daughters and five sons born of his first marriage survived; his second marriage produced three children with only two survivors.[209]

These then are the facts that go to make up the biological *ancien régime* we are discussing: a number of deaths roughly equivalent to the number of births; very high infant mortality, famine; chronic under-nourishment; and formidable epidemics. These pressures hardly relaxed even with the advances made in the eighteenth century, and then at different rates in different places of course. Only a certain section of Europe, and not even all of Western Europe, began to break free of them.

The advance was slow. We historians run the risk of exaggerating its pace. Renewed outbreaks of mortality still marked the whole of the eighteenth century in France as we have already mentioned. They are also evident in the decennial averages for Bremen (where deaths exceeded births from 1710 to 1729 and from 1740 to 1799); at Königsberg in Prussia where deaths ran at an average rate of 32·8 per 1000 for the period from 1782 to 1802 but reached 46·5 in 1772, 45 in 1775 and 46 in 1776.[210] Think of the repeated bereavements in the family of Johann Sebastian Bach. J.P. Süssmilch, the founder of social statistics, said in 1765: 'In Germany ... peasant and poor die without ever having employed the slightest remedy. No one ever thinks of the doctor, partly because he is too far away, partly ... because he is too expensive.'[211] The same story comes from Burgundy at the same period: 'The surgeons live in the town and never leave it without a fee.' At Cassy-les-Vitteaux, a visit from a doctor and medicaments cost forty-odd livres. 'The unfortunate inhabitants today would rather die than call in surgeons to help them.'[212]

And women were terribly vulnerable because of repeated childbirth. However, although boys were more numerous than girls at birth (102 boys are still being born for every 100 girls today) all the figures we possess since the sixteenth century show that there were more women than men in the towns and even in the country (with a few exceptions, including Venice for a short period and later St Petersburg). The villages of Castille, where investigations were made in 1575 and 1576, all had a surplus of widows.[213]

In any summing-up of the major characteristics of this *ancien régime*, the important thing to isolate is probably its capacity for short-term revival, which was as powerful if not as rapid as the sudden disasters that struck down the living. In the long term, compensatory movements set in imperceptibly but ultimately had the last word. The ebb never entirely removed what the preceding tide had brought in. This difficult and miraculous long-term rise was the triumph of the force of numbers, on which so much depended.

The many against the few

Numbers dictate the division and organization of the world. They give each mass of population its own particular weight, and thereby virtually command its levels of culture and efficiency, its biological (and even economic) patterns of growth, and indeed its pathological destiny: the densely populated countries of China, India and Europe are great reservoirs of disease, which may lie dormant or come to life, and are quick to spread.

But numbers also affect the relations between one population centre and another, relations reflected not only in the history of peacetime - trade, exchange and barter - but also in the long history of war. A book devoted to material life can scarcely ignore war. It is a multiform activity, always present, even at the earliest historical level. And numbers pre-determine its most obvious features, lines of force, repetitions and typologies. In battle, as in everyday life, there is no

Street scene in Goa, at the end of the sixteenth century. Bibliothèque Nationale, Paris, Cabinet des Estampes. (Photo Giraudon.)

equality of opportunity. Groups can be almost unerringly classified according to their numbers into masters and subjects, proletarians and privileged, faced with the possibilities, the normal opportunities of the time.

In this sphere as in others, numbers are certainly not the only factors at work. Technology weighs heavily in war, as well as in peace. But even if technology does not favour *all* dense populations equally, it is none the less always a product of numbers. These statements seem obvious to twentieth-century man. Numbers to him mean civilization, power, the future. But could the same be said of earlier times? Numerous examples immediately suggest the contrary. However paradoxical it may seem – and it seemed paradoxical to Fustel de Coulanges[214] examining the respective fates of Rome and Germania just before the barbarian invasions – the unsophisticated and less numerous side sometimes won or *seemed to win*, as Hans Delbrück demonstrated by calculating the ridiculously small number of barbarians who conquered Rome.[215]

Against the barbarians

When civilizations are defeated or seem to be defeated, the conqueror is always a 'barbarian'. It is a figure of speech. A barbarian to a Greek was anyone who was not Greek, to a Chinaman anyone not Chinese. The great pretext for

European colonization in the past was bringing 'civilization' to barbarians and primitive peoples. Of course, it was the civilized peoples who gave the barbarian his reputation, and at best he only half deserved it. We need not go to the other extreme and take literally the defence of Attila by the historian Rechid Saffet Atabinen,[216] but what certainly does require revision is the myth of barbarian strength. Whenever the barbarian won, it was because he was already more than half civilized. He had spent a long time in an antechamber and knocked not once but ten times before gaining admission to the house. He was, if not completely civilized, at least deeply imbued with the adjacent civilization.

This is what the classic case of the Teutons confronting the Roman Empire in the fifth century proves. But the process was also constantly repeated in the history of the Arabs, Turks, Mongols, Manchus and Tartars. The Turks and Turcomans were the transporters and caravaners *par excellence* on the routes from central Asia to the Caspian and Iran. They visited adjacent civilizations and often became completely integrated into them. The Mongols of Ghengis Khan and Kublai Khan, though barely (if at all) emerged from their Shamanism, do not give the impression of unsophisticated barbarism. They soon fell captive to Chinese civilization in the east and to visions of Islam in the west, and became divided and uprooted from their own destiny. The Manchus, who conquered Peking in 1644 and then the rest of China, were a mixed people. Mongol elements were numerous, but Chinese peasants had moved into Manchuria beyond the Great Wall of China very early on. Barbarians if you like, but imbued with Chinese influence beforehand, and driven to their conquest by the social and economic difficulties of the huge land of China by a sort of remote control.

Above all, the barbarian only triumphed in the short term. He was very rapidly absorbed by the conquered civilization. The Germans 'barbarized' the Empire and then drowned in the land of wine;[217] the Turks became the standard-bearers of Islam from the twelfth century; Mongols, then Manchus, were lost amongst the Chinese masses. The door of the conquered house closed behind the barbarian.

The disappearance of the great nomads before the seventeenth century

It must also be noted that the 'barbarians' who were a real danger to civilization belonged almost entirely to one category of men: the nomads of the deserts and steppes in the heart of the Old World – and it was *only* the Old World that experienced this extraordinary breed of humanity. These arid and abandoned lands formed an endless explosive fuse from the Atlantic to the waters of the Pacific. It burst into flames at the slightest spark and burned along its entire length. For when a dispute arose among these horse- and camel-men, as harsh on each other as they were on other peoples, or a drought or population increase drove them out from their pasturage, they invaded their neighbours' lands. As

Mongol horsemen hunting (fifteenth century). Topkapi Museum, Istanbul. (Photo Roland Michaud-Rapho.)

year followed year, the repercussions from these movements extended over thousands of miles.

They represented speed and surprise at a period when everything moved slowly. On the Polish frontier, the alarm that any threat of Tartar cavalry regularly set off, even in the seventeenth century, almost immediately caused a mass levy. Fortresses had to be equipped and stores laid in, and if there was still time, guns supplied, horsemen mobilized and barricades set up. If, as on so many occasions, the raid succeeded – across the mountains and the empty spaces of Transylvania for example – it hit town and countryside like a scourge, beyond comparison even with what the Turks did. At least the Turks customarily withdrew their troops at the start of winter, after Saint George's Day. The Tartars remained on the spot, wintering with their families, eating the countryside down to the root.[218]

Furthermore these raids (we can recapture the sense of terror they created from contemporary Western news-sheets) were nothing compared with the great

Caravan travelling to the desert. Illustration of al-Maqâmat, al Harîrî, Ms. ar. 5847, f° 31. (Photo Bibliothèque Nationale, Paris.)

nomad conquests in China and the Indies. Europe had the advantage of escaping them, despite various recorded episodes (Huns, Avars, Hungarians, Mongols). It was protected by the barrier of the Eastern peoples. Its peace was founded on their misfortunes.

The nomads' strength also lay in the carelessness and relative weakness of the men who held the approaches to the civilizations. Northern China was underpopulated before the eighteenth century – an empty space for anyone to enter. In India the Muslims took the Punjab early on – in the tenth century – and thenceforth the gates to Iran and the Khyber Pass stood open. The strength of the barriers in eastern and south-eastern Europe varied from century to century. The nomads' world rotated between these areas of negligence, weakness and sometimes ineffectual vigilance. A physical law drew them now westwards, now eastwards, according to whether their explosive life would ignite more easily in Europe, Islam, India or China. Eduard Fueter's classic work drew attention to the existence, in 1494, of a cyclonic zone, an enormous vacuum over the fragmented Italy of princes and urban republics.[219] All Europe was attracted towards this storm-creating area of low pressure. In the same way hurricanes persistently blew the peoples of the steppes eastwards or westwards, according to the lines of least resistance.

For example, China under the Mings drove the Mongols out in 1368 and burned their great centre at Karakorum in the Gobi desert.[220] But the long period of inertia that followed the victory caused a powerful nomad return eastwards. The space created behind the advance of their first waves tended to attract new ones and the movement had repercussions farther and farther westwards, at intervals of one, two, ten and twenty years. The Nogais crossed the Volga from west to east in about 1400, and it was then that the turn of the tide was felt in Europe. The peoples who had flowed towards the West and frail Europe for over two centuries now turned eastwards for the next two or three, attracted by the weakness of distant China. Our map summarizes this change of direction. Its decisive episodes were the conquest of northern India by Baber (1526) and the capture of Peking by the Manchus in 1644. The hurricane had once again struck India and China.

In the west, as a result, Europe was breathing more easily. The Russian seizure of Kazan and Astrakhan in 1551 and 1556 was not achieved solely by gunpowder and arquebuses; reduced nomadic pressure in southern Russia also facilitated the Russian drive towards the black earth country of the Volga, Don and Dniester. In the course of this action, old Muscovy lost a number of its peasants, who fled from the strict authority of their lords. The land they abandoned passed into the hands of new arrivals: peasants from the Baltic countries and Poland. The gaps this group left unoccupied were filled in their turn, and at the appropriate moment, by peasants from Brandenburg or Scotland. It was a sort of a relay race. This is the view that two distinguished historians, Alexandre and Eugène Kulischer, take of this silent history, this man-slide from Germany to China. Its currents run underground, as though concealed beneath the skin of history.

Later the conquest of China by the Manchus led to a new order in the 1680s. Northern China, protected and shielded by advance posts – Manchuria, where the conquerors had come from, then Mongolia, Turkestan and Tibet – was repopulated. The Russians, who had seized Siberia without opposition, met Chinese resistance along the valley of the Amur and were obliged to recognize the treaty of Nertchinsk (7 September 1689). The Chinese consequently reached from the Great Wall to the neighbourhood of the Caspian Sea. Even before this success, the manifold world of pastoral peoples had turned back towards the west, crossing in the opposite direction the narrow gateway of Dzungaria, the classic route for migration between Mongolia and Turkestan. Only this time the vast masses in flight no longer found a door open to receive them. In the west they met resistance from a new Russia under Peter the Great and the forts, strongholds and towns of Siberia and the lower Volga. Russian literature in the following century is full of accounts of these repeated battles.

In fact, this marked the end of the great career of the nomads. Gunpowder had triumphed over speed. Even before the end of the eighteenth century civilization had won at Peking and Moscow, Delhi and Teheran (after the lively

Afghan crisis). The nomads, condemned to stay at home, appeared in their true colours: a poor section of humanity, put in its place and from now on accepting it. In short, they represent an exceptional case of a long parasitical existence that came to an end once and for all. It is almost a marginal episode despite its very widespread repercussions.

The conquest of space

As a general rule, the civilizations played and won. They took over 'cultures' and primitive peoples. And they also took over unoccupied territory. In such cases, the most advantageous, everything had to be built up from scratch, but this was the Europeans' great good fortune in three-quarters of America. The Russians enjoyed the same advantage in Siberia, and the British in Australia and New Zealand. How lucky it would have been for the whites in South Africa if the Boers and the British had not been faced with a large and growing black population!

In Brazil the primitive Indian slipped away when the Portuguese appeared. The Paulist *bandeiras* scattered over more or less empty land. In less than a century the adventurers from São Paulo had overrun, although not colonized, half the South-American continent, from the Rio de la Plata to the Amazon and Andes, in their pursuit of slaves, precious stones and gold. They met no resistance until the Jesuits formed their Indian reserves, which the *paulistas* shamelessly pillaged.

The same process was repeated by the French and British in North America and the Spaniards in the north Mexican deserts, faced with a few primitive Chichimec Indians. They were still being systematically hunted down in the seventeenth century; every year, starting from November, they were run to earth 'like wild animals'. Things were more difficult in Argentina and particularly in Chile, because the Indian had at least acquired the horse from his conqueror; the Araucanians continued to be tough adversaries until the beginning of the twentieth century.[221] The real issue was not conquest of men (they were annihilated) but of space. From now on it was distance that had to be conquered. In the sixteenth century the means of this silent conquest were the slow carts from the Argentine pampas drawn by pairs of oxen, the caravans of mules from Iberian America or the covered wagons of the nineteenth-century westwards trek in the United States. The journey invariably ended at the colonial frontier, a pioneer zone from which everything sprang up. The colonists' life started from rock bottom in this distant border country: their numbers were too few for social life to impose itself; everyone was his own master. This attractive anarchy lasted for some time before order was established. Meanwhile the frontier would have moved a little farther towards the interior and the same temporary anarchic scenes would be re-enacted. This is the moving frontier that F.J. Turner

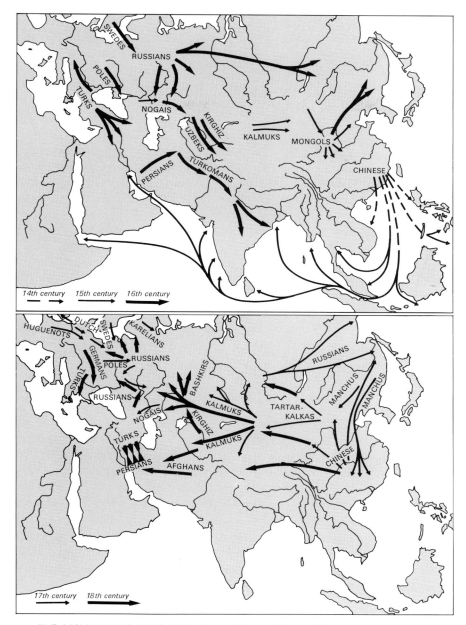

10 EURASSIAN MIGRATIONS FROM THE FOURTEENTH TO THE EIGHTEENTH CENTURY

The difference between the two maps is clear: on the first, overland migrations move from west to east, on the second from east to west. Note on the first map the Chinese *maritime* expansion, of such importance at the beginning of the fifteenth century, and the convergence of overland movements on India and China. On the second, the reestablishment of order by the Manchus in the seventeenth century (capture of Peking, 1644) leads to a huge Chinese expansion inland and the halt of the Russians. The nomads are pushed back towards the west and Russian Europe. (*After* A. & E. Kulischer.)

romantically interpreted (1921) as the real birth of America and of its strongest original characteristics.²²²

The easy conquest of empty or almost empty space also lay open to the great Russian expansion in the sixteenth century, when salt merchants, fur-hunters and Cossacks successfully took possession of Siberia. Sharp resistance broke out but soon collapsed. Towns sprang up – fortresses, road stations, bridges, staging-posts for carriages, horses and sledges (Tobolsk in 1587, Okhotsk in 1648, Irkutsk near Lake Baikal in 1652). For a certain doctor of Swiss origin with the Russian armies,²²³ Siberia even in 1815 was remembered only by exhausting days on horseback which could only end when a small stronghold or town offering the necessary accommodation had been reached. If a merchant travelling by sledge in winter missed his stopping point he ran the risk of being irretrievably buried beneath the snow with his retinue, animals and merchandise. A road and urban system slowly took shape. The Amur basin was reached in 1643, the immense Kamtchatka peninsula discovered in 1696. Russian explorers reached Alaska in the following century and colonists settled there in 1799. These were rapid but precarious acquisitions and all the more remarkable for that. When Bering moved to Okhotsk for his voyages of discovery in 1726 he found only a few Russian families in the citadel there. In 1719 John Bell travelled on a main road to Siberia and 'for six days saw neither houses nor inhabitants'.²²⁴

The resistance of cultures

When the advance was no longer into empty space everything became more complicated. This is quite a different story. There is no possibility of confusing the *Ostsiedlung*, the famous 'Germanic colonization' of eastern lands, and the saga of the American frontier, despite the efforts of comparative history. Colonists from Germania in the broad sense (often from Lorraine or the Netherlands) settled east of the Elbe from the twelfth to the thirteenth century and even in the fourteenth, by means of political or social arrangements, and also by force. The newcomers built their villages in the midst of vast forest clearings, laid out their houses along the roads, probably introduced heavy ploughs with iron ploughshares, created towns and imposed German law on both these and the Slav towns – the Magdeburg law for the mainland and the Lübeck for the seas. This involved an immense migration. But the colonization took place within an already established Slav people with fairly solid organizational structures capable of resisting the newcomers, and if necessary of swallowing them up. Germania's misfortune was its late formation and the fact that it only began its march eastwards after the settlement of the Slav peoples, who were more firmly attached to their land and established in their towns (this is proved by excavations) than was formerly believed.²²⁵

The same process recurs in connection with Russian expansion, not in

Siberia, which was almost empty, but again in the sixteenth century towards the southern rivers,[226] Volga, Don and Dniester. This expansion was also marked by widespread peasant colonization. The steppe between the Volga and the Black Sea was not densely settled but was overrun by nomad peoples – the Nogais and Tartars from the Crimea. These formidable horsemen were the vanguard of Islam and of the vast Turkish empire that supported them and occasionally threw them forward. It had even saved them from the Russians by supplying them with firearms, an asset the defenders of the khanates of Kazan and Astrakhan had lacked.[227] They were therefore not adversaries to be scorned. Tartar raids took them to the near-by lands of Transylvania, Hungary, Poland and Muscovy, which they cruelly devastated. In 1572, one of their raids captured Moscow. The Tartars sold innumerable Slav prisoners (Russians and Poles) as slaves on the Istanbul market. It is known that Peter the Great's attempt to open 'a window' on the Black Sea in 1696 failed; the failure was not made good until Catherine II's reign a hundred years later. Even then the Tartars were not eliminated; they remained in occupation until the Second World War.

Colonization by Russian peasants would in any case have been unthinkable without the strongholds and military 'marches' and without the help of those outlaws the Cossacks. As horsemen, they could counter an adversary with extreme mobility; as boatmen, they went up and down the rivers, carrying their boats from one reach to another; some 800 of them came from the Tanais in about 1690 to throw their canoes into the Volga in pursuit of the 'Kalmyck Tartars'; as sailors, they pirated the Black Sea in boats crammed with sail, from the end of the sixteenth century.[228] This side of modern Russia was therefore not built on a *tabula rasa* – any more than the Russian advance into the Caucasus or Turkestan in the nineteenth century (which once again brought it face to face with Islam) took place effortlessly or without surprise.

Other examples could support this account: the late and ephemeral colonization of Black Africa by the European powers in the nineteenth century or the conquest of Mexico and Peru by the Spaniards. These immature civilizations, which were really cultures, collapsed in the face of a small number of men. Today these countries are once more Indian or African.

A culture is a civilization that has not yet achieved maturity, its greatest potential, nor consolidated its growth. Meanwhile – and the waiting period can be protracted – adjacent civilizations exploit it in a thousand ways, which is natural if not particularly just. History is full of examples of this type of economic exploitation; the trade along the coasts of the Gulf of Guinea, a familiar feature from the sixteenth century, is typical. The Kaffirs of Mozambique on the shores of the Indian Ocean claimed that if the monkeys 'do not talk it is because they are afraid that they will be made to work'.[229] But they themselves made the mistake of talking and buying cotton goods and selling gold dust. The strong always adopted the same very simple tactics: the Phoenicians and Greeks in their trading-posts and colonies; the Arab merchants on the Zanzibar coast from the eleventh century; the Venetians and Genoese at Caffa and Tana in the thirteenth century; and the Chinese in the Indian Archipelago, which had been their market for gold dust, spices, pepper, slaves, precious woods and swallows' nests even before the thirteenth century. During the period covered by this book, a host of Chinese transporters, merchants, usurers, pedlars and middlemen exploited these 'colonial' markets. If China remained so uninventive and so backward at the capitalist level, despite its intellectual power and its discoveries (paper money for example), it is to the extent that this exploitation was so easy and widespread. The Chinese had things too easy.

It is only a step from market to colony. The exploited have only to cheat, or to protest, and conquest immediately follows. But it has been proved that the cultures, the semi-civilizations (the term is even applicable to the Tartars in the Crimea) were no mean adversaries. They were pushed back but they reappeared; they were stubborn enough to survive. They could not be permanently deprived of their future.

Civilization against civilization

When civilizations clash the consequences are dramatic. Today's world is still embroiled in them. One civilization can get the better of another: India's tragedy resulted from the British victory at Plassey (1757), which marked the beginning of a new era for Britain and the whole world. Not that Plassey (or rather Palassy, near present-day Calcutta) was an exceptional victory. The French could claim that Dupleix or Bussy were just as successful. But Plassey had immense consequences, which is how great events are recognized: they have a sequel. In the same way the absurd Opium War (1840-2) marked the beginning of a century of 'inequality' for China, colonized without really being so. As for Islam, it foundered completely in the nineteenth century, with the possible exception of Turkey. But China, India and Islam (or rather its various parts) recovered their independence with the series of decolonization measures after 1945.

So certain stormy conquests looked at retrospectively, through the eyes of men today, seem like episodes, whatever their duration. They are achieved quickly or slowly. Then, one fine day, they collapse like stage sets.

I am not suggesting that the path of history, thus telescoped and simplified, has been entirely dominated by numbers. It is not simply a question of strength or sheer weight. But numbers have mattered, throughout the centuries and we would do well to remember it. They provide one of the regular explanations, or rather constraints or constants of material life. If one neglects the role played by war for instance, a whole social, political and cultural (religious) area is immediately left out of account. And exchanges lose their meaning, since they are often unequal. Europe cannot be understood without its slaves and its subject economies. China similarly cannot be understood if we ignore the savage cultures within the country that defied it and the distant conquered lands outside it that lived in its orbit. All these things figure in the balance of material life.

We have used numbers to give a first glimpse of the different destinies of the world between the fifteenth and the eighteenth centuries. Men were divided into great masses as unevenly equipped to deal with their material life as the different groups within a given society. Thus the collective personalities who will be introduced in the pages that follow are presented on a world scale. They will appear even more in the second volume, which will be devoted to the pre-eminence of economic life and capitalism; categories that probably separate the world more sharply than material life, into developed and backward regions, according to a classification with which the dramatic reality of the present world has made us familiar.

2

Daily Bread

MEN'S DIET between the fifteenth and the eighteenth centuries essentially consisted of vegetable foods. This was clearly the case in pre-Columbian America and Black Africa, and strikingly so in the Asiatic rice-growing civilizations, not only in earlier times but today. The early settlement and then the spectacular increase in population in the Far East were only possible because of the small amount of meat eaten. The reasons for this are very simple. If the choices of an economy are determined solely by adding up calories, agriculture on a given surface area will always have the advantage over stock-raising; one way or another it feeds ten to twenty times as many people. Montesquieu made the point with reference to the rice-growing countries: 'Land which elsewhere is used to feed animals there directly serves as sustenance for men.'[1]

But everywhere in the world, and not only from the fifteenth to the eighteenth centuries, any population-increase beyond a certain level means greater recourse to vegetable foods. The choice between cereals and meat depends on the number of people. This is one of the great tests of material life: 'Tell me what you eat, and I will tell you who you are.' A German proverb using a play on words, says the same thing: *Der Mensch ist was er isst* (man is what he eats).[2] His food bears witness to his social status and his civilization or culture.

A journey from a culture to a civilization, or from a low density of population to a relatively high one (or vice versa), can mean significant changes in diet for a traveller. Jenkinson, the leading merchant of the Muscovy Company, arrived in Moscow in 1558 from distant Archangel and proceeded down the Volga. Before reaching Astrakhan, he saw on the river bank 'a great heard of Nagay Tartars'. These were nomadic shepherds ('towne or house they had none') who robbed and murdered and knew none but the skills of war, who neither ploughed nor sowed, and who had nothing but scorn for the Russians they fought. How could such Christians, they said, be men, since they not only ate wheat, 'the top of a weede', but drank it too (since beer and vodka were made from grain). The Nagays drank milk and ate meat, which was quite different. Jenkinson continued his journey across the deserts of Turkestan, risking death from thirst or hunger. When he reached the valley of the Amu Dar'ya, he found fresh water, mares' milk and meat from wild horses, but no bread.³ The same differences and the same exchange of insults between herdsmen and husbandmen were just as likely to be found in the West, between the graziers of Bray and the cereal-growers of the Beauvaisis, for instance,⁴ or between the Castilians and the cattle-farmers of the Béarn, 'cowherds' as the southerners called them – but they gave as good as they got. More spectacular, and particularly visible in Peking, was the contrast between the eating habits of the Mongols – and later Manchus – who ate meat in large slices, in the European style, and the attitude towards food of the Chinese. For the Chinese, cooking was an almost ritual art, in which basic cereals – *fan* – were always served with an accompaniment known as the *ts'ai*, in which vegetables, sauces and spices were skilfully combined with a little meat or fish, which had to be cut up into small pieces.⁵

Europe was on the whole a region of meat-eaters: 'butchers had catered for the belly of Europe for over a thousand years'.⁶ For centuries during the middle ages, its tables had been loaded with meat and drink worthy of Argentina in the nineteenth century. This was because the European countryside, beyond the Mediterranean shores, had long remained half empty with vast lands for pasturing animals, and even in later times its agriculture left plenty of room for livestock. But Europe's advantage declined after the seventeenth century. The general rule of vegetable supremacy seemed to be re-asserting itself with the increase in population in Europe up to at least the middle of the nineteenth century.⁷ Then and only then, scientific stock-raising and massive arrivals of meat from America, salted and then frozen, enabled it to break its fast.

Furthermore the European, true to his long-established tastes, regularly and promptly demanded they be catered for when he was overseas. Abroad, the lords and masters ate meat. They stuffed themselves with it unrestrainedly in the New World, recently populated by herds from the Old. Their appetite for meat roused opprobium and astonishment in the Far East: 'One has to be a very great lord in Sumatra,' said one seventeenth-century traveller, 'to have a boiled or roast chicken, which moreover has to last for the whole day. Therefore they say that two thousand Christians [meaning Westerners] on their island would soon exhaust the supply of cattle and poultry.'⁸

These dietary choices and the conflicts they implied were the result of very long-term processes. Maurizio goes so far as to write: 'A thousand years bring scarcely any changes in the history of diet.'⁹ In fact the broad outlines of man's dietary history were laid down and directed by two ancient revolutions. At the end of the Paleolithic Age the 'omnivores' moved on to hunting large animals. 'Great carnivorism' was born and the taste for it has never disappeared: 'a craving for flesh and blood, a "hunger for nitrogen", in other words for animal protein.'¹⁰

The second revolution, in the seventh or sixth millennium before the Christian era, was neolithic agriculture with the arrival of cultivated cereals. Now fields were cultivated, at the expense of hunting-ground and extensive grazing.

The Harvesters' Meal, by Brueghel the Younger, private collection, Brussels. (Photo Giraudon.)

As the centuries passed, the expanding population was reduced to eating vegetable foods, raw or cooked, often insipid and always monotonous whether they were fermented or not: gruels, sops and bread. From now on, history records two opposing species of humanity: the few who ate meat and the many who fed on bread, gruel, roots and cooked tubers. In China in the second millennium, 'the administrators of the great provinces were designated ... meat-eaters'.[11] In ancient Greece it was said that 'the eaters of barley gruel have no desire to make war'.¹² An Englishman centuries later (1776) stated: 'Vigour and Fortitude of Heart are much more generally found in Persons that live on Flesh, than in such as live on lighter Meat.'¹³

Having said this, we will concentrate first on the food of the majority between the fifteenth and the eighteenth centuries and therefore on those foods supplied by agriculture, the oldest industry of all. Wherever it began, agriculture had from the start been obliged to opt for one of the major food-plants; and had been built up around this initial choice of priority on which everything or almost everything would thereafter depend. Three of these plants were brilliantly successful: wheat, rice and maize. They continue to share world arable land between them today. The 'plants of civilization',¹⁴ they have profoundly organized man's material and sometimes his spiritual life, to the point where they have become almost ineradicable structures. Their history and the 'determinism of civilization'¹⁵ they have exercised over the world's peasantry and human life in general are the subject of the present chapter. Our journey from one to the other of these cereals will take us round the world.

Harvest-time in India in the sixteenth century, on the Malabar Coast. (Photo F. Quilici.)

Wheat

Wheat is primarily – but not only – found in the West. Well before the fifteenth century, it was growing on the plains of northern China side by side with millet and sorghum. It was 'planted in holes' there and not reaped but 'uprooted with its whole stem', with a hoe. It was exported by the Yun Leang Ho – 'the grain-bearing river' – up to Peking. It was even found from time to time in Japan and southern China where, according to Father de Las Cortes (1626), the peasant sometimes succeeded in obtaining a wheat harvest between two harvests of rice.[16] This was simply an extra, because the Chinese 'did not know how to knead bread any more than they knew how to roast meat' and because, as a minor product, 'wheat [in China] is always cheap'. Sometimes they made a sort of bread from it, cooked in steam over a cauldron and mixed 'with finely chopped onions'. The result, according to one Western traveller, was 'a very heavy dough that lay like a stone on the stomach'.[17] Biscuit was made at Canton in the sixteenth century, but it was for Macao and the Philippines. Wheat also provided the Chinese with vermicelli, gruels and lard cakes, but not bread.[18]

An excellent type of wheat was also grown in the dry plains of the Indus and in the upper Ganges, and immense caravans of oxen effected exchanges of rice and wheat across all India. In Persia a rudimentary type of bread, a plain biscuit made without leaven, was generally on sale at a low price. It was often the result of enormous peasant labour. In the neighbourhood of Ispahan for example, 'the wheat lands are heavy and need four or even six oxen to till them. And a child is placed on the yoke of the first pair to drive them on with a stick'.[19] And of course wheat grew all round the Mediterranean, even in the oases of the Sahara, and especially in Egypt. As the Nile floods in summer, the crops there are always produced in winter, when the water has receded from the land. The climate at this time of year is scarcely favourable to tropical plants but it suits wheat, which is also found in Ethiopia.

From Europe, wheat travelled far and made many conquests. Russian colonization carried it eastwards to Siberia, beyond Tomsk and Irkutsk; as early as the sixteenth century, the Russian peasant established its success in the black earth country of the Ukraine (where Catherine II eventually completed her conquests in 1793). Wheat had triumphed there well before that date, even somewhat inopportunely: 'At present,' states a report of 1771, 'piles of grain the size of houses, enough to feed all Europe, are again rotting in Podolia and Volhynia.'[20] The same catastrophic superabundance happened in 1784. Wheat was 'at such a low price in the Ukraine that many landowners have abandoned its cultivation', noted a French agent.[21] 'However, stocks of this grain are already so plentiful that they not only feed a large part of Turkey but even supply exports for Spain and Portugal.' And for France as well, via Marseilles. Boats from Marseilles took on grain from the Black Sea either in the Aegean islands or in the Crimea, for example at Gozlev, the future Eupatoria, the crossing of the Turkish straits being effected, one surmises, by administrative collusion.

In fact, the great period of 'Russian' wheat was still to come. The arrival in Italy of boats loaded with Ukrainian wheat in 1803 seemed like a disaster to the landowners. The same threat was denounced in the French Chamber of Deputies a little later in 1818.[22]

Wheat had crossed the Atlantic from Europe well before these events. In Latin America it had to contend with excessively hot climates, destructive insects and rival crops (maize and manioc). Its success in America came later on, in Chile; on the banks of the St Lawrence; in Mexico; and later still in the English colonies in America, in the seventeenth and particularly the eighteenth centuries. At that time Boston sailing ships were carrying flour and grain to the sugar islands of the Caribbean, then to Europe and the Mediterranean. From 1739, American ships were unloading grain and flour in Marseilles.[23] In the nineteenth century, wheat triumphed in Argentina, southern Africa, Australia, the Canadian prairies and the Middle West, everywhere asserting by its presence the expansion of European civilization.

Wheat and other grains

To return to Europe: as soon as one looks at the question of grain, one realizes what a complicated phenomenon it is. It would be better to put it in the plural – *los panes*, as so many Spanish texts say. In the first place there were different qualities of grain: in France the best was often called 'the head of the corn': sold side by side with it were medium-quality wheat, 'small corn' or maslin, a mixture of wheat and another cereal, often rye. Moreover, wheat was never grown by itself. Despite its great age, even older cereals grew alongside it. Spelt, a cereal with a 'dressed grain', was still grown in the fourteenth century in Italy; in 1700 in Alsace, the Palatinate, Swabia and the Swiss uplands, where it was regarded as suitable for making bread; and in the late eighteenth century in Gelders and the county of Namur (where it was chiefly used, like barley, for pig-feed and to make beer); and until the early nineteenth century in the Rhône valley.[24] Millet was even more widely grown.[25] When Venice was besieged by the Genoese in 1372, it was saved by its stocks of millet. In the sixteenth century, the Venetian government deliberately kept stocks of this long-lasting cereal (it could sometimes be kept for twenty or so years) in the fortified towns of the Terra Firma. And millet rather than wheat was sent to the *presidios* in Dalmatia or the islands of the Levant when they were short of food.[26] Millet was still grown in Gascony, Italy and central Europe in the eighteenth century. But it produced a very coarse foodstuff to judge by the comments of a Jesuit at the end of the century. He admired the use the Chinese made of their various millets and exclaimed: 'With all our progress in the sciences of curiosity, vanity and uselessness, our peasants in Gascony and the Bordelais *Landes* are as little advanced as they were three centuries ago in methods of making their millet into a less uncivilized and less unhealthy food'.[27]

Wheat had other and more important associates; for example barley, which was used to feed horses in the south. 'No barley harvest, no war', could have been said in the sixteenth century and later, of the long Hungarian frontier where battles between Turks and Christians were inconceivable without cavalry.[28] Towards the north, hard grains gave way to soft grains, barley to oats and more especially rye, which came late to the north – probably not before the great invasions of the fifth century; after this it seems to have become established and spread there at the same time as triennial rotation.[29] Boats from the Baltic, very soon attracted farther and farther from home by hungry Europe, carried as much rye as wheat. First they came as far as the North Sea and the Channel, then to the Iberian ports on the Atlantic and finally, on a massive scale at the time of the great crisis of 1590, as far as the Mediterranean.[30] All these cereals were used to make bread, even in the eighteenth century, whenever wheat was in short supply. 'Rye bread,' wrote a doctor, Louis Lemery, in 1702, 'is not as nourishing as wheat and loosens the bowels a little.' Barley bread, he added, 'is refreshing but less nourishing than wheat or rye bread'; only the northern peoples make bread from oats 'which suits them very well'.[31] But it is a harsh fact that throughout the eighteenth century, in France, arable land was almost equally divided between *'bled'* (that is bread cereals, wheat and rye) and *'menus grains'* (or lesser cereals: barley, oats, buckwheat, millet); and that rye, which was about equal to wheat in 1715, was grown in a ratio of two to one in 1792.[32]

Another expedient was rice, which had been imported from the Indian Ocean since classical antiquity. Traders in the middle ages rediscovered it in the commercial ports of the Levant, and in Spain where the Arabs had established the crop very early on: rice from Majorca was sold at fairs in Champagne in the fourteenth century; and rice from Valencia was exported as far afield as the Netherlands.[33] From the fifteenth century onwards it was grown in Italy and sold at a low price on the market at Ferrara. A person who laughed easily was said to have eaten rice soup – a play on words: *Che aveva mangiato la minestra di riso*.

Rice later spread into the lands of the peninsula, bringing into being vast estates (up to 1000 hectares) in Lombardy, Piedmont, even in Venetia, Romagna, Tuscany, Naples and Sicily. When these rice fields succeeded, their capitalist organization turned the peasant labour force into a proletariat. It had already become *il riso amaro*, bitter rice, harsh taskmaster to the men who produced it. Similarly rice played an important role in the Turkish Balkans.[34] It also reached America; at the end of the seventeenth century Carolina became a great exporter via England.[35]

But it was an emergency foodstuff in the West, barely tempting the rich, although they sometimes ate rice cooked in milk. Boats laden with rice from Alexandria in Egypt were 'an expedient to feed the poor' in France in 1694 and

1709.³⁶ As early as the sixteenth century, rice flour was mixed with other flours to make bread for the people during famines in Venice.³⁷ In France it was eaten in hospitals, military barracks and ships. Distributions to the people by Paris churches often included 'economical rice' mixed with mashed turnips, pumpkins and carrots, cooked in water. The saucepans were never washed so as not to waste the leftovers and 'deposit'.³⁸ According to the experts, cheap bread could be made from rice mixed with millet and distributed to the poor 'so that they could be satisfied from one meal to the next'. This was somewhat equivalent to China's provision for its poor 'who could not buy tea': hot water in which beans and vegetables had been cooked, plus cakes of 'crushed beans made into a paste'. The same beans, boiled as usual, 'providing a sauce to soak the food. . . .' Can these have been soya beans? In any case the product was inferior, intended to satisfy the hunger of the poor, like rice or millet in the West.³⁹

Everywhere, one finds a clear correlation between wheat and supplementary cereals. It already appears in the curves that can be drawn for English prices after the thirteenth century:⁴⁰ grain prices tended to move in unison during a fall; during a rise, the relationship was not quite so close, as rye, the food of the poor, rose sharply during periods of scarcity to even higher points than wheat at times. Oats, on the other hand, lagged behind. 'The price of wheat always increases much more than that of oats,' taught Dupré de Saint-Maur (1746) because of 'our custom of living on wheaten bread [the rich at least – my correction] while horses are put to graze in the countryside as soon as the price of oats rises'.⁴¹ Talking about wheat and oats amounted to saying people and horses. The normal ratio was three to two, according to Dupré de Saint-Maur (he called it a 'natural' ratio like the old economists who wanted all prices to be in a natural relationship, of one to twelve in the case of gold and silver). 'In a given period, whenever a *setier* [approximately eight pints] of oats . . . was selling at about a third less than a *setier* of wheat, things were in their natural relationship.' A breakdown in this ratio was a sign of famine, and the greater the discrepancy the more serious the famine. 'In 1351 a *setier* of oats was worth a quarter of a *setier* of wheat, in 1709 a fifth, in 1740 a third. Thus prices were higher in 1709 than in 1351, and in 1351 than in 1740.'

This argument is probably sound within the limits of the facts immediately available to the author. To say that it amounts to a law during the period from 1400 to 1800 is another matter. For example, between 1596 and 1635 and probably during the greater part of the sixteenth century, oats were worth roughly half what wheat was worth in France.⁴² The 'natural' ratio of three to two only appeared in 1635. It would be too simple to follow Dupré de Saint-Maur and conclude that there was a concealed scarcity in the sixteenth century and to blame this on the troubles of the period, arguing that things returned to normal in about 1635 with the return of relative *internal* peace. It could just be as well be argued that France under Richelieu entered what the textbooks call the Thirty Years War in 1635; therefore the price of oats – without which there

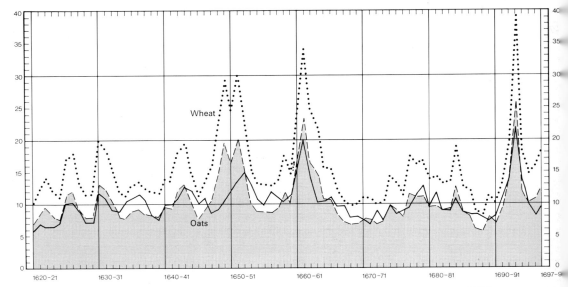

11 THE PRICE OF WHEAT AND OATS ACCORDING TO THE PARIS MARKET LISTINGS

The dotted line represents what the price of oats *would have been* according to the relationship Dupré de Saint-Maur considered 'natural' (i.e. ⅔ the price of wheat).

could be no horses, cavalry or artillery trains – rose sharply.

All the bread crops added together never created abundance; Western man had to adapt himself to chronic scarcities. He compensated for them in the first place by the regular consumption of vegetables or flour substitutes made from chestnuts or buckwheat, which was grown in Normandy and Brittany from the sixteenth century, being sown after the corn harvest and ripening before winter.[43] Buckwheat, incidentally, is not one of the gramineae but a 'pseudo-cereal' belonging to the polygonaceae; it was known, however, as *blé noir* (black wheat). Chestnuts yielded flour, and biscuit known as 'tree bread' in the Cévennes and Corsica. In Aquitaine (where they were called *ballotes*) and elsewhere, they often filled the role taken over by potatoes in the nineteenth century.[44] People relied on chestnuts to a larger degree in southern countries than is usually thought. Charles v's major-domo, living with his master at Jarandilla near Yuste in the Castilian Estremadura (1556), noted: 'It is the chestnuts that are good here, not the wheat, and what wheat there is is horribly expensive.'[45]

On the other hand consumption of 'acorns and roots' as in Dauphiné during the winter of 1674-6 was quite abnormal, and a symptom of terrible famine. Lemery incredulously reported in 1702 that 'there are still places where these acorns are used for the same purpose'.[46]

Pulses, lentils, beans, black, white and greyish-brown peas and chick-peas

Gathering chestnuts in the fourteenth century. Illustration from *Tacuinum sanitatis in medicina*. (Photo B.N., Paris.)

were really supplementary cereals and also a cheap source of protein. The Venetian documents called them *menudi* or *minuti* (minor foods). When a village in Terra Firma lost its *menudi* following a summer tornado, as frequently happened, the misfortune was immediately reported to the Venetian authorities and induced their intervention. The thousands of documents that place these minor foodstuffs on an equal footing with wheat itself prove that they were considered 'cereals'. For instance a boat from Venice or Ragusa could be commissioned to load either wheat or beans at Alexandria in Egypt. A Captain-General of Grenada looking for chick-peas and beans for the fleet wrote that they were difficult to come by in sufficient quantity and that their 'price was the same as wheat' (2 December 1539).[47] A Spanish letter from a *presidio* in Africa about 1536 mentioned that the soldiers there preferred *garbanzos* (chick-peas) to wheat or biscuit.[48] The *Biave*, the Venetian Corn Exchange, always took account in its forecasts and estimates of the harvest, of the supply of cereals and pulses as a whole. The wheat harvest had been good, it noted for example in 1739, but it was a poor season for *minuti* or minor foods, which at the time included beans and millet.[49] Excavations of early medieval villages in Bohemia have shown that peas rather than wheat provided the staple diet. The *Preis-courant* for Bremen in 1758 gives prices for cereals and pulses one after another (*Getreide* and *Hülsenfrüchte*). Similarly, the market records of Namur and

Luxemburg in the seventeenth and eighteenth centuries show that rye, buckwheat, barley, oats, spelt and peas figured alongside wheat.[50]

Wheat and crop rotation

Wheat cannot be cultivated on the same land for two years running without serious harmful effects. It has to be rotated. Hence the amazement of Westerners in China at the sight of rice growing continually 'on the same ground', wrote Father de Las Cortes (1626), 'which they never leave fallow any year, as in our Spain'.[51] In Europe, and wherever it was cultivated, wheat was sown in a different field from one year to the next. The space it required had to be two or three times the surface area it occupied, according to whether it could return to the same 'break' one year in two or three. It was therefore caught up in a two- or three-year rotation.

Very roughly, if we leave aside a few limited areas of advanced agriculture with virtually no fallow land, Europe was divided between two systems. In the south, wheat and other bread grains took half of the cultivated land in turn, the other half lying fallow, in *barbechos* as they say in Spain. In the north the land was divided into three fields: winter cereals, spring-sown cereals (also known as *mars, marsage, carêmes, trémis, trémois*) and fallow. In Lorraine, even quite recently one could still see around the village which formed the central point, the three fields (wheat, oats and fallow) dividing the land like the sectors of a roughly drawn circle extending to the near-by forest. In successive years, wheat replaced fallow, oats replaced wheat and fallow replaced oats. This was the cycle of triennial rotation; after three years the situation was the same as at the beginning. There were therefore two systems: on one, land under wheat lay fallow for a longer period; in the other it always covered a larger area, proportionately, as long as it was entirely sown to wheat – which was in fact never the case. The grain in the south was richer in gluten; in the north the yield was higher, but the quality of the soil and the climate also played a part.

Such an outline is only very roughly true: there was some cultivation 'in thirds' (fallow for two years) in the south, in the same way as biennial rotation persisted in certain places in the north (for example in northern Alsace, from Strasbourg to Wissemburg).[52] Triennial rotation had developed later than biennial rotation, which continued to exist over quite large areas, like old writing showing through on a palimpsest.

One could find mixtures of the two, of course, on the boundaries of the two great European systems. A survey of Limagnes in the sixteenth century[53] notes the tangle of biennial and triennial rotations depending on soil, labour force and level of peasant population. There was even a small region of three-yearly rotation in the extreme south of the 'biennial' zone, around Seville, in about 1755, which seems similar to northern rotation.

But setting such variations aside, as a general rule there was always a dead

Ploughing, from the *Heures de la Bienheureuse Vierge Marie*, fourteenth-century miniature. (Photo Bulloz.)

period, a rest from cultivation of grain, whether rotation revolved on a two- or three-yearly basis. This dead period enabled the soil lying fallow to regain its richness in nourishing salts, especially when it was manured and then tilled. Repeated tilling was supposed to aerate the soil, prevent weeds and prepare the ground for abundant harvests. Jethro Tull (1674-1741), one of the apostles of the English agricultural revolution, recommended repeated tilling as strongly as manuring and rotation of crops.[54] Documents even mention seven tillings, including those preceding sowing. Three tillings (in spring, autumn and winter) were already the rule in England and Normandy in the fourteenth century. In Artois (1328), the land reserved for wheat was 'well worked with four furrows (tillings), one in winter and three in summer'.[55] In Bohemia on the Czernin domains in 1648, three or four tillings, depending on whether the land was intended for rye or wheat were the general rule. Here are the words of a Savoy

Seedtime. British Museum, Mss 90089, thirteenth century. (Photo by the museum.)

landowner (1771): 'In certain places we wear ourselves out with incessant tilling and we till four or five times in order to have a single harvest of wheat – which is often of very mediocre quality.'[56]

Moreover, wheat requires careful manuring. This treatment was never given to oats or to any 'spring sowing', with the result that the yield from oats, which were sown more closely, was normally half that of wheat – the reverse of present results. Manure intended for wheat was so important that it was closely supervised by the landowner. A lease granted by the Carthusian monks in Picardy in 1325 provided for arbitration by men of experience and integrity in case of dispute in this matter. A *Düngerregister* (a register of dunghills) was kept on the large (too-large no doubt) estates of Bohemia. Even around St Petersburg 'they manure with dung mixed with straw: they till the soil twice for all cereals, three times for *Winterroggen*'[57] (winter rye – the source is a German observer). In Basse-Provence in the seventeenth and eighteenth centuries, calculations were continually made and remade of the loads of manure required, of what had been spread, and also of what the *mège*, the farmer, had not supplied. One lease even provided that manure should be checked by authorized persons before being spread and that its production should be supervised.[58]

There were substitute manures – manure crops, ashes and dead leaves kept in peasants' courtyards or village streets – but the principal source of manure remained livestock – never human beings, as in the towns and countryside of the Far East (in the West urban refuse was, however, used around certain towns, such as Valencia in Spain, certain Flemish cities, and even around Paris).[59]

In short, grain and grazing were complementary, particularly when the use of harnessed animals was necessary. It would have been impossible for a man who could dig two hectares a year at most[60] (he comes far below horses and oxen in the league of strength) to prepare the vast areas of arable unaided. Harnessed animals were necessary – horses in the north, oxen and mules (an increasing number of mules) in the south.

Thus there became established in Europe, with certain regional variations, 'a complicated system of relationships and habits', based on wheat and other grains, which was 'so firmly cemented together that no fissure was possible' according to Ferdinand Lot.[61] Plants, animals and people each had their place in it. In fact the whole system was inconceivable without the peasants, the harnessed teams of animals, and the seasonal labourers at harvest and threshing time, since reaping and threshing was all done by hand. The fertile lowlands called on labour from poor land, inevitably wild highland regions. Innumerable examples (the southern Jura and Dombes, the Massif Central and Languedoc) demonstrate that the partnership was a basic rule of life, repeated on many occasions. An immense crowd of harvesters arrived every summer in the Tuscan Maremma, where fever was so prevalent, in search of high wages (up to five *paoli* a day in 1796). Malaria regularly claimed innumerable victims there. The sick were then left to fend for themselves in huts near the animals, with a little straw, some foul water, coarse bread and an onion or a head of garlic. 'Many die without medicine and without a priest.'[62]

However, it is clear that arable land, even when well organized, with its open fields, its regular and in fact rather rapid rotation, and the reluctance of its farmers to take land out of cereal-growing, was caught in a vicious circle. If its productivity was to be increased, then more fertilizer was needed, and this meant giving more land over to livestock, horses and cattle, at the expense naturally of arable. Quesnay's 14th maxim recommends the farmer 'to multiply his livestock, for it is this which will give the land the manure that produces rich harvests'. Triennial rotation, which rests the land for a year before sowing wheat on it, without allowing much to grow on the fallow field, and which gives an absolute priority to cereal production, generally results in fairly low yields. Wheat fields are not admittedly, as rice-fields are, completely closed systems, sufficient to themselves: the necessary livestock could always be pastured in forests, newly cleared land, hayfields or even eat the grass by the roadside. But these resources were not sufficient. A solution had been discovered and put into practice but only in a few limited areas: in Artois, northern Italy and Flanders in the fourteenth century, in some parts of Germany in the sixteenth century and later in Holland and England. This consisted of having cereals and forage crops alternate, at long intervals which reduced or even eliminated fallow periods; it had the double advantage of providing fodder for horses and cattle and of increasing cereal yields by restoring to the land its mineral riches.[63] But in spite of the advice of experts on agriculture, who were becoming more numerous, this 'agricultural revolution', which began to make headway after 1750, took another hundred years or so to become accepted in a country like France, where the wheat-fields are concentrated mainly north of the Loire. This was because the cereal-growing culture really acted as a straitjacket; it had its own structures which farmers were extremely reluctant to forsake. In the Beauce, which had always been regarded as a successful wheat-growing area, farm contracts continued for a long time to insist on respecting the three seasons or *soles*. 'Modern' agriculture took time to penetrate here.

Hence the pessimistic opinions of eighteenth-century agronomists, who saw the elimination of fallow and the adoption of artificial prairies as the primary, indeed the essential, condition for agricultural progress. This is the criterion they unfailingly use to pronounce on the level of rural modernization. In 1777, the author of a topographical dictionary of the Maine in France, tells us that 'near Mayenne the soil is black and hard to cultivate; it is even worse near Laval where . . . the best ploughmen with six oxen and four horses can plough no more than 15 or 16 *arpents* in a year. Consequently they let the land rest for 8, 10, or 12 years at a stretch'.[64] Things were equally unpromising in Finistère in Brittany, where 'fallow can last for 25 years on poor land and 3 to 6 years on good'. When Arthur Young travelled through Brittany, he thought it was like the wilds of Canada.[65]

But this was a grotesque error of judgement and perspective, as a recent article by Jacques Mulliez has shown with an abundance of illustrative evidence. In France, as elsewhere in Europe, there were in fact many large areas where there was more grass than wheat, and where livestock was the predominant form of wealth, the commercial 'surplus' off which peasants lived. Such were the rocky massifs, the foothills of mountains, damp or marshy regions, the wooded *bocages*, or the sea-coasts (which in France means the long stretch from Bayonne to Dunkerque). Wherever it was to be found, this grassland was another aspect of the Western countryside which agronomists of the eighteenth and early nineteenth century totally misjudged, obsessed as they were with their desire to increase cereal yields at any price in order to meet the needs of a growing population. And historians have naturally followed in their footsteps. But it is clear that in these regions, fallow land if fallow there was, was a productive element, not a deadweight or a waste of time.[66] The grass fed the flocks, whether to provide meat for slaughter, dairy goods, draught animals or beasts of burden – ponies, horses, calves, cattle, oxen, donkeys or mules. And without this other France, how could Paris have been fed? Where would the great livestock markets of Sceaux and Poissy have got their supplies? And where would the thousands of draught animals have come from for the army and transport?

The basic mistake is to confuse fallow land in cereal-growing areas with fallow in livestock regions. The very word is inappropriate outside the context of arable land under rotation. Near Mayenne or Laval, as elsewhere (around Rome for instance), ploughing a pasture under from time to time and sowing cereals on it for a year or two is simply a way of resting the pasture – and indeed

Van Gogh's *Harvester* (Nuenen, 1885), The Van Gogh Foundation, Amsterdam.

Compare it with the harvester in the *Heures de Notre-Dame*, known as the Hennessy Heures (sixteenth century). Although more than two centuries separate them, they are using the same gesture and identical implements (*pick en hak*) – admittedly in the same region.

(Photos Gemeentemusea van Amsterdam and Bibliothèque royale, Brussels.)

it is still done today. The so-called fallow in such cases is far from being 'wasted', or lying dead and uncultivated as it so often is under triennial rotation. It bears natural grazing, restored from time to time by ploughing, but it also bears cultivated pasture. In Finistère, for instance, a kind of gorse (*ajonc*) called *jan* has always been planted; despite appearances, it is actually a forage crop. Arthur Young was unaware of this and took for scandalous wasteland the artificially created *ajoncières*. In the Vendée or the Gâtine in Poitou, broom was used for the same purpose.[67] Here again use was made, probably from the very earliest times, of local plants. But it is not surprising that in these so-called 'backward' areas, maize, which can be used both as animal fodder and for human consumption, was widely adopted, and that turnips, beet and cabbages – the modern forage crops of the 'agricultural revolution' – spread in these areas from a fairly early date, viz. the latter half of the eighteenth century.[68]

So in France, and elsewhere in Europe, no doubt, there were regions that were poor in cereals but rich in livestock, contrasting with those that were rich in cereals and poor in livestock. They both contrasted with and complemented each other, since cereal crops required draught teams and manure, and the livestock areas were short of grain. So the 'vegetable' determinism of Western civilization was not the result of wheat alone, but of wheat and grazing together. Finally, the appearance in men's lives of domestic animals as a reserve of meat and energy, proved to be a continuing originality of the West. Rice-growing China may have ignored and even rejected the possibilities offered by livestock, and by so doing chosen not to settle and farm her mountain areas. But as far as Europe is concerned, we ought to revise our ways of thinking. Livestock areas, regarded by agronomists of the past as backward and condemned to toil on poor land, now appear according to J. Mulliez's article, to have been more efficient than the 'good' cereal-growing land at feeding their peasant population[69] – which was, it is true, much smaller. If I had to choose a place to live in the past, I should probably prefer the Bray to the Beauvaisis, the woods and fields of the Ardennes to the great plains further south, and even perhaps, despite the cold winters, the country around Riga or Reval to the great windswept stretches of the Paris Basin.

Low yields, compensations and disasters

Wheat's unpardonable fault was its low yield: it did not provide for its people adequately. All recent studies establish the fact with an overwhelming abundance of detail and figures. Wherever one looks, from the fifteenth to the eighteenth century, the results were disappointing. For every grain sown, the harvest was usually no more than five and sometimes less. As the grain required for the next sowing had to be deducted, four grains were therefore produced for consumption from every one sown. What does this yield represent in quintals and hectares? Before embarking on these simple calculations, we must warn the reader to be wary of their simplicity. Probability in these matters is not enough and, furthermore, everything varied with the fertility of the land, the methods of cultivation and changes in climate from year to year. *Productivity*, the relationship between what is produced and the total effort expended to produce it (labour is not the only factor involved), is a difficult value to calculate, and certainly a variable.

Having said this, we will assume that, as today, between one and two hectolitres of wheat were sown per hectare (without taking into account the fact that the grains were smaller and that therefore the number in a hectolitre used to be larger) and start from an average of 1·5 hectolitres of seed. At 5 to 1, 7·5 hectolitres, or about 6 quintals would be obtained. It is a very low figure. But Olivier de Serres confirms it: 'The farmer generally has something to be happy about when his land yields him an average of five or six to one'.[70] Quesnay (1757) says the same about 'small-scale farming', which was still very much the predominant system in France in his own period: 'Each *arpent* giving on an average four to one ... the seed deducted and not including the tithe.'[71] In the eighteenth century in Burgundy, according to a modern historian, 'the normal yield from an average soil, seed deducted, was generally five or six quintals to the hectare'.[72] Such figures are very probable. France had perhaps 25 million inhabitants around 1775. It more or less managed to live from its wheat, what it exported equalling what it imported over the years. If we accept the figure of four hectolitres per inhabitant per year for the consumption of bread grain, the country needed to produce 100 million hectolitres or 80 million quintals. In fact production had in addition to supply grain for sowing and for feeding animals and had therefore to be far above this figure. According to a high estimate by J.C. Toutain, it was in the order of 100 million quintals.[73] If we accept a figure of 15 million hectares for the area sown, we come back to a production figure of six quintals. We therefore remain within the limits of our first estimate, in the neighbourhood of five to six quintals (a pessimistic figure, hardly open to charges of exaggeration).

But although the answer seems reasonable it far from indicates the whole complexity of the problem. Chance samples of reliable book-keeping present us with figures far above or far below our approximate average of five or six quintals to the hectare.

Hans-Helmut Wächter's impressive calculations for the *Vorwerk-Domänen* – large estates owned by the Teutonic Order and then by the Duke of Prussia (1550 to 1695) – which deal with almost 3000 totals, give average yields as follows (quintals per hectare): wheat 8·7 (but only a minute crop was involved); rye 7·6 (in view of the latitude, rye tended to become the most important grain); barley 7; and oats only 3·7. Higher figures, although they are still low, were given by a survey in Brunswick (for the seventeenth and eighteenth centuries this time): wheat 8·5; rye 8·2; barley 7·5; and oats 5.[74] One might think that these were record figures for a later period. But an Artois landowner at the beginning of the fourteenth century, Thierry d'Hireçon,[75] who was concerned with the good administration of his estates, obtained the following yields from one grain sown on one of his properties at Roquestor (for 7 known years between 1319 and 1327): 7.5; 9.7; 11.6; 8; 8.7; 7; 8.1; that is approximately between 12 and 17 quintals per hectare. Similarly, Quesnay indicated that the large-scale farming he advocated produced yields of 16 quintals per hectare, a record amount to notch up to the credit of modern capitalist agriculture. But we will return to this later.[76]

As opposed to these unusually high figures, which are not averages, there are many sadder tales to tell. Leonid Zytkowicz's study[77] has established how low yields were in Poland. On average, between 1550 and 1650, 60% of the rye-harvests yielded only 2 or 4 grains to 1 (for 10% of the harvests, the figure was less than 2); during the next century, the figures fell even lower. There was no real improvement until the end of the eighteenth century, when yields of between 4 and 7 to 1 represented 50% of the total. Wheat and barley yields were a little higher, but the pattern was similar. In Bohemia, on the contrary, there was a clear improvement in yields as early as the second part of the seventeenth century. But Hungary and Slovakia were as badly off as Poland.[78] Hungary of course only became a great grain-producing country in the nineteenth century. But it would be wrong to suppose that the old farmland in the West always showed a higher yield. In Languedoc,[79] from the sixteenth to the eighteenth century, the sower's 'hand was heavy', often two and even three hectolitres of seed to the hectare. Oats, barley, rye or wheat were grown too closely together and choked each other, as Alexander von Humboldt was still able to observe across the whole of Europe.[80] These massive sowings only produced wretched yields in Languedoc: less than 3 to 1 in about 1580-5; 4 or 5 to 1 on average during the peak period of the sixteenth century, 1660-70; then it dropped again and began the long climb back after 1730, reaching an average of 6 to 1 only after 1750.[81]

Increased cultivation and higher yields

These low averages did not prevent a slow and continuous advance, as wide investigations undertaken by B.H. Slicher van Bath (1963)[82] prove. What he accomplished was to group together all the known figures for cereal yields, which were almost meaningless in isolation. Compared, they point to a long-term advance. This slow-motion race gives us the opportunity to distinguish groups of runners who moved at the same pace. Four groups emerge: (1) England, Ireland and the Netherlands; (2) France, Spain and Italy; (3) Germany, the Swiss Cantons, Denmark, Norway and Sweden; (4) Bohemia in the wide sense, Poland, the Baltic countries and Russia.

If a single yield is calculated for the four principal cereals (wheat, rye, barley and oats) – so many grains harvested from one sown – it is possible to distinguish four phases, A, B, C, D, according to group and yield obtained:

CEREAL YIELDS IN EUROPE (1200-1820)

A	Before 1200-49 *Yield of 3 to 3·7 from 1*	
	1. England 1200-49	3·7
	2. France before 1200	3
B	1250-1820 *Yield of 4·1 to 4·7*	
	1. England 1250-1499	4·7
	2. France 1300-1499	4·3
	3. Germany, Scandinavian countries 1500-1699	4·2
	4. Eastern Europe 1550-1820	4·1
C	1500-1820 *Yield of 6.3 to 7*	
	1. England, Netherlands 1500-1700	7
	2. France, Spain, Italy 1500-1820	6·3
	3. Germany, Scandinavian countries 1700-1820	6·4
D	1750-1820 *Yield above 10*	
	1. England, Ireland, Netherlands 1750-1820	10·6

Source: B.H. Slicher van Bath.

So there was a series of slow and modest advances from A to B, from B to C and C to D. They do not exclude relapses of fairly long duration, for example from 1300 to 1350, from 1400 to 1500, and from 1600 to 1700 (the dates are approximate). Neither do they exclude sometimes quite marked variations from one year to another. But the main thing to remember is the long-term advance of 60% to 65%. It will also be noted that progress in the last phase, 1750-1820, was made in the most densely populated countries, England, Ireland and the Netherlands. A correlation obviously exists between the rise in yields and the rise in population. One last point: the initial advances were relatively the strongest, as calculations would show; the advance from A to B was proportionally greater than from B to C. The transition from 3:1 to 4:1 represented a decisive step, the establishment (roughly speaking) of the first towns in Europe, or the revival of those that had not gone under during the high middle ages. For towns obviously depended on a surplus of cereal production.

DECLINES IN CEREALS (1250-1750)

		Yields from 1 grain sown	Decreases %
England	1250-99	4·7	16
	1300-49	4·1	
	1350-99	5·2	14
	1400-49	4·6	
	1550-99	7·3	13
Netherlands	1600-49	6·5	
Germany	1500-99	4·4	18
Scandinavia	1700-49	3·8	
Eastern Europe	1550-99	4·5	17
	1650-99	3·9	

Source: B.H. Slicher van Bath.

Not surprisingly the area sown was often extended, particularly during each population-increase. Sixteenth-century Italy was a hive of intensive land-improvement schemes in which Genoese, Florentine and Venetian capitalists invested enormous sums. The slow toil of winning back land from water – from rivers, lagoons and swamps – from forests and heathland, tortured Europe incessantly and condemned it to superhuman effort. All too often these exertions were accomplished to the detriment of peasant life. The peasants were slaves to the crops as much as to the nobility.

Agriculture has often been called the largest industry of pre-industrial Europe. But it was an industry that was always in difficulty. Even in the large food-producing regions of the north, the newly cultivated lands were only makeshift economic ventures that proved inefficient in the long run. To extend the cultivation of corn was to meet with decreasing yields (we have already mentioned this for Poland; a graph by Heinrich Wächter shows the same thing in precise terms for Prussia;[83] it was also true of Sicily). It was, on the contrary, by opting for forage crops and livestock farming that eighteenth-century England achieved a revolutionary improvement in cereal yields.

Local and international trade in grain

As the countryside lived off its harvests and the cities off the surplus, it was sensible for a town to obtain its provisions from within striking distance – 'from its own possessions', as a council-meeting in Bologna was already advising as early as 1305.[84] This provisioning from within a radius of between twenty and thirty kilometres avoided the difficulties of transport as well as the always hazardous recourse to foreign suppliers. It functioned all the better because towns almost everywhere controlled the adjacent countryside. In France until Turgot and 'the Flour War', even until the Revolution, the peasant was obliged to sell his grain at the market of the nearby town. During the troubles accompanying the summer famine of 1789 the rioters knew where to lay their hands on those grain merchants reputed to be hoarders: everybody knew them. This was probably true all over Europe. For instance, there was no place in eighteenth-century Germany without measures against 'usurers', grain hoarders, *Getreidewucher*.

This life based on local exchanges did not go on without hitches. Every bad harvest obliged the towns to appeal to more fortunate areas. Wheat and rye from the north probably reached the Mediterranean as early as the fourteenth century.[85] Even earlier than this, Italy was receiving Byzantine and later Turkish wheat Sicily had always been a great supplier – equivalent to Canada, Argentina or the Ukraine in a later period.

These suppliers on which the large towns depended had to be easily accessible – on the sea or the banks of navigable rivers, since water transport was preferable for heavy goods. Picardy and the Vermandois exported to Flanders by the Scheldt and to Paris by the Oise, in years of good harvests, up to the end of the fifteenth century. Champagne and Barrois supplied Paris in the sixteenth century, the grain leaving Vitry-le-François to make the sometimes perilous journey down the Marne.[86] At the same period, barrels of grain left Burgundy by the Saône and Rhône, with Arles as a corn exchange for these consignments from upstream. When Marseilles feared famine it turned to its good friends the Consuls of Arles.[87] Later, particularly in the eighteenth century, it became a great port itself for 'grain from the sea'. Then it was to Marseilles that the whole of Provence appealed in difficult times. But for their own consumption, the Marseillais preferred good local grain to imported cereals, which usually deteriorated somewhat during the voyage.[88] Genoa, similarly, ate the expensive grain from the Romagna and exported the cheap grain she bought in the Levant.[89]

From the sixteenth century on northern grain played a growing part in international trade in cereals – often to the disadvantage of the exporting country itself. The large quantity of grain that Poland exports every year, a dictionary of commerce explains (1797),[90] would give the impression that this country is one of the most fertile in Europe. But those who know it and its inhabitants will judge otherwise, because even if there are fertile and well-cultivated regions there, elsewhere there are more fertile regions which are even better cultivated and which still do not export grain. 'The truth is that the nobles are the only landowners there and the peasants are slaves, and the former, in order to maintain themselves, appropriate the toil and products of the latter, who form at least seven eighths of the population and are reduced to eating bread made from barley and oats. Whereas the other peoples of Europe consume the major

Transporting grain by mule in Italy. Pinacoteca, Sienna. (Photo Scala.)

part of their best grain, the Poles retain only a small portion of their wheat and rye so that one might think they only harvest it for foreign lands. Thrifty nobles and bourgeois eat rye bread themselves, wheaten bread being only for the tables of the great lords. It is no exaggeration to say that a single town in other European states consumes more wheat than the whole realm of Poland.'

These underpopulated or underdeveloped countries able to supply Europe with the grain it lacked were almost always on the margins to the north, or east (the Turkish empire), or even to the south (Barbary Coast, Sardinia, Sicily). The process was subject to frequent revision. One granary closed and another opened. In the first part of the seventeenth century it was Sweden[91] (Livonia, Estonia, Scania); then from 1697 until 1760, England, under the impetus of export subsidies which encouraged enclosure; in the eighteenth century, the English colonies in America.[92]

The attraction in each case was ready cash. The rich always paid cash down in the grain trade. The poor succumbed to the temptation and, of course, those who made the biggest profits were the middle-men, like the merchants who speculated on wheat 'in the blade' in the kingdom of Naples as elsewhere. Venice in 1227 was already paying for grain from Apulia in gold bullion.[93] Similarly the tiny Breton boats that usually carried the grain needed by Seville and particularly Lisbon, in the sixteenth and seventeenth centuries, carried away its counterpart either in silver or in 'red gold' from Portugal, a practice forbidden in any other trade.[94] Exports of grain from Amsterdam to France and Spain in the seventeenth century were also paid for 'in cash'. A 'pseudo-Englishman' wrote in 1754 that 'in recent years it is the abundance of our grain harvests and their export that has maintained our balance of trade'.[95] In 1795, France was on the verge of famine. Envoys sent to Italy could find no other way of obtaining grain than to send from Marseilles to Leghorn some silver coffers, 'which were sold for the weight of silver alone, without counting the craftsmanship which was worth quite as much as the metal'.[96]

None the less the quantities involved in this essential commerce were never as large as might at first be thought. There were about 60 million people in the Mediterranean area in the sixteenth century. At a rate of three hectolitres per head, total consumption would have been 180 million hectolitres each year, or 145 million quintals. A rough calculation indicates that maritime trade involved one or two million quintals or barely 1% of total consumption. If we start with a consumption figure of four hectolitres per inhabitant, the percentage would be even lower.

The situation was probably much the same in the seventeenth century. Danzig, the chief grain port, exported 1,382,000 quintals in 1618, and 1,200,000 in 1649 (in round figures).[97] If we assume that the north as a whole was the equivalent of three or four Danzigs, her providential grain exports would have amounted to between three and five million quintals. Add the million or so quintals which could be provided by the Mediterranean and one has an approximate maximum for the European grain trade of six million quintals at the outside. It may sound a large figure, but it is negligible in relation to the 240 million quintals consumed by the Europeans (100 million inhabitants, 3 hectolitres each). And even these record exports were not kept up: in 1753-4, Danzig exported only 52,000 *lasts* (624,000 quintals).[98] Turgot estimated the international grain trade at this time at four or five million quintals, a figure considered excessive by Sombart.[99] Finally, one should not forget that these supplementary cereal supplies travelled almost entirely by water, so that only maritime powers were able to use them to alleviate recurrent famine.[100]

Of course, given the means available at the time, this long-distance trade seems to us a fascinating achievement. It is extraordinary to think that the Bardi of Florence, in the service of Pope Benedict XII, succeeded in sending grain from Apulia to Armenia in 1336;[101] that Florentine merchants managed to handle between five and ten thousand tons of Sicilian grain every year in the fourteenth century;[102] that the Grand-Dukes of Tuscany, Venice and Genoa moved tens of thousands of tons of grain from the Baltic and the Black Sea, through the agency

The international grain trade: boats carrying Polish grain arriving in Danzig after travelling up the Vistula. Detail of the painting reproduced in Vol. III.

of international merchants and letters of exchange on Nuremberg and Antwerp, to make up for shortages during the calamitous 1590s in the Mediterranean;[103] that wealthy but still backward Moldavia sent 350,000 hectolitres on an annual average to Istanbul in the sixteenth century; and that a boat from Boston arrived at Istanbul loaded with American flour and grain at the end of the eighteenth century.[104]

We may also find very impressive the docks and warehouses set up at departure points (in the Sicilian *caricatori*,[105] in Danzig, Antwerp – important from 1544 – Lübeck and Amsterdam) and at arrival points like Genoa or Venice (forty-four warehouses in Venice in 1602). And we may admire the facilities available for this trade: the tickets, the grain *cedole* for the Sicilian *caricatori* for example.[106]

However, taking everything into account, this trade remained marginal, spasmodic and 'more closely supervised than anything subjected to the attentions of the Inquisition'. Large-scale systems of purchase, warehousing and distribution – essential for regular long-distance trade in heavy and perishable merchandise – did not appear until the eighteenth century, if then. Even in the sixteenth century, neither Venice, Genoa nor Florence had big independent merchants specializing even to a small extent in trade in grain (except possibly the Florentine Bardi Corsi). They engaged in it during times of great crisis when the opportunity offered. It is true that the great Portuguese firms, including the Ximenes, who financed the vast movement of northern grain to the Mediterranean during the massive crisis of 1590 earned a return of between 300% and 400%;[107] but they were not necessarily typical. Generally, big merchants found little profit in this risky and restrictive trade. In fact no concentration appeared in the grain trade until the eighteenth century. Thus during the food shortage of 1773, the grain trade in Marseilles was virtually monopolized by a small number of merchants, who were able to dictate their terms.[108]

We know of various large transactions in grain, for instance important purchases by Gustavus Adolphus in Russia; purchases by Louis XIV on the Amsterdam market just before his invasion of Holland in 1672; and Frederick II's urgent order to buy 150,000 to 200,000 bushels of rye immediately in Poland, Mecklenburg, Silesia, Danzig and other foreign places (which led to difficulties with Russia) issued on 27 October 1740, the day after he learned of the death of of Emperor Charles VI. In these large transactions, much depended on the military policy of the states. And the example of Frederick II shows that in cases of emergency it was necessary to approach all the grain-producers at the same time because of the lack of substantial stocks. Furthermore, obstacles to free trade were endlessly multiplied, so that movement became even more difficult. The case of France during the last years of the *ancien régime* demonstrates this. In its efforts to do the right thing, the royal administration brushed aside too-free private initiative and created a monopoly of trade in grain to its own advantage, or rather the advantage of its agents and the merchants in its service, all at its own expense and to its own greatest prejudice. But the antiquated system was incapable of providing for the supply of the enlarged towns and gave rise to monstrous abuses and repeated extortion, from which the legend of the Famine Pact[109] was born. In this case we can say that there was truly no smoke without fire.

All this was very serious. Grain was France's whole life, as it was of all the West. We know about the 'Flour War'[110] which followed Turgot's untimely measures in support of the free movement of grain. 'When they have pillaged the markets and the bakers' shops,' said a contemporary, 'they can pillage our houses and slit our throats.' He added: 'They are beginning to ransack the farms, why not ransack the châteaux?'[111]

Grain and calories

A man today requires 3500 to 4000 calories a day if he belongs to a rich country and a privileged class. These levels were not unknown before the eighteenth century. But they were less frequently the norm than today. None the less as we need a reference point for our calculations we will use this figure of 3500 calories. Earl J. Hamilton in fact arrives at the same high level in his calculations of the nutritive value of the meals intended for the crews of the Spanish fleet in the Indies in about 1560.[112] This was certainly a record, that is if we are prepared to accept without hesitation (despite Courteline's warnings about listening to the bureaucracy) the official figures given by the Administration, in whose eyes the rations were always satisfactory.

We know of even higher levels at the tables of princes or privileged classes (for example at Pavia at the Collegio Borromeo at the beginning of the seventeenth century); but such isolated cases should not deceive us. As soon as we begin to calculate the averages (for the great urban masses, for example) the level often falls to around 2000 calories. This was the case in Paris just before the Revolution. Of course the few figures we possess never hold the exact answer to the problems that concern us, especially as there is dispute over the reliability of calories as the test of a healthy diet (which demands a balance between carbohydrates, fats and protein). For example, should wine and alcohol be included in the calory intake? It has become established practice never to attribute more than 10% of the calory intake to drink. What is drunk over and above that percentage is not included in the calculations – which does not mean that the surplus did not count as far as the health and expenditure of the drinker were concerned.

None the less general rules do become apparent (Figure 12). For example, the distribution of the various types of foodstuffs reveals the diversity or, much more often, the monotony of diet. Monotony is obvious whenever the share of carbohydrates (cereals in nearly every case) is *far* in excess of 60% of intake expressed in calories. The share of meat, fish and dairy products is then fairly limited and monotony sets in. Eating consists of a lifetime of consuming bread, more bread, and gruel.

On these criteria, it would appear that northern Europe was characterized by a larger consumption of meat, and southern Europe by a larger share of carbohydrates, except obviously in the case of military convoys when meals were improved by barrels of salted meat and tunny fish.

Not surprisingly the tables of the rich were more varied than those of the poor, the difference being marked by quality rather than quantity.[113] Cereals only represented 53% of calories on the Spinolas' luxurious table at Genoa around 1614-15. At the same date they formed 81% of the diet of the poor at the Hospital for Incurables (one kilogram of wheat is equivalent to 3000 calories and one kilogram of bread to 2500). If other dietary categories are compared, the Spinolas ate hardly any more meat and fish, but twice as much dairy produce and fats as the inmates of the hospital, and their much more varied diet included plenty of fruit, vegetables and sugar (3% of expenditure). Similarly we can be sure that if the boarders at the Collegio Borromeo (1609-18) were overfed (their

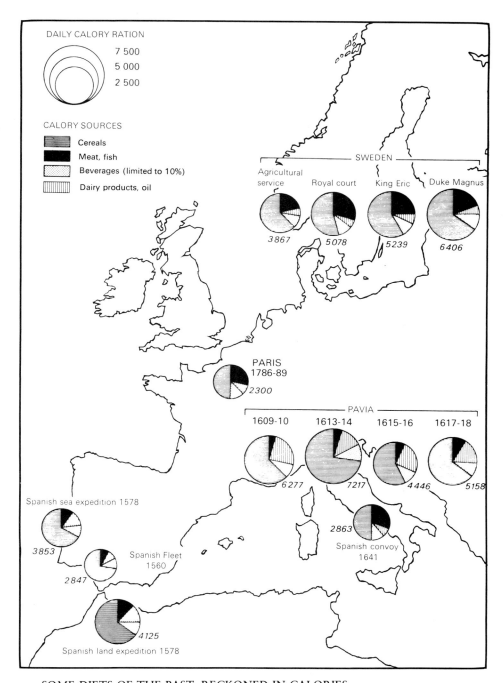

12 SOME DIETS OF THE PAST, RECKONED IN CALORIES
The map is based on a few relatively privileged menus. It would be necessary to find thousands of examples, from different periods and every social level, to establish a valid map for Europe. (From F. Spooner, *Régimes alimentaires d'autrefois*.)

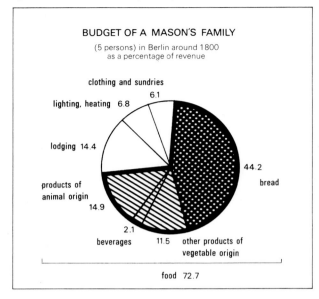

13 BUDGET OF A MASON'S FAMILY IN BERLIN ABOUT 1800
Compare it with the calculations of the *average* expenditure on food of the Parisian in 1788 and 1854 (p. 133). Bread here represents considerably more than half the family's food budget, an enormous proportion in view of the relative price of cereals. So this is a precise example of what a monotonous and difficult diet was like.

almost incredibly large intake of food amounted to between 5500 and 7000 calories daily) they were not overfed in a particularly varied way. Cereals represented up to 73% of the total. Their food was not, could not be, particularly interesting.

Sooner or later a more varied diet became common in towns everywhere where assessment is possible, at the very least more varied than in the countryside. In Paris, where as we have seen, per capita consumption in 1780 was about 2000 calories, only 58% of the total was accounted for by cereals: about a pound of bread a day.[114] And this corresponds to figures (both earlier and later) for average Parisian bread consumption: 540 grams in 1637; 556 in 1728–30; 462 in 1770; 587 in 1788; 463 in 1810; 500 in 1820; and 493 in 1854.[115] We certainly cannot vouch for these quantities – any more than we can vouch for the figure of 180 kilograms per person, which *seems* (though the calculation is doubtful) to have been the annual consumption in Venice at the beginning of the seventeenth century.[116] However, other indications suggest that the Venetian working class was both well paid and demanding, and that the better-off had the extravagant habits of long-standing town-dwellers.

In general there is no doubt whatsoever that bread was consumed on a substantial scale in the country, much more so than in the town, and amongst the lowest levels of the working classes. According to Le Grand d'Aussy in 1782, a working man or a peasant in France ate two or three pounds of bread a day, 'but people who have anything else to eat do not consume this quantity'. However, one can see construction workers in southern Italy even today dining on enormous loaves accompanied, almost as a flavouring, by a few tomatoes and onions significantly called the *companatico*: something to go with the bread.

The triumph of bread arose of course because grain – and also alcohol made from grain, as a Polish historian has pointed out,[117] thus vindicating the propensity of peasants in his country to drink and not only eat their grain – was the least expensive foodstuff in relation to its calorific content. In about 1780 it cost eleven times less than meat, sixty-five times less than fresh sea fish, nine times less than fresh-water fish, six times less than eggs, three times less than butter and oil. Grain, the primary source of energy, came only third in expenditure, after meat and wine, in budgets calculated for the average Parisian in 1788 and 1854 (only 17% of total expenditure in both cases).[118]

So grain is rehabilitated, after we have spoken so dismissively of it. It was the manna of the poor, and 'its price was the most sensitive general index of the food market'. 'This,' wrote Sébastien Mercier in 1770, 'is the third consecutive winter when bread has been dear. During the past year, half the peasants needed public charity and this winter will be the last straw, because those who until now have lived by selling their effects now have nothing left to sell.'[119] For the poor, if the cereal supply gave out, everything gave out. We should not forget this dramatic aspect of the problem: the slavery in which grain held producers, middlemen, transporters and consumers. There were constant mobilizations and alarms. 'The grain which feeds man has also been his executioner,' as Sébastien Mercier said, or rather repeated.

The price of grain and the standard of living

Mercier's remark is hardly an exaggeration. In Europe, grain represented approximately half man's daily existence. Its price varied incessantly, at the mercy of stocks, transport, bad weather preceding and therefore governing harvests, at the mercy of the harvests themselves, and finally according to the time of year. Our retrospective graphs of grain prices look like the oscillations of a seismograph. The lives of the poor were all the more affected by these variations, because they were rarely able to escape seasonal increases in price by laying in large stocks at the right time. Can we take the variations in grain prices as a sort of barometer of the standard of living of the masses in the short and long term?

We have the choice of few, invariably imperfect, methods of working this out. We can compare the price of grain with wages, but many wages were paid in kind or partly in kind, partly in money. We can calculate wages in terms of wheat or rye as Abel has, in the graph in Figure 14. We can fix the average price of one typical 'shopping basket', as Phelps Brown and Sheila Hopkins have.[120] Or we can adopt as our unit the hourly wage of the most underprivileged workers, usually hodmen or plasterers' labourers. This last method, employed by Jean Fourastié and his pupils, notably René Grandamy, has its advantages.

What do these 'real' prices ultimately show? They certainly indicate that a quintal of grain (if we convert the old measures for this purpose) cost the equivalent of 100 hours' work until about 1543, then remained above that critical line until about 1883. This, in very general terms, is what French conditions (and conditions outside France, in the West, which were similar) suggest. A worker does approximately 3000 hours of work every year; his family (of four) consumes approximately twelve quintals a year. It is always serious when the 100-hours-for-one-quintal line is crossed; to cross the 200 is a danger signal; 300 is famine. In René Grandamy's opinion the 100 line was always crossed because of some sharp fluctuation, either by a rocketing rise, as in the middle of the sixteenth century, or by a sharp drop, as in 1883. Once the line was crossed in either direction the movement always proceeded rapidly. Thus for the centuries covered by this book, real prices moved in an unfavourable direction. The only favourable period seems to have followed the Black Death; this discovery makes it necessary to revise systematically all previous assumptions.

The conclusion therefore points to a low level of town wages, and to the poverty of the people in the country, where wages in kind fluctuated to almost the same rhythm. The rule for the poor was therefore fairly plain: they were obliged to fall back on secondary cereals, 'on less expensive products which still provided a sufficient number of calories, to abandon foods rich in protein in order to consume foodstuffs based on starch'. In Burgundy, on the eve of the French Revolution, 'the peasant, apart from the small farmer, eats little wheat. This luxury cereal is reserved for sale, for small children and for a few rare celebrations. It supplies the purse rather than the table ... Secondary cereals make up the main part of the peasant's food: *conceau* or maslin, rye in fairly rich homes, barley and oats in the poorest, maize in Bresse and in the Saône valley, rye and buckwheat in Morvan.'[121] Average consumption in Piedmont in about 1750 was as follows (in hectolitres): wheat 0·94; rye 0·91; other grains 0·41; chestnuts 0·45,[122] a total of 2·71 hectolitres a year. In this rather inadequate diet, wheat played only a modest part.

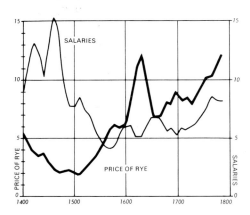

14 WAGES AND THE PRICE OF RYE IN GÖTTINGEN, FIFTEENTH TO NINETEENTH CENTURY

The price of rye is calculated in silver reichmarks, and wages (based on those of a woodcutter-joiner) are expressed in kilograms of rye. There is an obvious correlation between the rise in the price of rye and the drop in real wages, and vice versa. (After W. Abel.)

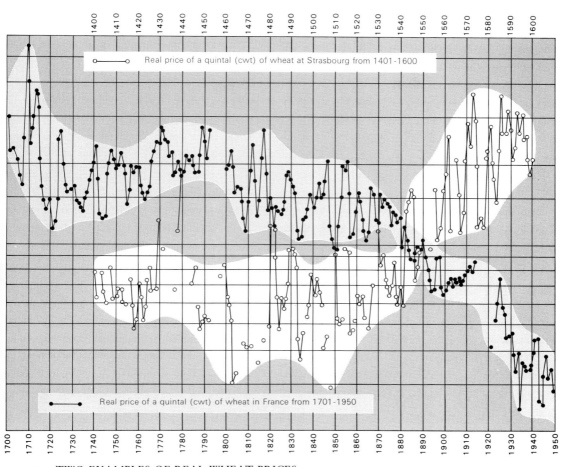

15 TWO EXAMPLES OF REAL WHEAT PRICES
This graph seeks to show the significance of the trend in real wages (expressed in wheat). Old-style measures have been converted into present-day quintals and the price of wheat calculated in tens of hours of manual labour.

The line marked 10 (i.e. 100 hours of work) represents the dangerous ceiling above which life becomes difficult for the workers; it becomes desperate at 200 hours and famine occurs at 300 hours (the record was reached in 1709: 500 hours).

The interest of the graph lies in the area where the two curves cross: in 1540-50, the 100 hour line was crossed and there was not to be a return to this low level until 1880-90, after a very long period of high prices. The crossing of the 100 hour line appears to happen very precipitately, whether the movement is up or down; whenever it happens, it marks a shift in the entire economy.

This graph is one more piece of evidence pointing to a relatively good standard of living for ordinary people in the fifteenth century, despite a few sharp alarms, evidently the result of bad harvests. (From R. Grandamy's article in J. Fourastié, *Prix de vente et prix de revient*, 14th series.)

Bread of the rich, bread and gruel of the poor

There are different grades of bread just as there are various types of corn. In Poitiers in December 1362, 'when the price of a *setier* of wheat reached twenty-four sous, there were four types of bread: *choyne* bread without salt, salted *choyne* bread, *safleur* bread and *reboulet* bread'. *Choyne* bread, with or without salt, was superior-quality white bread made from sifted flour. *Safleur* bread (the name is still used) contained the full flour, not subjected to sifting. *Reboulet* was probably made from 90% whole flour, and contained that fine bran 'which is still called *riboulet* in the Poitou dialect'. These four qualities corresponded to calm periods of moderate grain prices. Only three categories were authorized when prices were low, or rather reasonable, but seven widely different qualities could be manufactured when they rose; which meant in effect a whole range of inferior bread.[123] Nothing is more typical of the extent to which social inequality was the general rule (we have taken Poitiers from amongst thousands of other examples). Bread was sometimes bread in name alone. Often there was none at all.

Europe remained faithful to an old tradition and continued to feed on coarse soups and gruels until the eighteenth century. These were older than Europe itself. The *puls* of the Etruscans and ancient Romans were basically millet. *Alica*, another gruel, had a starch or bread basis; there was also something known as Punic *alica*, a luxury dish containing cheese, honey and eggs.[124] Before it was made with maize, *polenta* was a gruel of barley grains, toasted and then ground and often mixed with millet. Oats were used in Artois in the fourteenth century (probably earlier and certainly later) 'to prepare a sort of porridge or gruel very common among the rural population'.[125] A gruel made of millet was current in Sologne, Champagne and Gascony in the fourteenth century and until the eighteenth. In Brittany there was also a thick gruel called *grou* made from buckwheat and water or milk.[126] Doctors in France at the beginning of the eighteenth century recommended gruel on condition that it was 'made with rich oats'.

These old practices have not entirely disappeared today. Scots and English porridge is a gruel made from oats; *kasha* in Poland and Russia is made from ground and toasted rye, cooked like rice. A British grenadier in the Peninsula campaign in 1809 cooking a makeshift dinner was unwittingly linked to an old tradition: 'We prepared this wheat,' he tells, 'by boiling it like rice or, if it were more convenient, we crushed the grain between two flat stones and then boiled it so that we had a sort of thick dough.'[127] A young Turkish *sipahi*, Osman Aga, captured by the Germans at the time of the taking of Limova near Temesvar in 1688, was even more resourceful, much to his guards' surprise. The regular bread, the *kommissbrot*, being exhausted, the quartermaster distributed rations of flour to the soldiers (they had been without supplies for two days). Osman Aga was the only person who knew how to knead it with a little water and cook it under the hot ashes of the fire, having been, he said, in similar circumstances before.[128] It was almost like bread – or at any rate the unleavened bread, kneaded and cooked under ashes that is often eaten in Turkey and Persia.

White bread was therefore a rarity and a luxury. 'In all French, Spanish and English homes,' wrote Dupré de Saint-Maur, 'there are not more than two million men eating wheaten bread,'[129] If the statement is accurate it would mean that no more than 4% of the European population ate white bread. Even at the beginning of the eighteenth century, half the rural population fed on non-bread-making cereals and rye, and a lot of bran was left in the mixture of grains that went to make the bread for the poor. Wheaten bread and white bread, *choyne* bread (probably the bread eaten by canons, the word being a corruption of *chanoine*), remained a luxury for a long time. A French proverb says 'Don't eat the *choyne* bread first'.[130] It existed early on, but for the exclusive use of the rich. In 1581, young Venetians on the road to Compostela in Spain broke into an isolated house near the Duero to appease their hunger. There they found 'neither real bread, nor wine, nothing but five eggs and a large loaf made of rye and other mixtures which we could scarcely bear to look at, and of which some of us were able to eat one or two mouthfuls'.[131]

Of even higher quality than white bread, 'soft bread' became popular in Paris fairly early on. It was made from the finest flour, with the addition of brewer's yeast (in place of 'true' yeast). When milk was added to the mixture it became the 'Queen's bread' that Maria de Medici adored.[132] In 1668 the Faculty of Medicine vainly condemned the use of brewer's yeast but it continued to be used for 'rolls'. Women carried bushels full of them 'balanced on their heads in the manner of milkmaids' to the bakers' shops each morning. Soft bread of course remained a luxury. As a Parisian said (1788): 'with its firm golden crust it seems to rebuke the Limousin cob ... it looks like a noble amongst rustics'.[133] These luxuries, however, were only available in times of abundance. In times of dearth, as in Paris in September 1740, two decrees of the Parlement promptly forbade 'the making of any types of bread except second quality'. Soft bread and rolls were prohibited; so was the use of powder with a flour base, widely used on wigs at that period.[134]

The real revolution in white bread only occurred between 1750 and 1850. At that period wheat took the place of other cereals (as in England) and bread was increasingly made from flours that had had most of the bran removed. At the same time the view gained ground that only bread, a fermented foodstuff, suited the health of the consumer. Diderot considered all gruel indigestible 'not having yet been fermented'.[135] In France, where the revolution in white bread began early, a National School of Bakery was founded in 1780.[136] Shortly afterwards Napoleon's soldiers introduced this 'previous commodity, white bread' all over Europe. None the less, taking the continent as a whole, the revolution was amazingly slow and not completed before 1850. But its influence on what kind of crops were grown was felt well before its final success, because of the

A meal of gruel in a peasant family in Holland (1653). The single dish is set on a stool. On the right the fireplace; on the left a ladder serves as a staircase. Engraving by A. Van Ostade, Bibliothèque Nationale, Paris. (Photo B.N.)

traditional demand of the rich and the new demand of the poor. Wheat was predominant near Paris in the Multien and the Vexin, from the beginning of the seventeenth century, but not until the end of the century in the Valois, Brie and Beauvaisis. And western France remained loyal to rye.

The French led the way then, on the matter of white bread. Where is good bread eaten if not in Paris? asked Sébastien Mercier: 'I like good bread, I know it and I can tell it at a glance.'[137]

To buy bread, or bake it at home?

The price of bread did not vary; its weight did. Roughly speaking, variable weight was the general rule throughout the Western world. The average weight of bread sold in the bakers' shops in Saint Mark's Square or on the Rialto in Venice varied in an inverse ratio to the price of grain as Figure 16 demonstrates. Regulations published at Cracow in 1561, 1589 and 1592 indicate the same practices: unvarying prices and variable weights. They fixed what must have been the equivalents in bread, of variable quality and weight, of one *grosz* (a coin) – six pounds of rye bread or two pounds of wheaten bread in 1592.[138]

There were exceptions to this, including Paris. The regulation of July 1372 distinguished three types of bread: *Chailli* bread, blistered or *bourgeois* bread and *brode* bread (a brown bread). Their respective weights for the same price were one, two and four *onces*. At this period, therefore, the usual system of constant prices and variable weights was in force. But after 1439[139] the respective weights of the three types of bread were fixed once and for all at half a pound, one pound and two pounds. 'After that, it was the price of bread that changed with the price of grain.' This was probably because of the authorization to sell 'cooked bread' by weight granted at a very early date to bakers working outside the capital – at Gonesse, Pontoise, Argenteuil, Charenton, Corbeil, etc. Bread in Paris, as in London, was bought at one of the ten to fifteen markets in the town much more than at bakers' shops.[140]

Bakers throughout Europe were then important people, more important even than the millers, because they bought grain direct and therefore played the part of merchants. But their production was intended only for a part of the consuming public. Domestic ovens, even in towns, must be taken into account in the production and public sale of household bread. In Cologne in the fifteenth century, in Castile in the sixteenth and even today, peasants from the neighbouring countryside arrived in the towns at daybreak to sell bread. In Venice it was the ambassadors' privilege to be supplied with country bread from the outskirts. It was reputed to be superior to the produce of the Venetian bakers. And numerous wealthy houses in Venice, Genoa and elsewhere had their own granaries and ovens. Even more modest householders often baked their own bread, judging by a painting of the town market in Augsburg in the sixteenth century: grain is being sold in small measures (which can indeed still be seen in the town museum).

In Venice in 1606, according to perfectly credible official calculations, bakers only handled 182,000 *stara* of the city's total grain consumption of 483,000. Markets accounted for another 109,500, and 'households which buy their own provisions'[141] for 144,000. The rest was used for the manufacture of biscuit for the fleet. So the bread sold by bakers amounted to only a little more than the total of bread baked at home – even in Venice.[142]

The market on the Perlachplatz in Augsburg, in the sixteenth century. The different activities represent different months: on the left, October, the sale of game; November, wood, hay, slaughtering a pig; December, grain is sold in small quantities. On the right a long procession

of fur-clad bourgeois coming from the Town Hall. In the background the countryside. (Städtlische Kunstsammlungen, Augsburg.)

142   *The Structures of Everyday Life*

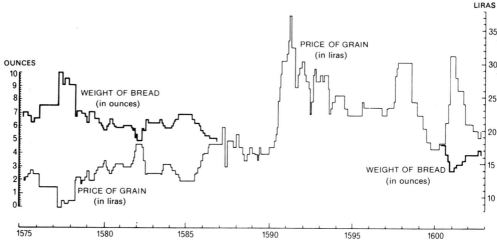

16   BREAD WEIGHTS AND GRAIN PRICES IN VENICE AT THE END OF THE SIXTEENTH CENTURY
(From F. Braudel, 'La vita economica di Venezia nel secolo XVI', in *La Civiltà veneziana del Rinascimento*.)

There was much commotion in Genoa in August 1673, when there was talk of forbidding domestic baking. 'The people are grumbling,' explained the French consul. 'It seems that [the nobles of the town] want to force everyone to buy bread at the markets and it is said that there are gentlemen [i.e. local businessmen] who offer one hundred and eighty thousand écus a year to have this privilege of making bread because ... the custom is that everyone makes his own bread at home, and with this law passed no one will be able to do so, which will be a very great expense because bread is sold at the markets ... at a price of forty lires a *mina* and is only worth about eighteen, besides which the aforesaid bread sold is good on the day it is made and is bitter and cannot be eaten on the next. This affair is causing a great stir and yesterday morning a notice was found stuck up on Saint-Sire Square where the ancient nobility assembles, which spoke strongly against the government and threatened that its tyranny would be evaded.'[143]

According to Parmentier, it was only in the 1770s that the practice of baking bread at home died out 'in most of the large towns in France'.[144] Jean Meyer notes that home-baking had entirely disappeared in Nantes by 1771, and puts it down to the adoption of white wheatmeal bread.[145]

We may wonder where the grain bought for family baking was ground. In fact all towns had mills close at hand, for if grain kept fairly well (even so it was often stored on the ear and several threshings took place throughout the year) flour hardly kept any time. It had to be ground almost daily then, all through the year, in the mills which were then to be seen on the outskirts of every village

A bread-oven, Cracow, fifteenth century. Codex of Balthasar Behem. Jagiellonska Library, Cracow. (Photo Marek Rostworowski.)

and town, and sometimes even in the centre, wherever there was a stream. Any breakdown in the mills – such as happened in Paris, for instance, when the Seine froze or even flooded – brought immediate supply problems. So it is hardly surprising that windmills were built on the fortifications of Paris and that hand-powered mills still survived and had their advocates.

Grain rules Europe

The trinity of grain, flour, bread is to be found everywhere in the history of Europe. It was the major preoccupation of towns, states, merchants, and ordinary people for whom life meant 'eating one's daily bread'. Bread is an insistent presence in all the correspondence of the period. Whenever the price began to go up, there was much agitation and threats of revolt. Necker's observation was equally true everywhere, from London to Paris or Naples: 'the people will never listen to reason on the subject of dear bread'.[146]

At every alert, the mass of small consumers, those who would suffer most, were quick to resort to violence. In Naples, in 1585, large-scale exports of grain to Spain had caused domestic famine. The people had to eat bread *di castagne*

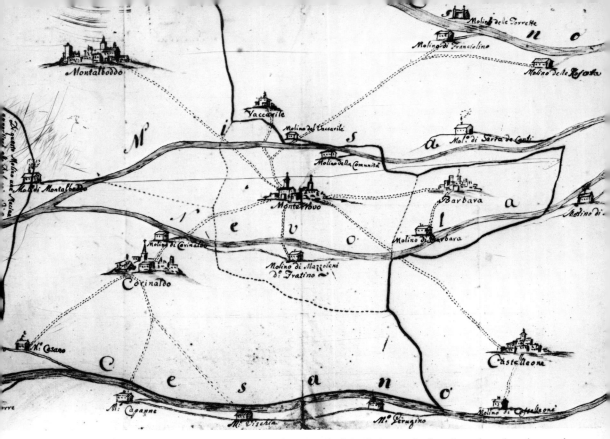

The high density of mills. This map of 1782 (which is disconcertingly oriented so that the south is at the top, the north at the bottom, the Adriatic on the left and the Apennines on the right) shows five large villages one of which is a double village Montalboddo-plus-Vaccarile, lying between four streams in the Marches behind Ancona. The total population of 15,971 inhabitants, spread out over an area of 450 km² has access to 18 mills, i.e. one mill for 880 inhabitants; the average in France was of the order of one to 400 (cf. p. 358). But a lot depended on the power of the mills, the number of wheels and millstones and this we do not know. (Photo Sergio Anselmi.)

e legumi – made with chestnuts and pulses. The grain-hoarding merchant Giovanni Vicenzo Storaci faced with a crowd who were shouting that they would not eat that bread, insolently replied: *Mangiate pietre* ('Eat stones'). The Neapolitans hurled themselves at him and murdered him, dragged his mutilated body round the city and finally chopped the corpse into pieces. The viceroy subsequently had 37 men hanged, drawn and quartered, and sent another 100 to the galleys.[147] In Paris, in 1692, the bakers' shops on the Place Maubert were looted. The repression was prompt and brutal: two of the ringleaders were hanged, the others sent to the galleys, put in chains or flogged,[148] and the trouble died down at least apparently. But thousands of similar bread-riots occurred between the fifteenth and the eighteenth century. And it was of course with one such that the French Revolution began.

A very good harvest, on the other hand, was greeted as a divine godsend. In Rome, on 11 August 1649, a solemn mass was celebrated to thank God for the good harvest that had just been brought home. Pallavicini, the official in charge of supply, became a hero overnight: 'He has doubled the size of a loaf of bread.'[149] The reader will have grasped the meaning of this apparently puzzling expression: as we have seen, in Rome as virtually everywhere else, the price of bread never changed; but the size of a loaf did. So Pallavicini had indeed (though only for a short while) at a stroke increased by 110% the buying power of the very poorest people, those who hardly ate anything but bread.

Rice

Rice is an even more tyrannical and enslaving crop than wheat. Readers of a recent history of China by a distinguished historian[150] may have been amused at the author's constant comparisons: one emperor was the Hugues Capet of China, another the Louis XI, or the Louis XIV, or the Chinese Napoleon. To understand the world of the Far East, the Westerner has to refer to his own circumstances. So we will refer to wheat when talking of rice. Both plants are gramineae and both natives of dry countries. Rice was later adapted to a semi-aquatic cultivation, which ensured its high yields and popularity. But one characteristic still reveals its origin: like wheat its roots require a rich supply of oxygen, which stagnant water cannot give. Consequently, however static the water in a rice field may appear, it is always in motion at some time so that oxygenation is possible. Hydraulic technology has therefore to be used alternately to create and suspend the movement of the water.

Compared to wheat, rice can be considered both more and less important. More in the sense that it accounts not, as wheat does, for 50% to 70% of the diet of the millions who eat it – but for 80% or 90%, or even more. Unhusked, it keeps better than wheat. On the other hand in the world as a whole, wheat cultivation is more extensive, accounting for 232 million hectares in 1977 to rice's 142. However, wheat yields much less to the hectare than rice (16·6 quintals against 26, on average) and the total production figures are roughly equal: 366 million tons of rice to 386 of wheat (and 349 of maize).[151] But the figures for rice are subject to adjustment, since they apply to unpolished rice: it loses 20% to 25% of its weight when it is husked. So the total production figure drops to 290 million tons, far below wheat and maize where the outer covering is retained. Another disadvantage of rice is that it holds the world record for the amount of man-handling it requires.

It must be added that, despite spreading in Europe, Africa and America, rice is still largely limited to the Far East, to the tune of 95% of present production; and that it is usually consumed locally, so that there is no trade in rice comparable to the grain trade. The only important trade before the eighteenth century was from southern to northern China, by the Imperial Canal, for the benefit of the Court at Peking; rice also travelled from Tonkin, present-day Cochin China, and Siam, to India, which always suffered from a shortage of food. There was only one exporting area in India: Bengal.

Rice cultivated dry and in paddy-fields

Rice and wheat like so many other cultivated plants, are natives of the dry valleys of central Asia. But wheat became popular much earlier than rice, possibly in about 5000 BC as compared with 2000 BC. Wheat therefore had a lead of tens of centuries. For a long time rice made a poor showing amongst dry-land plants. The earliest Chinese civilization did not know of rice at all: its staple crops were three gramineae grown on the vast windswept lands of northern China. They are still standard crops today: sorghum, with stems four to five metres high, wheat and millet. This, according to an English traveller (1793), was 'the Barbadoes millet distinguished by the Chinese under the name of *Kow leang* or lofty corn. It is cheaper than rice in all the northern provinces where it was probably the grain first cultivated, as it appears in ancient Chinese books, that measures of capacity were originally ascertained by the numbers of this grain which they contained. Thus one hundred grains would fill a *choo*.'[152] European travellers in northern China, who arrived exhausted in Peking in 1794, found that all the inn could offer was 'some wretched sugar and a dish of half-cooked millet'.[153] Even today, gruels made of wheat, millet and sorghum are still regularly eaten, alongside soya and sweet potatoes.[154]

Compared with this early progress, southern China, tropical, wooded and swampy, long remained a poor region. Like the Pacific islanders today, its inhabitants lived on yams – liana tubers used to make a nourishing flour – or taro (colocasia), a plant similar to beetroot. Its leaves are still a characteristic of the small earthbanks in China today, proof that taro was once important there. The American plants – sweet potato, manioc, potato and maize – did not cross the sea to join yam and colocasia until after the European discovery of the New World. They met resistance from the rice-growing civilization, well established by then. Manioc only became established in the region of Travancore in the Deccan, and the sweet potato in China in the eighteenth century, in Ceylon and on the distant Sandwich Islands of the Pacific Ocean. Today, tubers are still not much eaten in the Far East. Cereals are far more important, above all rice: 220 million tons in Asia as a whole in 1966, as against 140 million tons of grain (wheat, millet, maize, barley).[155]

Aquatic rice is thought to have become established in India first and then to have reached southern China overland or by sea, possibly in about 2150 or 2000 BC. It settled in slowly, in the standard form in which we now know it, and as it spread, the hourglass of Chinese life turned: the new south took over the dominance of the old north – especially as the north had the misfortune to open on the deserts and routes of central Asia and would later suffer invasions and devastation. From China (and India) rice-growing spead widely into Tibet, Indonesia and Japan. For the countries that adopted it, 'it was a way of showing that they were civilised'.[156] In Japan, the acceptance of rice must have been very slow, since it was already there in the first century AD, but did not play a very large part in the Japanese diet until the seventeenth century.[157]

Even today paddy-fields cover very small areas in the Far East (probably 95% of the total land devoted to aquatic rice in the world but still only 100 million hectares in 1966).[158] Outside this zone, rice managed to spread over enormous spaces somehow or other as a dry-land plant. This poor-quality rice is the staple foodstuff of certain underdeveloped peoples. Imagine a burnt and cleared corner of a forest in Sumatra, Ceylon or the highlands of Annam. The grain is sown broadcast on the cleared earth without any preparatory work (the tree stumps are left where they are and the ground is not tilled; the ashes serve as fertiliser). It ripens in five and a half months. A few crops – tubers, aubergines, various vegetables – can then be tried in its wake. This system completely exhausts the poor soil. The following year another section of the forest has to be cleared. With *decennial* rotation, this type of cultivation theoretically demands one square kilometre for fifty inhabitants, in fact for about twenty-five, as a good half of the mountainous ground is unusable. If the rotation necessary to restore the forest is not ten but twenty-five years (as is most frequently the case), the density should be ten to the square kilometre.

The 'fallow forest' invariably yields a fine soil easily worked by primitive tools. The system works well, provided, obviously, that the population does not increase excessively and that the destroyed forest grows again after each successive burning. This system of cultivation has various local names: *ladang* in Malaysia and Indonesia, *ray* or *rai* in the Vietnam mountains, *djoung* in India, and *tavy* in Madagascar where rice was introduced by Arab sailors in about the tenth century. They are all simple forms of life, supplemented by 'the farinaceous marrow of the sago palms', or the produce of the bread-fruit tree. They are a far cry from the methodical production of the paddy-fields but very far also from the exhausting labour they demand.

The miracle of the paddy-fields

So much has been written about the paddy-fields that we should be able to give a fairly complete account of them. Drawings in a Chinese work of 1210, the *Keng Tche Tou*, already show the chequered pattern of the paddies, divided into small patches, irrigation pumps worked by pedals, the planting and harvesting

Rice seedlings, nineteenth-century China. (Photo B.N., Paris.)

of the rice, and 'the same plough as today, yoked to a single buffalo'.¹⁵⁹ The picture is the same whatever the date, even today. Nothing seems to have changed.

What is striking at first glance is the extraordinarily intensive utilization of these precious lands: 'All the plains are cultivated,' wrote the Jesuit Father du Halde (1735).¹⁶⁰ 'One sees neither hedges, ditches nor almost any trees, so afraid are they of losing an inch of land.' That other admirable Jesuit, Father de Las Cortes, had said the same thing a century before: 'there was not an inch of land ... not the smallest corner that was not cultivated'.¹⁶¹ The paddies are divided by flimsy earthbanks into sections some fifty metres along each side. Water flows in and out of them. The water is muddy – which is a good thing, as mud restores the fertility of the soil and does not suit the malaria-carrying mosquito. The clear water in hills and mountains, on the other hand, favours mosquitoes; so the *ladangs* and *ray* are regions of endemic malaria and therefore of limited demographic growth. In the fifteenth century Angkor Wat was a thriving capital, with rice-fields irrigated by muddy water. Siamese attacks were not themselves responsible for its destruction; but they threw daily life and agriculture into confusion. The water of the canals cleared and malaria triumphed, and, with it, the invading forest.[162] Similar dramas seem to have occurred in seventeenth-century Bengal. If the rice-field was too small and flooded by adjacent clear water, the destructive onslaught of malaria was unleashed. Malaria was omnipresent in the depression between the Himalayas and the Siwalik hills, where there are so many clear springs.[163]

Water is certainly the great problem. It can submerge the plants: in Siam and Cambodia the unparalleled adaptability of floating rice, capable of growing stems nine to ten metres long, had to be used to combat the enormous variations in water level. The harvesting is done from boats, by cutting the heads and leaving the stalks, which are sometimes of incredible length.[164] Bringing in and then draining off water is another difficulty. Sometimes it is brought along bamboo conduits from high-ground springs; sometimes drawn from wells, as in the Ganges plain and often in China; or, as in Ceylon, from large reservoirs – but the tanks that collect the water are almost always at a low level, sometimes sunk deeply into the ground. In some places it was therefore necessary to carry water to a paddy-field on higher ground, hence the rudimentary norias and pedal pumps that can still be seen today. To replace them by steam pumps or electric pumps would be to forfeit cheap human labour. Father de Las Cortes saw them functioning: 'They sometimes draw water,' he noted, 'with a handy little machine, a sort of noria that does not require horses. It is the easiest thing in the world [according to him] for a single Chinaman to make this device rotate with his feet all day'.[165] Sluices were also needed to make the water flow from one paddy to the next. Of course, the system chosen depends on local conditions. When no type of irrigation is possible, the earthbanks of the rice fields serve to retain rainwater, which is enough to support a very large area of cultivation in the plains of the monsoon lands of Asia.

All in all, an enormous concentration of work, human capital and careful adaptation was involved. Even then nothing would have held together if the broad lines of this irrigation system had not been firmly integrated and supervised from above. This implies a stable society, state authority and constant large-scale works. The Imperial Canal of the Blue River at Peking was also a vast irrigation system.[166] The increase in the number of rice-fields implied an increase in state control. It also implied the concentration of villages, as much because of the collective requirements of irrigation as because of the insecurity of the Chinese countryside.

The rice-fields therefore brought high populations and strict social discipline to the regions where they prospered. If southern China was dominant in about 1100, it was because of rice. As early as 1380, the population of the south was two and a half times that of the north: 38 million to 15, according to the official figures.[167] And the real achievement of the rice-fields was not their continuous use of the same cultivable area, nor their water technology designed to safeguard the yield, but the two or sometimes three harvests they produced every year.

This can be illustrated by the present-day calendar of Lower Tonkin: the farming year begins with the January planting-out; the harvest comes five months later in June: this is the 'five-month crop'. In order to make sure of another, five months later, in the tenth month, all speed must be made. The harvest is hastily taken to the barns, the rice-fields must be ploughed again, levelled, manured and flooded. There is no time to sow broadcast – germination would take too long. The young plants are taken from a seed-bed where they have been thickly sown on a well-manured soil. Then they are planted out at intervals of 10 to 12 cm. The seed-bed, which is abundantly manured with both human excrement and domestic refuse, is vital to the operation: it saves time and produces strong seedlings. The harvest of the tenth month – which is the important one – is in full swing by November. Immediately afterwards begins the ploughing for the January planting.[168]

The sequence of these hurried labours is fixed by a strict agricultural timetable everywhere. In Cambodia[169] the first tilling after the rains, which leave pools of water, 'wakes up the rice-field'. The ground is tilled once from the circumference inwards and then from the centre outwards. The peasant walks beside his buffalo so as not to leave hollows behind him that would fill with water. He draws one or many diagonal channels across the furrows to drain off excessive water; he also has to pull up the weeds and leave them to rot, drive away the crabs that infest insufficiently deep water and take the precaution of pulling out the seedlings with his right hand and beating them against his left foot 'to knock the earth from the roots, which are further cleansed by being rinsed in water'.

Proverbs and familiar figures of speech bear witness to these tasks. In Cambodia, when the water is brought into the fields of seedlings, they call it the 'drowning of partridges and turtledoves'; when the first panicles appear they say that 'the plant is pregnant'; the rice-field then takes on a golden hue the 'colour of a parrot's wing'. A few weeks later, at harvest-time, when the grain 'where the milk has formed becomes heavy', comes the game (or almost a game) of stacking the sheaves in 'mattresses', 'lintels', 'flying pelicans', 'dogs' tails' or 'elephants' feet'. Threshing completed, the grain is winnowed to remove 'the promise of the paddy' (the strict meaning of *paddy* is 'rice in the husk').

To a Westerner, the *chevalier* Chardin, who saw rice being grown in Persia, the most striking thing was the speed at which it grew: 'This grain ripens in three months, although it is moved after shooting up; for ... it is transplanted, ear by ear in a well watered and muddy soil ... A week's drying and the grain is ripe.'[170] It was the speed that explained the two harvests, both of rice, or farther north one of rice and the other of wheat, rye or millet. Sometimes three harvests are possible, two of rice and one in between of wheat, barley, buckwheat or vegetables (turnips, carrots, beans, Nankin cabbages). The rice-field is thus a factory. In Lavoisier's time one hectare of land under wheat in France produced an average of five quintals; one hectare of rice-field often bears thirty quintals of rice in the husk. After milling, this means twenty-one quintals of edible rice at 3500 calories per kilogram, or the colossal total of 7,350,000 calories per hectare, as compared with 1,500,000 for wheat and only 340,000 animal calories if that hectare were devoted to stock-raising and produced 150 kilograms of meat.[171] These figures demonstrate the enormous advantage of the rice-field and of vegetable foodstuffs. The Far Eastern civilizations' preference for vegetarianism certainly does not spring from idealism.

Rice lightly boiled in water is daily food, like bread in the West. One cannot help thinking of the Italian *pane e companatico* when noting the meagre accompaniment to the rice ration of a well-fed peasant in the Tonkin delta in modern times: 'five grams of pork, ten grams of *nuoc mam* (fish sauce), twenty grams of salt and a quantity of green leaves with no calorific value' to 1000 grams of white rice (representing 3500 calories out of a total of 3565).[172] The daily ration of a rice-eating Indian in 1940 was more varied, but equally vegetarian: '560 grams of rice, 30 grams of peas and beans, 125 grams of fresh vegetables, 9 grams of oil or vegetable fat, 14 grams of fish, meat and eggs and a negligible quantity of milk'.[173] And the workers of Peking were equally short of protein in 1928, since 80% of their expenditure on food went on cereals, 15.8% on vegetables and spices and only 3.2% on meat.[174]

Present-day reality is not far removed from the past. In seventeenth-century Ceylon, a traveller noted with amazement that 'some rice cooked in water and salt, with a few green leaves and the juice of a lemon, passes for a good meal'. Even 'the great' ate very little meat or fish.[175] In 1735, Father du Halde mentions that a Chinaman who had spent the day working incessantly 'often in water up to his knees, in the evening ... would think himself lucky to find rice, cooked herbs, with a little tea. It must be noted that rice in China is always cooked in water and is to the Chinese what bread is to the European, never giving rise to distaste.'[176] The ration, according to Father de Las Cortes, was: 'a small bowl of rice and water without salt, which is the usual bread in these regions' – or rather four or five of these bowls 'which they raise to their lips with their left hand, holding two sticks in their right, hastily conveying it to their stomachs, as if they were throwing it into a bag, blowing on it first of all'. There was no point in mentioning bread or biscuit to these Chinese. When they had wheat they ate it in cakes kneaded with lard.[177]

These Chinese 'rolls' delighted Guignes and his fellow travellers in 1794. They improved them with 'a little butter' and thus 'made up for the fasts the mandarins had imposed on us'.[178] What one has here is surely choice of an entire civilization, a dominant taste or rather passion, in terms of diet, the result of a conscious preference, the recognition of excellence. To stop cultivating rice would be to slide down the scale. 'The men in the monsoon lands of Asia,' says

Pierre Gourou, 'prefer rice to tubers and gruel cereals' or bread. Japanese peasants today cultivate barley, corn, oats and millet, but only between rice harvests or when only dry cultivation is possible. They never eat these cereals – 'which they think dreary' – except from necessity. This explains why rice at present extends as far towards the Asiatic north as possible, up to the 49th parallel, in regions where we would expect other crops.[179]

The entire Far East lived on a diet of rice and its by-products, even the European settlers in Goa. The Portuguese women of the town, writes Mandelslo in 1639, prefer rice to bread 'now that they have got used to it'.[180] A wine made from rice in China was 'as intoxicating as the best Spanish wine', 'tending toward the colour of amber'. Either in imitation, or perhaps because rice was so cheap in the West, 'in certain places in Europe [in the eighteenth century] a very strong liquor was distilled from it, but it is forbidden in France as are spirits made from grain or molasses'.[181]

Diet therefore consisted of a great deal of rice, and little meat or no meat at all. Its overwhelming importance in these circumstances can be imagined; variations in its price in China affected everything, including the daily pay of the soldiers, which rose and fell with it on a kind of sliding scale.[182] It was even more marked in Japan, where rice was actually currency before the crucial reforms and changes of the seventeenth century. The price of rice on the Japanese market, with additional pressures from monetary devaluations, multiplied by ten between 1642-3 and 1713-15.[183]

Rice's greatest claim to fame is the second harvest. When does this date from? It must already have been established for several centuries by the time Father de Las Cortes admired the multiple harvest in the Canton area in 1626. He noted that from the same land, 'they obtain three consecutive harvests in one year, two of rice and one of wheat, with a yield of 40 or 50 to 1, because of the moderate heat, atmospheric conditions and most excellent soil, much better and more fertile than any soil in Spain or Mexico'.[184] We may doubt the '40 or 50 to 1' and perhaps the third harvest (of wheat), but the impression of abundance remains. As for the precise date of this crucial revolution, it was at the beginning of the eleventh century that varieties of early-maturing rice (which ripened in winter and thus made the double harvest possible) were first imported from Champa (the centre and south of Annam). Gradually the innovation reached all the warm provinces, one by one.[185] By the thirteenth century, the system had been established. And thus the great demographic expansion of southern China began.

The importance of rice

The success of and preference for rice raises a series of problems, as indeed does wheat as the dominant foodplant of Europe. Boiled rice, like the European loaf of bread, is a 'staple foodstuff' – that is, the entire nourishment of an enormous

Threshing rice by hand. Drawing by Hanabusa Itchô (1652-1724). Galerie Jeannette Ostier, Paris. (Photo Nelly Delay.)

population depends upon the monotonous daily consumption of this single food. Cookery is the art of improving, making more attractive, the basic foodstuff: this was common to both cultures. But historical information about Asia is often lacking.

The success of rice brought it many obvious and far-reaching responsibilities. For one thing, rice-fields occupy a very small area of ground. Secondly, their high productivity enables them to feed a large and densely settled population. According to the perhaps over-optimistic view of one historian, every Chinese inhabitant over the last six or seven centuries would have been supplied with 300 kilograms of rice or other cereals, amounting to 2000 calories a day.[186] Even if these figures are probably too high and even if the continuity of this well-being is contradicted by unequivocal evidence of poverty and peasant revolts,[187] rice nevertheless does seem to have provided a degree of security of food supply to those who grew it. How else could they have kept their numbers up?

However, the concentration of the rice-fields and of the labour force in the lowland regions led to some missed opportunities. So it was that in China, where by contrast with Java or the Philippines, mountain rice was the exception until at least the eighteenth century, a traveller could still in 1734 find the highlands virtually deserted when he crossed from Ning Po to Peking.[188] As a result, all the resources that Europe drew from her mountain regions – men, livestock, a whole

154 *The Structures of Everyday Life*

active capital of energy which was put to good use – was foregone and even deliberately rejected in the Far East. What an opportunity was lost there! But then how could the Chinese be expected to develop their mountain regions, when they had no experience of forestry or livestock farming, when they consumed no milk or cheese, very little meat, and had never attempted to incorporate the mountain-dwelling population where it existed (indeed the contrary). To paraphrase Pierre Gourou, we should imagine the Jura or Savoy without flocks, with haphazard forest clearings, and with the active population concentrated in the plains, by the shores of the lakes and rivers. The cultivation of rice, its very abundance and the eating habits of the Chinese population were partly responsible for this state of affairs.

The explanation is also to be sought in a long and still obscure history. While irrigation is not as ancient as Chinese tradition teaches, it was certainly introduced on a large scale in the fourth and third centuries BC, along with a government policy of intensive land-clearing and the development of more sophisticated agronomy.[189] It was during this age that China turned to hydraulics and intensive cereal-production and created her classic historical landscape, under the Han dynasty. Even so this landscape, which by Western chronology appeared during the age of Pericles, cannot have been complete before the successful introduction of the early-maturing varieties of rice in the south, which

Threshing rice with a flail in Japan. Galerie Jeannette Ostier, Paris. (Photo Nelly Delay.)

takes us to the time of the Crusades (eleventh to twelfth centuries). It was only comparatively recently then, by the very slow standards of civilizations, that classical China emerged in recognizable form, from a long agricultural revolution which broke up and rebuilt her structures and which was undoubtedly the most important event in the history of mankind in the Far East.

There is nothing comparable to this in Europe where, long before the Homeric legends, an agrarian civilization was already established in the Mediterranean region – wheat, olives, vines and livestock, with herds of sheep that moved from one level of the mountains to another, or down on to the plains. Telemachus remembered living among the mud-stained mountain-dwellers of the Peloponnese, who lived on acorns.[190] Rural life in Europe was based on both agriculture and stock-farming, *labourage et pâturage*, the latter providing not only the manure vital to the crops, but also animal energy which was put to constant use, and a substantial share of human diet. On the other hand, a hectare of arable land in Europe, under crop rotation, could nourish far fewer people than a hectare in China.

In the rice-growing south, the Chinese were preoccupied with their own problems: they did not try, and fail, to conquer the mountain regions: they never attempted it. Having eliminated almost all domestic animals and closed his doors to the wretched mountain-dwellers, who grew rice on dry land, the lowlander prospered, but had to become a jack-of-all-trades, pulling the plough if necessary, hauling along the boats or hoisting them from one reach to another, carrying timber, and footing it along the roads with news and letters. The buffaloes of the rice-fields, who were fed on short rations, hardly worked at all. Horses, mules and camels were only to be found in the north (but the north was not rice-growing China). In the last resort, the China of the paddy-fields represents the triumph of a peasantry turned in upon itself. Rice-growing was not initially directed towards outlying areas and new land, but became established around the already existing towns. It was the domestic rubbish and human excrement of the towns, and the mud of the streets that fertilized the first rice-fields. So there was a constant coming and going of peasants to collect from the towns the precious fertilizer 'which they pay for with herbs, vinegar or money'.[191] And that also explains the unbearable smells that wafted over the towns and country villages. The symbiosis between town and countryside was even greater than in the West, which is saying a good deal. Rice, or rather the immense success of rice-growing, was responsible for this.

It took the substantial demographic increase of the eighteenth century to bring into cultivation the hills and certain mountain-slopes, along with the revolutionary expansion of maize and sweet potatoes which had in fact been imported two hundred years earlier from America. For important as it was, rice did not rule out other crops – either in China, India or Japan.

Japan under the Tokugawa (1600–1868) experienced during the seventeenth century, at a time when it was cut off, or virtually so, from foreign trade (after

Two aspects of rice cultivation: Ploughing with a buffalo, 'to make the water soak in and penetrate the earth'.

1638), a spectacular development of both its economy and its population, which rose to 30 million. The capital Edo (Tokyo), alone, had a population of a million in about 1700. Progress on this scale was possible only because of a constant rise in the agricultural production which supported these 30 million people on a surface area which 'could only have supported 5 or 10 million people in Europe'.[192] First of all, there was gradual progress in rice production, as a result of improvements in seeds, in irrigation networks and drainage systems, and in the manual implements used by the peasants (in particular the invention of the *senbakoki*, a sort of giant comb used for raking the rice);[193] and even more as a result of the commercialization of richer and more plentiful fertilizers than human or animal excrement: dried sardines, colza, soya or cotton cake, for instance. These fertilizers often represented 30% to 50% of working expenses.[194] In addition, the increasing commercialization of agricultural products led to the establishment of a considerable trade in rice, with merchants who hoarded stocks; and also an increase of complementary crops like cotton, colza, hemp, tobacco, pulses, mulberries, sugar cane, sesame and wheat. Cotton and colza were the most important, colza in association with rice-growing, cotton with wheat. These crops increased gross income from agriculture but required double or triple the amount of fertilizer used in the rice paddies and twice as much manpower. Outside the rice paddies, in the 'fields', barley, buckwheat and

Irrigating the rice-field. Engravings from paintings in the *Keng Che Too* (Cabinet des Estampes, B.N., Paris). (Photo B.N.)

turnips were often combined in a three-crop system. While rice was still subject to a very heavy rent in kind (50% to 60% of the harvest was paid to the landowner) these new crops led to the payment of rents in money. They linked the rural world to a modern economy and account for the appearance of peasants who were if not rich at least comfortably off, though the properties were and remained tiny.[195] This is proof enough, if proof is needed, that rice too is a complex phenomenon with features which we Western historians are only beginning to recognize.

As there were two Chinas, so there were two Indias: rice was grown all round the peninsular part of India, to some extent in the lower Indus valley, and throughout the broad delta and lower valley of the Ganges, but left an enormous area to wheat and in particular to millet, which could be grown on infertile soil. According to recent work by historians of India, there was a great burst of agricultural activity, beginning with the Empire of Delhi, which undertook many land-clearing and irrigation projects, diversified production, and encouraged industrial crops like indigo, sugar cane, cotton and mulberry trees for silkworms.[196] In the seventeenth century, there was considerable demographic expansion in the towns. As in Japan, production increased too, and trade, particularly in grain and rice, was organized over very long distances, by land, sea and river. But unlike Japan, it seems, there was no equivalent progress in agricultural techniques. Animals, oxen and buffalo, played an important role as beasts of burden or as draught animals, but their dried dung was used as fuel, not as fertilizer. For religious reasons, human excrement was not used as manure, as in China. Above all, of course, the great herds of cattle were not used for food, apart from milk and ghee (and these were only produced in small quantities because of the poor condition of the animals, which were not usually kept under cover and hardly fed at all).

All in all, rice and other grains could only provide inadequately for life in the great subcontinent. As in Japan,[197] the demographic surplus of the eighteenth century was to lead to dramatic famine in India. Rice cannot be blamed for that of course, since it was not the only agent in India or elsewhere, of the over-population, past or present. It only contributed to make it possible.

Maize

Maize is a fascinating subject to complete our study of the dominant food plants. I decided after reflection not to include manioc, which only serves as a basis for primitive and generally small-scale cultures in America. Maize, on the other hand, sustained the brilliance of the Inca, Maya and Aztec civilizations or semi-civilizations, all of which were its authentic creations. It then rose to remarkable popularity on a world scale.

Well-ascertained origins

Everything is straightforward in this case, even the question of origins. As a result of some doubtful texts and interpretations, eighteenth-century naturalists thought that maize had come both from the Far East (yet again) and from America, where Europeans discovered it at the time of Columbus' first voyage.[198] The first proposition is unquestionably wrong. Maize only reached Asia and Africa (where certain remains, even certain Yoruba sculptures, might still be misleading) from America. Archaeology has inevitably had the last word on the question. Although ears of maize are not preserved in ancient layers, its pollen can be fossilized. Fossilized pollen has been found around Mexico City, where deep excavations have been carried out. The town in the past was on the edge of a lagoon which was drained so that the ground subsided and considerable settlement occurred. Numerous excavations of the old swampy soil of the town have revealed grains of maize pollen at a depth of fifty to sixty metres – that is dating from thousands of years ago. Some of the pollen is of the same type as the maize cultivated today, some from at least two species of wild maize.

The problem has been elucidated by recent excavations in the valley of

Tehuacan, 200 kilometres south of Mexico City. The dryness of this region, which becomes an immense desert every winter, has preserved grains of ancient maize, chewed-up leaves and the stalks of ears. These plants, together with human remains, were found near points where underground water rose to the surface. Cave dwellings have supplied the excavators with considerable material and in one stroke yielded up the whole retrospective history of maize.

> In the older layers you can see all the modern types of maize disappear one by one.... Only a primitive maize is present in the very oldest, from seven or eight thousand years ago, and everything suggests that it was not yet cultivated. This wild maize was a small plant.... The ripe ear only measured two to three centimetres, with only fifty or so grains, situated at the axil of feeble bracts. The ear has a very fragile axis and the leaves surrounding it do not form a lasting sheath, so that the seeds must have been easily disseminated.[199]

Wild maize was thus able to ensure its survival. In cultivated maize, on the other hand, the grains are imprisoned by leaves that do not open when the grain is ripe. Man has to lend a hand.

Of course the mystery is not entirely solved. Why did this wild maize disappear? The herds, notably of goats, brought in by the Europeans may have been responsible. In what country did it originate? That it was America is accepted, but research still has to fix the exact birthplace in the New World of this plant so marvellously transformed by man. Paraguay, Peru and Guatemala have been suggested; Mexico has just shown a more ancient claim. But archaeology too may have some surprises in store. And as if these fascinating questions are destined to remain unsolved, some experts still talk or at least speculate about a second possible place of origin of maize: the mountains of Asia, cradle of almost all world cereals, or perhaps Burma.

Maize and American civilizations

In any case maize had long been part of the American landscape by the fifteenth century, when the Aztec and Inca civilizations were becoming established. Sometimes it was combined with manioc, as in eastern South America; sometimes it was grown alone, either as a dry crop or on the irrigated terraces of Peru and the shores of the Mexican lakes. As far as dry cultivation is concerned, the system is much the same as the cultivation of rice in *ladang* or *ray*. It is enough to have seen the great brushwood fires on the Mexican plateau, the Anahuac, and the immense clouds of smoke, in which aeroplanes (flying at only two or three thousand feet above these highlands) sometimes go into alarming vertical drops because of the pockets of warm air – to imagine the rotation of maize crops on this dry terrain, a new section of forest or brush being cleared every year. The system is called *milpa*. Gemelli Careri noticed it in the mountains near Cuer-

Woman grinding maize. Mexican sculpture, Museum of Anthropology, Guadalajara. (Photo Giraudon.)

navaca a little way from Mexico in 1697: 'There was only grass,' he noted, 'so dry that the peasants burned it to fertilise the land.'[200]

Intensive cultivation of maize is found on the shores of the Mexican lakes, and even more spectacularly on terraces in Peru. When the Incas came down by the Andes valleys from the heights of Lake Titicaca they had to find land for their increasing population. The mountain was cut out in steps, linked by stairways and irrigated by a series of canals. Iconographic documents are very evocative of this culture: they show peasants with digging sticks and women planting the seeds; in another picture, the quickly ripening grain has to be defended against the apparently countless birds and an animal, probably a llama, which is eating a cob. At harvest-time the ear was pulled out with the stalk, which was rich in sugar and a valuable foodstuff. It is instructive to compare such naïve drawings by Poma de Ayala with some photographs taken in upper Peru in 1959. They show the same peasant vigorously driving in an enormous digging stick and hoisting up large lumps of earth while the woman plants the grain. In the seventeenth century in Florida, Coreal saw the natives burning off brush and twice a year, in March and July, using 'pointed sticks' to bury the seed.[201]

Maize is a miraculous plant; it grows quickly and its grain is edible even before it is ripe.[202] The harvest from one grain sown was between 70 and 80 in the dry zone of colonial Mexico; in the Michoacan, a yield of 150 to one was considered low. Almost incredible record yields are mentioned of 800 to one on very good land near Queretaro. It was even possible to obtain two harvests in Mexico in hot or temperate country; one of *riego* (with irrigation), the other of *temporal* (as a result of rainfall).[203] Thus, in the colonial period, we can imagine yields of between five and six quintals a hectare, similar to those on small properties today. Easily obtained, what is more, for maize has always been a crop that demands little effort. The archaeologist Fernando Márquez Miranda has given us an excellent account of the advantages enjoyed by peasants cultivating maize: it required them to work only fifty days in the year, one day in seven or eight, according to season.[204] They were therefore free, perhaps a little too free. The maize-growing societies on the irrigated terraces of the Andes or on the lakesides of the Mexican plateaux resulted in theocratic totalitarian systems and all the leisure of the peasants was used for gigantic public works of the Egyptian type. (It is arguable whether the cause was indeed maize, or irrigation, or the dense population of societies which became oppressive from sheer weight of numbers.) Without maize, the giant Mayan or Aztec pyramids, the cyclopean walls of Cuzco or the wonders of Machu Pichu would have been impossible. They were achieved because maize virtually produces itself.

The problem then is that on one hand we have a series of striking achievements, on the other, human misery. As usual we must ask: who is to blame? Man of course. But maize as well.

What did all that suffering achieve? An unsatisfactory daily bread made from cornflour, cornmeal cakes cooked on earthenware dishes over low heat, or corn popped over the fire. None of these is an adequate food. They need to be supplemented by a meat ration, but that was never possible. Even today, the maize-growing peasants in the Indian regions are only too often in a wretched condition, particularly in the Andes. Their food consists of maize, more maize and dried potatoes (our potatoes are known to have originated in Peru). Cooking is done in the open air on a hearth built of stones. The one room in the low hut is shared by animals and people alike. Their unchanging clothes are woven from llama wool on primitive looms. Their only resort is to chew coca leaves, which numb the pangs of hunger, thirst, cold and fatigue; or to drink beer made from sprouted (or mashed) maize, *chicha*, which the Spaniards discovered in the West Indies and propagated, at least in name, throughout Indian America. Even more popular is *sora*, the strong Peruvian beer. Both were dangerous drinks vainly forbidden by sensible authorities. They enabled these sad and enfeebled populations to escape from themselves in Goyaesque scenes of drunkenness.[205]

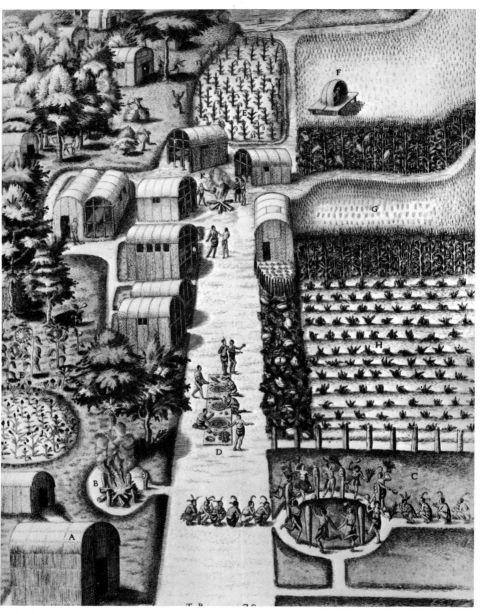

An Indian maize plantation: the Indian camp of Secota in Virginia, on the edge of a forest, with cabins, hunters, ritual dances, tobacco-fields (E) and maize (H and G) in widely spaced rows, as de Bry explains, because of the importance of this plant 'with broad leaves like those of great reeds'. Theodore de Bry, *Admiranda Narratio...*, 1590, plate XX. (Photo Giraudon.)

Maize has one serious disadvantage: it is not always within easy reach. It stops half-way up the slopes of the Andes, because of the cold. Elsewhere it occupies limited areas. The grain must therefore be moved around, whatever the cost. The dramatic migration of the Yura Indians south of the Potosi, even today, takes them down from the inhuman heights where they live – at an altitude of 4000 metres – towards the maize regions. The providential saltmines in the mountains which they work like stone quarries, provide them with exchange currency. Every year, in March, men, women and children, all on foot, embark on a journey of at least three months there and back in search of maize, coca and alcohol; bags of salt stand like ramparts near their camps. This is a small and modest example of one of the ways in which maize or maize flour have been moved around since the very distant past.[206]

In the nineteenth century, Alexander von Humboldt[207] in New Spain and Auguste de Saint-Hilaire[208] in Brazil noted the transport of maize by mules, with its stopping places, ranches, stations and fixed routes. Everything depended on it, even the mines. There is no saying who profited most: the miners in search of silver, the gold-washers – or the food merchants. Any stoppage in the traffic and the consequences immediately affected the mainstream of history, as we can tell from the memoirs of Rodrigo Vivero, Captain-General of the port of Panama at the beginning of the seventeenth century: silver from the Potosi mines arrived at the port of Panama from Arica, via Callao. The valuable cargo then crossed the isthmus and travelled to Porto Belo on the Caribbean Sea, first by caravans of mules and then by boat on the river Chagres. But muleteers and boatmen had to be fed, otherwise there would be no transport. And Panama lived solely on imported maize, either from Nicaragua or Caldera (Chile). In 1626, during a barren year, the situation was only saved by the dispatch of a boat from Peru loaded with 2000 to 3000 *fanegas* of maize (100 to 150 tons) which enabled the silver to travel over the heights of the isthmus.[209]

The dietary revolutions of the eighteenth century

Cultivated food plants are constantly reaching new areas where they can completely alter people's lives. But their natural movements can take centuries or millennia. After the discovery of America, however, such movements became more frequent and faster. The plants of the Old World travelled to the New, and in return New World plants reached the Old: in one direction went rice, wheat, sugar cane and the coffee bush; in the other maize, potatoes, haricot beans, tomatoes,[210] manioc and tobacco.

Wherever they went, the newcomers met resistance from existing crops and eating habits: Europeans considered potatoes a sticky and indigestible food; maize is still despised in south-east China where rice still rules. But despite these entrenched attachments and the slow pace at which new experiences were absorbed, all these plants in the end became widespread and accepted. In Europe, in any case, it was the poor who first opened their doors to them; and demographic growth subsequently turned them into desperate necessities. And if the world population increased, or was able to increase, was this not after all at least partly the result of the increased production of foodstuffs which the new crops made possible?

Maize outside America

Whatever the arguments put forward, it seems unlikely that maize had strayed beyond its American home before the voyage of Columbus, who brought back some grains when he first returned in 1493. It also seems unlikely that it originally came from Africa. To cite the different names by which maize is known throughout the world as evidence of origin is not very convincing: it has been called just about every name under the sun. In Lorraine, for instance, it is known as 'Rhodes corn'; in the Pyrenees 'Spanish corn'; in Bayonne 'Indian corn'; in Tuscany 'Syrian *doura*', elsewhere in Italy it was called *il gran turco* and in both Germany and Holland it was also called 'Turkish corn'; in Russia *kukuru* – which is in fact the Turkish word for it, but in Turkey itself it was also known as 'Roums (i.e. Christian) corn'; and in Franche-Comté 'turky'. In the Garonne valley and the Lauragais, it had an even more unexpected change of name: it appeared in the marshes of Castelnaudary in 1637 and round Toulouse in 1639, under the name of 'Spanish millet', while millet, which was much grown in the area, began to be listed in market records as 'French millet'; then the two cereals were known as 'coarse millet' and 'fine millet' until maize finally ousted millet altogether and took its name: so by 1655, it was simply known as 'millet'. And so it was called for over a century, until the Revolution, when the word *maïs* (maize) finally appears on the market lists.[211]

After the discovery of America, we can very approximately trace the career of maize in Europe and beyond: it was a very slow one, with really widespread success only in the eighteenth century.

Botanists had, however, begun to note the plant in their herbals as early as 1536 (Jean Ruel); and Leonhart Fuchs (1542) gives an accurate drawing of it, adding that it is to be found in any garden.[212] But what interests us is when it left the kitchen-garden – which is usually an experimental laboratory – and conquered the fields and markets. The peasants had to become used to the new plant, learn to use it and in particular to eat it. Maize is often associated in this respect with haricot beans, which also came from America and which enriched the soil: *fagioli* and *grano turco* invaded Italy together. Olivier de Serres noted that they had both arrived in his native Vivarais by 1590.[213] But it all took a very long time. As late as 1700, an agronomist was still surprised that maize was so little grown in France.[214] Similarly, in the Balkans, maize became established

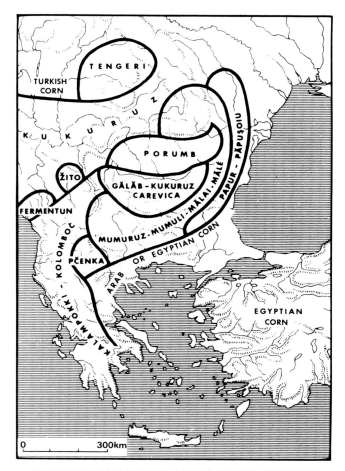

17 DIFFERENT NAMES FOR MAIZE IN THE BALKANS
(From Traian Stoyanovitch, in *Annales E.S.C.*, 1966, p. 1031.)

under at least ten different names, but in order to evade taxation and seigneurial dues, it was restricted to gardens and land far off the main roads. It did not take over the wide open spaces until the eighteenth century, two hundred years after the discovery of America.[215] It was only in the eighteenth century, in any case, that maize really took hold in Europe as a whole.

This is quite surprising, since locally there were exceptions, where there was early and spectacular success. Maize travelled from Andalusia, where it was to be found in 1500, and from Catalonia, Portugal and Galicia where it was growing by 1520, to Italy and to south-western France.

It was spectacularly successful in Venetia. Maize-growing is thought to have been introduced there in about 1539, and had spread to the entire Terra Firma some time between the end of the century and the beginning of the next. It had developed even earlier in the Polesina, a narrow region near Venice where there was much capital investment in the sixteenth century, and where farmers were experimenting with new cereals in whole fields: it is hardly surprising then that the *grano turco* should have taken hold rapidly here from about 1554.[216]

In south-west France, Béarn was the first place to grow maize. By 1523 in the Bayonne region, and 1563 in the country round Navarrenx,[217] maize was being used as a green fodder crop. It took longer to become accepted as a food for the peasants. The decline of woad-growing in the Toulouse area probably helped.[218]

In the valley of the Garonne, in Venetia, and in general wherever it was grown, it was inevitably the poor, whether in town or country, who had to take without enthusiasm to eating cornmeal cakes instead of bread. We read of the Béarn in 1698, for instance: '*Milloc* (i.e. maize) is a sort of grain from the Indies, which the people eat.'[219] 'It is the principal food of the poor people in Lisbon,'[220] according to the Russian consul there. In Burgundy, '*gaudes*, cornflour cakes cooked in the oven, are the food eaten by the peasants and are taken to be sold in Dijon'.[221] But nowhere did the upper classes take to eating maize: they probably had the same reaction to it as the twentieth-century traveller to Montanegro who commented on 'the heavy cornballs one sees everywhere here: their golden yellow flour is pleasing to the eye but unpalatable to the stomach'.[222]

Maize had one very persuasive argument in its favour: its high yield. In spite of the risks (a diet too dependent on maize can produce pellagra) it did after all put an end to the previously recurrent famines in Venetia. The *millasse* of southern France, the *polenta* of Italy and the *mamaliga* of Roumania thus all became well known to the tables of the masses, who had experience, as we should not forget, of much less palatable famine foods. No taboo in eating habits stands up to famine. In addition, maize could also be used to feed livestock, and once it began to be grown on fallow land, effected a revolution comparable to that of the first forage crops which had also used the fallow. Finally, the growing proportion of harvests accounted for by this abundant crop increased the production of saleable wheat. The peasant ate maize and sold his wheat, for which he could get about double the price. It is a fact that in eighteenth-century Venetia, thanks to maize, between 15 and 20% of the cereal crop was exported – a proportion comparable to that of England in 1745-55.[223] France, during this period, was consuming to within 1 or 2% of all the cereals it produced. But in the Lauraguais too, 'in the seventeenth and particularly the eighteenth centuries, maize by supplying the bulk of the peasants' food, makes it possible for wheat to become a marketable crop'.[224]

In the Congo, maize, which was imported from America by the Portuguese in the early sixteenth century, and was known as Masa ma Mputa, 'Portuguese grain', was not originally adopted with any more enthusiasm than in Europe. In 1597, Pigafetta reported that it was less highly prized than other cereals and was used not to feed men, but for pigs.[225] But this was an early reaction. Gradually maize came to occupy the first place among food plants north of the Congo, in Benin and among the Yoruba. And the ultimate accolade, it has been incorporated into the cycle of legends, which also reminds us that food is not a reality confined to material life.[226]

Reaching Europe and even Africa was fairly easy. But for maize to penetrate India, Burma, Japan and China was an achievement of quite a different order. It arrived early on in China, by the first half of the sixteenth century, both by the continental route, and over the Burmese frontier, thus reaching Yunan where it became established; and by the sea route to Fukien whose ports had close links with the East Indies. It was by the same ports incidentally (and through the intermediary of either the Portuguese or the Chinese merchants who traded with the Moluccas) that the groundnut arrived in the sixteenth century, and a little later the sweet potato. However, until 1762, maize was not widely grown in China, being confined to Yunan, a few districts in Szechwan, and Fukien. It did not in fact take hold until the rapid population expansion of the eighteenth century made it necessary to clear more land in the hills and mountains, outside the rice-growing plains. Here again, it was from necessity, not choice that the Chinese people had to give up their favourite food. Maize became widely established in the north and spread even further towards Korea. It joined the traditional northern crops, millet and sorghum, and this extension of maize-growing restored the demographic balance between northern and southern China, the south having been much more populous hitherto.[227] Japan, too, welcomed maize along with a whole range of new plants some of which reached it by way of China.

Potatoes: a great future

Potatoes are known to have been growing in the Andes regions of America since about 2000 BC, at altitudes where maize cannot thrive. They were a life-saving standby, usually in dried form in order to keep longer.[228]

The spread of potatoes to the Old World did not follow quite the same pattern as that of maize: it was as slow, or even slower, but not as far-reaching. China, Japan, India and Muslim countries were hardly affected. Potatoes became a New World crop – spreading all over America – and above all a European one. The potato thoroughly colonized Europe, and this new plant caused what amounted to a revolution in eating habits. One economist, Wilhelm Roscher[229] (1817-94), even maintained, perhaps rather rashly, that the potato was the cause of the population growth in Europe. We may be a little more cautious and grant that it may have been one of the causes. The expansion of the European population had occurred before the new plant could have had much effect. In 1764, we find one of the King of Poland's advisers saying 'I should like to introduce [to our country] potato-growing, which is almost unknown.'[230] In 1790, around St Petersburg, only German colonists were cultivating potatoes.[231]

And yet the population was already growing in Russia and in Poland, as it was everywhere else, before these dates.

As seems to be a general rule, the spread of the new crop was very slow. The Spanish had encountered it in Peru in 1539; Spanish merchants even provided dried potatoes for the Indian miners at Potosi, but the plant seems to have crossed the Iberian peninsula without any immediate consequences. In Italy, which may have been more ready to welcome new foods than Spain since it was more populated, it aroused interest much more quickly, was grown experimentally and was given one of its first European names; *tartuffoli*, one of the dozens it received: *turma de tierra, papa, patata*, in Spain; *batata, batateira* in Portugal; *patata, tartuffo, tartuffola* in Italy; *cartoufle, truffe, patate, pomme de terre* in France; American potato in England; Irish potato in the United States; *Kartoffel* in Germany; *Erdtapfel* in Vienna – and I will spare the reader the Slavonic, Hungarian, Chinese and Japanese names.[232] Olivier de Serres mentions it and gives a detailed account of how it is grown in 1600. The first botanical

Incas planting and harvesting potatoes. Their tools are digging sticks and hoes. Peruvian Codex of sixteenth century. (Photothèque A. Colin.)

description of the plant was by Carolus Clusius in 1601, by which time, according to him, it was already grown in most English gardens. Traditionally, Sir Walter Raleigh is supposed to have introduced the potato to England a little earlier than this, in 1588, the year of the Spanish Armada. This prosaic event, it could be argued, probably had more consequences in the long run than the clash of the two fleets in the English Channel.

The potato did not really take hold in Europe as a whole until the eighteenth or even nineteenth century. But like maize, it was locally successful at earlier dates. In France, which was particularly backward in this respect, the only areas to grow it early were the Dauphiné; Alsace, where potatoes were growing in the fields by 1660;[233] and Lorraine where it was established in about 1680, and where although still criticized and disliked in 1760, it had by 1787 become 'the principal healthy nourishment' of the country people.[234] It had reached Ireland earlier than this, in the first half of the seventeenth century and by the eighteenth it had become, with a little milk and cheese, the almost exclusive diet of the peasants

– with at first happy and later disastrous results.[235] It made progress in England too, but for a long time it was grown for export rather than for home consumption.[236] Adam Smith deplored the English disdain for a crop which had apparently proved its value as a food in Ireland.[237]

The new crop had more substantial success in Switzerland, Sweden and Germany. It was indeed in Prussia, where he was a prisoner during the Seven Years War, that Parmentier (1737-1813) 'discovered' the potato for France.[238] However, in the Elbe region in 1781, not a valet or servant would deign to eat *tartoffeln* '*Lieber gehn sie ausser Dienst*': they prefer to change masters.[239]

In fact wherever the potato was grown and suggested as a rival to bread, there was resistance to it. Some claimed that it transmitted leprosy. Others that it caused flatulence, which was admitted by the *Encyclopédie* in 1765, with the comment: 'But what is a little wind to the vigorous organs of the peasants and workers!' So it is not surprising that in those countries where it spread widely and rapidly, its victory is to be explained by peculiarly dramatic circumstances: the threat of famine, for instance, as in Ireland, since the piece of land which could grow enough to feed one person on wheat, could feed two on potatoes.[240] Sometimes it was the threat of war, which could destroy the wheat-fields. The peasants value the potato, a document explains apropos of Alsace, 'because it is never exposed ... to the ravages of war': an army could camp all summer on a potato field without destroying the autumn crop.[241] Indeed every war seems to have encouraged potato-growing: it happened in Alsace during the second half of the seventeenth century; in Flanders during the war of the Augsburg League (1688-97), then during the War of the Spanish Succession and finally during the War of the Austrian Succession, which coincided with the cereal crisis of 1740; it happened in Germany during the Seven Years War and especially during the War of the Bavarian Succession (1778-9), which was known as 'the potato war'.[242] Finally, it had one particular advantage: in some areas the new crop was not subject to tithes and indeed it is through the lawsuits brought by landowners that it is possible for us to trace the early introduction of the potato to the southern Netherlands after about 1680, and in the United Provinces from about 1730.

Still in Flanders, C. Vandenbroeke has calculated the revolutionary rise in potato consumption indirectly, from the fall in grain consumption which it caused. The latter fell from 0·816 kilos per person per day in 1693 to 0·758 in 1710; 0·680 in 1740; 0·476 in 1781; 0·475 in 1791. This drop in grain consumption meant that potatoes had replaced 40% of cereal consumption in Flanders. This is corroborated by the fact that in France, which did not on the whole welcome the potato, the grain ration went up rather than down during the eighteenth century.[243] The potato revolution took place there, as elsewhere in Europe, only in the nineteenth century.

In fact it was part of a larger-scale revolution which drove a great variety of vegetables and pulses from kitchen-gardens to fields: it occurred earliest in

Potatoes were the food of the humble. Charity offered to the poor of Seville in 1645 consisted of a cauldron of potatoes. Detail of the picture on p. 79. (Photo Giraudon.)

England and did not escape the attention of Adam Smith: 'Potatoes ... turnips, carrots and cabbages,' he wrote in 1776, 'things which were formerly never raised but by the spade, but which are now commonly raised by the plough. All sorts of garden stuff too, has become cheaper.'[244] Thirty years later, a Frenchman in London noted the abundance of homegrown vegetables, 'which are served in the unadorned simplicity of their natural state, like hay to horses'.[245]

Eating other people's bread

To convince oneself of the reality of the revolution in European eating habits in the eighteenth century (even if it took two hundred years before it was fully accomplished) one has only to look at the conflict that occurs whenever two different diets meet – that is when an individual finds himself away from home and from his usual foods and eating customs, and obliged to eat something else. Europeans provide the best examples: their experiences reveal with unfailing regularity the dietary frontiers and the difficulties of crossing them. In the countries opened up to their curiosity or their exploitation they never abandoned their customs: wine, alcohol, meat, ham that came from Europe and sold like gold in the Indies, even when worm-eaten. They had to have their bread at any price. In China Gemelli Careri procured wheat and had it made into biscuits and cakes 'when biscuit was lacking, because rice cooked dry, as it is served in this country, and with no seasoning whatsoever, does not suit my stomach'.[246] In the Panama isthmus, where wheat would not grow, flour came from Europe. Bread was therefore a luxury. 'It is scarcely to be found except amongst Europeans settled in the towns and rich Creoles, and they only use it when taking chocolate or eating caramel sweets.' At all other meals they served maize cakes, a sort of *polenta*, and even cassava 'flavoured with honey'.[247]

When that indefatigable traveller Gemelli Careri arrived at Acapulco from the Philippines in February 1697, he naturally did not find wheaten bread. This happy surprise was reserved for a later occasion, on the road to Mexico City in the Massatlan *trapiche*, where 'we found ... good bread, which is no small thing in these mountains where all the inhabitants eat only maize cakes'.[248] This is an occasion to recall the considerable cultivation of wheat on irrigated or non-irrigated land (*riego* or *secano*) in New Spain, intended for export to the towns. On Tuesday, 12 March 1697, Careri actually witnessed a popular commotion in Mexico City: 'A sort of uprising occurred today; the populace went to ask for bread under the Viceroy's windows.' Measures were immediately taken to prevent the people from burning the Palace, 'as had been done at the time of the Count of Galoe in 1692'.[249] Was this 'populace' composed of whites only, as seems quite likely? If so, it suggests that one can make the simple equation: white bread, white man (in the American context, of course). If on the other hand, *mestizos*, Indians and black slaves from the town were involved, then it is most probable that what they were demanding under the always ambiguous name of 'bread' was only maize.

The rest of the world

However important they may be, the dominant food plants we have been considering only occupy a small place in the world: they coincide with the zones of dense population, and developed or fast-developing civilizations. And we should not be misled by the very expression 'dominant food plants': they were indeed adopted by the human masses and incorporated into their way of life to the point of determining it and locking it into a sometimes irreversible series of choices, but the relationship was reciprocal: it was the dominant civilizations which established these crops and made their fortune. Wheat, rice, maize and potatoes were transformed by those who used them. Pre-Columbian America had five or six varieties of potato: scientific agriculture has now produced about a thousand. There is nothing in common between the maize of the earliest farmers and the maize now grown in the corn belt of the United States.

Wheat introduced to America by the Spaniards. The Indian labourers are using the same tools in its cultivation as the European peasant. (Photo Mas.)

In short, what we may think of as the success of a plant may also, perhaps, largely be the success of a culture. For a triumph of this order to be achieved, the 'development techniques' of the society achieving it have inevitably played a part. If manioc, for instance, is not considered a major food plant, it is not because cassava (the flour obtained when the manioc root is cut, washed, dried and grated) is an inferior foodstuff. On the contrary, in many African countries today, it is a bulwark against famine. But having originally been adopted into primitive cultures, it has always remained among them. In America, as in Africa, it remained the food of the local people, and never climbed up the social scale in the same way that maize and potatoes did. Even in its countries of origin, it

174 *The Structures of Everyday Life*

had to face competition from cereals imported from Europe. Plants, like men, only survive when circumstances favour them. In this case, the mainstream of history passed them by. Manioc and tropical tubers, a certain kind of maize, and the providential tropical fruit trees - the banana trees, bread-fruit trees, coconut palms and oil palms - were at the disposal of human communities less privileged than the rice- or wheat-growers, but who occupied, with perseverance, very large areas. We can call them the people of the hoe.

The people of the hoe

What is striking even today is the vast extent of the land where work is done mainly with either a digging stick (a sort of primitive hoe) or a hoe. These lands form a belt round the whole world (Figure 18) including Oceania, pre-Columbian America, Black Africa and a large part of south and south-east Asia (where they border and sometimes cross the territory of the plough). In the south-east particularly (Indochina in the broad sense) there is a mixture of the two types of agriculture.

We can say: (1) that this feature of the globe is extremely old and applies over the whole chronological range of this book; (2) that the people involved are remarkably homogeneous, with inevitable local variations; but (3) that as the centuries go by they naturally find themselves less and less protected from outside influences.

(1) *A feature of ancient times*

If prehistorians and ethnologists - who are still arguing the point amongst themselves - are to be believed, cultivation with the hoe was the result of a very ancient agricultural revolution, even earlier than the revolution that gave birth to agriculture with harnessed animals in about the fourth millennium BC. It may go back to the fifth millennium and be lost in the darkness of prehistory. Like the other revolution, it is said to have originated in peninsular India or more probably ancient Mesopotamia - in any case, from experience that had been passed on from earliest times and had continued as the result of the endless repetition of a lesson learned.

From our point of view it is unimportant whether the distinction between agriculture with or without the plough is valid, because what is involved in either case is the determination of tools. An original book by Ester Boserup (1966)[250] explains that in systems of the *ladang* type, described above, if space is restricted, any increase in mouths to be fed results in a shorter fallow period for the reconstitution of the forest. And the change of tempo in its turn will make the transition from one tool to another necessary. The tool, according to this theory, is the result and no longer the cause. The digging stick is adequate - and sometimes not even needed - for sowing broadcast and planting seeds or

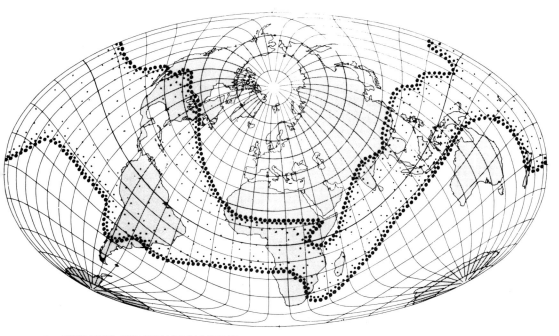

18 THE HOE-CULTIVATION BELT
Note how broad this zone is over the Americas and the Pacific islands. (From E. Werth.) According to Hubert Deschamps, in a letter (7/1/1970) Werth is mistaken when he includes Madagascar in the zone of cultivation by hoe. The implement used there is a very long spade, probably of Indonesian origin, called an *angady*.

cuttings amidst ashes and charred wood (remember that the tree stumps are left in the ground). But if the forest does not grow again, because of the rapid return of cultivation, grass moves in. Burning it is not enough because fire does not destroy the roots. The hoe is then essential for weeding. We see this happening in Black Africa where cultivation takes place both on patches of burnt forest and patches of burnt savannah. Finally, when the tempo of harvest is increasingly accelerated, making necessary constant preparation of the land, the spade and swingplough move in on the vast expanses laid bare and cleared of all shrub formation.

This amounts to saying that our peasants with their hoes are backward communities, that because demographic pressure is still light they have not been forced into the skills and oppressive toil reserved to the drivers of harnessed animals. Father Jean François of Rome (1648) gives us an accurate picture of the agricultural activity of the Congo peasants during the rainy season: 'Their manner of cultivating the land,' he wrote, 'demands little work because of the great fertility of the soil [we need not of course accept this reason]; they do not plough or dig, but scratch the earth a little with a hoe to cover the seed. In return for this slight effort, they reap abundant harvests, provided that rainfall is not deficient.'[251] We can conclude that the labour of the peasant with a hoe was more productive (considering time and effort spent) than that of the tillers in Europe or the rice-growers in Asia, but that it was not conducive to dense human settlement. It was neither soil nor climate that encouraged this primitive agriculture, but rather the vast area of fallow land (available precisely because of the scattered population) and types of society which made up a network of habits that were hard to break – what Pierre Gourou has called the 'technical parameters'.

(2) *A homogeneous humanity*

The world of men with hoes was characterized – and this is the most striking fact about it – by a fairly marked homogeneity of goods, plants, animals, tools and customs. We can say that the house of the peasant with a hoe, wherever it may be, is almost invariably rectangular and has only one storey. He is able to make coarse pottery, uses a rudimentary hand loom for weaving, prepares and consumes fermented drinks (but not alcohol), and raises small domestic animals – goats, sheep, pigs, dogs, chickens and sometimes bees (but not cattle). He lives off the vegetable world round about him: bananas, bread-fruit trees, oil palms, calabashes, taros and yams. In Tahiti, in 1824, what should one of the Tsar's sailors find but bread-fruit trees, coconut palms, plantations of banana trees, and 'little patches of yams and sweet potatoes'.[252]

Naturally variations occur between the large zones of cultivation with the hoe. For example we find cattle, buffalo and oxen in the African steppes and savannahs, probably as the result of transmission in ancient times via the Abyssinian tillers. The banana tree, which has always been cultivated (the fact that it cannot reproduce by seeds but only by cuttings proves the antiquity of its cultivation) and is characteristic of zones under the hoe, is absent in marginal regions. It does not grow in the Sudan, north of the Niger or in New Zealand, where the severity of the climate surprised the Polynesians (Maoris) who arrived there in their outrigger canoes after their adventurous voyages between the ninth and the fourteenth centuries AD.

But the main exception concerns pre-Columbian America. The peasants with hoes who were responsible for the late-flowering and fragile civilizations of the Andes and the Mexican plateaux, were descended from populations of Asian origin, who reached America very early, by the Bering Straits, in several waves. The oldest human remains so far found are thought to go back as far as 48000 or 46000 BC. But archaeological excavacations are still going on, and these dates may well be amended. What seems beyond question is the fact that men were in America from the very earliest times, that they were of evident Mongolian type and that a very long time elapsed before the most striking successes of Amerindian civilization. Hunting and fishing accounted for the wanderings, which to us seem extraordinary, of these little groups of prehistoric men. They travelled the whole continent from north to south and may have arrived in Tierra del Fuego by about the sixth millennium BC. Oddly enough, in this remote corner there were still wild horses, a form of game which had vanished centuries earlier from the other regions of the New World.[253]

In the great open spaces of the American continent, these men from the north (with perhaps the addition of a few boatloads of people from the Chinese and Japanese coasts and Polynesia who had been driven across the Pacific by storms) split up into tiny groups which developed in their own way in isolation, building up their own cultures and languages without making contact with each other. The amazing thing is that geographically some of these languages are to be found as islands in other linguistically foreign zones.[254] The small numbers of the original Asian immigrants helps to explain why, apart from a few cultural features that echo the ancestral origins, everything was created from scratch. The newcomers used and developed local resources in the course of a very long process of acclimatization. It was only much later that agriculture became established on a foundation of manioc, potatoes, sweet potatoes, and above all maize: the latter, which probably originated in Mexico, led to the spread of the hoe into the temperate zones in the north and south of the continent, far beyond its usual habitat in the tropical or warm manioc zone.

(3) *Absorption of new elements*

With the social mixing set in motion by the maritime integration of the world, modifications became increasingly numerous and new combinations of crops appeared. I have already mentioned the arrival in the Congo of manioc, sweet potatoes, groundnuts and maize, some of the benefits resulting from Portuguese navigation and trade. The newcomers grew only moderately well among the established plants: maize and manioc side by side with various kinds of millet, white or red. Millet was mixed with water to give a sort of *polenta* which when dried would keep for two or three days. 'It serves as bread and is in no way harmful to the health.'[255] Similarly vegetables, also imported by the Portuguese – cabbages, gourds, lettuces, parsley, chicory, garlic – did not usually prosper by the side of the native peas, red haricots and beans. But they did not disappear.

The African food-producing trees formed the most distinctive setting: kolas, banana trees, and particularly palm trees. There were many different varieties of palm, providing oil, wine, vinegar, textile fibres and leaves. 'The products of the palm are to be found everywhere: in fences and roofs of houses, in traps for game and in the fisherman's eel-pot, in the public treasury [pieces of material served as money in the Congo], in clothing, cosmetics, therapeutics and foodstuffs.' 'Symbolically, [palms] are *male* trees, and thus in a certain sense noble.'[256]

In short, these populations and societies dependent on rudimentary but long-established agriculture should not be underestimated. Think of Polynesian expansion, for example, which occupied an enormous maritime triangle, from Hawaii to Easter Island and New Zealand in the thirteenth century: no mean achievement. But civilized man has driven them far into the background. He has obliterated, devalued their achievement.

The primitive peoples

The users of the hoe are not on the lowest rung of the cultural ladder. Their plants, implements, crops, houses, navigation skills, domestic animals and successes are an indication of a cultural level which is far from negligible. The lowest level is occupied by peoples who subsist without agriculture and live by gathering plants, hunting and fishing. These 'predators' occupy categories 1 to 27 of Gordon Hewes's map – covering quite a large area. Indeed they occupy vast expanses of land, but their rule is challenged by forests, lakes, meandering rivers, wild animals, thousands of birds, ice and extremes of temperature. They do not control their environment: at best they manage to slip in between the obstacles and constraints it offers. Such peoples are at a minimum level in history; it has even been said, wrongly, that they have no history.

We should, however, find a place for them in a 'synchronic' representation of the world between the fifteenth and eighteenth centuries. Without them our categorical and explanatory framework would not possess its full range, and would lose its meaning. But how difficult it is to see them in historical terms, as we might for instance the French peasant or the Russian settler in Siberia. All the data is missing, except for what anthropologists of the past can tell us, or travellers who observed their way of life and tried to understand the mechanisms of their existence. And such explorers and voyagers, who were all Europeans and in search of strange and picturesque images, were perhaps over-inclined to apply their own experience and attitudes to other people. They judged by comparison and contrast. And even these accounts, for what they are worth, are incomplete and few in number. It is not always easy to discover from them whether they are referring to really primitive people, living virtually in the Stone Age, or to the people who lived by the hoe, whom we have already discussed and who were as far removed from 'savages' as they were from the 'civilized' people of more populous societies. The Chichimec Indians, of northern Mexico, who gave the Spanish so much trouble were already the enemies of the sedentary Aztecs, before the arrival of Cortes.[257]

To read the journals of the famous voyages round the world, from Magellan to Tasman, Bougainville or Cook, is to find oneself lost in the monotonous and limitless expanses of the sea, especially the southern seas which cover half the planet. They tell us above all about the concerns of the sailors, the different latitudes, the rations – especially water – the state of the rigging and steering, the sicknesses and the mood of the crew. The lands they describe, briefly glimpsed

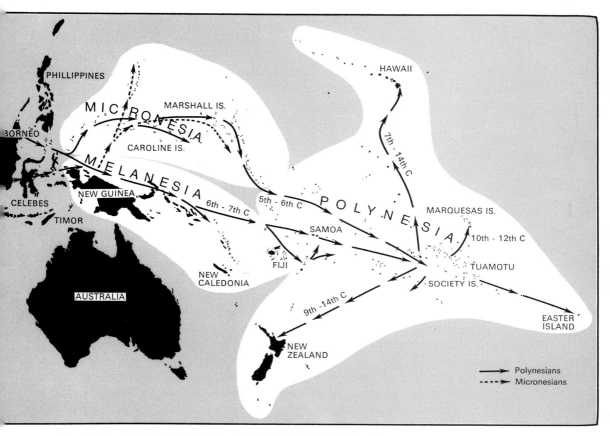

19 MELANESIAN AND POLYNESIAN MIGRATIONS BEFORE
THE FOURTEENTH CENTURY
Note the huge triangle outlined by the voyages of Polynesian sailors, from Hawaii to Easter Island and New Zealand.

when the ship puts in to port, were sometimes lost again as soon as they had been discovered or rediscovered. Descriptions of them are vague.

This was not so, however, in the case of Tahiti, the Pacific paradise discovered by the Portuguese in 1605, and rediscovered by the Englishman Samuel Wallis in 1767. Bougainville put in there the following year, on 6 April 1768, and James Cook almost a year to the day later, on 13 April 1769: between them they established the reputation of the original model of the 'South Sea island myth'. But were the savages they described really primitive people? Far from it. 'More than a hundred canoes of various sizes, all with an outrigger, surrounded the two vessels [of Bougainville, a day before they dropped anchor at the island]. They were laden with coconuts, bananas and other local fruits. They exchanged these delicious fruits for all kinds of trinkets which we gave them, in good faith.'[258] The scene was repeated when Cook arrived on board the *Endeavour*:

'We had no sooner come to anchor', the ship's log relates, 'than a great number of the natives in their canoes came off to the Ship and brought with them cocoanuts & cᵃ.'[259] They swarmed aboard the ships like monkeys, and pilfered whatever they could get their hands on, but agreed to peaceful exchanges. These promising welcomes, the willingness to barter and exchange goods without hesitation, are evidence of an established culture, and of the presence of social discipline. The Tahitians were not in fact 'primitive' people at all: in spite of the comparative abundance of wild plants and fruits, they cultivated gourds and sweet potatoes (imported no doubt by the Portuguese), as well as yams and sugar cane, which they ate raw. They reared pigs and poultry in abundance.[260]

The crew of the *Endeavour* was to meet some truly primitive people later, when they landed in the Magellan Straits, or on the way round Cape Horn, possibly when they touched the coast of the south island of New Zealand, and certainly when they dropped anchor off the shores of Australia, to go in search of wood and water or to careen the ship's hull. They did so, in fact, whenever they had sailed outside the hoe-civilization belt.

So it was that Cook and his men encountered in the Le Maire Strait, at the southernmost tip of America, a handful of wretched savages, deprived of everything, and with whom the Europeans were unable to make any real contact. Clad in sealskin, and possessing no other tools than harpoons, bows and arrows, sheltering in rough cabins which were poor protection against the cold, they were 'in a word, ... perhaps as miserable a set of People as are this day upon Earth'.[261] Two years earlier, in 1767, Samuel Wallis had met the same savages. '[One of our sailors] who was catching fish, gave to one of these Americans a live fish which he had just caught, a little larger than a herring. The American seized it as avidly as a dog does a bone that is thrown it: he killed it first by biting it near the gills, then began to eat it starting with the head and proceeding to the tail without discarding the bones, fins, scales or guts.'[262]

And the Australian aborigines, whom Cook and his companions had leisure to observe, were primitive people too. They lived a nomadic existence, without possessions, hunting a little but living mostly from fishing in the mudflats at low tide. 'We never saw an inch of cultivated land in their country.'

And of course more numerous and equally representative cases could be quoted from the northern hemisphere in inland regions. Siberia, of which more later, remained an unparalleled anthropological museum until our own times.

But perhaps the outstanding field of observation is North America, with its great expanses, against which European colonization pitted itself, bringing destruction and enlightenment. I know of no more evocative general view than the Abbé Prévost's *Observations générales sur l'Amérique*.[263] For since he brings together haphazardly the work of Fr. Charlevoix, the observations of Champlain, Lescarbot, La Hontan and de Potherie, the Abbé Prévost has painted an impossibly large picture, where over the vast expanses between Louisiana and Hudson Bay, the Indians divide up into distinct groupings. There are 'absolute

In New Zealand an English sailor barters a handkerchief for a crayfish. The drawing is taken from the journal of a member of the Cook expedition in 1769. (Photo British Library.)

differences' between them, as can be seen from the rituals and beliefs and the infinite variety of customs of these 'savage nations'. For us the crucial difference is not whether they were cannibals or not, but whether they cultivated the earth. Wherever the Indians are described as growing maize or other plants (tasks usually left to the women, incidentally), whenever there is a mention of a hoe or even a digging stick, or a long spade which cannot be described as autochthonous, every time we hear of the various native methods of preparing maize, or of the adoption of the potato in Louisiana for instance, or further west even of Indians growing 'wild oats', we are in the presence of a settled or semi-settled peasant community, however unsophisticated it may be. And from our point of view, these peasants have nothing in common with the hunting and fishing Indian tribes. (Who in fact did less and less fishing, as the European invasion, without specifically aiming to, systematically drove them further from the fish of the Atlantic seaboard and the eastern rivers, before later harassing them on their hunting-grounds as well.) The Basques, for instance, gave up their original trade of whale-harpooning and quickly turned to fur-trapping, which 'does not demand so much expense and fatigue and brings greater profit'.[264] Even though at this time, whales were still coming up the Saint-Lawrence, 'sometimes in large numbers'. So the Indian hunters were chased out by the fur traders, who were master-minded from the forts on the Hudson Bay or stations on the Saint-Lawrence, and who dispersed their poor nomadic settlements in order to surprise the animals 'which can be caught in the snow' with traps and snares: deer, lynxes, martens, squirrels, ermine, otters, beavers, hares and rabbits. So it was that European capitalism laid hands on the great stocks of furs and skins of America – enough to challenge before long the hunters of the forests of Siberia.

One could multiply images like this to show convincingly that the story of mankind, with all its halts and false starts stretching over thousands of years, is one: that synchrony and diachrony join hands. The 'agricultural revolution' did not take place only in a few privileged areas like the Middle East in the seventh or eighth millennium BC. It had to spread to new regions and its progress was not accomplished in a single movement; far from it. Varieties of human experience are spread out over a single itinerary, but at several centuries distance. In today's world, the civilizations of the hoe have not yet been eliminated. And a few primitive people still survive, here and there, protected by the inhospitable lands which have become their sanctuaries.

3

Superfluity and Sufficiency: Food and Drink

WHEAT, RICE AND MAIZE – the staple foods of the majority of the world's inhabitants – represent problems of a comparatively simple type. As soon as we begin to consider less ordinary foodstuffs (meat, for example), or needs of a more diversified nature such as clothing and shelter, we are moving into a much more complex area. For here necessity and luxury are constantly found side by side.

Perhaps it will help to clarify the problem if we distinguish from the start between the condition of the majority – the food, clothing and lodging of the general run of mankind – and that of the minority, the privileged, whom we may regard as living in luxury. To make such a distinction, between the average and the exceptional, means applying a necessary but difficult dialectic. We shall have to move to and fro across the dividing line, since our classification can never be perfect: luxury is an elusive, complex and contradictory concept, by definition constantly changing: it can never be identified once and for all.

Sugar, for example, was a luxury before the sixteenth century; pepper was still a luxury in the closing years of the seventeenth; so were alcohol and the first 'aperitifs' at the time of Catherine de Medici, or the swansdown beds and silver cups of the Russian boyars before Peter the Great. The first flat plates, which Francis I ordered from a goldsmith in Antwerp in 1538, were also a luxury. The first deep plates, known as 'Italian', were mentioned in the inventory of Cardinal Mazarin's possessions in 1653. Other sixteenth- and seventeenth-century luxuries were forks (ordinary table forks) and glass window panes, both of which originated in Venice. But the manufacture of glass panes – the glass was no longer made with potassium after the fifteenth century but with soda, which gave a more transparent material, easy to smooth – became widespread in England in the following century thanks to coal-firing. So one present-day historian likes to think that the Venetian fork and English glass met somewhere in France.[1] It is also surprising to think that the chair is still a luxury, a rarity in Islam and India even today. Indian troops stationed in southern Italy during the

Second World War were amazed at the wealth they saw: there were chairs in all the houses! Handkerchiefs were another luxury. Erasmus in his *Civility* explains: 'To wipe the nose on the cap or sleeve belongs to rustics; to wipe the nose on the arm or elbow to pastrycooks; and to wipe the nose with the hand, if by chance at the same instant you hold it to your gown, is not much more civil. But to receive the excreta of the nose with a handkerchief turning slightly away from noble people is an honest thing.'[2] Oranges likewise were still a luxury in England in the Stuart period: they appeared around Christmas and were preciously guarded until April or May. And we have said nothing yet on the inexhaustible subject of dress.

Luxury then can take on many guises, depending on the period, the country or the civilization. What does not change, by contrast, is the unending social drama of which luxury is both the prize and the theme, a choice spectacle for sociologist, psychologist, economist and historian. A certain amount of connivance is of course required between the privileged and the onlookers – the watching masses. Luxury does not only represent rarity and vanity, but also social success, fascination, the dream that one day becomes reality for the poor, and in so doing immediately loses its old glamour. Not long ago a medical historian wrote: 'When a food that has been rare and long desired finally arrives within reach of the masses, consumption rises sharply, as if a long-repressed appetite had exploded. Once popularised [in both senses of the word – becoming "less exclusive" and "more widespread"] the food quickly loses its attraction ... The appetite becomes sated.'[3] The rich are thus doomed to prepare the future life of the poor. It is, after all, their justification: they try out the pleasures that the masses will sooner or later grasp.

This affords plenty of scope for futility, pretentiousness and caprice. 'We find extravagant praise of turtle soup amongst English eighteenth-century authors: it is delicious, a sovereign remedy for consumption and weakness, it arouses the appetite. No state dinner [like the Lord Mayor's banquet in the City of London] was without turtle soup.'[4] Also in London we hear of 'roast mutton stuffed with oysters'. Economically extravagant, Spain paid silver coin for wigs manufactured for her by the wicked countries of the north. 'But what can we do about it?' asked Ustariz in 1717.[5] At the same time the Spaniards were buying the loyalty of a few sheikhs in North Africa with black tobacco from Brazil. And if we believe Laffemas, adviser to Henry IV, many of the French were, like savages, willing to take 'baubles and strange merchandise in exchange for their treasures'.[6]

Similarly Indochina and the East Indies provided gold dust, spices, precious woods – sandalwood and rosewood – slaves and rice in exchange for Chinese trifles: combs, lacquer boxes, and coins made of copper mixed with lead. But it is comforting to find that China, in its turn, committed similar acts of folly for swallows' nests from Tonkin, Cochin China and Java, or 'paws of bears and various other wild animals which arrive salted from Siam, Cambodia, or Tar-

Luxury at a Venetian banquet: detail of 'The Wedding at Cana' by Veronese, 1563. (Photo Giraudon.)

tary'.[7] Finally, to return to Europe: 'What a wretched luxury porcelains are!' exclaimed Sébastian Mercier in 1771. 'A cat, with one tap of its paw, can do more damage than the devastation of twenty arpents of land.'[8] However, the price of Chinese porcelains was falling at that time and soon they no longer served as anything but common ballast for boats returning to Europe. The moral is not surprising: every luxury dates and goes out of fashion. But luxury is reborn from its own ashes and from its very defeats. It is really the reflection of a difference in social levels that nothing can compensate for and that every movement recreates. An eternal 'class struggle'.

This was a conflict waged not only by classes, but by civilizations. Civilizations were incessantly eyeing each other, acting out the same drama as the rich played in relation to the poor. But this time it was reciprocal, and therefore created currents and led to accelerated exchanges, from near and far. In short, as Marcel Mauss wrote, 'it was not in production that society found its driving force: luxury is the great stimulus'. According to Gaston Bachelard 'the attainment of the superfluous causes greater spiritual excitement than the attainment of necessities. Man is a creature of desire and not a creature of need.' Jacques Rueff, the economist, goes so far as to repeat that 'production is the daughter of desire'. Probably few would deny the existence of such drives and cravings even in present-day societies with their mass luxuries. For there is no society without a hierarchy. And the slightest social prestige is associated with luxury, today as in the past.

Does that mean one should accept the view, advanced most forcefully by Werner Sombart,[9] that the luxury displayed by the princely courts of the West (of which the papal court of Avignon was the prototype) laid the foundations of early modern capitalism? Or rather should one say that before the innovations of the nineteenth century, the many forms of luxury were not so much an element of growth as a sign of an economy failing to engage with anything, one that was incapable of finding a meaningful use for its accumulated capital? In this sense, one could suggest that a *certain* kind of luxury was, and could only be, a phenomenon or sign of sickness peculiar to the *ancien régime*; that until the Industrial Revolution it was (and in some cases still is) the unjust, unhealthy, conspicuous and wasteful consumption of the 'surplus' produced by a society with fixed limits on its growth. In reply to the unconditional defenders of luxury and its creative capacity, the American biologist Theodosius Dobzhansky has written: 'I for one do not lament the passing of social organizations that used the many as a manured soil in which to grow a few graceful flowers of refined culture.'[10]

Eating habits:
luxury and the foods of the masses

The two sides are clearly visible at first glance: luxury and poverty, superabundance and penury. Luxury is the more conspicuous spectacle, the better documented and also the more attractive to the armchair observer today. The other side cannot but be depressing, however unwilling one may be to accept a Michelet-type romanticism, all too natural in the circumstances.

A belated luxury

We can risk the generalization that there was no real luxury or sophistication of eating habits in Europe before the fifteenth or sixteenth centuries. In this respect the West lagged behind the other Old World civilizations.

Chinese cookery, which has taken over so many restaurants in the West today, belongs to a very ancient tradition, over a thousand years old, with its unchanged rules, rituals, elaborate recipes: one that is extremely attentive both in a sensual and a literary sense to the range of tastes and their combinations, displaying a respect for the art of eating which is shared perhaps only by the French (though in a completely different style). An interesting book, recently published,[11] stresses the little-known riches of the Chinese diet, its variety and the balance it maintains – with many illustrations. But I would be inclined to temper the enthusiasm of F.W. Mote's contribution with the essays by K.C. Chang and J. Spencer. It is quite true that Chinese food is healthy, tasty, varied and inventive; it makes admirable use of the available ingredients, and it provides a balanced diet, with fresh vegetables and soya proteins compensating for the scarcity of meat. But one could equally well sing the praises of French provincial culinary tradition, and point to the inventiveness, taste and ingenuity developed in France over the last four or five hundred years in the use of local resources: meat, poultry, game, cereals, wines, cheeses, homegrown fruit and vegetables, not to mention the distinct tastes of butter, lard, goosegrease, olive or walnut oil, or the traditional methods of home preserving. But the real question is: was this what most people ate? And in France, the answer is no. The peasant often sold more than his 'surpluses', and above all, he never ate his best produce: he ate millet and maize and sold his wheat; he ate salt pork once a week and took his poultry, eggs, kids, calves and lambs to market. As in China, feasting on special occasions interrupted the monotony and shortages of everyday life. And such feasts undoubtedly kept alive the popular tradition of cookery. But the diet of the peasants, that is the vast majority of the population, had nothing in common with the cookery books written for the rich, any more than it would with the following list, drawn up by a gourmet in 1788 of the gastronomic resources of France: turkey with truffles from the Périgord; pâté de foie gras from Toulouse, partridge pâtés from Nérac, fresh tunny pâtés from Toulon, skylarks from Pézénas, brawn from Troyes, woodcock from the Dombes, capons from the Caux, Bayonne hams, cooked tongue from Vierzon – and even 'the sauerkraut of Strasbourg'.[12] Exactly the same must have been true of China: refinement, variety or even having enough to eat were for the rich. From popular proverbs, it is possible to deduce that meat and wine were for the rich; for a poor man, having enough to live on meant 'having grains to chew'. Chang and Spencer are agreed that Sir John Barrow was not mistaken when he stated in 1805 that in culinary matters nowhere in the world was the disparity between rich and poor as great as in China. To illustrate this, Spencer quotes from a famous eighteenth-century novel, *The Dream of the Scarlet Pavilion*: the rich young hero happens by chance to visit the humble home of one of his serving-women. The servant, as she offers him a tray on which she has carefully laid out the best food in the house – cakes, fruit and nuts – sadly realizes 'that there was nothing there which Pao-yü could possibly be expected to eat'.[13]

Whenever we talk about elaborate cooking in the past, we are invariably referring to a luxury. Though in fact this sophisticated cuisine, typical of all advanced civilizations, and found in China in the fifth century and in the Muslim world from the eleventh or twelfth centuries, did not appear in the West until the fifteenth century, and then in the rich city-states of Italy where it became a costly art with its own precepts and etiquette. The Senate in Venice was very early on protesting at the expensive feasts the young nobles held; in 1460 it forbade banquets costing half a ducat a head. The *banchetti*, of course, continued. Marin Sanudo's *Diarii* have preserved some of the menus and prices from these princely meals, on gala days of the Carnival. As if fortuitously, they ritually contained the dishes forbidden by the Venetian government: partridges, pheasants, peacocks, and so on. A little later, Ortensio Lando in his *Commentario delle più notabili e mostruose cose d'Italia* (printed and reprinted in Venice from 1550 to 1559) attempted to list foods available to charm gourmet palates in the towns of Italy; he had a bewildering range to choose from: sausages and saveloys from Bologna, *zampone* (stuffed bacon hock) from Modena, round pies from Ferrara, *cotognata* (quince jam) from Reggio, cheese and *gnocchi* with garlic from Piacenza, marzipan from Sienna, *caci marzolini* (March cheeses) from Florence, *luganica sottile* (fine sausage) and *tomarelle* (mince) from Monza, *fagiani* (pheasant) and chestnuts from Chiavenna, fish and oysters from Venice, even *eccellentissimo* bread (a luxury in itself) from Padua, not forgetting the wines whose reputation later grew.[14]

But even at this time, France had become the homeland of fine fare, where precious recipes were created and others collected from the four corners of Europe and the world; the place where the presentation and the ceremonial of those profane festivals of gourmandizing and *bon ton* were perfected. The abundance and variety of French resources, were able to surprise even a Venetian. Girolamo Lippomano, ambassador in Paris in 1557, went into ecstasies over the omnipresent opulence: 'There are innkeepers who will feed you at their houses at all prices: for one *tester*, for two, for one écu, for four, for ten, for even twenty per person, if you so wish. But for twenty-five écus, you will be given manna in soup or roast phoenix: in fact everything that is most precious on earth.'[15] However, great French cooking was perhaps only established later, with the Regency and the active good taste of the Regent; or even later still, in 1746, when 'Menon's *Cuisinière bourgeoise* finally appeared, a valuable book which rightly or wrongly has certainly run through more editions than Pascal's *Provinciales*'.[16] From then on, France, or rather Paris, prided itself on culinary fashion. 'People have only known how to eat delicately,' claimed a Parisian in 1782, 'for the last half-century.'[17] However, another, writing in 1827, argued that 'the art of cookery has made more progress in the last thirty years than it did in the whole preceding century'.[18] The later writer had before him, it is true, the magnificent spectacle of a few great 'restaurants' of Paris (only recently had the '*traitants*' or 'suppliers' become '*restaurateurs*'). In fact fashion governs cooking like clothing. Famous sauces fall into disrepute one day and after that elicit nothing but condescending smiles. 'The new cooking,' wrote the author of the *Dictionnaire Sentencieux* (1768), who seems to have had a dry sense of humour, 'is all juice and jelly.' '*Soup*,' says the same dictionary, 'which everyone ate in former times is rejected today as too bourgeois and too old-fashioned a dish, on the pretext that stock relaxes the fibres of the stomach.' The same went for 'pot herbs', the vegetables which the 'refinement of the century has almost banished as a vulgar food! . . . Cabbages are no less healthy, nor less excellent', for all that, the writer continues, and all the peasants eat them throughout their lives.[19]

Other small changes gradually occurred. Turkeys came from America in the sixteenth century. A Dutch painter, Joachim Buedkalaer (1530–73) was probably among the first to include one in a still life, today in the Rijksmuseum, Amsterdam. We are told that turkeys multiplied in France with the restoration of internal peace in the reign of Henry IV! I do not know quite what to make of this new version of the famous '*poule-au-pot*' but by the late eighteenth century, they had certainly caught on: 'Turkeys,' wrote a Frenchman in 1779, 'have made geese more or less disappear from our tables, on which they formerly held the place of honour.'[20] Do the fat geese of Rabelais' period belong to a past age of European gluttony?

We might also follow fashion in food through the revealing history of certain words which are still in use but which have changed in meaning several times: *entrées*, *entremets*, *ragoûts*, etc. Similarly with 'good' and 'bad' ways of roasting meat – but that is another, and very long, story.

Carnivorous Europe

There was, as we have said, no sophisticated cooking in Europe before the fifteenth century. The reader must not let himself be dazzled by feasts like those given by the ostentatious court of the Valois of the house of Burgundy: fountains of wine, set-pieces, and children disguised as angels descending from the sky on cables. Ostentatious quantity prevailed over quality. At best, this was an orgy of greed. Its striking feature was the riot of meat – a long-lasting feature of the tables of the rich.

Meat, in all its forms, boiled or roasted, mixed with vegetables and even with fish, was served 'in a pyramid' on immense dishes called *mets* in France. 'Thus all the roasts placed on top of one another formed a single *mets*, and the very varied sauces for them were offered separately. They did not even think twice about piling up the whole meal on a single vessel and this dreadful hotchpotch was also called a *mets*.'[21] We have French cookery books dated 1361 and 1391 mentioning *assiettes* (plates) in the same sense: a meal of six *assiettes* or *mets* consisted of what we would call six courses. All of them were lavish and to our eyes often unexpected. A single *mets*, of four described in succession in the *Ménagier de Paris* (1393), consisted of the following: *pâtés* of beef, rissoles, lamprey, two broths with meat, white fish sauce, plus an *arboulastre*, a sauce made with butter, cream, sugar and fruit juice.[22] The book gives the recipe for each of these items but we would not advise a cook today to take them literally. All experiments have turned out badly.

Consumption of meat on this scale does not seem to have been a luxury reserved to the very rich in the fifteenth and sixteenth centuries. Even in 1580, Montaigne noted dish-stands in inns in Upper Germany equipped with several compartments to enable the servants to offer at least two dishes of meat at the same time and replenish them easily up to the seven dishes Montaigne observed on certain days.[23] Meat abounded in butchers' shops and eating houses: beef, mutton, pork, poultry, pigeon, goat and lamb. As for game, a treatise on cooking, possibly dating from 1306, gave a fairly long list available in France; wild boar was so common in Sicily in the fifteenth century that it cost less than butcher's meat; Rabelais' list of feathered game is interminable: herons, egrets, wild swans, bitterns, cranes, partridges, francolins, quails, wood pigeons, turtledoves, pheasants, blackbirds, larks, flamingoes, water fowl, divers, etc.[24] Except for large items (boar, stag, roe deer) the long price list for the Orleans market (from 1391 to 1560) indicates regular and abundant supplies of game: hare, rabbit, heron, partridge, woodcock, lark, plover, teal.[25] The description of the Venice markets in the sixteenth century is equally rich. This was perhaps only to be expected in a Europe so sparsely populated. A news item from Berlin appeared in the *Gazette de France* on 9 May 1763: 'Since livestock is very scarce here', the king had ordered 'a hundred head of deer and twenty boar' to be driven into the city 'every week, for the inhabitants' consumption'.[26]

Feast given in Paris by the Duke of Alva in honour of the birth of the Prince of the Asturias, 1707. Engraving by G.I.B. Scotin Ainé after Desmaretz. (Photo Roger-Viollet.)

We should not accept too readily the complaints, often in literary form, about the food of the poor peasants, robbed by the rich of 'wine, wheat, oats, oxen, sheep and calves, leaving them only rye bread'. There is proof to the contrary.

In the Netherlands in the fifteenth century, 'meat was *so commonly eaten* that even in times of famine, demand scarcely fell'; consumption went on rising during the first half of the sixteenth century (in the infirmary at the convent of Lierre, for instance).[27] In Germany an ordinance by the Dukes of Saxony in 1482 ran 'let it be understood by all that the craftsmen must receive a total of four courses at their midday and evening meals; on a meat day: one of soup, two of meat, one of vegetables; for a Friday or a meat-less day: one of soup, one of fresh or salted fish and two of vegetables. If the fast has to be extended, five courses: one of soup, two sorts of fish and two vegetables. And in addition, bread, morning and night.' And again with the addition of *kofent*, a light beer. It might be argued that this menu was for craftsmen, who were citizens. But in Oberhergheim in Alsace in 1429 if a peasant doing statute labour did not want to eat with the others in the *Maier*'s (the steward's) farm, the *Maier* had to send 'two pieces of beef, two pieces of roast meat, a measure of wine and two pfennig-worth of bread' to the man's house.[28] There is more evidence on the same subject. A foreign observer in Paris in 1557 said that 'pork is the habitual food of poor people, those who are really poor. But every craftsman and every merchant, however wretched he may be, likes eating venison and partridge at Shrovetide just as much as the rich.'[29] Of course these rich and prejudiced observers begrudged the poor the slightest luxury they indulged, and, as if it were all part of the same thing: 'there is no labourer nowadays,' wrote Thoinot Arbeau (1588), 'who does not want oboes and sackbuts (a type of trumpet with four branches) at his wedding.'[30]

Tables laden with meat presuppose regular supplies from the countryside or from nearby mountains (the Swiss Cantons); Germany and northern Italy were supplied even more plentifully from the eastern regions of Poland, Hungary and the Balkan countries, which still sent half-wild cattle westwards on the hoof in the sixteenth century. No one turned a hair at the sight of 'extraordinary herds of 16,000 and even 20,000 oxen' at a time pouring into the largest cattle fair in Germany at Buttstedt near Weimar.[31] In Venice herds from the East arrived overland or via shipping points in Dalmatia; they were rested before slaughter on the Lido island, which was also used for testing artillery pieces and as quarantine for suspect boats. Offal, particularly tripe, was one of the everyday foods of the Venetian poor. In 1498, Marseilles butchers bought sheep from as far afield as Saint-Flour, in the Auvergne. Butchers as well as animals were imported from these distant regions. In the eighteenth century the butchers of Venice were often mountain-dwellers from the Grisons, quick to cheat on the selling price of offal; from the Balkans, Albanian and later Epirot butchers and tripe merchants have continued to emigrate to far-off lands up to the present day.[32]

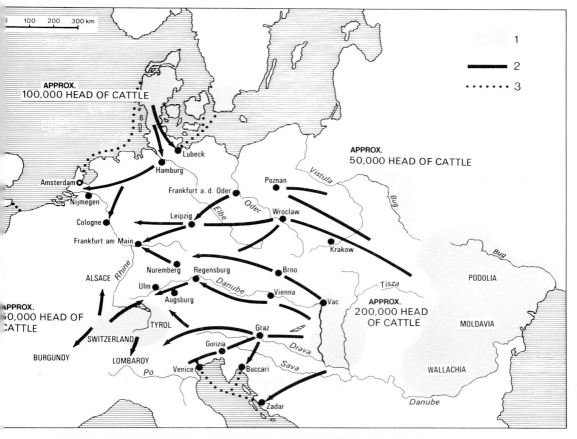

20 THE CATTLE TRADE IN NORTHERN AND EASTERN EUROPE IN ABOUT 1600
1. Place of origin. 2. Overland routes. 3. Sea routes. Bakar is the former Buccari. The cattle trade by both overland and sea routes to the slaughterhouses of central Europe was substantial (400,000 head). But in the Paris markets alone, in 1707 (see Vol. II) almost 70,000 cattle were sold annually; proof that the long-distance supplies were supplemented by local and regional trade which provided for basic meat consumption in Europe. (Wolfgang von Stromer, 'Wildwest in Europa', in *Kultur und Technik*, no. 2, 1979, p. 42, after Othmar Pickl.)

From 1350 to 1550 Europe probably experienced a favourable period as far as *individual* living standards were concerned. Following the catastrophes of the Black Death, living conditions for workers were inevitably good as manpower had become scarce. *Real* salaries have never been as high as they were then. In 1388, canons in Normandy complained that they could not find anyone to cultivate their land 'who did not demand more than six servants would have been paid at the beginning of the century'.[33] The paradox must be emphasized since it is often thought that hardship increases the farther back towards the middle ages one goes. In fact the opposite is true of the standard of living of the

Butchers' stalls in Holland in the seventeenth century. The customers must surely have been prosperous? Engraving. (Viollet Collection.)

common people – the majority. Before 1520-40, peasants and craftsmen in Languedoc (still little populated) ate white bread, a tell-tale detail.[34] But with the passage of time, after the 'waning' of the middle ages, the deterioration becomes progressively worse, lasting well into the nineteenth century. In some regions of Eastern Europe, certainly in the Balkans, the downward movement continued for another century, to the middle of the twentieth.

The decline in meat consumption after 1550

Things had begun to change in the West by the middle of the sixteenth century. Heinrich Müller wrote in 1550 that in Swabia 'in the past they ate differently at the peasant's house. Then, there was meat and food in profusion every day; tables at village fairs and feasts sank under their load. Today, everything has truly changed. Indeed, for some years now, what a calamitous time, what high

Food and Drink   195

prices! And the food of the most comfortably-off peasants is almost worse than that of day-labourers and valets in the old days.'[35] Historians have been wrong in not taking account of this repeated evidence or in persistently interpreting it as man's morbid need to praise the past. 'How far away is the time, oh comrades,' explained an old Breton peasant (1548), 'when it was difficult for an ordinary feast day to pass by without someone from the village inviting all the rest to dinner, to eat his chicken, his gosling, his ham, his first lamb and his pig's heart.'[36] 'In my father's time,' a Norman gentleman wrote in 1560, 'we ate meat every day, dishes were abundant, we gulped down wine as if it were water.'[37] Before the Religious Wars, another witness noted, the 'village people (in France) were so rich and endowed with all possessions, their houses so well furnished,

This peasant meal in the latter half of the seventeenth century consists of a single dish without meat. And things could be worse still: a meal could consist entirely of gruel (1653, cf. p. 138). Painting by Egbert van Heemskerck.
(Photo A. Dingjan.)

so well stocked with poultry and animals that they were noblemen'.[38] Things had indeed changed. In about 1600, the workers in the copper mines in Mansfeld, Upper Saxony, could only afford, on their wages, to eat bread, gruel and vegetables. And even the privileged journeymen weavers of Nuremberg complained in 1601 that they were only receiving three times a week the meat-ration which was supposed to be supplied to them every day. To which their masters replied that the allowance of six kreutzers did not permit them to provide meat for the journeymen every day.[39]

From now on, cereals would be at a premium on the market. Their prices rose to such high levels that people had no money left to buy extras. Meat consumption diminished over the long term, and things did not change, as we have seen, until about 1850. This was an extraordinary step backwards. It is true that there were breathing spaces and exceptions. In Germany, for example, just after the Thirty Years War, livestock quickly built up its strength again in a land often empty of people; in the important agricultural regions of Auge and Bessin (Normandy) constantly rising meat prices and constantly falling wheat prices between 1770 and 1780 led to the substitution of stock-raising for the cultivation of grain, at least until the great fodder crisis of 1785. The result of course was unemployment, and the reduction to beggary and vagabondage of a considerable mass of the small peasantry, at that time going through a period of demographic growth which was to have far-reaching consequences.[40] But the respites did not last long and the exceptions do not invalidate the rule. The obsession with ploughing the fields and scattering continued. The number of butchers in the small town of Montpezat in the Bas-Quercy steadily decreased: eighteen in 1550, ten in 1556; six in 1641; two in 1660; one in 1763. Even if its inhabitants also decreased during that period they did not decline in a ratio of eighteen to one.[41]

Figures for Paris indicate an average annual consumption per head of between 51 and 65 kilograms of meat from 1751 to 1854. But Paris is Paris. Lavoisier, who estimated per capita meat consumption in the capital at the high figure of 72·6 kilograms in 1789, put average consumption in France at the same time at 48·5 pounds (each of 488 grams), i.e. 23·5 kilograms – and experts think this is still optimistic.[42] Annual consumption in Hamburg (but the town is on the threshold of Denmark, a source of livestock supplies) in the eighteenth century was 60 kilograms of meat per capita – although it is true that this only included 20 kilograms of fresh meat. But in Germany as a whole, in the early nineteenth century, it was less than 20 kilograms per head per year (as compared to 100 during the late middle ages).[43] The essential fact is the inequality between one city and another (Paris, for example, was obviously privileged even in 1851) and between town and countryside. In 1829, one observer flatly stated that 'in nine-tenths of France, the poor and the small farmers eat meat, and only salt meat at that, no more than once a week'.[44]

In the modern period then, Europe's privileged status as a meat-eating area declined, and real remedies were only found in the middle of the nineteenth century as a result of the widespread creation of artificial pastures, the development of scientific stock-raising, and the exploitation of distant stock-raising areas in the New World. Europe remained hungry for a long time. Of the territory of Melun, covering 18,800 hectares in the Brie, 14,400 hectares were given over to arable in 1717 and an almost negligible 814 to pasture. And 'the farmers only keep what is absolutely indispensable for their agricultural needs', selling fodder at a good price in Paris (for the numerous horses in the capital). It is true that wheat on the tilled land yielded twelve to seventeen quintals per hectare in a good harvest. This kind of competition proved an irresistible temptation.[45]

There were, as we have said, degrees of regression. It was more pronounced in the Mediterranean countries than in the northern regions, with their rich pasturage. Poles, Germans, Hungarians and English seem to have been less rationed than others. In England, there was even a real revolution in meat in the eighteenth century, within the agricultural revolution. A Spanish ambassador is said to have remarked about the great London market of Leadenhall (1778): 'More meat is sold in a month than is eaten in the whole of Spain during a year.' However, even in a country like Holland where 'official' rations were high[46] (if not strictly apportioned), diet remained unbalanced before the improvements of the end of the eighteenth century: beans, a little salted meat, bread (made from barley or rye), fish, a small quantity of bacon, occasionally game. But game was normally for peasants or nobles. Poor townspeople rarely saw it: for them there were 'turnips, fried onions, dry if not mouldy bread' or sticky rye bread and 'small beer' (the 'double' was for the rich or for drunkards). The Dutch middle classes also lived frugally. The *hutsepot*, the national dish, did of course contain meat, either beef or mutton, but it was finely minced and always used sparingly. The evening meal was often only gruel made from left-over bread soaked in milk.[47] Amongst doctors, the discussion opened at about this time as to whether a meat diet was good or harmful. 'As far as I am concerned,' Louis Lemery wrote, with his tongue in his cheek, in 1702, 'without entering into what seem to me to be fruitless debates, I believe one can say that the use of animal flesh can be advisable, provided it is in moderation.'[48]

Concomitant with the decrease in the meat ration, consumption of smoked and salted meat clearly increased. Werner Sombart spoke, not without justification, of a revolution in salting at the end of the fifteenth century to feed ships' companies at sea. In the Mediterranean, salt fish and above all the traditional biscuit long remained the basic fare of sailors on board ship. It was only at Cadiz, the gateway to the vast Atlantic, that the salt-beef zone began: *vaca salada* was supplied by the Spanish administration from the sixteenth century onwards. Salt beef came primarily from the north, particularly Ireland, which was also an exporter of salted butter. But the administration was not the only interested party. As meat grew to be a luxury, salted foods became the ordinary diet of the poor (which soon included the black slaves in America). 'Salt beef was the standard winter dish' in England, in the absence of fresh food after the summer season. In Burgundy in the eighteenth century, 'pork provides the greatest part of the meat consumed in the peasant's household. Few inventories do not mention a few portions of bacon in the salting tub. Fresh meat is a luxury reserved to convalescents, and moreover so expensive that one cannot always satisfy this requirement.'[49] In Italy and Germany, sausage pedlars (*Wursthändler*) were familiar figures in the towns. From Naples to Hamburg, from France to the vicinity of St Petersburg, salt beef and above all salt pork furnished the poor of Europe with their meagre meat ration.

There were exceptions to this of course. The most outstanding was England, where they 'eat nothing but meat', according to P.J. Grosley in 1770. 'The amount of bread one Frenchman eats in a day would be sufficient for four Englishmen.'[50] Britain was the only 'developed' country in Europe where this would have been true. But it shared the privilege with certain comparatively

The sale of salt meat, *Tacuinum sanitatis in mediciina* (early fifteenth century). (Photo B.N., Paris.)

backward areas. Mademoiselle de Montpensier, tells us in 1658 that her peasants in the Dombes 'are well-dressed ... have never paid taxes' and adds 'they eat meat four times a day'.[51] Although we have only her word for it, this is possible, since the Dombes in the seventeenth century was a wild and unhealthy region; and it was precisely in such regions, untamed by man, that animals, both wild and domestic, were most plentiful. And it is probably true that we of the twentieth century would have found the ordinary fare in Riga in the days of Peter the Great, or in Belgrade (where Tavernier found everything 'excellent' although 'very cheap' – bread, wine, meat and the great carp and pike from the Danube or Sava)[52] better than the equivalent in Berlin, Vienna or even Paris. Many backward countries are no more deprived in human terms than richer places. Living standards are always a question of the number of people and the total resources at their disposal.

Europe's privileged position

Europe remained in a privileged position, though less so than in the past. It is enough to compare it with other civilizations. 'In Japan,' said a Spaniard (1609), 'the only meat they eat is game which they kill by hunting.'[53] In India the population fortunately regarded meat with horror. The soldiers of the Great Mogul Aurangzeb were very undemanding, according to a French doctor: 'Provided they have their *kicheris* or a mixture of rice and other vegetables over which they pour browned butter ... they are content.' This mixture was actually made of 'cooked rice, beans and lentils mashed up together'.[54]

In China, meat was rare. There were hardly any animals for slaughter: just the household pig (fed at home on scraps and rice), poultry, game, and even dogs, which could be found in special butchers' shops or offered on doorsteps, 'skinned and prepared', or else transported in crates, like sucking-pigs or young goats in Spain, according to Father de Las Cortes: the meagre sum total of these beasts would not have satisfied the appetite of a resolutely meat-eating nation. Except in Mongolia, where boiled mutton was common, meat was never served on its own. It was chopped into tiny pieces, the size of a a mouthful, or even minced, as a contribution to the *ts'ai* – the many dishes combining meat and fish with vegetables, sauces and spices which were the traditional accompaniment to rice. Refined and sophisticated though it was, this style of cookery surprised Europeans, who considered it a sign of poverty. Even the rich mandarins, Father de Las Cortes noted, 'only nibble a few mouthfuls of pork or chicken or some other meat, as if to whet their appetites ... For however rich and mighty they are, they eat only tiny quantities of meat; and if they ate it as we Europeans do, all the types of meat they possess would in no way suffice to feed them ... the fertility of their China could not meet the challenge.'[55] The Neapolitan, Gemelli Careri, who crossed China from Canton to Peking and back in 1696, was infuriated by the vegetable dishes, in his opinion badly cooked, that were served to him in the inns; whenever he could, he bought chickens or eggs, pheasants, hares, ham or partridges in local markets.[56] In about 1735, a European observer noted: 'The Chinese eat very little butcher's meat' and added, 'they therefore need less land to graze their animals'. A missionary in Peking, about forty years later, gave a more detailed explanation. 'The surplus of population, of which modern European philosophers have not realised the inconveniences and consequences', obliges the Chinese 'to do without the aid of oxen and herds, because the land on which they would live is required to feed the people'. Consequently there is no 'manure for the fields, no meat on the tables, no horses for battle' and 'more labour and more men are required to obtain the same quantity of grain as in other countries'. 'All in all,' he concluded, 'there are at least ten oxen in France for every one in China.'[57]

Chinese literature provides similar evidence. Under the Tsing dynasty, a proud father-in-law confides: 'The other day my son-in-law came bringing me two pounds of dried venison, and here it is on this dish.' A butcher is full of admiration for a high personage 'who had more money than the Emperor

The sophistication of Chinese cookery. Painting on silk. (Photo Roger-Viollet.)

himself' and whose house harboured scores of relatives and servants. Irrefutable proof of his wealth: he 'buys 4000 to 5000 pounds of meat in a year even when there are no ceremonies!' The complete menu for one feast consisted of 'swallows' nests, chicken, duck, cuttlefish, and bitter cucumbers from Kwang Tung ...' And there was no end to the dietary requirements of one young and capricious widow: eight *fen* of medicaments daily, duck one day, fish the next, fresh vegetables and soup made of bamboo shoots on another occasion, or again oranges, biscuits, water-lilies, fruit, salted crawfish and, naturally, wine, 'the wine of a hundred flowers'.[58] The shortage of meat did not prevent – indeed it encouraged – extreme sophistication, often at great cost, in the preparation of food. But if the luxury of Chinese cooking was so misunderstood by Europeans, it was because for them meat was synonymous with luxury. No traveller describes any accumulation of meat except in Peking, in front of the Emperor's palace and in certain squares of the city. And there it consisted entirely of heaps of game sent from Tartary and preserved by the cold winter weather for two or three months: it was so cheap 'that a deer or a wild boar was sold for a piece of eight'.[59]

The same moderation and frugality existed in Turkey where dried beef, *pasterme*, was not only food for soldiers in the field. Apart from the enormous consumption of mutton in the Seraglio, the average in Istanbul from the sixteenth to the eighteenth century was about one sheep or a third of a sheep per person per year. And Istanbul was well off.[60] In Egypt, which seems at first glance the granary of plenty, 'the way the Turks live,' said a traveller in 1693, 'is one continual penance. The meals, even of the richest, are composed of bad bread, garlic, onion and sour cheese; when they add boiled mutton it is a great feast for them. They never eat chicken or other fowl, although they are cheap in that country.'[61]

If the Europeans' privilege was in the process of diminishing on their own continent, it was making a fresh start for some of them elsewhere, bringing back the good times of the middle ages. This was true both of East Europe – Hungary for example – and of colonial America: Mexico, Brazil (the São Francisco valley, for instance, which was invaded by wild herds and where a thriving meat-eating civilization was established to the advantage of whites and halfbreeds). Farther south, around Montevideo and Buenos Aires, horsemen would kill a wild animal for a single meal. Such massacres did not cancel out the extraordinarily rapid increase in free livestock in Argentina, but they did in the north of Chile. All that survived around Coquimbo at the end of the sixteenth century were dogs which had returned to the wild state.

Meat dried in the sun (the *carne do sol* of Brazil) quickly became a standby for coastal towns and the black slaves on the plantations. *Charque*, boned and dried meat produced in the *saladeros* of Argentina (once again intended for slaves and the European poor), was to all practical purposes invented at the beginning of the sixteenth century. However in 1696, on the galleon from Manila to Acapulco, by the end of the seven or eight months of the interminable journey a traveller with little stomach for it was obliged 'on meat days' to eat 'slices of cows and buffalo dried in the sun.... They are so hard that one cannot chew them without beating them thoroughly with a piece of wood, from which they do not greatly differ, nor digest them without a strong purgative'. The worms swarming in this awful food were a further source of disgust.[62] But carnivorous necessity obviously knew few laws. Thus despite a certain repugnance, the filibusters of the West Indies, like the Africans, killed and ate monkeys (preferably young ones); unfortunates and poor Jews in Rome bought buffalo meat, sold in special butchers' shops and viewed with horror by the majority. Oxen were not killed and eaten in Aix-en-Provence until before about 1690, as such 'coarse meat' was long reputed to be unhealthy.[63] And in Denmark, 'horseflesh is sold in the market', a French traveller noted with some disgust.[64]

The extravagances of the table

After the fifteenth and sixteenth centuries, only a few privileged people in Europe ate luxuriously. They consumed huge quantities of rare dishes. What was left went to their servants, and what was left after that was sold to food-dealers, even if it had gone rotten. Typical of such extravagance was the transport of a turtle to Paris from London; 'this is a dish (1782) which cost a thousand écus; seven or eight gluttons can gorge themselves on it'. By comparison wild boar grilled over a fire seems commonplace. 'Yes,' the same witness tells us, 'I saw it with my own eyes on a gridiron as big as St. Laurence's. It was surrounded with live coals, larded with *foie gras*, flamed with fine fats, doused with the fullest-flavoured wines, and served in one piece with its head.'[65] The guests then barely sampled the various quarters of the animal. These were the whims of princes. For the king and the wealthy houses, the caterers filled their baskets with the best of the meat, game and fish on the market. Smaller fry were sold low-quality cuts and at higher prices than the rich paid. What is worse, this merchandise was generally adulterated. 'The butchers of Paris on the eve of the Revolution were supplying the large houses with the best of the beef; they sold the people the worst and even then added bones, which were ironically called *réjouissances* (a *double-entendre* which meant either rejoicings or make-weights).' The very worst pieces, which the poor ate, were sold outside butchers' shops.[66]

Hazel grouse and ortolans were other rare dishes. Some sixteen thousand livres' worth of these birds were consumed at the Princess of Conti's wedding (1680).[67] The ortolan, a bird of the vineyard, abounded in Cyprus (from where it was exported to Venice preserved in vinegar in the sixteenth century); it was also found in Italy, Provence and Languedoc.[68] There were also green oysters, and new oysters from Dieppe or Cancale which arrived in October, and strawberries and pineapples grown in greenhouses in the Paris region. The rich also indulged in elaborate – often over-elaborate – sauces, which mingled all conceivable ingredients: pepper, spices, almonds, amber, musk, rose water ... And let us not forget the costly cooks from Languedoc, the best in Paris, who sold their services at enormous prices. If the poor wanted to participate in these feasts they had to make friends with the servants or go to the *regrat* at Versailles where left-overs from the royal table were sold. A quarter of the town fed on them without any compunction. A gentleman might 'step in, with his sword at his side, and buy a turbot and a head of salmon, a rare and delicate morsel'.[69] He might have done better to have gone to an eating house in the Rue de la Huchette in the Latin Quarter, or to the Quai de la Vallée (the quay for poultry and game), and treated himself to a capon *au gros sel* fished out of 'the ever-ready pot' hanging from a wide pot-hanger, where it would be boiling with a mass of other capons. He could eat it piping hot at home, 'or four steps away, washing it down with a Burgundy wine'.[70] But such 'ways' were confined to the bourgeois!

Laying the table

Table luxury also included crockery, silver, tablecloths, napkins, lighted candles and the whole setting of the dining-room. It was customary in Paris in the sixteenth century to rent a grand house, or better still gain admittance to one through the paid collusion of the caretaker. The caterer would then deliver the dishes for the temporary host to entertain his friends. Sometimes he settled in until the real owner dislodged him. 'In my time,' said an ambassador (1557), 'Mgr Salviati, the Papal Nuncio, was forced to move house three times in two months.'[71]

There were sumptuous inns as well as sumptuous houses. At Châlons (sur-Marne), 'we lodged at *La Couronne*,' Montaigne noted (1580), 'which is a beautiful hostelry and the food is served on silver plates'.[72]

It must have posed quite a problem to lay a table for 'a company of thirty persons of high estate whom one wishes to entertain lavishly'. The answer is given in a cookery book with an unexpected title, *Les Délices de la campagne* (The Pleasures of the Countryside) by Nicolas de Bonnefons, published in 1654. It is: lay fourteen places on one side, fourteen on the other and, as the table is rectangular, one person at the 'top end' plus 'one or two at the bottom'. The guests will be 'the space of a chair apart'. 'The tablecloth [must] reach to the ground on all sides. There will be several salt cellars and table mats in the centre for the extra dishes.' The meal will have eight courses, the eighth and last, by way of example, being composed of 'dry or liquid' jams, crystallised sweets, musk pastilles, sugared almonds from Verdun, musky and amber-scented sugar ...' The maître d'hôtel, sword at side, will order the plates to be changed 'at least at every course and the napkins at every two'. But this careful description, which even specifies the way the dishes will be 'rotated' on the table at each course, omits to say how the table should be laid for each guest. At this period he would certainly be given a plate, spoon and knife, possibly an individual fork,

The Wedding at Cana, with the table laid for a feast. Painting by Hieronymus Bosch. Boymans-Van Beuningen Museum, Rotterdam.

but no glass or bottle would be placed in front of him. The rules of propriety remain uncertain; the author recommends a deep plate for soup as an elegance, so that the guests could serve themselves with all they wanted at one time 'without having to take spoonful after spoonful from the dish, because of the disgust some might feel for others'.

A table laid in the modern way and our present table manners are the results of many details that custom has imposed slowly, one by one, and in ways that vary according to region. Spoon and knife are fairly old customs. However, the use of a spoon did not become widespread until the sixteenth century, and the custom of providing knives dates from the same time – before that the guests brought along their own. Individual glasses for each guest also appeared at about this time. Courtesy formerly dictated that one emptied the glass and passed it on to one's neighbour, who did the same. Or else, when requested, the manservant brought the required drink, wine or water, from the pantry or the dresser near the guest table. When Montaigne crossed southern Germany in 1580, he noted that 'everyone has his goblet or silver cup at his place; the man serving takes care to refill this goblet immediately it is empty, without moving it from its place, pouring wine into it from a distance away out of a pewter or wooden vessel with a long spout'.[73] This elegant solution economized on the effort demanded of the staff, but it required every guest to have a personal goblet in front of him. In Germany in Montaigne's time every guest also had his own plate, either pewter or wooden; sometimes a wooden bowl underneath and a pewter plate on top. We have proof that wooden plates continued to be used in some places in the German countryside, and probably elsewhere, until the nineteenth century.

But for a long time before these more or less tardy refinements, guests were satisfied with a wooden board or a 'trencher', a slice of bread on which the meat was placed.[74] The large dish then sufficed for everything and everybody: each guest selected the morsel he wanted and picked it up with his fingers. Montaigne noted that the Swiss 'use as many wooden spoons with silver handles as there are people [note that each guest had his own spoon] and a Swiss is never without a knife, with which he takes everything; and he scarcely ever puts his hand in the dish'.[75] Wooden spoons with metal handles (not necessarily silver) are preserved in museums, together with various types of knife. But these were old implements.

This is not the case with forks. The very large fork with two prongs, used to serve meat to the guests and to manipulate it on the stove or in the kitchen, probably goes back a long way, but the individual fork, with one or two exceptions, does not.

The individual fork dates from about the sixteenth century; it spread from Venice and Italy in general, though not very quickly. A German preacher condemned it as a diabolical luxury: God would not have given us fingers if he had wished us to use such an instrument. We know that Montaigne did not use a fork, since he accuses himself of eating too quickly so that 'I sometimes bite my fingers in my haste'. Indeed he says he rarely 'makes use of spoon or fork'.[76] The lord of Villamont, describing in great detail the culinary and eating habits of the Turks in 1609, adds 'they do not use forks as the Lombards and Venetians do'. (Note that he does not say 'the French' for the good reason that they did not.) An English traveller at about the same time, Thomas Coryate, came across the table fork in Italy: he made fun of it at first, then adopted it – to the great amusement of his friends who christened him *furciferus* (fork-handler, or to be more precise pitchfork-handler).[77] Was it the fashion of wearing ruffs that led rich diners to use forks? Probably not, since in England, for example, there is no mention of table forks in any inventory before 1660. Their use only became general in about 1750. Anne of Austria ate her meat with her fingers all her life.[78] And so did the Court of Vienna until at least 1651. Who used a fork at the Court of Louis XIV? The Duke of Montausier, whom Saint-Simon describes as being 'of formidable cleanliness'. Not the king, whose skill at eating chicken stew with his fingers without spilling it is praised by the same Saint-Simon! When the Duke of Burgundy and his brothers were admitted to sup with the king and took up the forks they had been taught to use, the king forbade them to use them. This anecdote is told by the Princess Palatine, with great satisfaction: she has 'always used her knife and fingers to eat with'.[79] This accounts for the many napkins offered to table-guests in the seventeenth century although the custom had only reached private households in Montaigne's lifetime, as he himself tells us.[80] It also explains the custom of hand-washing several times during a meal, using a jug and bowl of water.

The slow adoption of good manners

Such changes, representing a new code of behaviour, were adopted gradually. Even the luxury of a separate dining-room did not become current in France until the sixteenth century, and then only among the rich. Before then the nobleman ate in his vast kitchen.

The whole ceremonial of the meal meant large numbers of servants in the kitchen and around the guests, and not only at Versailles where the *Grand* and *Petit Commun* were mobilized for the meal or 'the King's meat', as it was called. All this new luxury only reached the whole of France or England with the eighteenth century. 'If people who died sixty years ago came back,' wrote Duclos in about 1765, 'they would not recognise Paris as far as its tables, costumes and customs are concerned.'[81] The same was probably true of all Europe, in the grip of an omnipresent luxury, and also of its colonies where it had always tried to establish its own customs. Hence Western travellers thought even less of the customs and habits of the wide world and looked down on them more than ever. Gemelli Careri was surprised when his host, a Persian of high rank, received him at his table (1694) and used 'his right hand instead of a spoon to pick up rice so as to put it on the plate [of his guests]'.[82] Or read what Father Labat (1728)

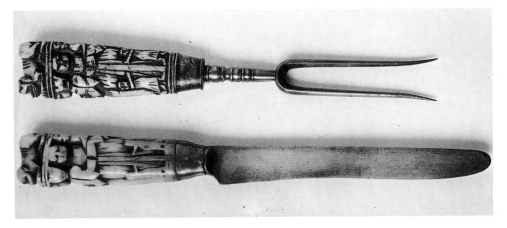

Ivory-handled cutlery, seventeenth century. (Bayerisches Nationalmuseum, Munich.)

has to say about the Arabs in Senegal: 'They do not know what it is to eat off tables.'[83] No one found favour with these fastidious arbiters except the refined Chinese, who sat down at tables, ate out of glazed bowls, and carried in their belts the knife and chopsticks (in a special case) that they used to eat with. The Baron de Tott has left a humorous description of a reception in the country house near Istanbul of 'Madame the wife of the First Dragoman', in 1760. This class of rich Greeks in the service of the Grand Turk adopted local customs, but liked to make some difference felt. 'A circular table, with chairs all round it, spoons, forks – nothing was missing except the habit of using them. But they did not wish to omit any of our manners which were just becoming as fashionable among the Greeks as English manners are among ourselves, and I saw one woman throughout the dinner taking olives with her fingers and then impaling them on her fork in order to eat them in the French manner'.[84]

However, an Austrian ordinance of 1624 for the landgraviate of Alsace still laid down for the use of young officers the rules to be observed when invited to an archduke's table: to present themselves in clean uniform, not to arrive half drunk, not to drink after every mouthful, to wipe moustache and mouth clean before drinking, not to lick the fingers, not to spit in the plate, not to wipe the nose on the tablecloth, not to gulp drink like animals. Such instructions make the reader wonder at the state of manners in Richelieu's Europe.[85]

At the table of Christ

It is extremely instructive on these journeys into the past to look at pictures painted before these refinements came into use. Meals were a favourite subject

The Last Supper. Tapestry, fragment of an antependium, Nuremberg, fifteenth century. (Bayerische Nationalmuseum, Munich.)

with painters – particularly the Last Supper, which has been depicted thousands of times by Western artists; or Christ's meal with Simon, the wedding at Cana, the table of the pilgrims of Emmaus. If we forget the figures for a moment and look at the tables, the embroidered tablecloths, the seats (stools, chairs, benches), and above all the plates, dishes and knives, we can see that no fork appears before 1600 and almost no spoons either. Instead of plates there are slices of bread, round or oval pieces of wood or pewter discs only slightly hollowed: they are the spots of blue which appear on the majority of south German tables. The trencher of stale bread, often placed on a wooden or metal slab, was intended to soak up the juice from the carved joint. This 'bread plate' was then distributed to the poor. There is always at least one knife – sometimes extra large when it is the only one available and has to serve for all the guests – and often small individual knives. Of course, wine, bread and lamb appear on the table at this sacred feast. And of course the Last Supper is not a lavish or luxurious meal; the event transcends earthly sustenance. None the less, Christ and his apostles eat like Ulm or Augsburg bourgeois; for the scene is almost the same whether it represents the marriage at Cana, Herod's feast, or the meals served to some master of Basle, surrounded by family and attentive servants, or the Nuremberg practitioner painted with his friends at his house-warming in 1593. As far as I know, Jacopo Bassano (1599) painted one of the first forks to figure in a Last Supper.

Everyday foods: salt

It is time to turn from luxuries to everyday foods. Salt calls us to order very effectively, since this ultra-common commodity was the subject of an essential and world-wide trade. It was essential both to humans and to animals, and for preserving meat and fish; and was all the more important as governments had an interest in it. Salt was a major source of income to states and merchants, in Europe and China alike, as we shall see. As salt was such an indispensable commodity, trade in it overcame all obstacles and took advantage of all facilities. As a heavy good, it was carried by river traffic (going up the Rhône, for instance) and by shipping in the Atlantic. Not a single rock salt mine remained unexploited. It so happened that all the salt-pans of the Mediterranean and Atlantic, needing a sunny climate, were in Catholic countries, while their salt, from Brouage, Setubal and San Lucar de Barrameda, was in much demand among the northern fishermen, who were Protestants. The trade was always carried on, regardless of wars, and to the great profit of large consortia of merchants. Similarly, blocks of salt from the Sahara braved the desert, carried by camel to Black Africa – in return it is true for gold dust, elephants' tusks and black slaves. Nothing is a clearer indication of the irresistible pressure of this trade.

The small Swiss canton of Valais demonstrates the same thing in terms of economy and distances to be covered. Resources and population in these lands flanking the upper Rhône valley were in perfect balance, except for iron and salt – particularly salt, which the inhabitants needed for stock-raising, cheeses and salting. Salt had to cover great distances to reach these Alpine cantons: it came from Peccais (Languedoc) 870 kilometres away, via Lyons; from Barletta, 1300 kilometres away, via Venice; and, also via Venice, from Trapani, 2300 kilometres away.[86]

Essential, irreplaceable, salt was a sacred food ('salted food is synonymous with holy food both in ancient Hebrew and the current Malagasy language'). In the Europe of insipid farinaceous gruels consumption of salt was large (twenty grams daily per person, double the present figure). One medical historian even thinks that the peasant uprisings against the *gabelle*, the salt tax, in western France in the sixteenth century, can be explained by a hunger for salt which the tax thwarted.[87] Furthermore, an odd detail here and there informs us – or fortuitously reminds us – of numerous uses of salt which are not immediately obvious: for example, for making botargo in Provence or for domestic preserving which spread in the eighteenth century: asparagus, fresh peas, mushrooms, morels, artichoke hearts and so on.

Everyday foods: dairy products, fats, eggs

Cheese, eggs, milk and butter would certainly not be classed luxuries. Cheeses arrived in Paris from Brie and Normandy (*angelots* from Bray, *livarots*, and the cheese of Pont-L'Évêque); from Auvergne, Touraine and Picardy. They could be bought from *regrattiers*, those all-purpose retail merchants in touch with convents and the neighbouring countryside. Cheese from Montreuil and Vincennes was sold there 'freshly curdled and drained, in little baskets woven from wicker or rushes', *jonchées*.[88] In the Mediterranean, Sardinian cheeses, *cacio cavallo*[89] or *salso*, were exported everywhere – to Naples, Rome, Leghorn, Marseilles and Barcelona. They left Cagliari in boatloads and sold even more cheaply than the cheeses from Holland, which were invading the markets of Europe and the whole world by the eighteenth century. As early as 1572, thousands of Dutch cheeses were unlawfully reaching Spanish America. Cheeses from Dalmatia and enormous wheels of cheese from Candia were sold in Venice. Cheese consumed in Marseilles in 1543 included some from the Auvergne,[90] where it was so plentiful that it formed the principal basis of diet in the sixteenth century. In the previous century, cheese from the Grande-Chartreuse in Dauphiné was considered excellent and was used to make *fondues* and cheese on toast. Large quantities of Swiss gruyère were already being consumed before the eighteenth century. In about 1750, France was importing 30,000 quintals of it annually. It was 'counterfeited in Franche-Comté, Lorraine, Savoy and Dauphiné,' and while these imitations may not have been as reputable or as expensive as the original, they were widely sold. Attempts to imitate Parmesan cheese, in Normandy for instance, were however unsuccessful.[91]

Cheese, a source of cheap protein, was one of the great foods of the people in Europe, greatly missed by any European forced to live far away and unable to get it. French peasants made fortunes in about 1698 by carrying cheeses to the armies fighting in Italy and Germany. Nevertheless, particularly in France, cheese had not yet won its great reputation. Cookery books gave it only a small place, describing neither its qualities nor its individual names. Goats' cheese was scorned and considered inferior to cows' or ewes'. As late as 1702, the medical writer Lemery recognized only three great cheeses: 'Roquefort, Parmesan and those from Sassenage in Dauphiné ... served at the most refined tables.'[92]

Roquefort at that time recorded a sale of over 6000 quintals every year. Sassenage was a mixture of cows', goats' and ewes' milk, boiled together. Parmesan (like the 'marsolin' of Florence which later went out of fashion) had been an acquisition of the Italian wars, after the return of Charles VIII.

Despite what Lemery says, however, when Cardinal Dubois was in London on a mission, what did he ask his nephew to send him from Paris? Three dozen Pont-L'Évêque cheeses, and the same number of *marolles* and Bries (as well as a wig).[93] So there were already connoisseurs who favoured certain regional cheeses.

Mention must be made of the great place these humble but nutritionally rich foodstuffs – milk, butter, cheese – occupied throughout Islam as far as the Indies. A traveller noted in 1694 that the Persians spent little; they 'are satisfied with a little cheese and sour milk in which they soak the local bread, which is as thin as a wafer, tasteless and very brown; in the morning they add rice to this (or pilau) sometimes only cooked with water'.[94] But pilau, often a stew with rice, distinguished the tables of the comfortably-off. In Turkey, milk products were almost the sole food of the poor: sour milk (yoghourt) accompanied, according to the season, by cucumbers or melons, an onion, a leek, or stewed dried fruit. Along with yoghourt, mention must also be made of *kaymak*, a slightly salted boiled cream, and the cheeses preserved in leather bottles (*tulum*), in wheels (*tekerlek*), or in balls, like the famous *cascaval* which the Wallachian mountain-dwellers exported to Istanbul and even to Italy. This was a cheese made of ewes' milk subjected to repeated boiling, like *cacio cavallo* in Sardinia and Italy.

In the East, however, there was one huge and persistent exception: China. The Chinese systematically ignored milk, cheese and butter. Cows, goats and sheep were raised purely for meat. So what was the 'butter' M. de Guignes'[95] thought he was eating? It was only used in China to make rare pastries. Japan shared China's repugnance on this score. Even in villages where oxen and cows are used to work the land, the Japanese peasant still does not eat dairy products and thinks them 'unwholesome'; he draws the small quantities of oil he requires from soya.

Milk was consumed in such large quantities, on the other hand, in the towns of the West that problems of supply appeared very early on. In London, consumption increased every winter, when all the wealthy families moved to the capital; it decreased in summer for the opposite reason. But, winter or summer, it was the subject of gigantic fraud. Milk was watered on a wide scale by dairy farmers and retailers. 'A considerable Cow-keeper in Surrey has a pump of this kind, which goes by the name of the *Famous Black Cow* (from the circumstances of its being painted black), *and is said to yield more than all the rest put together.*'[96] We may prefer to think of Valladolid a century earlier: the streets were daily thronged with hundreds of donkeys bringing milk from the neighbouring countryside and supplying the town with curd cheeses, butter and cream. A Portuguese traveller praised the quality and cheapness of these products. Everything was plentiful in Valladolid, a capital which Philip III was soon to abandon for Madrid. Over seven thousand birds were sold daily on the poultry market; the mutton there was the best in the world, the bread excellent, the wine perfect, and its supply of dairy products was a luxury in Spain, where such goods were particularly scarce.[97]

Butter remained limited to Northern Europe, except for the wide zone where rancid butter was used, from northern Africa to Alexandria in Egypt and beyond. The rest of Europe used lard, bacon fat and olive oil. France clearly demonstrates this geographical division of culinary resources. A veritable river of butter flowed through the lands of the Loire, in Paris and beyond. 'Practically no sauce is made without it in France,' said Louis Lemery (1702). 'The Dutch and the northern peoples use it even more than we do and it is claimed that it contributes to the freshness of their complexion.'[98] Actually the use of butter did not really spread until the eighteenth century, even in Holland. It characterized the cooking of the rich. It distressed Mediterranean people when they were obliged to live in or cross these strange countries; they thought that butter increased the number of lepers. The wealthy cardinal of Aragon was careful to take his own cook when he travelled to the Netherlands in 1516, and carried a sufficient quantity of olive oil in his luggage.[99]

Eighteenth-century Paris, so well set in its comforts, had an ample supply of butter at its disposal – fresh, salted (from Ireland and Brittany), and even clarified in the Lorraine manner. A good part of its fresh butter arrived from Gournay, a small town near Dieppe where merchants received the butter unrefined and then kneaded it again in order to eliminate the whey it still contained. 'They then make it into large blocks, of between forty and sixty pounds, and send it to Paris.'[100] As snobbery is always with us, according to the *Dictionnaire Sentencieux* (1778) 'there are only two types of butter which the fashionable world dares mention: butter from Vanvre (Vanves) and butter from the Frévalais',[101] in the vicinity of Paris.

Eggs were widely eaten. Doctors repeated the old precepts of the Salerno School – let them be eaten fresh and not overcooked: *Si sumas ovum, molle sit atque novum*. And there were numerous recipes for keeping eggs fresh. Their market price is a valuable indicator: eggs were a cheap commodity and their price accurately followed the fluctuations of the economic situation. A statistician[102] can reconstruct the movement of the cost of living in the sixteenth century from a few eggs sold in Florence. Their price alone is a valid measure of the standard of living or the value of money in any given town in any given country. At one time in seventeenth-century Egypt, 'one had the choice of thirty eggs, two pigeons or one fowl for a sou'; on the road from Magnesia to Brusa (1694) 'provisions are not dear: seven eggs can be bought for one *para* (one sou), a fowl for ten, a good winter melon for two, and as much bread as you can eat in a day for the same price'. In February 1697 the same traveller, this time near Acapulco in New Spain, noted: 'The innkeeper made me pay a piece of eight (thirty-two

Old woman with eggs, painted by Velasquez in 1618 before he left his native city of Seville. (National Gallery of Scotland, The Cooper Bridgeman Library, Ziolo.)

sous) for a fowl, and eggs were one sou each.'[103] Eggs were an everyday food for Europeans. Montaigne's surprise in the German inns was therefore understandable: they never served eggs there, he wrote, 'except hard-boiled cut into quarters in salads'.[104] Montesquieu, leaving Naples and returning to Rome (1729), was astonished 'that in this ancient Latium the traveller finds neither a chicken nor a young pigeon, nor often an egg'.[105]

But in Europe these were exceptions and not the rule that applied to the vegetarian Far East, where China, Japan and India never made use of this rich and commonplace item of diet. Eggs were very rare there and formed no part of ordinary people's fare. The famous Chinese ducks' eggs, preserved in pickling brine for thirty days, were a delicacy of the rich.

Everyday seafoods

The sea was an extremely important source of nourishment and could have been even more so. Whole regions were barely aware of the existence of seafoods, even when they were close at hand.

This was more or less the case in the New World, despite the huge shoals in the fishing grounds of the Caribbean where boats often made miraculous hauls on the way to Vera Cruz; despite the great wealth of the coasts and banks of Newfoundland, which supplied food almost exclusively to Europe (although barrels of cod reached the eighteenth-century English colonies and the American plantations in the southern states); despite the salmon that swam up the cold rivers of Canada and Alaska; despite the resources of the Bay of Bahia where an influx of cold waters from the south made whale-hunting possible and accounts for the presence of Basque harpooners as early as the seventeenth century. In Asia, only Japan and southern China from the mouth of the Yang-tse-Kiang to the island of Hainan went in for fishing. Elsewhere it would seem that only a few boats, as in Malaysia or around Ceylon, were so engaged – if we except some oddities like the pearl fishermen in the Persian Gulf, near Bandar Abass (1694) who 'preferred their sardines [dried in the sun, these were their daily fare] to the pearls the merchants bought, as more reliable and easier to fish'.[106]

In China, where fresh-water fishing and fish-breeding yielded large profits (sturgeon were caught in the lakes of the Yang-tse-Kiang and in the Pei Ho), fish was often preserved in the form of a sauce obtained by spontaneous fermentation, as in Tonkin. But even today consumption there is insignificant (0·6 kilograms per person per year). The sea does not manage to penetrate the continental mass. Only Japan was widely fish-eating. It has kept this characteristic and today is on a par with carnivorous Europe (forty kilograms per person per year and the leading fishing fleet in the world after Peru). The abundance comes from the richness of its internal sea, and still more from the proximity of the Yeso and Sakhaline fisheries, at the meeting point of enormous masses of cold waters from Oya Shivo and warm waters from Kuro-shivo – just as Newfoundland is at the confluence of the Gulf Stream and the Labrador current in the north Atlantic. The meeting of plankton from hot and cold waters helps the rapid breeding of fish.

Europe is not so well provided for but it has many sources of supply at short and long range. Fish was all the more important here as religious rulings multiplied the number of fast days: 166 days, including Lent, observed extremely strictly until the reign of Louis XIV. Meat, eggs and poultry could not be sold during those forty days except to invalids and with a double certificate from doctor and priest. To facilitate control, the 'Lent butcher' was the only person authorized to sell prohibited foods at that time in Paris, and only inside the area of the Hôtel Dieu.[107] This led to a huge demand for fresh, smoked and salted fish.

However, fish was not always plentiful around the coasts of Europe. The much-vaunted Mediterranean had only limited resources – tunny from the Bosporus, caviar from the Russian rivers (choice food for Christian fasts as far afield as Abyssinia), dried squids and octopus, always a providential food for the Greek archipelago, sardines and anchovies from Provence. Tunny was also trapped in the madragues of North Africa, Sicily, Andalusia and the Portuguese Algarve. Lagos was a great shipping point for whole boatloads of barrels of salted tunny bound for the Mediterranean and the north.

By comparison, the resources of those narrow northerly inland seas – the Channel, North Sea and Baltic – and even more those of the Atlantic, were superabundant. The Atlantic coasts of Europe were the scene of an active fishing industry in the middle ages (salmon, mackerel, cod). The Baltic and North Sea have been centres of large herring fisheries since the eleventh century; they were the making of the Hanse and then of fishermen from Holland and Zealand. A Dutchman, William Beukelszoon, is said to have discovered in about 1350 the rapid method of gutting herrings and salting them on the boat where the fishermen could barrel them immediately.[108] But the herring disappeared from the Baltic between the fourteenth and fifteenth century.[109] After that, boats from Holland and Zealand fished on the barely covered sands of the Dogger Bank and in the open sea off the English and Scottish coasts, as far as the Orkneys. Other fleets gathered at these rich grounds. In the sixteenth century, at the height of the conflicts between Valois and Hapsburgs, herring truces were duly concluded to ensure Europe's continued supplies.

Herrings were exported to western and southern Europe by sea, along rivers, by carriage and by pack animals. Bloaters and red and white herrings arrived in Venice: white herrings were salted, the red were smoked, and bloaters had been bloated, that is slightly smoked and slightly salted. The *chasse-marées*, carriers of fresh sea fish, could often be seen hurrying towards large towns like Paris – poor fellows urging on wretched horses weighed down with fish and oysters. Their cry: 'Herrings fresh last night' can be heard in *Les cris de Paris* by the musician Janequin. In London, eating a barrel of oysters with wife and friends was a minor luxury and one the young and economical Samuel Pepys could treat himself to.

But sea fishing was hardly sufficient to satisfy Europe's hunger. Recourse to fresh-water fish becomes more and more essential as we move farther away from sea coasts, towards the central and eastern continental lands. No river, no stream, not even the Seine at Paris, was without its authorized fishermen. The distant Volga was a colossal reserve. The Loire was famous for salmon and carp; the Rhine for perch. A Portuguese traveller to Valladolid in the first years of the seventeenth century found supplies of sea fish rather deficient and not always of high quality, in view of the time they took to reach the city. There were sole, *escabèches* of sardines and oysters, and sometimes coalfish, all the year round; and excellent dorado came from Santander during Lent. But our traveller was startled by the unbelievable number of magnificent trout coming from Burgos and Medina de Rioseco and sold daily on the markets, sometimes so many that half the town, which was at that time the capital of Spain, could be fed on them.[110] Artificial ponds and the fish-breeding on the large estates in the south of Bohemia have already been mentioned. Carp was commonly eaten in Germany.

Cod fishing

It was something of a revolution when, as early as the end of the fifteenth century, the large-scale fishing of cod began on the Newfoundland banks. It provoked a scuffle between Basques, French, Dutch and English, the strongest driving out the less protected. The Spanish Basques were eliminated and access to the fishing grounds remained in the hands of the powers with the strongest navies: England, Holland and France.

The great problem was how to preserve and transport the fish. The cod was either prepared and salted on board the Newfoundland boat, or dried on land. Salted cod was the 'green cod' 'which has just been salted and is still wet'. Boats specializing in green cod were of light tonnage with ten or twelve fishermen on board, plus sailors who cut, cleaned and salted the fish in the hold – often full to the beams of the bridge. Their practice was to drift with the tide once they had 'embanked' (arrived on the Newfoundland banks). On the other hand, quite large sailing ships were used to bring back dried or dressed cod. They dropped anchor when they arrived off the coast of Newfoundland and the fishing expedition was continued in boats. The fish was dried on land by complicated processes, described at length by Savary.[111]

Every sailing ship, whatever sort of cod it carried, had to be 'victualled' before it set out – to take on board salt, naval stores, flour, wine, alcohol, lines and fish-hooks. Fishermen from Norway and Denmark still went to San Lucar de Barrameda near Seville at the beginning of the seventeenth century to obtain their salt. Naturally the merchants advanced it to them; the borrowers had to pay it back in fish when they returned from America.[112]

This was the custom at La Rochelle during its period of prosperity in the sixteenth and seventeenth centuries. Numerous sailing ships, often of a hundred tons because quite large holds were required ('Cod is bulky rather than heavy'), put into port there every spring. They had twenty to twenty-five men on board, which shows the importance of manpower in this thankless job. The 'bourgeois victualler' advanced the owner flour, tools, drink and salt, according to the terms of a 'charter-party', legalized by a notary. Near La Rochelle, the little port of Olonne alone equipped up to a hundred sailing ships and sent several thousand men to the other side of the Atlantic every year. As the town numbered 3000 inhabitants the owners had to engage sailors from as far afield as Spain. In any case once the boats had left, the money the bourgeois had advanced 'on bot-

Whale-fishing. Plate, Delft, eighteenth century. Musée Carnavalet, Paris. (Photo Marine Nationale.)

tomry' floated at the whims of the fish and the sea. No repayment would be made until the return, after June. Furthermore a valuable bonus awaited the first boats to put in. The victorious skipper was mobbed in the inn by the townsfolk amidst arguments, brawls and solicitations. It was a singularly profitable victory. Everyone would be waiting for the new fish. The winning captain might be able to sell his 'little hundred' cod (110 to the 100 according to custom) for as much as 60 livres, while the 'thousand' a few days later would be selling for no more than 30 livres. One of the boats from Olonne itself usually won the race, since they were used to making two trips a year – for the early and late season (which might mean 'disembanking' from Newfoundland in a hurry if they were caught there by bad weather).[113]

The fishing there was inexhaustible: on the great shoulder of Newfoundland, an undersea plateau very near the surface, the cod 'congregate . . . they hold their assemblies here so to speak, and their numbers are so great that the fishermen of all nations who come here do nothing all day but throw in their lines, haul them up, gut the cod and put the guts back on the hook as bait for the next. One man can sometimes catch as many as three or four hundred in a day. When the food that tempts them to this feeding-ground is exhausted, the cod leave and start looking for whiting, to which they are very partial. The whiting run ahead of them, and it is this chase which brings the whiting so often to our shores [in Europe].'[114]

'It is God who gives us cod in Newfoundland,' wrote a native of Marseilles in 1739. A century earlier a French traveller had already explained: 'One can truly say that the best trade in Europe is to go and fish cod because it costs nothing [he meant by this no cash outlay, which is both true and false] to have the aforesaid cod, except the effort of fishing and selling; you make good Spanish coin out of it and a million men live on it in France.'[115]

The last figure is obviously exaggerated. A late-eighteenth-century register gives a few scattered figures on cod-fishing in France, England and the United States. In 1773, there are records of 264 French boats (25,000 tons and 10,000 crewmen); in 1775, there were 400 English boats (36,000 tons and 20,000 crewmen) and 665 'American' boats (25,000 and 25,000 crewmen). That gives a possible annual total of 1,329 ships, 86,000 tons and 55,000 crewmen, for a total haul of about 80,000 tons of fish. By adding to this the Dutch and other European cod fishers, one might end up with something like 1,500 ships and 90,000 tons of cod.[116]

The correspondence of a Honfleur merchant[117] (a contemporary of Colbert) acquaints us with the requisite distinctions in quality: 'gaff' cod, which was exceptionally large, and 'merchant', ling and codling, small green cod, which were, however, still better than the rejects – the enormous mass of 'spoilt' goods, either salted too much or too little, or damaged by the stackers' heels. As green cod was sold in pieces and not by weight (like dried cod), sorters able to distinguish between merchandise at a single glance and to gauge quantities had to be employed. One of the problems facing these cod merchants was to prevent the arrival on the Honfleur market of herrings from Holland (subjected to 'stiff duties') and even more, herrings caught at banned periods, particularly after Christmas, by a few wretched fishermen from Normandy. The fish at that time of year was not good quality, and as it was caught in quantity, sold at low prices: 'As soon as this herring appears, it is difficult to sell a cod's tail.' Hence a royal prohibition which the honest cod fishermen approved.

Every port specialized in a type of fish, depending on the preferences of the zone it supplied. Dieppe, Le Havre and Honfleur supplied Paris, which ate green cod; Nantes supplied the varied tastes of the Loire region; Marseilles absorbed half the French catch of dried cod on an average but re-exported part of it to Italy. Numerous vessels from Saint Malo also sailed directly to Italian ports, notably Genoa, from the seventeenth century.

Much is known about the way Paris was supplied with green (or, as it is still called, white) cod. The first fishing fleets (leaving in January, returning in July), and then the second (leaving in March, returning in November and December), led to two lots of supplies, the first small, the second more abundant but exhausted by about April. There followed a shortage which lasted for three months – April, May, June – and affected the whole of France. And 'moreover this is a season when vegetables are still scarce, eggs dear and little fresh-water fish is eaten'. Hence the sudden value and high price of the green cod which the English fished off their own coasts and which was redistributed to Paris through the port of Dieppe, a mere intermediary on this occasion.[118]

Nearly all the fleets suspended their fishing operations during the great maritime quarrels for world domination: wars of succession in Spain and Austria, the Seven Years War, the War of American Independence. Only the strongest powers continued to enjoy their cod.

A gradual increase in the catch is perceptible, though not calculable; and there was certainly a rise in average tonnage, although barely any change in the duration of the round trip (a month to six weeks). The miracle of Newfoundland was the continual reconstitution and superabundance of supplies. The banks of cod fed on plankton and were also particularly fond of whiting, driving them out of Newfoundland waters and towards the coasts of Europe where fishermen caught them. It would even seem that cod was numerous on the coasts of Europe in the middle ages. Later it seems to have moved westwards.

Europeans rushed to eat this providential food. In March 1791, 54 English ships, with a cargo of 48,110 quintals of cod, arrived in Lisbon. 'What a profit for the English from this one commodity.'[119] In Spain, the total spent annually on cod consumption in about 1717 was over 2,400,000 piastres.[120] But like all fish, cod spoils quickly in transit and becomes quite disgusting. Even the water used to soak salted cod soon became so smelly that people were allowed to throw it into the drains only at night.[121] So it is easy to understand the bitter remarks attributed to a serving-girl in 1636: 'I like meat-eating better than Lent ... I would rather see a good solid sausage in the pan and four hams, than a rotten side of cod.'[122]

Cod-fishing. The various operations carried out on land to produce 'dried cod'. Eighteenth century. (Biarritz, Maritime Museum.)

Cod was indeed chiefly eaten during Lent, when it was unavoidable, or by poor people. 'It is a food left to labourers,' says one sixteenth-century author. The same had once applied to whale meat and fat, which were very much coarser (except for the tongue, which was delicious according to Ambroise Paré) but were nevertheless eaten by poor people during Lent,[123] until the time when the fat was converted into oil and widely used for lighting, soap and various manufactured products. Whale meat then disappeared from the market. It was no longer eaten except 'by Kaffirs near the Cape of Good Hope, a semi-savage people', said a treatise of 1619, which none the less mentioned the use in Italy of fat from salted whales, known as 'Lenten lard'.[124] In any case, industrial requirements were sufficient to maintain an increasingly active whale-hunt: for example the Dutch sent 6995 ships to the Spitsbergen area between 1675 and 1721 and harpooned 32,908 whales, depopulating the adjacent seas.[125] Boats from Hamburg looking for whale oil regularly traversed the seas of Greenland.[126]

The decline in the vogue for pepper after 1650

Pepper occupies a peculiar position in the history of food. An ordinary seasoning we are far from considering indispensable today, it was for many centuries associated with spice, the primary object of trade with the Levant. Everything depended on it, even the dreams of the fifteenth-century explorers. 'As dear as pepper' was a common saying.[127]

Europe had had a very old passion for pepper and spices – cinnamon, cloves, nutmeg and ginger. We must not be too quick to call it a mania. Islam, China and India shared the taste, and every society has its crazes for particular foods that become almost indispensable. They express the need to break the monotony of diet. A Hindu writer said: 'When the palate revolts against the insipidness of rice boiled with no other ingredients, we dream of fat, salt and spices.'[128]

It is a fact that the poorest and most monotonous diets in underdeveloped countries today are those which most readily resort to spices. By spices we mean all types of seasoning in use in our period (including pimento, which came from America under many names) and not merely the glorious spices of the Levant. There were spices on the tables of the poor in Europe in the middle ages: thyme, marjoram, bay leaves, savory, aniseed, coriander and particularly garlic, which Arnaud de Villeneuve, a famous thirteenth-century doctor, called the peasants' theriac. The only luxury product amongst these local spices was saffron.

The Roman world from the time of Plautus and the older Cato was passionately fond of *silphium*, a mysterious plant from Libya which disappeared in the first century of the Empire. When Caesar emptied the public treasury in 49 he found over 1500 pounds (490 kilograms) of *silphium*. Later came the fashion for a Persian spice, *asa foetida*: 'its alliaceous and fetid smell earned it the name of *stercus diaboli*, devil's dung.' It is still used in Persian cooking today. Pepper and spices came late to Rome, 'not before Varro and Horace, and Pliny was surprised by the favour pepper found'. In his time its use was widespread and prices were relatively modest. According to Pliny fine spices were even cheaper than pepper, which was not the case in later years. Pepper ultimately had its own specialized storehouses in Rome, *horrea piperataria*, and when Alaric seized the town in 410 he captured five thousand pounds of pepper with it.[129]

The West inherited spices and pepper from Rome. It is probable that both were later in short supply, in Charlemagne's time, when the Mediterranean was all but closed to Christianity. But compensation followed rapidly. In the twelfth century the craze for spices was in full swing. The West sacrificed its precious metals for them and engaged in the difficult Levant trade which meant travelling half-way round the world. The passion was so great that along with black and white pepper (both genuine peppers, the colour depending on whether or not the dark coating was left on) Westerners bought 'long pepper', also from India, and a substitute product like the bogus pepper or *malaguetta* which came from the Guinea coast from the fifteenth century onwards.[130] Ferdinand of Spain tried in vain to prevent the importing of cinnamon and pepper from Portugal (it meant letting silver out of the country in return) arguing that *'buena especia es el ajo'* – garlic is a perfectly good spice.[131]

Cookery books show that the mania for spices affected everything: meat, fish, jam, soup, luxury drinks. Who would dare cook game without using 'hot pepper', as Douet d'Arcy counselled as early as the beginning of the fourteenth century? The advice of *Le Ménagier de Paris* (1393) was to 'put in the spices as late as possible'. Its recipe for black pudding ran as follows: 'take ginger, clove and a little pepper and crush together'. In this booklet, *oille*, 'a dish brought back from Spain' and consisting of a mixture of various meats, duck, partridge, pigeon, quail and chicken (to all appearances the popular *olla podrida* of today), also becomes a mixture of spices, 'aromatic drugs', eastern or otherwise, nutmeg, pepper, thyme, ginger and basil. Spices were also consumed in the form of preserved fruits and elaborate powders to treat any disease medicine might diagnose. They were all reputed 'to drive off wind' and 'favour the seed'.[132] In the West Indies, black pepper was often replaced by red pepper, 'axi or chili', which was so liberally sprinkled over meat that new arrivals could not swallow a mouthful.[133]

In fact there was nothing in common between this spice-orgy and the late and moderate consumption known to the Roman world. It is true that the Romans ate little meat (even in Cicero's time it was the object of sumptuary laws). The medieval West, on the other hand, was carnivorous. We might assume that the badly preserved and not always tender meat cried out for the seasoning of strong peppers and spicy sauces, which disguised its poor quality. Some doctors argue today that the sense of smell has some curious psychological features. They claim that there is a sort of mutual exclusion between the taste for seasonings 'with a bitter smell, like garlic and onion ... and the taste for more delicate seasonings with sweet and aromatic smells, reminiscent of the scent of flowers'.[134] In the middle ages, the former may have predominated.

Things were probably not so simple. In any case consumption of spice increased in the sixteenth century (until then, it had been a great luxury) with the sharp rise in deliveries following Vasco da Gama's voyage. The increase was particularly marked in the north, where purchases of spices far exceeded those in the Mediterranean regions. The spice-market shifted from Venice and its *Fondaco dei Tedeschi* to Antwerp (with a short sojourn at Lisbon) and then to Amsterdam, so the trade was not governed by simple considerations of commerce and navigation. Luther, who exaggerated, claimed that there was more spice than grain in Germany. The large consumers were in the north and east. In Holland, in 1697, it was thought that after coin, the best merchandise 'for cold countries' was spice, consumed 'in prodigious quantities' in Russia and Poland.[135] Perhaps pepper and spices were more sought after in places where they had been late arrivals and were still a new luxury. When Abbé Mably reached Cracow he was served with wine from Hungary and 'a very plentiful meal which might have been very good if the Russians and the Confederates had destroyed all those aromatic herbs used in such quantities here, like the cinnamon and nutmeg that poison travellers in Germany'.[136] It would seem therefore that in eastern Europe the taste for strong seasoning and spices was still medieval in style at that date, while the ancient culinary customs were to some extent disappearing in the West. But this is conjecture and not fact.

It seems at any rate that when spices began to fall in price and to appear on all tables, so that they were no longer a symbol of wealth and luxury, they were used less and their prestige declined. Or so a cookery book of 1651 (by François-Pierre de La Varenne) would suggest, as does Boileau's satire (1665) ridiculing the misuse of spices.[137]

As soon as the Dutch reached the Indian Ocean and the Indian Archipelago they did their utmost to restore and then maintain for their own profit the monopoly in pepper and spices against the Portuguese (whose trade was gradually eliminated) and soon against English competition and later French and Danish. They also tried to control supplies to China, Japan, Bengal and Persia, and were able to compensate for a slack period in Europe by a sharp rise in their trade with Asia. The quantities of pepper reaching Europe via Amsterdam (and outside its market) probably increased, at least until the middle of the seventeenth century, and then were maintained at a high level. Annual arrivals in about 1600 before the Dutch success were possibly of the order of 20,000 present-day quintals, hence an annual quota of 20 grams per inhabitant for 100 million Europeans. Consumption may well have been of the order of 50,000 quintals in about 1680, more than double the figure at the time of the Portuguese monopoly. The sales of the *Oost Indische Companie* from 1715 to 1732 suggest that a limit was reached. What is certain is that pepper ceased being the dominant spice-trade commodity it was in the days of Priuli and Sanudo and the undisputed supremacy of Venice. Pepper still held first place in the trade of the Company in

The transport of spices by natives. *Cosmographie universelle*, by G. Le Testu, f⁰ 32 v⁰, sixteenth century. Paris, Library of the Musée de la Guerre. (Photo Giraudon.)

Amsterdam in 1648-50 (33% of the total). It fell to fourth in 1778-80 (11%) after textiles (silk and cotton, 32.66%), spices (24.43%) and tea and coffee (22.92%).[138] Was this a typical case of the ending of a luxury consumption and the beginning of a general one? Or the decline of excessive use?

For this decline the popularity of new luxuries – coffee, chocolate, alcohol and tobacco – can legitimately be blamed; perhaps also the spread of new vegetables which gradually began to vary Western diet (asparagus, spinach, lettuce, artichokes, peas, green beans, cauliflower, tomatoes, pimentoes, melons). These vegetables were mostly the product of European, and especially Italian, gardens. (Charles VIII brought the melon back from Italy.) Some, like the cantaloupe, came from Armenia, others, like the tomato, haricot bean and potato, from America.

One last but rather unconvincing explanation remains. A general decrease in meat consumption took place after 1600 or even earlier, which meant a break with former diet. Concurrently the rich adopted a simpler style of cooking, in France at least. German and Polish cooking may have been behindhand and have also had better supplies of meat and therefore a greater need for pepper and spices. But this explanation is only conjectural and those given before will have to satisfy us until fuller information is available.

There is evidence of a certain saturation of the European market; a German economist (1722) and an 'English' witness (1754) both reported that the Dutch had 'sometimes to burn large quantities of pepper and nutmeg ... or throw them into the sea to maintain the price'.[139] Furthermore, Europeans had no control over the fields of pepper trees outside Java, and Pierre Poivre's efforts in the islands of Mauritius and Réunion where he was governor (1767) only seem to have been of passing interest; the same was true of similar attempts in French Guiana.

As nothing is ever simple, the seventeenth century which saw the break with spices in France fell madly in love with perfumes. They invaded stews, pastries, liqueurs and sauces: amber, iris, rose water, orange-flower water, marjoram, musk, and so on. 'Scented waters' were even spooned over eggs!

Sugar conquers the world

Sugar cane is native to the Bengal coast, between the Ganges delta and Assam. The wild plant later reached gardens where for a long time it was cultivated for its sugar water and then sugar, regarded as a cure at that period: it appears in doctors' prescriptions in Sassanid Persia. Similarly, medicinal sugar vied with honey in general prescriptions in Byzantium. It appears in the pharmacopaea of the Salerno School in the tenth century. Before that date it had begun to be used as a foodstuff in India and in China where the cane was imported in about the eighth century AD. It quickly adapted itself to the hilly area of Kwang Tung, in the neighbourhood of Canton – predictably enough, because Canton was already the largest port in ancient China and had a wooded hinterland (sugar production required a great deal of fuel). For many centuries Kwang Tung provided the main part of Chinese production, and in the seventeenth century the *Oost Indische Companie* had no difficulty in organizing exports to Europe of sugar from China and Taiwan.[140] By the end of the next century, China was herself importing sugar from Cochinchina, at very low prices, and yet this luxury does not seem to have been known in northern China.[141]

Cane was in Egypt by the tenth century and sugar was already being produced by an advanced process. The Crusaders met it in Syria. After the fall of Acre, with Syria lost (1291), sugar passed into the hands of the Christians and rapidly established itself in Cyprus. The beautiful Catherine Cornaro, wife of the last of the Lusignans and last queen of the island (the Venetians seized it in 1479) was descended from the Cornaros, Venetian patricians and in their day 'sugar kings'.

Even before its success in Cyprus, sugar had been brought by the Arabs to Sicily and later Valencia, where it prospered. It had reached the Moroccan Sousse by the end of the fifteenth century and spread to Madeira, then the Azores, the Canaries, the island of São Tomé and Prince's Island in the Gulf of Guinea. In about 1520, it reached Brazil, where its prosperity was consolidated in the latter half of the sixteenth century. From now on, sugar never looked

Sugar loaves and the manufacture of syrup in the fifteenth century. Modena, Estense Library. (Photo Giraudon.)

back. 'Whereas before, sugar was only obtainable in the shops of apothecaries, who kept it exclusively for invalids,' writes Ortelius in the *Théâtre de l'Universe* (1572), today 'people devour it out of gluttony ... What used to be a medicine is nowadays eaten as a food.'[142]

From Brazil, as a result of the Dutch expulsion from Recife in 1654 and the Holy Office's persecutions of the Portuguese *marranos*,[143] cane and sugar mills in the seventeenth century reached Martinique, Guadeloupe, Dutch Curaçao, Jamaica and Santo Domingo. The great period for these producers began in about 1680, and from then on production showed an uninterrupted increase. If I am not much mistaken, sugar production in Cyprus in the fifteenth century was reckoned only in hundreds or at most in a few thousand 'light' quintals (= 50 kilograms).[144] But Santo Domingo alone was producing 70,000 at its peak in the eighteenth century. In 1800 England consumed 150,000 tons of sugar annually, almost fifteen times more than in 1700, and Lord Sheffield was right when he noted in 1783: 'The consumption of sugar may increase considerably. It is scarcely known in half of Europe.'[145] Consumption in Paris just before the Revolution was 5 kilograms per person per year (on the doubtful reckoning of a population of 600,000); in 1846 (and this figure is more reliable) consumption was only 3·62 kilograms. An estimate for the whole of France in 1788 gives a theoretical average consumption of one kilogram.[146] We can be certain that sugar was still a luxury item despite public favour and the relative fall in its price. The sugar loaf hung over tables in many peasant households in France. Directions for use: hold your glass up to it briefly so that the sugar can melt into it. In fact, if one were to draw a map of sugar consumption, it would be very irregular. In sixteenth-century Egypt, for instance, there was a minor industry in preserves and sweetmeats, and sugar was such a predominant crop that cane-straw was used for melting gold.[147] Two centuries later, there were still great tracts of Europe where sugar was quite unknown.

The low level of production was also the result of the late establishment of sugar beet. It was known, however, as early as 1575 and the German chemist Markgraff had isolated sugar from it in solid form in 1747. Its career only began with the Continental Blockade and required almost another century to reach its full extent.

Sugar cane cultivation was limited to hot climates, which was why it did not cross to the north of the Yang-tse-Kiang in China. It also had special marketing and industrial requirements. Sugar demanded a large labour force (in America the black slaves) and expensive installations – the *yngenios* in Cuba, New Spain and Peru, equivalent to the *engenhos de assucar* in Brazil, the *engins* or sugar mills in the French islands, and the English 'engines'. The cane had to be crushed by rollers arranged in various ways and worked by animals, waterpower, wind; in China they were powered by elbow-grease, and in Japan where no rollers were used, the cane was twisted by hand. The sap of the plants required treatment, preparation, precautions and long heating in copper vats. When crystallized in clay moulds it produced raw sugar or *muscovado*; when filtered in white clay, clayed sugar or moist sugar. It was then possible to obtain ten different products, plus alcohol. Raw sugar was very often refined in Europe, at Antwerp, Venice, Amsterdam, London, Paris, Bordeaux, Nantes, Dresden, etc. The operation was almost as profitable as the production of the raw material. This gave rise to conflicts between refiners and sugar growers, the colonists of the islands who dreamed of manufacturing everything on the spot, or as they said 'setting themselves up in white' (in white sugar). Cultivation and production therefore required capital and chains of intermediaries. Where intermediaries did not exist, sales rarely went beyond the local market; this remained the case in Peru, New Spain and Cuba until the nineteenth century. If the sugar islands and the coast of Brazil prospered, it was because they were situated within easy reach of Europe, given the speed and capacity of contemporary ships.

There was an additional obstacle: 'To feed a colony in America,' Abbé Raynal explains, 'it is necessary to cultivate a province in Europe.'[148] For the sugar-growing colonies could not feed themselves, as the cane left little space for food crops. This is the characteristic of sugar as a monoculture in north-east

Brazil, the West Indies, and Moroccan Sousse (where archaeology is bringing to light vast installations from the past). In 1783 England sent 16,526 tons of salt meat, beef and pork, 5188 flitches of bacon and 2559 tons of preserved tripe to its own West Indies (Jamaica particularly).[149] Food for the slaves in Brazil was secured by importing tons of cod from Newfoundland, *carne do sol* from the interior (*sertão*), and soon by *charque* (dried meat) shipped from Rio Grande do Sul. The saving of the West Indies was salt beef and flour from the English colonies in America: in exchange the colonies obtained sugar and rum – rum which very shortly afterwards they would be able to produce for themselves.

To sum up: we must not be too quick to talk about a sugar revolution. Sugar was established very early but progressed extremely slowly. It was still not widespread on the threshold of the nineteenth century. We cannot conclude that sugar graced every table in the world. Scarcely is that statement uttered, however, than we think of the agitation provoked by lack of sugar in revolutionary Paris at the time of *le maximum*.

Drinks, stimulants and drugs

Even a short history of drinks must discuss the old and the new, the popular and the refined, together with the various changes that occurred with the passage of time. Drinks are not only foodstuffs: they have always served as drugs, a means of escape. Sometimes, as with certain Indian tribes, drunkenness is even a means of communication with the supernatural. Be that as it may, the rise of alcoholism was continuous in Europe during the centuries that concern us. And then exotic stimulants were coming in: tea, coffee and, not least, tobacco in all its forms, an unclassifiable 'dope', neither food nor drink.

Water

Paradoxically we must begin with water. It was not always readily available and, despite specific advice from doctors who claimed that one sort of water was preferable to another for a particular disease, people had to be content with what was on hand: rain, river, fountain, cistern, well, barrel or a copper receptacle in which it was wise to keep some in reserve in every provident household. There were some extreme cases. Sea water was distilled by alembic in the Spanish *presidios* in North Africa in the sixteenth century; otherwise water would have been brought from Spain or Italy. And we hear of the desperate plight of some travellers across the Congo in 1648 who, starving, tired to death and sleeping on the bare ground, had to 'drink water [which] resembled horse's urine'.[150] Another great problem was the lack of fresh water on board ship. There was no way of keeping it drinkable, despite so many recipes and jealously guarded secrets.

Whole towns – and very wealthy ones at that – were poorly supplied with water. This applied to Venice where the wells in the public squares or the courtyards of palaces were not (as is often thought) dug right down to the underground fresh-water level, below the bed of the lagoon. They were cisterns half-filled with fine sand through which rain water was filtered and decanted and then oozed into the well running down through the centre. When no rain fell for weeks on end, the cisterns ran dry; this happened when Stendhal was staying in the city. If there was a storm they were tainted with salt water. Even in normal weather they were inadequate for the enormous population of the town. Fresh water had to be brought from outside, not by aqueduct but by boats filled in the Brenta and sent to Venice daily. These *acquaroli* of the river even formed an autonomous guild at Venice. The same unpleasant situation prevailed in all the towns of Holland, reduced to using cisterns, shallow wells and dubious canal waters.[151]

There were few aqueducts in use: the deservedly famous ones at Istanbul, and the one at Segovia, the *puente* (repaired in 1481), which dated from Roman times and astounded visitors. Portugal had aqueducts at Coimbra, Tomar, Villa do Conde and Elvas all functioning in the seventeenth century. The new Spring Water aqueduct built in Lisbon between 1729 and 1748, took water to the outlying square of the Rato. The water of this fountain was much sought after, and it was here that the water carriers came to fill the red casks with iron handles which they carried on the backs of their necks.[152] Sensibly, Martin v's first concern when he reoccupied the Vatican after the Great Schism was to restore one of the demolished aqueducts of Rome. Two new aqueducts had to be built to supply the great city at the end of the sixteenth century: the *Aqua Felice* and the *Aqua Paola*. The fountains of Genoa were chiefly supplied by the aqueduct of La Scuffara, whose water also powered the mill-wheels inside the city walls and was then distributed among the different quarters of the town. The western side, however, drew on water from springs and cisterns.[153] In Paris the Belleville aqueduct was repaired in 1457; in conjunction with the one at Pré-Saint-Gervais it supplied the town until the seventeenth century. The Arcueil aqueduct, reconstructed by Maria de Medici, brought water from Rungis to the Luxembourg Palace.[154] Large hydraulic wheels raised river water to supply towns in some places (Toledo 1526; Augsburg 1548) and drove powerful lift-and-force pumps for this purpose. The Samaritaine pump, built between 1603 and 1608, yielded 700 cubic metres of water every day, drawn from the Seine and redistributed to the Louvre and the Tuileries; in 1670 the pumps of the Notre Dame bridge drew 2000 cubic metres from the same source. Water from aqueducts and pumps was distributed about the towns through terracotta pipes (as in Roman times) or wooden pipes (hollowed tree trunks fixed together, as in northern Italy from the fourteenth century and at Breslau from 1471. There was even some lead piping, but although the use of lead is recorded in England in 1236, it remained limited. In 1770, Thames water 'which is not good' was carried to all the houses in

Food and Drink 229

London by underground wooden pipes, but this was not what we would usually think of as running water: it was 'distributed regularly three times a week, according to the amount consumed per household ... it was received and kept in great pipes bound with iron'.[155]

In Paris, the chief source of water remained the Seine. Its water, which was sold by carriers, was reputed to have all the virtues: it was supposed to bear boats well, being muddy and therefore heavy, as a Portuguese envoy reported in 1641 – not that this quality would recommend itself to drinkers; and it was considered excellent for the health – which we may be allowed to doubt. 'A number of dyers pour their dye three times a week into the branch of the river which washes the Pelletier quay and between the two bridges,' said an eye witness (1771). 'The arch which forms the Gêvres quai is a seat of pestilence. All that part of the town drinks infected water.'[156] It is true that this was soon remedied. And after all Seine water was better than water from the wells on the Left Bank, which were never protected from terrible infiltrations and with which

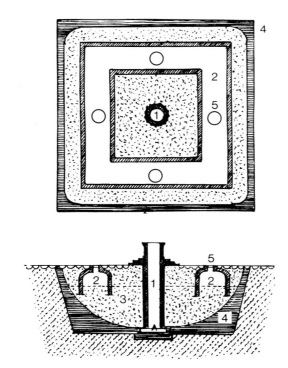

21 A WELL-CISTERN IN VENICE: SECTION AND ELEVATION
1. Central well-shaft. 2. Rain-water tanks. 3. Sand for filtering. 4. Clay surround. 5. Mouths of rain-water tank, commonly known as *pilele* (literally fonts). The filtered water reappeared in the central well-shaft. Nowadays Venice has water mains, but the Venetian wells can still be seen in public squares or inside houses. (After E.R. Trincanato.)

the bakers made their bread. This river water was a natural purgative and of course 'unpleasant for foreigners' but they could always add a few drops of vinegar or buy filtered and 'improved' water – or better still, a product called the King's water, or the best and most expensive, the so-called Bristol water. These refinements were unknown before about 1760. 'One drank water [from the Seine] without really bothering about it.'[157]

Twenty thousand carriers earned a living (though a poor one) supplying Paris with water, taking some thirty 'loads' (two buckets at a time) even to the top floors at two sous a load. It was therefore the beginning of a revolution when the Périer brothers installed two steam pumps at Chaillot in 1782, 'very curious machines' which raised water 110 feet from the low level of the Seine 'by ordinary steam from boiling water'. This was in imitation of London, which had had nine such pumps for several years. The Saint-Honoré district, the wealthiest and therefore the most able to pay for such progress, was the first to be served. But people were worried: what would happen to the twenty thousand water carriers if the number of machines increased? And furthermore, the venture shortly turned into a financial scandal (1788). But all the same, with the eighteenth century the problem of supplying drinkable water was clearly posed and the solutions seen and sometimes achieved. And as the proposed water supply for Ulm (1713) proves, this was not confined to capital cities.

Despite everything, progress was slow. In every town in the world the water carrier was indispensable. One Portuguese traveller in Valladolid in Philip III's time praised the excellent water sold in delightful demi-johns and ceramic jugs of all shapes and colours.[158] In China the water carrier used two pails, as in Paris, balancing them at each end of his pole. But a drawing of Peking in 1800 also shows a large barrel on wheels, with a bung at the back. An engraving of about the same period explains 'the way in which women carry water in Egypt' in two jars, reminiscent of ancient amphorae: a large one on the head supported by the left hand, a small one held flat on the right hand by a graceful movement of the bent arm. Many fountains were built in Istanbul as a result of the religious requirement to wash frequently every day under running water. The water drunk there was probably purer than anywhere else; which may be why Turks today still pride themselves on being able to recognize the taste of the water from the different springs – just as Frenchmen boast that they can tell the wine from different vineyards.

As for the Chinese, not only did they attribute different qualities to water according to its origin: ordinary rain water, storm water (dangerous), rainfall in the early spring (beneficial), water from melted hailstones or frost in winter, water collected from stalactites in caves (a sovereign remedy), water from river, well or spring – but they were also concerned about the dangers of pollution and recommended boiling any suspect water.[159] Hot drinks were in any case the rule in China (vendors sold boiling water in the streets)[160] and this habit no doubt considerably contributed to the health of the Chinese population.

Seventeenth-century comfort. Water is drawn up straight into the kitchen. Painting by Velasquez. (Photo Giraudon.)

In Istanbul, by contrast, snow water was sold everywhere in the streets for a small sum. It was also available in Valladolid where a Portuguese, Bartolomé Pinheiro da Veiga, at the beginning of the seventeenth century was amazed that it was possible to treat oneself to 'cold water and iced fruit' during the hot months.[161] But snow water was mostly a great luxury, reserved for the wealthy. This was the case in France, which only developed a taste for it at the time of Henri III, and around the Mediterranean where boats loaded with snow sometimes made quite long voyages. The Knights of Malta were supplied by Naples; one of their requests, in 1754, stated that they would die if they did not have 'this sovereign remedy' to break their fevers.[162]

Wine

The whole of Europe drank wine; only a part of Europe produced it. Although the vine (if not wine) had its successes in Asia, Africa and more still in the New

World – zealously remodelled in the obsessive image of the Old – only Europe really counted.

Wine-producing Europe consisted of all its Mediterranean countries and an area to the north added to it by the perseverance of the vine-growers. As Jean Bodin says: 'The vine cannot grow beyond the forty-ninth parallel because of the cold.'[163] A line drawn from the mouth of the Loire on the Atlantic coast up to the Crimea and beyond as far as Georgia and Trans-Caucasia sets the northern boundary of the commercial cultivation of the vine – one of the great hinges in the economic life of Europe and its eastern extensions. At the latitude of the Crimea, the wine belt was very narrow, and would only come to life in the nineteenth century.[164] None the less it was a very old implantation and in ancient times they used to bury the vine stumps before the beginning of winter to protect them from the cold winds of the Ukraine.

Outside Europe, wine followed in the wake of Europeans. Great feats were accomplished in acclimatizing the vine in Mexico, Peru, Chile (reached in 1541) and in Argentina, after the second foundation of Buenos Aires in 1580. In Peru vineyards rapidly prospered in the hot and fever-ridden valleys because of their proximity to Lima, an exceptionally wealthy town. They prospered still more in Chile where the soil and climate were propitious; vines were already growing amongst the *cuadras*, the blocks of the first houses of the growing town of Santiago. In 1578 Drake seized a boat loaded with Chilean wine in the open sea off Valparaiso.[165] The same wine, carried on the backs of mules or llamas, reached the high point of Potosi. But vines were not planted in California until the end of the seventeenth and in the eighteenth centuries, during the last northward thrust of the Spanish empire.

However, its most brilliant success was in mid-Atlantic, between the Old and the New World, in the islands (both new Europes and pre-Americas), and notably Madeira, where the production of red wine was increasingly substituted for sugar. Then came the Azores, a half-way point where ships could take on board good wines with a high alcohol content. When politics intervened (John Methuen's treaty with Portugal was in 1704), it was more convenient to carry them than French wines from La Rochelle or Bordeaux. Finally the Canaries, notably Tenerife, exported white wine on a large scale to Anglo-Saxon and Iberian America, and even to England.

In southern and eastern Europe wine came up against the unyielding obstacle of Islam. It is true that the vine maintained itself throughout the land controlled by Islam, and wine proved an indefatigable clandestine traveller. Innkeepers near the Arsenal in Istanbul sold it daily to Greek sailors, while Selim, son of Suleiman the Magnificent, was only too fond of Cyprus liqueur wine. In Persia (where the Capuchin friars had vine arbours and wines – which were not used solely for mass), wines from Shiraz and Ispahan had a reputation and customers. They travelled as far as the Indies in enormous glass demi-johns protected by wicker, actually manufactured in Ispahan.[166] What a pity that the Great Moguls

'Drinking to get drunk.' Choirstall in the church at Montréal-sur-Serein, by the brothers Rigoley (sixteenth century). (Photo Giraudon.)

who succeeded the Sultans of Delhi after 1526 were not content with these strong Persian wines instead of taking to rice spirit, arak!

On the whole then, the subject of wine is best summed up in the context of Europe, and we must go back to that long line from the Loire to the Crimea, the northern limit of the vine. On one side of it there were the peasant producers and consumers, accustomed to local wine, to its treachery and its benefits alike; on the other, eager customers – not always experienced drinkers, but with specific requirements and generally a partiality for wines with a high alcoholic strength. Englishmen very early on established the great reputation of Malmsey, liqueur wines from Candia and the Greek islands.[167] Later they launched port, malaga, madeira, sherry and marsala, all famous wines with a high alcohol content. The Dutch created the popularity of all types of spirits from the seventeenth century onwards. Thus northerners had their own special palates and tastes. The southern people looked jeeringly upon these drinkers who, in their opinion, did not know how to drink and emptied their glasses in one gulp. Jean d'Auton, chronicler of Louis XII, saw German soldiers suddenly start drinking (*trinken*) like this when they pillaged the castle of Forli.[168] And there they were again staving in the barrels and rapidly becoming dead drunk during the terrible sacking of Rome in 1527. Sixteenth- and seventeenth-century German engravings of peasant festivities almost invariably show one of the guests turning round on his bench to throw up his excess of drink. When Felix Platter from Basle stayed in Montpellier in 1556 he admitted that 'all the boozers' in the town were German and were to be found snoring under barrels, the chosen victims of countless tricks.[169]

This large northern consumption gave rise to large-scale trade with the south: by sea, from Seville and Andalusia to England and Flanders; or along the Dordogne and the Garonne to Bordeaux and the Gironde; from La Rochelle or the Loire estuary; along the Yonne, from Burgundy to Paris, and then beyond as far as Rouen; along the Rhine; across the Alps (large German carriages, which the Italians called *carretoni*, arrived immediately after every wine harvest to look for new wines from the Tyrol, Brescia, Vicenza, Friuli and Istria); from Moravia and Hungary to Poland;[170] a little later by Baltic routes, from Portugal, Spain and France, right up to St Petersburg and the violent but undiscriminating Russian thirst. Of course the whole population of northern Europe did not drink wine. Only the rich did as a rule; then there were a few bourgeois, the odd prebendal monk in Flanders in the thirteenth century; or the Polish nobleman in the sixteenth who thought he would lose caste if he were satisfied with the same home-brewed beer as his peasants. When Bayard was a prisoner in the Netherlands in 1513, and held open house, the wine was so dear that 'sometimes he spent twenty crowns on wine in a day'.[171]

The wine that travelled about in this way and was awaited and greeted with joy everywhere was new wine. For wine did not keep well from one year to the next: it turned sour. And clarifying, bottling and the regular use of corks were still unknown in the sixteenth century and possibly even the seventeenth.[172] So that in 1500, a cask of old Bordeaux cost only 6 livres tournois, while a cask of good new wine was worth 50.[173] But by the eighteenth century, the whole system was in working order, and collecting old empty bottles for wine merchants was one of the lucrative activities of London thieves. On the other hand, for a very long time wine was transported in wooden barrels (with dove-tailed and ringed staves), no longer in the amphorae of Roman times (in spite of persistent survivals here and there). The wine did not always keep well in these barrels, which had been invented in Roman Gaul. The Duke of Mondejar advised Charles V on 2 December 1539 that large quantities of wines should not be bought for the navy. If they 'are to turn into vinegar, it is better that they remain with their owners than with your Majesty'.[174] As late as the eighteenth century a dictionary of commerce was surprised that the Romans had considered 'the age of wines as their claim to excellence, while in France wines are thought to be stale (even those from Dijon, Nuits and Orleans, the most suitable of all for keeping) when they reach the fifth or sixth *feuille*' [year]. The *Encyclopédie*

A monastery meal: the fare is frugal, but does not exclude wine which was part of everyday life in the Mediterranean. Fresco by Signorelli, fifteenth century, Sienna, Abbey of Monte Oliveto. (Photo Scala.)

firmly states: 'The wines of four or five years standing which some people talk of so highly are past their best.'[175] However, when Gui Patin, to celebrate his becoming a deacon, offered a feast to thirty-six of his colleagues, 'I never saw serious people laugh and drink more,' he tells us: 'It was the best *old Burgundy*, which I had saved for the banquet.'[176]

The vintage wines did not establish themselves before the eighteenth century. The best-known possibly owed their reputation less to their merits than to the convenience of the routes in their vicinity and particularly to their proximity to a large town or waterways (this was just as true of the small vineyard of Frontignan on the coast of Languedoc as of the large vineyards in Andalusia, Portugal, Bordeaux and La Rochelle). Paris alone absorbed the 100,000 or so barrels (1698) produced by the vines of Orleans; wines from the Kingdom of Naples – *greco*, *latino*, *mangiaguerra*, *lacryma christi* – were near the enormous clientele of Naples and even Rome. Champagne, which began to be produced during the first half of the eighteenth century, took time to displace the old local red, 'grey' and white vines. But the job was done by the middle of the eighteenth century when all the great vintages of today had established their eminence. 'Taste the wines of the Romanée,' wrote Sébastien Mercier in 1788, Saint-Vivant,

Cîteaux and Graves, both red and white ... and insist on Tokay if you meet it. In my opinion, it is the greatest wine in the world and only the masters of the world should drink it.'[177] Savary's *Dictionnaire de Commerce* lists all the wines in France in 1762 and places 'those of Champagne and Burgundy' at the top. It also mentions: 'Chablis, Pomar, Chambertin, Beaune, le Clos de Vougeau, Volleney, la Romanée, Nuits, Mursault.'[178] Obviously with the increasing differentiation of vintages, wine was developing more and more into a luxury product. This was the time when according to the *Dictionnaire sentencieux* (1768) the new expression *sabler le vin de champagne* (meaning to toss off a drink) was coming into fashion amongst the smarter set.[179]

But here, we are interested more in the ever-increasing number of ordinary drinkers than in these refinements and their history, which could easily lead us too far out of our way. Drunkenness increased everywhere in the sixteenth century. Consumption in Valladolid reached 100 litres per person per year in the middle of the century;[180] in Venice, the Signoria was obliged to take new and severe action against public drunkenness in 1598; in France, Laffemas was quite positive on that point at the beginning of the seventeenth century. This widespread urban drunkenness never required high-quality wine; coarse types of vines with high yields were becoming general in commercial vineyards. In the eighteenth century, the movement reached the countryside itself (the taverns there were the ruin of the peasants) and became more pronounced in the towns. Mass consumption became general with the establishment of the *guingettes* at the gates of Paris, outside the boundaries of the town, where the *aides*, the tax of 'four sous admittance for one bottle which intrinsically is only worth three',[181] was not chargeable.

> Commoners, artisans, grisettes,
> All leave Paris and run to the guingettes.
> Two pints for the price of a single booze
> On two boat's benches, without cloth or serviettes,
> You'll drink so much in these Bacchic stews
> That out of your eyes the wine will ooze.

This prospectus for the poor, below a contemporary engraving, was not without some truth. Hence the popularity of the suburban taverns: the famous Courtille, near the Belleville 'gate', founded by Ramponeau whose name, according to a contemporary, 'is a thousand times better known to the multitude than Voltaire's and Buffon's'; or 'the famous beggars' saloon' at Vaugirard where men and women danced barefoot in a tumult of dust and noise. 'When Vaugirard is full the people [on a Sunday] stream back to the Petit Gentilly, the Porcherons and the Courtille: the next day you see empty barrels by the dozen in front of wine merchants' stalls. These people drink enough for the whole week.'[182] In Madrid too, 'good wine can be drunk cheaply outside the town, because you do not pay the taxes there which amount to more than the price of the wine'.[183]

The most famous of the *guingettes* outside the Paris city walls: the Courtille. Eighteenth century. (Photo Bulloz.)

Were there extenuating circumstances for this over-indulgence in wine? Consumption in Paris on the eve of the Revolution was of the order of 120 litres per person per year, which is not scandalous in itself.[184] In fact wine, principally low-quality wine, had become a cheap foodstuff. Its price even fell relatively every time grain became too expensive. One historian, Witold Kula, has suggested that wine could have been a compensation (like other forms of alcohol) – that is to say, cheap calories every time bread was short. Or is the explanation more simply that purses emptied by the high prices during famine periods left fewer customers for wine and therefore its price inevitably dropped? In any case we should not measure the standard of living by those conspicuous debaucheries. And we should remember that wine, calories or not, was often a means of escape; what the Castilian peasant still calls a *quita-penas*, drowner of sorrows. This is the red wine that Velasquez's two comrades are drinking (Museum of Budapest) or the golden yellow wine that looks even more precious in the long fluted glasses and the magnificent rounded glaucous goblets of Dutch paintings; here, wine, tobacco, women of easy virtue and the music of violinists (which became fashionable in the seventeenth century) are combined for the drinker's delight.

Beer

With beer we will still stay in Europe – if we leave out the American maize beer which we have mentioned in passing, and the millet beer which for the black peoples of Africa filled the ritual role of 'bread and wine with Westerners', and also if we do not inquire too much into the distant origins of this very old beverage. For in fact beer was known in both ancient Babylon and Egypt, and in China, by the end of the second millennium, under the Shangs.[185] The Roman Empire did not like beer much, and encountered it generally far away from the Mediterranean, at Numantia for example, which Scipio besieged in 133 BC; or in Gaul. The Emperor Julian the Apostate (361-363) only tasted it once and immediately scorned it. But there were barrels of beer at Trèves in the fourth century,[186] where it was the drink of the poor and the Barbarians. In Charlemagne's time, it was drunk throughout his empire, and even in his palaces, where master brewers were instructed to make good beer: *cervisam bonam ... facere debeant*.[187]

Beer can be made by brewing wheat or oats, barley, rye or millet, or even spelt. The grain is never treated by itself: today brewers add hops and rice to the sprouted barley (malt). But old recipes added all sorts of things: poppy seeds, mushrooms, aromatics, honey, sugar, bay leaves. The Chinese also added aromatic or even medicinal ingredients to their millet or rice 'wines'. The addition of hops, which is now universal in the West (adding a bitter taste and acting as a preservative) is thought to have originated in the monasteries in the eighth or ninth century. The first mention is 822; hops are recorded in Germany in the twelfth century;[188] in the Netherlands in the early fourteenth;[189] and reached England later, in the early fifteenth century. As the rhyme has it, with a little exaggeration (though hops were forbidden until 1556):

> Hops, Reformation, bays and beer
> Came into England all in one year.[190]

Beer became established outside the vine-growing region and was really at home in the vast zone consisting of the northern lands, from England to the Netherlands, Germany, Bohemia, Poland and Muscovy. It was produced in the towns and on noblemen's estates in central Europe where 'the brewers are generally liable to cheat their masters'. The peasants on the Polish estates consumed up to three litres of beer a day. Naturally the beer region had no precise western or southern boundaries. It even fairly rapidly extended southwards, particularly in the seventeenth century with the Dutch advance. In Bordeaux, a wine-growing region where breweries were vigorously opposed,[191] imported beer flowed copiously in the taverns in the suburb of Chartrons which had been colonized by Dutchmen and other foreigners.[192] There was even a brewery in Seville, which was not only the centre of local wine production but of the international wine trade, in 1542. In the West, with a large and indistinct frontier zone, the introduction of breweries did not constitute a real revolution. This was so in Lorraine, for instance, where vineyards were mediocre and yields uncertain; and in Paris too. Le Grand d'Aussy (*La vie privée des Français*, 1782) thought that as beer was the drink of the poor every difficult period saw an extension of its consumption; conversely, good times, economically speaking, turned beer drinkers into wine drinkers. He appended a few examples drawn from the past, adding: 'Have we ourselves not seen the disasters of the Seven Years War (1756-63) produce similar effects? Towns which had only known wine before that time began to drink beer, and I myself know certain places in Champagne where four breweries were set up in the same town in a single year.'[193]

However, between 1750 and 1780 (the contradiction is only an apparent one, since *in the long term* this period was economically favourable) beer production in Paris went through a prolonged crisis. The number of brewers fell from 75 to 23 and production from 75,000 hogsheads (one hogshead equals 286 litres) to 26,000. The poor brewers then had to worry about the apple crop every year and try to make up their losses from beer by their earnings from cider.[194] Their situation had not improved by the time of the Revolution. Wine remained the great winner: its consumption in Paris from 1781 to 1786 rose to an annual round figure of 730,000 hectolitres, as compared with 54,000 of beer (or a ratio of 1 to 13). But Le Grand d'Aussy's theory was confirmed during the period of obvious economic difficulty from 1821 to 1830, when wine consumption in Paris fell and the ratio of beer to wine consumed was 1 to 6·9 with a comparative rise in beer-drinking.[195]

But beer was not always a mark of poverty - as in the case of English small beer brewed at home to wash down the daily ration of cold meat and oatcakes. By the sixteenth century, the Netherlands had a luxury beer for the rich, imported from Leipzig, as well as a popular cheap brew. In 1687, the French ambassador in London was sending to the marquis de Seignelay regular consignments of English ale, 'known as Lambeth ale' and not 'strong ale, the taste of which is not liked in France and which makes men as drunk as wine and costs just as much'.[196] Beer of superior quality was being exported as far as the East Indies from Brunswick and Bremen by the end of the seventeenth century.[197] In Germany, Bohemia and Poland, a large growth in urban brewing pushed the light beer made by lord and peasant, often without hops, into second place. There is an immense literature on this subject. Beer, as well as the shops where it was consumed, was the object of legislation.[198] The towns supervised its production; for example, brewing was only allowed between Michaelmas and Palm Sunday in Nuremberg. Books appeared praising the virtues of different and increasing varieties of beer. One by Heinrich Knaust[199] in 1575 listed the names and nicknames of famous beers and described their medicinal qualities for drinkers. But like all reputations, these could change. In Muscovy, where everything was behind the times, the consumer still obtained his 'barley-beer' from the 'public canteen' in 1655, at the same time as he bought his spirits, salted fish, caviar and black sheepskins imported from Astrakhan and Persia – all these purchases destined to fill the coffers of a commercial and monopolist state.[200]

So there were millions of 'beer bellies' all over the world. But wine-drinkers from the vineyard regions made mock of this northern drink. A Spanish soldier who fought at the battle of Nordlingen had nothing but scorn for beer and would not touch it 'because it always looks to me like the urine of a sick horse'. Five years later, however, he took the plunge: unfortunately what he had been drinking all evening were *'potes de purga'*, pots of purgative.[201] Charles v was a true Fleming, as is proved by his passion for beer: he did not give it up even after he retired to Yuste, despite the warnings of his Italian doctor.[202]

Cider

A few words about cider. It originated in Biscay where the cider apple trees came from; they appeared in Cotentin, the Caen region and the Pays d'Auge towards the eleventh or twelfth century. Cider was mentioned in these regions in the following century. It should be noted that the vine was also present there, although to the north of its commercial boundary. The newcomer did not

The brewery 'De Drye Lelyen' in Haarlem in 1627, by J.A. Matham. Franz Hals Museum, Haarlem. (Photo by the museum.)

interfere with wine; it competed with beer and met with some success, since beer was made from grain and drinking it sometimes meant going without bread.[203]

Then apple trees and cider extended their territory. They arrived in eastern Normandy (lower Seine and Pays de Caux) at the end of the fifteenth and the beginning of the sixteenth centuries. A representative sent by the province to the States General could still say in 1484 that the great difference between lower and upper Normandy (eastern Normandy) was that one had apple trees and the other did not. Furthermore beer and more particularly wine (such as the wine from the vineyards in the sheltered bends of the Seine) were holding their own in upper Normandy. Cider only made headway in about 1550, and, of course, amongst people of small account.[204] Its success was more evident in Lower Maine since it became the drink of the rich there from the fifteenth century onwards (at least in the south-west of the province), beer remaining the drink of the poor. At Laval, however, the rich resisted until the seventeenth century. For a long time before they succumbed they preferred bad wine to cider, which they left to masons, servants and chambermaids.[205] Perhaps this minor change can be attributed to the recession in the seventeenth century. Naturally Normandy was too near to Paris for cider's success not to affect the capital. But a Parisian consumed an average of 121·76 litres of wine between 1781 and 1786; 8·96 of beer and 2·73 of cider.[206] Cider came well and truly last and in Germany, for example, met competition from cider made from wild apples, a very second-rate drink.

The belated popularity of alcohol in Europe

The great innovation, the revolution in Europe was the appearance of brandy and spirits made from grain – in a word: alcohol. The sixteenth century created it; the seventeenth consolidated it; the eighteenth popularized it.

Brandy was obtained by distilling, 'burning' wine. The operation required an apparatus, the still or alembic (*al*, the Arab definite article, and *ambicos* from the Greek, a vase with a long neck for distilling liquid). Neither the Greeks nor the Romans can have had more than a primitive version of this at best. But we do know that there were stills in the West before the twelfth century and therefore that the possibility of distilling various kinds of alcoholic liquors existed. But for a long time, the distillation of wine was practised only by apothecaries. Brandy, resulting from the first distillation, and spirit of wine, resulting from the second (theoretically 'free from all humidity') were medicines. Alcohol was possibly discovered in about 1100, in southern Italy 'where the Salerno school of medicine was the most important centre of chemical research' of the period.[207] The first distillation had been attributed (probably wrongly) to Raymond Lull who died in 1315, or to a curious itinerant doctor, Arnaud de Villeneuve, who taught at Montpellier and Paris and died in 1313 on a journey from Sicily to Provence. He wrote a work entitled *La conservation de la jeunesse*.

Beer, wine and tobacco. Still-life by J. Jansz van de Velde (1660). The Mauritshuis, in The Hague. (Photo A. Dingjan.)

According to him, brandy, *aqua vitae*, accomplished the miracle of preserving youth, dissipated superfluous body fluids, revived the heart, cured colic, dropsy, paralysis, quartan ague, calmed toothache and gave protection against plague. But his miracle cure brought Charles the Bad, of execrable memory, to a terrible end (1387); doctors had enveloped him in a brandy-soaked sheet sewn up with large stitches for greater efficiency so that it fitted tightly round the patient. A servant held a candle up close to try to break one of the threads, and sheet and invalid went up in flames.[208]

Brandy remained as a medicine for a long time, particularly against plague, gout and loss of voice. As late as 1735, a chemical treatise stated that 'spirits of wine rightly used is a sort of panacea'.[209] By this date, it had long been used for the manufacture of liqueurs. However, the liqueurs made in Germany with decoctions of spices were still pharmaceutical products in the fifteenth century. The change only became apparent in the last years of that century and the first years of the next. Brandy must have had other patrons besides the sick at Nuremberg in 1496, because the town was obliged to forbid the free sale of alcohol on feast days. A Nuremberg doctor in about 1493 even wrote: 'In view of the fact that everyone at present has got into the habit of drinking *aqua vitae* it is necessary to remember the quantity that one can permit oneself to drink and learn to drink it according to one's capacities, if one wishes to behave like a gentleman.' There is therefore no doubt that by then *geprant Wein*, 'burnt' wine, *vinum ardens* or, as other texts call it, *vinum sublimatum*, had been born.[210]

Brandy only broke away from doctors and apothecaries very slowly. Louis XII did not grant the guild of vinegar-makers the privilege of distilling it until 1514. This was the first step towards making the 'remedy' more widely available. In 1537 Francis I divided the privilege between vinegar-makers and victuallers – giving rise to quarrels indicating that the game was already worth the candle. At Colmar the movement took place earlier. From 1506 the town controlled wine distillers and brandy merchants, and their product thereafter figured in its fiscal and customs returns. Brandy rapidly took on the appearance of a national industry. At first it was entrusted to the wet coopers, a powerful trade association in a land of prosperous vineyards. But, as was to be expected, the wet coopers did excellent business and the merchants attempted to seize it after 1511. It was fifty years before they succeeded. The quarrel continued because the wet coopers again obtained the right to distil in 1650, though on condition that they handed over their production to the merchants, among whom we find many of the Colmar patriciate. The trade already had a high standing.[211]

Unfortunately we do not have enough evidence to enable us to sketch out the geography and chronology of the first brandy industry. Some indications relating to the Bordeaux region suggest that an early distillery was operating at Gaillac in the sixteenth century and that brandy was sent to Antwerp as early as 1521;[212] but we cannot be sure. *Acquavite* only made its appearance in Venice – at least in customs tariffs – in 1596.[213] There is hardly any question of it before the seventeenth century in Barcelona. Beyond these indications it would indeed seem that as far as brandy is concerned the northern countries – Germany, the Netherlands and France north of the Loire – were in advance of the Mediterranean lands. The role of promoters, if not of inventors, was really played by Dutch merchants and sailors, who made the distilling of wines general on the Atlantic coasts of Europe in the seventeenth century. Engaged in the largest wine-trade of the period, they had got to grips with the many problems posed by transport, preservation and sweetening. The addition of spirits gave even the most feeble wines new body. As they were more valuable than the same volume of wine, transport costs were correspondingly less. And contemporary taste was beginning to favour brandy.

Helped by demand, distillation of wines spread far inland, the question of transport being less important for spirits than for wine. Thus distillation was established in the vineyards of the Loire, Poitou, Bordeaux, Périgord and Béarn (Jurançon wine is a mixture of wine and brandy). Thus evolved the international reputations of Cognac and Armagnac in the seventeenth century. Everything helped in this success: the type of vine (such as *Enrageant* or *Folle Blanche* in Charente), supplies of wood available, proximity to navigable waterways. By 1728, some 27,000 casks of brandy from Cognac were being sent through the port of Tonnay-Charente.[214] Even poor wine from the Meuse region in Lorraine was distilled in about 1690 (and perhaps earlier) in the same way as grape *marc* (to make white brandy), and all these products travelled along the river to reach the Netherlands.[215] Brandy gradually came to be made wherever the raw material was available. Inevitably it poured out of the vine-growing lands of the south: Andalusia near Jerez, Catalonia, Languedoc.

Production rose rapidly. Sète only exported 2250 hectolitres of brandy in 1698. By 1725 it was exporting 37,500 hectolitres (the product of the distillation of 168,750 hectolitres of wine); and by 1755 65,926 hectolitres (from 296,667 hectolitres of wine). The last was a record export figure reached on the eve of the Seven Years War, which was disastrous for exports. At the same time the price fell: 25 francs per *verge* (equal to 7·6 litres) in 1595; 12 in 1698; 7 in 1701; 5 in 1725. A slow increase after 1731 brought prices back to 15 in 1758.[216]

Of course prices depended on the various qualities[217] – above the lowest limit fixed by the 'Dutch test': a sample was removed during the distillation process and a phial half filled with the specimen. A thumb was placed over the phial and it was turned upside down and shaken. If the air entering the liquid formed bubbles of a certain shape the brandy had the alcoholic content necessary to make it of marketable quality (47 to 50 degrees). Below the specified limit it had to be thrown out or subjected to fresh distillation. Average quality was called three-five and contained 79 to 80 degrees of alcohol; three-eight, at the top of the scale, was pure spirit with 92 to 93 degrees.

Production remained difficult and the technology was primitive. Stills were only inadequately and empirically modified until Weigert's (1773), which made continuous cooling by a double current possible.[218] The crucial changes that made it possible to distil wine in one operation came even later. They were the work of a little-known inventor, born in 1768, Edouard Adam. They lowered manufacturing costs and contributed to the enormous spread of alcohol in the nineteenth century.[219]

Consumption, however, increased by leaps and bounds. It soon became the custom to give alcohol to soldiers before battle. According to a doctor in 1702, this did not produce 'a bad effect'.[220] The soldier became a habitual drinker and the production of brandy, when the need arose, a war-time industry. An English military doctor even stated (1763) that wine and alcoholic beverages tended to suppress 'putrid diseases' and were thus indispensable for the good health of the troops.[221] Similarly the porters at the *Halles*, both men and women, became accustomed to drinking brandy diluted with water, but flavoured with long pepper, a good means of contending with the tax on wine entering Paris. The clientele of smoking-rooms – popular taverns where 'idle' working-class smokers

The *kvass*-seller in Russia. *Kvass* was the poor man's alcohol in Russia. It was obtained by the fermentation of barley and sometimes even of left-over bread or rancid fruit. Engraving by J.-B. Le Prince. (Author's personal collection.)

took their pleasure – did the same.²²²

Alcohol was also in demand for 'apéritifs' (known at that time as *ratafias*) which we would call liqueurs. 'Inflammable spirits,' wrote Doctor Louis Lemery in his *Traité des Aliments*, 'have a slightly pungent and often empyreumatic taste ... To remove the disagreeable taste, several compositions have been invented, which have been given the name of ratafia and which are nothing more than brandy or spirit of wine flavoured with a mixture of different ingredients.'²²³ The taste for such liqueurs had become fashionable in the seventeenth century. Gui Patin, who was always quick to ridicule the fads of his contemporaries, did not fail to mention the famous *rossolis* from Italy: 'This *ros solis* [i.e. sun dew in Latin] *nihil habet solare sed igneum*,' he wrote.²²⁴ But sweet liqueurs had definitely found their way into drinking habits, and by the end of the century books of household advice to the solid bourgeois such as *La Maison réglée* took it upon themselves to describe 'the true way to make all kinds of liqueurs ... in the Italian fashion'.²²⁵ In eighteenth-century Paris, there was a baffling profusion of alcoholic mixtures: 'Sète waters', aniseed, frangipane and claret waters (made like 'claret' wine, that is strengthened by spices soaked in them), ratafias with a fruit base, Barbados waters, with a sugar and rum base, celery water, fennel water, *mille fleurs* water, lily water, 'divine' waters, coffee waters, and so on. The great centre for the production of these 'waters' was Montpellier, near the brandy supplies of Languedoc. Paris was obviously the big customer. Montpellier merchants set up a vast warehouse in the Rue de la Huchette where taverners obtained supplies wholesale.²²⁶ What had been a luxury in the sixteenth century had become an everyday amenity.

Brandy was not the only drink to spread through Europe and the world. A product of West Indian sugar cane, rum had become popular in England, Holland and the English colonies in America more than in the rest of Europe. It was an honourable adversary. In Europe, brandy made from wine met brandies made from cider (which produced the incomparable calvados²²⁷ in the seventeenth century), or from pears, plums and cherries (kirsch, which came from Alsace, Lorraine and Franche-Comté, was used as a medicine in Paris in about 1760). Maraschino from Zara, famous in about 1740, was the jealously guarded monopoly of Venice. Marc-brandy and alcohols made from grain were lesser but still formidable opponents: grain brandy was the contemporary description. The distillation of grape marc began in about 1690 in Lorraine. In contrast to brandy, which needed a low heat, it required a high temperature and therefore large quantities of wood. The plentiful forests in Lorraine played their part. But this type of distillation gradually spread, for instance in Burgundy (the marc produced there was soon the best known of all) and also in all the vineyards of Italy each of which had its *grappa*.

The great competitors (rather like beer versus wine) were alcohols made from grain: *kornbrand*, vodka, whisky, Hollands and gin, which became established north of the commercial boundaries of the vine without our knowing exactly when they began to spread.²²⁸ Their great advantage was their modest price. By the early eighteenth century, the whole of London society, from top to bottom, was determinedly getting drunk on gin.

The lands along the northern boundaries of the vine-countries naturally presented a mixture of tastes: England, which was open to brandy from the continent and rum from America (punch began to enjoy success there), drank its own gin as well as whisky from Scotland and Ireland. Holland was exactly at the meeting point of all the wine brandies and all the grain-based alcohols in the world, to say nothing of rum from Curaçao and Guiana. All these alcoholic drinks were quoted on the Amsterdam Stock Exchange: rum at the head, followed by brandy, and then, far behind these noble leaders, grain alcohols. Germany between the Rhine and the Elbe also had a two-fold consumption: in 1760 Hamburg received 4000 casks of brandy from France (500 litres per cask, making about 20,000 hectolitres). The region where alcohol made from grain was consumed almost exclusively only really began beyond the Elbe and around the Baltic. At the same date, in 1760, Lübeck was importing only 400 casks of French brandy, Königsberg 100, Stockholm 100, the Lübeck total being 'very little and in any case only for Prussia'. For Poland and Sweden, Savary explains, although no more 'reserved than anyone else about this fiery drink ... prefer grain alcohols to wine alcohols'.[229]

Alcohol succeeded all too well in Europe, which discovered in it one of its everyday stimulants, a cheap source of calories and certainly an easily accessible luxury, with vicious consequences. And the watchful state soon found that it too could profit.

Alcoholism outside Europe

Every civilization found its own answer or answers to the problem of drinks, particularly alcoholic drinks. Any fermentation of a vegetable product produces alcohol. The Indians in Canada found their solace in maple juice; the Mexicans, before and after Cortes, in *pulque* made from agaves which 'intoxicates like wine'; the poorest Indians in the West Indies or South America, in maize or manioc. Even the simple Tupinambas, whom Jean de Léry met in the bay of Rio de Janeiro in 1556, on feast days drank a beverage made from manioc chewed up and then left to ferment.[230] Elsewhere there was palm wine, a fermented sap. Northern Europe had its own saps of birch trees and its beers made from cereals; it was responsible for the success of mead (fermented honey water) until the fifteenth century. Very early on, the Far East had wine made from rice, preferably glutinous rice.

Did the still give Europe the advantage over all these peoples – the possibility of making any super-alcoholic beverage it chose? Rum, whisky, *kornbrand*, vodka, calvados, marc, brandy, and gin all had to go through the cooled tube of the still. To answer this question, one would have to know more about the origins of rice and millet alcohol in the Far East, whether they were in existence before or after the Western still, which dates roughly from the eleventh or twelfth century.

European travellers cannot of course tell us the answer. They do establish the presence of arak (*arrequi*) in Algiers under the corsairs in the seventeenth century.[231] Mandelslo, a traveller to Gujerat in 1638, claims that 'the *terri* from coconut palms is a sweet liqueur and pleasant to drink', and adds, 'from rice, sugar and dates they make *arac*, which is a kind of brandy much stronger and more agreeable than what is made in Europe'.[232] An experienced doctor, Kämpfer, described the *sacki* he drank in Japan (1691) as a sort of beer made from rice, 'as strong as Spanish wine'; on the other hand the *lau* he tasted in Siam was a sort of burnt wine, a *Branntwein*, which travellers mentioned along with araka.[233] And Chinese wine was a 'real beer' made from 'coarse millet' or rice, according to a Jesuit correspondent. Fruit was often added to it, 'either fresh or preserved or dried in the sun'; hence the names of 'quince, cherry or grape wine'. But the Chinese also drank a sort of brandy 'which has been distilled in the alembic and is so strong that it burns almost like spirits of wine'.[234] A little later, in 1793, George Staunton when in China drank 'a yellow vinous liquor' (rice wine) and also distilled spirit. The spirit seems to have been of better quality than the wine which was generally cloudy, had a flat taste and turned sour quite quickly. The spirit was 'clear and seldom partook of any empyreumatic odour'. Sometimes it was so strong that it was 'above the common proof for ardent spirits'.[235] Finally, Gmelin, a German explorer of Siberia, gives us a description – but only in 1738 – of the kind of still used by the Chinese.[236]

But we are still no nearer to the answer to the problem: when did distilling begin? It seems fairly certain that Persia under the Sassanids already had stills. Al Kindi, in the ninth century, speaks not only of the distillation of perfumes, but also describes the apparatus used for the purpose. He speaks of camphor, which is obtained from the distillation of camphor wood.[237] Now camphor was being produced from very early times in China. There is no reason why spirits should not have been produced by the Chinese in the ninth century (and two poems dating from the T'ang dynasty mention the famous *shao chiu* or burnt wine of Szechwan in the ninth century). But the experts are not agreed on the question, since in the same collective publication (1977) in which E.H. Schafer mentions this early appearance, M. Freeman dates the first development of distilling techniques from the early twelfth century, while F.W. Mote describes them as a novelty in the twelfth or thirteenth century.[238]

So it would be difficult for anyone to establish either that the West led the way or that China did. Perhaps Persia was the real country of origin: one of the Chinese words for spirit comes from the Arabic *araq*.

On the other hand, it is undeniable that brandy, rum and *agua ardiente* (alcohol made from cane) were Europe's poisoned gifts to the civilizations of America. All probability suggests that this was also the case with *mezcal*, produced by distilling the heart of the agave and much more alcoholic than the *pulque* made from the same plant. The Indian peoples suffered tremendously from the alcoholism in which they were encouraged to indulge. It would really seem as if the civilization of the Mexican plateau, losing its ancient framework and taboos, abandoned itself to a temptation which wrought havoc with it after 1600. State revenue from *pulque* in New Spain was equal to half the revenue from the silver mines![239] It was deliberate policy on the part of the new masters. In 1786 the Viceroy of Mexico, Bernardo de Galvez, expressed his satisfaction at its results and, noting the Indian's taste for drink, recommended that it be spread amongst the still innocent Apaches in the north of Mexico. Apart from the profits to be expected, there was no better way of creating 'a new need which forces them to recognize very clearly their obligatory dependence with regard to ourselves'.[240] The English and French had already done the same in north America, the French propagating brandy, despite all royal prohibitions, the English rum.

Chocolate, tea, coffee

At nearly the same time as the discovery of alcohol, Europe, at the centre of the innovations of the world, discovered three new drinks, stimulants and tonics: coffee, tea and chocolate. All three came from abroad: coffee was Arab (originally Ethiopian); tea, Chinese; chocolate, Mexican.

Chocolate came to Spain from Mexico, from New Spain, in about 1520 in the form of loaves and tablets. Not surprisingly it was in the Spanish Netherlands slightly earlier (1606) than in France. The anecdote about Maria Theresa (her marriage to Louis XIV took place in 1659) drinking chocolate on the sly, a Spanish habit she was never able to lose, may well be true.[241] The person who really introduced it into France a few years earlier was said to have been Cardinal Richelieu (brother of the minister, he was archbishop of Lyons and died in 1653). This is possible, though chocolate at that time was regarded as a medicine quite as much as a foodstuff: 'I have heard one of his servants say,' reported a witness later, 'that he [the cardinal] took it to moderate the vapours of his spleen and that he got this secret from some Spanish nuns who brought it to France.'[242] Chocolate reached England from France in about 1657.

These first appearances were discreet and fleeting. Madame de Sévigné's letters mention that chocolate was either all the rage at court or out of favour, according to the day or the gossip.[243] She herself worried about the dangers of the new beverage, having like others got into the habit of mixing it with milk. In fact chocolate did not become established until the French Regency. The Regent made it popular. At that time 'to go to the chocolate' meant to attend the prince's levée, to be in his good books.[244] Nevertheless its popularity should not be exaggerated. We are told that in Paris in 1768 'the great take it sometimes, the old often, the people never'. The only area where it triumphed was Spain: every foreigner made fun of the thick chocolates, perfumed with cinnamon, which were the delight of the inhabitants of Madrid. A Jewish merchant, Aaron Colace, whose correspondence has been preserved, had good reason to settle in Bayonne in about 1727. From this town he was able to watch the Peninsular market while maintaining business connections with Amsterdam and its market in colonial goods (notably cocoa from Caracas, which often made this unexpected detour).[245]

In December 1693 Gemelli Careri offered chocolate to a Turkish Aga at Smyrna, and had cause to regret it. The Aga 'was either intoxicated by it [which

Drinking chocolate in Spain: The breakfast chocolate, by Zurbaran (1568-1664). Besançon Museum. (Photo Bulloz.)

is unlikely] or smoke from the tobacco produced that effect, for he flared up at me violently, saying that I had made him drink a liquor to upset him and take away his powers of judgment'.[246]

Tea came with the Portuguese, Dutch and English from China where its use had spread ten or twelve centuries earlier. The transfer to Europe was long and difficult: leaves, teapots and porcelain cups had to be imported, together with a taste for this exotic drink, which Europeans had first known in the Indies where tea was very widely used. The first cargoes of tea are thought to have arrived at Amsterdam in 1610 on the initiative of the *Oost Indische Companie*.[247]

The tea plant was a bush from which the Chinese peasant plucked leaves. The first small and tender leaves – the smaller the better – produced imperial tea. Tea leaves were dried either by heat from a fire (green tea) or in the heat of the sun (the tea then fermented and blackened to form black tea). Both types were rolled by hand and sent out in 'large chests lined with lead or tin'.

In France, the new drink is not mentioned until 1635 or 1636, according to Delamare, but it was by no means generally welcomed, as a medical student found to his cost: he defended a thesis on tea in 1648: 'Some of our doctors burned a copy of the thesis,' reports Gui Patin, 'and the dean was criticized for having approved it. You will see it and be able to laugh at it.' But ten years later, another thesis, under the patronage of the Chancellor Séguier (who was himself a fervent tea addict) celebrated the virtues of the new drink.[248]

Food and Drink

Tea arrived in England by way of Holland and the café proprietors of London who launched the fashion in about 1657. Samuel Pepys drank it for the first time on 25 September 1660.²⁴⁹ But the East India Company only began to import it from Asia in 1669.²⁵⁰ In fact European tea consumption did not become considerable until 1720-30 when direct trade between Europe and China began. Until then the major part of this trade had been carried on via Batavia, founded by the Dutch in 1617. Chinese junks bringing their usual cargoes to Batavia also carried a small quantity of rough tea which was the only variety that would keep and survive the long journey. The Dutch for a time succeeded in paying for this tea from Fukien with bales of sage instead of silver. Sage was also used in Europe to prepare a drink, one with highly praised medicinal qualities. But the Chinese were not won over; tea fared better in Europe.²⁵¹

The English very quickly overtook the Dutch. Exports from Canton in 1766 were as follows: 6 million pounds (weight) on English boats, 4·5 on Dutch, 2·4 on Swedish, 2·1 on French; making a total of 15 million pounds, about 7000 tons. Veritable tea fleets gradually grew up. Increasing quantities of dried leaves were unloaded at all ports with 'Indies quays': Lisbon, Lorient, London, Ostend, Amsterdam, Gothenburg, sometimes Genoa and Leghorn. The figures rose enormously; 28,000 'pics' (one picul equals about 60 kilograms) left Canton annually between 1730 and 1740; 115,000 from 1760 to 1770; 172,000 from 1780 to 1785.²⁵² George Staunton, taking 1693 as the starting point, could infer that 'an increase of four hundredfold' had occurred a century later. In his day it was estimated that in England, 'more than a pound weight each, in the course of a

Drinking chocolate in Italy: *La cioccolata* by Longhi (1702-85). (Photo Anderson-Giraudon.)

year, for the individuals of all ranks, ages and sexes' was consumed.[253] This adds a final touch to the portrait of this extravagant trade: only a tiny part of Western Europe – Holland and England – had taken to the new drink on a large scale. France consumed a tenth of its own cargoes at the most. Germany preferred coffee. Spain hardly tried it.

Is it true to say that the new drink replaced gin in England? (The English government had taken the tax off gin production to combat the invasion of imports from the continent.) Was it a remedy for the undeniable drunkenness of London society in the reign of George II? Or did the sudden taxation of gin in 1751[254] on the one hand and the general rise in grain prices on the other favour the newcomer – reputed in addition to be an excellent remedy for colds, scurvy and fevers? Such might have been the end of Hogarth's 'gin alley'. In any case tea won the day and the State subjected it to vigilant taxation (as in the American colonies which later used it as a pretext for revolt). In fact an unprecedented contraband trade brought in six or seven million pounds from the continent every year, via the North Sea, the Channel and the Irish Sea. All the ports and Indies companies as well as high finance in Amsterdam and elsewhere participated in the smuggling. Everyone was in on it, including the English consumer.[255]

This picture covers only north-west Europe and one important customer is missing – Russia. Tea may perhaps have been known there in 1567, though it hardly came into general use before the treaty of Nertchinsk (1689) and more particularly before the establishment of the Kiatka fair, south of Irkutsk, very much later in 1763. A document in the archives at Leningrad dating from the end of the century and written in French states that:

> [The goods] that the Chinese bring ... are a few silk fabrics, a few varnished objects, not many porcelains, large quantities of material from Canton which we call *nankins* and the Russians call *chitri*, and very considerable quantities

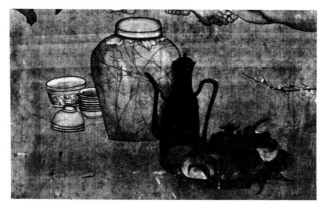

Tea: detail from an eighteenth-century Chinese painting. Musée Guimet, Paris. (Photo Giraudon.)

Dutchmen sitting at table with the Chinese, seen by the Japanese at Deshima in the eighteenth century: they are drinking tea. Bibliothèque Nationale, Paris, Cabinet des Estampes. (Photo B.N.)

> of green tea. It is infinitely superior to the tea Europe receives across the immense seas, and thus the Russians are forced to pay as much as twenty francs a pound for it although they rarely resell it for more than fifteen or sixteen. To compensate for the loss, they never fail to raise the price of their furs, almost the sole commodity they supply to the Chinese, but the trick turns much less to their advantage than to the profit of the Russian government, which levies a tax of twenty-five per cent on everything bought and sold.[256]

However, Russia was importing less than 500 tons of tea at the end of the eighteenth century. It was a far cry from the 7000 tons consumed by the West.

To conclude this chapter on tea in the West, note that it took Europe a very long time to find out how to lay hands on the plant. The first tea shrubs in Java were only planted in 1827 and in Ceylon from 1877, immediately after the island's coffee shrubs had practically been destroyed.

The popularity of tea in Europe – even limited to Russia, the Netherlands and England – was an immense innovation. But the event is insignificant when measured on a world scale. Even today the essential business of tea is carried on in China, the largest consumer and producer. Tea there plays the same kind of role as the vine on the shores of the Mediterranean. Both vine and tea have their geographical zones where their very ancient cultivation has been gradually changed and perfected. Minute and repeated attentions are necessary to satisfy the requirements of generations of knowledgeable consumers. Tea, which was known about in Szechwan long before, had spread throughout China by the eighth century AD.[257] According to Pierre Gourou, the Chinese 'have sharpened their taste to the point of being able to distinguish between teas from the various localities, and to establish a subtle hierarchy.... All this is strangely reminiscent of viticulture at the other extremity of the Old World, also the result of thousands of years of progress accomplished by a civilisation of sedentary peasants.'[258]

Every plant of civilization creates a state of strict bondage. The soil of the tea plantations has to be prepared, the seeds sown, the tea plants pruned so that they remain shrubs instead of growing into trees 'which they are in the wild state'; the leaves carefully plucked then treated on the same day, dried either naturally or by heating, rolled and then dried again. In Japan the drying/rolling operation can be repeated six or seven times. Certain qualities can then sell for huge prices – the quality of the product depending on its type, on the soil, even more on the season when it is picked (the young spring leaves are more scented than the others), and finally on the treatment that differentiates green teas from black. The best green teas are used for the powdered tea the Japanese dissolve in boiling water (instead of simple infusion) according to an old Chinese method (forgotten in China itself) which is reserved for the famous tea ceremony, the *Cha-no-yu*. According to an eighteenth-century memoir, this was such a complicated ceremony that to learn the art of it properly 'you need a teacher, just as in Europe you need one to learn to dance, to bow, etc.'.[259]

For tea certainly had its ritual – like wine, like any self-respecting plant of civilization. Even in poor households in China and Japan boiling water was always in readiness to make tea at all hours of the day.[260] No guest would ever be received without being offered a cup of tea. In well-off Chinese homes, a source informs us in 1762:

> There are very suitable implements for that purpose, such as a decorated table [the traditional low table], with a small stove beside it, boxes with drawers, bowls, cups, saucers, spoons for jam, crystallised sugar in pieces shaped like nuts, to hold in the mouth whilst drinking the tea, for this has least effect on its good taste, and uses up less sugar. All this is accompanied by various preserves, both dry and liquid, the Chinese having a much better understanding of how to make them dainty and attractive[261] than European confectioners.

It must, however, be added that according to a nineteenth-century traveller in northern China where tea did not grow well, 'the members of the lower classes only know it as a luxury and sip hot water with as much pleasure as the well-to-do take their infusion of green tea – they are content to give it the name of tea'.[262] Was it the social custom of tea that spread this strange *ersatz* of hot water? Or was everything generally drunk hot in China, as in Japan – tea, saké, alcohol made from rice or millet, and even water? When Father de Las Cortes drank a cup of cold water, he shocked all the Chinese accompanying him, who tried to

Food and Drink 255

dissuade him from such a dangerous practice.²⁶³ 'If the Spaniards, who have a passion for drinking everything iced at all seasons, did as the Chinese do,' remarks a very sensible book (1762), 'they would not see so many diseases prevalent in their midst, nor so much dryness in their temperament.'²⁶⁴

Tea, the universal drink in China and Japan, was adopted far less generally by the rest of the Far East. It was made into compact briquettes for long journeys and very early on carried from the Yang-tse-Kiang to Tibet by caravans of yaks, following what was probably the worst route in the world. Caravans of camels took the briquettes to Russia until the railway line was laid, and briquettes of tea are still in general consumption in certain regions of the USSR today.

Tea was also a success in Islam. Very sweet mint tea became a national drink in Morocco, but it only appeared there in the eighteenth century, introduced by the English, and did not become widespread until the following century. We do not know much about its travels in the rest of Islam. But it is a remarkable fact that all tea's successes occurred in countries where the vine was unknown:

Interior of a Turkish café in Istanbul. Bibliothèque Nationale, Paris, Cabinet des Estampes. (Photo B.N.)

northern Europe, Russia, Islam. Should we infer that the plants of civilization are mutually exclusive? Ustáriz seemed to think so in 1724, saying that he did not fear that tea would spread throughout Spain, since it was only used in the north 'to compensate for the scarcity of wine'.[265] By the same token perhaps, European wines and spirits did not conquer the Far East.

There is a danger that the history of coffee may lead us astray. The anecdotal, the picturesque and the unreliable play an enormous part in it.

The coffee shrub[266] was once thought to be a native of Persia but more probably came from Ethiopia. In any case coffee shrub and coffee scarcely appeared before 1470. Coffee was being drunk in Aden at that date. It had reached Mecca by 1511 since in that year its consumption was forbidden there; the prohibition was repeated in 1524. It is recorded in Cairo in 1510 and Istanbul in 1517; after this it was forbidden and re-authorized at regular intervals. Meanwhile it spread widely within the Turkish Empire, to Damascus, Aleppo (1532) and Algiers. By the end of the century, it had installed itself virtually throughout the Muslim world – though it was still rare in the Islamic regions of India in Tavernier's time.[267]

It was certainly in Islam that coffee was first encountered by such Western travellers as Prospero Alpini,[268] an Italian doctor, who stayed in Egypt in about 1590, or the swaggering Pietro della Valle, who was in Constantinople in 1615:

> The Turks [wrote della Valle] also have another beverage, black in colour, which is very refreshing in summer and very warming in winter, without however changing its nature and always remaining the same drink, which is swallowed hot.... They drink it in long draughts, not during the meal but afterwards, as a sort of delicacy and to converse in comfort in the company of friends. One hardly sees a gathering where it is not drunk. A large fire is kept going for this purpose and little porcelain bowls are kept by it ready-filled with the mixture; when it is hot enough there are men entrusted with the office who do nothing else but carry these little bowls to all the company, as hot as possible, also giving each person a few melon seeds to chew to pass the time. And with the seeds and this beverage, which they call *kafoue*, they amuse themselves while conversing ... sometimes for a period of seven or eight hours.[269]

Coffee reached Venice in about 1615. In 1644, a merchant of Marseilles, de La Roque, brought the first coffee beans to his native city, along with some precious cups and coffee-pots.[270] By 1643, the new drug was making its first appearance in Paris,[271] and possibly by 1651 in London.[272] But all these dates refer to the first rather clandestine arrivals rather than to the beginning of a popular taste or public consumption.

In fact it was in Paris that coffee first met with the welcome which made its fortune. In 1669, a Turkish ambassador, an arrogant but sociable man, Soliman Mustapha Raca, who entertained a great deal, offered coffee to his Parisian guests. The embassy failed, but the coffee succeeded.[273] Like tea, coffee was thought to be a marvel remedy. A treatise on the *Usage du caphé, du thé et du chocolate* which appeared anonymously in Lyon in 1671, and may have been by Jacob Spon, listed all the virtues attributed to the new drink:

> It dries up all cold and damp humours, drives away wind, strengthens the liver, relieves dropsies by its purifying quality; sovereign equally for scabies and impurity of the blood, it revives the heart and its vital beat, relieves those who have stomach ache and have lost their appetite; it is equally good for those who have a cold in the head, streaming or heavy.... The vapour which rises from it [helps] watering eyes and noises in the ears, sovereign remedy also for short breath, colds which attack the lungs, pains in the spleen, worms; extraordinary relief after over-eating or over-drinking. Nothing better for those who eat a lot of fruit.[274]

However, other doctors, and public rumour, claimed that coffee was an anti-aphrodisiac and a 'eunuch's drink'.[275]

As a result of this publicity and despite these accusations, coffee made ground in Paris.[276] Pedlars appeared on the scene during the last years of the seventeenth century, Armenians dressed as Turks and wearing turbans, who carried trays in front of them with coffee pot, lighted stove and cups. Hatarioun, an Armenian known by the name of Pascal, opened the first stall to sell coffee in 1672 in one of the booths of the Saint-Germain fair (held for centuries near the abbey on which it depended, on the site of the present Rue du Four and Rue Saint Sulpice). Business was not good for Pascal and he moved to the Right Bank of the Seine to the quai de l'Ecole du Louvre where at one time his customers consisted of a few Levantines and Knights of Malta. He then moved on to England. Despite his failure, other cafés opened. One of these was the Malibar café, with premises first in the Rue de Buci and then in Rue Férou, owned by another Armenian. The most famous was established in the modern style by a former waiter of Pascal's, called Francesco Procopio Coltelli: he was born in Sicily in 1650 and later took the name Procope Couteau. He set up at the Saint-Germain fair, then in the Rue de Tournon, and finally in 1686 in the Rue des Fossés-Saint-Germain. This last café, the *Procope* – it is still there today – was near the elegant and busy centre of the town, at that ti)e (before it moved to the Palais Royal in the eighteenth century) the Buci crossroads, or more properly the Pont Neuf. He had another piece of luck when the Comédie Française started up opposite his newly opened café. The Sicilian's ability to set the right tone ensured his success. He knocked down the partitions between two adjoining houses, hung tapestries and mirrors on the walls, chandeliers from the ceilings, and sold preserved fruit and drinks as well as coffee. His stall was the rendezvous of the idle, of gossips, conversationalists, wits (Charles Duclos, future secretary of the Académie Française was one of the pillars of the establishment) and beautiful women. The theatre was near at hand and *Procope* also sold refreshments in a booth there.

The modern café could not remain the prerogative of one district or one street. In addition the movement of the town gradually militated against the Left

Bank to the advantage of the Right, which was livelier, as a summary map of Parisian cafés in the eighteenth century demonstrates – a total of six to seven hundred.[277] The reputation of the Café de la Régence, founded in 1681 in the Palais-Royal square, grew up at that time (later its fame became even greater and it moved to its present position in the Rue Saint-Honoré). The vogue the cafés enjoyed gradually lowered the social status of the taverns. The fashion was the same in Germany, Italy and Portugal. Brazilian coffee was cheap in Lisbon, and so was sugar, which was poured so copiously into it that, to quote one Englishman, the spoon stood up in the cup.[278]

This fashionable drink was not fated to remain limited to the fashionable world. While all other prices were rising, superabundant production in the islands maintained the cost of a cup of coffee almost unchanged. In 1782 Le Grand d'Aussy explained that:

> Consumption has tripled in France; there is no bourgeois household where you are not offered coffee, no shopkeeper, no cook, no chambermaid who does not breakfast on coffee with milk in the morning. In public markets and in certain streets and alleys in the capital, women have set themselves up selling what they call *café au lait* to the populace, that is to say poor milk coloured with coffee grounds which they buy from the kitchens of big houses or from café proprietors. This beverage is in a tin urn equipped with a tap to serve it and a stove to keep it hot. There is usually a wooden bench near the merchant's stall or shop. Suddenly, to your surprise, you see a woman from Les Halles or a porter arrive and ask for coffee. It is served in large pottery cups. These elegant people take it standing up, basket on back, unless as a sensuous refinement they want to place their burden on the bench and sit down. From my windows overlooking the beautiful quai where I live [the Quai du Louvre in the neighbourhood of the Pont Neuf] I often see this spectacle in one of the wooden booths that have been built from the Pont Neuf to the Louvre. And sometimes I have seen scenes which make me regret that I am not Teniers or Callot.[279]

To correct this picture by an awful Parisian bourgeois, it must be said that perhaps the most picturesque or rather the most moving sight was the woman pedlars standing at street corners when the workmen went to work at daybreak. They carried the tin urns on their backs and served *café au lait* 'in earthenware pots for two sous. Sugar was not much in evidence.' It was, however, enormously popular; the workmen 'have found more economy, more sustenance, more flavour in this foodstuff than in any other. As a result, they drink it in prodigious quantities, saying that it generally sustains them until the evening. Thus they eat only two meals, a large breakfast, and beef salad in the evening'; which meant slices of cold beef with parsley, oil and vinegar.[280]

If there was such an increase in consumption – and not only in Paris and France – from the middle of the eighteenth century, it was because Europe had organized production itself. So long as the world market had depended solely on coffee shrubs around Mocha, in Arabia, European imports had perforce been

Food and Drink 259

limited. But coffee shrubs were planted in Java from 1712; on Bourbon island (Réunion) from 1716; on the island of Cayenne in 1722 (it had therefore crossed the Atlantic); in Martinique in 1723-30; in Jamaica in 1730; in Santo Domingo in 1731. These dates do not apply to production because the coffee shrubs had to grow and spread. Imports of coffee to France from the islands began in 1730.[281] Father Charlevoix writes in 1731: 'We are delighted to see coffee enriching our island [Santo Domingo]. The tree which produces it is already becoming as fine ... as if it were native to the country, but it needs time to get accustomed to the soil.'[282] The last to come on to the market, coffee from Santo Domingo remained the least mentioned and the most plentiful of all: some 40 million pounds were produced in 1789, when European consumption fifty years before was perhaps 4 million pounds. Mocha always headed the list as far as price and quality were concerned, followed by coffee from Java and Bourbon Island ('a small, bluish bean, like that of Java') when its quality was good, then by the products of Martinique, Guadeloupe and finally Santo Domingo.[283]

The Café Procope, a fashionable meeting-place, with portraits of some of its famous customers: Buffon, Gilbert, Diderot, D'Alembert, Marmontel, Le Kain, J.-B. Rousseau, Voltaire, Piron, D'Holbach.

Careful checks, however, warn us against exaggerating the figures for consumption.[284] In 1787, France imported 38,000 tons of coffee (half of it from Santo Domingo). Of this, 36,000 tons were re-exported and Paris only kept about a thousand tons for its own use.[285] Some provincial towns still did not welcome the new beverage. The Limoges bourgeois only drank coffee 'as a medicine'. Only certain social categories – the postmasters in the north, for example – followed the fashion.

It was therefore necessary to go in search of new markets. Through Marseilles, coffee from Martinique conquered the Levant after 1730, at the expense of Arabian coffee.[286] The *Oost Indische Companie*, which supplied coffee to Persia and Muslim regions of India, which had remained loyal to mocha, wanted to sell its surpluses from Java there as well. If the 150 million Muslims are added to the 150 million Europeans, there was a possible market of 300 million – perhaps a third of all human beings – actual or potential coffee drinkers in the eighteenth century. Coffee had become a 'national commodity' like tea, a means of making money. An active capitalist sector had a financial interest in its production, distribution and success. It had a significant impact on Parisian social and cultural life. The café (the shop where the new drink was sold) became the rendezvous for men of fashion and the leisured, as well as a shelter for the poor. 'There are men,' wrote Sébastien Mercier (1782), 'who arrive at the café at ten in the morning and do not leave until eleven at night [the compulsory closing time, supervised by the police]; they dine on a cup of coffee with milk, and sup on Bavarian cream' [a mixture of syrup, sugar, milk and sometimes tea].[287]

An anecdote illustrates the slow infiltration of coffee amongst the people. When Cartouche was about to be put to death (29 November 1721), his 'judge' who was drinking white coffee offered him a cup. 'He replied that this was not his drink and that he would prefer a glass of wine with a little bread.'[288]

Stimulants: the glories of tobacco

Diatribes against the new drinks were numerous. Some wrote that England would be ruined by its possessions in the Indies, meaning 'the stupid luxury of tea'.[289] Sébastien Mercier on his moralizing walk across Paris in the year 2440 is conducted by a 'sage' who reprovingly tells him:

> We have banished three poisons of which you used to make perpetual use – tobacco, coffee and tea. You used to put an evil powder in your noses that took away from you Frenchmen what little memory you had. You burned your stomachs with destructive liquors that hastened digestive action. Your common nervous diseases were due to that effeminate washing which removed the nourishing essence of animal life.[290]

In reality every civilization needs dietary luxuries and stimulants. In the twelfth and thirteenth centuries the craze was for spices and pepper; in the sixteenth century for alcohol; then it was tea and coffee, not to mention tobacco. The nineteenth and twentieth centuries were destined to have new luxuries of their own, their good and evil drugs. In any case I like the Venetian text dating from the beginning of the seventeenth century which sensibly and not unhumorously specified that the tax on *acque gelate*, coffee and other *bevande* applied to all similar things *inventate o da inventarsi*, invented or yet to be invented.[291] Michelet's view that coffee as early as the French Regency was the 'drink of the Revolution'[292] was certainly exaggerated. But more prudent historians also misrepresent the reality when they talk about the *Grand Siècle* and the eighteenth century without mentioning the shortage of meat, the excesses of alcohol and the coming of coffee.

It may be an error of perspective on my part, but it seems to me that with the increase – or at least the continuation – of very serious dietary difficulties, humanity had need of compensation, according to a constant rule of its life.

Tobacco was one of these compensations. How should it be classified? Louis Lemery, 'Doctor Regent in the Faculty of Medicine of Paris, of the Royal Academy of Sciences', did not hesitate to include it in his *Traité des Aliments* (1702). The plant, he specified, 'is taken either by the nose, or in smoke or by chewing'. He also spoke of coca leaves, similar to myrtle leaves, which 'appease hunger and pain, and give energy'. He did not mention quinine, although he alluded to opium, consumed amongst the Turks even more than in the West, a drug which it was 'dangerous to use'.[293] What did escape him was the immense opium venture spreading from India to the East Indies (along one of the major lines of Islamic expansion) and already reaching China. The great turning point came after 1765, just after the conquest of Bengal, when a monopoly of poppy fields was established to the advantage of the East India Company; they had formerly been a source of income for the Great Mogul. Louis Lemery did not of course possess any of these facts in the early years of the century. Nor did he know about Indian hemp. Stupefacients, foods or medicines, these were great factors destined to transform and disturb men's daily lives.

We shall confine ourselves to tobacco. Between the sixteenth and seventeenth centuries it conquered the whole world, and enjoyed even greater popularity than tea or coffee, which was no mean achievement.

Tobacco originated in the New World. When Columbus arrived in Cuba on 2 November 1492 he saw the natives smoking rolled tobacco leaves. The plant and its name (either Caribbean or Brazilian) moved to Europe where it was for a fairly long time an object of curiosity in botanical gardens or known because of supposedly medicinal qualities. Jean Nicot, French ambassador at Lisbon (1560), sent Catherine of Medici tobacco powder to use against migraine, according to Portuguese practice. Jean Thevet, who also brought the plant to France, asserted that the natives of Brazil used it to eliminate superfluous fluids from the brain.[294] Naturally at one point in Paris a certain Jacques Gohory (died 1576) attributed to it the virtues of a universal panacea.[295]

The plant was cultivated in Spain in 1558 and spread rapidly to France, England (about 1565), Italy, the Balkans and Russia. It was in the Philippines by 1575, having arrived with the 'Manila galleon'. By 1588 it was in Virginia, where production began to soar after 1612; in Macao after 1600, in Java in 1601, in India and Ceylon in about 1605-10.[296] Its diffusion was all the more remarkable as there was no producer market – that is to say no civilization – behind tobacco comparable to that for pepper at its distant beginnings (India), tea (China), coffee (Islam), even chocolate, which had the advantage of a high-quality culture in New Spain. Tobacco came from 'savage' areas in America; the production of the plant had therefore to be ensured before its blessings could be enjoyed. But it had one unique advantage: its great flexibility in adapting itself to the most varied climates and soils. In England, its cultivation spread rapidly among the small peasant-farmers.[297]

The outlines of the history of commercialized tobacco do not appear before the first years of the seventeenth century in Lisbon, Seville and above all Amsterdam, although snuff had begun to be popular in Lisbon at least from 1558. The first two of the three ways of using tobacco (snuff, smoking, chewing) were the most important. 'Powdered tobacco' rapidly acquired several forms, depending on the ingredients added: musk, amber, bergamot, orange blossom. There was a 'Spanish type' tobacco, and tobacco with 'perfume of Malta' or 'perfume of Rome', 'illustrious ladies taking as much as great lords'. Meanwhile 'smoking tobacco' was taken by pipes, later in cigars (the rolled leaves 'the length of a candle'[298] that the natives of Spanish America smoked were not immediately imitated in Europe); except in Spain, where Savary mentions as an apparent rarity leaves of Cuban tobacco 'which are smoked without pipes, by rolling them up into the shape of a cornet'.[299] Later still came cigarettes. The latter first appeared it seems in the New World, since a French document of 1708 refers to 'the infinite quantity of paper' imported from Europe for 'the little rolls in which they wrap chopped tobacco to smoke it'.[300] Cigarettes spread outside Spain during the Napoleonic Wars: it became the custom at that time to roll tobacco in a small piece of paper, a *papelito*. The *papelito* then reached France, where it became popular among the French youth. Meanwhile the paper became thinner and the cigarette came into general use in the Romantic period. George Sand, referring to the doctor who treated Musset in Venice, said 'All his pipes are not worth one of my cigarettes'.[301]

We get our information about the early use of tobacco from violent government prohibitions (governments later came to realize the attractive possibilities of financial return and the Tobacco Monopoly was established in France in 1674). These prohibitions encircled the world: England 1604, Japan 1607-9, the Ottoman Empire 1611, the Mogul Empire 1617, Sweden and Denmark 1632, Russia 1634, Naples 1637, Sicily 1640, China 1642, the Papal States 1642, the

'The solid enjoyment of bottle and friend', English engraving of 1774. The tobacco and port have triumphed over the conversation. (Photo Snark.)

Electorate of Cologne 1649, Wurttemberg 1651.³⁰² Of course they were ignored, particularly in China where they continued in force until 1776. The use of tobacco was already universal in the Tche-li in 1640. In Fukien (1664) 'everyone has a long pipe in his mouth, lights up, inhales and blows out the smoke'.³⁰³ Vast regions were planted with tobacco and China exported it to Siberia and Russia. By the end of the eighteenth century everyone in China smoked – men and women, mandarins and poor, 'down to toddlers two feet high'. How quickly habits change! as a letter from Che Kiang says.³⁰⁴ The same was true of Korea in 1668: tobacco had been introduced here from Japan in about 1620.³⁰⁵ (In eighteenth-century Lisbon small boys took snuff, it must be said.)³⁰⁶ All types of tobacco and all the ways they could be used were known and accepted in China, including, from the seventeenth century, the consumption of tobacco mixed with opium, which came from the Indian Archipelago and Formosa through the medium of the *Oost Indische Companie*. 'The best commodity to take to the East Indies,' says a report of 1727, 'is powdered tobacco, either from Seville or Brazil.' In any case the temporary decline in the popularity of tobacco in Europe in the eighteenth century, about which we have very little information, had no parallel in China or India. It goes without saying that the disfavour was only temporary. All the peasants in Burgundy³⁰⁷ were apparently indulging in smoking at about this time, and all the rich people in St Petersburg. In 1723, the Virginia and Maryland tobacco, which England imported only to re-export two-thirds of

The merry drinker, by J. Leyster (1629) with the full kit of the perfect smoker: pipe, tobacco, long matches and brasero. Rijksmuseum, Amsterdam. (Photo by the museum.)

it to Holland, Germany, Sweden and Denmark, already amounted to 30,000 kegs a year and required the services of 200 ships.[308]

In Africa the vogue grew. The success of large plaits of black tobacco from Bahia whose inferior quality was disguised by an admixture of molasses continued until the nineteenth century to stimulate a lively trade between Brazil and the gulf of Benin, where an active clandestine black slave trade lasted until about 1850.[309]

4

Superfluity and Sufficiency: Houses, Clothes and Fashion

IN THE LAST CHAPTER we tried to draw the line between superfluity and sufficiency in an area ranging from meat to tobacco. To complete the picture and give us a further opportunity of studying the differences between rich and poor it remains to describe housing and costume. After all, where is luxury more conspicious than in house, furniture and dress? At the same time we shall be able to make comparisons between civilizations, for no two were alike.

Houses throughout the world

We cannot hope to look at all the kinds of houses in existence between the fifteenth and eighteenth centuries. We can do little more than pick out a few obvious general characteristics.

Fortunately, almost everywhere we turn, we shall be looking at something that changed only very slowly, if at all. Many houses standing today, preserved or restored, refer us back not only to the eighteenth century but to the sixteenth and fifteenth or even earlier, as we can see in the Golden Street of the Hradčany in Prague, or in the breathtaking village of Santillana, near Santander. An observer remarked in 1842 that Beauvais retained more of its ancient dwellings at that time than any other town; he described 'some forty wooden houses going back to the sixteenth and seventeenth centuries'.[1]

Furthermore, houses are built or rebuilt according to traditional patterns. Here more than anywhere else the strength of precedent makes itself felt. The masons called in to rebuild the houses of the rich at Valladolid after the terrible fire of 1564 were the unconscious representatives of the old Muslim crafts,[2] and their beautiful new houses were archaic in design. The influence of custom and tradition is always present, for these are ancient legacies that can never be discarded. Traditionally, for instance, Islamic houses are closed in on themselves. The traveller was right when he said that all well-off homes in Persia in 1694 'are of the same architecture. There is always a room about thirty feet square in the middle of the building, at its centre a hollow full of water in the form of a small pond and surrounded by carpets.'[3] The force of tradition is even more present in the case of country-dwellers throughout the world. To have seen a very poor peasant's house being built from its frail wooden frame in the region of Vitoria north of Rio de Janeiro in 1937[4] is to possess an ageless document, valid for centuries before the present day. The same applies to the nomad's simple tent: it has come down through the centuries without change, often woven on the same primitive loom as in the past.

In short, a 'house', wherever it may be, is an enduring thing, and it bears perpetual witness to the slow pace of civilizations, of cultures bent on preserving, maintaining and repeating.

Rich building materials: stone and brick

Repetition was all the more natural as building material varied little and imposed certain limitations on every region. That is not to say that civilizations were absolutely imprisoned inside the restrictions imposed by stone, brick, wood or earth. But these materials often did constitute long-lasting limitations. 'It is lack of stone,' a traveller noted, (and lack of wood too, we might add) 'that obliges [the Persians] to build walls and houses of earth.' In fact they were built of sun-dried, or sometimes baked bricks. 'Rich people decorate the outside walls with a mixture of whitewash, Muscovy green and gum which makes them look silvery.'[5] They were still walls of clay, for all that: geography explains why, but it does not explain everything. Human beings also had a say in the matter.

Stone was a luxury which had to be paid for; otherwise it was necessary to accept compromises, like mixing brick with stone, as Roman and Byzantine masons had already done and as Turkish and Chinese masons still regularly did; or using wood and stone; or reserving stone solely for the houses of princes and gods. Stone buildings were the rule in the Inca city of Cuzco, but only observatories, temples and stadiums enjoyed this privilege in the Maya kingdoms. Side by side with these monuments we must imagine the everyday huts made of branches and *pisé*, like those still to be seen around the ruins of Chichen Itza or Palenque in Yucatan today. Similarly, the striking stone architecture of the rectangular towns in the Indian Deccan stretches northwards only as far as the soft earth of the Indus-Ganges plain.

In the West and in the Mediterranean, civilizations that built with stone took centuries to evolve. Quarries had to be worked and stone selected that was both easy to cut and hardened in contact with the air. It meant a human investment for centuries on end.

There are innumerable sandstone, sand, rough limestone and gypsum quarries around Paris. The town cleared its own site in advance. Paris was built on enormous excavations, which ran out 'towards Chaillot, Passy and the old road from Orléans', and under 'the whole suburb of Saint-Jacques, the Rue de la Harpe and the Rue de Tournon.'[6] Rough limestone was widely quarried until the First World War, sawn up in yards in the suburbs and transported across Paris by heavy horse-drawn drays. Nevertheless we should not be misled: Paris was not always a stone city: to turn it into one was an immense labour, starting in the fifteenth century and requiring troops of carpenters from Normandy, roofers, makers of edge tools, masons from the Limousin (who were accustomed to heavy labour), tapestry-makers specializing in fine work, and large armies of plasterers. In Sébastien Mercier's day, the road these plasterers took to return to their lodgings every evening was marked by the trail of their white footprints.[7] And a great many houses of that period only had a stone foundation while the upper floors were still of wood. In the Petit-Pont fire on 27 April 1727 the wooden houses blazed fiercely like a 'great limekiln [into which] one saw whole beams fall'. The few stone houses formed protective barriers stopping the advance of the fire. 'The Petit Châtelet, which is very well built,' noted a witness, 'saved the Rue de la Huchette and the Rue Galande.'[8]

So Paris was for a long time a wooden town, like so many others – like Troyes, which went up in flames in the vast fire of 1547; like Dijon, which still had wooden houses with thatched roofs in the seventeenth century. It was only then that stone began to be widely used, together with tiles, and in particular glazed tiles, which were beginning to make their appearance.[9] Houses in Lorraine towns and villages were covered with wooden shingles: round tiles, regarded by a persistent but erroneous tradition as a Roman survival, were adopted only slowly.[10] In the seventeenth century, it was necessary to forbid the use of straw and even irregular shingles to roof houses in certain villages of Wetterau near the Main, because of the fire risk no doubt. Fires were so frequent in Savoy that the king of Sardinia's administration proposed in 1772 to grant aid to those who had lost their homes 'in towns, settlements and villages' only on condition that the new roofs were made of tile or slate.[11] In other words, the use of stone and tile was only achieved in some places by coercion or subsidy. A tiled roof remained 'a sign of wealth' in the Saône valley even in the eighteenth century,[12] and was still exceptional in peasant dwellings in 1815.[13] There is a drawing in the museum at Nuremberg in which all the houses in a village are clearly shown, with tiled roofs coloured red and thatched roofs grey: we can be sure that this was one way of telling the houses of well-off farmers from those of poor peasants.

Brick gradually replaced wood in buildings, from England to Poland, but it did not predominate immediately. In Germany, its success began precociously, though slowly, in the twelfth century.

London began to adopt brick in the Elizabethan period, at about the same time as Paris became a stone city. The transformation was completed after the fire of 1666 – which consumed three-quarters of the town, over twelve thousand houses – in the massive work of rebuilding that followed and which was, perhaps inevitably, disorganized and unmethodical. Similarly in Amsterdam, all the new

A street in Delft in about 1659: brick houses, wooden shutters, and fixed windows with glass panes. Amsterdam, the Rijksmuseum. (Photo by the museum.)

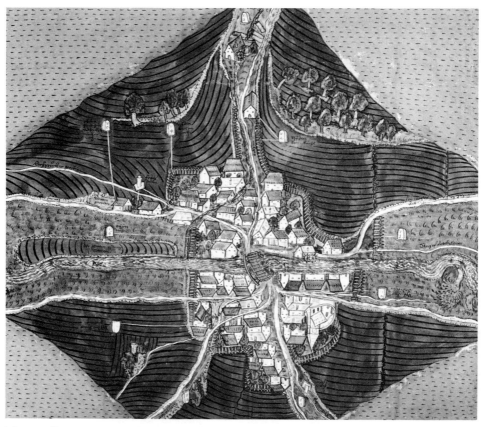

A large village near Nuremberg in 1600: there are about fifty houses, of which about forty have thatched roofs (the darker ones) and about ten tiled roofs (the lighter ones); also in the picture are two mills, one with two wheels, meadows and ploughed fields. The village is surrounded by a palisade. (Hauptamt für Hochbauwesen Nürnberg.)

buildings in the seventeenth century were made of brick – a brick darkened by protective coatings of tar, contrasting with the white stone of pediments and cornices. And in Moscow, a traveller of 1662 tells us, although the houses were usually made of wood, during the previous few years, 'whether out of vanity or for greater security against fire... which is very frequent', a 'fairly large number' of brick houses had been built.[14]

So one kind of building material could succeed another, and the change marked the advance of progress and prosperity. But almost everywhere, different kinds of building material co-existed side by side as well. In China, for example, alongside the much-used wood and *pisé*, brick was considerably in evidence in the domestic architecture of the towns and certain prosperous areas of the countryside. Town walls were generally made of brick, bridges often of stone,

Houses, Clothes and Fashion 271

and some roads were paved. In Canton, the low single-storeyed houses which were the norm in China were very lightly constructed, almost without foundations, and the material used was brick, either fired or unfired, and covered with a mortar of straw and plaster.[15] There was no stone or marble: these were reserved for princely dwellings. In the huge enclosure containing the palaces of Peking, terraces, staircases and balustrades of white marble stretched far into the distance and 'all the buildings are constructed on a foundation of reddish-grey marble', up to the height of a man.[16] The roofs with upcurved ends, covered with the famous varnished tiles, were supported by wooden columns and 'by a forest of wooden joists, plates and bars, coated with green lacquer intermingled with golden figures'.[17] In Chinese architecture, this mixture of wood and marble is hardly mentioned as occurring anywhere other than the imperial palace or rather city, which was indeed an exception, a city to itself. Describing Chou-King-fu, a town in Che-kiang province, 'situated in one of the most beautiful plains in the world, and greatly resembling Venice', with its canals crossed by bridges and its streets 'paved with white stone', a traveller adds: 'Some of the houses are built of dressed stone of an extraordinary whiteness, something almost unheard of in the other towns of China.'[18]

The wooden Pont de la Tournelle in Paris, in 1620. Drawing by Mathan. (Photo by the author.)

Less favoured building materials: wood, earth, fabric

Whether combined with clay or *pisé*, or used alone, wood was the predominant building material wherever geography or tradition encouraged its use: in Picardy, Champagne, the Scandinavian countries, Muscovy, the Rhineland – anywhere where a degree of backwardness preserved the tradition. Painters of the Cologne school in the fifteenth century regularly depict houses built of daub and half-timbered. In Moscow, prefabricated wooden houses could be erected in a few hours, or moved wherever the purchaser desired.[19] The ever-present forest, dominating the landscape and the horizon, offered, indeed urged its resources on men – why look any further? In Poland or Muscovy, where massive forests loomed in every direction, the peasant in order to build his house, 'cuts down pine trees, and carries off their trunks, which he splits in half lengthways, places them on four large stones set at the four corners of a square to form the base, taking care to turn the flat side inwards. He indents them at the ends so that they can be fitted to each other at the corners without leaving too much space; and in this way he builds a cage about six feet high and twelve feet wide, in which two openings are left: one about a foot high for light, and the other about four or five feet high for the doorway. Two or three panes of glass or oiled paper are used to seal the window. At one of the corners of the base, four rods are set in such a way as to form the skeleton of a reduced pyramid, interwoven with branches covered in clay, to act as a catchment for the smoke of an oven which is built inside.' All this work was carried out with the help of a single implement: an axe.[20] This model was not unique to Eastern Europe: it is also found in the French or Italian Alps; and the log cabin of the American pioneers, built under very similar conditions, is much the same sort of thing.

Wherever there was not enough wood – and here it inevitably became a luxury – earth, clay and straw were the only recourse. Near Portuguese Goa in 1639, the houses 'are all made of straw, and very small, having no opening except a low and narrow doorway. The furniture consists of a few rush mats, on which the people lie down to sleep or take their meals ... They coat their houses with cattle-dung, because they think it keeps the fleas away.'[21] This picture would still be accurate even today in many parts of India, where the houses are remarkably small, and have no fireplace or window; and where the narrow village street is often blocked by wandering cattle which have no shelter.

The houses in villages in northern China, as described by Macartney or Guignes,

> consisted mostly of indurated mud; or of masses of earth baked imperfectly in the sun, or moulded between planks ... or of wicker-work, defended by a coating of clay. The roofs were covered generally with straw, rarely with green turf. The apartments are divided by lattice-work hung with broad paper containing either the figures of deities or columns of moral sentences. A court or vacant space around the house, is enclosed with wattles or the stems of the *kow leang* [sorghum].[22]

The style of the present-day house is reminiscent of these ancient descriptions. In its simplest form, it is one narrow rectangle, at most two or three rectangles, arranged around a courtyard closed by a wall. The doors and windows (when they exist) draw their light from this courtyard. Generally speaking, the materials used are brick and tile in the south (a sign of wealth or tradition), cob (*pisé*) and thatch (sorghum or wheat-straw) in the north.

But whether made of bricks or of mud, the houses were almost always built on a wood frame. The Chinese expression for a building (even in our own time) is an 'enterprise of earth and wood'. But wood was rare, especially in the bare country of northern China, and for a building of any size, the necessary supply of wood represented 'extravagant expense' in both men and money. A sixteenth-century official quoted a popular saying in the province of Szechwan: 'For every thousand people who go into the mountains in search of wood, five hundred come back.' According to the same witness, at every proclamation demanding wood for imperial buildings, the peasants in the Hupeh and Szechwan provinces 'wept with despair until they choked'.[23]

In general, China – and the surrounding regions which to some extent came under her cultural influence – built houses on the ground, 'on solid foundations' – everything being relative. In South-East Asia by contrast (in Laos, Cambodia, and Siam, apart from the Chinese-influenced areas of Vietnam) dwellings and storehouses were on the whole built on piles, and were therefore necessarily rather flimsy constructions of wood and bamboo, with wood and mud lattices and roofs of 'grass stalks', the equivalent of a Western thatch.[24] Was the comparative solidity of Chinese construction proof of the solidity of its rural economy, a symbol of deep-seated strength?

In Islam, the buildings were built straight on the ground too. The *chevalier* Chardin, whose exhaustive descriptions are fascinating and tiresome by turns, confirms that this was the case in Persia, of which he was an unparalleled observer, inspired by admiration and enthusiasm. Although there was no real shortage of stone in Persia, bricks were the principal material: laid flat or on end, they could be used for everything, as even the domes on top of the houses were made of masonry. Only very large buildings might have the ceilings supported by wooden columns or pilasters. But whether the bricks had been fired hard to a dark-red colour (in which case they cost a crown a hundred) or whether they had merely been dried in the sun (and therefore only cost a few sous a hundred) they were a fragile building material. So the houses 'which are far from having the fine appearance that ours do', deteriorated rapidly, even palaces, unless they were well maintained. Rich or poor, if they inherited a house, the Persians usually preferred to demolish it and build a new one.[25] It seems clear that there was a hierarchy of building materials throughout the world which determined the classification of different types of architecture in relation to each other.

The frailest dwelling of all is still the nomad tent. Its substance (felt, woven

Japanese house; *old-style* Chinese houses were built on this model. (Galerie Janette Ostier, Paris.)

goat- or camel-hair), its shape and its proportions may vary. Yet this fragile object has persisted through the centuries. Can one call it a necessity or only a makeshift? Often a change in circumstances or opportunity has been enough to make the nomad settle down and change his style of dwelling. This probably occurred to some extent at the end of the Roman Empire; it happened more certainly during the Turkish conquests and the forced settlements which accompanied them in the Balkans; it could be observed in colonial Algeria in recent years and may still be seen in all the Islamic countries today.

Rural dwellings in Europe

The two broad categories of houses throughout the world are obvious: rural and urban. The former, clearly the most numerous, were shelters rather than houses, intended to meet the rudimentary needs of men and domestic animals. It is hard for a Westerner to imagine the rural habitat of Islam or Asia as it must have been in its day-to-day reality. Here, as in other respects, Europe is the continent of which we have the most historical knowledge – and even that is limited.

The peasant house in Europe hardly figures at all in literary documents. The classic description by Noël du Fail is only a rapid sketch of a Breton house of the middle of the sixteenth century.[26] The same is true of a description – though an unusually detailed one – of a Finnish farm near St Petersburg (1790). It mentions the group of wooden huts, most of them in a state of collapse, that made up the farm: the house, with its single smoky room, two small byres, a Russian bath (a *sauna*), a stove to dry wheat or rye. The furniture consisted of a table, a bench, a cast-iron pot, a cauldron, a basin, a pail, some barrels, tubs, wooden or earthenware plates, an axe, a spade, a knife for slicing cabbages.[27]

Drawings and paintings can usually add a little more to our knowledge of the appearance of whole villages or the interiors of large houses where men and beasts lived together. We learn even more by studying the regulations governing village buildings.

A village house could only be built or repaired with the authorization of the community or the seigneurial authority – which controlled access to the stone or clay quarries and to the forests where the wood for building grew. Five large trees had to be cut down for one house in Alsace in the fifteenth century and the same for a barn.[28] These regulations also contain information on the way in which rushes, reeds or straw were woven at the top of a roof; on the stones that were added to shingles (wooden tiles) in the mountains so that the wind should not blow them off; on the relatively small fire risk represented by a thatched roof which had been exposed to the elements for a long time; on the excellent fertilizer provided by old straw roofs that had been replaced; on the food that such roofs could provide for cattle in times of distress (as in Savoy in the eighteenth century);[29] on methods of mixing wood and clay or of arranging planks for the main room; on the custom of indicating inns by signs, either the hoop of a cask or a crown, as in Germany. Many details did not change until the nineteenth century, and even later – for example the village square; the wall which often surrounded the cluster of houses; the church, which often served as a fortress; the water supplies (rivers, fountains, wells); and the arrangement of the peasant house into quarters for humans and animals and the barn for harvests. At Varzy (Nièvre), a small town in Burgundy, the houses of the rich

Peasant houses in Germany (sixteenth century) with thatched roofs. In the foreground, a cart and a well with plunger. Woodcut from Sebastian Münster's *Cosmography*, 1543. Germanisches Nationalmuseum, Nuremberg. (Photo by the museum.)

were peasant in style and the inventories describing them in the seventeenth century scarcely mention more than one large habitable room, which was kitchen, bedroom and living-room all in one.[30]

Excavations undertaken in the past twenty years on sites of deserted villages in the USSR, Poland, Hungary, Germany, Denmark, Holland, England and, recently, in France, are gradually making good a previously chronic lack of information. Ancient village houses discovered in the earth of the Hungarian *puzta* and elsewhere reveal shapes and details (for example the brick furnace) which were destined to endure. The first French excavations (1964 and 1965) concentrated on three abandoned villages: Montaigut (Aveyron), Saint-Jean-le-Froid (Tarn) and Dracy (Côte-d'Or). The first was fairly large, the third rich in various objects, the second has now been sufficiently cleared for us to visualize it with its rampart, ditch, approach road, paved streets equipped with gutters, one of its residential districts, its cemetery, two and probably three churches all built on the same site and of more striking dimensions than the last chapel, which is still visible.[31]

The lesson of these excavations is the relative mobility of villages and hamlets; they grew up, expanded, contracted, and also shifted their sites. Sometimes these 'desertions' were total and final – the *Wüstungen* mentioned by German historians and geographers. More often the centre of gravity within a given cultivated area shifted, and everything – furniture, people, animals, stones – was moved out of the abandoned village to a site a few kilometres away. Even the form of the village could change in the course of these vicissitudes. The large compact village in Lorraine *apparently* dates from the seventeenth century.[32] The *bocage vendéen*, the pattern of woods and hedges in the Gâtine area of the Vendée, was created in the same period, with the establishment of large farms, isolated from each other, which reshaped the landscape.[33]

Many villages or houses have come down, sometimes altered of course, to our own time. There are museum villages as well as museum towns where it is possible to go back towards a distant past. The great problem is dating the various stages with any precision. But a substantial body of research – the results have been published for Italy[34] and the French results are still awaiting publication (a total of 1634 unpublished monographs)[35] – is now providing the elements of a possible reconstruction. In places where life has not followed too precipitous a course, as in Sardinia, peasant dwellings can often be found intact, variously adapted to their functions of housing people and animals according to the different regions of the island.[36]

Any traveller or tourist can see for himself without learned inquiry the interiors of mountain houses preserved in the Innsbruck museum, for example; or the occasional house in the Savoy that has not been converted into a holiday home, and still has its wooden chimney, known as the *borne*, where ham and sausages are smoked. Similarly, large seventeenth-century peasant houses can be seen in Lombardy, and there is a magnificent fifteenth-century *masia* in

Dracy, a village on the vine-growing slopes of Burgundy, which was deserted between 1400 and 1420. Excavations have revealed about 25 dwellings. Shown here are two houses: the one in the foreground is typical: it has a cellar (which would have had a grain-store overhead) and a living-room with a beaten earth floor; small windows, set on the slant, and a niche in the wall. (Photo by the medieval archaeology group of the EPHESS.)

Catalonia with Roman vaults, arches and beautiful stone masonry.[37] In both cases the houses in question undoubtedly belonged to that rare being, the comfortably-off peasant.

Urban houses and dwellings

It is even easier to visit the urban rich – in Europe of course, because outside Europe, apart from princely palaces, practically nothing of the old houses has been preserved – the fault of their poor materials; and good eye-witness accounts are lacking. So our examples will all have to be European.

The *Musée de Cluny* (hostel of the abbots of Cluny), opposite the Sorbonne in Paris, was completed in 1498 (in less than thirteen years) by Jacques d'Amboise, brother of the cardinal who was Louis XII's minister for a long time. It gave temporary shelter to Louis XII's very young widow, Mary of England, in 1515. The residence of the Guise family between 1553 and 1697 in the Marais district now holds the *Archives Nationales*, while in 1643-9 Mazarin lived in what is now the *Bibliothèque Nationale*. Jacques-Samuel, Comte de Coubert, son of Samuel Bernard (the richest merchant in Europe in Louis XIV's time) lived at 46, Rue du Bac a few metres away from the present-day Boulevard Saint-Germain, in a house built between 1741 and 1744. Nine years later in 1753 its owner went bankrupt and Voltaire was one of the victims.[38] If one goes to a beautifully preserved town like Cracow one can still visit the home of Prince Czartoryski, or that of the rich fourteenth-century merchant, Wierzynek, in whose house in the Market Square (the Rynek) it is still possible to dine today. In Prague, if one is prepared to lose the way inside, one can visit Wallenstein's immense and arrogant house on the banks of the Moldau. In Toledo, the museum of the Dukes of Lerma is probably more authentic than El Greco's house.

At a more modest level we can trace the plans of sixteenth-century Parisian apartments from the files of the legal Archives. Such dwellings were not, however, for everyone.[39] When their numbers increased – inordinately as it seemed to seventeenth- and eighteenth-century Parisians – the poor continued to be housed even more wretchedly than they are today, which is saying a great deal.

Furnished rooms in Paris, generally kept by wine merchants or wigmakers, were dirty, infested with fleas and bugs, and served as a home for prostitutes, delinquents, foreigners and penniless youths recently arrived from the country. The police searched them remorselessly. People who were scarcely better off lived in the new *entresols* (built on the cheap by the architects, 'like cellars') or on the top floors of houses. Normally the social condition of the lodger deteriorated the higher he climbed. Poverty was the rule on the sixth or seventh floors, in attics and garrets. Certain individuals managed to emerge from it; Greuze, Fragonard and Vernet lived like that and 'did not blush for it', but what became of the others? In 1782, in the 'faubourg Saint-Marcel', the worst district of all, 'a whole family [often] occupies one single room ... where the wretched beds have no curtains, where cooking utensils lie side by side with chamber pots'. When rent quarter came round there were many hasty and furtive removals. The Christmas quarter, in the winter cold, was particularly severe. 'A porter puts the sum total of a poor fellow's household possessions on his crochet: bed, mattress, chairs, table, cupboard, cooking utensils; he brings all his property down from a fifth floor [in one place] and takes it up to a sixth [in another] ... So true is it that there is as much money in a single house in the Faubourg Saint-Honoré [in about 1782] as in the whole of the Saint-Marcel district.' And the district was periodically exposed to flooding from the Bièvre, 'the river of the Gobelins'[40] It was the same story in the closely packed houses of small towns, like Beauvais: they were built of poor half-timbering, 'two up, two down and one family per room'.[41] Or the houses in Dijon, which 'are all at the back, having only a narrow façade on to the street', with pointed gables 'like dunces' caps', made of beams and plaster.[42]

Indeed the story was the same everywhere. In Dutch towns, even in Amsterdam, the poor were lodged in low houses or in basement rooms. These poor houses – which were the rule before the general prosperity of the seventeenth

1. HOUSE WITH TWO SETS OF BUILDINGS AND GALLERY, BELONGING TO THE HOTELIER JEAN ALAIRE

(Arch. Nat.; Mrn. Centr. XIX-269 9 July 1540)

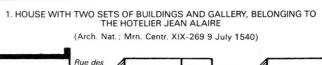
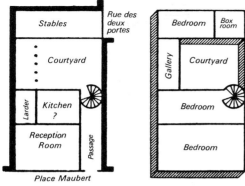
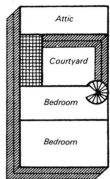

2. HOUSE WITH TWO SETS OF BUILDINGS, BELONGING TO NICOLAS BRAHIER. *PROCUREUR* AT THE CHATELET

(Arch. Nat.; Min. Centr. LIV-2 28 May 1528)

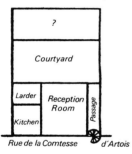
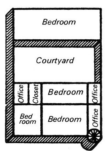
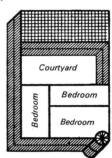

3. HOUSE WITH SINGLE BUILDING, BELONGING TO GEORGES DESQUELOT, APOTHECARY, HERBALIST

(Arch. Nat.; Min. Centr. CXXII-56 4 August 1541)

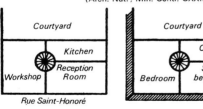

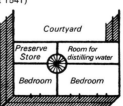

Ground floor   1st floor   2nd floor

A.N. = Archives Nationales, Paris
Min. Centr. = Minutier Central (legal records)

Diagram by E.P.H.E.

century – consisted of two rooms: 'the front room and the back room'. When wealth increased and houses became 'bourgeois', they generally only housed one family but they still had their narrow frontages. So they were extended in every possible way: upwards and downwards, in basements and upper storeys, in 'hanging rooms', in recesses and annexes. The rooms were linked by steps or narrow staircases like ladders.[43] Behind the drawing-room in Rembrandt's house was a bedroom with a bed in the alcove, where Saskia lay when she was ill.

The new luxury that came with the eighteenth century meant above all the separation of the living habitats of the rich. The poor felt its consequences, but that is another question. On the one hand there was the home, the place for eating, sleeping, bringing up children. Here, the woman had nothing to do but exercise her role as mistress of the house, which (given the abundance of manpower) was crowded with a chattering domestic staff working or pretending to work, disloyal, but also frightened: one word, one suspicion, one theft meant prison or even the gibbet. On the other hand there was the house where the man worked, the shop where he sold, or the office where he spent the best part of his days.[44] Until then there had been no such division: the master had his shop or his workshop in his own home, and housed his workmen and apprentices there. This gave merchants' and artisans' houses in Paris their characteristic form – narrow (in view of the price of land) and high: the shop was on the lower floors; the master's dwelling overhead, and above that the workmen's rooms. Similarly, in 1619, every baker in London had his children, his servants and his apprentices under his own roof. The group constituted the 'family', with the master baker at its head.[45] Even the king's secretaries in Louis XIV's reign sometimes had their ministerial offices in their own homes.

The change came in the eighteenth century. And we must assume that it came because of the very nature of large towns, since, oddly enough, we find the same thing in Canton (as well as in Paris and London): in the eighteenth century, Chinese merchants in communication with Europeans had their shops in one place, their houses in another. And the same was just as true of Peking, where well-to-do merchants would leave their shops every evening to return to the quarter where their wives and children lived.[46]

It is unfortunate for a fair appreciation of the world that we know so little of the evolution of life outside Europe. The plans and pictures we give of the houses of Islam, China and India may seem – indeed are – of no particular age. Even the towns – the reader should refer to what we have to say about Peking – do not yield up their real image, especially as the travellers who give us our information did not have Montaigne's meticulous curiosity: they chased after the great spectacles their potential readers expected, not the houses of Cairo, but the Pyramids; not the streets, shops or houses of notables in Peking or Delhi, but the forbidden imperial city with its yellow walls, and the palace of the Great Mogul.

The urbanized countryside

It is obvious, however, that on a world scale the division between town and country houses is too categorical. The two species come together in the dwellings of the rich, because – apart from a few changes like those which so spectacularly transformed English villages in the sixteenth and seventeenth centuries[47] – changes in the countryside were a reflection and a consequence of the wealth of the town. The town that had accumulated too much money invested it in the nearby countryside. It would have done so even if the rich had not been attracted by land, which carried a title to nobility, by the profitable or at least reliable income from rural jurisdiction, and by the comforts of seigneurial residences.

This return to the land was a prominent feature in the West. In the seventeenth century, when the economic situation changed, it became a craze. Noble and bourgeois property gradually spread out round the towns. Only outlying regions sheltered from these raging appetites remained archaic and peasant in character. For the town proprietor supervised his possessions, rents and rights; he drew corn, wine and poultry from his lands; occasionally he stayed there and often had part of the buildings reconstructed for his own use, joining up plots of land and making enclosures.[48]

The many seigneurial farms, landowners' dwellings and country houses

The Villa Medici in Trebbio in the Val di Sieve, a branch of the Arno, with its chapel, gardens and outbuildings: a fortified dwelling in the medieval style, which could serve as a refuge if necessary. It belonged to Giovanni delle Bande Nere (d. 1528) the father of Cosimo, first Grand Duke of Tuscany. (Photo Scala.)

around Paris can be accounted for in this way. So can the *bastides* in the Provençal countryside; or the Florentine residences which in the sixteenth century created a second and equally rich Florence outside the main town; or the Venetian residences in the Brenta valley that drained the old city of its resources. In the eighteenth century, urban palaces were scorned in favour of villas. The profit motive obviously played a part in all this, whether in the neighbourhood of Lisbon, Ragusa, Dijon, Marseilles, Bordeaux, Ulm, Nuremberg, Cologne, Hamburg, The Hague or London. Expensive residences were built throughout the English countryside in the eighteenth century. A 1779 miscellany[49] gives descriptions with reproductions of eighty-four of these 'castles', notably the Earl of Orford's seat at Houghton in Norfolk, begun by Walpole in 1722 and completed in 1735, with its immense rooms, marbles and galleries. One of the most beautiful journeys still to be made today is a search for eighteenth-century neo-classical villas in the outskirts of Naples, as far as Torre del Greco; from Barra to S. Giorgio, from Cremano to Portici in the vicinity of the Royal Palace; from Resina to Torre Annunziata. All these villas are luxurious, marvellous summer residences between the slopes of Vesuvius and the sea.

The urban colonization of the countryside, so obvious in the West, also occurred in other places; witness the residences built by the rich of Istanbul on both banks of the Bosporus,[50] or the *raïs* of Algiers on the Sahel hills, where the gardens are 'the most beautiful in the world'.[51] If the phenomenon is not as obvious in the Far East, it is because of the unsafe nature of the countryside, and more still the inadequacy of our documentation. A book by Bernardino de Escalante (1577) speaks (on the basis of what he had read and heard from other travellers) of the 'pleasure houses' of wealthy Chinese, 'with their gardens, groves of trees, aviaries, ponds'.[52] An ambassador from Moscow arriving in the neighbourhood of Peking in November 1693 admired 'a great number of pleasure houses, or magnificent castles, which belong to the mandarins and the inhabitants of the capital ... with a broad canal running in front of each house and a little stone bridge to cross by'.[53] This was an ancient tradition. A whole series of known Chinese texts, dating from at least the eleventh century, celebrate the charms and pleasures of these houses, in the midst of running water, always near an artificial pond with the 'purple and scarlet' blossoms of water lilies. To build up a library in such a place, to watch the swans or 'storks waging war against the fishes', or to 'stalk rabbits' and pierce them with arrows 'at the entrance to their holes' were among the greatest pleasures life had to offer.[54]

Interiors

Houses viewed from the outside are one thing, from within, another. Interiors are equally difficult to study though: we shall meet the same problems of classification and description in a frame of reference that must cover the whole world. Here again we can sketch the broad outlines of the picture by looking at what remains of it today, at things that are slow to change. Interiors change hardly at all in the world of the poor, wherever they are, or in static, inward-looking – that is poor – civilizations. Only the West is distinguished by uninterrupted change. Such is the ruler's privilege.

The lack of possessions of the poor

The first rule goes almost without saying: poor people had few possessions. If it is established for Europe, the richest civilization and the one most ready to change, it will apply *a fortiori* to the rest. The poor in the towns and countryside of the West lived in a state of almost complete deprivation. Their furniture consisted of next to nothing, at least before the eighteenth century, when a rudimentary luxury began to spread (chairs, where before people had been content with benches,[55] woollen mattresses, feather beds) together with decorative peasant furniture, painted or painstakingly carved, in certain regions. But this was still exceptional. Inventories made after death, which are reliable documents, testify almost invariably to the general destitution. Apart from a very small number of well-to-do peasants, the furniture of the day labourer and the small farmer in Burgundy even in the eighteenth century was identical in its poverty: 'the pot-hanger, the pot in the hearth, the frying pans, the *quasses* (dripping pans), the *meix* (for kneading bread) ... the chest, the bedstead with four pillars, the feather pillow and *guédon* (eiderdown), the bolster, sometimes a tapestry (cover) for the bed, the drugget trousers, the coat, the gaiters, a few tools (shovels, pickaxe)'. But before the eighteenth century, the same inventories mention only a few old clothes, a stool, a table, a bench, the planks of a bed, sacks filled with straw. Official reports for Burgundy between the sixteenth and the eighteenth centuries are full of 'references to people [sleeping] on straw ... with no bed or furniture' who were only separated 'from the pigs by a screen'.[56] And we can see it for ourselves. A picture by Adrien Brouwer (1605-38) shows four peasants singing in chorus in a poorly furnished room: a few stools, a bench and a barrel doing service as a table, on which is a dishcloth, a crust of bread and a jug. This was not by chance. Old barrels cut in half served all purposes in the village taverns, so dear to seventeenth-century Dutch painters. They were even cut away to form armchairs with backs. A canvas by J. Steen shows a young peasant being given a writing lesson by his mother, who stands near him; his desk is a plank laid over a barrel. And he did not even belong to the most wretched class, since the people around him knew how to read and write! A few words in an old thirteenth-century text provide another eloquent testimony: in Gascony, although 'rich in white bread and excellent red wine', the peasants 'seated round the fire, are accustomed to eat without a table and to drink out of the same goblet'.[57]

None of this should surprise us of course: poverty was all around. A typical French ordinance of 1669 orders the demolition of 'houses built on poles by vagabonds and useless members of society', on the edges of forests.[58] These huts are reminiscent of those built by a few Englishmen who escaped the plague of London in 1665-6 and took refuge in the woods.[59] The situation in the towns was just as depressing: in Paris, in the suburbs of Saint-Marcel and even Saint-Antoine, only a few craftsmen-joiners were comfortably off; in Le Mans and

'Russian soup': in this *isba* in the eighteenth century, there is hardly any furniture at all: just a cradle hanging from the ceiling. Engraving by Le Prince.
Bibliothèque Nationale, Paris, Cabinet des Estampes. (Photo B.N.)

Beauvais the weavers lived in penury. But in Pescara on the Adriatic, a small town with about a thousand inhabitants, an inquiry in 1564 revealed that three-quarters of the families in the town, who had come from the nearby mountains or from the Balkans, were virtually homeless, living in makeshift shelters (what we should call shanty-towns). And yet this was in a town which, although small, had its fortress, garrison, fairs, harbour, salt works and was, after all, situated in Italy in the second half of the sixteenth century when it was linked with the Atlantic and the wealth of Spain.[60] In the very rich town of Genoa, the homeless poor sold themselves as galley slaves every winter.[61] In Venice, poor wretches lived with their families on miserable boats, near the quays (the *fondamenta*) or under the bridges of the canals. They were the counterpart of the Chinese artisans who lived on board junks or sampans on the waterways of the cities, endlessly travelling upstream or down in search of work with their families, domestic animals and poultry.

Traditional civilizations and unchanging interiors

Rule number two: traditional civilizations remain faithful to their accustomed décor. A Chinese interior of the fifteenth century could equally well date from the eighteenth, if one ignores certain variations – porcelains, paintings and bronzes. The traditional Japanese house looked in the sixteenth or the seventeenth century much as it does today, except for the coloured prints that came in during the eighteenth century. The same applies to the Indies. And Muslim interiors of the past can be imagined from those of the present.

Non-European civilizations, except for the Chinese, were in any case poor in furniture. There were practically no chairs in India and no tables: in Tamil the word for table – *mecei* – derives from the Portuguese (*mesa*). There were no chairs in Black Africa where Benin artists were content to imitate European chairs. Neither were there chairs or for that matter high tables in Islam or the countries under its influence. An item in the invective against the Moriscoes in the *Antialcorán* by the Spanish writer Pérez de Chinchón (1532) is this odd claim to superiority: 'We Christians sit at a proper height, not on the ground like animals.'[62] In the Muslim part of Yugoslavia, in Mostar for instance, it was still normal some twenty years ago for guests to sit on cushions around a low table. The custom is still kept up in certain families attached to tradition, and in many villages.[63] In 1699, Dutch merchants were advised to take very strong paper to Muscovy; having few tables, the Russians wrote mostly on their knees and so had to have a tough type of paper.[64]

The West was not, of course, superior in every respect to the rest of the world. Other civilizations adopted ingenious solutions to the problems of housing and furniture that were often less expensive than the European. The East had various points of superiority to its credit: Islam had its public baths (though inherited from Rome); Japan had the elegance and cleanliness of its most ordinary interiors and the ingenuity of its storage space.

In spring 1699, Osman Aga passed through Buda (recaptured by the Christians in 1686) on his difficult journey home to freedom (he had been taken prisoner, or rather reduced to slavery by the Germans at the capture of Lipova ten years earlier). There, he was thoroughly happy to be able to make his way to 'the magnificent baths of the town'.[65] They were of course the Turkish baths on the bank of the Danube below the fortified town and had admitted everyone, without charge, since the time of the Ottoman domination.

Rodrigo Vivero[66] considered that the Japanese houses he saw in 1609 did not look as beautiful from the street as houses in Spain, but their interiors were more beautiful. Everything in the most modest Japanese house was put away first thing in the morning as if to be removed from inquisitive eyes – the cushions from the bed, for example. Straw mats were placed everywhere, the partitions of the rooms let in the light and everything was in order.

And yet, there were also considerable disadvantages. There was no heating. For the most part the sun had to provide that, as in Mediterranean Europe. But it did not always provide it very successfully. There was not even a fireplace in the whole of Turkish Islam (with the exception of the monumental fireplace in the Seraglio in Istanbul). A brazier was the only solution when supplies of charcoal for it were available. Muslim houses in present-day Yugoslavia are still without fireplaces. They did exist in Persia and in all the rooms of the rich, but in a narrow form 'because to avoid smoke and save wood, which is very expensive, the Persians burn it standing on end'.[67] Neither were there fireplaces in India or the Indian Archipelago (where they would not often have been necessary). Nor in Japan, though the cold there was acute: smoke from the hearth in the kitchen 'could escape only through a hole in the roof'; braziers were not very effective at heating the rooms which were not sealed against draughts,[68] and the baths taken by the Japanese in piping hot water, in the tubs heated by wood fires which every house possessed, were a way of keeping warm as much as keeping clean.

In northern China, on the other hand, which can be as cold as Siberia, the communal living-room was heated by 'lighting a fire in the small stove at the front of the platform at the back of the room, which was used for sleeping on. In the houses of rich people in Peking the stoves are bigger: they have pipes underneath the floors of the rooms and are stoked from outside' – a kind of central heating. But in poor houses, a primitive brazier was often the only form of heating: 'a charcoal stove.'[69] The same was also true of Persia where it could be very cold indeed.[70]

With few exceptions then, there was little or no heating – and almost no furniture. In Islam, there were a few chests made of precious cedar-wood, used to store clothing, materials and the household valuables. Low tables were occasionally in use, and sometimes large copper trays balanced on wooden frames. In Turkish and Persian houses, at least, recesses in the walls of the rooms

Chinese bowl from the early eighteenth century showing a scholar sitting on a chair in a pavilion and reading. Probably a scene from a novel. Musée Guimet, Paris. (Photo M. Cabaud.)

could be used as cupboards. But 'they have no beds or chairs as we do; no mirrors, tables, washstands, cupboards or pictures'. There was nothing but the mattresses which were laid out at night and put away in the morning, plenty of cushions and the beautiful woollen carpets of many colours, sometimes piled one on top of another[71] which have always been so passionately sought after in Christendom. These were the belongings of a race of nomads.

Istanbul museums contain little furniture: their treasures are of another kind: precious fabrics, often embroidered with stylized tulips; spiral glasses (known as nightingales' eyes); magnificent spoons made of rock crystal, ivory or pepper wood and encrusted with copper, silver, mother of pearl or coral; porcelains from Cyprus and China; magnificent jewellery; and two or three extraordinary thrones completely encrusted with rubies, emeralds, turquoises and pearls. A detailed inventory of the treasures seized from a Kurdish prince by the Turkish army in July 1655 and put up for auction gives the same impression: ivory, ebony and cedar-wood boxes; chests encrusted with precious stones; flagons of rose-water studded with gems; perfume-pans; books printed in the West; copies of the Koran in jewelled covers; calligraphy by famous artists; silver candlesticks; porcelains from China; agate cups; plates and bowls from Iznik; weapons worthy of the *Arabian Nights* – sabres with sought-after silver blades and golden scabbards; masses of solid silver; gold-embroidered saddles; hundreds of tiger skins and innumerable carpets.[72]

The double pattern of Chinese furniture

No sudden change occurred in China during the centuries which concern us, but one characteristic distinguished it from all other non-European countries – its abundant and refined furniture, its precious woods often imported from very far afield, lacquers, cupboards, cabinets with ingeniously contrived shelving, high and low tables, chairs, benches and stools, beds, generally with curtains, rather like those in the West in earlier days. Its most marked originality (because it implied a whole way of life) was certainly the use of a table, with chair, stool or bench. It should be noted, however, that this had not come down from primitive China. At the time when Japan borrowed and meticulously copied all the artefacts of the T'ang civilization of China (618–907), neither chair nor high table was to be found there. In fact present-day Japanese furniture exactly corresponds to ancient Chinese furniture: low tables, elbow-rests for arms to make the squatting position more comfortable, mats (the Japanese *tatami*) on platforms of varying heights, low storage furniture (cabinets and chests set beside each other), cushions. Everything is adapted to life at floor level.

Two ways of sitting down. The miniaturist, Persian copy of a portrait of a Turkish painter attributed to Gentile Bellini (1424–1507). J. Doucet collection. (Photo Giraudon.)

... And the writer, by Chardin (eighteenth century). Bibliothèque Nationale, Paris, Cabinet des Estampes. (Photo B.N.)

The chair probably arrived in China in the second or third century AD, but took a very long time to become a general item of furniture (the first known representation of it is in 535–40: a sculptured stele now in Kansas City Museum in the United States). It was probably European in origin, whatever detours it may have made to arrive in China (via Persia, India or northern China). Moreover, its original Chinese name, still current today, means 'barbarian bed'. It was probably first used as a seat of honour, either for lay or religious purposes. And even recently in China chairs were reserved for guests of honour and old people, while stools were used much more frequently, as in Europe in the middle ages.

But the important thing is the sitting-up position that chair and stool imply, and therefore a way of life unlike that of ancient China and the other Asiatic countries, indeed unlike all non-European countries. If the chair travelled via Persia or India, it met with no popular success on its way through those countries. But a thirteenth-century Chinese scroll, depicting a journey along a country road then through a Chinese town, shows high tables with benches and various seats both in the country inns and the town shops.

For China this acquisition corresponded to a new art of living, which was all the more original in that it did not exclude the old way of life. As a result, China possessed two forms of furniture, low furniture and high furniture. The large communal living-room, so characteristic of northern China, had two levels: on the lower level would be found chairs, stools and benches, alongside a high table and a high cupboard (sometimes with drawers, though the Chinese did not have chiffoniers or chests consisting entirely of drawers until much later, and then only occasionally, in imitation of nineteenth-century Europe). Furniture of the old or Japanese variety was arranged on the higher level, on a brick platform the height of a bench, above the other part of the room. This was the *kang*, heated by interior piping, covered with mats or felt, cushions and brightly coloured carpet, with a very low table and equally low cupboards and chests. This was where people slept in winter, protected from the cold, and where they received visitors, seated on the floor and drinking tea; here, the women sewed or wove their carpets. One took off one's shoes before going up on the *kang*, and wore only boots made of blue cloth with white padded soles (which self-respect demanded be always worn impeccably clean). Heating was not necessary in southern China but the two types of furniture were also to be found there. The scenes Father de Las Cortes sketched in the Canton region at the beginning of the seventeenth century show the Chinese seated on their chairs around a square table eating a meal. And the sedan chair he depicted was conceived on the same principle as the European sedan chair, however different its flimsy wood may have made it.

The rapid summary we have just given indicates but does not resolve the problems of what was, after all, a very striking change. To see it merely as the story of the chair and the numerous consequences of its introduction is one of those over-simple explanations that abound in past histories of technology. The reality was always much more complex (we will return to its broader implications in the following chapter). In fact, there must have taken place in China (some time before the thirteenth century) a major expansion of life-styles, accompanied by a separation between seated life and squatting life at ground level, the latter domestic, the former official: the sovereign's throne, the mandarin's seat, benches and chairs in schools. The subject would require research and analysis beyond our present scope; nevertheless it is worth while noting these two types of behaviour in the everyday life of the world: the seated position and the squatting position. The latter is omnipresent except in the West, and the two only came together in China. To find the origins of this behaviour in Europe would take us back to antiquity and the very roots of Western civilization.

We must be content for the present to sum it up in a few examples. As one might expect, the traveller in the Japanese ox-drawn cart had no seat. A Persian miniature shows a prince sitting cross-legged on a wide throne. Until very recently the Cairo cabman who sat with a bundle of straw in front of his seat pulled up his legs even though he could have stretched them out. Ultimately, an almost biological difference[73] is involved: resting on the heels in a kneeling position in the Japanese manner, sitting cross-legged as people do in Islam and

'Women of Hindustan', eating a meal; miniature illustrating Manucci's *History of India*. (Photo B.N.)

Turkey, or squatting as the Hindus so often do, is impossible or at best difficult for a European. And the Japanese regard our way of sitting as so surprising that they call it 'hanging up the legs'. Gemelli Careri found no seat in the Turkish or rather Bulgarian coach in which he was travelling from Gallipoli to Adrianople in the winter of 1693. 'As I was not at all accustomed,' he wrote, 'to being seated on the ground, legs crossed Turkish fashion, I was very uncomfortable in this carriage, which had no seats and was made in such a way that there is no European who would not have been likewise inconvenienced.' The same traveller two years later was in a palanquin in the Indies and 'obliged to keep stretched out as in a bed'.[74] An obligation which we would consider less of a hardship! But there were often no seats in the carriages in Peking either, and John Barrow grumbled like Gemelli Careri, 'They are to a European, who must sit on his haunches in the bottom, the most uneasy vehicle that can be imagined'.[75]

Only the Chinese were equally at home with both postures (though Chinese of Tartar origin made little use of chairs and tables as a rule; there was indeed a difference in life-style in Peking between the Tartar and Chinese quarters). A Frenchman who visited Peking in 1795 as a member of a Dutch embassy writes: 'The mandarins had assumed we would sit cross-legged on the floor. But seeing that we found this posture very uncomfortable, they took us into a great pavilion ... furnished with tables and chairs' in luxurious fashion. 'The platform had a thick carpet and they had lit a fire underneath.'[76] In the West, the superimposition of two cultures, the Iberian and the Islamic, resulted in a similar situation in Spain for a while. We have already mentioned a quotation from Pérez de Chinchón to the effect that the Muslims 'sit on the ground like animals'; he repeats the remark in another form, at first sight incomprehensible: 'they sit on the ground

A stag-hunt at Aranjuez in 1665: the ladies of the Court are present, sitting on cushions, Muslim-fashion. It was underneath the platform where the ladies are sitting that the animals would be driven by beaters and slaughtered. Detail of a painting by Martínez del Mazo, *La cacería del Tabladillo en Aranjuez*, Prado Museum. (Photo Mas.)

like women.' And indeed Spanish women did sit on the floor, on cushions, Arab-style, for a long time (until the seventeenth century). Hence the expression *tomar la almohadilla* (literally: to take the cushion) which signified that a lady of the Court had received permission to be seated in the queen's presence. In the days of Charles v, a platform furnished with cushions and low seats was reserved for women in reception rooms.[77] It was almost like being in China.

In Black Africa

Whether the poverty of individuals or the poverty of civilizations, the result was the same. In what I have called 'cultures',[78] both combined to give a double poverty; and this deprivation could be maintained for centuries. This was undoubtedly the case in Black Africa, as a brief inquiry quickly confirms.

There were no compact towns of the Western or Chinese type on the fringes of the Gulf of Guinea, where European trade had established itself and penetrated inland. The peasantry was if not unhappy (for how can one define that?) certainly deprived, as one can see from the earliest descriptions of villages in travellers' tales. The people lived in mud huts made with poles and reeds, 'round like dovecotes', seldom whitewashed, without furniture (except mud vases and baskets), without windows, carefully filled with smoke every night to drive out gnats, the *maringouins*, which stung painfully. 'Not everyone is accustomed as they are,' wrote Father Labat (1728), 'to be smoked like hams and to be smitten with a smell of smoke which makes people sick when they first start to associate with the Negroes.'[79] We need not pay too much attention to his squeamishness. After all, historians and sociologists in Brazil tell us (though no one is obliged to believe them) that runaway slaves living in the *sertão* (rough, open country) in independent republics, and even the town blacks in their urban hovels (*mucambos*), lived a healthier life in the nineteenth century than their masters on the plantations or in the towns.[80]

There were a few whitewashed huts alongside the ordinary huts in Africa, and this was already a luxury, however slight, compared with the common lot. The 'Portuguese-style' houses (so called because they derived from the ancient conquerors, whose language the 'princes' still spoke) marked an even greater progress, though there were very few of them. These houses had 'open vestibules', 'small very clean wooden stools' (so that visitors could sit down) and even tables; and certainly palm wine for special guests. It was in houses like these that the beautiful mulattas lived who held the hearts of the chiefs of the land or those of the rich English merchants, which amounted to the same thing. The courtesan who ruled over the 'king' of Barre was clad in 'a little satin bodice in the Portuguese style' and wore 'as a skirt, one of those beautiful loin cloths from the island of Saint Yague, one of the Cape Verde islands ... these are loin cloths of some consequence, as only distinguished people wear them; they are very beautiful and very fine'.[81] This interesting sidelight proves that the usual opposing modes were also to be found in the vast expanse of Africa – destitution and luxury.

The West and its many different types of furniture

Compared with China and the rest of the world, the characteristic of the West in matters of furniture and interior decoration was undoubtedly its taste for change, a relative rapidity of development which China never knew. In the West, everything was constantly changing. Not of course from one day to the next; but nothing escaped a complex evolution. Each new step in a museum takes one to a new room, a changed scene. The scene of course changed quite differently in the different regions of Europe; only the major transformations were common to all, over and above considerable time-lags, imitations, and the more or less conscious assimilations of other styles.

The common life of Europe thus consisted of a medley of obstinately different colours: the north was not the same as the south, the European West was not the New World, nor was the old Europe the same as the new – now expanding eastwards as far as wild Siberia. Furniture bears witness to these contrasts, affirming the identity of the small countries and the different social groups into which the Western world was divided. Finally, the furniture or rather the whole décor of houses bore witness to a broad economic and cultural movement carrying Europe towards what it itself christened the Enlightenment, progress.

Floors, walls, ceilings, doors and windows

Everything in the familiar setting of our present-day lives can be seen, if one thinks about it, as a heritage, an ancient acquisition: the desk I write on, the linen cupboard, the paper pasted on the walls, the seats, the wooden floor, the plaster ceiling, the arrangement of the rooms, the fireplace, staircase, the ornaments, engravings and pictures. I can mentally reconstruct the ancient evolution from a simple present-day interior and as it were run the film backwards to take the reader back towards ancient luxuries which were, however ancient, slow to emerge. This will at least fix the landmarks, outline the main points of a history of furniture.

A room for human habitation has always had four walls, a ceiling, a floor, one or more windows and one or more doors.

For a long time, floors at ground level were made of beaten earth: later they were paved or tiled. Ancient miniatures often show magnificent tiling – an inexpensive luxury. Inlaid tiles were in use in the fourteenth century. 'Leaded' tiles (covered with an enamel with a graphite base) appeared in the sixteenth. By the seventeenth, ceramic tiling was everywhere, even in modest homes. Nevertheless there was no mosaic, at least in France, before the end of the seventeenth century. As for parquet in the modern sense, it appeared in the fourteenth century but only became really fashionable in the eighteenth, with many variations (bonded parquets, inlaid, in Hungarian points).[82] The need for wood increased. Voltaire could write: 'Once oaks used to rot in the forests; today they are made into parquet floors.'

Ceilings were originally only the boarding of the floor above or the attic, with exposed beams and joists left bare in ordinary houses, planed down, decorated or concealed in richer dwellings. In the early seventeenth century, the fashion spread from Italy of enclosing the beams in wooden cases which might be carved, gilded or painted with scenes from mythology. The taste for light-coloured ceilings only came with the eighteenth century. Plaster and stucco covered up the wooden timbers and in some old houses one can still find underneath their successive layers the beams that were painted with flowers and emblems three hundred years ago.[83]

The most curious ancient custom, which continued until the sixteenth cen-

Houses, Clothes and Fashion 295

tury (and even later), was to cover the floors of the ground-floor rooms and the bedrooms with straw in winter and herbs and flowers in summer. 'The Rue du Fouarre, cradle of our Faculties of Letters and Sciences, owes its name to the straw with which the floors of the lecture rooms used to be covered.'[84] The same custom prevailed in royal residences. Care was taken at a banquet given by the town of Paris for Catherine de Medici in June 1549 to 'scatter the room with fine aromatic herbs'.[85] A picture (1581-2) of the ball on the duc de Joyeuse's wedding night shows the floor strewn with flowers. All the same, these flowers, herbs and rushes had to be changed. This was not always the case in England, at least according to Erasmus, so that dirt and refuse tended to collect there. Despite such disadvantages, a doctor still recommends the use of scattered green herbs in 1613, 'in a handsome room, well-matted or hung with tapestries all round and paved below with rosemary, pennyroyal, oregano, marjoram, lavender, sage and other similar herbs'.[86] The straw and herbs, with rushes or swordgrass arranged decoratively along the walls, disappeared before the woven straw mats which had always been known and were made in varied colours,

A bourgeois interior, southern Germany, in the fifteenth century. Anonymous master, Bâle, Kunstmuseum. (Photo Oeffentliche Kunstsammlung, Basel.)

with arabesques. They were soon replaced in turn by carpets. Thick and brightly coloured, they covered the ground, tables (right down to the floor), chests, and even the tops of cupboards.

Flowers and rushes on the walls of rooms (painted with oils or size) gave way to tapestries which could 'be made from all sorts of material, such as velvet, damask, brocade, brocatelle, Bruges satin, caddis'. But Savary (1762) recommends that the description 'tapestry' should perhaps be limited to 'Bergamot tapestries, gilded leathers (the *guadameciles* of Spain, known for centuries), tapestries made from wool shearings in Paris and Rouen, and other tapestries of quite new invention made of thick woven cloth where the figures and landscapes of high-warp tapestry are well copied in various colours'.[87] The fashion for these high-warp tapestries with figures goes back to the fifteenth century and is ascribed to the craftsmen of Flanders. The Gobelins workshops later brought them to technical perfection. But their high production costs were against them; in addition furniture, which became more widespread in the eighteenth century, limited their use: a chest of drawers or sideboard placed in front of them and as Sébastien Mercier explained, there were your beautiful figures cut in two.

Wallpaper (it was known as *domino*) made definite progress, helped by its cheapness. It was printed by *dominotiers*, by the same process used to make playing-cards.

> This type of paper tapestry ... had for a long time only been used by country folk and the common people in Paris to decorate and to hang here and there in their huts, shops and rooms; at the end of the seventeenth century, however, it had been brought to such a degree of perfection and attractiveness that in addition to the large consignments sent to foreign countries and the principal towns of the realm there is no house in Paris, however magnificent, which has not got somewhere, either closet or some still more secret place, hung with it and quite pleasantly decorated (1762).[88]

Besides, wallpaper was invariably found at the level of the attics, sometimes very simple with black and white stripes. For there was wallpaper and wallpaper: not all was like the expensive specimen (1770) in the Munich National Museum, which is in the Chinese style.

Occasionally walls were also covered with wood panelling. From the fourteenth century, English joiners had produced panels in Danish oak to cover walls and combat the cold.[89] Examples range from the neat and simple panels found in the small study of one of the Fugger's houses (sixteenth century) in Germany, to the large, lavishly carved, painted and gilded panels of eighteenth-century French salons, whose décor served as a model for all Europe, Russia included.

From walls, let us turn to doors and windows. Until the seventeenth century, doors were narrow, opened inwards and only let one person at a time pass through. Large double doors came later. Windows were often, in their earliest form, simple solid wood shutters, as we can see from peasant dwellings even in the eighteenth century. When the leaded glass window, the privilege of the church, spread to houses, the irregular glass set in lead was too heavy and also too valuable for the leaf to be movable. The problem was solved in various ways: in Germany a single opening leaf in a window with fixed glass was used. The Dutch solution combined fixed glazed panels with movable wooden panels. In France, the glazed frames were often fixed; Montaigne noted that 'what makes the glass [in Germany] shine so brightly is that they have no fixed windows in our fashion', so that they can 'polish them very often'.[90] Some opening windows also had panes made of parchment, canvas treated with turpentine, oiled paper or sheets of gypsum. It was really only in the sixteenth century that transparent panes appeared, and they spread only haphazardly. Their progress was rapid in England, for instance, where peasant houses had glass panes in the 1560s with the increase in agricultural prosperity and the development of the glass industry.[91] But at about the same time (1556) Charles V, who was coming from Flanders to Estremadura, was anxious to buy panes of glass before reaching the journey's end.[92] Montaigne, on the road to Germany, noted that from Epinal onwards, 'there is no village house however small, that has not glazed windows'.[93] And the Strasburger Brackenhoffer[94] said the same thing sixty years later of Nevers and Bourges. But two travellers from the Netherlands to Spain in 1633 noticed a southern demarcation line: after crossing the Loire at Saumur, they saw no more glass in the windows of the houses.[95] Meanwhile further east, in Geneva, at about the same time, even the grandest houses were content to use paper[96] and even in 1779, when glass was letting the daylight in to the rooms of the humblest Parisian workers, oiled paper was still being used in Lyons and certain provinces, particularly for silk workers according to our informant, because the light it gave was 'softer'.[97] Panes of glass were not commonly seen in Serbia until the nineteenth century, and they were still a rarity in Belgrade in 1808.[98]

Another feature slow to disappear was the use of several wooden crosspieces, necessary because of the small size of the panes and the weight of the frame. It was not until the eighteenth century that large windows became the general rule, at least in the houses of the rich.

Painters, as we would expect, offer plenty of varied evidence of this belated modernization. There was never at any given moment a typical Dutch-style window common to the whole of Europe, with fixed panes (upper part) and opening solid wood (lower part). There is such a window in an Annunciation by Schöngauer, but another painted at the same period only has one narrow panel of opening glass; yet another has an external wooden shutter closing over the fixed window. The wooden leaf could be either double or single. Sometimes there were curtains inside, sometimes none. All in all, there were many solutions to the problem of ventilating and lighting houses, and also of mitigating the effects of cold and stopping daylight disturbing the sleeper. Everything depended on climate and custom. Montaigne was not pleased that in Germany he had no 'defence against the evening dew or the wind except ordinary glass, which was

The Spanish *brasero*. The birth of St Eloy by P. Nunyes (detail). Museo de Arte de Catalunya, Barcelona. (Photo Mas.)

not in any way covered with wood' (therefore without external or internal shutters), and moreover the beds in German inns had no curtains![99]

Chimneys and fireplaces

There were no fireplaces set in the wall before about the twelfth century. Until then, the round hearth in the centre of the room was used only for cooking. Braziers or *'chaufferettes'* were used for warmth.[100] But from Venice, whose tall chimneys have so often been painted by artists, to the North Sea, and from Muscovy to the Atlantic, chimneys very quickly became established in the main room of the house, where everyone took refuge from the cold.

At first the hearth had a brick base; later, in the seventeenth century, a metal plate. Andirons supported the logs. A vertical cast-iron plate called the backplate and often decorated (some were very beautiful) stood on the hearth. In the chimney itself the pothanger, which enabled a pot – or more often a cauldron in which water was kept permanently hot – to be hung over the fire, was attached to a ring and equipped with notches allowing adjustments of height. Cooking was done on the hearth in front of the fire near the flames, or glowing embers were used to cover the lid of an iron pan. Frying pans with long handles made it possible to use the hottest part of the fire in comfort.

In rich households the fireplace naturally became the main decorative element of a room. Mantels were decorated with bas-reliefs, hoods with frescoes, and bases were moulded to terminate in consoles or capitals with human heads. The hood of a Bruges chimney dating from the end of the fifteenth century was decorated with an Annunciation from the school of Gérard David.[101]

But these beautiful fireplaces long remained of very rudimentary design, technically much like those of peasant households at the beginning of the twentieth century: the vertical flue, which was too wide, with room for two chimney-sweeps at a time, caused such draughts that anyone sitting by the fire was likely to be roasted on one side and frozen on the other. Hence the tendency to build fireplaces ever bigger, so that stone seats could be set in on either side of the hearth under the hood.[102] It was here that people could sit when the fire had died down to its embers, and chat 'under the mantel'.

Such a system may possibly have been acceptable for cooking, but it was a deplorable means of heating. The area round the fire offered the only refuge in a cold house when winter set in. The two fireplaces at the extremities of the Hall of Mirrors at Versailles did not succeed in heating its enormous expanse. It was advisable to wear furs for added protection. But even they were hardly sufficient. On 3 February 1695 the Princess Palatine wrote: 'At the king's table the wine and water froze in the glasses.' The detail (there are many more that could be cited) is enough to evoke the discomfort of a seventeenth-century house. Cold weather, at that period, could be a public disaster, freezing rivers, halting mills, bringing packs of dangerous wolves out into the countryside, multiplying epidemics. When the severity of the weather increased, as in Paris in 1709, 'the people died of cold like flies' (2 March). In the absence of heating since January (again according to the Princess Palatine) 'all entertainments have ceased as well as law suits'.[103]

But everything changed in about 1720: 'Since the Regent, we can claim that we manage to keep warm during the winter.' It was achieved as a result of an advance in 'caminology' for which chimney-sweeps and stove-setters were responsible. The secrets of the 'draught' had been discovered. The hearth of the chimney was made narrower and deepened, the mantel lowered, the chimney shaft curved, as the straight chimney had had a persistent tendency to smoke.[104] (One wonders how the great Raphael was able to cope with his appointed task of preventing the Duke of Este's chimneys from smoking.) With a better draught it was possible to heat reasonably sized rooms – not the apartments in Mansard's palaces, but certainly those in the town houses built by Gabriel. Chimneys with several hearths (at least two, said to be in the style of Popelinière) even made it possible to heat the servants' quarters. A revolution in heating thus belatedly took place.

But we must not suppose that there was any saving in fuel (as a book called *L'épargne-bois* had foreseen a century earlier in 1619). Having become more efficient, hearths increased astonishingly in number. Before winter set in, every town was filled with the activity of transporting and sawing up wood for heating. In Paris from the middle of October on the very eve of the Revolution:

> There is a new problem in all districts of the town. The roads are cluttered up with thousands of carts laden with wood, which, as it is thrown down, sawn up and transported, puts all passers-by in danger of being crushed, bowled over or having their legs broken. The carters unload roughly and hurriedly, throwing the logs off the top of the cart. The cobbles resound. Deaf and blind to everything, the men only want to unload their wood promptly, to the danger of passing heads. Then comes the sawyer, plies his saw rapidly and throws the wood around him, without taking heed of anybody.[105]

The same performance was repeated in every town. In Rome the wood merchant offered to deliver his merchandise to the door by donkey-cart. Although Nuremberg was situated amidst vast and accessible forests, an order of 24 October 1702 bade the peasants within its jurisdiction deliver half their stocks of wood to its market.[106] And in the streets of Bologna, the log-splitter was plying for hire.

Furnaces and stoves

Montaigne rather hastily asserted that there were 'no fireplaces' in Germany. Specifically, there were no fireplaces in the bedrooms or living-rooms of inns. There was always one in the kitchen. But Germans 'do not like anyone going into their kitchens'. The traveller could only warm himself in the vast living-room where meals were taken and where the earthenware stove, the *Kachelhofen*[107] stood. The chimney did not fit 'our style of life': 'They build hearths in the middle or in the corner of a kitchen and the chimney shaft runs along almost its whole width; it is a large opening, seven or eight feet square and ending right at the top of the building; this gives them the space to accommodate in one place their large sail, which in our houses would take up so much space in our shafts as to prevent the passage of the smoke.'[108] This 'sail' or smoke-jack was like a small windmill which moved as the smoke and hot air rose, and caused the spit to turn. A glance at the illustration on p. 302 will tell the reader more about German stoves, if not about this particular mechanism, at least about the spit, the high oven and advantages of being able to do the cooking without bending down as one had to in France, Geneva[109] or the Netherlands.

Stoves were also found well beyond Germany – in Hungary, Poland, Russia and soon in Siberia. They were ordinary ovens made of stone, brick and sometimes clay. In Germany, from the fourteenth century, the furnace was built in a lighter material – potters' clay (*Töpferthon*). The earthenware tiles covering it

Woman in front of the stove, etching by Rembrandt, Holland, seventeenth century. Bibliothèque Nationale, Paris, Cabinet des Estampes. (Photo B.N.)

were often decorated. A bench stood in front for sitting or sleeping upon. Erasmus explained (1527): 'In the stove [that is in the room it heated] you take off your boots, you put on your shoes, you change your shirt, if you wish; you hang up your clothes, damp from the rain, near the fire and you draw near to dry yourself.'[110] 'At least,' as Montaigne said, 'you burn neither your boots nor your face and you are free of the smoke of France.'[111] In the private houses in Poland, where all travellers had to stay since there were no inns, Francis of Pavia and all his family, as well as passing guests, slept on wide benches covered with pillows and furs, set all round the room in which the stove was kept. The Italian gentleman Octavian took advantage of this arrangement, choosing a place near one or other of the women of the house 'by whom he was sometimes well received and sometimes got his face scratched' – all in silence of course, without waking anyone else![112]

Stoves made of glazed earthenware only appeared in France in about 1520, five years after Marignan. Their success began in the seventeenth century and was consolidated in the next. Fireplaces were still rare in Paris in 1571.[113] It was often necessary to use a brazier for warmth. The poor of Paris continued to use braziers in the eighteenth century. They burned coal in them, which gave rise to frequent cases of poisoning by fumes.[114] Fireplaces finally played a larger role in France than stoves, which continued to be used more in the cold eastern and northern countries. Sébastien Mercier noted in 1788: 'What a difference between a stove and a fireplace! The sight of a stove extinguishes my imagination.'[115]

In Spain, there were neither stoves nor fireplaces 'in any of the apartments ... They only use braziers'. The comtesse d'Aulnoy, who tells us this adds: 'it is lucky that in a country like this which is short of wood, they do not need it'.[116]

As for England, it occupies a special place in the history of chimneys, since from the sixteenth century on, the shortage of wood led to the increased use of coal as a fuel. This in turn brought about a series of developments in fireplaces, of which the most important was Rumford's design, which was devised so as to reflect the heat into the room.[117]

Cooking without bending down: the German fireplace with raised hearth (1663). From the *Mendelsche Bruderbucher* (*Books of the Companions of the Mendel Foundation*), Stadtbibliotek Nurnberg, Nuremberg. (Photo Armin Schmidt.)

Furniture makers and the vanities of buyers

Interiors and furniture never changed very quickly, however pronounced the taste for change amongst the rich. Fashion evolved, but in slow motion. There were several reasons. The expense occasioned by renovation and refurnishing was enormous; more important, production possibilities remained limited. The mechanical saw worked by water did not exist until at least 1250;[118] no material except oak was in general use until the sixteenth century, when the fashion for walnut and exotic woods began in Antwerp. More important still, everything depended on the crafts, which developed slowly. Joiners – who worked on smaller-scale pieces – became independent from carpenters between the fifteenth and the sixteenth centuries; then cabinet-makers, long called 'marquetry and veneering joiners', appeared from the ranks of the joiners themselves, in the seventeenth century.[119]

Carpenters had produced furniture and houses for centuries on end. The result was the large scale, the solidity and a certain unashamed roughness of 'Gothic' furniture – heavy cupboards hung from walls, enormous narrow tables, benches more often than stools or chairs, chests made from large, ill-squared planks 'fitted together with a flat joint and held by nailed iron bands' with heavy locks.[120] Such things were storage quite as much as furniture. Planks were smoothed with an axe: the plane, an old tool known in Egypt, Greece and Rome, only resumed its role in northern Europe in the thirteenth century. Planks were joined with iron nails. Mortise and tenon and dovetail joints slowly reappeared later, then wooden nails, pegs (a late technique), and iron screws, always known but never fully utilized until the eighteenth century.

All the tools – axes, hatchets, chisels, mallets, hammers, crossbow-lathes (for large pieces; to turn the foot of a table, for example), handle- or pedal-lathes (for fine pieces) – had always been known and were in fact a heritage from far back, before the Roman world.[121] The ancient tools and processes had been preserved in Italy, where there exists the only furniture we have dating from before 1400. There again, Italy had a lead and an advantage; it produced and propagated furniture, models for furniture and means of constructing furniture. For proof of this one need only look at the sixteenth-century Italian chests in the National Museum in Munich. With their complicated carving, stands, polished wood and sophisticated shapes, they are very different from chests of the same period in the rest of Europe. The drawers that belatedly appeared north of the Alps also arrived from the south via the Rhine valley. They only reached England in the fifteenth century.

It was the general practice until the sixteenth century and on into the seventeenth to paint furniture, ceilings and walls. We have to imagine the ancient furniture with its carvings painted gold, silver, red and green, in palace, house and church alike. It indicates a desperate hunger for light and bright colours in poorly lit, dark interiors. Furniture was sometimes covered with a fine cloth and plaster before it was painted so that the colour should not bring out any of the faults in the wood. Objects began to be plainly waxed and varnished at the end of the sixteenth century.

How can we follow the complicated biography of each of these pieces of furniture? They appeared, changed, but scarcely ever disappeared, constantly sustaining the tyrannies of architectural style and the arrangement of interiors.

The habit of placing the bench in front of the fireplace probably gave rise to the narrow rectangular table; the guests sat on only one side of it, 'with their backs to the fire and their stomachs to the table'. According to the legend of King Arthur, the round table overcame the problem of precedence. But round tables could only become popular when there were chairs to go with them, and chairs were late acquiring their form and production on any large scale. The earliest were monumental singletons reserved for the medieval seigneur; other people made do with benches and stools. Chairs for them only came much later.[122]

Society – we might as well say vanity – was the arbiter in this matter of furniture. For example, the dresser started life in the kitchen as an ordinary table on which were placed the dishes and loads of crockery required to serve a meal. In seigneurial houses a second dresser made its way into the drawing-room: on it were displayed the gold, silver and vermeil services, the bowls, *aiguières* and goblets. Etiquette prescribed the number of shelves it should have according to the status of the master of the house – two for a baron, the number increasing with rank.[123] A painting which takes as its subject the feast of Herod shows a dresser with eight rows, marking the supreme royal dignity. The dresser finally moved out to the street itself on Corpus Christi day 'in front of the tapestries with which the houses were hung'. An English traveller, Thomas Coryate, was amazed to see so many dressers with silverware in 1608 in the streets of Paris.[124]

To take another example, it is possible to trace the history of cupboards, from the heavy ancient cupboards strengthened with iron bands to the seventeenth-century models already becoming 'bourgeois' (according to a historian who has no great love for the 'frontons, entablatures, columns and pilasters' of the Louis XIII style).[125] Cupboards were by this time often reaching considerable proportions, sometimes so vast that it was desirable to cut them in half. This created a new piece of furniture, the low cupboard, which never became really popular. Cupboards thus became a piece of ostentation, occasionally richly carved and embellished. They lost this role in the eighteenth century, at least in luxurious houses and, relegated to the function of wardrobes, no longer appeared in reception rooms.[126] But for centuries on end they remained the pride of peasant and working-class homes.

Importance and then insignificance; fashion moved relentlessly on, as one sees in the case of the cabinet, a piece of furniture with drawers or compartments to hold toilet articles, writing equipment, packs of cards and jewellery. There are examples of it in the Gothic style. Its popularity began in the sixteenth

Fifteenth-century dresser with gold vessels. Histoire du Grand Alexandre, f° 88. Paris, Musée du Petit-Palais. (Photo Bulloz.)

century. Renaissance cabinets decorated with *pietra dura* and German-style cabinets both enjoyed a vogue in France. Some of the cabinets in the time of Louis XIV were very large. In the eighteenth century the *secrétaire* was launched on its successful career.

It is perhaps even more instructive to follow the fortunes of the chest-of-drawers, which would soon take pride of place. This was the piece of furniture that really ousted the cupboard. It first appeared in France at the very beginning of the eighteenth century. And just as the appearance of Breton peasant chests, and certain Milanese furniture, suggests that the first cupboards were probably chests stood on end, the idea behind the chest-of-drawers was probably that of several small chests placed on top of each other. But both idea and achievement came rather late in time.

Launched by a new fashion into a century of refined elegance, the chest-of-drawers was immediately an item of luxury furniture. Its shape – rectilinear or curved, straight or bulging, bulky or slim – the marquetry, precious woods, bronzes and lacquers, closely followed the dictates of changing fashion, including the vogue for *chinoiserie*, displaying all the differences between the Louis XIV, Louis XV and Louis XVI styles with which we are familiar. Whether a simple piece of furniture or a rich man's luxury, the chest-of-drawers only came into general use in the nineteenth century.

But are the several histories of these items of furniture really the history of furnishing?

The domestic interior seen whole

However characteristic it may be, one piece of furniture does not reveal a whole picture; and the whole picture is what matters most.[127] Museums, with their isolated objects, generally only teach the basic elements of a complex history. The essential is not contained within these pieces of furniture themselves but is in their arrangement, whether free or formal, in an atmosphere, an art of living both in the room containing them and outside it, in the house of which the room is a part. How then did people live, eat and sleep in these furnished interiors of the past – which were of course havens of luxury?

The first precise evidence concerns late Gothic, and comes to us through Dutch and German pictures in particular, where furniture and objects are painted as lovingly as people, like a series of still lives. The Birth of Saint John by Jan van Eyck or an Annunciation by van der Weyden give a concrete idea of the atmosphere of the fifteenth-century living-room. A door open on to the succession of other rooms is enough to conjure up the kitchen or the bustle of the servants. It is true that the subject helps – Annunciations and Nativities, whether by Carpaccio, the older Holbein or Schöngauer, with their beds, chests, a beautiful open window, a bench in front of the fireplace, the wooden tub in which the new-born child is bathed, the bowl of soup carried to the woman after her confinement, are as evocative of the domestic scene as the subject of the Last Supper is of mealtime ritual.

Despite the very few pieces of furniture and their robust rusticity, these late Gothic homes have, at least in northern countries, the warm intimacy of very cosy rooms, enclosed in folds of luxurious fabrics in bright and iridescent colours. Their only real luxuries are the curtains and covers for the beds, hangings on the walls and silky cushions. Fifteenth-century tapestries with their pure colours and luminous backgrounds strewn with flowers and animals also bear witness to this taste, this need for colour. It was as though the houses of the period were a response to the external world and like 'the cloister, the fortified castle, the walled town, the walled garden' acted as a protection against the dimly apprehended difficulties of material life.

However, once Renaissance Italy, the most economically advanced region of Europe, began to produce the new and magnificent settings for princely courts, a completely different framework began to appear. It was solemn and more formal; its architecture and furniture (which repeated the same motifs and the same monumental lines in pediments, cornices, medallions and sculptures) aimed at a kind of social magnificence, at the grandiose. Fifteenth-century Italian interiors, with their colonnades, immense carved and canopied beds and monumental staircases, already give a strange foretaste of the *Grand Siècle* of Louis XIV, and of that court life which was to be a sort of parade, a theatrical spectacle. Luxury was already unquestionably becoming a means of government.

Let us jump two hundred years. In the seventeenth century, the decoration of the house sacrificed everything to fashion, to social significance – in France, England and even the Catholic Netherlands. (There were of course exceptions including Germany and Holland, where greater simplicity was the rule.) Reception-rooms became immense, with very high ceilings, more open to the exterior, deliberately solemn, with a superabundance of ornaments, sculptures, decorative

A bourgeois interior in Holland, seventeenth century: lightness and order, a large communal room containing both a harpsichord and a four-poster bed; and a series of rooms opening off each other. Boymans van Benningen, Rotterdam. (Photo A. Frequin.)

furniture (buffets, heavily carved sideboards), which supported equally decorative pieces of silverware. Plates, dishes and pictures hung on the walls, and the walls themselves were painted with complex motifs (as in the Rubens room with its decoration of grotesque figures). Tapestries, always in high favour, had changed their style and were also moving towards a certain grandiloquence and costly, subtle complication.

All the same, the grand reception-chamber was still an all-purpose room: in the same hall, with its imposing décor which appears in so many Flemish paintings from Van de Bassen to Abraham Bosse or Hieronymus Janssen, the guests are shown gathering for a lavish banquet while the bed stands heavily curtained, usually near the fireplace. And seventeenth-century luxury was not aware of thousands of amenities – heating for a start. Neither did it recognize privacy. When Louis XIV himself, in his palace at Versailles, wanted to visit Madame de Montespan, he had to go through the bedroom of Mademoiselle de la Vallière, the previous royal favourite.[128] Similarly, in a Parisian town house of the seventeenth century, on the first floor, which was the noble storey, reserved for the owners of the house, all the rooms – antechambers, salons, galleries and bedrooms – opened off each other and were sometimes hard to tell apart. Everyone, including servants on domestic errands, had to go through them to reach the stairs.

Privacy was an eighteenth-century innovation. Not that Europe abandoned fashionable display at that time; it made even greater sacrifices for the sake of social appearances. But the individual was soon to have his revenge. Housing and furniture changed because individuals wanted them to and because the large town favoured their inclination. In the rapidly growing towns – London, Paris, St Petersburg – everything became more and more expensive, luxury unrestrained. Space was in short supply and architects had to utilize to the maximum limited spaces bought at sky-high prices.[129] The modern town house, the modern apartment, conceived for a less grandiose but also a more agreeable life, then became indispensable. An advertisement from the reign of Louis XV offers a rented apartment in Paris 'with ten rooms, divided into an ante-chamber, dining room, reception room, second reception room arranged for winter [therefore with heating], a small library, a small social room and bedrooms with closets'.[130] Such an advertisement would have been unthinkable in Louis XIV's time.

As a contemporary author explained, from now on a house was divided into three kinds of apartment: reception rooms for polite society, where one could entertain one's friends agreeably; the public room for display and ostentation; and the private or family apartments.[131] With this subdivision of the household, people could choose more how they would live. The pantry was distinct from the kitchen, the dining-room from the drawing-room; the bedroom was established as a realm apart. Lewis Mumford thinks that from being a summer activity love then became an all-the-year-round pastime![132] We do not need to believe him (dates of births in the records even prove the contrary) but it is true that in

Flemish interior, seventeeth century: this immense reception room, with its heavy and luxurious décor, contains everything: huge fireplace, four-poster bed, the table at which the guests are feasting. Paris, Musée des Arts Décoratifs. (Photo by the museum.)

about 1725 there came about an 'internal allocation of apartments' which had not existed in Rome, or in Tuscany under the Medicis, or in France under Louis XIV. This new disposition of rooms, 'which arranges an apartment so skilfully and makes it more convenient for both master and servant'[133] was not simply a matter of fashion. 'Small houses with more sections [rooms], are more convenient; one has a lot of things in little space.'[134] 'Our small apartments,' wrote Sébastien Mercier, 'are fashioned and arranged like round and polished seashells, and one lives with light and pleasure in spaces hitherto lost and really quite dark.'[135] 'Moreover', added a sage, 'the ancient manner [immense houses] would be too dear; nowadays people are not rich enough.'[136]

To compensate, the desire for luxury turned towards furniture: an infinity of finely wrought delicate pieces, less clumsy than the old furniture, adapted to the new dimensions of boudoir, drawing-room and bedchamber, but also highly specialized to meet the new requirements of comfort and intimacy. This was when all those little tables began to appear – the gaming tables, card tables, night tables, bureaux, centre tables, dumb waiters, etc., as well as the chest-of-drawers in the early years of the century and whole range of soft armchairs. In France, new names were invented for all these novelties: the *bergère, marquise, duchesse, turquoise, veilleuse, voyeuse, athénienne, fauteuil cabriolet* or *volant*.[137] The same taste was employed on ornamentation: sculpted and painted panelling, sumptuous and sometimes top-heavy silver decorations, bronze and lacquer in the Louis xv style, exotic and precious woods, mirrors, mouldings and chandeliers, pier-glasses, silk hangings, Chinese vases and German crockery. This was the age of the Franco-German rococo which in one way or another influenced the whole of Europe; the age of the great English collectors, of the stucco arabesques of a Robert Adam, and of the joint reign of *chinoiserie* and what was described as Gothic ornamentation 'in a happy mixture of the two styles' as an article in *The World* put it in 1774.[138] In short, the new simplicity in architecture did not lead to sobriety of decoration, indeed the reverse. The grandiose had disappeared; but it was often replaced by the fussy.

Luxury and comfort

Such luxury seems all the more false to us because it was not always accompanied by what we would call comfort. Heating was still poor, ventilation derisory, cooking done in a rustic manner, sometimes on a portable charcoal stove. Apartments did not always include English-style water-closets, although Sir John Harington had invented them in 1596. When they did exist, the house still had to be cleared of pestilential odours, which called for the perfecting of the valve and siphon, or at the least the ventilating stack.[139] The problems posed by the defective emptying of cesspools in Paris even worried the Academy of Sciences in 1788. And chamber pots, as always, continued to be emptied out of windows; the streets were sewers. For a long time Parisians 'relieved themselves under a row of yews' in the Tuileries; driven from there by the Swiss guards, they betook themselves to the banks of the Seine, which 'is equally revolting to eye and nose'.[140] This picture is from Louis xvi's reign. And it was more or less the same in all towns, large and small, from Liège to Cadiz, from Madrid to the little towns of the Haute-Auvergne, which usually had a stream or canal running through the middle, known as the 'merderel', which took 'everything that was put into it'.[141]

A bathroom was a very rare luxury in these seventeenth- and eighteenth-century houses. Fleas, lice and bugs conquered London as well as Paris, rich interiors as well as poor. As for lighting, candles and oil lamps continued to be used in houses until the blue flame of gas lighting appeared in about 1808. But even the thousands of ingenious methods of early lighting from torch to lantern, sconce, flat candlestick or chandelier, as we see them in old pictures, were late in coming. A study has established that in Toulouse they only really became widespread in about 1527.[142] Until then lighting had been almost non-existent. And one paid dearly for this 'victory over the night', which was such an object of pride and even ostentation. It required wax, tallow, olive oil (or rather a by-product of it known as 'hell oil') and increasingly in the eighteenth century, whale oil – which made the fortunes of the fishermen of Holland and Hamburg, and later in the nineteenth century of the American seaports which Melville was to describe.

So if we moderns were to enter into an interior of the past, we would very soon feel uncomfortable. However beautiful it might be – and it was often wonderfully so – what seemed like luxury to the people of the past would not be enough for us.

Costume and fashion

The history of costume is less anecdotal than would appear. It touches on every issue – raw materials, production processes, manufacturing costs, cultural stability, fashion and social hierarchy. Subject to incessant change, costume everywhere is a persistent reminder of social position. The sumptuary laws were therefore an expression of the wisdom of governments – but even more of the resentment of the upper classes when they saw the *nouveaux riches* imitate them. Neither Henry IV nor his nobility could consent to the wives and daughters of the Parisian bourgeoisie dressing in silk. But nothing has ever been effective against the passion to move up in the world or the desire to wear those clothes which, in the West, symbolized the least degree of social promotion. Nor did governments ever prevent the ostentatious luxury of the great lords, the extraordinary shows of finery by newly delivered mothers in Venice, or the displays in Naples when burials took place.

It was the same in the poorest environments. At Rumegies, a village in Flanders, near Valenciennes, in 1696, a priest's journal tells us that the rich peasants sacrificed everything to luxury of dress 'the young men with hats trimmed with gold or silver, and the rest to match; the girls with coiffures a foot high and their other clothes in proportion'. There they were, with 'unheard-of insolence frequenting taverns every Sunday'. But a little later the same priest wrote: 'Except for Sundays when they are in church or at the tavern, they [rich and poor] are so dirty that the girls are a cure for the men's concupiscence and the men for the girls'.[143] This puts the situation in the right light, against the backcloth of everyday life. In June 1680, Madame de Sévigné, half admiring, half indignant, granted an interview to 'the beautiful little wife of a tenant-farmer from Bodégat (Brittany) with her gown of Holland cloth cut away to show watered silk, and slashed sleeves'. Alas, the tenant's wife owed her 8000 francs.[144] But she was an exception, as were the peasants wearing ruffs at the parish feast in a German village in 1680. Usually all went barefoot, or almost so, and one glance even at a town market was enough to differentiate between middle and lower classes.

When society stood still

If a society remained more or less stable, fashion was less likely to change – and this could be true at all levels, even the highest in established hierarchies. The mandarin's costume in China was the same from the outskirts of Peking, the new capital (1421), to the pioneer provinces of Szechwan and Yunan and had been so from well before the fifteenth century. And the silk costume with golden embroidery drawn by Father de Las Cortes in 1626 was the same shown in so many eighteenth-century engravings, with the same 'many-coloured silk boots'. At home, mandarins dressed in simple cotton clothes. Their brilliant costumes were donned in the course of their duties and served as a social mask, an authentification of their official personality. The mask scarcely changed in the course of centuries, but then Chinese society itself scarcely moved at all. Even the upheaval of the Tartar conquest in 1644 hardly interfered with a centuries'-old stability. The new masters forced their subjects to wear their hair close-cropped (except for one lock) and altered the large robe of former times. But that was all and it did not amount to very much. 'Dress is seldom altered in China from fancy or fashion,' wrote a traveller in 1793. 'Whatever is thought suitable to the condition of the wearer, or to the season of the year continues generally, under similar circumstances, to be the same. Even among the ladies, there is little variety in their dresses, except, perhaps, in the disposition of the flowers or other ornaments of the head.'[145] Japan was also conservative, possibly despite itself after Hideyoshi's harsh reaction. For centuries it remained faithful to the *kimono*, an indoor garment hardly any different from the present-day kimono, and to the '*jinbaori*, a leather garment painted on the back' which was regulation wear for walking in the streets.[146]

As a general rule no changes took place in these societies except as a result of political upheavals which affected the whole social order. When India was more or less conquered by the Muslims, the costume of the Mogul conquerors (the *pyjama* and the *chapkan*) became the rule, at least for the rich. 'All the portraits of the Rajput princes [with one exception] show them in court dress, an incontestable proof that in general the high Hindu nobility had accepted the customs and manners of the Mogul sovereigns.'[147] The same conclusions apply to the Turkish empire. Wherever the strength and influence of the Osmanli sultans made itself felt, the upper classes adopted their costume – in far-off Algeria and in Christian Poland, where Turkish fashion only belatedly gave way (and then imperfectly) to French fashion in the eighteenth century. All these imitations, once adopted, scarcely changed over the centuries. Mouradj d'Ohsson confirms the impression in the *Tableau général de l'Empire ottoman*, which appeared in 1741. 'Fashions which tyrannise European women hardly disturb the fair sex in the east; hair styles, cut of clothing and type of fabric there are almost always the same.'[148] It is certainly true that in Algiers, which had been Turkish since 1516 and remained so until 1830, female fashion changed

A Chinese mandarin, eighteenth century. Bibliothèque Nationale, Paris, Cabinet des Estampes. (Photo B.N.)

little in three centuries. The detailed description supplied by a prisoner, Father Haedo, in about 1580, 'could be used, with very little correction, as a caption to engravings of 1830'.[149]

If all the world were poor ...

The question would not even arise. Everything would stay fixed. No wealth, no freedom of movement, no possible change. To be ignorant of fashion was the lot of the poor the world over. Their costumes, whether beautiful or homespun, remained the same. The beautiful was represented by the feast-day costume, often handed down from parent to child. It remained identical for centuries on end, despite the infinite variety of national and provincial popular costumes. Crude homespun was the everyday working garb, made from the least expensive local resources: it varied even less.

The Indian women in New Spain in Cortes' day wore long tunics, sometimes embroidered, made of cotton and later of wool: and so they did still in the eighteenth century. Male costume, on the other hand, changed – but only to the extent that the conquerors and missionaries demanded clothing decently concealing the nudity of the past. Peruvian Indians of today are clad in the same fashion as in the eighteenth century: a square of homespun llama wool with an opening in the centre for the head – the *poncho*. The same applies, and has always done, to India: the Hindu continues to wear a *dhoti*, today as in the past. In China 'the villagers and lower classes have always worn cotton clothing in every sort of colour'[150] – a long shirt, gathered in at the waist. In 1609, and probably for centuries before, Japanese peasants were wearing kimonos lined with cotton.[151] In his *Voyage d'Egypte* (1783) Volney expressed surprise at the Egyptian costume: 'The bundle of material, rolled in folds round a shaven head; the long garment which falls from neck to heels, concealing the body rather than clothing it.'[152] This is an even older garment than the one worn by the rich Mamelukes and dating from the twelfth century. As for the costume which Father Labat describes the poor Muslims in Black Africa as wearing, it could hardly change when it was so meagre. 'They have no shirts; they wrap their bodies above their breeches with a piece of material fixed to the belt; most of them go bare-headed and barefoot.'[153]

The poor in Europe were more covered, but made no greater concession to caprice. Jean-Baptiste Say wrote in 1828: 'I confess that the unchanging fashions of the Turks and the other Eastern peoples do not attract me. It seems that their fashions tend to preserve their stupid despotism [...] Our villagers are to some extent Turkish in respect of fashions; they are slaves to routine and one sees old pictures of the wars of Louis XIV where male and female peasants are represented in clothes barely differing from those we see today.'[154] We can demonstrate the validity of the comment for an earlier period by a comparison of three items at the Munich Pinakothek: a picture by Pieter Aertsen (1508–75) and two canvases by Jan Breughel (1568–1625), all three depicting crowds at a market. A single glance is enough in every case to distinguish the humble vendors and fishermen from the groups of bourgeois customers and passers-by. Their costumes immediately give them away. A second fact to emerge is more curious. During the half-century or so separating the two painters, bourgeois costume changed considerably: Aertsen's Spanish-style high collars edged with simple fluting have been replaced by the true ruffs which both men and women are wearing in the Breughel, while the popular female costume (turned-down open collar, bodice, apron over a gathered skirt) has remained exactly the same, except for the headdress, but that was probably regional. A widow living in a village in the upper Jura in 1631 received under the terms of her husband's will 'one pair of shoes and a chemise every two years and a dress of coarse cloth every three'.[155]

Although peasant costume remained similar in appearance, certain important details did change. Thus, underwear came into general use, inside and outside France, towards the thirteenth century. It was customary in eighteenth-century Sardinia to wear the same shirt for a period of a year as a sign of mourning, which at least shows that the peasant was used to wearing shirts and that not to change them was a sacrifice. On the other hand we see from many pictures that in the past – even in the fourteenth century – rich and poor slept naked in their beds.

Furthermore, an eighteenth-century demographer remarks that 'scabies, ringworm, all the skin diseases and others originating from lack of cleanliness were so common in the past only because of lack of linen'.[156] In fact medical and surgical books prove that these diseases had not entirely disappeared in the eighteenth century, but they were on the retreat. The same eighteenth-century observer also mentions the spread of thick woollen clothing among the peasants of his own day.

> A French peasant [he writes] is badly dressed and the rags which cover his nudity are poor protection against the harshness of the seasons: however it appears that his state, in respect of clothing, is less deplorable than in the past. Dress for the poor is not an object of luxury but a necessary defence against the cold: coarse linen, the clothing of many peasants, does not protect them adequately ... but for some years ... a very much larger number of peasants have been wearing woollen clothes. The proof of this is simple, because it is certain that for some time a larger quantity of rough woollen cloth has been produced in the realm; and as it is not exported, it must necessarily be used to clothe a larger number of Frenchmen.[157]

These were belated and limited improvements. The change in the French peasant's dress lagged behind that of the English peasant. Nor should one assume that the change was general. On the eve of the French Revolution peasants in the Chalonnais and the Bresse were still wearing 'coarse cloth dyed black' with the aid of oak bark, and 'this custom was so widespread that the woods all suffered thereby'. Moreover 'in Burgundy, clothing was not [at that time] a significant item in the [peasant] budget'.[158] This was true of Germany as well, where the peasant was still dressed in coarse cloth at the beginning of the nineteenth century. The shepherds depicted as characters in a manger scene in the Tyrol in 1750 have homespun smocks to their knees, their legs and feet being bare or merely shod with a sole held on by a leather strap wound round the leg. In Tuscany, supposed to be a rich land, the countryman, even in the eighteenth century, was dressed exclusively in homespun fabrics, hempen cloth and cloth made of equal parts of hemp and wool (*mezzelane*).[159]

Europe and the craze for fashion

We can now approach the Europe of the rich and of changing fashions without risk of losing ourselves in its caprices. First of all we know that fashionable whims only affected a very small number of people, but that they made a great deal of noise and show, perhaps because the rest, even the most wretched, looked on and encouraged them in their extravagance.

We also know that the craze for change year after year took some time to become really established. It is true that a Venetian ambassador at the court of

Peasants in conversation, Flanders, sixteenth century. Attributed to Breughel the Elder. Besançon Museum. (Photo Giraudon.)

Henri IV was already saying: 'A man ... is not considered rich unless he has twenty-five to thirty suits of different types, and he must change them every day.'!¹⁶⁰ But fashion is not only a matter of abundance, quantity, profusion. It also consists of making a quick change at the right moment. It is a question of season, day and hour. In fact one cannot really talk of fashion becoming all-powerful before about 1700. At that time the word gained a new lease of life and spread everywhere with its new meaning: keeping up with the times. From then on fashion in the modern sense began to influence everything: the pace of change had never been as swift in earlier times.

In fact, the further back in time one goes, even in Europe, one is more likely to find the still waters of ancient situations like those we have described in India, China and Islam. The general rule was changelessness. Until towards the beginning of the twelfth century costumes in Europe remained entirely as they had been in Roman times: long tunics falling straight to the feet for women and to the knees for men. For century upon century, costume had remained unchanged. Any innovation, such as the lengthening of men's clothes in the twelfth century was strongly criticized. Orderic Vitalis (1075-1142) deplored the follies of fashion of his time, which he thought quite unnecessary: 'The old way of dressing has been almost completely thrown over,' he writes, 'by the new inventions.'[161] He exaggerates a good deal. Even the influence of the crusades was not as great as people thought: they introduced the use of silks and the luxury of furs, but did not fundamentally alter the shape of costumes in the twelfth and thirteenth centuries.

The really big change came in about 1350 with the sudden shortening of men's costume, which was viewed as scandalous by the old, the prudent and the defenders of tradition. 'Around that year,' writes the continuer of Guillaume de Nangis's chronicle, 'men, in particular noblemen and their squires, and a few bourgeois and their servants, took to wearing tunics so short and tight that they revealed what modesty bids us hide. This was a most astonishing thing for the people.'[162] This figure-hugging costume was to last, and men never went back to wearing long robes. As for women, their bodices too became more close-fitting, and were cut with a large décolleté – another cause for censure.

In a way, one could say that fashion began here. For after this, ways of dressing became subject to change in Europe. At the same time, whereas the traditional costume had been much the same all over the continent, the spread of the shorter costume was irregular, subject to resistance and variation, so that eventually *national* styles of dressing were evolved, all influencing each other to a greater or lesser extent – the French, Burgundian, Italian or English costume, etc. Eastern Europe, after the fall of Byzantium, came increasingly under the influence of Turkish dress.[163] So Europe became and remained a patchwork of costumes, until at least the nineteenth century, although from time to time it was willing to accept the leadership of some advanced region.

In the sixteenth century, for example, the European upper classes adopted the black costume of Spanish inspiration. This was a sign of the political preponderance of the Catholic King's 'world-wide' empire. The sumptuous costumes of Renaissance Italy, with their low-cut bodices, wide sleeves, hairnets, gold and silver embroidery, figured brocades, satins and crimson velvets, which had set the fashion for much of Europe, were replaced by Spanish sobriety with dark material, close-fitting doublets, padded hose, short capes and high collars edged with a small ruff. In the seventeenth century, on the other hand, brightly coloured French costumes gradually took over, even in the Spanish territories. Spain itself was of course the last to give way. Philip IV (1621-65), who was hostile to the luxuries of the Baroque, forced his aristocracy to observe the austere costume inherited from the time of Philip II. The court for a long time obstructed the *vestido de color*; a foreigner was only received there if properly 'dressed in black'. An envoy from the Prince de Condé (then an ally of the Spaniards) could only obtain an audience after he had changed into the compulsory dark clothing. It was not until about 1670, after Philip IV's death, that foreign fashions penetrated Spain to its heart in Madrid, where Philip IV's bastard son, the second Don John of Austria was to assure its success.[164] Catalonia, however, had been won over to the new styles of dress by 1630, ten years before it revolted against Madrid. The Stadtholder's court in Holland yielded to the craze at about the same date, though there were still a number who held out against it: a portrait of Bicker, the burgomaster of Amsterdam in 1642, now in the Rijksmuseum, shows him wearing a traditional costume in the Spanish style. Perhaps this was also a question of generations, since in a picture by D. van Sanvoort, of the Burgomaster Dirk Bas Jacobsz and his family, father and mother are both wearing ruffs in the old style, while their children are all dressed in the new fashion (see illustration on p. 331). The clash between the two fashions could also be seen in Milan, but there it had a different meaning: Milan was then a Spanish possession and in a mid-century caricature, a traditionally dressed Spaniard seems to be teasing a Milanese resident who has opted for the French fashion. Could the spread of the new fashion throughout Europe be interpreted as a sign of Spanish decline?

Such successive dominating influences suggest the same explanation we advanced for the expansion of Mogul costume in India or Osmanli costume in the Turkish empire. Europe was a single family, despite or because of its quarrels. The law was laid down by the most admired, not necessarily by the strongest, or, as the French believed, by the most loved or the most refined. Clearly, the political influences which affected the whole body of Europe – making it seem to change its direction or its very centre of gravity from one day to the next – did not affect the whole realm of fashion immediately. There were time-lags, aberrations, gaps, delays. French fashion was predominant in the seventeenth century but really only established its sovereignty in the eighteenth. In 1716, even in Peru, where the extravagance of the Spanish was of unheard of proportions, the men were dressing 'in the French style, usually in silk [imported from Europe] in a strange mixture of bright colours'.[165] Paris set the fashion for the four corners of Enlightened Europe with its mannequin dolls. They appeared very early on and thereafter reigned undisputed. In Venice, long regarded as the capital of fashion and good taste in the fifteenth and sixteenth centuries, one of the oldest shops was and still is called 'The Doll of France' (*La Piavola de Franza*). As early as 1642, the Queen of Poland (who was a sister of the emperor) was asking a Spanish courier, if he should be passing through the Netherlands, to bring her 'a doll dressed in the French style', for her dressmaker to copy, since she was dissatisfied with Polish fashions.[166]

Obedience to a dominant fashion did not take place, of course, without any resistance. There was, as we have seen, the large-scale inertia of the poor, who lived entirely outside the world of fashion. And there were also islands of regional resistance standing out above the sea of conformity. These instances of dissidence and aberration are headaches for the historian of costume. The court of the Valois in Burgundy was both too near Germany and too independent to follow the fashion of the French court. While the farthingale may have been in

The black costume in the Spanish style, worn by Lord Darnley and his young brother (1563). (Portrait by Hans Eworth, Windsor Castle.)

Zocoli, a kind of miniature stilts worn by women to protect their feet from puddles in the streets of Venice: the fashion spread beyond Venice for a while in the sixteenth century. (Bayerisches Nationalmuseum, Munich.)

general use in the sixteenth century, and furs enjoyed a long vogue everywhere, there were many different ways of wearing them. Ruffs, for instance, could vary from discreet ruching to the enormous lace ruff worn by Isabella Brandt in the portrait by Rubens which depicts her at his side; or the ruff worn by Cornelis de Vos's wife in the picture in the Brussels Museum in which she is shown with the painter and her two small daughters.

One evening in May 1581, *doppo disnar*, there arrived in Saragossa three young Venetian noblemen, handsome, impressionable, intelligent, glad to be alive and very pleased with themselves. A procession passed with the Holy Sacrament, followed by a crowd of men and women. 'The women were very ugly,' says the narrator mischievously, 'their faces painted in every colour, so that the effect was most strange, and they were wearing very high shoes or rather *zocoli*,[167] in the Venetian fashion, and mantillas in the fashion of all Spain.' Curiosity drew the travellers towards the spectacle. But whoever looks at other people must expect to be observed, noticed and pointed out in turn. Men and women passing in front of them began to shriek with laughter and shout at them. 'All this simply,' writes our Francesco Contarini, 'because we were wearing *nimphe* (lace collarettes) broader than Spanish custom decreed. Some said: "All Holland has come to our town" (i.e. all Holland cloth, or some other play of words on *olanda*, the fabric used to make sheets and linen); others remarked: "What enormous lettuces!" From this we derived great amusement.'[168]

The abbé Locatelli, who arrived in Lyon from Italy in 1664 had less self-confidence: he did not stand out for long against the children who called after him in the street. 'I had to give up my sugar-loaf [a sort of top hat with a wide brim] ... my coloured stockings and began to dress entirely in the French fashion', with 'a Zani hat with a narrow brim, a wide collar which made me look more like a doctor than a priest, a cassock which reached only to mid-thigh, black stockings and narrow shoes ... with silver buckles instead of laces. In this costume, ... I could hardly believe I was a priest any more.'[169]

Is fashion frivolous?

Fashion seems to enjoy freedom to act and to pursue its whims. In fact, its path is largely ordained in advance and its range of choice limited.

Its mechanism depends on the rules governing cultural transfers. And all diffusion of this type is by nature slow, involving a whole series of processes and constraints. The dramatist Thomas Dekker (1572-1632) amused himself by reflecting on the sartorial borrowings his compatriots had made from other nations – 'his Codpeece is in Denmarke, the collar, his Duble and the belly in France, the wing and narrow sleeve in Italy: the short waste hangs over a Dutch Botchers stall in Utrich: his huge Sloppes speakes Spanish: Polonia give him the Bootes'.[170] The pedigrees were not necessarily exact, but the diversity of the ingredients probably was, and it was not in one season that a recipe acceptable to all was to be produced.

Everything moved faster in the eighteenth century and therefore became more lively, but for all that, frivolity did not become the general rule in this boundless kingdom so enthusiastically described by witnesses and participants. Listen to Sébastien Mercier (without necessarily believing all he says), a good observer and talented diarist but certainly not a very great intellect: 'I fear,' he wrote in 1771, 'the approach of winter because of the harshness of the weather. . . . It is then that are born the noisy and insipid gatherings where all the useless passions exercise their ridiculous authority. The taste for frivolity dictates the judgements of fashion. All the men are turned into effeminate slaves, all subordinated to the whims of the women.' Here, let loose, is 'that flood of fashions, fantasies, amusements, not one of which will last'. 'If it took my fancy,' he goes on, 'to give a treatise on the art of curling, into what state of astonishment would I throw my readers by proving that there are three or four hundred ways of cutting a gentleman's hair.' The tone is typical of Mercier, decidedly moralistic though always anxious to entertain. So it is tempting to take him more seriously when he appraises the development of feminine fashion in his period. Of women and the outmoded farthingale he wrote:

> The hoops enclosing the women of our mothers' generation, their multitude of beauty spots, some of which really looked like plasters, – all that has disappeared, except for the immoderate height of their *coiffures*; ridicule has not been able to correct this last custom, but the defect is tempered by

Duchess Madeleine of Bavaria, by Pieter de Witte (known as Candid), 1548-1628. Her sumptuous costume is made of silk, gold ornaments, precious stones, pearls, embroidery and fine lace. Munich Art Gallery. (Photo Bayerisches Staatsgemaldesammlung.)

the taste and grace which direct the construction of the elegant edifice. Women, taking everything into account, are better dressed today than they have ever been; their attire combines lightness, decency, freshness and charm. These gowns made of light fabric [printed calico] are renewed more frequently than the gowns that glittered with gold and silver; they follow as it were the colours of the flowers of the different seasons.[171]

Here is telling evidence, showing how fashion eliminates one style and imposes another – a double role representing a double difficulty. The innovation in question was the arrival of printed calicos, relatively inexpensive cotton fabrics. But even they did not reach Europe overnight. And the history of textiles shows that in the field of fashion everything depends on everything else; participants have less freedom than they imagine.

Is fashion in fact such a trifling thing? Or is it, as I prefer to think, rather an indication of deeper phenomena – of the energies, possibilities, demands and *joie de vivre* of a given society, economy and civilization? In 1609, Rodrigo Vivero, returning from Manila where he had been acting Captain-General, aboard a large ship (two thousand tons) making for Acapulco in New Spain, was shipwrecked off the coast of Japan. The castaway almost immediately became an honoured guest of the islanders (who were curious about the foreigner) and then a sort of ambassador extraordinary. (He tried, but to no avail, to close the islands to Dutch trade and also, equally vainly, considered attracting miners from New Spain, so that the silver and copper mines of the archipelago might be better exploited.) This rather appealing character was also a good and intelligent observer. One day he was chatting idly with the Shogun's secretary at Yedo. The secretary criticized the Spaniards for their pride, their reserve. He then proceeded to discuss their way of dressing, 'the variety of their costumes, a realm in which they are so inconstant that they are dressed in a different way every two years'. These changes could only be ascribed to their levity and the levity of the governments which permitted such abuse. As for him, he would show 'by the evidence of traditions and of old papers that his nation had not changed its costume for over a thousand years'.[172]

Chardin, after living ten years in Persia, was equally categorical in 1686: 'I have seen Tamberlaine's costume, which is kept in the treasury of Ispahan,' he wrote, 'and it is cut exactly like the clothes worn here today, without any difference.' For 'dress in the East is not subject to fashion; it is always made in the same way and ... the Persians ... do not vary the colours, shades and types of material any more than the style'.[173]

I do not regard these as idle remarks. Can it have been merely by coincidence that the future was to belong to the societies fickle enough to care about changing the colours, materials and shapes of costume, as well as the social order and the map of the world – societies, that is, which were ready to break with their traditions? There is a connection. Did not Chardin also say of the Persians, who 'are not anxious for new discoveries and inventions,' that 'they believe they possess all that is required in the way of necessities and conveniences for living, and are content to remain so'.[174] Tradition was both a strength and a straitjacket. Perhaps if the door is to be opened to innovation, the source of all progress, there must be first some restlessness which may express itself in such trifles as dress, the shape of shoes and hairstyles? Perhaps too, a degree of prosperity is needed to foster any innovating movement?

But fashion can have other meanings too. I have always thought that fashion resulted to a large extent from the desire of the privileged to distinguish themselves, whatever the cost, from the masses who followed them; to set up a barrier. 'Nothing makes noble persons despise the gilded costume so much [according to a Sicilian who passed through Paris in 1714] as to see it on the bodies of the lowest men in the world.'[175] So the upper classes had to invent new 'gilded costumes', or new distinctive signs, whatever they might be, every time complaining that 'things have changed indeed, and the new clothes being worn by the bourgeois, both men and women, cannot be distinguished from those of persons of quality' (1779).[176] Pressure from followers and imitators obviously made the pace quicken. And if this was the case, it was because prosperity granted privileges to a certain number of *nouveaux riches* and pushed them to the fore. Social mobility was occurring – and this was an affirmation of a certain level of material well-being. Material progress was occurring: without it nothing would have changed so quickly.

And indeed fashion was consciously used by the world of trade. Nicholas Barbon sang its praises in 1690: 'Fashion or the alteration of Dress ... is the spirit and life of Trade'; thanks to fashion, 'the great body of trade remains in movement' and man lives a perpetual springtime, 'without ever seeing the autumn of his clothes'.[177] The Lyons silk traders in the eighteenth century exploited the tyranny of French fashions to impose their products on foreign markets and eliminate competition. Their silks were indeed magnificent, but the Italian craftsmen could easily copy them, especially when the practice spread of sending samples. The silk merchants of Lyons found the answer to this: they paid designers known as 'silk illustrators', who changed the patterns every year. When the copies reached the market, they were already out of date. Carlo Poni has published correspondence which leaves one in no doubt about the Lyonnais tactics.[178]

Fashion is also a search for a new language to discredit the old, a way in which each generation can repudiate its immediate predecessor and distinguish itself from it (at least in the case of a society where there is conflict between generations). 'The tailors,' ran a text in 1714, 'have more trouble inventing than sewing.'[179] But the problem in Europe was precisely that of inventing, of pushing out obsolete languages. The stable values – Church, Monarchy – made all the greater effort to preserve the same appearance; nuns wore the costume of women in the middle ages; Benedictines, Dominicans and Franciscans remained faithful to their ancient style of dress. The ceremonial costume of the English monarchy

These Turks, drawn by Bellini in the fifteenth century, might almost come from a nineteenth-century picture, so little had costume changed. Louvre, Rothschild collection. (Photo Roger-Viollet.)

went at least as far back as the Wars of the Roses. It was a deliberate reaction against the general current. Sébastien Mercier was not mistaken when he wrote (1782): 'When I see vergers I say to myself: everyone was dressed like that in Charles VI's reign.'[180]

The geography of textiles

Before we conclude, the history of costume should take us on to a history of textiles and fabrics, to a geography of production and exchange, to the slow work of the weavers and the regular crises resulting from the scarcity of raw materials. Europe lacked wool, cotton and silk; China, cotton; India and Islam, light wool; Black Africa bought foreign fabrics on the shores of the Atlantic or the Indian Ocean in exchange for gold or slaves. That was how poor peoples paid for their luxury purchases.

Production zones were, of course, to some extent fixed. For example, the world's wool-producing zone took shape and remained fairly static from the fifteenth to the eighteenth centuries, if one leaves out the production, peculiar to America, of vicuña wool (very fine) and llama wool (coarse). The static zone covered the Mediterranean, Europe, Iran, northern India and cold northern China.

So China did have sheep, 'and wool is quite common and cheap'. But 'they do not know how to make cloth in the European way' and admire that of England, although they do not buy much of it, since in China 'it is incomparably dearer than the finest silks. Their thick woollens are coarse, a kind of frieze.'[181] But they make a few serges, 'very fine and very precious ... worn generally by old men and persons of distinction in the winter'.[182] They did after all have plenty of choice: silk, cotton and two or three vegetable fibres that were easy to work, though not widespread. And when winter came in the north, mandarins and lords covered themselves with sables while even the poor wore sheepskins.[183]

Like the most humble cultural assets, textiles were always on the move, taking root in new regions. Wool found its promised land in Australia in the nineteenth century. It is likely that silk first reached the European world in the Trajan period (52-117). Cotton left India and spread like wildfire in China in the twelfth century; it reached the Mediterranean even earlier, in about the tenth century, via the Arab world.

Silk made the most striking of these journeys. Jealously guarded, it took centuries to reach the Mediterranean from China. The Chinese showed no desire to hasten its progress nor did the Sassanid Persians living between China and Byzantium and keeping vigilant watch in both directions. Justinian (527-65) was not only the builder of Saint Sophia, not only the author of the code which bore his name; he was the emperor of silk, having succeeded, after various vicissitudes, in introducing into Byzantium silk worms, white mulberries, the unwinding of cocoons and the weaving of the precious thread. Byzantium thereby earned a fortune which it jealously guarded for centuries.

However, in the fifteenth century, when this book begins, silk had been in Sicily and Andalusia for almost four hundred years. It spread in the sixteenth century - together with the mulberry - to Tuscany, Venetia, Lombardy, lower Piedmont and along the Rhône valley, reaching Savoy in the eighteenth century. Had it not been for this silent advance of trees and silk-worm rearing, the silk industry inside and outside Italy would not have experienced the remarkable success it enjoyed from the sixteenth century onwards.

The cotton plant and cotton made equally spectacular journeys. Europe was familiar with the valuable fabric quite early on, particularly after the thirteenth century, when wool became scarce following the decrease in sheep-raising. An ersatz cloth, fustian, made with a warp of flax and a woof of cotton, became widely used at about this time. It had a great vogue in Italy and an even greater one north of the Alps where *Barchent* began to achieve its great popularity in Ulm and Augsburg - the zone beyond the Alps which Venice dominated and inspired from afar: The great city was in fact the importing port for cotton - in the form of yarn or in bales of raw cotton (called cotton wool). Large ships left Venice twice a year in the fifteenth century to bring it back from Syria. It was, of course, also worked locally - in and around Aleppo, for example - and exported to Europe. This coarse blue cotton cloth, similar to the material used for kitchen aprons nowadays, served as clothing for the people in southern

England during the great days of the wool trade: a church brass from Northleach, Gloucestershire, representing the merchant William Midwinter, who died in 1501. His feet are resting on a sheep and a bale of wool bearing his trade mark. (Photothèque A. Colin.)

France in the seventeenth century. Later, in the eighteenth, cotton goods from India arrived on European markets. These were the fine printed fabrics, the 'calicos' which delighted female customers until the time when the industrial revolution enabled the English to do as well as the skilful Indian weavers, and then to ruin them.

Flax and hemp stayed more or less in their original environment, moving slightly eastwards towards Poland, the Baltic countries and Russia, but barely leaving Europe. (However, hemp did grow in China.) These textiles were not popular outside the Western countries (including America). Nevertheless they were extremely useful: sheets, table linen, underwear, sacks, overalls, peasant trousers, sailcloth and rope were all made from one or other or both of these textiles. Elsewhere, in Asia and even in America, cotton was inevitably substituted for them even for sails – although Chinese and Japanese junks preferred bamboo slats whose virtues continue to be praised by nautical experts.

To embark upon the history of cloth production and then the characteristics of the innumerable and varied fabrics would require many pages, as well as a dictionary of technical terms, since many of the expressions that have come down to us did not always designate the same product and sometimes designated products which we cannot identify reliably.

However, we shall have to return to the large subject of the textile industries in the second volume of this work. All things in good time.

Fashion in the broad sense: long-term change

Fashion does not only govern clothing. The *Dictionnaire sentencieux* defines the word thus: 'Ways of dressing, writing and behaving, which the French twist round and round in a thousand different ways to make themselves more gracious, more charming and often more ridiculous.' Fashion in this sense affects everything and is the way in which each civilization is orientated. It governs ideas as much as costume, the current phrase as much as the coquettish gesture, the manner of receiving at table, the care taken in sealing a letter. Fashion may govern the way one speaks: for example, it was said in 1768 that 'the bourgeois have servants, people of quality have lackeys, priests have valets'. And it may dictate eating habits: the times of meals in Europe varied according to place and social class but also according to fashion. Dinner in the eighteenth century was what we would call lunch. 'Artisans dine at nine o'clock [in the morning], provincials at twelve, Parisians at two, business people at half-past two, nobles at three.' As for 'supper' [our dinner], it 'is taken at seven in small towns, at eight in large, at nine in Paris and at ten at court. Nobles and financiers sup regularly, the judiciary never, adventurers when they get the chance'. This gave rise to the semi-proverbial expression: 'The Robe [the legal profession] dines and Finance sups.'[184]

Fashion may also concern the way of walking and of greeting one's acquaintances. Must the hat be raised or not? The custom of baring the head before kings in France is said to have come from the Neapolitan nobles, whose respect astonished Charles VIII and served as a lesson.

And the care of body, face and hair is also a question of fashion. If we pause a moment at these three items, it is because they are simpler to follow than others. And in observing them, we shall find that fashion could be capable of very slow oscillations, like the trends economists discern beneath the sharp and slightly incoherent movements of day-to-day prices. These rather slow backward and forward movements were also one of the facets, one of the realities of luxury and European fashion between the fifteenth and the eighteenth centuries.

Bodily cleanliness left much to be desired at all periods and for everyone. The privileged mention the repulsive dirtiness of the poor very early on. An Englishman (1776) was astonished at the 'unbelievable uncleanliness' of the poor in France, Spain and Italy: it 'makes them less healthy and more disfigured than they are in England'.[185] Let us add that the peasant practically everywhere hid behind his poverty, displayed it and used it to protect himself from nobleman or tax collector. But was the European privileged class itself so clean?

The custom for men 'to wear under-drawers which are changed every day and which maintain cleanliness' instead of simple lined breeches was hardly established until the second half of the eighteenth century. And, as we have already mentioned, there were few baths, except in the large towns. The West even experienced a significant regression from the point of view of body baths and bodily cleanliness from the fifteenth to the seventeenth centuries. Baths, which were an inheritance from Rome, were to be found throughout medieval Europe. There were private baths, of course, but also public baths, with their steam cabins, their tubs and beds for resting on, or their large pools in which both sexes bathed naked together. It was as commonplace to meet at the baths as at church and the bathing establishments were open to all classes, so much so that they were subject to seigneurial dues just like mills, smithies and houses selling drinks.[186] Rich houses all possessed their 'bathrooms' in the basement – which meant a steam-room with bathtubs, usually made of wood and bound with hoops like barrels. Charles the Bold possessed that rare luxury, a silver bath, which followed him to the battlefield: it was found in his camp after the disaster of Granson (1476).[187]

After the sixteenth century, public baths became less frequent and almost disappeared, it was said because of the risk of infection and in particular the terrible disease of syphilis. Another reason was no doubt the influence of preach-

The fifteenth-century bathtub, or how Liziart, Count of Forest, was able by a stratagem, and thanks to a hole in the wall made by a treacherous serving woman, to spy on the fair Euryant in her bath. Roman de la Violette, Bibliothèque Nationale, Paris. (Photo Giraudon.)

ers, both Catholic and Calvinist, who fulminated against the moral dangers and ignominy of the baths. Although rooms for bathing survived in private homes for a long time, the bath became a means of medication rather than a habit of cleanliness. At the court of Louis XIV, baths were taken only on exceptional occasions, in cases of sickness.[188] And those public baths that had survived in Paris eventually, in the seventeenth century, fell into the hands of the barber-surgeons. It was only in Eastern Europe that public baths remained in use, even in villages, where a sort of medieval innocence was retained. In the West, they often became brothels for rich customers.

From about 1760, baths in the Seine became fashionable, organized on board specially built boats. The *Chinese baths* near the Ile-St-Louis, subsequently had a vogue that lasted a long time. But such establishments continued to have a doubtful reputation and cleanliness did not make spectacular progress through them.[189] According to Restif de La Bretonne, hardly anyone in Paris took baths 'and those who did confined them to once or twice per summer that is per year' (1788).[190] There was not a single bathing establishment in London in 1800, and even later than that, the beautiful Lady Mary Montagu tells us how she once replied to someone who commented on the rather doubtful cleanness of her hands: 'If you call that dirty, you should see my feet!'[191]

The low level of soap production is hardly surprising in these conditions, although it had originated as far back as Roman Gaul. Scarcity of soap was a problem and was possibly one of the reasons for high infant mortality.[192] The hard soaps with soda from the Mediterranean were used for personal washing and included cakes of toilet soap, which had to be 'marbled and scented in order to enjoy the right to pass over the cheeks of all our dandies'.[193] Liquid soap made with potash (in the north) was intended for washing sheets and other fabrics. A poor tally on the whole – yet Europe was the continent *par excellence* for soap. It was not to be found in China; nor indeed was underwear.

We have to wait for the eighteenth century, and the discoveries it added to ancient heritages, for feminine beauty treatment. The coquette easily took five or six hours to dress, attended by her servants and in particular by her hairdresser, chatting with her priest or her 'lover'. Hair was the great problem. It was built up so high that the eyes of the beauties seemed to start out from the middle of their bodies. Make-up was an easier task, especially as foundations were spread on generously. Only the bright rouges obligatory at Versailles, offered a choice: 'Show me what rouge you wear and I will tell you who you are.' Perfumes were many: essences of violet or rose, jasmin, hyacinth, bergamot, iris or lily-of-the-valley, and Spain had long ago imposed a taste for strong perfumes with a musk and amber base.[194] An Englishman wrote in 1779 of French ladies at 'their toilets, where every Woman in France rests fully persuaded the Genius of Taste and Elegance in Apparel, and every Ornament that Invention contrives to grace the human Frame, appertains to them with an exclusive Right.'[195] The *Dictionnaire sentencieux* confirms that this sophistication was

Houses, Clothes and Fashion   331

already in an advanced state in the following definition: 'The toilette is the combination of all the powders, all the essences, all the cosmetics necessary to change a person's nature and make even ugliness and age young and beautiful. It is then that defects of the figure are made good, eyebrows put in shape, teeth replaced, faces made up, indeed when face and skin are changed.'[196]

But the most frivolous subject was still hairstyle, even for men.[197] Were they to wear their hair long or short? Were beard and moustache acceptable? It is surprising to see how much individual whims were held within bounds in such a personal matter.

At the beginning of the wars with Italy, Charles VIII and Louis XII wore their hair long and were clean-shaven. The new fashion of beard and moustache, but with short hair, came from Italy. It was launched, we are told, by Pope Julius II (which is open to doubt) and later imitated by Francis I (1521) and Charles V (1524). The dates are tentative. What is certain is that the fashion reached the whole of Europe. 'When François Olivier, who later became Chancellor, presented himself at the Parlement in 1536 to be received as Maître des Requêtes his beard frightened the assembled Chambers and caused a protest on their part.

Fashion and generation. In this family portrait of 1635 by D. van Sanvoort, the burgomaster Dirk Bas Jacobsz and his wife are still wearing Spanish dress: dark costumes, ruffs, the man with a long beard and flowing moustache. But their children are all dressed in the new Dutch-French style: short coloured breeches, large down-turned collars of linen and lace. The oldest son has a little moustache and the suspicion of a beard, again in the new style. Amsterdam Rijksmuseum. (Photo Roger-Viollet.)

Olivier was only received on condition that he abandoned his beard.' But the Church opposed even more vociferously than the Parlement the custom of 'fostering facial hair'. Royal jussive letters were still necessary in 1559 to impose a bearded bishop or archbishop on recalcitrant chapters, who had tradition and ancient fashion on their side.

Of course the chapters did not win. But the victors themselves tired of their success. In fact such fashions scarcely last a century at the most. Hair lengthened again and beards and moustaches shrank with the beginning of Louis XIII's reign. Once again, those who were behind the times suffered. The object of the conflict had changed, not its meaning. Very soon wearers of long beards became 'virtually foreigners in their own country. Seeing them it was tempting to believe that they came from a far-off land.' Sully's experience is an indication of the change. When he came to the court at the invitation of Louis XIII, who wanted to consult him on an important matter, the young courtiers could not restrain their laughter on seeing the hero with a long beard, a suit no longer in current fashion, a grave demeanour and manners suited to the old court. Beards dwindled away further until the logical conclusion: 'Louis XIV entirely abolished short beards. Only the Carthusian friars did not abandon them' (1773). For the Church, as always and in accordance with its nature, was reluctant to change: once it had accepted changes it inevitably retained them beyond their season. It protested against fashion in about 1629, at the beginning of the vogue for 'artificial hair', which shortly led to wigs and then to powdered wigs. Could a priest officiate in a wig that hid his tonsure? This was the subject of bitter controversy. The progress of wigs continued unaffected and at the beginning of the eighteenth century Constantinople even exported 'fashioned goat's hair for wigs' to Europe.

The point to note in these catalogues of trifles is the length of time successive fashions lasted: about a century. Beards, which disappeared in the time of Louis XIV, only came back into fashion with Romanticism, lasted until shortly after the First World War (about 1920) then vanished again. Would fashion take another hundred years to change? Apparently not: since 1968, long hair, beards and moustaches have reappeared. One should neither exaggerate nor minimize the importance of such things. England, with fewer than 10 million inhabitants in about 1800, counted 150,000 wearers of wigs, if the fiscal authorities are to be believed. To balance this, a document of 1779, which is no doubt accurate at least for France, says: 'The peasants and common people ... have always gone cleanshaven in a manner of speaking, and have worn their hair quite short and uncared for.'[198] Without taking this remark literally, one can hazard a guess that once again immobility was on one side, that of the majority, and change on the other, that of the privileged few.

Conclusions?

All these realities of material life – food, drink, housing, clothes and fashion – cannot be so closely correlated that the relationship can be taken for granted. The distinction between luxury and poverty is only a crude classification, one that recurs all the time, but does not in itself provide the necessary precision. One cannot indeed say that all these realities are the product of constraining necessity: man certainly finds food, shelter and clothing because he cannot do otherwise – but he could choose to feed, live and dress differently. Sudden changes in fashion demonstrate this in a 'diachronic' manner, and contrasts between different parts of the world, past and present, do so in a 'synchronic' manner. In fact, our investigation takes us at this point not simply into the realm of material 'things', but into a world of 'things and words' – interpreting the last term in a wider sense than usual, to mean *languages* with everything that man contributes or insinuates into them, as in the course of his everyday life he makes himself their unconscious prisoner, in front of his bowl of rice or slice of bread.

The important thing, if one is to follow such pioneering works as that of Mario Praz,[199] is to see both the material goods and the languages in an overall context: an economic context, of that there is no doubt; and a social context too, in all probability. If luxury is not a good way of supporting or promoting an economy, it is a means of holding, of fascinating a society. And those strange collections of commodities, symbols, illusions, fantasms and intellectual schemas that we call civilizations must also be invoked at this point. In short, at the very deepest levels of material life, there is at work a complex order, to which the assumptions, tendencies and unconscious pressures of economies, societies and civilizations all contribute.

5

The Spread of Technology: Sources of Energy, Metallurgy

IN A WAY, everything is technology: not only man's most strenuous endeavours but also his patient and monotonous efforts to make a mark on the external world; not only the rapid changes we are a little too ready to label revolutions (gunpowder, long-distance navigation, the printing-press, windmills and watermills, the first machines) but also the slow improvements in processes and tools, and those innumerable actions which may have no immediate innovating significance but which are the fruit of accumulated knowledge: the sailor rigging his boat, the miner digging a gallery, the peasant behind the plough or the smith at the anvil. 'What I call technology,' Marcel Mauss used to say, 'is a traditional action made effective':[1] in other words one which implies the action of one man or generation upon another, a kind of training which has been going on since the beginning of time.

Technology ultimately covers as wide a field as history and has, of necessity, history's slowness and ambiguities. Technology is explained by history and in turn explains history; but the correlation is in neither case fully satisfactory. In the realm of technology, co-extensive with the whole of history, there is no single onward movement, but many actions and reactions, many changes of gear. It is not a linear process. The mistake of Lefebvre des Noëttes, still in many ways an admirable writer, was to reduce the history of technology to a simple-minded materialism. It just will not do to say that the horse-collar, which replaced the yoke-harness from about the ninth century, thus increasing the traction-power of horses, 'progressively reduced man's slavery'. This particular over-simplification was criticized by Marc Bloch.[2] Nor did the centre-line rudder, which originated in the northern seas in the twelfth century, pave the way for, and then ensure, the success of the great maritime discoveries.[3] And Lynn White must have had his tongue in his cheek when he advanced his theory about spectacles for reading – namely that when they came into general use in the fifteenth century they assisted the intellectual advance of the Renaissance by increasing the numbers of readers.[4] There were of course a number of other factors present – the printing-press, for instance (or to answer White in the same coin, the spread of domestic lighting: imagine the hours gained for reading and writing!). Most important of all, one should investigate the motives behind the new passion for reading and knowledge – what economists would call the level of desired demand. After all, a desperate search for ancient manuscripts was already going on in Petrarch's time, well before many people were wearing spectacles.

In other words, one must always take account of history, or perhaps one should say society, in the broad sense; technology is never the only factor in the discussion. To say society is to speak of a history that is slow, mute and complicated; a memory that obstinately repeats known solutions, to avoid the difficulty and danger of imagining something else. Every invention that presents itself has to wait for years or even centuries before being introduced into real life. First comes the *inventio*, then, very much later, the application (*usurpatio*), society having attained the required degree of receptivity. The scythe is a good example. *Schnitter Tod*, death armed with a scythe, became an obsessive image following the epidemics that decimated the West in the fourteenth century. But the scythe was used exclusively to cut grass in meadows at that time. It was rarely the harvester's implement. The ears of corn were cut at varying heights, with a sickle. The straw was left standing for the flocks to eat, while leaves and branches from the forest served as their litter. In spite of the enormous urban growth, in spite of Europe's becoming a cereal-growing area (the *Vergetreidung* of German historians), the use of the scythe to harvest grain did not become general before the beginning of the nineteenth century.[5] Only then did the need for greater speed and a certain permissible degree of grain-wastage ensure the scythe's widespread predominance.

Hundreds of other examples show the same process. The steam engine, for example, was invented a long time before it launched the industrial revolution – or should one say before being launched by it? The history of inventions, taken by itself, is therefore a misleading hall of mirrors. A splendid sentence by Henri Pirenne neatly sums up the question: 'America [when the Vikings reached it] was lost as soon as it was discovered, because Europe did not yet need it.'[6]

In other words, there are times when technology represents the possible, which for various reasons – economic, social or psychological – men are not yet capable of achieving or fully utilizing; and other times when it is the *ceiling* which materially and technically blocks their efforts. In the latter case, when one day the ceiling can resist the pressure no longer, the technical breakthrough becomes the point of departure for a rapid acceleration. However, the force that overcomes the obstacle is never a simple *internal* development of technology or science, or at any rate not before the nineteenth century.

Harvesting with scythes in the Netherlands: still the exception at the end of the sixteenth century. Painting by Breughel the Younger (1565-1637). (Photo Giraudon.)

The key problem: sources of energy

Between the fifteenth and eighteenth centuries, man had at his disposal his own strength and that of his domestic animals; he also had the wind, running water, wood, charcoal and coal - varied but still only modest sources of energy. With the benefit of hindsight, we know that progress could only have been made by concentrating on coal, and particularly in using it systematically, in the form of coke, in iron metallurgy. Coal was in fact used in Europe from the eleventh and twelfth centuries, and in China, according to writings of the time, from the fourth millennium before the Christian era. But men took a very long time to realize that coal was anything more than a supplementary fuel. The discovery of coke itself did not immediately result in its use.[7]

The human engine

Man, using his muscles alone, is not a very powerful engine. His strength measured in horse-power (seventy-five kg to a height of one metre in one second) is derisory: between three and four hundredths of one horsepower against twenty-seven to fifty-seven hundredths for a cart horse.[8] In 1739, Forest de Belidor maintained that seven men were required to do the haulage work of one horse.[9] Other measurements in 1800 suggested that one man could 'till from 0·3 to 0·4 hectares, turn 0·4 hectares of meadow, harvest 0·2 hectares with a sickle, or thresh about 100 litres of grain in a day' – not a particularly impressive record.[10]

However, in the time of Louis XIII, a man's daily wage was not one-seventh but one-half of what one paid for a horse: eight sols to sixteen sols.[11] The tariff rightly over-estimated human labour because this not-very-powerful engine always had great flexibility. Man had many tools at his disposal, some of them dating from the distant past: hammers, axes, saws, tongs and spades; he also possessed rudimentary engines which he worked with his own strength: trepans, capstans, pulleys, cranes, jacks, levers, pedals, cranks and lathes. G. Haudricourt has suggested the appropriate term 'human engines' for the last three, which had come to the West from either India or China. The most complex human engine of all was the loom, which reduced everything to simple actions: the alternate movement of the feet worked the pedals, raising half the threads of the warp and then the other, while the hands threw the shuttle carrying the thread of the woof.

Man in himself therefore contains many possibilities; he combines skill and flexibility. A porter in Paris (according to an account dating from 1782) lifted on his back 'loads that would kill a horse'.[12] P.G. Poinsot, in *L'Ami des cultivateurs* (1806), gives advice which is flabbergasting in view of its late date:

> It would be most desirable if all the land could be tilled with a spade. The labour would certainly be much more profitable than with the plough and this implement is preferred in several cantons of France where great practice in handling it shortens the operation considerably, since one single man can turn over 487 [square] metres of earth at a depth of 65 centimetres in a fortnight, and such tilling is enough by itself, while tilling by plough must be repeated four times before heavy soil can be sown; furthermore the earth is never so well turned over nor crumbled up as with a spade.... It is clearly bad economy to till with a plough if a man has not a sizeable domain to cultivate, and this is the principal reason why almost all the small farmers are ruined.... Furthermore it has been proved that harvests from lands thus cultivated are triple those of the others. The spade used to cultivate the land must be at least double the length and strength of that used for gardens, which does not stand up to the efforts required to lift up compact earth and break it up sufficiently.[13]

Nor was this purely theoretical. Day labourers in the countryside often cultivated their plots with pick-axes, if not with spades. This, as they said in the eighteenth century, was farming 'by hand' or 'arm-labouring'.[14] It would be interesting to calculate what would have been the result if this absurd Chinese-type tillage had been the rule instead of the exception. Would Western towns have been able to subsist in such conditions? Could they even have been created? And what would have happened to the livestock?

The lone man working with bare hands is a recurring figure in China in modern times. A traveller notes (1793): not only is human labour there 'the least costly, but it is not spared at all, as long as it is sure of being put to good use' – a qualification we need not believe. The Chinese labourer dug with a pick-axe, drew the plough in the place of the buffalo, distributed water, worked 'chain pumps', husked grain with handmills ('this is the occupation of countless inhabitants'), carried travellers, lifted enormous burdens, transported weights balanced on a long wooden lever resting on his shoulders, turned the millstone at paper mills and hauled boats, whereas 'in many other countries horses are used for this'.[15] The highest lock on the Grand Canal from the Yang-tse-Kiang to Peking – called 'Tien Fi Cha, which means the Queen and the Mistress of the Sky' – was not worked by opening and closing the gates. The boats were hauled from one level to another by capstans and 'many cables and ropes pulled from both sides of the canal by 400 or 500 men, or even by a larger number, according to the weight and size of the boat'. Was Father de Magaillans, who stresses the difficulty and danger of the operation, therefore right (1678) to hold up as an

It took six Chinese hauliers on the tow-path to pull each of these boats carrying precious stones. Chinese painting of the eighteenth century.
Bibliothèque Nationale, Paris, Cabinet des Estampes. (Photo B.N.)

example the Chinese custom of accomplishing 'all sorts of mechanical work with many fewer instruments than we use'?[16] Gemelli Careri, some ten years later (1695) was also amazed at the speed of the chair-carriers who went trotting along as fast as 'little Tartary horses'.[17] A Jesuit father at Peking in 1657 produced a fire-engine capable of throwing 'water to a height of a hundred palms' by *manpower* and wind.[18] Yet even in India the noria and the sugar and oil mills were turned by teams of animals.[19] Another extreme example could be found in Japan in the nineteenth century: there is a picture by Hokusai that shows the almost incredible sight of sugar cane being milled solely by manpower.

The Jesuit fathers were still explaining matters in 1777:

> The question of the utility of machines and working animals is not so easy to decide, at least for a country where the land is barely sufficient to feed its inhabitants. What use would machines and working animals be there? - to turn part of the inhabitants into philosophists [sic], that is to say into men doing absolutely nothing for society and making it bear the burden of their needs, their well-being, and what is even worse their comical and ridiculous ideas. When our country folk [the writer is a Chinese Jesuit] find themselves either supernumerary or unemployed in a few cantons, they decide to go away and work in Tartary, in the newly-conquered countries where our agriculture is making progress.[20]

How reasonable it sounds. It is moreover true that at that time Chinese agriculture was being extensively developed. However, it is also true that agricultural progress was incapable of keeping pace with, let alone overtaking, demographic progress.

Human labour was widely used in Black Africa and India, as the reader will hardly need reminding. When Aurangzeb made his journey to Kashmir, the camels had to be unloaded at the first slopes of the Himalayas; they were relieved by 15,000 to 20,000 porters, some forced to serve, others 'attracted by the alluring pay of ten crowns per hundred pounds in weight'.[21] This might be regarded as wasteful - or on the other hand as a saving and an economy. At the house of correction in Bicêtre (1788), water used to be drawn from the wells by twelve horses, 'but tough and powerful prisoners have since been employed at this work, a wise and most advantageous economy'.[22] And this is the moralist Sébastien Mercier talking! Similarly black slaves could be seen even later than this, replacing horses in the towns of Brazil, pulling heavily laden carts.

The precondition for progress was probably a reasonable balance between human labour and other sources of power. The advantage was illusory when man competed with machines inordinately, as in the ancient world and China, where mechanization was ultimately blocked by cheap labour. There were slaves in Greece and Rome, and too many highly efficient coolies in China. In fact there is never any progress unless a higher value is set on human labour. When man has a certain cost price as a source of energy, then it is necessary to think about aiding him or, better still, replacing him.

Detail of the silver mine of Kutna Hora, about 1490. The baskets of ore were hauled to the surface by a windlass worked by two men. The same mine possessed giant windlasses worked by horses. But these were still only elementary means. Fifty years later, in the time of Agricola, huge hydraulic wheels were being used for lifting.
(Vienna, Aus dem Bildarchiv d. Ost. Nationalbibliothek.)

Animal power

Man was relieved by domestic animals early on, though the luxury was very unfairly distributed over the world. The history of these 'engines' will be clearer if we distinguish between Old and New Worlds from the beginning.

In America, the situation was comparatively straightforward. Llamas, 'the sheep of the Andes', were the only important heritage from the Amerindians. They were fairly poor carriers but unique in being able to adapt to the rarefied air of the high Cordillera. All the other animals (except for vicuñas and turkeys) came from Europe: oxen, sheep, goats, horses, dogs and poultry. The most important for economic life were mules, which gradually became indispensable as carriers – except in North America, certain areas of colonial Brazil, and in the Argentine pampas where wooden carts with high wheels, drawn by teams of oxen, remained the general rule until the twentieth century.

Elsewhere, caravans of mules with their noisy bells covered immense distances. In New Spain in 1808, Alexander von Humboldt noted their importance for the transport of merchandise and maize flour,[23] indispensable to life in every town, above all the rich capital, Mexico City. The same was true of Brazil, where Auguste de Saint-Hilaire was an observant witness some twelve years later. This traffic, with its compulsory stops and fixed routes, required mule 'stations' – as at Porto da Estrella,[24] at the foot of the Serra do Mar near Rio de Janeiro. The owners of the convoys, the Brazilian *tropeiros*, financed cotton production and later coffee. They were the pioneers of an early form of capitalism.

In the vast kingdom of Peru, in 1776, 500,000 mules were employed for trading along the coast or through the Andes and for drawing coaches in Lima. The kingdom imported about 50,000 of them a year from the Argentine pampas in the south. There they roved in the wild, watched over at a distance, and were driven northwards by *peones* on horseback in enormous herds of several thousand animals as far as Tucuman and Salta, where they were brutally broken in. They finally arrived in either Peru or Brazil, and would often end up at the enormous fair of Sorocaba, in São Paulo province.[25] This production and trade reminded Marcel Bataillon of the automobile industry today and 'its internal market in a continent open to motorization'.[26]

The commerce gave primitive Argentina the chance to share in the silver of Peru and the gold of Brazil. Add the 500,000 mules in Peru to possibly the same number in Brazil and those in New Spain and elsewhere – Caracas, Santa Fé de Bogota, central America – and we have anything up to two million beasts, of burden or for saddle (rarely for hauling). Say one animal to every five or ten inhabitants; that represents an enormous 'mechanization' effort in the service of precious metals, sugar or maize. There was nothing comparable anywhere else in the world, with the exception of Europe. But even there, Spain only counted 250,000 mules for 10 million inhabitants (or almost the whole population of

A caravan of llamas in Peru. Théodore de Bry. Bibliothèque Nationale, Paris, Cabinet des Estampes. (Photo Giraudon.)

Iberian America) in 1797.[27] Even if more accurate research were to modify the statistics for America, the disproportion would still be considerable.

Other European domestic animals also proliferated in the New World, particularly oxen and horses. Yoked oxen drew the heavy cart of the pampas and the *carro de boi*, with solid wheels and creaking wooden axle, typical of colonial Brazil. They also formed wild herds. This was the case in the Rio São Francisco Valley in Brazil, where a 'leather civilization' is reminiscent of similar scenes in the Argentine pampas and the Rio Grande do Sul, with orgies of eating meat roasted over an open fire.

Despite their superabundance, here as everywhere else in the world horses represented a sort of violent and virile aristocracy, that of the masters and the *peones* leading the herds of animals. The most astounding horsemen in the world, the *gauchos*, were already riding the pampas at the end of the eighteenth century. But a horse cost practically nothing – two reals: for there was no shortage of horseflesh. An ox did not even have a market price; it belonged to whoever caught it with a *lasso* or *bola*. A mule, however, sold for up to nine pesos in Salta.[28] As a black slave in Buenos Aires was often worth 200 pesos, the New World had it seems both raised the price of man – and placed the whole animal kingdom in his power.

In the Old World, by contrast with the New, very old and complicated patterns had been inherited from ancient times.

Yet nothing could have been more logical – or so it seems *a posteriori* at least – than the spread of camels and dromedaries to all the empty parts of the Old World, that interminable chain of hot and cold desert lands running uninterrupted from the Atlantic Sahara to the Gobi desert. The hot deserts were the domain of dromedaries, animals susceptible to the cold and also unadapted to mountainous country. The cold deserts and mountains were the domain of camels, the division between them being on either side of Anatolia and Iran. As a traveller put it (1694): 'Providence has made two types of camel, one for hot countries, the other for cold.'[29]

But this providential division was in fact the result of a long process. Dromedaries only arrived in the Sahara at about the beginning of the Christian era[30] and did not appear there in strength until the Arab conquests of the seventh and eighth centuries, and then the arrival of the 'great nomads' during the eleventh and twelfth centuries. Camels colonized the West between the eleventh and the sixteenth centuries, with the Turkish advances into Asia Minor and the Balkans. Of course camels and dromedaries could both be found outside their respective regions.[31] Dromedaries crossed Iran and went as far as India where they sold at high prices, like horses. They penetrated south of the Sahara to the borders of Black Africa where canoes and carriers took over from them. At one time they even pushed as far northwards as Merovingian Gaul, while in the east, camels penetrated the Balkans: although their presence there was intermittent, they were still crossing the Balkans until the nineteenth century. In 1529 they brought supplies to the Turkish army under the walls of Vienna. Northern China, at the other end of the Old World, was likewise affected by the camel invasion. A traveller near Peking (1775) noticed alongside the rickshaws a camel 'carrying sheep' on its back.[32]

In the camel, Islam possessed a near-monopoly in a powerful pack-animal which could be used for local transport, tilling the land and working norias (though donkeys had long been used for these purposes in the Mediterranean region) as well as for long-distance caravan connections with the Sahara, the Near East, and central Asia – a network of communications to be attributed to a resourceful ancient capitalism.[33] Dromedaries and camels carried fairly heavy loads – 700 pounds for less powerful animals, quite often 800 (around Erzerum, for example), and 1000 to 1500 between Tabriz and Istanbul, according to a document of 1708.[34] The pounds concerned must have been the so-called light pounds (under 500 grams) and the average load would have been roughly 4 or 5 present-day quintals. A caravan of 6000 camels could carry 2400 to 3000 tons, or the load of 4 to 6 reasonable-sized sailing ships of that period. For Islam, which thus controlled – over a long period – the bulk of inland communications in the Old World, the camel was the crucial element in commercial supremacy.

As for oxen (together with buffaloes and zebus) they spread throughout the Old World halted only by the Siberian forest in the north, where reindeer (wild or domestic) predominated; and in the south by the African tropical forest, home of the tsetse fly.

In India they were sometimes not put to work at all; some, however, were harnessed to ploughs, pulled gilded carriages, turned mills or were ridden by soldiers and nobles; enormous convoys of up to ten thousand animals under the command of caravaneers of the curious Mouris caste would even be used to transport corn and rice. In case of attack, men and women defended themselves with volleys of arrows. When two caravans crossed on the narrow north Indian roads flanked by trees and walls, one line would wait for the other to pass by to avoid confusion. Other travellers might be blocked for two or three days, unable to move forward or backwards because of the animals.[35] These Indian oxen were ill-fed and never stabled. Buffaloes in China, which were much rarer, worked very little, but were hardly fed at all, and had to fend for themselves. They were rather wild and easily frightened by travellers.

A common sight, particularly in Europe, was a pair of yoked oxen; even today, in places like Galicia in Spain, they can still be seen drawing wooden carts with solid wheels. Oxen could also be harnessed like horses: this was done by the Japanese and Chinese, who used the yoke harness, and sometimes by north Europeans who used the collar-harness. Oxen have immense possibilities as draught animals. Alonso de Herrera, a Spanish agriculturalist whose book appeared in 1513, advocated harnessing oxen and was not in favour of mules: mules were faster but oxen tilled more deeply and economically.[36] In France, on the contrary, Charles Estienne and Jean Liébaut sang the praises of the horse: 'Three of the best oxen of the Bourbonnais or the Forez cannot do as much as one good horse of France [i.e. the Ile-de-France] or the Beauce', they wrote in 1564.[37] François Quesnay took up the old discussion in 1758. In his time, capitalist agriculture using horses was driving out traditional agriculture which primarily employed oxen.[38] All things considered, however (the horse is quicker and its working day longer, but it eats more and depreciates in value much more in old age than the ox destined for the butcher's shop), the ox costs 30% more than its rival for an equal amount of work. A unit used to measure land in Poland in the seventeenth century corresponded to the surface that could be worked by one horse or a pair of oxen.

The horse has a long history. There were horses in France in the Neolithic Age, as is proved by the vast ossuary discovered at Solutré near Mâcon which covers more than a hectare. There were horses in Egypt in the eighteenth century BC and they crossed the Sahara in the Roman period. Did they perhaps originate in the regions surrounding the gates of Dzungaria, in the very heart of Asia? In any case they became so well distributed over Europe that by the sixteenth and seventeenth centuries AD, wild horses, or rather horses that had returned to a wild state, were to be found in the forests and thickets of north-west Germany, the Swiss mountains, Alsace and the Vosges. A cartographer, Daniel Spekle, mentions these wild horses in 1576 'in the forests of the Vosges, reproducing

Egyptian water-wheel in the last years of the eighteenth century. From the *Description de l'Égypte. État moderne*, a collection of documents made by the team of scholars who accompanied Bonaparte on the Egyptian expedition, published by the imperial government in 1812. (Photo B.N.)

themselves, feeding themselves in all seasons. In winter, they shelter beneath rocks.... Extremely wild, they are very sure-footed on the narrow, slippery rocks.'[39]

So the horse had long been known in Europe. This centuries-old familiarity helped to bring about the gradual improvement in harnessing (the horse-collar in the West in the ninth century, soon to be followed by saddles, stirrups, bits, reins, harness, tandem teams, shoes). In the Roman period horses were badly harnessed (the yoke harness throttled them) and they could only draw a relatively light load: in terms of work they were not worth more than four slaves. In the twelfth century, their performance suddenly improved, like an engine increased to four or five times its power, as a result of the invention of the horse-collar. Until then they had been animals of war; thereafter they played a very large part in harrowing, tilling and transport. This important transformation was one of a series of changes which included demographic expansion, the spread of the heavy plough, the propagation of triennial rotation in the north, and increased crop yields – all factors in the rise of northern Europe.

However, horses remained very unevenly distributed. There were relatively few in China: 'We have scarcely seen them,' said Father de Las Cortes (1626), 'in the Kingdom of Chanchinfu, and those we have seen are very small animals with short legs; they do not shoe them and do not use spurs. The saddles and bits are not as ours. [The Chinese were still using wooden saddles and ordinary ropes instead of reins in the eighteenth century.] We have seen a few more in the Kingdoms of Fuchinsu and Canton, but never in large numbers. I have been told that there are many horses in the mountains who have returned to wild life, and that it is the practice to capture them and break them in.'[40] As for mules, they were few in number and conspicuously 'small', according to another traveller, although they were sold at a higher price than horses 'because they are easier to feed and they do not tire so easily'.[41] If a traveller wanted to travel on horseback in China he would have been well advised to choose a good horse to start off with, since he would not have been able to change it; relay-points were reserved solely for the emperor's use. The sensible choice remained the sedan chair – light, quick and comfortable, with eight men taking it in turns to carry it. As for the transport of baggage and merchandise, which was very well organized – they could be left at a goods office and would be found in the corresponding office on reaching one's destination – this was often effected by porters or by one-wheeled carts pushed by one or two men, less frequently by pack-mules or donkeys.[42] True, the Emperor of China was described as 'the most powerful prince in the world in cavalry' and Magaillans in 1668 gives some apparently precise figures: 389,000 horses for the army, 175,000 for the staging-posts[43] reserved for the Emperor's service throughout the Empire. Even so, in 1690, when an expedition was launched against the khan of the Eluths, all privately owned horses in Peking, even those of the mandarins, were requisitioned for the army.[44] One may wonder, however, whether all the Emperor's subjects put together owned many more horses than their sovereign. Indeed, with a few exceptions (like the little horses of Szechwan) China's horses were supplied from outside her frontiers, at the special fairs held on the frontiers of Mongolia and Manchuria: the fairs of Ka Yüan or Kuang Min; after 1467, the fairs of Fu Shun.[45] According to an early eighteenth-century source, the Emperor bought about 7000 horses a year at the fairs, while 'the lords, and civilian and military mandarins' and the rest of the population bought in all only 'twice or three times this number'. In other words a maximum of 28,000 horses a year was bought in the north: quite a low figure.

Horses were even rarer in India and Black Africa. Moroccan horses were indeed objects of great luxury, bartered for gold dust, ivory and slaves in the Sudan: twelve slaves for one horse at the beginning of the sixteenth century, and still as many as five later on.[46] Fleets loaded with horses bought in Persia sailed for the Indies from Hormuz. A horse at Goa sold for as much as 500 *pardoes* or 1000 of the Great Mogul's rupees, whereas a young slave at the same period was worth between 20 and 25 *pardoes*.[47]

How did these expensive horses live with neither barley nor hay?

> For food [wrote Tavernier in 1664] the horses are given a species of large pea that is crushed between two small millstones and then left to soak because its hardness makes its digestion very lengthy. These peas are given to the horses morning and evening; they are made to swallow two pounds of rough black sugar, crushed with the same amount of flour, and a pound of butter in small balls which are pushed down their throats; after which their mouths are carefully washed out because they have an aversion to this food. In the daytime they are only given certain herbs from the fields which are pulled up by the root and which are also carefully washed so that no earth or sand remains.[48]

In Japan, where carriages were normally harnessed to oxen (from Korea), horses were primarily nobles' mounts.

In Muslim countries, horses were the aristocracy of the animal world. They constituted Islam's great military weapon almost from the beginning, certainly after its first great successes. Giovanni Botero recognized the superiority of the Wallachian, Polish, Hungarian and Turkish cavalry in 1590: 'If they have broken your lines you cannot escape them by fleeing, and if you have succeeded in scattering them you cannot catch them, for they are as swift as hawks and can either swoop down on you or vanish in a moment.'[49] And they were plentiful: a traveller (1694) saw caravans of 1000 horses in Persia.[50] From a military point of view, the Ottoman Empire in 1585 consisted of 40,000 horses in Asia and 100,000 in Europe; according to an ambassador, hostile Persia had 80,000.[51] These were formidable reserves. In fact Asia won the race to produce war-horses – witness the vast numbers of them assembled at Scutari and then shipped to Istanbul.[52]

Théophile Gautier in nineteenth-century Istanbul marvelled at the sight of so many thoroughbreds from Nedj, Hedjaz and Kurdistan. He also described the 'Turkish cabs' or *arabas* stationed opposite the landing stage in Scutari. These were 'gilded and painted carriages', covered 'with cloth fitted over a frame' and harnessed to 'black buffaloes or silver-grey oxen'.[53] In fact in the nineteenth century horses were still reserved for soldiers, the rich, and nobles. In Istanbul horses might certainly turn the mills; and small horses, their feet shod in solid iron soles, provided transport in the Western Balkans. But they were menials, and it was not to horses like these that a traveller was referring when he said as recently as 1881 that a horse was worth 40 or 50 ducats at Mazagan in Morocco, while a black slave of eighteen years fetched sixteen ducats and a child seven.[54] Horses did not finally replace oxen and camels for tilling in Asia Minor until after the First World War, in about 1920.

To its cost, Europe was slow to develop its own resources when faced with this world of horsemen. After the battle of Poitiers (732) it had to increase its numbers of horses and horsemen to protect itself and survive: the great charger the armed horseman rode in battle, the palfrey which carried him in times of peace, and his valet's common nag. This period witnessed a war effort on the part of both Islam and Christendom, with tensions and occasional respites. The Swiss victory over Charles the Bold's cavalry, for example, marked a return in the West to infantry, pikemen and later to arquebusiers. The Spanish *tercio* in the sixteenth century was the most effective development of the foot-soldier. Similarly the janissary inaugurated the reign of the unmounted soldier on the Turkish side. However, the Turkish cavalry, the Sipahis, continued to fight alongside the janissaries and long remained incomparably superior to Western cavalry.

Good horses sold for high prices in Europe. When Cosimo de Medici was reinstalled at Florence in 1531 and created a guard of two thousand horsemen, the ostentatious magnificence ruined him. In 1580, the Spanish cavalry briskly achieved an easy conquest of Portugal, but immediately afterwards the Duke of Alva was complaining of a lack of horses and carriages. The same shortage occurred in the following century, for example during the war of Catalonia (1640-59), and throughout Louis XIV's reign, when the French depended on the 20,000 or 30,000 horses they could rely on buying abroad during an average year. The stud farms established in France by Louis XIV, which made systematic

Eighteenth-century Manchuria: wild horses are caught by lasso as in the Argentine pampas. This was to supply the Emperor with cavalry - there was practically no horse-breeding in China. Musée Guimet, Paris. (Photo by the museum.)

purchases of stallions from Friesia, Holland, Denmark and the Barbary coast,[55] did not eliminate the need to buy foreign horses throughout the eighteenth century.[56]

The best horses were bred in Naples and Andalusia: the large Neapolitan breed and the Spanish jennets. But it was impossible to buy one at any price without the gracious consent of the King of Naples or the King of Spain. Of course smuggling was rife on both sides; the *passador de cavalls* on the Catalonian frontier was even risking the thunderbolts of the Inquisition, which had been entrusted with this unwonted supervision. In any case it took a very rich man, like the Marquis of Mantua, to have his own agents engaged in prospecting markets in Castile and as far afield as Turkey and North Africa in order to buy thoroughbred horses, pedigree dogs and falcons.[57] The Grand Duke of Tuscany, whose galleys (the Order of Saint-Stephen, founded in 1562) pirated the Mediterranean, often helped out Barbary privateers in return for gifts of good horses.[58] When relations with North Africa became easier in the seventeenth century, Barbary horses were shipped to Marseilles and sold at the Beaucaire fairs. Attempts were made to breed thoroughbreds from imported Arab horses, first in England in Henry VIII's reign, then in France in Louis XIV's and in Germany, where stud farms increased in the eighteenth century.[59] Buffon explained that 'it is from them [the Arab horses] that, either directly or indirectly, the best horses in the world are bred'. Breeds therefore gradually improved in the West; and numbers also increased. At the beginning of the eighteenth century, the Austrian cavalry which made possible Prince Eugène's successes against the Turks were in part the result of this progress.

Concurrently with the breeding of cavalry horses for Western armies, came the increased use of the draught-horse, which was indispensable for military transports and for hauling artillery. In 1580, the Duke of Alva's invading army made rapid progress through Portugal thanks to the requisition of many carts and carriages.[60] Almost a century earlier, Charles VIII's army had already surprised the Italian population when its pieces of field artillery passed quickly by, drawn not by oxen but by large horses 'clipped in the French style without tail or ears'.[61] A manual of Louis XIII's day[62] listed everything needed to mobilize a troop of 20,000 men equipped with artillery. It included among other things an enormous number of horses for the transport of cooking utensils, luggage and crockery belonging to the various officers, the field blacksmith's tools, the carpenter's, the surgeon's chests, but above all for the transport of pieces of artillery and their ammunition. The largest required at least twenty-five horses to carry the piece itself, plus at least a dozen for powder and shot.

Such were the duties of the large horses from the north which were increasingly exported southwards. Milan bought them from German merchants from the beginning of the sixteenth century; France from the Jewish dealers of Metz; they were in great demand in Languedoc. Clearly defined breeding areas developed in France – Brittany, Normandy (Guibray fair), the Limousin and the Jura.

We do not know whether the price of horses showed a relative fall in the eighteenth century. Whatever the case, Europe was equipped and even overburdened with horses. In England, horse thieves and receivers formed a social category of their own at the beginning of the nineteenth century. In France, just before the Revolution, Lavoisier calculated that there were 3 million oxen and 1,780,000 horses, including 1,560,000 engaged in agriculture (960,000 in regions where only horses were used, 600,000 where work was also done by oxen).[63] And France at that time had 25 million inhabitants. If proportions were constant, Europe would have had 14 million horses and 24 million oxen at its disposal – an important contribution to the continent's power supply.

Mules were also used in Europe; in Spanish agriculture, in Languedoc and elsewhere. Quiqueran de Beaujeu mentions mules in Provence 'whose price is often higher than that of horses'.[64] A historian has deduced the tempo of economic life in Provence in the seventeenth century from the number of mules and muleteers and their movements.[65] Since carriages could only cross the Alps at certain points, like the Brenner pass, the other paths were left exclusively to mule transport. These animals were even described as 'large transports' at Susa and all the other mule stations in the Alps. French Poitou should be noted among the important regions where asses and mules were reared. Every town depended on its horses for its daily provisioning, its internal communications, coaches and hired carriages. In about 1789, there were some 21,000 horses in Paris.[66] And the supply had constantly to be renewed. Convoys of horses, known as 'horse-trains', were always arriving in the city. They consisted of files of ten to twelve animals, each attached to the tail of the one in front, with a blanket on its back and shafts along each side. They were assembled in the district of Saint-Victor or on the Montagne Saint-Geneviève, and for many years there was a horse market in the rue Saint-Honoré.

Except for Sundays when boats took sightseers to Sèvres or Saint-Cloud (not always safely), the Seine was scarcely used for public transport, which moreover was almost non-existent. The vehicle for someone in a hurry was a hired carriage. At the end of the century two thousand seedy cabs plied for trade in the town; they were drawn by broken-down horses and driven by foul-mouthed coachmen who had to pay out twenty sous a day for 'the right to drive on the highway'. Congestion was notorious and we have many descriptions of it. 'When the cabs are empty,' said a Parisian, 'they are fairly docile; around midday they are more difficult, in the evening they are unmanageable.' And they were unobtainable at rush hours, for example at dinner time (for such it was) around two o'clock in the afternoon. 'You open the door of the cab, someone else does the same on the other side; he gets in, you get in. It is then necessary to go to the commissioner [of police] for him to decide who shall have it.' At such times a gilded carriage might be seen blocked by a cab crawling slowly along in front of it, at a slow and measured pace, 'all broken down, covered with burnt leather and with planks in place of glass'.[67]

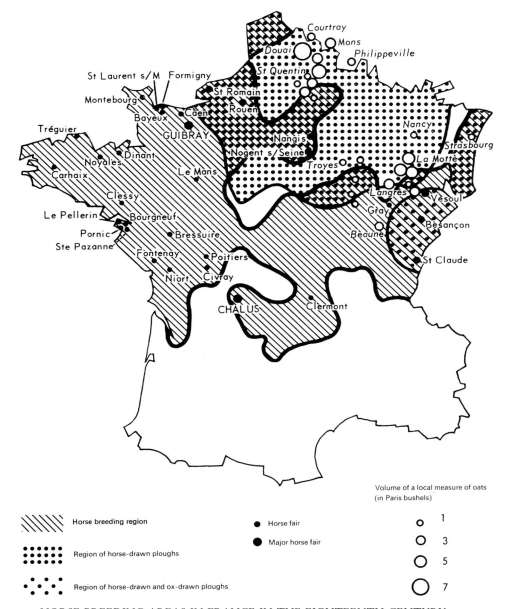

23 HORSE-BREEDING AREAS IN FRANCE IN THE EIGHTEENTH CENTURY

Note 1. the horse-breeding regions; 2. the approximate boundaries of the north-east region, the country of open fields, triennial crop rotation, with large supplies of oats and where horses were the animals most used for ploughing. These were distinct zones, but there were areas of overlap (Normandy, the Jura, Alsace, etc.). Outside north-east France, teams of oxen were used for ploughing, if one excepts a few places where they were replaced by mules (Provence, part of Languedoc and Dauphiné).

The real responsibility for such congestion lay with Old Paris, that network of narrow streets often lined with sordid houses into which the population was crowded – particularly as Louis XIV had opposed further development of the city (by the ordinance of 1672). Paris had not changed since the days of Louis XI. There had never been any catastrophe to wipe out the old city, as happened in London in 1666 or in Lisbon with the earthquake of 1755. The idea that some such disaster might not have been altogether a bad thing seems to have crossed the mind of Sébastien Mercier when he writes that the destruction of Paris is sooner or later 'inevitable', and mentions Lisbon as a huge ugly town where 'three minutes sufficed to destroy what would have taken human effort much longer ... And the city arose from its ashes mighty and magnificent'.[68]

Carriages had more room for manœuvre on the road from Paris to Versailles and back; they were drawn by horses that were nothing but skin and bone, but urged recklessly on 'all dripping with sweat'; these cabs were known as the *enragés*. 'Versailles is the land of horses.' They showed 'the same differences as exist amongst the inhabitants of the town: some are fat, well fed, well trained ... others ... with drooping neck and withers, only drawing carriages of court valets or provincials.'[69]

The scene would have been the same in St Petersburg and London, where we have only to follow day by day Samuel Pepys' drives and excursions in hired coaches in Charles II's reign. Later he treated himself to the luxury of a private carriage.

It is difficult to imagine what these problems of transport meant, for goods as much as people. Every town was full of stables. The shoeing smith was a person of substance, his establishment being rather like the present-day garage. Nor should the provision of oats, barley, hay and straw be forgotten. In Paris 'anyone who does not like the smell of new-mown hay,' wrote Sébastien Mercier in 1788, 'does not know the pleasantest of perfumes; anyone who likes this smell should go in the direction of the Porte d'Enfer [it is still there today, south of the Place Denfert-Rochereau] twice a week. There he will find long lines of carts overloaded with hay: they ... are awaiting purchasers ... suppliers to houses which keep horses and carriages are there, examining the quality of the produce; all of a sudden they pull out a fistful of hay, feel it, smell it, and chew it; they are cup-bearers for the horses of Madame la Marquise.'[70] But the Seine remained the great supply route. The fire that broke out on 28 April 1718, setting light to the arches of the Petit Pont and burning houses on it and neighbouring dwellings, started on a boat loaded with hay.[71] In London hay was bought at a market just outside Whitechapel bar. At the Perlachplatz market in Augsburg in the sixteenth century, October saw peasants offering piles of hay side by side with supplies of wood and game, and in Nuremberg pedlars with wheelbarrows sold the straw needed for the stables of the town.

Wind engines and water engines

The West experienced its first mechanical revolution in the eleventh, twelfth and thirteenth centuries. Not so much a revolution, perhaps, as a whole series of slow changes brought about by the increased numbers of wind- and watermills. The power from these 'primary engines' was probably not very great – from two to five horse-power from a water-wheel,[72] sometimes five, at most ten, from the sails of a windmill. But they represented a considerable increase of power in

A curious representation, quite late in date (1430), of a horizontal water-wheel. But this mill was in Bohemia, where the horizontal system was maintained for many years (cf. the illustration of the French Bible, *infra*, Vol. III, chapter 5, where the wheel is already shown as vertical). (Document in the author's collection.)

Mechanism of a watermill (1607): a perfect representation of the transformation of the vertical movement of the wheel into the horizontal movement of the millstone (a discovery already several centuries old by this period). From V. Zonca, *Novo teatro di machine*. (Photo B.N.)

an economy where power supplies were poor. And they undoubtedly played a part in Europe's first age of growth.

Watermills were both older and of much greater importance than windmills. They did not depend on the irregularities of the wind, but on water which is on the whole less capricious. They were more widespread because they had been in existence for a long time, and also on account of the large number of streams and rivers, dams, diversions and aqueducts which could turn a wheel fitted with blades or paddles. The force of the current was used by 'boat-mills' on the Seine in Paris, the Garonne at Toulouse, etc. Nor should power from the tides be forgotten; it was harnessed, both in Islam and the West, even in places where the tides were slight. In 1533 a French traveller to the lagoon at Venice was full of admiration for the only watermill he could have seen on the island of Murano, moved 'by water from the sea on a wheel when the sea swells and subsides'.[73]

The first watermill was horizontal, a sort of rudimentary turbine: it is sometimes called the Greek mill (because it appeared in ancient Greece) or the Scandinavian mill (because it was used in Scandinavia for a long time). It might just as well be described as Chinese or Corsican, or Brazilian, or Japanese, or as coming from the Faroe Islands or central Asia, because water-wheels turned horizontally there until variously the eighteenth or twentieth centuries, developing a small amount of power able to move millstones slowly. It is no surprise to find these primitive wheels in Bohemia in the fifteenth century or in Rumania in about 1850. This type of mill, with vanes, even functioned up to about 1920 near Berchtesgaden.

It was a stroke of genius to move the wheel to the vertical position, which Roman engineers did in the first century BC. The energy was transmitted by gear wheels to a horizontal plane for the purpose of turning the millstone – which turned five times faster than the propelling wheel, thanks to the use of gears. These first engines were not always rudimentary. Archaeologists have discovered impressive Roman installations in Barbegal near Arles: an aqueduct over ten kilometres long in which the water was 'forced along' culminated in a series of eighteen wheels – a set of early engines.

Nevertheless, the appearance of this Roman equipment was both late and limited to a few points in the Empire and was used solely to grind corn. Whereas the twelfth- and thirteenth-century revolution that increased the number of water-wheels also extended their use to other purposes. The Cistercians built them in association with their iron-works in France, England and Denmark. Centuries went by until the day when no village in Europe, from the Atlantic to Muscovy, was without a miller and a wheel turning with the current, except where a piping system brought water from higher up.

The uses of the water-wheel had become manifold; it worked pounding devices for crushing minerals, heavy tilt hammers used in iron-forging, enormous beaters used by cloth fullers, bellows at iron-works; also pumps, grindstones, tanning mills and paper mills, which were the last to appear. We should also mention the mechanical saws that appeared in the thirteenth century – as shown in a sketch made about 1235 by that strange 'engineer' Villard de Honnecourt. With the extraordinary development of mining in the fifteenth century, the best mills worked for the mines: treadmills powering winches with a reversible action to raise buckets of ore, machines to ventilate galleries or to pump water by norias, bucket chains or even by lift-and-force pumps, and controls operating levers that could set in motion mechanisms which were already complicated and which were to remain unchanged until and after the eighteenth century. These impressive mechanisms with wheels sometimes up to ten metres in diameter are shown in the magnificent plates in *De re metallica* by Georg Agricola (Basle 1556) which summed up earlier work and brought it up to date.

For mechanical saws, fullers' beaters, tilt hammers and bellows, the problem had been the transformation of a circular movement into an alternating movement: this was made possible by the use of the camshaft. A whole book could be written (and indeed one was) on the necessary gear mechanisms. The astonishing thing, to our eyes, is that such complicated solutions should have been possible using wood as the only construction material. These mechanical marvels were not, I hasten to say, everyday sights in the past. When Barthélemy Joly crossed the Jura and arrived at Geneva in 1603 he noticed mills in the Neyrolles valley at the outlet of the lake of Silan handling 'pine and fir wood which is thrown from the top of the precipitous mountains to the bottom; they have a pleasing device by which several movements from bottom to top and in the opposite direction [these were made by the saw] proceed from a single wheel turned by water, the wood moving forward of its own accord ... and another tree following in its place with as much method as if it were done by men's hands'.[74] It is obvious that this was indeed an unusual sight, worthy of inclusion in a traveller's tale.

Mills had, however, become universally used machines, so that water power, from rivers, whether exploited to the full or not, was absolutely necessary. The 'industrial' towns (and what town at that time was not?) adapted themselves to the courses of rivers, moving near them, controlling the running water and taking on a Venetian appearance, at least along three or four distinctive streets. Troyes was typical; Bar-le-Duc still has its *Rue des Tanneurs* on an offshoot of the river; Châlons, the cloth centre, used the Marne (over which there is a bridge called the Cinq Moulins - the Five Mills); Rheims the Vesle; Colmar the Ill; Toulouse the Garonne, where a fleet of 'floating mills', that is boats with wheels turned by the current, existed very early on and long remained in use; and Prague was built round several loops of the Moldau. The Pegnitz made it possible for the many wheels of Nuremberg to turn inside the city walls and in the nearby countryside (180 were still operating in 1900). In and around Paris, about twenty windmills afforded extra power, but even if there had been enough wind to turn their sails every day of the year, they could have supplied no more than a twentieth of the flour consumed by Paris bakers. There were 1200 watermills (mostly reserved for grinding grain) along the banks of the Seine, the Oise, the Marne and smaller rivers like the Yvette or the Bièvre (where the royal manufacture of the Gobelins was set up in 1667). Smaller rivers, flowing from a nearby source, had the advantage that they rarely froze in winter.

Was the takeover of the mills by the towns a second-stage development? In a thesis yet to be published, Robert Philippe has shown how in the preceding phase, the first mills were built on sites dictated by the flow of water to be used, in the countryside, near villages, where the source of energy thus became established and remained for centuries. The mill, whose primary function was to grind grain, was thus the essential tool of the *manorial economy*. The lord of the manor bought the millstones, and provided wood and stone; the peasants contributed their labour. The manorial economy consisted of a series of basic units, capable of self-sufficiency. But the exchange economy, which concentrated and distributed commodities, operated on behalf of the towns and led to the towns: it eventually imposed its own system on the preceding pattern and created a new series of mills, corresponding to its many requirements.⁷⁵

The mill thus becomes a sort of standard measure of the energy supply in pre-industrial Europe. When the Westphalian doctor Kämpfer landed in 1690 on an insignificant island in the Gulf of Siam, he wrote of the river, to give some idea of its flow, that it was abundant enough to turn three windmills.⁷⁶ Towards the end of the eighteenth century there were, according to records for Galicia (which had come under Austrian rule), 5243 watermills (and only 12 windmills) in an area of 2000 square leagues and for a population of 2 million. This looks an enormous figure at first sight, but then the Domesday Book of 1086 records 5624 mills serving a mere 3000 settlements south of the Severn and the Trent,⁷⁷ and one has only to look out for the innumerable little wheels visible in so many paintings, drawings and town plans to understand how widespread they had become. If the ratio of watermills to population was the same elsewhere as in

A windmill: wooden choir-stall, fourteenth century. Musée de Cluny, Paris. (Photo Jean Roubier.)

Poland, there would have been 60,000 in France[78] and not far off 500,000 to 600,000 in Europe on the eve of the industrial revolution.

In a meticulous article, to my mind as brilliant as Marc Bloch's classic article on the watermill, Lazlo Makkai confirms these estimates: '500,000 to 600,000 mills, the equivalent of one and a half million to three million horse-power'. His calculations are based on the number of leases; the dimensions of the wheels (two or three metres diameter) and the numbers of paddles or blades they had (about twenty on average); the number of wheels per mill (1·2 or more); a comparison between the mills of East and West Europe (roughly the same, at least as far as flour mills are concerned); and the almost constant ratio of mills to population: on average from actual records, 1 to 29. Since the number of mills or the size of the wheels increased with the population, the supply of mill-power more or less doubled between the twelfth and the eighteenth century. As a rule, every village had its mill. Where there was not enough running water, on the Hungarian plains for instance, mills were operated by horses or even manual labour.[79]

Windmills appeared very much later than water-wheels. They were previously thought to have originated in China; more probably they came from the highlands of Iran or from Tibet.

Mills were probably operating in Iran from the seventh century AD and certainly by the ninth century. They were moved by vertical sails fitted to a wheel turning horizontally. The momentum from the wheel was transmitted to a central axis and set in motion a millstone to grind grain. Nothing was simpler: there was no need to adjust the direction of the wheel since it was always situated in the path of the wind. It had another advantage; no gear-wheel was required to transmit the energy to the millstone. The problem in the case of a grain mill was always to power a horizontal millstone, the *mola versatilis*, which crushed the grain on a stationary millstone placed beneath it. The Muslims were said to have spread these mills to China and the Mediterranean. Tarragona, at the northern limit of Muslim Spain, possessed windmills in the tenth century. But we do not know how they turned.[80]

The great event in the West – as opposed to China where mills turned horizontally for centuries – was the transformation of the windmill into a wheel fitted vertically, as had happened to watermills. Engineers say that the modification was a stroke of genius and that power was greatly increased. It was this new style of mill, a creation in itself, that spread in Christendom.

The statutes of Arles record its presence in the twelfth century. It was in England and Flanders by the same period, and the whole of France welcomed it in the thirteenth century. There were already windmills in Poland and Muscovy in the fourteenth century; they had come via Germany. A point of detail: the Crusaders did not, as has been said, find windmills in Syria; they took them there.[81] Timelags were numerous, but in general northern Europe was more advanced than southern. For example, the windmill arrived late in certain regions of Spain, notably La Mancha, so much so that according to one historian Don Quixote's alarm was quite natural: the great monsters were new to him. The same did not apply in Italy; in 1319, in Dante's *Inferno*, Satan stretches out his enormous arms *come un molin che il vento gira*.[82]

Windmills were more expensive to maintain than other mills and costlier for the same amount of work, notably flour-milling. But they had other uses. The major role of the *Wipmolen* in the Netherlands in the fifteenth century (and still more after 1600) was to drive the bucket chains that drained water from the soil and poured it into canals.[83] So the mill became one of the instruments used in the patient reclamation of the Low Countries' soil; mills were located behind the dykes built up against the sea and along the lakes formed on the sites of over-exploited peatbogs. Another reason why Holland was the homeland of windmills was its situation in the centre of a great area of permanent westerly winds from the Atlantic to the Baltic.

Originally[84] the whole mill pivoted on itself to align its sails in the direction of the wind, like the Brittany mills, called by the distinctive name of *chandeliers*. The whole mill was mounted on a central mast and a directing bar or 'tail-pole' enabled the body to pivot. It was best if the sails were situated as high as possible above ground level to catch the strongest wind, so the machinery of gear-wheels and millstones was placed at the top of the building (hence the need for sack-hoists). One small detail is worthy of note: the axis of the sails was never strictly horizontal, the tilt being regulated by trial and error. We can understand these simple machines from plans (like that of Ramelli, 1588) and mills still in existence – how they transmitted momentum, their braking systems, the possibility of substituting two lateral pairs of millstones for the single central pair, and so on.

It is scarcely more complicated to explain the working of a *Wipmolen*, which took its driving power from the top of the mill and retransmitted it to the base and the bucket chain that acted as a pump. The momentum was transmitted by a shaft through a hollow central mast. This gave rise to certain difficulties when *Wipmolen* were, as the opportunity offered, converted for the purpose of milling grain, but they were not insurmountable.

Quite soon, certainly in the sixteenth century, thanks to Dutch engineers, tower mills became widespread: their sails were adjusted at the top of the building, the only movable part. The difficulty with these mills, sometimes called 'smock mills' (because from a distance they looked like a peasant clad in his smock), was to facilitate the movement of the 'cap' on the fixed part of the mill by the use of wooden runners or various types of rollers. Inside, the problems to be solved remained the same: to adjust, control and stop the movement of the sails, to organize the slow descent from the mill-hopper of the grain, which passed through the upper turning part of the millstone by the 'mouth'; the basic problem was to convert the momentum from the vertical plane of the sails to the horizontal plane of the millstones by gear-wheels.

Wooden machines and gears: this enormous tread-mill was a cage operated by three men standing inside. (Lichtbildstelle, Deutsches Museum, Munich.)

A windmill, with special sails turning round a vertical axis: they do not therefore have to be re-aligned to catch the wind. The transmission of the movement is in this case the opposite of that in a watermill: the initial horizontal movement is transmitted to a vertical bucket chain which is hauling up water (this mill was a draining-machine developed in 1652 in the English fens). In Dutch mills, there was a double transformation of the momentum: it began as horizontal, with the movement of the sails, became vertical through the transmission of the main shaft, then horizontal again for the pump. Drawing by W. Blith, from *The English Improver improved*, 1652. (Photothèque A. Colin.)

More generally the great advance was the discovery that a single engine, a single wheel – whether wind- or watermill – could transmit its momentum to several implements: not to one millstone but to two or three; not to one saw but to a saw plus a tilt-hammer; not to one pile but to a whole series, as in a curious model (in the Tyrol) which 'pounded' corn instead of milling it[85] (in this case the roughly crushed grain was used to make wholemeal bread which was more like biscuit than bread).

Sails: the European fleets

It is not my intention here to discuss the question of sailing-rigs in general, only to convey some idea of the power that sails put at the service of man. The sail was in fact one of the most powerful engines at his disposal, as the European example convincingly demonstrates. In about 1600 Europe had some 600,000 to 700,000 tons of merchant shipping (a figure to be treated with the usual caution, and best regarded as an order of magnitude). According to reliable statistics established in France probably in 1786, the European fleet had by then reached 3,372,029 tons.[86] Its volume had therefore possibly quintupled in two centuries. At an average of three voyages a year this would represent a trade of ten million tons, equivalent to that of a large port today.

These figures do not enable us to calculate the power of the wind engines that shifted such a volume with the same reliability we would have in the case of a fleet of steam-driven cargo boats. It is true that around 1840, when sailing ships and steam ships existed side by side, it was estimated that steam did the work of about five sailing ships for equal tonnage. The European fleet was therefore equivalent to 600,000 to 700,000 tons of steam-driven cargo boats, and we can hazard a figure of between 150,000 and 233,000 horse-power, according to whether the power needed to propel a nautical ton in about 1840 is estimated at a third or a quarter of one horse-power. The figure would have to be considerably increased if we included war-time fleets.[87]

Wood, an everyday source of energy

Calculations of energy today leave out work by animals and to some extent manual work by men; and often they ignore wood and its derivatives as well. But wood, the first material to be in general use, was an important source of energy before the eighteenth century. Civilizations before the eighteenth century were civilizations of wood and charcoal, as those of the nineteenth were civilizations of coal.

Everything in the European scene points to it. Wood was much used in buildings, even stone ones; all overland and sea transport was made of wood, as were machines and tools, the metal parts always being kept to a minimum; looms and spinning wheels, wine-presses and pumps were made of wood, and most ploughing implements were wooden; the swing plough was made entirely of wood, the plough usually had a wooden ploughshare fitted with a thin iron blade. To our eyes nothing is more extraordinary than some of the complicated gear-wheels with their precision-fitting wooden pieces that can be seen, for example, in the Deutsches Museum, the museum of technology in Munich. Exhibits there even include several eighteenth-century clocks, made in the Black Forest, with works entirely of wood, as well as a rarer item, a round wooden watch.

The fact that wood was used everywhere carried enormous significance in the past. One of the reasons for Europe's power lay in its being so plentifully endowed with forests. Against it, Islam was in the long run undermined by the poverty of its wood resources and their gradual exhaustion.[88]

Strictly speaking, we should here be concerned only with the wood directly transformed into power for heating houses and for industries using heat, iron furnaces, glass works, tile works and charcoal workshops, and salt mines, which often used firing processes. But, apart from the fact that supplies of wood available for burning were limited by the other uses of wood, these other uses exerted a major influence on the manufacture of all the implements producing energy.

The forest enabled man not only to warm and house himself but to build his furniture, tools, carriages and boats.

The type of wood he required varied. He used oak for houses; ten different woods, ranging from fir to oak or walnut, were used for galleys;[89] elm was used for gun carriages. The result was enormous devastation. No transport was too long or too costly for the needs of the arsenals: every forest was affected. Planks and timber loaded in the Baltic and Holland were being imported to Lisbon and Seville in the sixteenth century; so were rather heavy but cheap ready-made boats which the Spaniards sent to America with no intention of bringing them back, leaving them to finish their career in the Caribbean or sometimes abandoning them to the ship-breakers as soon as they arrived. These were the lost boats, *los navios al través*.

Every fleet, in no matter what country, required for its construction the destruction of enormous expanses of forest. Ship-building in Colbert's time exploited the forestry resources of the entire kingdom; timber was transported by every navigable route, even small waterways like the Adour or the Charente. Fir from the Vosges was floated along the Meurthe and then transported by road to Bar-le-Duc where the tree trunks were assembled into rafts on the Ornain. Next the Saulx, Marne and finally the Seine were used.[90] For the crucial supplies of masts for warships, France found itself excluded from the Baltic trade which primarily supplied England (via Riga and later St Petersburg). France did not think of exploiting the forests in the New World, particularly those of Canada (as the British did later).

The French navy was therefore obliged to use 'assembly masts' made of pieces of jointed wood ringed with iron, but they lacked flexibility and broke if overloaded with sail. Compared with the English, French ships could never show an extra turn of speed. We can judge better by looking at the time when the situation was momentarily reversed during the War of American Independence: the English had to resort to the inferior type of mast, for the League of Neutrals closed the Baltic to them, and the advantage passed to their opponents.[91]

This was not the only way in which forest reserves were wasted, nor even the most dangerous in the long run. The peasant, particularly in Europe, was continually uprooting trees to extend his tillage. Common land was the enemy of the forest. The forest of Orléans measured 140,000 arpents in François I's reign and only 70,000, it was said, a century later. The figures are not reliable, but certainly land clearance from the end of the Hundred Years War (which had favoured the invasion of field by forest) until Louis XIV's reign reduced wooded expanses to their lowest limits, which correspond more or less to those of today.[92] Everything conspired against the forest; in 1519 a hurricane destroyed fifty to sixty thousand trees in the forest of Bleu, which linked the Lyons massif with the woods of Gisors in the middle ages; peasants with ploughs moved quickly into the breach and the forest was never united again.[93] Today the view of the land on an aeroplane journey from Warsaw to Cracow still shows the way in which the long fields thrust into the forest areas. If French forests were stabilized in the sixteenth and seventeenth centuries, was it the result of careful legislation (for example, the great ordinance of 1573 and Colbert's measures); or was a balance naturally reached because the land that was still unexploited was too poor and not worth the effort?

Some historians, thinking primarily of the New World, have said that those who burned forests and set up cultivated zones in their place were much misled, since they were destroying one kind of wealth which already existed, in favour of another, yet to be created and not necessarily worth more. There is a clear fallacy in this argument: forest wealth only existed when incorporated into the economy through intermediaries – shepherds tending their flocks (not only the pigs at acorn time), woodcutters, charcoal-burners, carters: a whole community whose profession it was to exploit, to utilize and to destroy. The forest was worth nothing unless it was used.

Immense forest areas still remained outside the clutches of civilizations before the nineteenth century: there were the Scandinavian forests; the Finnish forests; the almost uninterrupted forest between Moscow and Archangel, crossed by a narrow network of roads; the Canadian forest; the Siberian forest linked by trappers to the markets of China and Europe; the tropical forests of the New World and the Indian Archipelago, where precious woods were pursued instead of furs: campeachy wood in present-day Honduras, *pau brasil* ('brazil', which gave a red dye and was cut down on the coasts of north-east Brazil), teak from the Deccan, sandalwood and rosewood elsewhere.

Wood was also used for cooking, for heating houses, and for all the industries that needed fire-power – for which demand was increasing with alarming speed even before the sixteenth century. A striking example is recorded near Dijon in 1315-17: to feed the six furnaces producing terracotta tiles, 423 woodcutters were employed in the forest of Lesayes and 334 drovers were needed to transport the wood.[94] There were many eager takers for the forest wealth which was bitterly fought over – since its abundance was only apparent. A forest was not a fuel reserve in any sense comparable to the most modest coal-mine, even at this time. It took twenty or thirty years to grow again once it had been harvested.

Woodcutters at work: paper cut-out. Probably Lower Brittany in about 1800. Museum of popular arts and traditions, Paris. (Photo A. Colin.)

During the Thirty Years War, the Swedes, who needed money, cut down vast areas of forest in Pomerania with the result that many regions were afterwards invaded by sand-dunes.[95] When the fuel situation became difficult in France in the eighteenth century, it was said that a single forge used as much wood as a town the size of Châlons-sur-Marne. Enraged villagers complained of the forges and foundries which devoured the trees of the forests, not even leaving enough for the bakers' ovens.[96] In Wieliczka in Poland, the heat-process for the saline water of the huge mine often had to be abandoned after 1724, and mining restricted to slabs of rock salt, because of the devastation of the surrounding forests.[97]

Because of its bulk, wood for burning had indeed to be close at hand. It was ruinous to transport it more than thirty kilometres – unless, that is, it could float on its own by waterway or sea. Tree trunks thrown into the Doubs could travel all the way to Marseilles in the seventeenth century. 'New' wood arrived in Paris in boatloads and 'floated' wood began to arrive from Morvan along the Cure and Yonne after 1549. Twelve years later it was floating down the Marne and its tributaries from Lorraine and the Barrois. It took extraordinary skill to manœuvre these floats, up to 250 feet long, under the arches of the bridges. Charcoal reached Paris in the sixteenth century by way of Sens from the forest of Othe; by the eighteenth century, it was arriving from all accessible forests, sometimes in carts or on pack animals, usually by the rivers – the Yonne, the Seine, the Marne and the Loire – in boats 'piled high, with hurdles along the sides of the boat to keep the charcoal in'.[98]

Great rafts of wood were coming down the Polish rivers to the Baltic from the fourteenth century onwards.[99] The same sight, on an even more grandiose scale, was to be seen in distant China. Rafts of wood from Szechwan, the trunks tied together with a sort of 'wicker rope', were taken down to Peking. 'The richer the merchant, the longer the rafts; some of them are half a league long.'[100]

Wood was also transported over long distances by sea. There were the 'black sailing ships' that carried charcoal from Cape Corse to Genoa, and the boats from Istria and Quarnero that brought Venice its winter wood. The ships from Asia Minor that supplied Cyprus and Egypt sometimes towed tree trunks behind them. Even slender galleys were used to carry firewood to Egypt, where the fuel shortage was acute.[101]

However, there were limits to this form of supply and most towns had to be content with what they could find close at hand. Thomas Platter, a citizen of Basle who finished his medical studies in 1595 at Montpellier, noted the absence of forests around the town.

> The nearest is at the Saint-Paul glass works, a good three miles in the direction of Celleneuve. The firewood is brought from there in winter and sold by weight. One wonders where they would get it if the winter lasted a long time because they consume an enormous quantity of it in their fireplaces, while shivering beside them. Stoves are unknown in this region; unlike at home, the shortage of wood is so great that bakers fill their ovens with rosemary, kermes-oak and other bushes.[102]

The shortage increased the farther south one went. Antonio de Guevara, the Spanish humanist, was right: fuel in Medina del Campo was more expensive than what was cooked in the pot.[103] In Egypt the straw from the sugar cane was burned for want of anything better; in Corfu the residue from squeezed olives, made into bricks and immediately put to dry, was used as fuel.

To supply fuel on this huge scale required a vast transport organization, regular maintenance of the waterways used for floating, extensive commercial networks and the supervision of stocks – to which end governments increased the number of regulations and prohibitions. None the less wood became rarer every day, even in richly endowed countries. The problem was to utilize it better. But it would appear that no attempt was made to economize on fuel in either glass- or iron-works. As soon as the radius from which a wood-burning factory drew its supplies became too large and costs increased, the response was if anything to move the factory. Or else to reduce its activity. A blast furnace 'built in Dolgyne in Wales in 1717' was not fired until four years later when 'enough charcoal had been accumulated for thirty-six and a half weeks' work'. It only operated for an average of fifteen weeks a year, again because of lack of fuel. Furthermore, it was the general rule, in view of this constant shortage of supplies,

Sources of Energy, Metallurgy 367

for 'blast furnaces only to function one year in every two or three, or even one year in five, seven or ten'.[104] According to calculations by one expert, an average iron-works where the furnace was working two years on and two years off, in the period before the eighteenth century, absorbed the production of 2000 hectares of forest. The pressures this produced were aggravated by the industrial progress of the eighteenth-century. 'In the Vosges, trade in wood has become the trade of all the inhabitants: it is a case of who can fell more trees, and in a short time the forests will be completely destroyed.'[105] It was from this crisis – latent in England from the sixteenth century – that in the course of time the coal revolution emerged.

And, of course, there was also the pressure of prices. In his *Oeconomies Royales* Sully went so far as to say 'that the price of all the commodities necessary for life would constantly increase and the growing scarcity of firewood would be the cause'.[106] The rise in price accelerated in 1715 and 'shot up with the last twenty years of the *ancien régime*'. In Burgundy 'timber can no longer be found' and 'the poor do without fires'.[107]

It is very difficult to present the matter statistically, but we do have at least three rough estimates at our disposal. In 1942, when France was reduced to heating with wood, the country is said to have used 18 million tons, about half of it in the form of firewood. In 1840, French consumption was of the order of 10 million tons in firewood and charcoal alone (not counting wood used for building).[108] And in 1789, it was about 20 million tons. In Paris alone, on the eve of the Revolution, charcoal and firewood represented more than 2 million tons,[109] that is 2 tons per head. That is a very high figure, but at this time Paris was receiving only insignificant quantities of coal – the figure for wood was 140 times that for coal. The difference between 1789 and 1840 is of course accounted for by the increasing use of coal. If France is reckoned to account for one-tenth of European consumption, Europe as a whole must have been burning 200 million tons of wood in 1789 and 100 million in 1840.

It is on the basis of this figure of 200 million tons that we must try to conduct the hazardous calculation of the value in horse-power of wood as a source of energy. Two tons of wood are equal to a ton of coal. If we assume that one horse-power hour represents the combustion of two kilograms of coal and that energy was used at the rate of about three thousand hours per year, the energy available will be in the order of 16 million horse-power. These calculations, which I have shown to specialists, only give a very approximate order of magnitude and the reduction to horse-power is both outmoded and risky. It should also be borne in mind that there was a very low return on the energy invested – about 30%, which brings us to 4 or 5 million horse-power. This figure is still comparatively high, given the scale of pre-industrial energy, but it is not to be ruled out of court: after all, more serious calculations than mine have shown that coal did not overtake wood in the economy of the United States until 1887!

Seventeenth-century Lyon still had wooden bridges. Drawing by Johannes Lingelbach. Albertina, Vienna. (Photo by the library.)

Coal

Coal was not unknown to either China or Europe. In China it was used in Peking for domestic heating (and had been for four thousand years according to Father de Magaillans), for cooking food in the houses of the mandarins and those in high positions, and also by 'blacksmiths, bakers, dyers and the like'.[110] In Europe it was extracted in the eleventh and twelfth centuries – from the shallow basins in England, for example, in the Liège basin, in the Saar, and in the small coal basins of the Lyonnais, Forez and Anjou – for lime kilns, domestic heating and for some processes in the iron-works (not all, at least not until anthracite or coke were available, coke coming in at the end of the eighteenth century). However, well before that date coal was fulfilling the minor functions charcoal left it, in chaferies and splitting mills (where the iron was split up) and wire mills where the wire was drawn. And coal was transported over quite long distances.

The excise authorities in Marseilles in 1543 noted the arrival of 'brocz' of coal by the Rhône, probably from Alès.[111] At the same period, a peasant mine at La Machine, near Decize, yielded barrels (they called them 'fish' or 'loads') of coal, which were taken up to the small port of La Loge on the Loire. From there they were sent on by boat to Moulins, Orléans and Tours.[112] Admittedly these were all small-scale enterprises. So too was the coal-firing employed at the Saulnot salt mines, near Montbéliard, as early as the sixteenth century. When wood was short in Paris in the autumn of 1714, the import firm Galabin & Co. made public experiments in the city hall with 'Scottish fuel'. They obtained a licence to import this foreign fuel.¹¹³ The Ruhr itself had to wait until the first years of the eighteenth century before coal became really significant. Similarly, it was only at this time that coal from Anzin was exported beyond Dunkirk to Brest and La Rochelle: that coal from the Boulonnais mines was used in Artois and Flanders in brickworks, breweries, lime-kilns and blacksmiths' forges, as well as for keeping sentries warm; and that coal from the mines of the Lyonnais could be brought more quickly, after 1750, along the recently constructed Givors Canal to Lyon itself. The major obstacle to the spread of coal was indeed transport, usually effected by carts or pack animals.¹¹⁴

Within Europe there were only two achievements of any magnitude: in the Liège basin and in the Newcastle basin in England. Liège was already an 'arsenal', a metallurgical town, in the fifteenth century, and its coal was used to finish its products. Production tripled or quadrupled during the first half of the sixteenth century. Later its neutrality (Liège came under the authority of its bishop) helped it to prosper throughout the religious wars. The coal, which had already been extracted from deep galleries, was exported towards the North Sea and the Channel by the Meuse.¹¹⁵ Newcastle's success was on an even greater scale. It was an integral part of the coal revolution that modernized England after 1600, enabling fuel to be used in a series of industries with large outputs: the manufacture of salt by evaporating sea water; the production of sheets of glass, bricks, and tiles; sugar refining; the treatment of alum, previously imported from the Mediterranean but now developed on the Yorkshire coast; not to mention the bakers' ovens, breweries and the enormous amount of domestic heating that was to pollute London for centuries. Stimulated by rising consumption, production in Newcastle continually increased: 30,000 tons annually in 1563-4, 500,000 in 1658-9. Production around 1800 was probably in the neighbourhood of two million. The Tyne estuary was permanently filled with coal ships plying mainly between Newcastle and London. Their tonnage rose to 348,000 in 1786, at a rate of six round journeys a year. Part of this coal was exported; 'sea coal' travelled great distances, at least as far as Malta in the sixteenth century.¹¹⁶

Very early on it was thought necessary to refine the coal before using it in iron production, just as wood was burnt in primitive earth-covered furnaces to produce charcoal. The method of producing coke was known in England in 1627. The first combustion of coal in Derbyshire dates from 1642. Almost immediately the brewers in the region began to use coke instead of straw and ordinary coal for drying and heating the malt. The new fuel was to give Derby beer the 'paleness and sweetness which made its reputation',¹¹⁷ ridding it of the unpleasant smell of ordinary coal. It duly became the leading beer in England.

But coke did not achieve immediate popularity in metallurgy. '[Coal] can, with fire, be purged of the bitumen and sulphur it contains,' said an economist in 1754, 'so that by losing two-thirds of its weight and very little of its volume it remains a combustible substance but cleared of those parts that give off the unpleasant smoke for which it is criticised.'¹¹⁸ Nevertheless this 'coal cinder', as

A brass foundry in Thuringia belonging to the Nuremberg family of Pfinzing. In 1588 the fuel used was charcoal. The logs can be seen stacked in enormous piles.

the same eighteenth-century economist called it, only achieved its first metallurgical success around 1780. We will have to return to this apparently incomprehensible delay.[119] It is a good example of social inertia in the face of anything new.

The case of China is even more conclusive in this respect. We have indicated that coal played a part in domestic heating there, possibly several millennia before Christ, and in iron metallurgy from the fifth century BC. In fact the firing of coal made the production and utilization of cast iron possible very early on. This tremendous precocity did not lead to the systematic utilization of coke during the extraordinary Chinese advance in the thirteenth century, although it was probably known then.[120] Probably, not certainly. Otherwise, what an argument for our thesis: China, vigorous as it was in the thirteenth century, might have had the means to make the crucial breakthrough of the industrial revolution, and failed to do so! The achievement was left to England at the end of the eighteenth century – and England itself had taken some time to utilize what was under its nose. Technology is only an instrument and man does not always know how to use it.

Concluding remarks

Let us return to Europe at the end of the eighteenth century to formulate two connected remarks: the first on the subject of energy resources as a whole, the second on the machinery available.

(1) We can accurately classify available sources of energy in descending order of importance: first, animal traction; 14 million horses, 24 million oxen, each animal representing a quarter horse-power - that is roughly 10 million horse-power; next, wood, possibly equivalent to 4 or 5 million horse-power; then water-wheels, between 1·5 million and 3 million horse-power; then manpower (50 million workers), representing 900,000 horse-power; finally, sails, at most 233,000 horse-power, without counting the war fleet. This is obviously a far cry from the present-day energy supply, but that is not the point I wish to make. The interest of this incomplete calculation (in which, it should be pointed out, we have counted neither windmills, nor river boats, nor charcoal, nor even coal) is that it shows incontestably that the two principal sources of energy were draught-animals and wood combustion (windmills, which were not as numerous as watermills, cannot have represented more than a third or a quarter of the power of the water under control). If the mill was not more developed, it was partly for technical reasons (the widespread use of wood rather than metal) but chiefly because in the places where the mills were sited, there was no use for any greater energy supply, and at this time energy could not be transported. Lack of energy was the major handicap of *ancien régime* economies. The average watermill gave five times the yield of a hand mill operated by two men - and that was itself a revolution; but the first steam-driven mill would do five times the work of a watermill.[121]

(2) However, a preliminary stage was reached before the industrial revolution. The harnessing of horses, the flames from burning wood, rudimentary engines utilizing wind and river currents, plus an increased number of men at work, all provoked a certain amount of growth in Europe from the fifteenth to the eighteenth century, a slow increase in strength, power and practical understanding. Increasingly active progress in the 1730s and 1740s was built upon this gradual advance. There was thus an often imperceptible or unrecognized industrial pre-revolution in an accumulation of discoveries and technical advances, some of them spectacular, others almost invisible: various types of gear-wheels, jacks, articulated transmission belts, the 'ingenious system of reciprocating movement', the fly-wheel that regularized any momentum, rolling mills, more and more complicated machinery for the mines. And there were so many other innovations: looms for knitting and manufacturing ribbons, chemical processes. 'It was during the second half of the eighteenth century that the first attempts

were made to adapt lathes, borers and drilling machines [tools which had long been known] to industrial use.' It was the mechanization of weaving and spinning processes at the same time that launched the English economy.[122] Nevertheless what was lacking before these imagined or realized machines could be fully employed was a surplus of easily mobilized – and that means easily transportable – energy. But the machinery existed and was constantly being perfected. It is revealing to see how European travellers unfailingly comment on the contrast between the primitive machinery in use in India and China, and the quality and refinement of its products. 'One is amazed at the simplicity of the instruments used to make the finest silks in China,' writes one visitor,[123] and his words are echoed in almost identical terms by another writing about the famous cotton muslins of India.[124]

With the coming of steam, the pace of the West increased as if by magic. But the magic can be explained: it had been prepared and made possible in advance. To paraphrase a historian (Pierre Léon), first came evolution (a slow rise) and then revolution (an acceleration): two connected movements.

A French mine, in about 1600 (fireback). *'Pour parvenir il faut endurer'*: 'Endure to triumph'. (Lichtbildstelle, Deutsches Museum, Munich.)

Iron: a poor relation

Men the world over in the fifteenth century, and *a fortiori* in the eighteenth, would certainly not have thought the description of iron as 'a poor relation' either serious or in accordance with the facts. What would Buffon, iron-master at Montbard, have had to say about it? Nevertheless from our point of view the observation is true.

Iron smelting did use by and large the same basic processes as it does today – blast furnaces and power-hammers – but the difference is one of scale. Whereas a blast furnace today 'can consume the equivalent of three train-loads of coke and iron ore in twenty-four hours', the most perfected of these furnaces in the eighteenth century only functioned intermittently; then, flanked by a forge with two fires, for example, it barely produced 100 to 150 tons of iron a year. Today production is calculated in thousands of tons; 200 years ago they talked about 'hundredweights', which were quintals, the equivalent of fifty present-day kilograms. That is the difference in scale. It divides two civilizations. As Morgan wrote in 1877: 'When iron succeeded in becoming the most important production material, it was the event of events in the evolution of humanity.'[125] A Polish economist, Stefan Kurowski, goes as far as to maintain that all the vibrations of economic life can be grasped through the special case of the metallurgical industry: it summed everything up and paved the way for all that followed.[126]

But up to the beginning of the nineteenth century 'the event of events' had still not come to pass. In 1800, world production of the various forms of iron (cast iron, wrought iron, steel) had only risen at the very most to two million tons,[127] and even this figure, though there is some foundation for it, seems very inflated. Economic civilization at that time was dominated by textiles (it was cotton after all that launched the English revolution) much more than by iron.

Metallurgy remained traditional, out of date and precarious. It was an industry dependent on nature and its resources, on the fortunate abundance of ore, the always insufficient forest and the variable power of the waterways. In the sixteenth century, peasants in Sweden manufactured iron, but only during the rise of the spring waters; any fall in the rivers where the furnaces were built resulted in unemployment. And there were hardly any really specialized workmen – only, all too often, simple peasants, whether in Alsace, England or the Urals. Nor were there any entrepreneurs in the modern sense of the word. Many iron-masters in Europe were above all landowners and left their iron factories to stewards or farmers. A final hazard: demand was temporary, linked with wars that flared up and then died down.

The picture certainly did not appear in this light to contemporaries. They enthusiastically announced that iron was the most useful of metals, and all of them had had an opportunity to see iron-works (at least a village forge or the forge of a shoeing smith), a blast furnace, a chafery and a refinery. In fact local scattered production or supplying over short distances remained the general rule. Amiens in the seventeeth century bought iron from Thiérache, less than 100 kilometres from its markets, and redistributed it within a radius of 50 to 100 kilometres.[128] For the preceding century we have the journal of a merchant in the small Austrian town of Judenburg in the Obersteiermark[129] who brought together and shipped out iron, steel and metallurgical products from neighbouring iron-works and from the busy centre of Leoben. Details of purchases, sales, transports, prices and measures can be followed from day to day; there are bewildering lists of the innumerable grades, from raw and bar iron to various types of steel, wire (the heavy described as 'German', the thin as *Welsch*), not to mention needles, nails, chisels, stoves and 'white' iron utensils. And none of this went very far: even steel, a high-priced material, did not cross the Alps in the direction of Venice. Metallurgical products did not travel on a scale comparable to textiles, except for certain luxury items, like swords from Toledo, arms from Brescia or, to return to our Judenburg merchant, crossbows for hunting requested by Antwerp. The most developed trade in metallurgical products (from the Cantabrian region in the sixteenth century, from Sweden in the seventeenth, from Russia in the eighteenth) took advantage of sea and river routes and, as we will see, only involved modest quantities.

In short, until the eighteenth, or even the nineteenth century, in Europe (and naturally it was even truer outside Europe) the quantity of iron produced and used was not able to tip the balance of material civilization. We are speaking of

A seventeenth-century Japanese forge. (Photo B.N.)

The manufacture of sabres in Japan: forging and polishing. Eighteenth century. (Photo N. Bouvier.)

the period before the first smelting of steel, before the discovery of puddling, before the general use of coke for smelting, before the long sequence of famous names and processes: Bessemer, Siemens, Martin, Thomas. We are speaking of what was still another planet.

The beginnings of metallurgy

Iron smelting was discovered in the Old World and spread very early on, probably from the Caucasus, in the fifteenth century BC. All the Old World civilizations sooner or later learned this rudimentary skill, with varying degrees of efficiency. Only two spectacular advances occurred: the early advance in China, which appears doubly enigmatic (by its precocity on one hand, its stagnation after the thirteenth century on the other); and the later but crucial advance in Europe leading up to the industrial revolution.

China had the incontestable advantage of being first in the field. Cast iron and coal firing was known there perhaps as early as the fifth century BC; and the Chinese *may* have discovered how to smelt ore with coke by the thirteenth century. Now Europe was not familiar with casting molten iron before the fourteenth century, and smelting with coke, concerning which there had been conjectures in the seventeenth, only came into general use in England after about the 1780s.

The Chinese advance is hard to explain. The use of coal probably made very high temperatures possible; furthermore the ores used had a high phosphorus content and therefore melted at relatively low temperatures; finally, bellows with pistons worked by labourers or by paddle-wheels produced a continuous blast and thus created high temperatures inside the furnaces. The furnaces were quite unlike ours: they were in effect 'rectangular pits made of fire-bricks'. Inside were placed a number of crucibles which held the mineral ore and charcoal was piled up between the crucibles. The ore was not, therefore, in direct contact with the fuel and various substances could be added to it if desired, including charcoal. Successive smeltings in the crucible made it possible to obtain either malleable iron, almost entirely purified of its carbon content, or iron with variable carbon content, that is harder or softer steels. After two smeltings in the crucible, the product obtained enabled the Chinese to cast ploughshares or cooking pots in series – an art that the West discovered only some eighteen or twenty centuries later. A.G. Haudricourt has suggested, on the basis of philological data, that the *Flussofen*, for casting iron, which replaced the Styrian or Austrian *Stuckofen* or blast furnace in the fourteenth century, was the final stage in the transfer of Chinese technology which had come via central Asia, Siberia, Turkey and Russia.[130]

Another triumph of Asiatic smelting by crucible was the manufacture – thought by some to be of Indian origin, by others Chinese – of a special kind of steel, 'high quality carbonized steel', as good as the best hypereutectoid steels made today. The nature of this steel and the secrets of its manufacture remained a mystery to Europeans until the nineteenth century. It was known as Damascus or damask steel in Europe, *poulad jauherder* or 'watered steel' in Persia, *bulat* in Russia and later called wootz by the English, and was used above all to make sword-blades of amazing sharpness. It was already being made in India, in the kingdom of Golconda, when the Europeans arrived there and was sold in ingots which are described by Tavernier as being about the size of a small loaf of bread and weighing between six and seven hundred grammes. These were exported widely in the Far East, to Japan, Arabia, Syria, Russia and Persia. It was from this Indian steel, explained Chardin in 1690, that the Persians who regard their own steel 'less highly than this, and ours less highly than theirs'[131] made their finest sabres. Its particular characteristic was an undulating sheen, like watered silk, which was produced at the moment when the cooling process in the crucible crystallized into the mass of molten metal veins of white cementite, an iron carbonate of great hardness. So great was the reputation of this very valuable steel, that in 1591 the Portuguese captured a cargo of it off the Indian coast – but no blacksmith in Lisbon or Spain succeeded in forging it. Réaumur (1683-1757) was equally unsuccessful: he had a sample shipped from Cairo and entrusted to Parisian craftsmen. If wootz steel becomes red-hot, it breaks under the hammer and the sheen vanishes: it can in fact only be forged at low temperatures or resmelted in the crucible and cast. During the early decades of the nineteenth century, many Western scientists and Russian metallurgists endeavoured to discover the secrets of damask steel: the results of their research marked the birth of metallography.[132]

This combination of events explains why India was originally thought to be the home of damask steel. But in a brilliant article based on Arabic and Persian sources of the ninth and eleventh centuries and Chinese sources older still, Ali Mazaheri puts forward the hypothesis that 'Indian' steel was actually Chinese in origin (it was, like Chinese cast-iron, made in a crucible we should remember). He distinguishes between the Eastern sabre – associated with crucible-smelted Asian steel – and the Western sword, made of tempered and hammered steel, and traces the fantastic history of the Damascus sabre as it ran wild over Asia, into Turkestan and by way of the Scythian conquests into India, Persia, the Islamic countries and Muscovy. He suggests that the spectacular victories of the Sassanid Persians over the Roman legions, who fought with short swords of coarse iron, may have been achieved principally by the use by the Persian cavalry of damask steel sabres, far superior to any arms in the West. And 'it is to the sabre – and to China – that we must attribute the superiority of the Asian hordes which overran ... the Roman Empire and medieval Europe'.[133]

What is so extraordinary is that after this incredibly early start, Chinese metallurgy progressed no further after the thirteenth century. Chinese foundries and forges made no more discoveries, but simply repeated their old processes. Coke-smelting – if it was known at all – was not developed. It is difficult to ascertain this, let alone explain it. But Chinese development as a whole poses the same problem time after time: veiled in mystery, it has not yet been resolved.

Progress between the eleventh and fifteenth centuries in Styria and Dauphiné

A different kind of problem is raised by the lateness of the European success. The beginning of medieval metallurgy can be seen equally well in the Sieg or Saar Valleys or between the Seine and the Yonne. Iron ore was present almost everywhere; only almost pure (meteoric) iron, exploited in Europe from the La Tène period) was rare. The ore was broken up, washed and if necessary calcined, then placed inside an oven in successive layers alternating with layers of charcoal. The form the oven took varied greatly: excavations on a hillside in the forest of Othe, between the Seine and Yonne, have brought to light rudimentary ovens without walls, 'wind ovens'. At the end of two or three days, after firing, a small mass of spongy iron and a good deal of dross was obtained. The iron then had to be worked by hand in the forges, reheated (subjected to several firings), then beaten on an anvil.[134]

More complicated ovens, with walls but still not closed, appeared shortly. Natural ventilation (as in the case of an ordinary chimney) was no longer adequate. An example revealed by excavations in Landenthal, in the Saar, is the oven that was in use between 1000 and 1100. It had baked clay walls moulded on wooden slats, a height of 1·5 metres, a maximum diameter of 0·65 (it was shaped conically), and two bellows.[135] This example, with hardly any variations, was typical of a series of Corsican, Catalan and Norman ovens (the Norman for the treatment of *ossmurd*, the Swedish ore), all of them enclosed by walls but not shut at the top, worked by second-rate blowing machines and giving a low yield: ore with a 72% iron content would give a metallic mass in the order of 15%. Of course this applies to the metallurgy after the eleventh century practised by peasants in Europe (which lasted for such a long time) and by underdeveloped peoples in the Old World.[136]

The water-wheel resulted in decisive progress in iron-smelting in Europe after the eleventh and twelfth centuries. The advance was very slow, but for better or for worse finally established in all the great producing regions. Iron-works moved from forests to riversides. Water power worked enormous bellows, pounding devices that broke up the ore and hammers that beat the iron after its various firings. This progress began with the installation of blast furnaces at the end of the fourteenth century. They appeared in Germany (or perhaps the Netherlands) and were soon in eastern France and the upper valley of the Marne, while manual iron-works continued in the forests of Poitou, the lower Maine and the whole of western France until the sixteenth century.[137]

Styria was a good example of the new progress. The *Rennfeuer* (oven), entirely walled in, with hand bellows, appeared there in the thirteenth century. In the fourteenth century they had the *Stückofen* (bloomery furnace), higher than its predecessor and with a hydraulic blowing machine. At the end of the same century blast furnaces came in; they were similar to the *Stückofen* but even higher, with forehearths, and were grouped in the *Blähhaus* (the name appears in a document of 1389). The important thing was that smelting was achieved for the first time with the installation of enormous water-powered leather bellows and tunnels in the blast furnaces; which virtually means that cast iron was 'discovered' in the fourteenth century. Iron or steel could thereafter be obtained as required from cast iron, their common starting point, by extensive decarbonization (iron) or incomplete decarbonization (steel). In Styria they set out to produce steel.[138] But ancient metallurgy most frequently resulted in 'steeled iron' and not steel, until the innovations at the end of the eighteenth century.

Meanwhile the forge had moved away downstream from the blast furnace because in preserving its unity, the iron-works had become too large a fuel consumer and hampered in its supplies. A sketch of 1613 shows a *Blähhaus* in isolation, separated from the forge that functioned in association with it down-

Indian dagger with horse's head, seventeenth century. Damask steel and grey jade. Louvre, Department of Oriental antiquities. (Photo National Museums of France.)

river. The forge is equipped with a large water-powered hammer – the 'German hammer' or tilt-hammer. An enormous oak beam forms its handle. Its head, an iron mass which could weigh between 500 and 600 pounds, was raised by a wheel with a stopping-block and then let fall back on the anvil. This enormous striking power had become necessary to work the raw metal, which was now being produced in large quantities. However, as iron had to be reworked endlessly, small hammers with short, rapid blows were also used – they were called Italian hammers. Their prototype probably came from Brescia, the old iron capital, by way of workers from Friuli.[139]

Another example illustrating the advance takes us to the Alps. It has the advantage of pointing out the considerable role of the Carthusian monks throughout the early rise of metallurgy. They had settled in the Alps, in Styria, Lombardy, Carinthia and Piedmont by the twelfth century and were 'intimately connected with the invention of [pre-]modern iron smelting'. They are said to have invented cast iron at Allevard in Dauphiné in the twelfth century, in any case clearly before it appeared in Styria or elsewhere. This was the result of the early utilization of a fierce form of ventilation by means of enormous water blasts that harnessed a complete alpine torrent. With the arrival of Tyrolean workers (from 1172) a method of refining cast iron by charcoal fire and the addition of scrap iron was said to have allowed them to produce steel, called natural steel. None of this chronology is very reliable.[140]

In fact every centre had its individual stages, methods – particularly methods of refining – its secrets, customers, and its choices from amongst the various products. Techniques, however, have a tendency to become general whatever their origin, if only through the travels of craftsmen ready to move about. A tiny example of this occurred in about 1450 when two workers, 'natives of Liège', received a site on the Avelon near Senlis 'to make a waterfall to build a foundry or iron works'.[141]

All blast furnaces were sooner or later in continuous operation. The oven was immediately reloaded with ore and charcoal after each casting. Interruptions for repairs or supplies took place at increasingly long intervals. And blast furnaces grew in size: they doubled their capacity between 1500 and 1700 to reach as much as 4·5 cubic metres and a daily yield of two tons of molten iron.[142] The custom of retempering iron in molten iron to increase its carbon content also became general.

A mechanized forge in the Tyrol: both bellows and hammer are operated by a water-wheel, with a cog-wheel in the foreground. Sixteenth century.
(Bildarchiv der oesterreichischen Nationalbibliothek, Vienna.)

Semi-concentrations

Stimulated by wars, the demand for cuirasses, swords, pikes, arquebuses, cannons and iron bullets increased. Such urgent demands obviously did not last long. Reconversion remained difficult, but iron or cast iron was used to make cooking utensils, cauldrons, saucepans, grates, andirons, fire-backs and ploughshares. As these manifold demands used a considerable amount of material they led to concentrations or rather semi-concentrations, still rather uneven because problems of transport, fuel, the motive power available at any one point, supplies of victuals and the irregular pace of activity did not make highly intensive concentration possible.

At the end of the fifteenth century, Brescia had perhaps 200 arms factories – *botteghe*, workshops with a master and three or four workers. One document mentions sixty thousand people working iron. The figure is exaggerated even though we have to take into account workers at the ovens (*forni*), at the forges (*fucine*) and water-wheels (*mole*), diggers and miners who extracted ore, and carters responsible for its transport, all of them scattered within a radius of twenty to thirty kilometres around the town, as far as distant Val Camonica.[143]

Sources of Energy, Metallurgy

The situation was the same in Lyons, which collected the products of a multitude of small metallurgical centres, from over 100 kilometres around, in the sixteenth century. In Saint-Etienne, iron products in order of importance were: ironmongery, arquebuses, halberds, and, in lesser quantities, mountings for swords and daggers. In Saint-Chamond they manufactured ironmongery, arquebuses, buckles, rings, spurs, iron filings and implements required for throwing or for dying silk – copper basins, 'spindles for mills'. Secondary centres such as Saint-Paul-en-Jarez, Saint-Martin, Saint-Romain and Saint-Didier specialized in the manufacture of nails. Terre Noire manufactured domestic hardware; Saint-Symphorien '*ulles* or iron pots'; Saint-André agricultural implements: spades, iron parts for swing ploughs. Slightly farther away, Viverols produced 'bells for mules' (perhaps this was the place of origin of the bells the great Italian merchants of Lyons exported outside the kingdom). Saint-Bonnet-le-Château built up a reputation for the manufacture of 'clippers' (for shearing sheep).[144]

Craftsmen, such as the nail-smiths, took their merchandise to the large towns themselves, making up the load their animal carried with a small quantity of coal. This proves that the industry used coal, that Lyons knew of its use for domestic heating (even in the lime-kilns in the Vaise district), and that the finished products of the metallurgical industry circulated better, or less poorly, than the raw material.

The same conditions – small scale and relative dispersion of the production units, difficulty of transport – were the rule in the diversified hardware industry in and around Nuremberg, in seventeenth-century Swedish metallurgy, in the growth of industry in the Urals in the eighteenth century and in industrial methods in the Biscay or the Liège region. Concentration only took place where there were sea- or waterways: the Rhine, the Baltic, the Meuse, the Bay of Biscay, the Urals. The presence of the Atlantic at Biscay, together with rapid water courses, beech woods and rich mountain deposits, account for the early presence of an intensive metallurgical industry. Until the middle of the eighteenth century, Spain was still selling its iron to England and Spanish iron was used to equip the English ships that fought the Spanish fleets at sea.[145]

A few figures

I have already said that the world production figure of 2 million tons, which has been suggested for about 1800, appears excessive. Even supposing world production before the industrial revolution to have been two or three times that of Europe, the latter in 1525 was (according to John Nef) hardly more than 100,000 tons. In 1540 (according to Stefan Kurowski[146] from whom all the following figures are taken) European production was 150,000 tons; in 1700, 180,000 (of which 12,000 are accounted for by England and 50,000 by Sweden); in 1750, 250,000 (22,000 England, 25,000 Russia); in 1790, 600,000 (80,000 England, 125,000 France, 90,000 Sweden, 120,000 Russia), In 1810, total European prod-

A fifteenth-century inn: the men sitting at the table have hung up their arms behind them. Fresco in the castle of Issogne. (Photo Scala.)

uction was still only 1,100,000; and in 1840 it was 2,800,000 – almost half of which was accounted for by England. But by then the first industrial revolution had already taken place.

In the 1970s, Europe as a whole was producing 720 million tons of steel. In other words, the iron age had hardly begun for the entire chronological span of this book. The further back in time one goes from the great turning point of the industrial revolution, the smaller the role played by iron, and one can see how modest a place it had under the *ancien régime*. At the dawn of history, in the age of Homer, a warrior's armour was worth 'three pairs of oxen, a sword seven, and the bit of a horse's bridle more than the animal itself'.[147] The period covered by this book was still very much the age of wood.

Other metals

As historians, we tend to place large-scale production or trade in the foreground: we pay less attention to spices than to sugar, and *a fortiori* grain; less to precious or rare metals than to iron, the basis of everyday life, even in those centuries

Sources of Energy, Metallurgy 383

that were still not very eager to make use of it. The viewpoint is justified as far as rare metals of very modest use are concerned: antimony, tin, lead, zinc (which only came into use at the end of the eighteenth century); but the question is far from settled when precious metals – gold and silver – are involved. These metals gave rise to speculative enterprises with which proletarian iron was never concerned. A wealth of ingenuity was expended in the quest for silver – witness the beautiful diagrams in Agricola's book on mines, or the pits and galleries of Sainte-Marie-aux-Mines in the Vosges; it was for silver that the valuable deposits of mercury in Almaden in Spain were worked (the amalgam method made silver a metal of industrial production in the fifteenth century and particularly after the sixteenth century); for silver that mining progress (galleries, pumping out of water, ventilation) was accomplished.

It could even be maintained that copper played an equally great or perhaps more important role than iron at that time. Bronze pieces were the aristocrats of the artillery. Copper bottoms for boats became widespread in the eighteenth century. As early as the fifteenth, the double smelting of copper by the lead process made it possible to separate the silver mixed in its ore. Copper was the

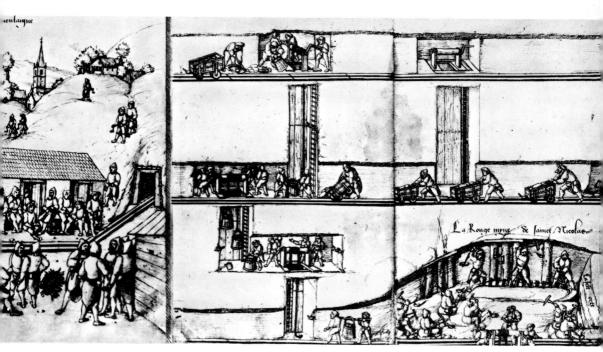

The Croix-de-Lorraine silver mines in the Vosges, first half of the sixteenth century: pits, ladders, windlasses, wagons for transporting the ore. These mines in the village of La Croix were worked until 1670. Bibliothèque Nationale, Paris, Cabinet des Estampes. (Photo B.N.)

third monetary metal, next to gold and silver. In addition it had the advantage of being relatively easy to smelt (one reverberatory furnace could yield thirty tons of copper daily). It was also favoured by early capitalism, which accounts for the amazing development of the copper mines at Mansfeld in Saxony in the sixteenth century, the boom in Swedish copper in the seventeenth, and the great speculation that Japanese copper (monopolized by the *Oost Indische Companie*) then represented. Jacques Coeur, and even more the Fuggers, were copper kings. On the Amsterdam stock market, even in later centuries, copper was the safest of investments.

6

The Spread of Technology: Revolutions and Delays

SUCH WERE the intractable technological foundations of society. Innovations penetrated them only slowly and with difficulty. The great technological 'revolutions' between the fifteenth and eighteenth centuries were artillery, printing and ocean navigation. But to speak of revolution here is to use a figure of speech. None of these was accomplished at breakneck speed, and only the third – ocean navigation – eventually led to an imbalance, or 'asymmetry' between different parts of the globe. It was more usual for new developments to spread gradually throughout the world: Arabic numerals, gunpowder, the compass, paper, silkworms, printing presses. No innovation remained for long at the service of one group, one state or one civilization. Or if it did, it was because other groups did not really need it. The new techniques were established so slowly in their place of origin that neighbouring groups had time to learn about them. Artillery made its appearance in some form in the West at the battle of Crécy; more reliably at Calais in 1347. But it was not a major element in European warfare until Charles VIII's expedition to Italy in September 1494, after a century and a half of gestation, experiment and discussion.

Above all, certain sectors remained stagnant: in transport (although the globe had been unified for the first time by Magellan's voyage) and in agriculture (where revolutionary progress was confined to certain sectors or submerged under the weight of routine), we shall continue to find the slow pace and the infuriating limitations on initiative of an *ancien régime* disrupted but not yet destroyed.

Three great technological innovations

The origins of gunpowder

A kind of 'Western nationalism' has led historians of science and technology to deny or minimize Europe's borrowings from China. The discovery of gunpowder by the Chinese was no 'legend', *pace* the otherwise excellent writer on the history of science, Aldo Mieli.[1] They were producing it with saltpetre, sulphur and crushed charcoal from the ninth century AD. The first firearms were also Chinese and are said to date from the eleventh century, though the first *dated* Chinese cannon is from the year 1356.[2]

Was it discovered independently in the West? The invention of gunpowder has been attributed – without evidence – to Roger Bacon (1214-93). The cannon was certainly in use in Flanders in about 1314 or 1319; at Metz in 1324; in Florence in 1326; in England in 1327;[3] at the siege of Cividale in Friuli in 1331;[4] cannon may have been used on the field of Crécy (1346), where Froissart tells us that the English *bombardiaux* merely 'flabbergasted' the French under Philip VI de Valois. And it was certainly employed a year later by Edward III at the siege of Calais.[5] But the new weapons really only made an impression in the following century, at the time of the dramatic Hussite wars in the very heart of Europe: the rebels had wagons carrying pieces of light artillery in 1427. Finally, artillery played a decisive role at the end of Charles VII's wars against the English – a good century after Calais – this time to the advantage of the French. Its new importance was linked to the development of corned gunpowder in about 1420.[6] This gave a sure and instantaneous combustion not obtained from the old mixture, which had to be packed into the gun, thus preventing air from circulating uniformly.

One should not, however, imagine that the presence of artillery now became the rule. There is some vague evidence that it was used in Spain and North Africa from the fourteenth century. But when Ceuta, a vital town on the Moroccan coast, occupied by the Portuguese since 1415, was under a new attack from the Moors, a soldier of fortune who had gone there to fight the Infidels

The first cannon bombarded the walls of towns at point-blank range. *Vigiles de Charles VII*, by Martial de Paris, *dit* d'Auvergne, 1484. Bibliothèque Nationale, Paris. (Photo B.N.)

wrote: 'We shot stones at them with our machines with a fair amount of success ... The Moors, for their part, had their marksmen armed with slings and arrows ... They were shooting with a few catapults during the whole day.'[7] Yet four years earlier, in 1453, the Turks had used a monstrous cannon under the walls of Constantinople. But even in Spain, trebuchets were still in use at the time of the siege of Burgos, in 1475-6. In addition, it may be noted that saltpetre was known in Egypt by the name of 'Chinese snow' in about 1248; that cannons were certainly in use in Cairo from 1366 and in Alexandria in 1376; and that they were common in Egypt and Syria in 1389. This chronology - Calais 1347, China 1356, etc. - still does not give first place to either Europe or China as far as the invention of the cannon is concerned. Carlo Cipolla does, however, think that in the early fifteenth century, Chinese cannon was equal or superior to that used in Europe. But by the end of the century, European artillery had become far superior to anything manufactured in Asia - hence the terror and alarm provoked by the appearance of European cannon in the Far East in the sixteenth century.[8] In the end, Chinese cannon failed to develop and adapt itself to the exigencies of war. In about 1630, a traveller remarked that in the outlying districts of Chinese cities 'they cast cannon, but have neither the experience nor the skill to handle them'.[9]

Artillery becomes mobile

In the beginning, pieces of artillery were short, light-weight weapons, only sparingly supplied with gunpowder (which was scarce and therefore expensive). We do not always know exactly what to make of their names. For example, the *ribaudequin* may have been a series of arquebus-like barrels assembled together (some commentators have described it as a sort of medieval machine-gun!).

Pieces then became larger - from 136 to 272 kilograms on average in the reign of Richard II (1377-99), according to specimens preserved in the Tower of London. They were sometimes enormous bombards in the fifteenth century, like the German *Donnerbüchsen*, monstrous bronze tubes, bedded in wooden cradles, which posed almost insoluble problems when they had to be moved. The miracle cannon - *der Strauss*, the ostrich - lent to Emperor Maximilian by the town of Strasbourg in 1499 to subdue the Swiss cantons, moved so slowly that it only just escaped the enemy clutches in time. A more commonplace accident occurred in March 1500 when Lodovico il Moro had 'six pieces of heavy artillery' brought for him to Milan from Germany: two of them broke on the journey.[10]

Relatively mobile, large-bore artillery, able to follow the movements of the troops, had made its appearance before this period - the Bureau brothers' artillery, for example, which was the instrument of Charles VII's victories at Formigny (1450) and Castillon (1453). Mobile artillery was drawn by teams of oxen in Italy: it was seen during the insignificant encounter of Molinacela in

1467.[11] But cannon mounted on gun-carriages, drawn by teams of powerful horses, only made its appearance in Italy with Charles VIII in September 1494. It shot iron cannon-balls (which quickly came into general use) instead of stone ones, and these missiles were no longer aimed only at the houses in a besieged town but also at its walls. No fortified city, where the action had hitherto consisted of defending or surrendering the gates, could stand up to such point-blank bombardments. For the guns were taken right up to the foot of the ramparts on the outer bank of the moats and immediately placed under protective *taudis* (hovels), according to Jean d'Auton, Louis XII's chronicler.

These weapons accounted for the chronic vulnerability of fortified towns for over thirty years: their ramparts were demolished like theatre sets. But counter-attack was gradually organized. Fragile stone ramparts were replaced by solid low-built earthworks, in which the shot lodged uselessly, and the defending artillery was set up on raised platforms - *cavaliers*. In about 1530, Mercurio Gattinara,[12] Charles V's chancellor, claimed that fifty pieces of artillery would be enough to protect the emperor's advantage in Italy from the French.[13] After all, in 1525 the fortified town of Pavia had immobilized François I's army, which was then surprised from the rear by the Imperial forces on 24 February. Marseilles resisted Charles V in the same way in 1524 and 1536; similarly, Vienna resisted the Turks in 1529, Metz the Imperial forces in 1552-3. This is not to say that towns could not still be taken by surprise: Düren was in 1544, Calais in 1558, Amiens in 1596. However, the fortress' revenge - the advent of skilled wars of siege and defence - was already foreshadowed, and it was only very much later that the strategies of men like Frederick II or Napoleon broke down this pattern, being no longer concerned with taking towns but with destroying enemy forces.

Meanwhile, artillery gradually improved. It was rationalized, reduced to seven sizes of calibre by Charles V in 1544, to six by Henry II. The heavier guns, earmarked for sieges or for defending towns, fired from 900 paces; the rest, called 'field' artillery, from only 400.[14] Later development was slow: in France, for example, General de Vallière's system, dating from Louis XV, lasted until Gribeauval's reform (1776). The impressive cannon then introduced served through the Revolutionary and Napoleonic Wars.

Artillery on board ship

Cannon were installed on ships very early on, but again in a very haphazard and irregular manner. In 1338 (that is *before* Crécy) they were already to be seen aboard the English ship, *Mary of the Tower*. But some thirty years later, '40 great ships' of Castile destroyed with their cannon a number of English vessels, in the open sea off La Rochelle. The English ships were entirely without artillery and unable to defend themselves.[15] Yet, according to experts, it had become the general rule for English ships to be armed with artillery by about 1373. In Venice,

The first mobile artillery. Charles VIII's field cannon, mounted on gun-carriages, accompanying the army along the roads of Italy. Bibliothèque Nationale, Paris. (Photo B.N.)

there is no evidence that there was naval artillery aboard the galleys during the relentless wars with Genoa (1378). But by 1440, and probably earlier, Venetian ships were carrying cannon, as no doubt were Turkish ships too. In 1498, at any rate, a Turkish *schierazo* of over 700 *botte* (350 tons) was firing stone shot, including one cannon-ball weighing 85 pounds, at the Venetians off the island of Mytilene (Lesbos).[16]

Naval artillery was not of course installed overnight, nor without difficulty. Long-barrelled cannon, shooting straight and with direct fire, were not to be found at sea before about 1550; cannon-ports were still not a regular feature of roundships in the sixteenth century. In spite of the danger, unarmed ships shared the seas with armed vessels. I have mentioned the English misadventure off La

Shipboard artillery: a ship bearing the arms of the admiral Louis Malet, Lord of Graville (died 1516). Olivier de la Marche, *Le Chevalier délibéré*, Condé Museum, Chantilly, MS. no. 507. (Photo Giraudon.)

Rochelle in 1372. But in 1520, at a time when French privateers on the Atlantic possessed artillery, Portuguese merchantmen still had none, very surprisingly for the date.

However, the increase in privateering in the sixteenth century soon forced all vessels to carry pieces of artillery and expert gunners to fire them. There was hardly any difference between war- and merchant-ships: they were all armed. This gave rise to some odd quarrels over etiquette in the seventeenth century: warships had the right to special salutes at the entrance to ports in the time of Louis XIV, on condition (and this was the subject of the dispute) that they did not carry merchandise – and of course they all did.

Revolution and Delays 391

Before long, the naval artillery now coming into general use was tending to conform to certain rules: so many men and so much artillery per ton capacity. In the sixteenth century, and still in the seventeenth, the scale was one piece for ten tons. Thus we can say that the English ship anchored at Bender Abassi on the scorching Persian coast in April 1638 was under-armed: it carried only 24 pieces for 300 tons. But this is only a rough and ready guide – there were all kinds of ships, all kinds of guns, and plenty of other measures of armament – size of crew, for instance. English ships in the Mediterranean and later on the long routes to the Indies from the end of the sixteenth century were usually over-armed, carrying more men and guns than others. Their half-decks were cleared of merchandise and therefore a more flexible defence was made possible. These were some of the reasons for their success.[17]

There were others. The large ship had ruled the waves for a long time because it was safer, better defended and equipped with a larger number of guns of a higher calibre. But by the sixteenth century, small ships had achieved staggering success in trade because they could be loaded quickly and did not

De Zeven Provincien, De Ruyter's flagship (1607–76), bristling with cannon. Rijksmuseum, Amsterdam. (Photo by the museum.)

remain idle for long in port; and in war because they had improved their firepower. The Chevalier de Razilly explained this to Richelieu on 26 November 1626: 'What made large ships formidable formerly was that they carried large cannon and the medium-sized ships could only carry small ones, which were not capable of piercing the side of a large ship. But now this new invention is the quintessence of the sea, so much so that a vessel of 200 tons can carry as heavy cannon as a vessel of eight hundred.'[18] In an encounter, a large vessel might well come off worst; the small one, faster and more manœuvrable, could fire away at its blind spots. The successful career of the English and Dutch navies on the seven seas was the triumph of small and middle-sized ships.

Arqueluses, muskets, rifles

It is impossible to say exactly when the arquebus appeared. Probably towards the end of the fifteenth century; it was certainly in use during the first years of the sixteenth. The defenders at the siege of Brescia in 1512 'sent shot from their artillery and their arquebutes [sic] as thick as flies', according to the *Loyal Serviteur*.[19] What got the better of the knights of yore was the arquebus, not the bombard or culverin. Heavy artillery caused the downfall of fortified castles and, at one time, towns. But it was a bullet from an arquebus that brought down the noble Seigneur Bayard in 1524. 'Would to God that these wretched instruments had never been invented,' Monluc wrote later, describing how, in 1527, he had raised 700 to 800 men in Gascony for M. de Lautrec and his expedition, which ended so unfortunately off Naples. 'This I did in a few days ... and they included four or five hundred arquebusiers; although there were but few in France at that time.'[20]

Such comments and others like them give the impression that the armies in the service of France lagged behind the German, Italian and particularly the Spanish forces at the beginning of this change. The French word was originally modelled on the German: *Hackenbüchse*; this produced *haquebute*. It then copied the Italian word: *archibugio*; which gave *arquebuse*. Perhaps the hesitancy is characteristic. There are many reasons for the French disaster at Pavia in 1525, but one was certainly the heavy bullet used by the Spanish arquebusiers. After this, the French increased the numbers of their arquebusiers (one for every two pikemen). The Duke of Alva went further and divided his infantry in the Netherlands into two equal bodies: the same number of arquebusiers as pikemen. The ratio in Germany in 1576 was five pikemen to three arquebusiers.

In fact it was impossible to abandon the pike – still described as 'the queen of weapons' in the seventeenth century – because arquebuses took a long time to manipulate. They had to be rested on prongs, loaded and reloaded, and the fuse lit. Even when muskets replaced arquebuses, Gustavus Adolphus still maintained one pikeman for every two musketeers. The coming of the rifle, an improved musket, first invented in 1630, and adopted by the French army in

1703, was one of the factors that made the changeover possible. Another was the introduction of paper cartridges, used by the Great Elector's army in 1670 but not until 1690 by the French. A final factor was the adoption of bayonets, which did away with the fundamental double nature of the infantry. By the end of the seventeenth century, all European infantry had rifles and bayonets; but this development had taken two centuries to come about.[21]

In Turkey, progress was even slower. At the battle of Lepanto (1571) the Turkish galleys carried more archers than arquebusiers. And even in 1603, a Portuguese ship which was attacked by Turkish galleys off Negropont found herself 'covered with arrows, up to the topmast'.[22]

Production and costs

Artillery and firearms quite transformed inter-state warfare, economic life and the capitalist organization of arms production.

A degree of concentration in the arms industry gradually took shape, but only on a modest scale, since the needs of war were so diverse. A single manufacturer could hardly produce gunpowder and arquebus barrels, side-arms and heavy artillery. And sources of energy were not readily concentrated at any given point. Industry had to be taken to them, near rivers or forests.

Only rich states were capable of bearing the enormous costs of the new warfare. They were eventually to eliminate the independent cities, which had nevertheless managed to preserve their autonomy over a long period. Montaigne, passing through Augsburg in 1580, could still visit the city's armoury, which he admired.[23] Had he been to Venice, he would also have been able to admire the arsenal there, an enormous factory with as many as three thousand workers at that time, summoned to work every morning by the great bell of Saint Mark's. Every major state had its own arsenal of course (François I founded eleven, and France possessed thirteen by the end of his reign). And they all had large arms depots. During the reign of Henry VIII, the principal arms stores in England were in the Tower of London, at Westminster and Greenwich. The policy of the Kings of Spain depended on the arsenals at Medina del Campo and Malaga.[24] The Grand Turk possessed arsenals at Top Hane and Galata.

But until the industrial revolution, European arsenals usually consisted of a series of workyards, and individual craft units, rather than factories with a rationalization of tasks. Artisans often even worked for the arsenal in their own homes, which might be some distance away. And it must have seemed prudent to locate the mills where gunpowder was manufactured far away from the towns. Mills were normally found in mountainous or sparsely populated areas such as Calabria, or near Cologne in the Eifel, and the Duchy of Berg. Twelve gunpowder mills had just been built in Malmédy in 1576 at the time of the uprising against the Spaniards. All mills – even those established in the eighteenth century along the Wupper, a tributary of the Rhine – produced their charcoal

Arquebusiers, detail of an imaginary representation of the battle of Pavia (1525) by Ruprecht Heller, a painter working in Germany in about 1529. Nationalmuseum, Stockholm. (Photo by the museum.)

from alder, *Faulbaum*, in preference to any other wood. The charcoal had to be triturated with sulphur and saltpetre, then sifted to obtain either coarse or fine powder.

Venice, economical as usual, persisted in using the coarse powder which was less expensive than the fine. However in 1588, the superintendent of its fortresses explained that it would have been better 'to use only the fine as do the English, French, Spaniards and Turks, who thus have only one single type of gunpowder for their arquebuses and cannon'. The Signoria had six million pounds of this coarse powder in magazines at that time, or 300 shots for each of its fortresses' 400 pieces. Two million more pounds or an expenditure of 600,000 ducats would have been necessary to supply 400 shots. To sieve the powder to make it fine would have meant an additional expense of a quarter again, or 150,000 ducats. But as the necessary charge of fine powder was less by a third than that of the coarse, the result would still have been a gain.[25]

Readers will excuse us for having dragged them into the bookkeeping of a past age. Its relevance is to show that Venice's security was 1,800,000 ducats' worth of powder at the lowest estimate, *or more than the equivalent of the annual receipts of the city itself.* This shows the huge scale of war expenditure, even when there was no war. And the figures increased with the years: in 1588, the Invincible Armada carried north with it 2431 cannon, 7000 arquebuses, 1000 muskets, 123,790 bullets and shot (or 50 per piece), plus the necessary powder. But in 1683, France had 5619 cast-iron cannon on board its fleets, and England 8396.[26]

Metallurgical war industries sprang up: at Brescia on the Venetian mainland from the fifteenth century; around Graz in Styria very early on; around Cologne, Ratisbon, Nordlingen, Nuremberg and Suhl (the arsenal for Germany and the most important centre in Europe until its destruction by Tilly in 1634);[27] at Saint-Etienne where over 700 workers were employed in the 'powerful arsenal of the lame husband of Venus' in 1605; and last but not least, the blast furnaces built in Sweden in the seventeenth century with capital from Holland or England. The Geer enterprises there were able to deliver in almost a single consignment the 400 pieces of artillery that enabled the United Provinces to block the advance of the Spanish south of the Rhine delta in 1627.[28]

The rapid progress of firearms stimulated the copper industries, as long as cannon were still being manufactured from bronze, and cast by the same process as church bells (the right combination – different from the one used for bells – eight parts of tin to ninety-two of copper, was already known in the fifteenth century). However, iron or rather cast-iron cannon appeared in the sixteenth century. Of the 2431 cannon of the Invincible Armada 934 were iron. This cheap cannon was to replace the expensive bronze pieces and to be manufactured on a large scale. There was a link between the development of artillery and the development of blast furnaces (like those set up by Colbert in Dauphiné).

But the cost of artillery did not end when it had been built and supplied with ammunition. It had also to be maintained and moved. The *monthly* bill for maintenance of the fifty pieces the Spaniards had in the Netherlands in 1554 (cannon, demi-cannon, culverins and serpentines) was over forty thousand ducats. To set such a mass in motion required a 'small train' of 473 horses for the mounted troops and a 'large train' of 1014 horses and 575 wagons (with 4 horses each), or 4777 horses in all, which meant almost 90 horses per piece.[29] At the same period a galley cost about 500 ducats a month to maintain.[30]

Artillery on a world scale

What mattered on a world scale was not only technology itself but the way it was used. The Turks – so skilled in earthworks, unequalled for digging pits during sieges, excellent gunners – had not succeeded in adopting the heavy cavalry pistols, manipulated with one hand, by 1550.[31] And they 'do not reload their arquebuses as promptly as our men', according to a witness who saw them at the siege of Malta in 1565. Rodrigo Vivero, who admired the Japanese, noted that they did not know how to use their artillery, and that their saltpetre was excellent but their gunpowder second-rate. Father de Las Cortes said the same of the Chinese (1626): they did not shoot their arquebus bullets with a sufficient charge of powder;[32] and this powder, another witness later said, was coarse, inferior stuff, at best good for firing salutes. Trade with Europeans introduced southern China to 'rifles seven palms long which took very small bullets, but they were more for pleasure than for use' (1695).[33]

This leads one to appreciate the significance of the artillery schools in the West. They were frequently found in the towns (particularly those that felt themselves threatened), with their apprentice gunners who marched off to the firing range and back, every Sunday, with a band leading the way. Despite the size of the demand, Europe was never short of gunners, arquebusiers or master smelters. Some of them wandered the world, to Turkey, North Africa, Persia, the Indies, Siam, the Indian Archipelago, and Muscovy. Until the death of Aurangzeb (1707), the Great Mogul's gunners in India were European mercenaries. They were then replaced, not very successfully, by Muslims.

As a result of these interchanges, technology in the end served all sides. This was true to a large extent in Europe where successes cancelled each other out. If Rocroi in 1643 marked the triumph of French artillery (which is not entirely certain) it was at best a tit-for-tat (in view of the arquebuses of Pavia). Certainly, artillery did not create any permanent imbalance of power in favour of one or another prince. It helped to raise the price of warfare and the efficiency of the state, and certainly entrepreneurs' profits. On a world scale, it put Europeans in a privileged position – on the Far Eastern maritime frontiers and in America, where the cannon was little used, but where the gunpowder of the arquebuses was of some significance.

Islam had more mixed fortunes. The taking of Grenada (1492) and the Spanish occupation of the North-African *presidios* (1497, 1505, 1509-10) were accomplished with artillery; so was Ivan the Terrible's capture of Kazan (1551) and Astrakhan (1556) from Islam. But there were Turkish rejoinders: the capture of Constantinople (1453), Belgrade (1521), and the victory of Mohacs (1526). The Turkish war effort was supplied by Christian artillery (5000 pieces seized in Hungary from 1521 to 1541). It used its firing-power with terrifying effectiveness for the time. At Mohacs, Turkish artillery drawn up in the centre of the battlefield cut the Hungarian line in two. At Malta (1565), 60,000 bullets were shot at the defenders, at Famagusta (1571-2), 118,000. Moreover, artillery gave the Turks a devastating advantage over the rest of the Islamic world (Syria 1516, Egypt 1517) and in their conflicts with Persia. In 1548, the large Persian town of Tabriz succumbed to an eight-day bombardment. We can also attribute to artillery the success of Baber's campaign when he destroyed India under the Sultans of Delhi with cannon and arquebuses on the battlefield of Panipat in 1526. And in a remarkable incident in 1636, three Portuguese cannon, hauled up on to the Great Wall of China, put the Manchurian army to flight, thus procuring an extra ten years or so of life for Ming rule in China.

The record is not complete but we can nevertheless draw our conclusions. If one balances advance against retreat, artillery did not materially change the frontiers of the great cultural groups. Islam stayed where it was. The Far East was not fundamentally touched (Plassey was not fought until 1757). Above all, artillery gradually spread everywhere of its own accord, as far afield as Japanese pirate ships in 1554. In the eighteenth century, no Malay pirate was without a cannon on board.

From paper to the printing press

Paper[34] came from very far afield, again from China, passed on to the West via the Islamic countries. The first paper mills were turning in Spain in the twelfth century. However, the European paper industry was not established in Italy until the beginning of the fourteenth century, when there was near Fabriano a water-wheel operating 'beaters' – enormous wooden pounders or mallets – fitted with anvil-cutters and nails which tore the rags to shreds.[35]

Water served both as motive power and ingredient. The production of paper required enormous quantities of clear water, so mills were sited on rapid rivers, up-stream of towns that might pollute it. Venetian paper was produced around Lake Garda. The Vosges had paper factories very early on; so did Champagne, with a large centre at Troyes; and Dauphiné.[36] Italian workers and capitalists played an important role in this expansion. Fortunately there was an abundance of old rags for raw material. Flax and hemp cultivation had increased in Europe from the thirteenth century. Linen cloth had replaced what woollen cloth there was. Old rope could also be used (as at Genoa).[37] Nevertheless the new industry prospered so much that crises of supply arose. Law-suits broke out between paper-makers and itinerant rag-and-bone men – attracted by the large towns or the reputation of the rags in a specific region, Burgundy for example.

Paper had neither the strength nor the beauty of parchment. Its sole advantage was its price. A 150-page manuscript on parchment required the skins of a dozen sheep[38] 'which meant that the actual copying was the smallest expense of the operation'. But the flexibility and uniform surface of the new material was bound to mark it out as the only solution to the problem of the printing press. As for the press itself, everything prepared the way for its success. The number

First folio of volume I of the Gutenberg Bible known as the '36-line Bible', with painted decorations. Bamberg, Gutenberg, about 1458-9. (Photo B.N.)

of readers in the universities of the West, and even outside them, had increased considerably since the twelfth century. An enthusiastic clientele had created an increase in the number of copyists' workshops and multiplied the numbers of correct copies; people were looking for rapid reproduction processes – for example, by tracing at least the main lines of illuminations. Virtual 'editions' of books appeared as a result of such methods. Two hundred and fifty copies of the *Voyage of Mandeville*, completed in 1356, have been preserved (73 in German and Dutch, 37 in French, 40 in English, 50 in Latin).[39]

The invention of moveable type

It does not really matter who invented moveable type in the West towards the middle of the fifteenth century. It could have been Gutenberg of Mainz and his collaborators – which still seems the most likely answer; or Procope Waldfogel, from Prague, who settled in Avignon; or Coster from Haarlem, if he existed; or perhaps someone completely unknown. The problem is rather to know whether the discovery was a revival, an imitation, or a rediscovery.

For China had been familiar with the printing press since the ninth century, and Japan was printing Buddhist texts by the eleventh. But this early printing, using blocks of engraved wood, each representing one page, was a very slow process. It was between 1040 and 1050 that Pi Cheng first devised the revolutionary idea of moveable characters. The first characters were made of pottery and fixed with wax into a metal forme. They were not much imitated; nor were the tin characters which followed them, and which deteriorated too quickly. But by the beginning of the fourteenth century, the use of moveable wooden characters had become widespread and had even reached Turkestan. Finally, during the first half of the fifteenth century, metal characters were perfected, either in China or Korea, and became widely used during the half-century preceding Gutenberg's 'invention'.[40] Were they brought to the West, as Loys Le Roy suggests – in 1576 it is true, that is some time after the event? The Portuguese 'who have sailed all over the world,' he writes, brought back from China 'books printed in the script of the country, saying that these have long been in use over there. Which has moved some to think that this invention was brought from there by way of Tartary and Muscovy to Germany, then communicated to the rest of the Christian world'.[41] This version of events is by no means proved. But there were certainly enough travellers – and travellers of some education – who had been to China and back for us to have serious doubts about the European origin of the invention.

Whether copy or re-invention, the European printing press became established after a good deal of experiment and difficulty in about 1440-50. The moveable type had to be cast from a mixture of precisely determined quantities of lead, tin and antimony (and antimony mines only seem to have been discovered in the sixteenth century) which would be sufficiently resistant without being too hard. There were three essential operations: a very hard steel punch was cut, bearing the character in relief; the character was then stamped into a copper (occasionally lead) die or matrix; finally, the moveable character itself was obtained by casting the alloy into the matrix. Then one could embark upon 'composing' lines of type which would be locked in a forme, inked and pressed on a sheet of paper. The bar press made its appearance towards the middle of the sixteenth century and was hardly altered until the eighteenth. The principal difficulty was that the letters wore out quickly. They had to be replaced by using the punches again and these in their turn wore out. In other words, the whole process had to start all over again. It really called for the craftsmanship of a goldsmith.[42] So it is not altogether surprising that the new invention emerged from this milieu, and not as some have maintained from the xylographers, or manufacturers of woodcuts – pages printed from blocks of carved and inked wood. On the contrary, these peddlers of popular pictures at first fought against the new invention. But in about 1461, Albrecht Pfister, a Bamberg printer, incorporated a woodcut in a printed book for the first time. From then on, wood was not a serious competitor.[43]

The printer's craft was slow to improve and was still virtually the same in the eighteenth century as when it began. 'Until 1787 (when François Ambroise Didot conceived the press which enabled a folio to be printed by one turn of the screw) methods of printing were such that if Gutenberg had come back to life and walked into a printing shop during the early years of Louis XVI's reign in France, he would immediately have felt at home in it, save for a few minor details.'[44]

The invention travelled round the world. Like gunners looking for hire, printing workers with makeshift equipment wandered at random, settled down when the opportunity offered and moved on again to accept the welcome of a new patron. Paris saw its first printed book in 1470, Lyon in 1473, Poitiers in 1479, Venice in 1470, Naples in 1471, Louvain in 1473 and Cracow in 1474. More than 110 European towns were known by their printing presses in 1480. Between 1480 and 1500, the process had reached Spain, spread throughout Germany and Italy, and touched the Scandinavian countries. By 1500, 236 towns in Europe had their own print shops.[45]

One calculation puts the total of *incunabula* (books printed before 1500) at 20 million. Europe had perhaps 70 million inhabitants at the time. The movement gathered speed in the sixteenth century: 25,000 titles were published in Paris, 13,000 in Lyon, 45,000 in Germany, 15,000 in Venice, 10,000 in England, perhaps 8000 in the Netherlands. An average of 1000 copies printed should be reckoned for every title, i.e. 140 to 200 million books, representing 140,000 to 200,000 titles or editions. And this when the population of Europe, including Muscovy, was even by the end of the century, little more than 100 million.[46]

Books and presses from Europe were exported to Africa, America, the Balkans (reached via Venice by itinerant printers from Montenegro) and Constantinople, where Western presses were taken by Jewish refugees. Presses and moveable type were taken on Portuguese ships to India, and naturally to the capital, Goa (1557); then to Macao (1589) on the doorstep of Canton, and Nagasaki (1590).[47] If the invention had indeed originated in China, the process had gone full circle.

Printing and history

Books were a luxury: as such they had from the start been subject to the strict laws of profit, supply and demand. A printer's materials had frequently to be renewed, the cost of labour was high, paper represented over double the other costs, and returns from outlay were slow. All this made the printing-house dependent upon money-lenders who soon controlled the distribution network. The publishing world had its Fuggers on a small scale, as far back as the fifteenth century: Barthélemy Buyer (died 1483) in Lyons; Antoine Vérard, master of a Paris workshop originally devoted to calligraphy and the illumination of manuscripts, who then adopted the new processes and specialized in illustrated books for France and England; the Giunta family from Florence; Anton Koberger, perhaps the largest publisher of his time, who brought out at least 236 works in Nuremberg between 1473 and 1513; Jean Petit, who controlled the Parisian book market in the early sixteenth century; the Venetian Aldo Manutio (died 1515); and one final famous example, the Frenchman Plantin, who was born in Touraine in 1514, but settled in 1549 in Antwerp where he made his fortune.[48]

As a commodity, books depended on routes, trade, and fairs; book fairs were held in Lyon and Frankfurt in the sixteenth century and in Leipzig in the seventeenth. The book trade as a whole was a source of power at the service of the West. All thought draws life from contacts and exchanges. Printed books accelerated and swelled the currents which the old manuscript books had kept within narrow channels. So printing hastened some developments, although there were times when advance was held back. In the fifteenth century, age of the *incunabula*, Latin predominated and with it a religious and devout literature. Not until the Latin and Greek editions of classical writings, appearing in the early sixteenth century, did printing serve the thrust of the humanist cause. Later still, the Reformation, then the Counter-Reformation, made use of books to further their ideas.

So it is hard to say whom the printing press really served. It expanded and invigorated everything. One particular consequence can perhaps be discerned. The great discovery which was to lead to the mathematical revolution of the seventeenth century was, to quote Spengler, the discovery of the number function: $y = f(x)$ in present-day terms. The notion of function implies the concepts of the *infinitesimal* and of the *limit*: both concepts already found in the thought of Archimedes. But how many people knew anything about Archimedes in the sixteenth century? A few privileged individuals. (Once or twice, Leonardo da Vinci went in search of an Archimedes manuscript after someone had talked to him about it.) Slow at first to engage in producing scientific works, printers gradually began to take them on, and little by little reinstated Greek mathematics. Alongside the works of Euclid, and of Apollonius of Perga (on conics) the seminal thought of Archimedes was for the first time made available to all.

It may be that the comparatively late date of such publications was responsible for the slow progress of modern mathematics between the end of the sixteenth century and the beginning of the seventeenth. Without them, however, progress might have been delayed even longer.

The triumph of the West: ocean navigation

The conquest of the high seas gave Europe a world supremacy that lasted for centuries. This time, technology – ocean navigation – did create 'asymmetry', an advantage on a world scale. In fact Europe's explosion on to all the seas of the world raises a major problem: how was it that ocean navigation was not *shared* by all the maritime civilizations of the world once the demonstration had been made? Theoretically they could all have entered the competition. But Europe remained alone in the race.

The navies of the Old World

It is all the more puzzling as the maritime civilizations had always known about each other: laid end to end, they covered the Old World in a continuous line from the European Atlantic to the Indian Ocean, the East Indies and the seas bordering the Pacific. Jean Poujade regarded the Mediterranean and the Indian Ocean as forming a single stretch of the sea which he appropriately called 'the route to the Indies'.[49] In fact 'the route to the Indies', the navigable axis of the Old World, was even longer, running, as it always had, from the Baltic and the English Channel as far as the Pacific.

The Suez isthmus did not cut it in two. Indeed a branch of the Nile joined the Red Sea for a period of several centuries (thus connecting it to the Mediterranean). This was Nechao's canal, as it was known, a 'Suez Canal' which was still functioning in St Louis' day but filled in soon afterwards. Venice and the Egyptians thought about opening it again at the beginning of the sixteenth century. In any case, men, animals and dismantled ships crossed the isthmus overland. The fleets the Turks launched on the Red Sea in 1538, 1539 and 1588 were taken there in pieces on the backs of camels and put together again.[50] Vasco da Gama's voyage (1498) did not destroy this ancient traffic between Europe and the Indian Ocean. It made a new route for it.

Such contact did not necessarily imply any mixing. No one is more attached to his own way of doing things than the sailor, wherever he may be. The Chinese junks, despite their many advantages (sails, rudders, hulls with watertight compartments, compasses after the eleventh century, and a large displacement volume from the fourteenth), went as far as Japan but did not venture beyond the Gulf of Tonkin to the south. From Tourane to the distant shores of Africa, only the less developed Indonesian, Indian and Arabian vessels with triangular sails were to be found. This, although it may be difficult to believe, was because the *maritime* frontiers of civilizations were as rigid as their continental frontiers. Nations kept to their own territory at sea as well as on land. Nevertheless neighbours visited each other: Chinese sails and junks were to be seen in the Gulf of Tonkin, because Tonkin was in effect under Chinese domination. If the Suez isthmus did not act as a frontier – although it appeared to have all the appearance and properties of one – it was because civilizations on either side were used to stepping over the border, as Islam did when it established itself over a large part of the Mediterranean, introducing incidentally the 'lateen' or fore-and-aft sail. This triangular sail, which was actually of Indian origin, came from the Sea of Oman where Islam had found it. Only through an act of historical trespassing did the sail we now think of as so typically Mediterranean reach the sea at all.[51]

The lateen rig was definitely a borrowing then, replacing the square sail previously used by all the peoples of the Mediterranean, from the Phoenicians to the Greeks, Carthaginians and Romans. Indeed, it met with some local opposition, on the coasts of Languedoc for instance, and even more so in Greek waters, as long as Byzantium held sway there with its powerful squadrons and its secret weapon, 'Greek fire'. It is not surprising though that triangular sails appeared on Portuguese ships, given the strong Islamic influence in Portugal.

In northern Europe, on the other hand, where a vigorous maritime revival took place before the thirteenth century, square sails remained the rule; hulls were clinker-built (with planks overlapping like tiles on a roof) which made for strength; and the pride and joy of northern shipbuilding was the axial rudder, operated from inside the ship and known as the centreline rudder.

All in all there were two different European navies, the Mediterranean and the northern: they were brought face to face and then intermingled by economic (not political) conquests. Genoan merchantmen,[52] the large ships of the Mediterranean, appropriated the best of the northern trade after 1297 with the first commercial voyage direct to Bruges. The process was one of capture, domination and education. Lisbon's rise in the thirteenth century was that of a port of call which gradually assimilated the lessons of an active, maritime, peripheral and capitalist economy. In these circumstances the long ships of the Mediterranean served as a pattern for the northern navies and suggested the precious lateen rig to them. Conversely, by a series of intermediaries, including the Basques, clinker construction and especially the centreline rudder of the northern ships, which

A fantastic representation of Venice, from the late fifteenth century, in which the Piazzetta with its two columns, the campanile and the Doges' palace are nevertheless recognizable. In the distance, between some imaginary islands and what seems to be the entrance of the lagoon, sail some square-rigged ships. Condé Museum, Chantilly. (Photo Giraudon.)

A boat with triangular sails, painted on a Byzantine plate. Corinth Museum. (Photo Roger-Viollet.)

improved their power to beat up to windward, were gradually introduced and accepted in Mediterranean yards. There were exchanges and mixtures and these in themselves indicate that a new unit of civilization was in the process of asserting itself: Europe.

The Portuguese caravel, dating from about 1430, was the issue of this marriage of north and south. It was a small clinker-built sailing ship with centreline rudder, three masts, two square sails and one lateen sail. The lateen sail, rigged sideways on to a mast whose yard was higher and longer on one side than the other, made it easy to slew the vessel round and steer it. The square sails ran across the width of the boat and were fitted to receive an astern wind. Once they had reached the Canaries, where trade winds blew uninterruptedly up to the Caribbean, caravels and other European ships could haul down their triangular sails and hoist square ones.

Early seventeenth-century merchantman, armed with cannon, on the Indies route. Flying fish seem to be raining around. Extract from Théodore de Bry, *Admiranda Narratio*, Frankfurt, 1590, 'Navigatio in Brasiliam Americae'. (Photo B.N.)

The water routes of the world

The prize of all such endeavours was victory over the water routes of the world. There was no apparent reason why any one of the many seafaring peoples of the world should out-distance the others in a race so often begun. After all, the Phoenicians had sailed round Africa at the bidding of an Egyptian Pharaoh, over 2000 years before Vasco de Gama. Irish sailors discovered the Faroes in about 690, centuries before Columbus, and Irish monks landed in Iceland in about 759; the Vikings rediscovered it in about 860. Eric the Red reached Greenland in 981 or 982 and Norsemen continued to be present there until the fifteenth or sixteenth centuries. The Vivaldi brothers passed through the straits of Gibraltar with two galleys in 1291, en route to the Indies, but were lost beyond Cape Juby. If they had succeeded in circumnavigating Africa they would have inaugurated the age of the great discoveries two centuries in advance.[53]

These were all European exploits. But in retrospect, the Chinese seem to have provided some formidable competition. They had had the compass since the eleventh century; by the fourteenth, they had large junks with four decks, divided into watertight compartments, rigged with four to six masts, able to carry twelve large sails, and manned by a thousand men. During the reign of the southern Sung dynasty, they ousted the small Arab ships from trade in the China Sea – making a clean sweep of their own doorstep, so to speak. In the fifteenth century, Chinese squadrons made some amazing voyages under the leadership of the great admiral Cheng Huo, a eunuch, a Muslim and a native of Yunan. His first expedition (1405–7) took him into the East Indies, with sixty-two large junks. The second (27,000 men, 48 ships, 1408–11) resulted in the conquest of Ceylon; the third (1413–17) in the conquest of Sumatra. The fourth (1417–19) and fifth (1421–2) were peaceful and led to exchanges of presents and ambassadors (the fourth to India, the fifth as far as Arabia and the Abyssinian coast). The sixth was a short trip, carrying letters from the emperor to the lord and master of Palembang in Sumatra. The seventh and last was perhaps the most spectacular. It left the port of Long Wan on 19 January 1431. For the rest of the year, the fleet was anchored at the most southerly ports of Chekiang and Fukien. The voyage was continued in 1432, via Java, Palembang, the Malaccan peninsula, Ceylon, Calicut and finally Hormuz, the end of the voyage. Here, on 17 January 1433, the fleet landed a Chinese ambassador of Muslim origin, who perhaps reached Mecca. It returned to Nanking on 22 July 1433.[54]

Then, as far as we know, everything stopped. It is true that China under the Mings had to face a renewed threat from the nomads of the north. The capital was transferred from Nanking to Peking (1421). This marked the end of an era. All the same, we can for a moment imagine what would have been the result of a possible spread of Chinese junks towards the Cape of Good Hope, or better still to Cape Agulhas which served as a southern gateway between the Indian and Atlantic Oceans.

We can cite another example of wasted opportunity. Arab geographers (starting with the tenth-century writer Masudi, who knew the Arab towns on the Zanzibar coast) had talked about the possibility of circumnavigating the African continent for centuries, contrary to Ptolemy's opinion. Their views coincided with the immutable opinion of the Christian Church which affirmed the unity of the liquid of the seas on the basis of the Bible. Certainly information from Arab travellers and sailors had percolated through to Christendom. Alexander von Humboldt was prepared to credit the remarkable voyage said to have been made in 1420 by an Arab ship, referred to in the legend on the map drawn in 1457 by Fra Mauro, the *geographicus imcomparabilis* of Venice. The ship is said to have sailed out into the 'Sea of Darkness' as the Arabs called the Atlantic Ocean, for forty days, covering 2000 miles 'between sea and sky', and to have taken seventy days to return.[55]

And yet it was to Europe that the credit finally went for solving the problem of the Atlantic, which held the key to all the other problems.

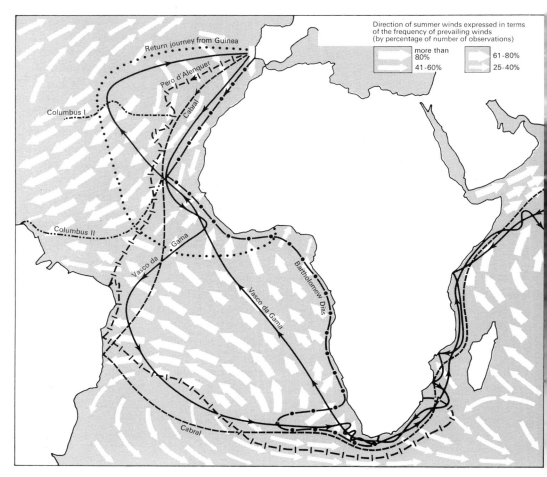

24 THE GREAT DISCOVERIES – THE ROUTES ACROSS THE ATLANTIC

This simplified map shows the summer positions of the northern and southern trade-winds, which change positions according to season. The routes to and from the Indies followed certain fairly simple rules. Ships were driven south by the northern winds and used the southern trades to reach the coasts of Brazil. On the return journey the southern trades drove them northwards and they cut across the northern trades to the winds of the middle latitudes. The dotted line showing the return from Guinea (or the return *da Mina*, as the Portuguese said) shows that it was necessary to avoid the African coast on the return journey to Europe. Bartolomeo Dias, whose voyage preceded Vasco da Gama's, made the mistake of hugging the coast of Africa when sailing southwards. The difficulties of the early navigations, during which these rules gradually came to be recognized, were greater than has been imagined. To complete the picture we ought to mention the role of ocean currents, which both helped and hindered navigation.

The simple problem of the Atlantic

The Atlantic consists of three large wind and sea circuits, shown on a map as three great ellipses. The currents and winds will take a boat in either direction with no effort on its part, as both the Vikings' circuit of the North Atlantic and the voyage of Columbus demonstrate. Columbus's three ships were driven as far as the Canaries, then to the West Indies; winds from the middle latitudes brought them home in the spring of 1493 via the Azores, after having taken them close to Newfoundland. To the south, another large circuit drove ships first towards the coast of South America, then on round to the Cape of Good Hope at the southern tip of Africa. There was only one rule for successful navigation: look for the right wind and never let it go when you find it. This usually meant taking to the open sea.

Nothing would have been simpler if ocean navigation had seemed a natural activity to sailors. But the early exploits of the Irish and the Vikings had vanished from memory. Before they could be revived, Europe had to be aroused to a more active material life, combine techniques from north and south, learn about the compass and navigational charts and above all conquer its instinctive fear. Portuguese discoverers reached Madeira by 1422 and the Azores by 1427; they simply followed the line of the African coast. It was child's play to reach Cape Bojador; but the return journey, with a head wind and against the northern trades was much more difficult. It was equally easy to reach Guinea, with its market in slaves, gold dust and pepper substitutes. But here again, the return trip meant cutting across the trade-winds and finding the way back to a westerly, which could only be done by sailing in the open sea for a month, as far as the Sargasso Sea. Similarly, the return journey from Mina (São Jorge de Mina was founded in 1487) made it necessary to beat against contrary winds for days on end as far as the Azores.

In fact the greatest difficulty was to conquer one's fear of the unknown, '*s'engoulfer*' as the French said (to take the plunge). The courage required for such an unwonted feat has been forgotten – as probably our grandchildren will know nothing about the bravery of the astronauts today. 'It is quite well known,' wrote Jean Bodin, 'that the kings of Portugal, having sailed the high seas for a hundred years,' seized 'the greatest riches of the Indies and filled Europe with the treasures of the East'.[56] They had 'taken the plunge' and reaped a rich reward.

Even in the seventeenth century seamen kept as close to the coast as possible. Tomé Cano, whose book appeared in Seville in 1611, says of the Italians: 'They are not sailors of the high seas.'[57] To Mediterranean sailors, who went from one seaport tavern to the next, taking the plunge meant at most going from Rhodes to Alexandria (four days in the open sea, out of sight of land, if all went well); or from Marseilles to Barcelona, following a chord of that dangerous semi-circle the Gulf of Lions; or making a bee-line from the Balearics to Italy, via Sardinia, and sometimes as far as Sicily. The most daring straight route, among European sea-passages during this *ancien régime* of ships and navigation, was however the journey from the Iberian peninsula to the mouth of the English Channel. It included the dramatic surprises of the stormy Bay of Biscay and the long swells of the Atlantic. When Ferdinand left his brother Charles V in 1518, the fleet carrying him from Laredo missed the Channel and found itself in Ireland.[58] When Dantiscus (ambassador of the King of Poland) crossed from England to Spain in 1522, it was the most dramatic voyage of his life.[59] Crossing the Bay of Biscay was certainly for centuries an apprenticeship to the savage high seas. This and other apprenticeships were perhaps necessary conditions for the opening-up of the world.

But why did none but Europeans take to the high seas? European observers and sailors were already wondering about this between the sixteenth and eighteenth centuries, when they had the very different navies of China or Japan before their eyes. Father Mendoza had an explanation in 1577: the Chinese were 'afraid of the sea, being people not accustomed to take risks'.[60] It was the custom in the Far East, as in the Mediterranean, to sail from one seaport tavern to the next. Rodrigo Vivero, travelling on the inland waterways of Japan between Osaka and Nagasaki – that is for twelve to fifteen days – declared 'that at sea, one sleeps almost every night on land'.[61] The Chinese, Father du Halde stated (1693), were 'good coastal pilots but pretty bad pilots on the high seas'.[62] 'The present system of Chinese navigation', wrote Barrow in 1805, 'is to keep as near the shore as possible; and never to lose sight of land unless in voyages that absolutely require it.'[63]

At the end of the eighteenth century, George Staunton gave more thought to the matter as he had the opportunity of examining at leisure Chinese junks in the Gulf of Tche-li beyond the Yellow Sea. He observed the 'curious contrast and singular spectacle of the towering masts and complicated tackling of European ships, in the midst of the low, simple and clumsy, but strong and roomy junks of the Chinese. Each of the latter was of the burden of about 200 tons.' He noted the way the hold was divided up into compartments, the abnormal size of the two masts, 'each of which consisted of a single tree or piece of timber; each carrying a square sail generally made of split bamboo, and sometimes of matting composed of straw or reeds. The junks are nearly of the same flat form at both extremities. At one is a rudder, of a breadth almost equal to that of a London lighter. It is guided by ropes passing from it along each side of the vessel's quarter.' *The Jackall* – the second English ship, which followed the ship of the line, *The Lion*, like a faithful servant – was only a hundred-tonner. In the Gulf of Tche-li it was outclassed by the junks with which it was competing. *The Jackall*, explained Staunton:

> was built for navigating with the variable and frequently adverse winds of the European seas; and drawing on that account double the quantity of water, or, in other words, sinking to double the depth of junks, or Chinese

Revolution and Delays 411

vessels of equal burden. The inconvenience of falling much to leeward with a side wind, to which the flat-bottomed vessels of Europe are liable, is not very much felt in the Chinese seas, where vessels sail generally with the monsoon directly in their favour [he means with a following wind]. The sails, too, of Chinese junks are made to go round the masts with so much ease, and to form so acute an angle with the sides of the vessel, that they turn well to windward, notwithstanding the little hold they have of the water.

His conclusions:

The Chinese, indeed, enjoy a similar advantage [to that of the Greeks], as their seas resemble the Mediterranean by the narrowness of their limits, and the numerous islands with which every part of them is studded. It is to be observed, likewise, that the art of navigation, improved among Europeans, dates its origins nearly from the same period when their passions, or their wants, impelled them to undertake long voyages over the boundless ocean.[64]

Chinese river boats. (Cabinet des Estampes. Print by courtesy of Bibliothèque Nationale.)

These observations bring us back to the problem we started with. Ocean navigation was the key to the seven seas of the world. But who is to say that the Chinese and Japanese were technically incapable of seizing this key and using it?

In fact both contemporaries and historians have been the prisoners of a search for a technical explanation, to be identified at all costs. But perhaps the explanation is not primarily technical. King John II ordered the Portuguese pilot who told him that it was possible to get back from the coast of Mina 'with any ship in good condition' to remain silent on threat of imprisonment. Another equally telling example dates from 1535: Diego Botelho had returned from the Indies in a simple *fuste*, which the King of Portugal immediately had burned.[65] Better still, there is the story of the Japanese junk which sailed from Japan to Acapulco in Mexico in 1610. A gift from the Japanese, it was carrying home Rodrigo Vivero and his fellow castaways. It was manned by a European crew, it is true. But two other junks, both with Japanese crews, later made the same voyage.[66] Such exploits prove that junks were technically quite equal to braving the high seas: so one would be on shaky ground to suggest that there was a purely technical reason why they did not.

Modern historians have even come up with the idea that the caravel did not owe its success so much to its sails and rudder as to its shallow draught which 'enabled it to explore coasts and estuaries', and even more to the fact that it was 'a ship of small dimensions, and so could be equipped relatively cheaply'.[67] This is to belittle its role.

It is no easier to explain why Muslim boats did not sail the high seas. Their voyages straight across the Indian Ocean were probably easy, with the alternation of the monsoons, but they none the less implied considerable knowledge, the use of the astrolabe or Jacob's staff; and these were high-quality ships. The story of Vasco da Gama's Arab pilot who took the small Portuguese fleet to Melinda and guided it straight to Calicut is very revealing. How was it, in these circumstances, that the adventures of Sinbad the Sailor and his successors did not lead to Arab domination of the world? How was it that, to borrow an idea of Vidal de la Blache's, Arab navigation south of Zanzibar and Madagascar stopped short just before the 'powerful current of Mozambique, which carries ships violently south' – towards the gateway of the 'Sea of Darkness'?[68] Let me reply in the first place by saying that the ancient navigational skills of the Arabs did lead Islam to dominate the Old World until the fifteenth century as I have had occasion to explain. Why then should they look for a route round the Cape when they had a Suez Canal (seventh to thirteenth centuries) at their disposal? And what would they want to find there? Islamic towns and merchants could already obtain gold, ivory and slaves on the coast of Zanzibar, and beyond the Sahara on the loop of the Niger. Some kind of 'need' for West Africa would have been the only possible stimulus. Perhaps the merit of the West, confined as it was on its narrow 'cape of Asia', was that it 'needed' the rest of the world, needed to venture outside its own front door. None of this could have happened,

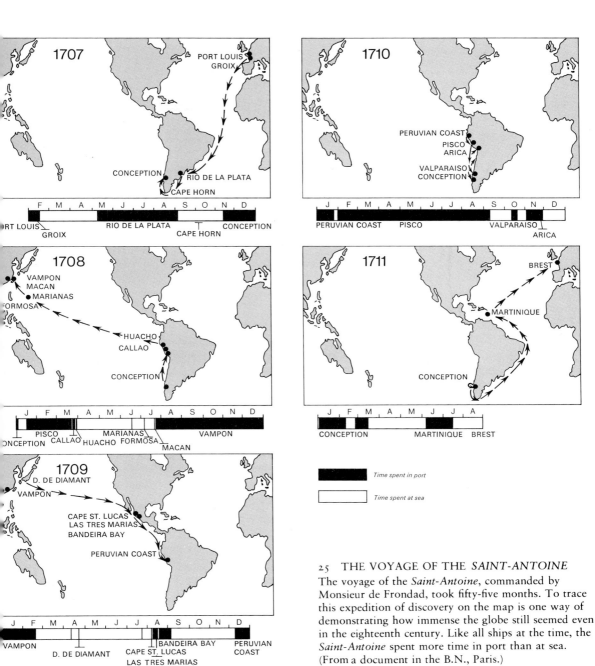

25 THE VOYAGE OF THE *SAINT-ANTOINE*
The voyage of the *Saint-Antoine*, commanded by Monsieur de Frondad, took fifty-five months. To trace this expedition of discovery on the map is one way of demonstrating how immense the globe still seemed even in the eighteenth century. Like all ships at the time, the *Saint-Antoine* spent more time in port than at sea. (From a document in the B.N., Paris.)

A seventeenth-century road – hardly visible at all. (From *Windmills*, by Breughel of Velours, fragment.)

according to an expert on Chinese history, without the growth of the *capitalist* towns of the West at that time.[69] They were the driving force. Without them technology would have been impotent.

To say this is not to explain the great discoveries entirely in terms of money or capital. On the contrary: China and Islam were both at the time rich societies; they even had what we would today call colonies. The West, by comparison, was still 'proletarian'. But the important thing was the long period of pressure after the thirteenth century which raised the level of its material life and transformed its whole psychology. What historians have called the hunger for gold, the hunger to conquer the world or the hunger for spices was accompanied in the technological sphere by a constant search for new inventions and utilitarian applications – utilitarian in the sense that they would actually serve mankind, making human labour both less wearisome and more efficient. The accumulation of practical discoveries showing a conscious will to master the world and a growing interest in every source of energy was already shaping the true face of Europe and hinting at things to come, well before that success was actually achieved.

Transport

The victory over the ocean was a great triumph and a great innovation which created a global network of communications. But it did so without altering the deficiencies and delays of traditional means of transport which remained permanent limitations on *ancien régime* economies. Up to the eighteenth century, sea journeys were interminable and overland transport went at snail's pace. We are told that Europe began to establish an enormous network of efficient roads in the thirteenth century. But we have only to look at the series of small paintings by Jan Breughel at the Pinakothek in Munich, for example, to realize that even in the seventeenth century, and even in flat open country, a road was not a clearly delineated strip along which traffic flowed smoothly. Its outline is generally barely perceptible in the pictures. It would certainly not be recognizable at first glance without the movement of those making use of it. And they are often peasants on foot, a cart taking a farmer's wife and her baskets to market, a pedestrian leading an animal by its halter. There is of course the occasional dashing horseman or a carriage containing an entire bourgeois family, pulled briskly along by three horses. But in the next picture the holes in the road are full of water, the horsemen are squelching along, their mounts up to their hocks in water; the carriages move painfully forward, their wheels sunk in the mud. Pedestrians, shepherds and pigs have wisely retired to the safer banks bordering the road. The same scenes, worse perhaps, were enacted in northern China. If the road 'is spoiled' or if it 'makes a considerable bend', 'coolies', carts and horses 'go across tilled land to shorten the route and make themselves a better one, not worrying overmuch whether the grain is risen or already tall'.[70] This report is a corrective to descriptions of other main roads in China, which were very well maintained, sanded and sometimes paved, according to the admiring remarks of European travellers.[71]

Nothing or very little would have changed in these matters between the time of Richelieu or Charles v, and China under the Sung dynasty or the Roman Empire. Such conditions governed and burdened commercial exchanges and even ordinary human relations. Mail took weeks, months, to reach its destination. The 'defeat of distance', as Ernst Wagemann calls it, was only to be achieved after 1875, with the laying of the first intercontinental cable. True mass communication on a world scale did not appear until the age of the railway, the steamship, telegraph and telephone.

Fixed itineraries

Imagine a road, anywhere, in any period: along it one will probably find some vehicles and beasts of burden, a few horsemen, inns, a forge, a village or town. However faintly it may appear to be marked, the track will in fact follow a fixed course, even in the Argentine pampas or eighteenth-century Siberia. Transporters and travellers remained prisoners of a limited range of choices. They would perhaps prefer to take one route rather than another, to avoid a toll or customs post, but might be obliged to turn back in case of difficulty. And they might follow one road in winter and another in spring according to the degree of frost or the number of potholes. But it was impossible to depart from established roads, for any travelling meant being dependent on services provided by other people.

In 1776, Jacob Fries, a Swiss doctor and a major in the Russian army, made the long journey from Omsk to Tomsk (890 kilometres) in 178 hours, an average speed of five kilometres an hour, changing horses regularly at each posting-house, in order to be sure of reaching the next one in good time: those who missed one in winter ended up buried beneath the snow.[72] In the Argentine interior, even in the eighteenth century, all travellers, whether on mules, on horseback – or aboard the heavy ox-carts which brought grain and hides to Buenos Aires and set off empty on the return trip to Mendoza, Santiago or Jujuy on the way to Peru – had to arrange their journeys so as to cross the *despoblados* (deserts) at convenient times, and to find at the necessary intervals houses, villages or watering-places, and supplies of eggs and fresh meat. If a traveller was tired of the narrow cabin of his carriole, he could mount a horse, load 'an adequate bed' on to another beast and set off at a gallop in front of the convoy, preferably at between two and ten in the morning to avoid the heat. 'The horses are so well accustomed to making these *crossings* in a short space of time that they gallop at full tilt without any urging.' The rider's reward was that he

The roadside inn, staging-post and scene of meetings and exchanges (watercolour by Thomas Rowlandson, 1824). In the sixteenth and seventeenth centuries, inns played an important part in the development of a free market in England, since they were not subject to the regulations which applied inside towns. (Whitworth Art Gallery, Manchester.)

quickly reached 'the post houses [which] are the best lodgings and where the traveller can rest as he pleases'.[73] He arrived and went straight to bed. This information makes it easier to understand the comments of an eighteenth-century writer on the first part of the road from Buenos Aires to Carcaranal: 'During these three-and-a-half days on the road, with the exception of two *crossings*, cows, sheep and goats will be found in abundance and at low prices.'[74]

These late pictures of 'new' lands (Siberia, the New World) are fairly accurate descriptions of journeys in the 'old' civilized lands in earlier centuries.

To reach Istanbul by way of the Balkans, advises Pierre Lescalopier (1574), 'it will be necessary to travel from morning to night, unless some stream or meadow gives you the means of putting foot to ground and taking some cold meat from your saddlebag and a bottle of wine from your saddlebow to take a light meal around midday, while your horses, unbridled and with hobbles on their feet, graze or eat what they are given'. The next caravanserai where food and drink were to be found had to be reached by evening. These were 'hospitals' (in the sense of hospices – hospitable houses) 'built to mark the limits of each day's journey ... Rich and poor lodge [there] for want of anything better; they are like very large barns; they have loopholes instead of windows'. The people were accommodated on 'projections' (platforms) arranged around this hall, to which the animals were attached. 'Thus everyone sees his horse and puts his food on the projections and to make him eat oats and barley [the Turks] use leather bags from which the horse eats while the straps of the bag are passed over his ears.'[75] A Neapolitan traveller described these inns more simply in 1693: 'They are nothing but ... long stables where the horses occupy the central part; the sides are left for the Masters.'[76]

In China a *Public Itinerary* printed in the seventeenth century indicated the roads out of Peking, with their outlines and their stopping places, where mandarins on mission were received at the emperor's expense, entertained, fed and refurnished with mounts, boats or porters. These stopping places, a day's journey away from each other, were large towns or 'second-order' towns, or castles, or *Ye* or *Chin* – places 'of lodging and guarding', 'formerly built in areas where there were no towns'. Towns often grew up there as a result.[77]

Travelling was only positively pleasant in regions where towns and villages were close together. *L'Ulysse françois* (1643) – the Blue Guide of its day – indicates the good inns (the *Faucon Royal* in Marseilles, the *Cardinal* hostelry in Amiens) and advises (revenge or wisdom?) against lodging at the *Cerf* inn in Péronne! Amenities and speed were the privileges of populated and firmly maintained, 'policed', lands: China, Japan, Europe, Islam. In Persia, 'good caravanserai are found every four leagues' and travelling there was 'cheap'. But the same traveller, having left Persia, was complaining about Hindustan in the following year (1695): no inns, no caravanserai, no animals to hire for carriages, no food outside 'the large towns of the Mogul's lands'; 'one sleeps beneath the stars or under a tree'.[78]

It may surprise us slightly more to learn that sea routes were also fixed in advance. But after all, ships were dependent on certain winds, currents and ports of call. Coasting was the rule, both in the China seas and the Mediterranean. The procession of coasting vessels steered by the line of the shore, to which they were constantly drawn as if by a magnet. As for voyages on the open sea, they too had their rules, dictated by experience. The route between Spain and the 'Castilian Indies' had been established by Columbus; it was only slightly modified by Alaminos[79] in 1519, and after that did not change until the nineteenth century. On the return journey, it went as far north as the forty-third parallel, bringing travellers into sudden contact with the rigours of the northern climate: 'The cold began to make itself severely felt,' noted one of them (1697), 'and certain knights clad in silk and without cloaks found it very hard to bear.'[80] Similarly, Urdaneta discovered the route from Acapulco to Manila, from New

Spain to the Philippines and back in 1565, and fixed it once and for all. The journey there was easy (three months); the return was difficult and long (six to eight months) and cost the traveller up to 500 pieces of eight (1696).[81]

All being well, the ship passed the points and stopped at the places where it was usual to pass and stop. Food and water were taken on at appointed ports of call. It could, if the need arose, careen, repair, replace a mast or remain for a long time in the calm bosom of the ports. Everything was provided for. If a gust of wind took a ship by surprise, before the sail was reefed, and broke her mast in the open sea off Guinea, where only low tonnages could reach the shallow coast, she sailed, if possible, to the Portuguese island 'of the Prince' – *a ilha do Principe* – to find a substitute mast, and to take on sugar and slaves. Near the Sunda straits, wisdom dictated that ships follow the coast of Sumatra as closely as possible and then make for the Malacca peninsula. The hilly coast of the large island would protect them against squalls and the water was not deep. When hurricanes blew up, as happened during Kämpfer's journey to Siam, in 1690, the ship had to drop anchor and, like other vessels in the vicinity, cling to the shallow sea floor until the squall had moved away.

On not exaggerating the importance of transport problems

Despite the attractions of the picturesque, we should be careful not to exaggerate the importance of incident on land and sea routes. There were always problems: sometimes they cancelled each other out and disappeared. It is tempting – but unwise – to see them as explanations. The decline of the Champagne fairs, for instance, cannot be explained by the action of the French authorities (particularly Louis X, 'the Headstrong', 1314-16) in placing administrative obstacles on the roads leading to the fairs. It cannot even be accounted for by the establishment of direct and regular maritime communication between the Mediterranean and Bruges by the big ships of Genoa after 1297. During these early decades of the fourteenth century, the structure of large-scale commerce was being transformed: the itinerant merchant was becoming a rare figure. Merchandise was beginning to travel alone: its movements between Italy and the Netherlands, the two poles of the European economy, were controlled from a distance by written correspondence, and there was no longer any need for merchants to meet and discuss matters half-way. The fairs of Champagne consequently lost their usefulness as a rendezvous. The success of the Geneva fairs, another meeting-place for settling accounts, did not become established until the fifteenth century.[82]

Likewise, one should not look for trivial explanations for the breakdown of the Mongolian route in about 1350. During the thirteenth century, the Mongol conquest had established direct overland contact between China, India and the West, skirting the borders of Islam. And the Polos, Marco's father and uncle, and Marco himself, were not the only ones to reach distant China or the Indies by long but surprisingly safe routes. The breakdown should be attributed to the

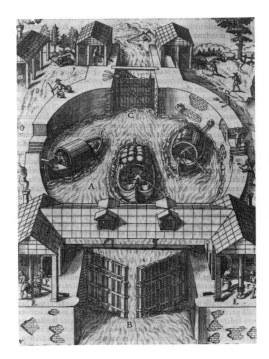

The workings of a lock, sketch by V. Zonca, 1607. The discovery of the principles of the lock, which T.S. Willan considers to have been as important as the discovery of steam, was certainly the sign of considerable technical advance in the West.

huge recession in the middle of the fourteenth century. For everything regressed at once, the West just as much as China under the Mongols. Neither did the discovery of the New World immediately transform the major trade routes of the globe. The Mediterranean was still the scene of active international trade a century after Columbus and Vasco da Gama. Its decline came later.

As for the patterns of short-distance routes, here too the ebb and flow of economic circumstances usually dictated their success or failure. For instance, it is doubtful that the 'free-trade policy' of the counts of Brabant was as crucial as has sometimes been suggested: it was apparently effective during the thirteenth century – when the Champagne fairs were at the height of their prosperity. Similarly, the agreement between Milan and Rudolph of Habsburg (1273-91) which secured a route untrammelled by tolls between Basle and Brabant was a great success: at this period, who could have failed to prosper? But later on, when a series of treaties between 1350 and 1640 restricted customs privileges to this same route, and when the city of Ghent had the road leading to the Champagne fairs repaired at its own expense, near Senlis,[83] such steps should be seen as the search for a remedy to a declining economic situation. On the other hand, in 1530, when trade was picking up again, the bishop of Salzburg had the mule-track over the Tauern made passable for vehicles, but failed to take traffic from the Saint-Gothard and the Brenner, which had the might of Milan and Venice behind them:[84] by then, there was enough trade for all the routes.

Water transport

A waterway brought animation to the land all around. It is easy to imagine life as it must have been. Looking at Gray, on the banks of the broad and now empty river Saône, one can picture the busy scenes of the past, with boats carrying wine and 'goods from Lyons' upstream, corn, hay and oats downstream. Without the Seine, Oise, Marne and Yonne, Paris would have had nothing to eat, drink or keep warm by. Without the Rhine, Cologne would not have been the largest town in Germany even before the fifteenth century.

A sixteenth-century geographer would have explained the existence of Venice in terms of the sea and the great waterways converging on its lagoons: the Brenta, the Po and the Adige. All kinds of small boats, some propelled by poles, were constantly arriving in the city along these rivers and the canals. But even the most unpromising stretches of water were everywhere exploited. Gunpowder, bullets, grenades and other ammunition manufactured in Navarre were transported down the Ebro, from 'Tudela to Tortosa and down to the sea', in flat-bottomed boats, even in the early eighteenth century, despite the many obstacles, in particular 'the Flix Falls, where the merchandise is unloaded and then re-loaded'.[85]

The great region for water transport in Europe, even more than Germany, was the zone beyond the Oder, Poland and Lithuania. River transport had developed there from the middle ages, with the aid of immense rafts of tree trunks. Each of them had a cabin for the sailors. This vast traffic led to the building of wharves – Torun (Thorn), Kovno, Brest-Litovsk – and aroused endless disputes.[86]

However, taking the world as a whole, there was nothing to equal southern China, from the Blue River to the borders of Yunan.

> The great internal trade of China, which has no equal in the world, depends on this traffic [noted a witness in about 1733]. One sees a perpetual movement of boats, barks, and rafts everywhere there (some of these rafts are half a league long and fold ingeniously because of the bends of the rivers) and they resemble so many moving towns. The drivers of these barks have their permanent home on them, having their wives and children with them there, so one can easily believe the report of most travellers that there are almost as many people on the water in that country as in the towns and countryside.[87]

'No country in the world,' according to Father de Magaillans, 'can equal China in navigation' (meaning water transport). In this country 'there are two empires, one on water, the other on land, and as many Venices as there are towns'.[88] An observer who went up the Yang-tse-Kiang 'which is called the Son of the sea' as far as Szechwan, over a period of four months in 1656, wrote: 'The Kiang which, like the sea, is limitless, is bottomless as well.' A few years later (1695), a traveller laid it down as a principle that 'the Chinese like to live in the water like ducks'. One sailed 'amid timber rafts' for hours, for half a day at a time, he explained. The canals and rivers of a town had to be negotiated infuriatingly slowly 'through great numbers of barks'.[89]

Antiquated means of transport

If I were to collect a series of pictures of means of transport from all over the world between the fifteenth and eighteenth centuries, mix them up thoroughly and present them to the reader, without telling him where they came from, he would easily be able to identify them geographically. No one could fail to recognize a Chinese sedan-chair or wheelbarrow (sometimes equipped with a sail); an Indian pack-ox or combat elephant; a Turkish *araba* from the Balkans (or indeed from Tunisia); the camel-trains of Islam; the files of bearers in Africa; or the two- and four-wheeled carts and carriages of Europe, pulled by oxen or horses.

But if one was asked to date the picture, one's troubles would begin. The means of transport scarcely developed at all. Father de Las Cortes saw Chinese porters 'lifting travellers' chairs on long bamboos' in the Canton region in 1626. George Staunton described the same thin coolies 'with their rags, straw hats and sandals' in 1793. When his barge had to change canals on the road from Peking it was lifted by arms and winches 'and is thus conveyed into the upper canal with less delay than can be done by locks, but by the exertion of much more human force; a force indeed which, in China, is always ready, of little cost, and constantly preferred to any other'.[90] Similarly, the descriptions left us of caravans in Africa and Asia by Ibn Batuta (1326); by an anonymous sixteenth-century Englishman; by René Caillé (1799-1838); or by the German explorer Georg Schweinfurth (1836-1925), are virtually interchangeable. The spectacle remained timeless and unchanging. I have myself seen convoys of narrow, four-wheeled peasant wagons on the roads of Cracow, in November 1957, going to town loaded with passengers and with pine-branches, their needles trailing like hair in the dust of the road behind them. This sight, by now no doubt a vanishing one, could have been seen in the fifteenth century.

The same could be said of the sea: the silhouettes of Chinese or Japanese junks, Malayan or Polynesian outrigger canoes, Arab boats on the Red Sea or Indian Ocean, have hardly changed over centuries. Ernst Sachau, the Babylonian expert, described in 1897-8 the boats of the Arabs in the same terms as Pierre Belon (1550) and Gemelli Careri (1695): they were made of planks tied together with palm fibre, without the aid of a single iron nail. Careri described the boat he saw being built at Daman, in India, as having 'wooden nails and cotton caulks'.⁹¹ Sailing-boats like this remained numerous until the introduction of the English steamboats, and here and there they still perform the same functions as they did in Sinbad's time.

Europe

Some chronological discrimination is obviously possible in Europe. We know that vehicles with a moveable front-axle, first used in gun-carriages, were really only employed after about 1470. The first, rather primitive coaches did not appear until the second half or the end of the sixteenth century (and had glass windows only in the seventeenth). Diligences were a product of the seventeenth century. Stagecoaches for travellers (*vetturini* as they were called in Italy) only appeared in any number in the Romantic period. The first canal locks date from the fourteenth century. But these innovations cannot conceal the many unchanging features that formed the basis of everyday life. In shipbuilding too, although this was the scene of much change, upper limits of tonnage and speed acted as a ceiling stifling further development.

Genoese carracks already had a tonnage of 1500 as far back as the fifteenth century, and 1000-ton Venetian ships were at the same period carrying bulky bales of cotton from Syria. In the sixteenth century, Ragusan cargo ships of 900 to 1000 tons specialized in the salt, wool and corn trades, as well as in carrying cases of sugar and bales of skins.⁹² At the same time the giant of the seas, the Portuguese carrack, had a displacement of up to 2000 tons. Counting both sailors and passengers, it carried a complement of 800 persons.⁹³ Consequently, if the wood used to build it had not been fully seasoned and it sprang a leak; if a storm threw it on the shallows off the coast of Mozambique; or if the nimble ships of privateers encircled, seized and set fire to it, the scale of the disaster was immense. When the English seized the *Madre de Dios* in 1587, they could not tow her up the Thames because of her draught. She was over 1800 tons and Sir John Burrough, Raleigh's lieutenant, who captured her, described her as a monster.⁹⁴

Broadly speaking, the art of shipbuilding had already produced its record tonnages a good century before the Invincible Armada sailed in 1588. Only heavy goods or long-distance trade, guaranteed by *de facto* or *de jure* monopolies, made the luxury of these large tonnages possible. The majestic Indiamen at the end of the eighteenth century (they specialized in trade with China, despite their name) had a displacement of barely more than 1900 tons. The upper limit was determined by the material used for construction, sails, and the armament on board.

But an upper limit is not an average. Very small ships of thirty, forty and fifty tons were sailing the seas until the last days of the sailing ships. The use of iron made the construction of larger hulls possible only in about 1840. A hull of 200 tons had until then been the general rule, one of 500 an exception, one of 1000 to 2000 an object of curiosity.

Low speeds and capacities

Bad roads, ridiculously low speeds: this is the conclusion modern man jumps to, and his point of view has its validity. He sees the enormous handicap hampering all active life in the past better than a contemporary, for whom it was an everyday fact. Paul Valéry pointed out that 'Napoleon moved no faster than Julius Caesar'. We can see this for ourselves from the three maps on pp. 426-427, showing the speed at which news travelled to Venice. For the period from 1496 to 1533 our source is the *Diarii* of Marin Sanudo, a patrician of Venice who kept day-to-day notes of the dates when letters were received by the Signoria as well as the dates when they were sent. After that we have hand-written gazettes circulated in Venice between 1686 and 1701 and between 1733 and 1735. Other calculations would give the same conclusions, namely that with horses, coaches, ships and runners, it was the general rule to cover *at most* 100 kilometres in 24 hours. Higher speeds were very infrequent and a great luxury. It was possible, if one was prepared to pay, to have an order taken from Nuremberg to Venice in four days at the beginning of the sixteenth century. If big cities attracted rapid news in their direction it was because they paid for speed and always had the means to create better communications, one of which was obviously to build stone or paved roads; but such things long remained exceptions.

The road from Paris to Orléans was entirely paved and thus allowed rapid communication with Orléans (although brigands were still feared in the seventeenth century near the forest of Torfou). Orléans was the main river port of France, equal or almost so to Paris, the Loire being the most convenient waterway of the realm, with 'the widest bed and the longest course ... on which one can sail for over a hundred and sixty leagues in the Kingdom, which is not found in any other river in France'. The road from Paris to Orléans was the 'King's highway', a great carriageway, *strada di carri* as an Italian said as early as 1581. The Stamboulyol, the road from Istanbul to Belgrade via Sofia, was also carrying carriages by the sixteenth century, and had its luxurious *arabas* in the eighteenth.[95]

One aspect of progress in eighteenth-century France was the extension of decently surfaced highways. The lease of the French posts rose from 1,220,000 livres in 1676 to 8,800,000 in 1776. The budget of the *Ponts et Chaussées* department was 700,000 under Louis XIV and 7 million as the Revolution drew near.[96] But this budget only took care of construction work – opening new roads. Old roads were maintained by the highway *corvée*, created in about 1730. It was annulled by Turgot in 1776, re-established in the same year and only disappeared in 1787. France then had approximately twelve thousand kilometres of completed road and twelve thousand under construction.[97]

The time had therefore come for the stagecoach, including the famous 'turgotines'. Contemporaries thought them dangerous, demoniacal. Their 'body is narrow,' said one of them, 'and seats get so crowded that everybody asks his neighbour for his leg or his arm back when it comes to getting down.... If by ill chance a traveller with a big stomach or wide shoulders appears ... one has to groan or desert'.[98] They went at an insane speed. Accidents were numerous, and no one compensated the victims. Furthermore, only a narrow central carriageway was paved on main routes. Two carriages could not pass at the same time without a wheel plunging into the mud at the side of the road.

Contemporary comments, some amazingly foolish, prefigured the reactions which later greeted the first railways. There were many protests in 1669 when a stagecoach covered the distance from Manchester to London in a day: it was the end of the noble art of horsemanship; it spelled ruination for saddle and spur manufacturers; it meant the disappearance of the Thames boatmen.[99]

But the trend continued. The first revolution in road travel was sketched out between 1745 and 1760. The price of transport fell, and what was more, 'a wave of small speculative capitalists' profited by it. They heralded the changing times.

But even these modest achievements only concerned highways. In France most of the time it was impossible to move heavy loads conveniently outside these 'postal' roads so admired by Arthur Young[100] and even, according to Adam Smith, 'to travel on horseback; mules are the only conveyance which can safely be trusted'.[101] The countryside, generally not well equipped with roads, remained condemned to partial suffocation.

Carriage and carriers

Carrying was the second occupation of millions of peasants in the West after the grain or grape harvest or during the winter months, and they were poorly paid for it. The seasons of the agricultural year dictated the ebb and flow of transport activity. Whether organized or not, this was handled by poor, or at any rate modest categories of people. Ships' crews too were recruited from among the wretched classes of Europe and the world. Dutch ships, which were victorious over all the seas in the seventeenth century, were no exception to the rule. The same was true of the amazing American sailors, 'Englishmen of the second kind' as the Chinese called them, who went off to conquer the seas at the end of the eighteenth century in tiny ships, sometimes of 50 to 100 tons, sailing from Philadelphia or New York to China, and getting drunk on every possible occasion according to report.[102]

And the transport entrepreneurs themselves were not as a rule large-scale capitalists: their profits were limited as we shall see later.[103]

But despite the small scale of costs and returns, carriage was expensive in itself: an average of 10% *ad valorem*, according to a historian of medieval Germany.[104] But the average varied according to period and country. We have records of the price of cloth bought in the Netherlands and sent to Florence in 1320 and 1321. The cost of carriage (for six known accounts) ranged from 11·7%

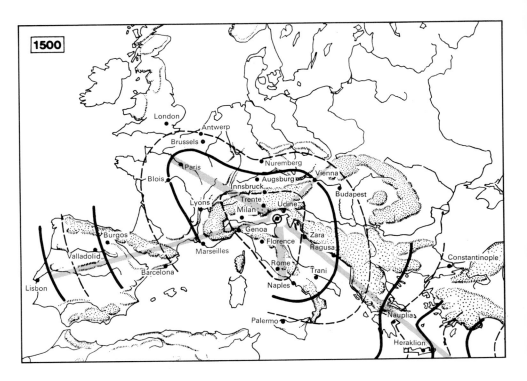

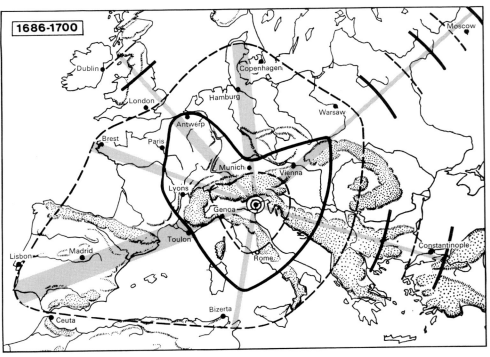

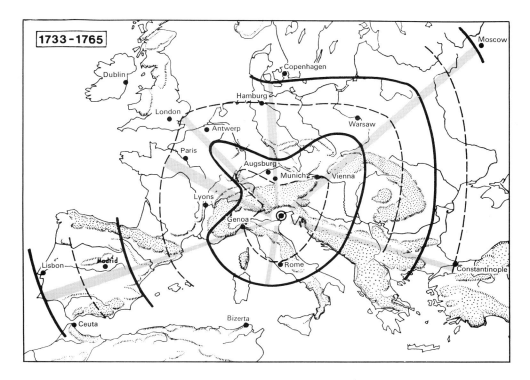

26 THE SPEED AT WHICH NEWS REACHED VENICE
The isochronic lines indicate on all three diagrams the time taken in weeks for letters to reach Venice.

Map 1 is based on P. Sardella's work on Sanudo's diaries, c. 1500 (in fact 1496-1533). Maps 2 and 3 are based on the manuscript Venetian gazettes in the Public Record Office in London. Calculations by F.C. Spooner.

The shaded grey lines are wider where average speeds were faster. Variations in speed from one map to another may be very great on certain routes. They were the result of employing more couriers in urgent circumstances. On the whole the slowest routes in Map 3 match the slowest routes in Map 1, whereas the times taken are sometimes much shorter in Map 2. There is nothing hard and fast about these calculations. In theory, speeds should be compared over areas bounded by isochronic contours of the same order of size. But it is not possible to define such areas with the necessary precision. However, if one attempts to superimpose them one on the other, they do seem to be roughly equivalent, extensions in one direction being compensated for by shortfalls in another. I need hardly add that calculating daily speeds from surface areas in kilometres requires some preliminary precautions.

of the value of the goods (the lowest rate) to 20·34% (the highest).[105] And this for merchandise which was not bulky and whose price was already high. Other goods rarely travelled over very long distances. In the seventeenth century, it was necessary 'to pay 100 to 120 francs to have a cask of wine, often not worth more than about 40 francs, carried from Beaune to Paris'.[106]

The expenses and problems were usually greater on land than on sea. This led to a certain lack of vitality in inland traffic, except for the waterways, but in that sector, nobles and towns imposed numerous tolls that led to many delays, visits and bribery and much waste of time. Merchants often chose overland roads, even in the Po valley or along the Rhine, in preference to waterways interrupted by chains stretched across from bank to bank to mark the tolls. There was also the not negligible risk of brigandage which remained common the world over – a marginal symbol of widespread and permanent economic and social malaise.

The sea route by contrast represented a sort of explosion of 'free trade', and brought a bonus to maritime economies. In the thirteenth century, the price of English grain increased by 15% for every eighty kilometres it travelled overland, whereas wine from Gascony shipped to Hull or Ireland via Bordeaux only cost an additional 10% despite the long sea journey.[107]

In 1828, Jean-Baptiste Say told his audience at the Collège de France that the inhabitants of the Atlantic towns in the United States 'warm themselves with coal from England which is over a thousand leagues away rather than with wood from their own forests, ten leagues away. Carriage over ten leagues overland is more expensive than transport over a thousand leagues by sea.'[108] Steam ships were not yet in use at the time when Jean-Baptiste Say was teaching these elementary ideas (repeating the similar remarks of Adam Smith). Nevertheless, maritime transport, with wood, sail and rudder, had long since attained its perfection, its limits of possibility, probably because of its increasing use.

This highlights the delay in road services and makes it all the more surprising. Roads had to wait for the first upsurge of the industrial revolution before their full potential was developed in the feverish years between 1830 and 1840 – just before the take-off of the railways. Between the stagecoach and the railway, as the latter prepared to take over, the tremendous changes taking place in road transport showed what it would have been possible to achieve *technically* very much earlier. Networks were extended at that time (from one to eight between 1800 and 1850 in the United States, where everything was already assuming enormous proportions; more than doubling in the Austrian Empire between 1830 and 1847). Vehicles and posting-houses were improved. Transport became more democratic. These changes were not the result of any precise technical discovery. They were simply the consequence of large-scale investment, of deliberate systematic improvement, because the economic growth of the time made them both 'profitable' and necessary.

Transport: a brake on the economy

The brief foregoing remarks are not intended as a description of transport – they cannot do justice, for example, to the very full account contained in Werner Sombart's classic book[109] – and I shall in any case be returning to certain aspects of the question.[110] They are simply meant as a rapid indication of the extent to which trade, the instrument of any developing economic society, was hampered

Warsaw, the left bank of the Vistula. There is a steady stream of craft along the river: sailing barges, small boats, log-rafts. Sketch by Z. Vogel, late eighteenth century. (Photo Alexandra Skarzynska.)

by the limits imposed by transport: it was invariably slow, inadequate, irregular and, not least, expensive. Everywhere, traders came up against this obstacle. Paul Valéry's remark bears repeating to remind us of this ancient and longstanding fact of life: 'Napoleon moved no faster than Julius Caesar.'

In the West, the horse, symbol of speed, was the classic means of combating the tyranny of distance – a means that seems derisory in retrospect. But the West tried hard to improve horse-drawn traffic: by increasing the numbers of horses; by harnessing teams of five, six or eight to pull heavy vehicles; by making fresh horses available at staging-posts along the roads, for the benefit of travellers and vehicles in a hurry; and even the roads themselves were improved. If all this took place, it was probably because overland transport was superior, by a long way, to transport by water along rivers and canals, which remained extremely slow.[111] Even coal from northern France was carried in wagons rather than in barges in the eighteenth century.[112]

The struggle against distance, apparently doomed in advance, could be seen in every region of the world. Travelling in China or Persia made Westerners more alive to the importance of horses – *a contrario*, since in the East human carriers were the rule. Chinese porters went as quickly, it was said, as the little horses of Tartary. There were magnificent horses in Persia, but they were reserved for warfare or treated as objects of luxury, with their 'harnesses of silver, gold and precious stones'. They were rarely used for transport or for communications. Human runners were used instead, and entrusted with urgent letters, money and precious goods. 'These special runners are called *chatirs*,' wrote Chardin in 1690, 'which is the name given to all foot-messengers and to those who can run and travel quickly. One recognizes them on the roads by the water-bottle and satchel they carry on their backs, which serves them as a sort of pilgrim's pack to carry provisions for the thirty or forty hours they are on the way: for in order to travel more quickly, they leave the main roads and take short cuts. They are also distinguished by their shoes and the bells they carry attached to their belts, like those of mules, whose purpose is to keep them awake. These people carry on their profession from father to son. They are taught to run quickly without losing breath, from the age of seven or eight years.' Similarly, 'the orders of the kings in India are carried by two men, on foot, running, who are relieved every two leagues. They carry the despatches on their heads, uncovered. They can be heard coming by their bells, like a postilion's horn; when they arrive, they fling themselves flat on the ground, the despatch is removed and given to two waiting men who carry it off in the same manner.' These express runners covered between ten and twenty leagues a day.[113]

Problems of the history of technology

First the accelerator, then the brake: the history of technology seems to consist of both processes, sometimes in quick succession: it propels human life onward, gradually reaches new forms of equilibrium on higher levels than in the past, only to remain there for a long time, since technology often stagnates, or advances only imperceptibly between one 'revolution' or innovation and another. It often seems as if the brakes are on all the time, and it is the force of the brakes that I had hoped to describe more successfully than I perhaps have. But maybe this is an impossible task: whether it is going forward or standing still, the history of technology is that of human history in all its diversity. That is why specialist historians of technology hardly ever manage to grasp it entirely in their hands.

Technology and agriculture

It is noticeable, for instance, how despite well-intentioned gestures and dense chapters into which they try to pack 'everything there is to know about it', historians of technology have devoted very little attention to the technology of agriculture. And yet, for thousands of years, agriculture was *the* great 'industry' of mankind. The history of technology, however, has usually been regarded as the pre-history of the industrial revolution. As a consequence, much attention is given to mechanics, metallurgy and energy sources, although agricultural technology both in its routine activities and its innovations (for agriculture did change, if slowly) was to have far-reaching consequences.

Planting out, for instance, is a technique; preparing for the plough land that has been long uncultivated is another: it requires heavy ploughs, strong teams and many hands, which means asking for help from the neighbours (*por favor* work, as it was called during land clearance in Portugal). Extending the crops, which meant clearing forest (with or without uprooting tree-stumps), burning, pulling down trees, or draining, irrigating, building dykes – all of these were aspects of agricultural technology, from China to Holland, or Italy, where 'land improvement and reclamation' was, from the fifteenth century at least, a major enterprise, soon calling upon the regular participation of *engineers*.

Moreover, as we have already seen, any increase in population, any rise in numbers, follows or at any rate accompanies a transformation in agriculture. In China (maize, ground nuts and sweet potatoes) or in Europe (maize, potatoes and beans) new plants from America marked major turning points in history. And all these new plants, of course, required new techniques which had to be invented, adapted and perfected – slowly, sometimes very slowly indeed, but in the end with massive momentum, since agriculture, work on the land is 'the mass of the masses'. And no innovation has any value except in relation to the social pressure which maintains and imposes it.

Technology in itself

So if one asks the question: is there such a thing as technology in itself, the answer is bound to be no. I have already made this point several times over about the period before the industrial revolution. Now the author of a recent book[114] has said the same thing of our own age: science and technology are indeed uniting today to dominate the world, but such unity necessarily depends upon the role played by present-day societies, which may encourage or restrain progress, today as in the past.

Moreover, before the eighteenth century, science was little inclined to concern itself with practical solutions and applications. There are some exceptions – Huygens' discoveries (the pendulum 1656-7; and the adjusting spiral, 1675) which revolutionized clock-making; or Pierre Bouguer's work on shipbuilding, the *Traité du navire de sa construction et de ses mouvements* (1746) – but they do no more than confirm the rule. Technology was a collection of tricks of the trade drawn from the experience of craftsmen, and it accumulated and developed at a leisurely pace. Good manuals were slow to appear: *De Re Metallica* by Georg Bauer (Agricola) only in 1556; Agostino Ramelli's *Le Diverse et Artificiose Machine* in 1588; Vittorio Zonca's *Nuovo Teatro di machine ed edifici* in 1621; Bernard Forest's *Dictionnaire portatif de l'ingénieur* or *Engineer's Handbook* in 1755. The profession of 'engineer' emerged only slowly. An 'engineer' of the fifteenth and sixteenth century would be concerned with military matters, or would hire out his services as architect, hydraulics expert, sculptor or painter. There was no systematic training before the eighteenth century. The *École des Ponts et Chaussées* was founded in Paris in 1743; the *École des Mines*, opened in 1783, was modelled on the *Bergakademie*, which had been set up in 1765 in Freiberg, the old mining centre of Saxony and training-ground of so many engineers who later worked in Russia.

Gradual specialization inevitably took place in the crafts. A Swiss artisan, Jost Amman, listed 90 different crafts in 1568. Diderot's *Encyclopédie* counted 250; the catalogue of the London firm of Pigot listed 826 different activities in the capital in 1826, some of them amusing and clearly marginal.[115] But despite everything such specialization was extremely slow. Existing practices constituted a barrier. Strikes of printing workers in France towards the middle of the sixteenth century were provoked by changes in the printing press which resulted in a reduction in the number of workers. No less characteristic was the workers'

The crane at Bruges, in the middle ages: a massive wooden construction with a huge wheel operated by three men. (Bayerisches Staatsbibliothek, Munich.)

The double crane in the port of Dunkirk in 1787. It had a gearing-down mechanism, and the apparatus could be moved easily, as it was mounted on wheels and could be pivoted; it was partly made of metal. Great advances had been made on the Bruges model, but the crane was still worked manually. Bibliothèque Nationale, Paris. (Photo M. Cabaud.)

resistance to the use of the 'beetle', an improvement which made 'spring shears', enormous scissors to cut fabrics, easier to handle. And if the textile industry showed little development from the fifteenth to the middle of the eighteenth century, it was because its economic and social organization, the elaborate division of operations and the low wages of its workers enabled it to face the exigencies of the market without any change. There were so many obstacles that we can agree with James Watt when he confided to his friend Snell (26 July 1769) 'that in life there is nothing more foolish than inventing'. The successful inventor had to have society on his side.

Nine times out of ten the patents of invention, serious or not, recorded on the pages of registers and dossiers in the Venetian Senate[116] corresponded to the particular problems of the city: they sought to make the waterways converging on the lagoon navigable; dig canals; raise water; drain swampy land; turn mills without resorting to hydraulic power (unobtainable in this world of stagnant waters); work saws, millstones, hammers to powder the tannin or raw materials used to produce glass. Social considerations were uppermost.

An inventor who had the good fortune to please the prince could obtain a 'patent of invention or, more accurately, a licence enabling him to exploit an invention as a monopoly'. Louis XIV's government distributed large numbers of them, 'affecting the most varied techniques. For example, the process of economical heating in which Madame de Maintenon invested some capital.'[117] But just as often real discoveries remained a dead letter because people did not need them – or did not think they needed them.

It was in vain that Baltasar de Rios, an ingenious inventor of the first years of Philip II's reign, proposed to build a large-calibre cannon that could be dismantled and transported in separate pieces on the backs of a few hundred soldiers.[118] The *Histoire naturelle de la fontaine qui brûle près de Grenoble* passed unnoticed in 1618; yet in this treatise, the author, Jean Tardin, a doctor from Tournon, studied the 'natural gas content of the fountain' and described the distillation of coal in a retort, two centuries before the invention of gas lighting. A doctor from Périgord, Jean Rey, explained the expansion of lead and tin after calcination by 'the incorporation of the heavy part of the air' in 1630, over a century before Lavoisier.[119] Schwenteer set out the principles of the electric telegraph as a result of which 'two individuals can communicate by means of the magnetic needle' in his *Délassements physico-mathématiques* in 1635. The magnetic needle had in fact to wait for Oersted's experiments in 1819. And 'to think that Schwenteer is less well known than the Chappe brothers!'[120] An American, Bushnell, invented the submarine, and a French military engineer, Duperron, the machine-gun, 'the military organ', in 1775.

All this was in vain. It was the same story with Newcomen's steam machine in 1711. Only one was in operation in England thirty years later, in 1742; on the continent two had been assembled. Success came in the following thirty years: sixty machines were built in Cornwall, to drain water from the tin mines. But only five were in use for iron-smelting in France at the end of the eighteenth century. The delays in coke-smelting we have already mentioned were no less typical.

Thousands of factors obstructed progress. What would happen to the labour force threatened with unemployment? Montesquieu was already criticizing the mills for taking work away from agricultural workers. A letter of 18 September 1754 from the marquis of Bonnac, French ambassador in Holland, asked for 'a good mechanic who can steal the secret of the different mills and machines in Amsterdam which avoid the expenditure of the labour of many men'.[121] But was it desirable to reduce this expenditure? The mechanic was not sent.

Finally there remains a matter of the greatest interest to the capitalist – the question of costs. Even when the industrial revolution in cotton was already well advanced English entrepreneurs continued to employ hand labour at home for spinning at a time when their mechanical weaving looms were already in full commission. This was because domestic production of thread was sufficient to supply the weaving looms at much lower cost. The tempo of demand had to increase immeasurably before the use of mechanical spinning became general, well after its invention. But since wages for hand-spinning then plummeted, employers continued to prefer it to the new processes for a long time, simply because it cost less. One might well wonder what would have happened if the boom in English cotton had stopped prematurely. Any innovation kept coming up against such obstacles. This was a battle of lost opportunities, as I shall have occasion to remind the reader apropos of the incredibly slow establishment of coke-smelting, a crucial but unconscious stage in the English industrial revolution.

Nevertheless, having pointed out the obvious limitations and circumstantial problems of technology, we should not underestimate its role, which was a vital one. Sooner or later, everything depended upon its necessary intervention. As long as daily life proceeded without too much difficulty in its appointed pathway, within the framework of its inherited structures, as long as society was content with its material surroundings and felt at ease, there was no economic motive for change. Inventors' blueprints (for there always were some) stayed in their drawers. It was only when things went wrong, when society came up against the ceiling of the possible that people turned of necessity to technology, and interest was aroused for the thousand potential inventions, out of which one would be recognized as the best, the one that would break through the obstacle and open the door to a different future. For there are always hundreds of possible innovations lying dormant; sooner or later, it becomes a matter of urgency to call one of them to life.

Our present situation, since the recession of the 1970s, tells this story better than any explanation. Among other problems – combined inflation and unemployment – the forecast that oil as a source of energy will soon be exhausted has provoked renewed interest in research into new alternatives – the only proper response, as Mensch has rightly remarked.[122] And yet all the alternative avenues of research were already well known before 1970: solar energy, the exploitation of bituminous schists, geothermal energy sources, gas from vegetable fermentation, alcohol-based petrol substitutes – were all explored during the last war, and rapidly developed by improvised methods. Then they fell into neglect. The difference is that today a major general crisis (one of the 'secular crises' to which I shall be referring again) has confronted all the developed economies with the dramatic choice between innovation, death or stagnation. They will undoubtedly choose the path of innovation. No doubt some such fear of disaster preceded each of the major advances in economic growth over the centuries – and technology always came up with an answer. In this sense, technology is indeed a queen: it does change the world.

7

Money

TO DEVOTE a chapter to money is to move to a higher level, apparently outside the scope of this volume. But viewed from a higher vantage point, the operation of the money supply can be seen as an instrument, a structure, a fundamental and regular phenomenon of any moderately developed commercial life. Above all, money everywhere contrives to insert itself into all economic and social relationships. This makes it an excellent indicator: by observing how fast it circulates or when it runs out, how complicated its channels are or how scarce the supply, a fairly accurate assessment can be made of all human activity, even the most humble.

Although it is an ancient fact of life, or rather an ancient technique, money has never ceased to surprise humanity. It seems mysterious and disturbing. In the first place, it must have seemed complicated in itself, for the monetary economy that goes with money was nowhere fully developed, even in a country like France in the sixteenth and seventeenth centuries, or indeed in the eighteenth. It only made its way into certain regions and certain sectors, and continued to disturb the others. It was a novelty more because of what it brought with it than what it was itself. What did it actually bring? Sharp variations in prices of essential foodstuffs; incomprehensible relationships in which man no longer recognized either himself, his customs or his ancient values. His work became a commodity, himself a 'thing'.

The words Noël du Fail put into the mouths of old Breton peasants (1548) expressed their astonishment and confusion. If there was so much less abundance inside peasant homes, it was because:

> chickens and goslings are hardly allowed to come to perfection before they are taken to sell [to the town market of course] for money to be given either to the lawyer or the doctor (people [formerly] almost unknown), to the one in return for dealing harshly with his neighbour, disinheriting him, having him put in prison; to the other for curing him of a fever, ordering him to be bled (which thank God I have never tried) or for a clyster; all of which our late Tiphaine La Bloye of fond memory [a bone setter] cured, without so much mumbling, fumbling and antidotes, and almost for a Paternoster.

But now they have 'transferred from the towns to our villages' those spices and sweetmeats ranging from pepper to 'sugar-coated leeks' quite 'unknown' to our predecessors and harmful to man's body, 'without which, however, a banquet in this century is tasteless, ill-arranged and graceless'. 'Upon my word,' replies one of the listeners, 'you speak true, my friend, and it seems to me I am in a new world.'[1] A bemused comment perhaps, but a revealing one, and similar reactions might have been found all over Europe.

For the same process can be observed everywhere: any society based on an ancient structure which opens its doors to money sooner or later loses its acquired equilibria and liberates forces that can never afterwards be adequately controlled. The new form of interchange disturbs the old order, benefits a few privileged individuals and hurts everyone else. Every society has to turn over a new leaf under the impact.

As a result, the extension of the monetary economy was a recurring drama quite as much in old countries accustomed to its presence as in those countries it reached without their immediately realizing it: Turkey under the Osmanlis at the close of the sixteenth century (when the *timars* or revocable fiefs granted to the *sipāhis* were replaced by outright private property); or Japan under the Tokugawas, which was at about the same time in the grip of a typical crisis affecting the cities and the bourgeoisie. We can get a good picture of these basic processes by examining what is still happening under our own eyes in certain underdeveloped countries today: in Africa, for example, where over 60% and even in some places 70% of transactions are completed without money changing hands. Man can still live in some places on the globe outside the market economy, 'like a snail in his shell'. But he is a condemned man on temporary reprieve.

History shows us an endless procession of these condemned men – men destined not to escape their fate. Naïve and astonishingly patient, they suffered the blows of life without really knowing where they were coming from. There were rents for farms and dwellings, tolls, the salt-tax, purchases which had to be made at the town market, and there were taxes. Somehow or other these demands had to be met in cash and, if silver money was lacking, in copper coins. A Breton tenant farmer brought his rent to Madame de Sévigné on 15 June 1680: an enormous weight of copper deniers amounting in all to thirty livres.[2] Salt-taxes had long been levied in kind, but the declaration of 9 March 1547, issued in France at the instigation of the large salt merchants, made collection in money compulsory.[3]

The 'jingle of coin' thus found its way into everyday life by many different paths. The modern state was the great provider (taxes, mercenaries' pay in money, office-holders' salaries) and recipient of these transfers; but not the only one. Many people were well placed to benefit: the tax-collector, the salt-tax farmer, the pawnbroker, the landowner, the large merchant entrepreneur and the 'financier'. Their net stretched everywhere. And naturally this new wealthy class, like their equivalent today, did not arouse sympathy. The faces of the

Two tax-collectors, by Martin van Reymerswade (sixteenth century), National Gallery, London. (Photo Giraudon.)

financiers look down on us from the museums. On more than one occasion the painter has conveyed the ordinary man's hatred and mistrust. But such feelings – the grievances both open and concealed which nourished a constant popular distrust of money itself, shared to some extent by the earliest economists – had little influence on the ultimate course of events. Over the whole world, the great monetary circuits organized transfer routes, and centres where profitable rendezvous could be arranged between money and the rich trades in 'royal commodities'. Magellan and del Cano sailed round the world in difficult and hazardous conditions. Francesco Carletti and Gemelli Careri, in 1590 and 1693 respectively, travelled round the globe with a bag containing pieces of eight and silver, and bundles of selected merchandise. What is more, they came back.[4]

Money is of course the symptom – as much as the cause – of the changes and revolutions in the monetary economy. It is inseparable from the movements that bring and create it. But explanations given in the past by Western observers too often considered money in isolation and resorted to metaphorical comparisons. Money was 'the blood of the social body' (a commonplace image well before Harvey's discovery);[5] it was a 'commodity', a view one finds repeated over the centuries. 'For Money,' according to William Petty (1655), 'is but the fat of the Body-politick, whereof too much doth as often hinder its Agility as too little makes it sick.'[6] In 1820, a French businessman explained that money 'is not the plough with which we till the ground and create goods': it merely assists the circulation of commodities 'just as oil makes a machine move more smoothly; when the wheels have been sufficiently greased, an excess can only harm their action'.[7] Even these images are better than the very questionable proposition advanced by John Locke, who was a better philosopher than he was an economist, and who in a book published in 1691 identified as one might say money with capital.[8] This comes close to confusing money with wealth, or measurement with the quantity measured.

All these definitions leave out the essential point – the monetary economy itself, the real reason for the existence of money. Money only becomes established where men need it and can bear the cost. Its flexibility and complexity are functions of the flexibility and complexity of the economy that it brings into being. There will ultimately be as many types of money and monetary systems as there are economic rhythms, systems and situations. All are connected in a process which is not after all so mysterious, if only we frequently remind ourselves that during the *ancien régime* there *was* a monetary economy: unlike that of today, it was very imperfectly realized, it existed on several levels, and it was by no means extended to all mankind.

Barter remained the general rule over enormous areas between the fifteenth and eighteenth centuries. But whenever the occasion demanded, it was eked out, as a sort of first step towards money, by the circulation of primitive or 'imperfect' currencies, such as cowrie shells. These are imperfect only in our eyes: the economies that resorted to them would hardly have been able to support any others. And often Europe's metal money proved very inadequate. Like barter, metal had shortcomings; there was not always enough of it for its task. When that happened, paper, or rather credit (*Herr Credit* as they mockingly said in Germany in the seventeeth century) offered its services, for better or for worse. Basically this is precisely the same process at a different level. Any active economy will in fact break away from its monetary language and innovate by very reason of its activity: all such innovations are then valuable as indications of the state of the economy concerned. Law's system and the contemporary English scandal of the South Sea Bubble were something quite different from post-war financial expedients, unscrupulous speculation, or share-outs between 'pressure groups'.[9] In France, innovation took the form of the confused and ineffectual but undeniable birth of credit, a difficult birth into the bargain. 'I have often wished that hell-fire would burn all these bills,' exclaimed the Princess Palatine, who claimed to understand nothing of the detestable system.[10] This uneasiness was the beginning of the awareness of a new language. For currencies are languages (if I too may be forgiven for using a metaphor): they make dialogue both necessary and possible and they only exist when the dialogue itself exists.

If China did not possess a complicated monetary system (apart from the long and strange interlude of its paper money) it was because it did not need one in its relations with the neighbouring regions it exploited: Mongolia, Tibet, the East Indies and Japan. If medieval Islam towered above the Old Continent, from the Atlantic to the Pacific for centuries on end, it was because no state (Byzantium apart) could compete with its gold and silver money, *dinars* and *dirhems*. They were the instruments of its power. If medieval Europe finally perfected its money, it was because it had to meet the challenge of the hostile Muslim world. Likewise the monetary revolution that gradually invaded the Turkish Empire in the sixteenth century was a result of its forced entry into the concert of Europe, which meant going beyond the largely ceremonial exchanges of ambassadors. Japan closed its doors to the external world after 1638, but only after a fashion: they stayed open to Chinese junks and Dutch liberty boats. The crack was wide enough for money and merchandise to make their way into the country and to force it to make the requisite response: the exploitation of its silver and copper mines. This effort was, at the same time, linked to its urban progress in the seventeenth century and the growth of a 'truly bourgeois civilization' in privileged towns. Everything was connected.

Such evidence reveals a sort of monetary foreign policy in which the foreigner sometimes dictated the terms, both by his strength and by his weakness. To hold a conversation one has to find a common language, some common ground. The merit of long-distance trade, of large-scale commercial capitalism, was its ability to speak the language of world trade. Even if this trade, as we will see in our second book, was not the most important in volume (trade in spices was much less – even in value – than trade in grain in Europe)[11] it was crucial because of its efficiency and the constructive change it introduced. Long-distance trade was the source of all rapid 'accumulation'. It controlled the world of the *ancien régime* and money was at its command, following or preceding it as necessary. Trade steered the economies.

One of many seventeenth-century caricatures of the death of 'Herr Credit' whose corpse lies in the foreground, with mourners all round. This refers to the everyday credit extended by shopkeepers to poor people, and was suspended when cash ran out. In the legend underneath this engraving, a baker is saying to a customer: *Wann du Geld hast, so hab ich Brod*, 'When you've got the money I've got the bread'. (Germanisches Nationalmuseum, Nuremberg.)

Imperfect currencies and economies

It would take too long to describe all the elementary forms of monetary exchange: many expedients were used, and some classification is required. Moreover, the dialogue between 'perfect' money (if such a thing exists) and 'imperfect' currencies can shed light on the very roots of the problem. If history can explain anything, this should be an ideal testing-ground – on condition that certain mistakes are avoided: such as assuming that perfection and imperfection cannot co-exist and even intermingle at times; or that these two levels of currency do not form one and the same problem; or failing to see that all forms of exchange necessarily depend on differences in voltage (as they still do today). Money too is a means of exploiting someone else, at home or abroad, and accelerating exchange.

A 'synchronic' view of the world in the eighteenth century bears this out to the point of obviousness. Vast areas and millions of people were still in the age of Homer when the value of Achilles' shield was calculated in oxen. Adam Smith was struck by this image: 'The armour of Diomede,' says Homer, 'cost only nine oxen; but that of Glaucus cost an hundred oxen.' An economist today would unhesitatingly call these simple types of humanity a Third World: there has always been a Third World. Its regular mistake was to agree to the terms of a dialogue which was always unfavourable to it. But it was often forced to.

Primitive currencies

A rudimentary form of money appears as soon as commodities are exchanged. A more sought-after or more plentiful commodity plays or tries to play the part of money, the standard of exchange. For example, salt was money in the 'kingdoms' of Upper Senegal and Upper Niger, and in Abyssinia, where cubes of salt, according to a French author in 1620, 'cut in the same way as rock crystal, the length of a finger', served indiscriminately as money and food, 'so that they can, with good reason, be said to eat their money in substance'. What a risk, this prudent Frenchman immediately exclaimed, 'of one day finding all their means melted and dissolved into water!'[12] Cotton cloth played the same role on the banks of the Monomotapa and the shores of the Gulf of Guinea where slave traders used the expression 'a piece of India' to designate the quantity of cotton goods (from the Indies) equivalent to the price of a man. Later the term came to designate the man himself, and professionals were soon saying that a 'piece of India' meant a male slave between fifteen and forty years old.

Copper bracelets, known as *manillas*, weighed quantities of gold dust and horses were all used as currency in this part of Africa. Father Labat (1728) spoke of the magnificent horses the Moors resold to the blacks. 'They price them,' he wrote, 'at fifteen slaves each. This is a quite absurd type of money, but every country has its own ways.'[13] The English merchants established an unbeatable tariff in the first years of the eighteenth century in order to oust their competitors: 'They set the captive "piece of India" at four ounces of gold or thirty piastres [of silver] or three-quarters of a pound of coral, or seven pieces of Scottish cloth.' Meanwhile chickens 'so fat and so tender that they are worth as much as capons and fowl in other countries' were so numerous in some black villages in the interior that their price was one chicken for a sheet of paper.[14]

Sea-shells were another form of money on the African coasts. They varied in size and colour but the best known are the *zimbos* of the Congo shores, and the cowries. 'The *zimbos*,' wrote a Portuguese in 1619, 'are very small sea snails having no use and no value in themselves. The barbarism of earlier times introduced this money which is still used today.'[15] (What is more it is still used in the twentieth century!) Cowries too are small sea-shells, blue streaked with red; they were strung together into ropes. Whole boatloads of them were sent from the 'lost islands' of the Indian Ocean, the Maldives and the Laccadives, to Africa, north-eastern India and Burma. Holland was importing them to Amsterdam in the seventeenth century, knowing very well to what use they could be put. Cowries formerly circulated in China by the routes Buddhism used to win the countries over to its faith. Moreover, cowries were not completely driven out by the Chinese *sapeke*; Yunan, the wood and copper country, was to retain them for a long time. Recent research there has indicated that at quite late dates contracts for hire and sale were still being drawn up in cowries.[16]

No less strange was the money discovered by an astonished Italian journalist who accompanied Queen Elizabeth and the Duke of Edinburgh on a visit to Africa: 'Natives in the interior of Nigeria,' he wrote, 'buy livestock, weapons, agricultural products, cloth, even their wives, not with Her Britannic Majesty's pounds sterling, but with strange coral money minted [or rather manufactured] in Europe. These coins ... come from Italy where they are called *olivette*; they are specially manufactured in Tuscany in a shop working Leghorn coral which has continued in existence to the present day.' *Olivette* are coral cylinders, perforated in the centre and milled on their outside surface. They are in circulation in Nigeria, Sierra Leone, on the Ivory Coast, in Liberia and even farther afield. In Africa the purchaser carries them at his belt on a string. Everybody can calculate his wealth at sight. Behanzin bought a specially manufactured *olivetta*, weighing a kilogram and exquisitely coloured for a thousand pounds sterling in 1902.[17]

It is impossible to draw up an exhaustive list of these unexpected forms of money. They are found everywhere. Iceland, according to regulations of 1413 and 1426 had a centuries-old market price list for commodities, payable in dried fish (1 fish for one horseshoe, 3 for a pair of women's shoes, 100 for a barrel of wine, 120 for a cask of butter, etc.).[18] In Alaska, and in Russia under Peter the Great, furs fulfilled the same role: sometimes these were ordinary squares of fur which piled up on the military paymasters' desks. But in Siberia, taxes were collected in the form of precious and marketable furs; and the Tsar effected many payments (notably officials' salaries) in furs – 'soft gold'. In colonial America tobacco, sugar, or cocoa, depending on the region, might be used as currency. The Indians in North America used little cylinders cut from blue or violet sea shells and threaded on a string. This was *wampum*, which European colonists continued to use legitimately until 1670 and which indeed continued to exist until at least 1725.[19] Similarly, the Congo in the broad sense (including Angola) witnessed the awakening of a series of markets and active trading networks between the sixteenth and eighteenth centuries, all no doubt operating in the vital service of barter, of trade with the whites and their agents, the *pombeiros*, often settled deep in the interior. Two types of pseudo-money were in circulation: *zimbos* and pieces of material.[20] The sea-shells were standardized: a gauged sieve was used to separate large from small (one large equalled ten small). The cloth money also varied in size; a *lubongo* was as large as a sheet of paper, a *mpusu* the size of a table napkin. This money was usually in sets of tens and therefore formed a scale of values, with multiples and sub-multiples like metallic money. It was thus possible to mobilize large sums. In 1649 the king of the Congo assembled 1500 loads of material, worth approximately 40 million Portuguese *reis*.[21]

444 *The Structures of Everyday Life*

The fate of this pseudo-money after the European impact (whether cowries in Bengal,[22] *wampum* after 1670, or the Congo *zimbos*) proves identical in every case where it can be investigated – monstrous and catastrophic inflation, caused by an increase in reserves, an accelerated and even hectic circulation, and a concomitant devaluation in relation to the dominant European money. And 'counterfeit' primitive money was even added to the confusion! The production of counterfeit *wampum* in glass paste in the nineteenth century by European workshops led to the total disappearance of the old money. The Portuguese had shown greater foresight; they had seized 'fishing grounds of money' (that is to say *zimbos*) off the coasts of Loanda island in Angola in about 1650. *Zimbos* had already been devalued by 10% between 1575 and 1650.[23]

From all this, one is obliged to conclude that primitive currencies were indeed forms of money, with all the appearances and properties of money. Their vicissitudes illustrate the history of the clash between primitive economies and advanced economies, brought about by the European invasion of the seven seas.

Barter within monetary economies

What is less well known is that almost equally uneven relationships were perpetuated inside the 'civilized' countries themselves. Under the thin surface of the

The emperor Kublai Khan, conqueror of China, having money struck in mulberry-tree bark stamped with the imperial seal. (*Livres de Merveilles*, MSS fr 2810, f° 45, Bibliothèque Nationale, Paris.)

monetary economies, primitive activities continued and blended into the others, in the regular meetings at town markets, or in the more concentrated atmosphere of trade fairs. Rudimentary economies survived in the heart of Europe, encircled by monetary life which did not destroy them but rather kept them as so many internal colonies within easy reach. Adam Smith (1775) spoke of a Scottish village 'where it is not uncommon, I am told, for a workman to carry nails instead of money to the baker's shop or the alehouse'.[24] At about the same time, in some isolated areas of the Catalan Pyrenees, villagers would come to the shop with small sacks of grain to pay for their goods.[25] There are later and even more convincing examples. Corsica, according to the evidence of ethnographers, was not annexed by a really efficient monetary economy until after the First World War. The change had hardly occurred in certain mountainous regions of 'French' Algeria before the Second World War. This was one of the underlying dramas of the Aurès up to the period around the 1930s.[26] We can imagine comparable dramas as the modern monetary order caught up with innumerable small closed worlds in certain rural or mountainous districts in eastern Europe or western America, at different times but by comparable processes whatever the date.

A seventeenth-century traveller, François La Boullaye, reports that in Circassia and Mingrelia, that is between the southern Caucasus and the Black Sea, 'minted money is not known'. Barter is the only form of exchange, and the tribute paid by the sovereign of Mingrelia to the Grand Turk is one of 'cloth and slaves'. The ambassador whose task it was to take the tribute to Istanbul had a particular problem: how could he pay his expenses in the Turkish capital? And indeed, being accompanied by a suite of some thirty or forty slaves, he was obliged to sell them one by one, except for his secretary, adds La Boullaye, from whom he was parted only as a last extremity! After which 'he returned home alone'.[27]

The example of Russia shows the same thing. At Novgorod at the beginning of the fifteenth century 'people were still only using ... small Tartar coins, scraps of marten's skin, bits of stamped leather. They only began to mint very coarse silver money in 1425. And Novgorod was advanced compared to the rest of the Russian economy, within which exchanges were made in kind for a long time.'[28] Money did not begin to be minted regularly until the arrival of German coins and ingots (because the Russian balance of trade was favourable) in the sixteenth century. And then only on a modest scale. And the minting of money still often depended on private initiative. Barter continued in places in this immense country. It only receded with the reign of Peter the Great. Regions until then isolated were put into contact with each other. Russia undeniably lagged behind the West: the crucial gold resources of Siberia were only really worked after 1820.[29]

Colonial America also presented a highly significant scene. The monetary economy only reached the large towns of the mining countries there – Mexico, Peru – and regions nearer Europe, such as the West Indies and Brazil (Brazil was soon to be in an advantageous position because of its gold mines). These were

A bronze counter with the mark of the Peruzzi (two pears), merchants of Florence. M. Bernocchi, who gave me this as a gift, has in his collection large numbers of similar counters which seem to have been issued by Florentine firms for internal use, since they often bear the marks of two families associated in business together. (Diameter 20 mm.) (Photo M. Cabaud.)

not perfect monetary economies; far from it. But prices in them did fluctuate – already a sign of a certain economic maturity – whereas up to the nineteenth century prices did not fluctuate in either Argentina or Chile (which nevertheless produced copper and silver).[30] Here they remained remarkably steady, having been so to speak stifled at birth. Exchanges of commodity for commodity were frequent throughout the American continent. The feudal or semi-feudal concessions of the colonial governments were a symptom of the scarcity of hard cash. Imperfect money therefore naturally played its part: pieces of copper in Chile, tobacco in Virginia, 'card money' in French Canada, *tlacos* in New Spain.[31] These *tlacos* (from a Mexican word) stood for an eighth of a *real*. They were small coins, created by retail dealers, proprietors of shops called *mestizas* which sold everything from bread and alcohol to silk fabrics from China. Each of these shop-owners issued small wood, lead or copper coinage with his own mark. The counters were occasionally exchanged against real silver *pesos* and circulated amongst a small public. Some of them got lost. All of them lent themselves to speculation, often sordid. Such a situation arose because silver money only consisted of large denominations, which in practice passed over the heads of people of small means. In addition every fleet that reached Spain drained the country of its silver. Finally, the attempt to create copper money in 1542 was a failure.[32] There was really no option but to be content with the defective system of almost primitive money. Was this so different from what happened in France in the fourteenth century? John the Good's ransom was enough to empty the country of its coin, so the king minted leather money which he bought back a few years later!

The same difficulties occurred in the English colonies, both before and after independence. In November 1721 a Philadelphia merchant wrote to one of his correspondents who had settled in Madeira: 'I had intended to send a little corn, but creditors here are reluctant and money so scarce that we begin to be, or rather we have for some time already been, racked by lack of a means of payment, without which trade is an occupation of much perplexity.'[33] In everyday transactions, people sought to escape such 'perplexity'. Clavière and Bris-

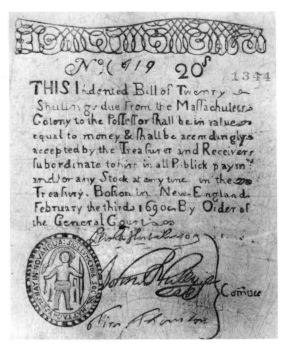

Note issued by the colony of Massachusetts in New England, 3 February 1690. The original is in the archives of Messrs Molson of Montreal who were so kind as to offer me this reproduction.

sot, well-known figures in the French Revolution, who wrote a book on the United States in 1791, remarked on the extraordinary extent of barter.

> Instead of money incessantly going backwards and forwards into the same hands, [they write admiringly] it is the practice here for country people to satisfy their needs by direct reciprocal exchanges. The tailor and bootmaker go and do the work of their calling at the home of the farmer who requires it and who, most frequently, provides the raw material for it and pays for the work in goods. These sorts of exchanges cover many objects; they write down what they give and what they receive on both sides and at the end of the year they settle with a very small quantity of coin, a large variety of exchanges, something which could only be done with a considerable quantity of money in Europe. [Thus] a means of wide circulation without coin.... [is created].[34]

This eulogy of barter and services paid for in kind, as a *progressive* innovation of young America, is amusing. In the seventeenth century, and even in the eighteenth, payments in kind were very frequent in Europe; they were the relics of a past in which they had been the general rule. One could draw up a long list (following the example of Alfons Dopsch)[35] - the cutlers of Solingen, miners and weavers of Pforzheim, peasant clock-makers of the Black Forest, were all paid in kind, in victuals, salt, cloth, brass wire, measures of grain, all of which were excessively priced. This was the 'Truck system' (barter) which existed in Holland, England and France just as much as in Germany in the fifteenth century. Even German 'officials' of the Empire, *a fortiori* municipal officials, received part of their salary in kind. And how many schoolmasters were still paid in poultry, butter and corn in the last century![36] Indian villages at all periods also paid their craftsmen (the craft was handed down from father to son in artisan castes) in foodstuffs; and *baratto* (barter) was whenever possible the prudent rule of all large merchants in the Levantine ports from the fifteenth century. Those experts in credit, the sixteenth-century Genoese, were probably following in the steps of this tradition of barter when they thought of turning the fairs known as 'Besançon fairs', where bills of exchange from all Europe were settled, into positive clearing-houses. A Venetian in 1602 was astounded by the millions of ducats which changed hands at Piacenza (the actual site of these fairs), with nothing to show for it in the end except a few handfuls of écus, '*di oro en oro*', in other words *real* money.[37]

Outside Europe: early economies and metallic money

Between Europe and the primitive economies, Japan, Islam, India and China represented intermediate stages half-way towards an active and complete monetary life.

Japan and the Turkish Empire

The monetary economy blossomed in Japan during the seventeenth century. However, the circulation of gold, silver and copper coins barely touched the masses. The old money – rice – continued in use. Loads of herrings were still exchanged for loads of rice. But the changeover gained ground. The peasants soon had enough copper coins to pay their dues in money on new fields not planted with rice (the old system of compulsory unpaid labour and allowances in kind being in force for the remaining fields). In the western part of Japan, on the *shogun's* domains, one-third of all peasant dues were paid in money. Certain *daimios* (great nobles) soon owned such large quantities of gold and silver that they even paid their own *samurais* (nobles in their service) with it. This development was slow because of interference by the government, hostile attitudes to the new system and the *samurais*' moral philosophy which forbade them to think, let alone speak, of money.[38] The monetary world of Japan, confronted with the peasant and feudal world, was at least threefold; governmental, merchant and urban – the stuff of revolution. And indisputable signs of a certain degree of maturity are provided by the known fluctuations of prices – in particular the price of rice and the peasants' money dues; or by the drastic devaluation of 1695, determined by the *shogun* in the hope of 'increasing money'.[39]

Islam had a monetary organization at its disposal from the Atlantic to India, but it was old and remained enclosed in its traditions. The only development benefited Persia, which was an active crossroads, the Ottoman Empire, and Istanbul, an exceptional case. In the enormous capital city during the eighteenth century, price lists fixed the prices of commodities and *ad valorem* customs duties in national currencies. Exchanges were effected on all the great markets of the West – Amsterdam, Leghorn, London, Marseilles, Venice and Vienna.

In currency at Istanbul were gold *sultanins* also known as *fonduc* or *fonducchi* (whole coins, halves and quarters); silver pieces – the Turkish piastres known as *grouck* or *grouch*; while the *para* and the *aspre* became moneys of account. A *sultanin* was worth five piastres, a piastre forty *paras*, a *para* three *aspres*; the *mekir* or *gieduki*, worth a quarter of an *aspre*, was the smallest real money (silver and copper) in circulation. This Istanbul currency was sent far afield to Egypt and the Indies via Basra, Baghdad, Mosul, Aleppo and Damascus, where colonies of Armenian merchants stimulated trade. A certain monetary deterioration is unmistakeable. Foreign coins were at a premium compared with Ottoman money; the venetian *sequin*, a golden coin, was worth 5·5 piastres; the Dutch *thaler* and Ragusan crown, silver coins, were quoted at 60 *paras*. The fine Austrian *thaler*, known as *Cara Grouch*, changed hands at 101, even 102 *paras*.[40] A Venetian document of 1688 already indicates that it was possible to make up to 30% on *reals* from Spain (sent to Egypt). Another showed that consignments of *sequins* or *ongari* bought in Venice made from 12% to 17·5% in Istanbul in 1671.[41] The Turkish Empire was thus luring in money from the West, which it required for its own circulation.

There is another aspect to the matter: in the Levant 'all money [which arrives] is melted down and sent to Persia and the Indies after having been converted into ingots'. They would then be minted in the form of Persian *larins* or Indian rupees.[42] That at any rate is what a French document of 1686 alleges. However, both before and after this date, Western coins were arriving intact in Ispahan or Delhi. The problem for merchants was that any coins brought into Persia had to be taken to the mint and restruck as *larins*. So they had to pay for the cost of minting. Until about 1620, the *larin*, which was a sort of international currency in the Far East, was in fact overvalued, so there was some compensation. But during the seventeenth century, it gradually lost this advantage to the *real*, so that by Tavernier's time merchants in Persia were anxious to obtain *reals* which they smuggled out for their dealings in India, either in the great caravan-trains or on the fleets of the Persian Gulf.[43]

India

The Indian subcontinent had long been familiar with gold and silver coin, since before the Christian era. During the centuries with which we are concerned, three expansions of the monetary economy took place, in the thirteenth, sixteenth and eighteenth centuries. None was complete or had the effect of standardization, and some kind of distinction was maintained between the north, with the Indus and Ganges valleys, which was the zone of Muslim rule, and the southern peninsula where Hindu kingdoms survived, including the long-prospering kingdom of Vijayanagar.

Where there was a system operating in the north it was a silver/copper bimetallism, the lower-ranking copper coins being far and away the most numerous. The silver coins – rupees (or their submultiples), sometimes round, sometimes square – appeared in the sixteenth century. They only affected the upper level of economic life: below this level one found copper, and also bitter almonds, a curious form of primitive money which originated in Persia. Gold coins, such as the *mohurs*, struck in the reign of Akbar, were virtually absent from circulation.[44] But this was not true of the south, where gold coins were the major currency in the Deccan; at lower levels a little silver and copper complemented sea-shell money.[45] The gold came in the form of what were known in the West as *pagodas*, very thick coins but with a narrow diameter, 'which were worth as much as the Venetian *sequin*' (in 1695), their metal being finer 'than that of the Spanish *pistole*'.[46]

Monetary chaos persisted in the eighteenth century. Coins were struck at innumerable mints, the one at Surat, the great port of Gujerat, being the largest. If quality and alloy were equal, local money was at a premium. Since minting was frequent, intervention with an eye to gain on the part of the princes increased the value of recent money even if, as was often the case, it was inferior to the old. Gemelli Careri advised the merchants in 1695 to strike (or rather restrike) their silver coins 'to the coinage of the land ... and above all the die should be of the same year otherwise a loss of half a per cent will be incurred. Facilities for minting money can be found in all the towns on the Great Mogul's frontiers.'[47]

Finally, as India in fact produced no gold, silver, copper or cowries, other countries' money came to it, passed through its ever-open door and provided it with the basis of its monetary raw material. Encouraged by the chaos, the Portuguese minted coins to compete with Indian coins. In the same way there were (until 1788) Batavian and Persian rupees. But a systematic drain on precious metals from the whole world continued, to the profit of the Great Mogul and his states.

> The reader must take into consideration [explained a traveller (1695)] that all the gold and silver which circulates in the world ultimately goes to the Great Mogul, as if to its centre. It is known that the metals that leave America go partly to Turkey and partly to Persia, via Smyrna, for silk, after

having roamed over several European kingdoms. But the Turks cannot do without coffee from Yemen or Arabia Felix. No more can the Arabs, Persians and Turks do without commodities from the Indies. This means that they send large sums of money by the Red Sea to Moka near Bab el Mandeb, to Basra at the bottom of the Persian Gulf, to Bandar Abessi and to Gommeron, and from there take it to the Indies on their ships.

The Dutch, English and Portuguese also made all their purchases in the Indies against gold and silver, because 'it is only by paying cash that we can obtain from the Indians the merchandise we want to transport to Europe'.[48]

The picture is hardly exaggerated. But, as nothing is free, India had to pay dearly for its precious metals. This was one of the reasons for its austere life and also for the rise of its compensating industries, notably the textiles of Gujerat, a real driving-force of the Indian economy even before the arrival of Vasco da Gama. A considerable export trade to countries near and far was carried on. Gujerat with its cotton weavers must have been like Netherlands wool centres in the middle ages. From the sixteenth century an enormous burst of industrialization began there and spread towards the Ganges. In the eighteenth century, cotton prints flooded into Europe. They were imported by merchants in large quantities until the moment came when Europe preferred to manufacture them itself and competed with them.

It was logical that the monetary history of India should correspond to movements in the West: its currency was remote-controlled. It appears that the resumption of the minting of silver coins in Delhi after 1542 had to wait for silver from America first to reach Europe and then to spread beyond it. V. Magalhaes Godinho has explained in detail how rupees were minted from Spanish *reals* and Persian *larins* – which were often themselves reminted *reals*. Similarly, Indian gold coins were actually reissues of Portuguese gold from Africa, Spanish gold from America and above all Venetian sequins.[49] The new influx completely altered the old monetary situation, which had been based on a comparatively modest supply of precious metals of Mediterranean (or rather Venetian) and Asian origin (gold from China, Sumatra, Monomotapa, silver from Japan and Persia); plus an equally modest amount of copper which came from the West via the Red Sea. And there was a plentiful supply of pseudomoney: cowries in Bengal and elsewhere, bitter almonds from Persia in Gujerat. Like that of gold and silver, the circulation of copper coin was greatly perturbed by the massive imports from Portugal, which were swallowed up in their entirety by Mogul India: that is until copper became scarce in Lisbon[50] before the supply completely dried up after 1580. After this, copper began to run out in India too, in spite of the appearance of some supplies from China and Japan. After the reign of Jahangir in about 1627, issues of copper coinage which had formerly been abundant, began to slow down in Mogul India, and silver began to play a larger part in transactions, while cowries were once more brought into common use to replace in part the copper *paysahs*.[51]

China

China can only be understood in the context of the primitive neighbouring economies linked to it and on which it depended: Tibet, Japan (almost up to the sixteenth century), the East Indies and Indochina. As exceptions prove the rule, we shall exclude certain areas from this general heading of primitive economies: Malacca, a market junction to which money flowed of its own accord; the western tip of Sumatra, with its gold towns and spices; and the island of Java, already fairly populated but where copper coins, *caixas*, followed the Chinese pattern. Java was still only at an elementary stage in its monetary life.

China thus lived near to countries that had remained in their infancy. In Japan rice had long served as money; in the East Indies and Indochina the usual currencies were Chinese *caixas* imported or imitated, copper 'gongs', gold dust by weight, or weights of tin or copper; in Tibet coral brought from the distant West, and gold dust.

All this accounts for the backwardness of China itself and at the same time a certain strength of its 'dominant' monetary system. It had been able to enjoy a lazy monetary history with no risks involved simply by preserving its status in relation to its neighbours. But let us not forget that stroke of genius – paper money – which lasted roughly from the ninth century to the fourteenth and was particularly effective in the Mongol period when China was simultaneously opened to the world of the steppes, Islam and the West by routes from central Asia. Paper money not only provided facilities for internal payments between provinces, but also made it possible to reserve silver for consignments of metal for trade with central Asia and the European West (note the paradox that China was an *exporter* of silver). The emperor collected certain taxes in notes, and foreign merchants, as Pegolotti recalls, had to change their coin into notes (it was restored to them when they left the country).[52] Paper money was the Chinese answer to the economic situation of the thirteenth and fourteenth centuries, a means of surmounting the difficulties inherent in the archaic circulation of heavy *caixas* of copper or iron and the animation of her external trade along the silk routes.

But with the fourteenth-century depression, and the victory of the peasant rising that brought to power the national dynasty of the Mings, the great Mongol route to the West was broken. Issues of notes continued but inflation was making itself felt. In 1378, seventeen paper *caixas* were worth thirteen copper *caixas*. Seventy years later, in 1448, one thousand notes were required for three *caixas* of cash. Inflation got the upper hand all the more easily because paper recalled the hated Mongol regime. The state abandoned it; only private banks still put paper for local needs into circulation.

From now on, China had only one type of money, *caixas*, *caches*, or copper *sapekes*, as the Europeans called them. These were an ancient creation, having appeared 200 years before the Christian era. They had changed slightly over the centuries but had been maintained in the face of strong competition from salt and grain, a more serious challenge from silk in the eighth century, and from rice which reappeared in the fifteenth century, when paper money went out.[53]

In the early days of the Ming dynasty these coins were always made of a mixture of copper and lead (four parts lead to six of copper) 'which means that they break very easily in the fingers'. They were circular, stamped on only one side and pierced by a square hole. A cord was threaded through the hole so that they could be made into strings of a hundred or a thousand. 'It is usual,' noted Father de Magaillans (who died in 1677 and whose book appeared in 1688), 'to give a cord of a thousand deniers for one *écu*, or Chinese *tael*; and this exchange is made in banks and public booths intended for that purpose.' Obviously Chinese 'deniers' were too small to fulfil every function. Silver, valued by weight,

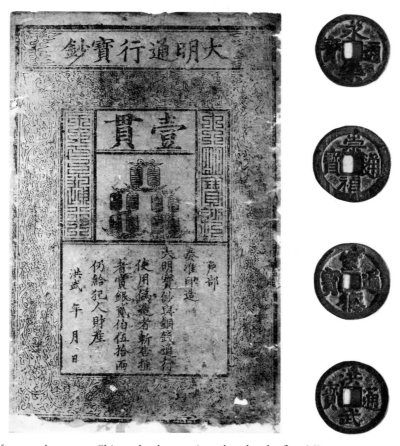

Left: A fourteenth-century Chinese bank note, issued under the first Ming emperor. Collection of G. Lion. (Photo Giraudon.)
Right, top to bottom: coins of the Ming period (fourteenth, fifteenth and seventeenth centuries). (Cernuschi Museum, Paris.)

was a sort of superior currency. Neither gold (very little used anyway) nor silver was made into coins: they occurred instead in ingots 'shaped like a small boat ... in Macao they are called *paes*, gold or silver "loaves" '. They were of different values, Father de Magaillans continued. 'The gold loaves are worth one, two, ten and up to twenty *écus*; the silver ones are half an *écu*, one *écu*, ten, twenty, fifty and sometimes one hundred and three hundred *écus*.'[54] The Portuguese Father persisted in talking in *deniers* and *écus* but his meaning is clear. We will only specify that the *tael* (the *écu*) was usually a money of account, an expression we will return to later.

In fact only the silver ingot was important at this upper level. 'White as snow' – because it was mixed with antimony, it was the basic instrument of large-scale transactions in China, the more so since under the Mings (1368-1644) a monetary and capitalist economy was coming to life, developing and extending its interests and services. One has only to think of the rush on the Chinese coalmines in 1596 and the enormous scandal that resulted in 1605. Silver was in such demand that it was exchanged for gold at rates of as much as five to one. When the Manila galleon set up its link with New Spain across the Pacific, Chinese junks hurried out to meet it. All goods in Manila changed hands in return exclusively for Mexican silver, a total turnover of something like a million *pesos* a year.[55] The Chinese 'would journey to hell' wrote Sebastien Manrique, to find new goods to exchange for the *reals* they so passionately desired. They even said, in their pidgin-Spanish, '*plata sa sangre*', 'silver is blood'.[56]

Silver loaves could not always be used whole in everyday life. Buyers 'cut them up with steel scissors they carry for this purpose, and divide them into pieces which are large or small according to the price of their purchase'. Each of these fragments had to be weighed. Buyer and seller used small Roman scales.

> There is scarcely a Chinaman [one European said (between 1733 and 1735)] however wretched he may be, who does not carry scissors and a precision scale around with him. The former is used to cut gold and silver and is called a *trapelin*; the latter which is used to weigh the materials, is called a *litan*. The Chinese are so adept at this operation that they will often cut two *liards*' [half an old farthing] worth of silver or five sous' worth of gold so accurately that they will not have to do it again.[57]

We find the same details described a century earlier by Father de las Cortes (1626) who was also amazed by the extraordinary familiarity displayed by all the Chinese with this strange method of payment. There is not a child, he writes, who does not know how to estimate the metal of the ingots and its degree of purity. The tiniest scrap of metal is picked up in a kind of bell which they wear at their waists, filled with wax. When they have accumulated enough scraps, all they have to do is melt the wax.[58] Should one admire this system? Our first informant certainly thought so:

> Reflecting [he writes] on the multiplicity of our coins in Europe, I deem it an advantage for the Chinese to have neither gold nor silver coins. The

reason for this, in my opinion, is that since these metals are considered as commodities in China, the quantity which gets in there cannot effect such a considerable rise in the prices of goods and merchandise as in a country where silver money is very common.... Moreover the price of everything is so well controlled in China that one hardly ever buys things at above their usual value in relation to each other. Only Europeans are the dupes of their good faith. Because it is a very common occurrence for the Chinese to sell them what they buy at above the price current in the country.[59]

It is certainly true that China, because of its size no doubt, was not inundated with silver, *pace* the many historians who have described it as a 'suction pump' for the world's silver supply. How do we know? Because of the huge purchasing-power of a single piece of eight. That it was worth from 700 to 1100 *caixas* according to province (and the many different currencies in circulation) may not tell us a great deal; but in 1695, a single one of these thin silver coins 'could buy the best bread in the world for six months'. The remark obviously refers to one person's consumption, in this case a traveller from the West who took advantage of the extraordinary cheapness of wheat flour, not appreciated in China. Yet the same small coin, handed over once a month, also enabled our traveller to hire a Chinese servant 'to do the cooking', and a *tael* (a *tael*, or 1000 *caixas*, still almost equivalent to a piece of eight at that period) bought him the services of a Chinese servant of 'mature' age, who received a further 'four pieces of eight [a lump sum] for the maintenance of his family' during the servant's absence when he followed Careri to Peking.[60]

The colossal hoarding of wealth in the imperial treasury must also be taken into account (not to mention hoarding by the rich and dishonest). Most of this mass of immobilized money depended on government decisions and measures, and the government used it to influence prices. This is explained in a correspondence between Jesuit fathers in 1779. According to them, the value of money in relation to goods varied under the Tsing dynasty, meaning that prices had on the whole risen. Moreover, whether silver was money in the strict sense or not (of course it was not), China lived under a sort of silver/copper bi-metallism. The internal rate of exchange was between *sapekes* on the one hand and on the other a Chinese 'ounce' of silver or a piece of eight sold by a Western merchant. But the silver/copper exchange rate varied from day to day, according to season, year and above all issues of silver and copper ordered by the imperial government. These issues were intended to maintain a normal monetary circulation and to bring the copper/silver relationship back into balance every time it was necessary, by releasing silver when silver was too highly priced, or copper when copper was. 'Our government,' said the Chinese Jesuit, 'makes the respective value of silver and money rise and fall ... it has organised this expedient for the whole Empire.' Control was all the easier in that the state owned all the copper mines in China.[61]

Money cannot therefore be said to have been a neutral tool in China, nor

In the streets of Peking: a merchant holding huge scissors used to cut up silver ingots; a pair of scales to weigh the fragments; a merchant selling cords to thread *sapekes*. Cf. the coins shown on p. 453, with holes in the middle, and the design on the bank note which shows groups of coins threaded together. (Cabinet des Estampes, Bibliothèque Nationale, Paris.)

prices always marvellously stable. The prices of some commodities – notably rice – did move. In the eighteenth century, prices rose in Canton under the impact of European trade, following a double revolution in money and credit which deeply permeated the old economy of the Middle Empire.[62] A seaboard economy linked to the 'piastre' overturned the internal economy linked to the *sapeke*. But the *sapeke* was not as fundamentally inert and calm as is generally supposed.

That said, the reader will perhaps be prepared to take my word for it: in monetary matters China was more primitive and less sophisticated than India. But its system had much more cohesion and obvious unity. China was not the recipient of coinage from all over the world.

Some rules of the currency game

Europe stood alone and was already something of a monetary monster. It experienced the whole gamut of currency experience. On the lowest level, and to a greater extent than is usually believed, were barter, self-sufficiency and primitive money – old expedients, indirect means of economizing on specie. At a higher level came relatively plentiful supplies of metallic money – gold, silver and copper. Finally there were many kinds of credit, from the pawnbroking activities of the Lombards and Jewish merchants to the bills of exchange and speculation of the great trading centres.

And these operations were not confined to Europe. The system was extended and introduced over the whole world like a vast net thrown over the wealth of the other continents. It was no minor detail that for Europe's gain the treasures of America were exported as far as the Far East in the sixteenth century to be converted into local money or ingots. Europe was beginning to devour, to digest the world. We can therefore have no sympathy with those economists of the past (and even some of the present) who seem to feel sorry for it, doubting its economic health and maintaining that it suffered a permanent monetary haemorrhage in the direction of the Far East. In the first place, Europe did not die of it. And in the second, one might as well feel sorry for the successful besieger of a town because he had to sacrifice powder, shot and time on it.

In the event, all the currencies of the world were enmeshed in the same net, if only because monetary policy in any one zone amounted to attracting or expelling one or another of the precious metals. Such monetary movements could sometimes have repercussions over immense distances. V. Magalhães Godinho has shown how even in the fifteenth century the currencies of Italy, Egypt and the Far East commanded each other's movements, as indeed did all the European currencies. Europe had no power to reshape for its own ends this world-wide monetary structure with its existing coherence. It had to bow to local practice wherever it wished to impose its rule. But to the extent that even before the conquest of America, Europe already possessed a comparatively large stock of precious metals, it often was able to see that the system operated to its advantage.

Competition between metals

A metal currency consists of a set of related coins: one is worth a tenth, a sixteenth, a twentieth of another, and so on. Usually several metals, precious or otherwise, are employed simultaneously. The West retained three metals: gold, silver and copper, with the inconveniences and advantages of such a mixture. The advantages were that it answered the varied requirements of exchange. Each metal with its coins dealt with a series of transactions. In a system exclusively of gold coins it would be difficult to settle small-scale everyday purchases. On the other hand large-scale payments would present difficulties in a system confined to copper. In fact every metal played its part: gold, reserved for princes, large merchants (even the Church); silver for ordinary transactions; copper naturally for the smallest. Copper was the 'black' money of people of small means and the poor. Mixed with a little silver it blackened quickly and deserved its name.

The character and the state of health of an economy can be guessed almost at first glance from its dominant metal. In Naples in 1751, gold was hoarded and silver left the country. Despite its small volume (1·5 million ducats against 6 million of silver and 10 of gold) copper was used to settle the bulk of transactions because it circulated rapidly and, inferior though it might be, 'it stayed where it was'.[63] It was the same story in Spain: in 1724 'the major part of payments is made ... in alloy [copper with a little silver added]; its transport is very cumbersome and expensive; moreover it is customary to accept it by weight'.[64] This was a deplorable custom at a time when alloy was used only as small change in France and Holland. But the other powers only permitted Spain to remain the apparent mistress of the silver of the New World on condition that it allowed these distant treasures to circulate as a money 'common to all nations', literally to drain itself for the benefit of others. Spain became 'a mere channel' for silver from its colonies, as Portugal was for gold. Careri called at Cadiz in 1694 with a fleet of galleons; in one day he saw 'over a hundred vessels arrive in the Bay coming to collect silver in return for the goods they had sent to the Indies'. 'The greater part of this metal which goes on the galleons,' he concluded, 'enters the purses of foreign nations.'[65]

In thriving economies, on the other hand, silver or gold became prominent. In 1699, the London Chamber of Commerce described silver money 'as more useful and of more employ than gold'. But the large-scale inflation of gold in the eighteenth century was not far distant. In 1774, England recognized gold as legal and common tender. From then on, silver played only a supplementary role.[66] France, however, continued to back silver, as we shall see.

This is, of course, a very rough outline of the rules in force. There were obvious exceptions. While the large stock markets were warding off copper money like the plague in the first part of the seventeenth century, Portugal was deliberately seeking it out – but with the intention of sending it beyond the Cape of Good Hope to the Indies, as was its custom. We should therefore be wary of appearances. Even gold can mislead us. Thus Turkey under the Osmanli dynasty belonged to a gold zone as far back as the fifteenth century (based on bullion from Africa and Egyptian coins). But gold was relatively plentiful in the Mediterranean and Europe before 1550; if it was also abundant in Turkey, this was because Turkey was merely a transit point for silver coins from Europe on their way east.

In any case, the predominance of one type of money (gold, silver, copper) came about principally as a result of constant interaction between the different metals. The structure of the system resulted in their being in competition with each other. Obviously copper normally played the least important role because the value of small change bore no exact relationship to its metal-content, indeed it often resembled low-denomination paper money. But surprises were always possible. Precisely because of its modest price, copper was the convenient medium for powerful and elementary inflations all over Europe in the seventeenth century. This was especially true of Germany[67] and Spain (up to 1680)[68] – economically sick countries that had found no other solution to their difficulties. Even outside Europe, for example in Persia in about 1660, copper small change – 'half scraped away, red as magpie's flesh' – invaded the markets and 'silver is becoming very scarce from day to day in Hispan (Ispahan)'.[69]

Having said this, let us leave copper out of the discussion. There remains the formidable aristocracy of gold and silver. Their production was irregular and never very flexible, so that depending on circumstances, one of the two metals would be relatively more plentiful than the other; then, with varying degrees of slowness, the situation would reverse, and so on. This resulted in upsets and disasters on the exchanges, and led above all to those slow but powerful fluctuations which were a feature of the monetary *ancien régime*. It is a well-known truth that 'silver and gold are hostile brothers'. Karl Marx adopted the formula for his own purposes: 'Wherever silver and gold exist side by side as legal money,' he wrote, 'the vain attempt has always been made to treat them as one and the same thing.'[70] The dispute has never ended.

Ancient theoreticians would have liked a fixed relationship giving gold twelve times the value of silver for equal weights. This was certainly not the general rule from the fifteenth to the eighteenth century. The ratio at that time varied frequently around and beyond this so-called 'natural' relationship. In the long term, the scales sometimes tipped towards one metal, sometimes towards the other (discounting temporary or local variations that need not detain us at present).

Thus *in the long term*, the value of silver increased from the thirteenth to the sixteenth century, until roughly 1550. At the risk of straining the meaning of the word, we might say that this was an age of gold inflation, which lasted for several centuries. The gold minted in Europe came from Hungary, the Alps, from the distant gold-washers of the Sudan, then from early colonial America. Gold coins were the easiest of all to gather together, so they were used by princes to further their designs: Charles VIII minted gold coins before his expedition to Italy[71] and Francis I and Charles V spent gold on their battles.

Who profited from this comparative abundance of gold? Inevitably the holders of silver bullion or coins, which means the Augsburg merchants, owners of the silver mines in Bohemia and the Alps. In their midst were those uncrowned kings, the Fuggers. Of the two, silver bullion was the stable value at that time.

Between 1550 and 1680 on the other hand, with the modern technique (amalgam) used in the American silver mines silver became superabundant and in turn fuelled a strong and sustained inflation. Gold became scarce and increased in value. Those who backed gold early, for example the Genoese in Antwerp from 1553, had picked a winner.[72]

The scales tilted back slightly again after 1680, with the beginning of gold-washing in Brazil. Until the end of the century, the situation could best be described as stable; then the slight movement became stronger. The relationship between the two metals in Germany, at the Frankfurt and Leipzig fairs, averaged 1 to 15·27 between 1701 and 1710. It moved to 1 to 14·93 between 1741 and 1750.[73] At least silver no longer fell in value as it had done before the gold from Brazil had come into circulation. This was because world production of gold had at least doubled between 1720 and 1760. A small but significant fact: gold reappeared in Burgundy in peasants' hands around 1756.[74]

In this slow, long-term process, every movement of one of the metals involved governed the movement of the other. This is a simple law. The relative abundance of gold in the last years of the fifteenth century 'launched' the silver mines of Germany. So too the first development of Brazilian gold around 1680 stimulated the silver mines of Potosi (which were in great need of stimulus) and even more the mines of New Spain, with the great wealth of Guanajuato and the Veta Madre vein.

In fact these oscillations simply come under the law known as Gresham's law – although Elizabeth I's counsellor was in no way its author. Its terms are well known: bad money drives out good. Gold or silver coins took turns, according to the long-term situation, to play the role of the less 'good' money driving the other, the better, into the hands of speculators or the woollen stockings of hoarders. Naturally such spontaneous activity could be precipitated by inopportune action on the part of governments who spent their time re-adjusting money, raising prices of gold or silver coins according to the oscillations of the market, in the hope (rarely realized) of re-establishing equilibrium.

If the rise was economically justified, the situation remained stable and nothing dramatic happened. If the rise was too high, when gold currency for example was concerned, all the gold coins from neighbouring countries flowed

Minting money: a picture by Hans Hesse (1521), probably painted to mark the occasion of the granting to the town of Annaberg the right in perpetuity to strike money, using the metal from its own mines. The painting is in the cathedral, not far from the miners' guild altar. (Photothèque A. Colin.)

to the country where they were at a premium, whether that country were France under Henry III, Titian's Venice or eighteenth-century England. If the situation persisted, the inordinately over-valued gold money played the role of bad money. It drove out silver money. This was often the case in Venice and, continuously from 1531 the bizarre situation in Sicily.[75] Since there were advantages to be gained from sending silver from Venice or Sicily to North Africa and even more to the Levant, we can be sure that these apparently absurd movements were never without reason, whatever one might think of them and whatever the theoreticians of the period tell us about them.

In these affairs, circumstances could change overnight. In Paris, Edmond Jean François Barbier noted in his journal in July 1723: 'One only sees gold in business; it has reached a point where it costs up to twenty sous ... to change one louis [into silver coins].... On the other hand we weigh out the louis ... and it is great nuisance. You need a precision scale in your pocket.'[76]

Flight, saving and hoarding

The monetary system in Europe suffered from two incurable diseases. On the one hand was the flight abroad of precious metals; on the other, metals were

The money-handler: Jacob Fugger by Lorenzo Lotto (detail). Budapest, Fine Arts Museum. (Photo Snark.)

immobilized by being saved and hoarded. As a result, the engine was constantly being deprived of fuel.

Precious metals had been leaving the Western circuits, primarily for the Indies and China, since the far-off times of the Roman Empire. Silk, pepper, spices, drugs and pearls from the Far East had to be paid for in either silver or gold to force them westwards. As a result, Europe's balance remained in deficit in this respect – until as late as the 1820s in the case of China.[77] This perennial flight became part of the economic structure of the world: precious metals flowed to the Far East by the Levant route, the Cape route, even across the Pacific. In the sixteenth century, they went in the form of Spanish pieces of eight, *reales de a ocho*; in the seventeenth and eighteenth, they took the form of *pesos duros*, 'strong' piastres, actually identical with *reales de a ocho* (only the name had changed) – another sign of continuity. Exit points were not hard to find: the Bay of Cadiz, so large that departures easily escaped detection; Bayonne, the centre for the active smuggling routes across the Pyrenees; or London and Amsterdam, meeting-places for the world's silver. American silver was even on occasion transported from the coasts of Peru directly to Asia by French boats.

Precious metals were also finding their way to East Europe, through the Baltic. The West was in fact gradually stimulating the circulation of money in these backward countries which supplied it with wheat, rye, wood, fish, hides and furs, and which bought very few goods in return. One can see the process beginning in the sixteenth century, with the trade through Narva, Muscovy's window on to the Baltic (opened in 1558 then closed in 1581), and with the White Sea trade at Archangel, initiated in 1553 by the English; and the same pattern still governed the St Petersburg trade in the eighteenth century. These infusions of foreign money were necessary so that the anticipated exports of raw materials could be arranged in exchange. The Dutch, who persisted in trying to pay for them in textile products, fabrics and herrings, eventually lost their leading position in trade with Russia.[78]

The second problem was that metal currency, being so much in demand, needed to flow ever more quickly. Yet it often stagnated, frequently in Europe itself, as a result of the many forms of saving, against which François Quesnay[79] and the physiocrats (like Keynes many years later) strongly protested; and also as a result of the illogical and widespread practice of hoarding, which was a perpetual drain on metals, comparable to India with its 'silver hunger'.

Medieval Europe had a passion for precious metals and gold ornaments. Later, in the thirteenth and fourteenth centuries, came the new 'capitalist' passion for minted coins. But the old attachment to precious objects persisted. Spanish grandees in the age of Philip II bequeathed chests of gold coins and innumerable objects in gold and silver work to their heirs. Even the Duke of Alva, who died in 1582 without a reputation for wealth, left his heirs 600 dozen silver plates and 800 silver platters.[80] Two centuries later Galiani estimated the reserves hoarded in the kingdom of Naples in 1751 at four times the monetary stock in circulation there. 'Luxury,' he explained, 'has made all silver objects – watches, snuff-boxes, sword and cane handles, forks and spoons, cups, plates – so common that it is unbelievable. The Neapolitans, like the Spaniards of yore in almost all their customs, derive very great pleasure from keeping ancient silver objects in their chests known as *scrittori* and *scarabattoli*.'[81] Sébastien Mercier spoke of the 'worthless and idle' wealth in Paris 'of gold and silver furniture, jewellery and plate dishes' (silver dishes).[82]

There are no reliable statistics on the subject of hoarding. A study made many years ago by W. Lexis assumes a ratio of three to four between precious metals hoarded and minted metal in circulation, at the beginning of the sixteenth century.[83] The ratio must have changed in the eighteenth century, perhaps not in the proportion of four to one suggested by Galiani, who was anxious to demonstrate that the demand for precious metals did not only depend on their monetary use. It is true that the world's stocks of metals increased enormously from the sixteenth to the eighteenth century – from one to fifteen according to a rough ratio suggested by W. Lexis,[84] and known examples do not contradict it. In 1670, the total amount of money in circulation in France was of the order of 120 million francs; a century later it was 2000 million. The stock of money in Naples in 1570 was 700,000 ducats; it was 18 million in 1751. Naples and Italy in the seventeenth and eighteenth centuries had huge reserves of unemployed currency. Bankers in Genoa in about 1680 were forced to offer their money to foreigners at 2% and 3%. Many religious orders borrowed from this miraculous source to pay off old debts, at 5%, 6% and 7%.[85]

And governments could be hoarders too, as certain well-known and much quoted examples show: Sixtus V's treasure, piled up in the Castel Sant Angelo, Sully's treasure at the Arsenal; the treasure of the Sergeant-King, Frederick William I, which he did not know how to use any more than he did his army (always ready to strike, *schlagfertig*, but never striking). There are other examples too, like the cautious banks created or re-created at the end of the sixteenth and beginning of the seventeenth century. A keen observer said of the prestigious Bank of Amsterdam in 1761: 'All the silver metal and coin is to be found in the bank ... this is not the place to examine whether the silver shut up there is not as useless to circulation as when it was buried in the mines. I am convinced that it could be made to circulate to the advantage of trade without altering credit or violating good faith.'[86] All the banks deserved this criticism, except the Bank of England, founded in 1694, which was revolutionary in its own way, as will be seen.

Money of account

The intermingling of currencies made it necessary to invent moneys of account or 'notional' units of currency. Some form of common measure was a logical requirement. Moneys of account are units of measurement, like the hours, minutes and seconds on a clock (the English guinea is one modern example).

When we say that on such and such a day in 1980, the *napoléon d'or* was quoted at 789.90 francs on the Paris Bourse, we are not making a statement difficult to grasp. But in the first place, the average Frenchman would not usually concern himself with such a quotation, nor does he meet with old gold coins every day of his life. In the second place, the franc, the actual money of account, really is in his wallet, in the form of bank notes. But if a Parisian bourgeois, in a certain month in the year 1602, were to note that the gold *écu* was worth 66 *sous* (or 3 *livres* 6 *sous*), the opposite would be the case: such a man would encounter gold and silver coins in his everyday life far more often than Frenchmen do today. On the other hand, he would never come across the *livre*, or the *sou* which was one-twentieth of it, nor the *denier*, one-twelfth of a *sou*: these were imaginary units, used for reckoning, for estimating the relative value of coins, for fixing prices and wages and for keeping commercial accounts which could later be translated into any kind of currency, local or foreign, when the time came to move from the ledger to actual cash payment. A debt of 100 *livres* could be paid in so many gold coins plus so many silver, with the addition of copper if necessary.

No contemporary of Louis XIV or Turgot had ever held a *livre* or a *sou tournois* in the palm of his hand (the last *deniers tournois* were minted in 1649). One would have to go back a very long way to find the coins corresponding to the money of account – but all such moneys of account had at some point in the past been real money. This is true of the *livre tournois*, the *livre parisis*, the pound sterling, the *lire* of the Italian city-states, the Venetian ducat (which became a money of account in 1517), or the Spanish ducat which ceased to be a real money in 1540, despite what has been written on the subject. The 'gros', the money of account of Flanders, was the old silver *gros* minted by Saint Louis in 1266, which had ceased to be real money. If one looks at an eighteenth-century trade note relating to India one sees that the country may be different but the problem is the same: 'All India reckons by the standard rupee which is worth thirty sous.' (As this is a Frenchman speaking, he means thirty *sous tournois*.) He adds: 'This is imaginary money like livres in France, the pound sterling in England or the "gros" livre of Flanders and Holland; such ideal money is used to settle the business one does and one has to state whether one is dealing in the standard rupee or rupees from some other country.'[87]

The explanation will be complete if it is added that real coins did not cease to rise in value, for governments were constantly putting up the price of currency and therefore devaluing money of account. If the reader has followed this reasoning he will find it easier to understand the fluctuating fortunes of the *livre tournois*.

The French example demonstrates how the device of money of account could be avoided. In 1577, Henry III, one of the most discredited French kings, decided to revalue the *livre tournois* under pressure from the Lyons merchants. Nothing was simpler than to link the money of account to gold. This was what the weak government succeeded in doing when it decided that accounts would from now on be kept in *écus* and no longer in *livres*. The *écu* was a real gold coin, one you could hold in your hand, valued at three *livres* or sixty *sous*. It was as if a French government were to decide tomorrow that the French fifty-franc note would in future be equivalent to a *louis d'or* and that all accounts would be kept in *louis d'or*. (Whether it would succeed is another matter.) The 1577 operation succeeded until the dark years which followed the assassination of Henry III (1589). Then things began to go wrong, as foreign exchange rates showed. The real *écu* broke away from the *écu* of account, which remained equivalent to 60 *sous;* the former was quoted at 63, 65, even over 70. The return to accounts in *livres tournois* in 1602 was the recognition of inflation; the money of account was again separated from gold.[88]

And this was so until 1726. Louis XV's government not only put an end to a long series of monetary movements. It tied the *livre tournois* to gold, and except for slight changes, the system no longer stirred. The last change came when the declaration of 30 October 1785 raised the ratio between gold and silver, on the pretext of the flight of gold. Until then it had been established at 1 to 14·5. Then it was fixed a point higher at 1 to 15·5.

Thus France did not completely abandon its preference for silver, since the ratio in both Spain and England was 1 to 16. This is no trifle. As gold was cheaper in France than England, it was a lucrative operation to take it across the Channel (from the French market) so that it could be coined in English mints. Silver left England in the opposite direction for the same reasons: between 1710 and 1717, to the value of 18 million pounds sterling.[89] English mints minted sixty times more gold (by value) than silver coins between 1714 and 1773.[90]

Eighteenth-century Europe could at last allow itself the luxury of these stabilizations. Until then all money of account, whether it had a high or low intrinsic value, had been subject to continual devaluation; some, like the *livre tournois* or the Polish *grosz*, more rapidly than others. These devaluations were probably not fortuitous for there was a sort of dumping of exports in countries like Poland and even France, which were primarily exporters of raw materials.

In any case, devaluation of money of account regularly stimulated the rise of prices. An economist (Luigi Einaudi) calculated that during the price rise in France between 1471 and 1598 the devaluation of the *livre tournois* was responsible for at least 209·6% of the total rise of 627·6%.[91] Devaluation of money of account did not stop until the eighteenth century. Etienne Pasquier, in a book published six years after his death, in 1621, said that he did not much care for the proverb: 'He is discredited like an old coin, to describe a man who has a bad reputation ... because as things go in France old money is better than new, which has been getting continually weaker for a hundred years.'[92]

Stocks of metal and the velocity of monetary circulation

France on the eve of the Revolution possessed a monetary stock of perhaps 2000 million *livres tournois*, or 100 livres per person for some 20 million inhabitants. Taking round figures for Naples – 18 million ducats and 3 million inhabitants in 1751 – one arrives at about 6 ducats per head. There had perhaps been 2000 tons of gold and 20,000 tons of silver in Europe in 1500 before the arrival of metals from America (figures derived, it should be said, from some highly questionable calculations):[93] the equivalent, if estimated in silver, of about 40,000 tons for 60 million inhabitants, or a little over 600 grammes per person – a

Some gold coins. *Left to right:* a Florentine florin, about 1300; a gold florin of Louis d'Anjou, fourteenth century; a gold genovino, thirteenth century.
(Photos A. Colin and Magyar Nemzeti Múzeum.)

derisory figure. Between 1500 and 1650, according to *official* figures, fleets from the Indies landed 180 tons of gold and 16,000 tons of silver at Seville. This was enormous and, yet again, very modest.

But the magnitude was relative. The point was that it stimulated channels of sluggish demand, despite what contemporaries imagined. And above all, the money passed from hand to hand, 'cascading' as a Portuguese economist said (1761).[94] It was multiplied by its velocity (the velocity of circulation suspected by Davanzati [1529-1606] and demonstrated by William Petty and Cantillon who was the first to use the expression).[95] Every rebound meant a new account settled, as money completed exchanges 'like a pin closing a joint', as a present-day economist has noted. It was never the whole price of sales or the whole price of purchases that was settled, only the difference between them.

In Naples, a total of almost 18 million ducats was in circulation in 1751: 1.5 million ducats in copper money, 6 million in silver coins and 10 million in gold coins (including 3 million in the banks). But total purchases and sales in one year can be estimated at *288 million ducats*. The figure can be reduced by 50% if auto-consumption, salaries in kind and sales by exchange are taken into account; if it is remembered, as Galiani explained, 'that the peasants who form three-quarters of our people do not settle a tenth of their consumption in hard cash'. That still leaves us with the following problem: how to settle payments of

144 million with a monetary stock of 18 million? Answer: each coin must change hands eight times.[96] The speed of circulation is therefore the quotient of total payments by the total of circulating currency. Must we assume that money would 'cascade' faster if total payments increased?

Irving Fisher's law helps to set out this problem. If the total of goods exchanged is Q, their average price P, total money M, its speed of circulation V, the equation for budding economists briefly reads: $MV = PQ$. If total payments increase and the monetary stock remains stationary, the velocity of circulation must rise, if everything is adjusted in the economy in question (Naples or any other).

Thus it seems that during the economic advance accompanied by the 'price revolution' in the sixteenth century the velocity of circulation increased at the same tempo as the other elements in Irving Fisher's equation. If, *lato sensu*, production, monetary mass and prices quintupled, the speed of circulation itself probably also quintupled. We are obviously dealing with averages which ignore short-term variations (such as a serious slump in business in 1580-4) and local variations.

On the other hand, circulation could achieve abnormal and exceptional speeds at certain points. A contemporary of Galiani's said that an *écu* could change hands fifty times in twenty-four hours in Paris: 'The whole world does not contain half the money spent in one year in the town of Paris alone, if one counts every statement of expenses made and paid for in currency from the first day of January to the last day in December, in all the orders of state, from the Royal Household to the beggars consuming a sou's worth of bread a day.'[97]

This circulation of money puzzled classical economists. They saw it as the fountain of all wealth, the explanation of absurd paradoxes. 'As communications were cut during the siege of Tournay in 1745 and for some time before,' one of them explained, 'lack of money made it difficult to pay the garrison. Someone thought of borrowing the sum of seven thousand florins from the canteens. It was all there was in them. By the end of the week, the seven thousand florins had returned to the canteens from which the same sum was once more borrowed. This was then repeated for seven weeks until the surrender, so that the same seven thousand florins had the effect of forty-nine thousand.'[98] There are other examples, like the 'siege money' of Mayence, May to July 1793.[99]

Outside the market economy

Let us return to the kingdom of Naples in 1751. Existing stocks of money, by circulating quickly, settled half the transactions. This was a great deal, but the residue was still enormous. The peasant population and all who received wages in kind (in bacon, salt, salt meat, wine or oil) were outside the money economy. The wages of workers in the textile industries, soap works and alcohol distilleries in Naples and elsewhere only made very short-term use of money: the workers were indeed paid in cash, but spent it almost immediately, in the time it took to go from hand to mouth, *della mano alla boca*. The German economist Schrötter as early as 1686 mentioned it as one of the advantages of factories that 'they make more money pass from hand to hand because in this way they provide food for more people'.[100] Transport was also paid in currency, however poorly. All this, in Naples as elsewhere, did not prevent the existence of a barter and subsistence economy of equal importance to the flexible market economy.

The key word is often *baratto*, or *barattare* or *dare a baratto*. *Baratto* was barter, a standard practice central even to the Levant trade: where since before the fifteenth century, the secret of success lay in obtaining spices, pepper or gall

The pawnbroker: whatever the currency, in every country of the world, the pawnbroker was at the heart of everyday life. *Heures de Rohan*, month of March.
(Photo Bibliothèque Nationale, Paris.)

nuts in exchange for fabrics or glass ornaments from Venice, thus avoiding paying cash. Commodities were commonly exchanged for one another in Naples in the eighteenth century, all parties agreeing to abide by prices which the authorities fixed later (prices called *alla voce*). Then each consignment of merchandise was valued in money, and exchanged according to the ratio of these values. What a mine of problems there was for the schoolboys who pored over the textbook *Arithmetica Pratica*, by Father Alessandro della Purificazione, which appeared in Rome in 1714. *Barattare* meant applying the rule of three – *la regola di tre* – but to one of the following: simple barter, wax against pepper, for example; barter half in money and half in kind; and barter with a time limit, 'when a date for settlement is fixed'. The fact that the operation figured in an arithmetic book indicates that merchants also practised barter and this, as we know, 'made it possible to cover up the price of interest', just like the bill of exchange.

All this reveals the inadequacies of monetary life even in the active eighteenth century which we tend to regard as a paradise in comparison with earlier times. But the bonds of money and market did not encompass all human life. The poor evaded them. It was possible to say in about 1713 that 'variations in money hardly interest the greater part of the peasants [in Burgundy], who do not possess currency'.[101] This was true almost always for peasants everywhere.

On the other hand, certain sectors of the economy were well advanced and already at grips with all the complications of credit. But these sectors were not the major ones.

Paper money and instruments of credit

To be found in circulation alongside metallic money (which we have discussed fully) were both fiduciary money (bank notes) and scriptural money (created by the process of book-keeping, by transferring money from one bank account to another: a practice known to the Germans as *Buchgeld*, book money. Economic historians would say there was an inflation of *Buchgeld* as early as the sixteenth century).

A clear frontier separates money (in all its forms) from credit (taking into consideration all instruments of credit). Credit is the exchange of two promises separated in time: I will do something for you, you will pay me later. The lord who advanced seed-corn to a peasant, on condition that he were repaid at harvest, was giving credit. So was the tavern-keeper who did not claim the price of his drinks from his customer immediately but put it down to the drinker's account by means of a chalk-mark on the wall ('chalking it up'); or the baker who delivered bread and marked up the payment to come by notching a double piece of wood (one part being kept by the giver, the other by the taker). Merchants in Segovia and elsewhere who bought standing corn from peasants, or wool from sheepbreeders before the sheep were shorn, were doing the same thing. And this is also the principle behind 'bills of exchange':[102] the seller of a bill on any market whatever – at a fair at Medina del Campo in the sixteenth century, for example – received the money immediately. The taker would be repaid at another market, three months later, according to the rate of exchange at the time. It was up to him to calculate his potential profit and work out the degree of risk.

If most contemporaries found money a 'difficult cabbala to understand'[103], this type of money that was not money at all, and this juggling of money and book-keeping to a point where the two became confused, seemed not only complicated but diabolical. Such things were a constant source of amazement. The Italian merchant who settled in Lyons in about 1555 with a table and an inkstand and made a fortune represented an absolute scandal, even in the eyes of people who understood the handling of money and the process of exchange fairly well. Even in 1752 a man of the intellectual calibre of David Hume (1711–76), philosopher, historian and moreover an economist, was a resolute opponent both of 'this new invention of paper bank-bills and chequer-notes', and of the national debt. He proposed nothing less than the suppression of the £12 million pounds' worth of paper money he presumed to be in circulation in England alongside the £18 millions in cash: this would be an infallible method, according to him, of attracting a new influx of precious metals into the kingdom.[104] What a pity, from the point of view of curiosity (but not from England's point of view), that this anti-Law system was never tried! Sébastien Mercier, on the other hand, regretted that Paris was not 'modelled on the Bank of London'. He describes the old-fashioned sight of cash payments in Paris: 'On the tenth, twentieth and thirtieth of the month, from ten in the morning until midday, one meets porters bent double under the burden of bags of money. They run as if an enemy army was about to surprise the city, which proves that we have not yet succeeded in creating that happy political symbol [the bank note] to replace all this metal, which should be represented by a symbol not requiring to be moved, instead of being transferred from cashbox to cashbox. Woe betide him who has a bill of exchange to pay on a certain date and has no funds!' The sight was the more impressive in that it was entirely concentrated on the Rue Vivienne, 'where there is more money', notes our informant, 'than in all the rest of the town put together; it is the pocket of the capital'.[105]

Old practices

These arrangements that by-passed money in the strict sense were old, sometimes very old inventions. They were techniques that really had only to be rediscovered. But they were on the whole more 'natural' than they seemed, if only on account of their very great age.

In fact as soon as men learnt to write and had coins to handle, they had replaced cash with written documents, notes, promises and orders. Notes and cheques between market traders and bankers were known in Babylon twenty centuries before the Christian era. There is no need to exaggerate the modernity of such systems to admire their ingenuity. The same devices were found in Greece and Hellenistic Egypt, where Alexandria became 'the most popular centre of international transit'. Rome was familiar with current accounts, and debit and credit figure in the books of the *argentarii*. Finally, all the instruments of credit – bills of exchange, promissory notes, letters of credit, bank notes, cheques – were known to the merchants of Islam, whether Muslim or not, as can be seen from the *geniza* documents of the tenth century AD, principally found in the Old Cairo synagogue.[106] And China was using bank notes by the ninth century AD.

These distant antecedents should warn us against the rather naïve amazement sometimes expressed. When the West rediscovered the old instruments, it was not like discovering America. In fact every economy that found itself restricted by metallic currency fairly quickly opened up instruments of credit of its own accord, as though in a logical and natural development. They sprang from its commitments, and no less from its shortcomings.[107]

So in the thirteenth century, the West rediscovered bills of exchange, a long-distance method of payment that spread through the whole length of the Mediterranean with the success of the Crusades. The bill of exchange came to be *endorsed* earlier than is usually thought. The recipient signed it and sold it. At the time of the first known endorsement, in 1410, the circulation of bills of exchange was not of course what it later became. A further advance came when the bill of exchange was no longer restricted to a simple journey from one market to another, as when it was first used. Businessmen caused it to be moved about from market to market, from fair to fair, known by the French as *le change et le rechange*, by the Italians as *ricorsa*. These advances, which meant prolonging credit, became widespread during the difficulties of the seventeenth century. Fictitious bills were in circulation at that time with the connivance of businessmen. It even became common for a man to draw upon his own credit – which left the door open to many abuses. In fact these abuses even preceded the seventeenth century. We know of re-exchanges to the profit of the Fuggers in 1590, on the Lyons market in 1592, and even more so in Genoa, the city of innovations, in the fifteenth century.

Neither can we say that the bank note made its first appearance in 1661 at the counters of the Bank of Stockholm – which in any case quickly suspended it in 1668 – or on the counters of the Bank of England in 1694, though this is more realistic. There are notes and notes. In the first place, governmental 'orders', prototypes of bank notes, had multiplied in England from 1667; and the use of 'goldsmiths' notes', later called bankers' notes, was common earlier, in the middle of the century, for the London goldsmiths received silver on deposit against notes. In 1666, one of these goldsmiths alone had the sum of 1,200,000

One of Law's bank notes. Bibliothèque Nationale, Paris. (Photo Giraudon.)

pounds sterling circulating in notes. Cromwell himself had recourse to their credit. The bank note was born almost spontaneously from commercial usage. It was a matter of urgent necessity. In 1640, when Charles I had seized the ingots deposited in the Tower of London by the city merchants, the merchants found asylum for their property with the goldsmiths, whose fortune they made until the Bank of England was created.

But England did not have a monopoly in these matters. The *Casa di San Giorgio* had its *biglietti* at least from 1586 and they were payable in gold or silver currency after 1606, according to the nature of the deposit which guaranteed them. In Venice the banks *di scritta* (of writing) had from the fifteenth century had their notes which could be exchanged and redeemed.

But the innovation of the Bank of England was that it added to the functions of deposit and clearing banks those of a deliberately organized issuing bank, capable of offering ample credit in notes (whose total amount in fact far exceeded actual deposits). By doing this, said Law, it did the greatest good to trade and the state, because it 'increased the quantity of money'.[108]

We will return later to scriptural money. It appeared with the very beginnings of the banking profession: one account was cleared against another, as the customer desired. There were even what we would call overdrawn accounts, if the banker consented to it. This form of money was, therefore, established from the beginning of the period covered in this book.

Cash and credit

Of course notes and paper did not always reach a wide public. David Hume's comment must not be forgotten. Even after the late foundation of the Bank of France (1801), its notes only interested a few Parisian merchants and bankers, practically no one in the provinces – no doubt because of the painful and persistent memory of the collapse of Law's system.

However, there were many kinds of paper and credit and in one way or another they incessantly rejoined and mingled in the stream of monetary circulation. A bill of exchange circulated *like real money* when it was endorsed, that is when it had been made over by its owner by means of a reference and a signature. (Contrary to the custom with present-day cheques, these endorsements were on the front of the paper on which the bill was drawn up, not on the back.) Even government bonds were sold wherever they were to be found – in Venice, Florence, Genoa, Naples, Amsterdam or London. So too in France with the *rente* certificates of the Hôtel de Ville de Paris, which were created in 1522 and suffered numerous vicissitudes. When the *connétable* of Montmorency bought an estate (the manor of Marigny) on 1 November 1555, he paid for it with Hôtel de Ville *rentes* or bonds.[109] Nine times out of ten, Philip II and his successors met their liabilities to the businessmen in *juros*, government bonds, reckoned at par. When the businessmen had been repaid in this way, they in their turn settled their debts to a third party in the same sort of 'money', making someone else bear the risks and disappointments of their profession. As far as they were concerned, this meant changing short-term debts (loans to the king, *asientos*) into funded perpetual or life debts. But shares in the *asientos* were themselves transferred, inherited and distributed. They were on the market, even if not quite openly.[110] 'Shares' in the Amsterdam Bourse were also on the market in their time and so were the innumerable rents that money from the towns had drawn in from peasant fields, vineyards and houses in all the lands of the West – a vast spectacle which is revealed whenever we find any detailed evidence. Even the *cedole* (the receipts) which Sicilian *caricatori* (grain warehouses) gave landowners who deposited their grain there, were sold. In addition, false *cedole* circulated with the complicity of the warehouse owners and the authorities.[111] One last detail: in Naples the viceroy issued *tratte*, authorizations to export cereals and even vegetables. He issued too many, and it was regular practice for Venetian merchants to buy them at below the nominal rate and thus pay their customs duties at a discount.[112] And we must also imagine a whole mass of other papers, of every size and description, taking part in the financial waltz. Every time there was a breakdown in metallic money anything was pressed into service and paper money flowed in or was invented.

In Paris 'it is worthy of note that there was such a shortage of currency in trade in 1647, 1648 and 1649 that people only gave a quarter in cash when they made a payment and three-quarters in notes or bills of exchange, which were signed uncompleted so as to serve as an endorsement and not as an order to pay. Thus merchants, traders and bankers had developed the custom amongst themselves of paying each other in this way.'[113] The text would call for comment (for example on the way they signed the bills uncompleted), but the interest of the document does not lie there. Cash was short and credit was resorted to: it was improvised. And, on the whole, this was William Petty's advice in his strange *Quantulumcumque Concerning Money* (1682), which may be freely translated as 'The least that can be said about Money'. He proceeded by question and answer. Question 26: 'What remedy is there if we have too little money?' Answer: 'We must erect a Bank', that is create a machine to produce credit, to increase the effect of the money in existence. As Louis XIV, grappling with continual wars, did not succeed in creating a bank, he had to manage with the help of financiers, 'tax farmers and partisans', who advanced him the enormous expenses of his armies abroad by way of bills of exchange. In fact these lenders advanced their own money and the money deposited with them by third parties. It was then up to them to get their money back in royal revenues. As for the king, how could he have acted otherwise when his kingdom was drained of precious metals?

For metal money was always the problem: slow to fulfil its functions or absent altogether (sitting in someone's woollen stocking) it had to be pushed into circulation or somehow replaced. To fill the gaps, or whenever there was a cash currency crisis, improvised solutions were repeatedly called for; and these in turn provoked reflections and hypotheses concerning the very nature of money. What began to happen very soon was the artificial manufacture of money, of ersatz or perhaps one might say 'manipulated and manipulable' money. All those bank promoters and eventually the Scot, John Law, gradually realized 'the business potentialities of the discovery that money – and hence capital in the monetary sense of the term – can be manufactured or created'.[114] This was both a sensational discovery (a lot better than the alchemists!) and a huge temptation. And what a revelation it is for us: it was the slow pace of the heavy metal money, its failure so to speak to keep the engine running, that created the necessary profession of banker, at the very dawn of economic life. He was the man who repaired or tried to repair the mechanical breakdown.

Schumpeter's diagnosis: everything is money and everything is credit

We come to the last and most difficult of our discussions. Is there really any absolute difference in kind between metal specie, substitute money and instruments of credit? It is normal to make initial distinctions between them; but thereafter should they not perhaps be related, even treated as identical? This problem, which opens the door to so much debate, is also the problem of modern capitalism: it was in these domains that capitalism first flexed its muscles, found its instruments and in seeking to define those instruments became 'conscious of its own existence'. It is of course a debate which I can only mention here without going into more fully. It will be treated at more length later.

Until at least 1760, all economists were extremely attentive to the phenomenon of money, as it appeared in its first manifestations. After that, for the whole of the nineteenth century and until the Keynesian revolution, they tended to consider money as a neutral element in economic exchange, or rather as a veil: to tear away the veil and observe what it concealed, was one of the standard objectives of 'real' economic analysis. The point was not to study money, with all its peculiar attributes, but the underlying realities: the exchange of goods and services, the flow of income and expenditure.

Let us start by adopting something like the old-fashioned (nominalist) approach of before 1760, and look at things through the deliberately mercantilist perspective of the preceding centuries. This perspective gave particular prominence to money, which was considered as wealth in its own right, like a river whose force alone could stimulate and complete exchanges, and whose mass could accelerate or slow them down. Money, or rather the monetary stock, combined mass and momentum. If the mass increased or the overall momentum was accelerated, the result was virtually the same: everything went up: prices, more slowly wages, and the total volume of transactions. If the opposite occurred, the whole process went into reverse. Under these conditions, if there is direct exchange of goods (barter); or if substitute money makes it possible for a deal to be concluded without cash changing hands; or if a transaction is facilitated by credit, it must be concluded that the volume in circulation has actually risen. In short, if all the instruments of capitalism are introduced into the monetary process, they are behaving like pseudo-money – or even real money. In other words, what one has is a general reconciliation, as Cantillon was the first to point out.

But if it is possible to say that everything is money, it is just as possible to claim that everything is, on the contrary, credit – promises, deferred reality. Even this *louis d'or* was given me as a promise, as a cheque (real cheques, drawn on specific accounts, only came into current use in England towards the middle of the eighteenth century). It is a cheque on the collection of tangible goods and services within my reach and amongst which, tomorrow or later, I will finally make my choice. It is only then that this coin will have fulfilled its purpose in the framework of my life. As Schumpeter said: 'Money in turn is but a credit instrument, a claim to the only final means of payment, the consumer's good. By now [1954] this theory, which of course is capable of taking many forms and stands in need of many elaborations, can be said to prevail.'[115] All in all, the brief can legitimately be argued either way.

Money and credit: a language

Like ocean navigation or printing, money and credit are techniques, which can be reproduced and perpetuated. They make up a single language, which every society speaks after its fashion, and which every individual is obliged to learn. He may not know how to read or write: only high culture depends on the written word. But not to know how to count would endanger one's survival. Daily life is ruled by sums: the vocabulary of debit and credit, barter, prices, the market and fluctuating currencies envelops and imprisons any society with a claim to development. Such techniques become inherited and are inevitably passed down through example and experience. They determine human life from day to day, lifetime to lifetime, generation to generation, century to century. They provide the environment of human history the world over.

So when a society becomes too populous, weighed down by the demands of cities and the expansion of exchange, the language becomes more complex, in order to solve the problems that arise. In other words, these all-invading techniques operate principally upon themselves, come into being of their own accord and are transformed by their own progress. If the bill of exchange, which had been familiar in the days of the Islamic triumphs of the ninth and tenth centuries, appeared in the West in the twelfth, it was because this was a time when money had to be transported over enormous distances, across the Mediterranean and through the Italian cities to the fairs of Champagne. If promissory notes, endorsement, exchanges, banks and discounting subsequently appeared one after another, this was because the system of fairs, with its fixed dates for long-term payments, had neither the flexibility nor the frequency required by an economy that was gathering speed. But such economic pressure was felt much later in East Europe. In about 1784, when the merchants of Marseilles were trying to set up trade with the Crimea, one of them noted, from the evidence of his own eyes that 'minted silver is not to be found in Kherson and in the Crimea: all one finds there are copper coins and some non-negotiable paper, since the means of discounting are absent'. This was because the Russians had only just occupied the Crimea and obtained the opening of the straits from Turkey. And it would take a good many more years before the wheat of the Ukraine was being regularly exported through the Black Sea. Until then, who would bother to organize discounting facilities at Kherson?

The techniques of money, like any other techniques, are therefore a response to express, insistent and often-repeated demand. The more developed an economy became, the wider the range of monetary instruments and credit facilities it employed. And in the wider international unity that money represented on a world scale, each society had its place, some favoured, some backward, some heavily handicapped. Money gave a certain unity to the world, but it was the unity of injustice.

Of this hierarchy and of the consequences it brought in turn (for money rushed to the service of monetary techniques), there was more awareness than one might think. An essayist, Van Ouder Meulen, remarked in 1778 that to read the authors of his day 'one would think that there are Nations who will become very powerful with the passage of time, and others who will be completely destitute'.[116] A century and a half earlier, in 1620, Scipion de Gramont had written: 'Money, said the seven sages of Greece, is the blood and soul of men and he who has none wanders dead among the living.'[117]

8

Towns and Cities

TOWNS ARE LIKE electric transformers. They increase tension, accelerate the rhythm of exchange and constantly recharge human life. They were born of the oldest and most revolutionary division of labour: between work in the fields on the one hand and the activities described as urban on the other. 'The antagonism between town and country begins with the transition from barbarism to civilization, from tribe to State, from locality to nation, and runs through the whole history of civilization to the present day,' wrote the young Marx.[1]

Towns, cities, are turning-points, watersheds of human history. When they first appeared, bringing with them the written word, they opened the door to what we now call *history*. Their revival in Europe in the eleventh century marked the beginning of the continent's rise to eminence. When they flourished in Italy, they brought the age of the Renaissance. So it has been since the city-states, the *poleis* of ancient Greece, the *medinas* of the Muslim conquest, to our own times. All major bursts of growth are expressed by an urban explosion.

To ask whether the towns were the origin or cause of growth is as meaningless as asking whether capitalism was responsible for the economic progress of the eighteenth century or the industrial revolution. What Georges Gurvitch used to call 'the reciprocity of perspectives' is relevant here. Towns generate expansion and are themselves generated by it. But even when towns do not create growth from scratch, they undoubtedly channel its course to their own advantage. And growth can be perceived in the towns and cities more clearly than anywhere else.

Towns: the problem of definition

Wherever it may be, a town is inseparable from certain realities and processes, certain regular and recurring features. Where there is a town, there will be division of labour, and where there is any marked division of labour, there will be a town. No town is without its market, and there can be no regional or

Aerial photograph of Brive (*département* of the Corrèze, France), an example of a town with a maze of narrow streets inherited from medieval times. (Photo French Ministry of Works.)

national markets without towns. One hears a great deal about the role of the town in the development and diversification of consumption, but very little about the extremely important fact that even the humblest town-dweller must of necessity obtain his food-supply through the market: the town in other words *generalizes* the market into a widespread phenomenon. Now the market provides the essential dividing-line running through the middle of societies and economies – a point to which I shall return later. Wherever there are towns, there will also be a form of power, protective and coercive, whatever the shape taken by that power or the social group identified with it. And while power may exist independently of towns, it acquires through them an extra dimension, a different field of application. Last of all, there can be no door to the rest of the world, no international trade without towns.

It was in this sense that I wrote ten years ago[2] and still maintain today, despite Philip Abrams' elegant criticism[3], that 'a town is always a town', wherever it is located, in time as well as in space. I do not mean that all towns are alike. But over and above their distinctive and original features, they all necessarily speak the same basic language: common to them all are the continuous dialogue with their rural surroundings, a prime necessity of everyday life; the supply of manpower, as indispensable as water to the mill; their self-consciousness – their desire to be distinguished from the others; their inevitable location at the centre of communications networks large and small; their relationship with their suburbs and with other cities. For a town never exists unaccompanied by other towns: some dominant, others subordinate or even enslaved, all are tied to each other forming a hierarchy, in Europe, in China, or anywhere else.

Minimum size, combined weight

The town, an unusual concentration of people, of houses close together, often joined wall to wall, is a demographic anomaly. Not that it is always full of people, a 'restless sea' of men, as Ibn Batuta said admiringly of Cairo, with its 12,000 water-carriers and thousands of camel-drivers plying for hire.[4] There are some towns that have barely begun being towns and some villages that exceed them in numbers of inhabitants. Examples of this are the enormous villages in Russia, past and present, the country towns of the Italian *Mezzogiorno* or the Andalusian south, or the loosely woven clusters of hamlets in Java, which has remained an 'island of villages up to the present time'. But these inflated villages, even when they were contiguous, were not necessarily destined to become towns.

For numbers are not everything. The town only exists as a town in relation to a form of life lower than its own. There are no exceptions to this rule. No privilege serves as a substitute. There is no town, no townlet without its villages, its scrap of rural life attached; no town that does not impose upon its hinterland the amenities of its market, the use of its shops, its weights and measures, its moneylenders, its lawyers, even its distractions. It has to dominate an empire, however tiny, in order to exist.

Varzy, in the present-day *département* of the Nièvre, barely numbered two thousand inhabitants at the beginning of the eighteenth century. But it was well and truly a town, with its own bourgeoisie. There were so many lawyers there that one wonders what they found to do – even when surrounded by an illiterate peasant population who obviously had to resort to the pens of others. But these lawyers were also landowners. Other members of the bourgeoisie were masters of ironworks or tanneries, or wood merchants profiting from the traffic in 'lost logs' along the rivers, sometimes involved in the colossal provisioning of Paris, and owning forests as far as the distant Barrois.[5] Varzy is a typical case of a small Western town. There are thousands of similar examples.

To make things clear, there ought to be some firm and indisputable lower limit to mark the minimum size of a town. Unfortunately it is impossible to reach agreement on this, particularly since the limit would change over time. Official statistics in France define a town as a settlement of at least 2000 inhabitants (the measurement still in use today) – which is exactly the size of Varzy in 1700. British statistics prefer the number 5000. So if we read that in 1801, towns accounted for 25% of the British population[6] we should bear in mind that if towns had been defined as communities of 2000 inhabitants and over, the percentage would have been 40.

Richard Gascon, thinking primarily of the sixteenth century, suggests that 'six hundred households (roughly 2,000 to 2,500 inhabitants) is probably a reasonable lower limit'.[7] However, I am inclined to think this far too high a figure, for the sixteenth century at least (Gascon may have been over-impressed by the comparative vitality of the towns around Lyons). In Germany as a whole in the late middle ages, 3000 places are reckoned to have been granted the status of cities: their average population was no more than 400 individuals.[8] So the minimum level for 'urban' life, in France and no doubt throughout the West, with some exceptions to confirm the rule, was well below the size of Varzy. Thus we find that Arcis-sur-Aube in Champagne for instance, the proud possessor of a salt-depot and an archidiaconate, which was given permission by Francis I in 1546 to erect city walls, still only had 228 households (900 inhabitants) at the beginning of the eighteenth century; Chaource, which had a hospital and a college, numbered 227 households in 1720; Eroy 265; Vendeuvre-sur-Barse 316 and Pont-sur-Seine 188.[9]

So urban history has to be extended to cover these small communities, for little towns, as Spengler observed,[10] eventually 'conquer' the surrounding countryside, penetrating it with 'urban consciousness', meanwhile being themselves devoured and subordinated by agglomerations more populous and more active. Such towns are thus caught up into urban systems orbiting regularly round some sun-city. But it would be a mistake only to count the sun-cities – Venice, Florence, Nuremberg, Lyons, Amsterdam, London, Delhi, Nanking,

Osaka. Towns form hierarchies everywhere, but the tip of the pyramid does not tell us everything, important though it may be. In China, urban hierarchies are defined by the suffix added to the name of a town: *fu* for a town of the first order, *chu* for one of the second, *hien* for the third, not counting the elementary towns, at a lower level still, which were built in the poor provinces because of 'the necessity of containing half-savage peoples who bear the yoke of authority with impatience'.[11] But it is this lowest network of elementary towns, in contact with the surrounding villages that we know least about, in China as elsewhere in the Far East. A German doctor, travelling in 1690 through a small town on the way to Yedo (Tokyo), counted 500 houses there (at least 2000 inhabitants) including the suburbs[12] – mention of the latter being proof enough that this was indeed a town. But such observations are rare.

It would be best of all if we could evaluate the entire mass of urban systems, estimate their overall weight, still taking as our base that minimum limit, the articulation between town and countryside. Overall figures would tell us more than particular statistics: to be able to place on one side of the scales all the towns, and on the other the total population of an empire, a nation or an economic region, then to calculate their relationship, would enable us to give a fairly reliable estimate of the social and economic structures of the unit under observation.

Or at least it would be fairly reliable if such percentages were easy to establish and satisfactory in themselves. Those Josef Kulischer puts forward in his book[13] seem over-optimistic and too high compared to recent calculations. And we can dismiss Cantillon's estimate altogether: 'It is generally supposed,' he writes, 'that half the inhabitants of a State subsist and have their homes in the town, the other half in the countryside.'[14] Recent calculations by Marcel Reinhardt conclude that in France in Cantillon's time, the urban population was only 16% of the total. And, of course, it all depends on the base level adopted. If towns are considered to be settlements of over 400 inhabitants, then 10% of the English population was living in towns in 1500, and 25% in 1700. But if 5000 is taken as the minimum definition, the figure would only be 13% in 1700, 16% in 1750, 25% in 1801. It is therefore evident that all the calculations would have to be repeated using identical criteria, before one could make a valid comparison of the degree of urbanization of the different regions of Europe. At present, all we can do is identify certain particularly low or high levels.

At the bottom of the scale, the lowest urbanization figures relate to Russia (2.5% in 1630; 3% in 1724; 4% in 1796; 13% in 1897).[15] So the figure of 10% for Germany in 1500 is not insignificant compared to the Russian figures. The same percentage is found in colonial America in 1700, when Boston had 7000 inhabitants, Philadelphia 4000, Newport 2600, Charlestown 1100 and New York 3900. And yet, in 1642, in New York (still known as New Amsterdam) 'modern' Dutch brick was already replacing wood in house-building, a clear sign of growing prosperity. The urban character of these centres where the population was still of modest size is clear to see. In 1690, they represented the degree of urban tension permitted by a total population of 200,000 or so, scattered over a vast area: about 9% of the whole. In about 1750, of the already dense population of Japan (26 million) 22% were already living in towns.[16]

At the top of the scale, it seems probable that the 50% mark was exceeded in Holland (140,180 town-dwellers in 1515, out of a total population of 274,810, that is 51%; 59% in 1627, and 65% in 1797). According to the 1795 census, even the province of Overijssel, certainly not in the van of progress, produced a figure of 45·6%.[17]

What one needs to know in order to interpret this scale of urbanization is the point (10% perhaps?) at which it attained a minimum degree of efficiency. And would there not be another significant landmark at about 50% or 40%, perhaps even lower? Are there, as Wagemann suggested, certain thresholds, marking levels at which self-generated transformations would occur?

The ever-changing division of labour

The essential problem, at the beginning and throughout the life of towns in Europe and elsewhere, remains the same: the division of labour between countryside and urban centres, a division that has never been perfectly defined and which has been subject to constant change. In theory, it is in the towns that one finds trade, the functions of political, religious and economic control, and craft activities. But only in theory, for the distinction is always being challenged from one side or another.

It should not be assumed that this version of the class struggle was automatically resolved in favour of the town, as the stronger partner. Nor should it be assumed that the countryside, as we are usually told, necessarily preceded the towns in time. It is of course frequently the case that the advance 'of the rural milieu, by the progress of production, permits the town to appear'.[18] But the town is not always a secondary development. Jane Jacobs, in a persuasive book[19] argues that the town appears at least simultaneously with rural settlement, if not before it. Thus in the sixth millennium BC, Jericho and Chatal Yüyük in Asia Minor were already towns, creating around them countrysides that could be called advanced or modern. They could do so to the extent, presumably, that the surrounding land was an empty uninhabited space, in which fields could be established virtually anywhere. This situation may have recurred in Europe in the eleventh century. Closer to our times, we can see it clearly in the New World, where Europeans built reproductions of their home cities and set them down literally in the middle of nowhere: their inhabitants, alone or with the aid of the local population, set about creating the countryside to supply them. In Buenos Aires, which was refounded in 1580, the local people were either hostile or (equally damaging) absent altogether, so the townspeople were obliged, as they complained, to earn their bread by the sweat of their brows. They were having

The town needs the countryside around: a market scene by Jean Michelin (1623-96): the sellers are peasants bringing their own produce to market. (Photo Giraudon.)

to create the countryside to meet the needs of the town. A very similar process is described by Morris Birkbeck, apropos the colonization of the mid-west by the American pioneers: 'On any spot where a few settlers cluster together ... some enterprising proprietor finds in his section what he deems a good scite [sic] for a town, he has it surveyed and laid out in lots which he sells or offers for sale by auction ... The new town then assumes the name of its founder: - a storekeeper builds a little framed store, and sends for a few cases of goods; and then a tavern starts up, which becomes the residence of a doctor and a lawyer, and the boarding-house of the storekeeper as well as the resort of the weary traveller; soon follow a blacksmith and other handicraftsmen in useful succession: a schoolmaster, who is also the minister of religion, becomes an important accession to this rising community ... Where once the neighbourhood ... was clad in "buckskin", now the men appear at church in good blue cloth and the women in fine calicoes and straw bonnets.' Once the town has got going, 'culture' (i.e. agriculture) spreads rapidly and becomes diversified in the surrounding countryside; and money flows in.[20]

The same could be said of Siberia, that other New World: in 1652, Irkutsk was founded before the country districts that would feed it.

The process had its own momentum: town and countryside obeyed the rule of 'reciprocity of perspectives': mutual creation, mutual domination, mutual exploitation according to the unchanging rules of co-existence.

The countryside surrounding the towns, even in China, gained from this proximity. In 1645, when Berlin was beginning to come to life again, the *Geheime Rat* remarked that 'the essential reason for the very low price of grain today is precisely that all the cities, with a few exceptions, have been devastated and have no need of the grain of the plains, but can provide for the needs of their few inhabitants from within their own territory'. The 'territory' referred to was in fact that of the countryside immediately surrounding the cities, and which they had developed in the last years of the Thirty Years War.[21]

True, the process could be reversed: the towns urbanized the countryside, but the countryside 'ruralized' the towns too. From 'the late sixteenth century,' writes Richard Gascon, 'the countryside was the abyss that swallowed up urban capital',[22] if only for the purchase of land, to build farms or countless country houses. Seventeenth-century Venice turned away from the profits of the sea and threw all her fortune into the countryside. Every city in the world has at one time or another seen similar transfers of wealth, whether London or Lyons, Milan or Leipzig, Algiers or Istanbul.

In fact town and countryside never separate like oil and water. They are at the same time separate yet drawn together, divided yet combined. Even in Islamic countries the town does not ignore or exclude the countryside, despite the apparently sharp divide between the two. It develops market-gardening activities around it. Certain water-channels along urban streets are extended to the gardens of nearby oases. The same symbiosis occurs in China where the countryside is fertilized with refuse and rubbish from the town.

But we need hardly demonstrate what is self-evident. Until very recently, every town had to have its foodstuffs within easy reach. An economic historian familiar with the statistics estimates that in the eleventh century, a town of 3000 inhabitants required, to survive, the land of some ten villages, or approximately 8·5 square kilometres, 'in view of the low yield of agriculture'.[23] In fact the countryside had to support the town if the town was not to live in a constant state of anxiety with regard to its subsistence. It could have recourse to long-distance trade only in exceptional circumstances, and only if it was a privileged city like Florence, Bruges, Venice, Naples, Rome, Peking, Istanbul, Delhi and Mecca.

Moreover, even the large towns continued to engage in rural activities up to the eighteenth century. They therefore housed shepherds, gamekeepers, agricultural workers and vine-growers (even in Paris). Every town generally owned a surrounding area of gardens and orchards inside and outside its walls, and fields farther away, sometimes with rotating crops, as in Frankfurt-am-Main, Worms, Basle and Munich. In the middle ages, the noise of the flail could be heard right up to the *Rathaus* in Ulm, Augsburg or Nuremberg. Pigs were reared in freedom in the streets. And the streets were so dirty and muddy that they had to be crossed on stilts, unless wooden bridges were thrown across from one side to the other. The main streets of Frankfurt were hurriedly covered with straw or wood shavings on the eve of the fairs.[24] As late as 1746, in Venice, it was apparently necessary to forbid the keeping of pigs 'in the city and in the monasteries'.[25]

As for the innumerable small towns, they could barely be distinguished from country life. The expression 'rural towns' has been used of them. All the same, Weinsberg, Heilbronn, Stuttgart and Esslingen in vine-growing lower Swabia took it upon themselves to send the wine they produced to the Danube;[26] and wine was an industry in itself. Jerez de la Frontera, near Seville, stated in answer to an inquiry in 1582 that 'the town has only its harvests of wine, corn, oil and meat', which were enough for its well-being and to keep its trade and its workers alive.[27] Algerian pirates were able to take Gibraltar by surprise in 1540, because they knew the customs of the place and chose the time of the grape harvest. All the inhabitants were outside the walls, sleeping in their vineyards.[28] Towns everywhere guarded their fields and vineyards jealously. Hundreds of municipal magistratures every year – in Rothenburg in Bavaria or in Bar-le-Duc, for example – proclaimed the opening of the grape-harvest when the 'vine leaves have taken on that yellow hue that proclaims ripeness'. Even a city like Florence received thousands of barrels every autumn, and was transformed into an enormous market for new wine.

The inhabitants of the towns often spent only part of their lives there: at harvest-time, artisans and others left their houses and trades behind them and went to work in the fields. This was true of busy, overpopulated Flanders in the sixteenth century. It was also true of England, even on the eve of its industrial revolution; and of Florence where the very important *Arte della Lana* operated chiefly in winter in the sixteenth century.[29] A diary kept by Jean Pussot, master-carpenter of Rheims, shows greater interest in vintages, harvests, the quality of the wine, and corn and bread prices, than in the events of political or guild life. At the time of the French Wars of Religion, the people of Rheims and the people of Epernay were not on the same side and both harvested their vines under military escort. But our carpenter notes, 'the thieves of Epernay took the herd of pigs away from the town [of Rheims] ... they took them to the aforesaid Epernay on Tuesday the thirtieth day of March 1593'.[30] It was not only a question of knowing who would win, the Leaguers or Henry IV, but of who would salt and eat the meat. Things had barely changed in 1722, when a treatise on economy deplores the fact that artisans instead of peasants were concerning themselves with agriculture in the small towns and princedoms of Germany. It would be better if everyone 'kept in his own station'. Towns would be cleaner and healthier if they were cleared of livestock and their 'piles of dung'. The solution would be 'to ban all farming in the towns, and to put it in the hands of those suited to it'.[31] Craftsmen would be able to sell goods to peasants; peasants would be sure of selling the regular equivalent to townspeople, and everyone would be better off.

If the town did not completely surrender the monopoly of crops or stock-raising to the countryside, conversely the countryside did not give up all its 'industrial' activities in favour of nearby towns. It had its share of them, although they were generally those activities the towns were glad enough to leave to them. In the first place, the villages had never been without craftsmen. Cartwheels were manufactured and repaired locally in the village itself by the wheelwright, and ringed with iron by the blacksmith (the technique spread at the end of the sixteenth century). Every large village had its shoeing smith. Such activities could still be seen in France until the beginning of the twentieth century. Moreover, in

Bilbao being supplied by boats and by mule-train. The goods were unloaded and put in store. Detail of the *Vista de la muy noble villa de Bilbao*, late eighteenth century, engraving by Francisco Antonio Richter. (Personal collection.)

Flanders and elsewhere, where the towns had established a sort of industrial monopoly in the eleventh and twelfth centuries, there was a massive exodus of urban industries to the outskirts of the towns in the fifteenth and sixteenth centuries, in search of cheaper manpower, outside the protection and hawk-eyed supervision of the urban craft guilds. The town lost nothing thereby, controlling as it did the wretched rural workers outside its walls and managing them as it wanted. In the seventeenth century and even more in the next, villages took upon their weak shoulders a very large burden of craft-working.

The same division was to be found elsewhere, but organized differently – in Russia, India and China, for example. In Russia, the greater part of industrial tasks fell upon the villages, which were self-supporting. Urban agglomerations did not dominate or disturb them as towns did in the West. There was as yet no real competition between townsmen and peasants. This is clearly explained by the slow rate of urban growth. There were a few large cities, despite the ills they were heir to (Moscow was burned down by the Tartars in 1571 and again by the Poles in 1611, but seems to have contained no fewer than 40,000 houses in 1636).[32] But in a poorly urbanized country, villages had no choice but to do everything for themselves. In addition, the owners of large estates, together with their serfs, set up a number of viable industries. The long Russian winter is not the only explanation for the industriousness of the countryside.[33]

The village in India was similarly self-sufficient. A thriving community, capable on occasion of moving en bloc to escape some danger or too heavy oppression, it paid taxes to the town but only called on it for rare commodities (iron tools, for example). In China, the country craftsman supplemented his hard life by work in silk or cotton. His low standard of living made him a formidable competitor for the town craftsman. An English traveller (1793) registered surprise and delight at the unwonted sight of peasant women near Peking breeding silk worms and spinning cotton: 'which is in general use for both sexes of the people, but the women are almost the sole weavers throughout the Empire'.[34]

The town and its newcomers: mainly the poor

A town would probably cease to exist without its supply of new people. It has to attract them. But they often come of their own accord towards its lights, its real or apparent freedom, and its higher wages. They come too because they have already been rejected first by the countryside, then by other towns. The standard stable partnership is between a poor region with regular emigration and an active town: such was the relationship between Friuli and Venice – the *Furlani* supplied it with its labourers and servants; Kabylia and Algiers under the corsairs – the mountain-dwellers came down to dig the gardens in the town and surrounding countryside; Marseilles and Corsica; the towns of Provence and the *gavots* of the Alps; London and the Irish. But every big town would have many different places of recruitment.

In Paris in 1788:

> The people known as common labourers are almost all foreigners [*sic*]. The Savoyards are decorators, floor polishers and sawyers: the Auvergnats ... almost all water-carriers; the natives of Limousin are masons; the Lyonnais are generally porters and chair-carriers; the Normans, stone cutters, pavers and pedlars, menders of crockery, rabbit-skin merchants; the Gascons, wigmakers or *carabins* [barbers' assistants]; the Lorrainers, travelling shoemakers or cobblers.... The Savoyards live in the suburbs; they are organised by *chambrées* [dormitories], each run by a head, sometimes an old Savoyard who is treasurer and tutor to the young children until they reach an age to govern themselves.

The Auvergnat who hawked rabbit skins, buying them individually and reselling them in quantity, travelled around 'so overloaded that one looks [in vain] for his head and arms'. And of course, all these poor people bought their clothes at the second-hand shops on the quai de la Ferraille or the Mégisserie where everything was bartered. 'A man [goes into] the shop as black as a crow and comes out green as a parrot.'[35]

But the cities did not only take in poor wretches such as these. They also drew high-quality recruits from the bourgeoisies of neighbouring or distant towns: rich merchants, masters and craftsmen (whose services were sometimes fought over), mercenaries, ships' pilots, professors and doctors, engineers, architects, painters. Thus the points from which apprentices and masters of its *Arte della Lana* came to Florence in the sixteenth century could be marked on the map of northern and central Italy. In the preceding century, they had come in a steady stream from the Netherlands.[36] The origins of new citizens in a lively town like Metz,[37] for instance, or even Amsterdam (from 1575 to 1614)[38] could equally well be marked on a map. In each case it would disclose a wide area associated with the life of the town concerned. Such an area might very well coincide with that marked out by the radius of its commercial relations, consisting of the villages, towns and markets that accepted its system of measures or money, or both, or which, failing that, spoke its dialect.

Such constant recruitment was a matter of necessity. Before the nineteenth century, cities had scarcely any excess of births over deaths. They were areas of high mortality.[39] If they were to expand, they could not do so unaided. Socially as well, they left the lowly tasks to new arrivals. Like our over-charged economies today, the big city needed North Africans or Puerto Ricans in its service, a proletariat which it quickly used up and had quickly to renew. 'The scum of the countryside becomes the scum of the cities', wrote Sébastien Mercier of the domestic servants in Paris – an army 150,000 strong apparently.[40] The existence of this wretched and lowly proletariat is a feature of any large town.

An average of 20,000 people died in Paris every year, even after the 1780s.

Some 4000 ended their days in the poor-house, either at the Hôtel-Dieu or the Bicêtre. The dead were 'sewn up in sacking' and buried unceremoniously in the paupers' grave at Clamart, which was sprinkled with quick lime. A hand-drawn cart carried the dead southwards from the Hôtel-Dieu every night. 'A mud-bespattered priest, a bell, a cross' – such was the only funeral procession of the poor. Everything about the poor-house 'is hard and cruel'; 1200 beds for 5000 to 6000 sick people. 'The newcomer is bedded down beside a dying man and a corpse.'[41]

And life was no kinder in its beginnings. Paris had 7000 to 8000 abandoned children out of some 30,000 births around 1780. Depositing these children at the poor-house was an occupation in itself. The man carried them on his back 'in a padded box which can hold three. They are propped upright in their swaddling clothes, breathing through the top ... When [the carrier] opens his box, he often finds one of them dead; he completes his journey with the other two, impatient to be rid of the load.... He immediately sets off once more to start the same task, which is his livelihood, over again.'[42] Many of these abandoned children came from the provinces. Strange immigrants indeed.

The self-consciousness of towns

Every town is and wants to be a world apart. It is a striking fact that all or nearly all of them between the fifteenth and eighteenth centuries had ramparts. They were held in a restrictive and distinctive geometry, cut off even from their own immediate surroundings.

The primary reason was security. Protection was only superfluous in a few countries; in the British Isles, for example, there were practically no urban fortifications. Towns there were thus spared a lot of useless investment, according to economists. The old city walls in London had only an administrative function, although temporary fear on the part of the Parliamentarians in 1643 caused fortifications to be hurriedly built around the town. Nor were there any fortifications in the Japanese archipelago, which was also protected by the sea, nor in Venice, an island in itself. There were no walls in self-confident countries like the vast Osmanli Empire which had ramparted towns only on its threatened frontiers – in Hungary facing Europe, in Armenia facing Persia. Both Erivan (where there was a small force of artillery) and Erzerum (crowded by its suburbs) were surrounded by double walls (though not earthworks) in 1694. Everywhere else the *pax turcica* led the ancient ramparts to fall into disrepair. They deteriorated like the walls of abandoned estates, even the splendid ramparts at Istanbul inherited from Byzantium. Opposite, in Galata, in 1694, 'the walls [are] half-ruined and the Turks do not seem to be thinking of rebuilding them'.[43] By 1574 at Philippopoli, on the road to Adrianople, there was 'no longer even the appearance of a gate'.[44]

No such confidence was to be found anywhere else. Urban fortification became the general rule across continental Europe (Russian towns were ramparted to a greater or lesser degree and depended on a fortress as Moscow depended on the Kremlin), across colonial America, Persia, India and China. Furetière's *Dictionnaire* (1690) defined a town as the 'home of a large number of people which is normally enclosed by walls'. For many Western towns, this 'ring of stone' built in the thirteenth and fourteenth centuries, was the 'outward sign of a conscious effort for independence and freedom', which marked urban expansion in the middle ages. But it was also, in Europe and elsewhere, often the work of a prince, a protection against an external enemy.[45]

In China, only second-rate or declining towns no longer had or never had had walls. Ramparts were usually impressive, and so high that they concealed 'the tops of the houses' from view. Towns there

> were all built in the same way and in a square [said a traveller (1639)] with fine brick walls which they cover with the same clay from which they make porcelain; this hardens so much in the course of time that it is impossible to break it with a hammer.... The walls are very wide and flanked with towers built in the ancient style, almost in the same fashion as one sees Roman fortifications depicted. Two large wide roads generally cut the town crosswise and they are so straight that, although they run the whole length of a town, however large it may be, the four gates are always visible from the crossroads.

The wall of Peking, said the same traveller, is, unlike the walls of European towns, 'so wide that twelve horses could gallop abreast on it at full speed without colliding [not that we should take his word for it: another traveller describes them as being '20 feet wide at the base and about twelve feet wide at the top'.[46]] It is guarded at night as if it were war-time, but by day the gates are not guarded except by Eunuchs who stay there rather to collect entrance fees than for the safety of the town.'[47] On 17 August 1668 a torrential flood submerged the countryside around the capital and 'a quantity of villages and country houses [were carried away] by the momentum of the water'. The new town thereby lost a third of its houses, 'and countless wretched people were drowned and buried under the ruins' but the old town escaped. 'Its gates were promptly closed ... and all holes and all cracks were stuffed with lime and bitumen mixed together.' Here is proof of the almost impervious stability of the walls of Chinese towns.[48]

It is interesting to note that during these centuries of *pax sinica*, when danger no longer threatened the towns from outside, the walls virtually became a system for supervising the townspeople themselves. Soldiers and horsemen could be mobilized in an instant up the wide ramps giving access from within to the top of the ramparts where they could overlook the whole town. There is no doubt that the city was firmly controlled by the authorities. Moreover, every street in both China and Japan had its own gates and internal jurisdiction. Any incident whatever, any misdeed, and the gates of the street were closed and the guilty or

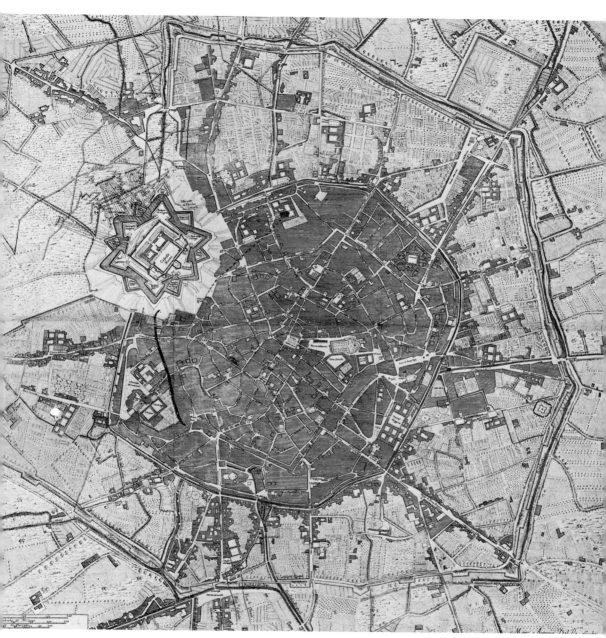

Plan of Milan after the building of the new Spanish fortifications in the sixteenth century. They added to the old town (the dark-shaded sections) new territory relatively undeveloped, still largely gardens and fields. The *Castello* commanding the city was a town in itself. (Milan, Archivio di Stato.)

Walls and gate of Peking, early eighteenth century. Cabinet des Estampes, Bibliothèque Nationale, Paris.

arrested person immediately, often bloodily, punished. What made the system even stricter was that everywhere in China the square outline of the Tartar town stood alongside the Chinese town and watched closely over it.

The wall frequently enclosed a portion of fields and gardens together with the town. The reason was of course the need for supplies in time of war. There is a place in Castile where ramparts were rapidly constructed in the eleventh and twelfth centuries around a group of villages at some distance from each other, with enough space left in between to hold the flocks in case of emergency.[49] The rule holds wherever, in anticipation of a siege, ramparts enclosed meadows and gardens, as in Florence; or arable land, orchards and vineyards, as in Poitiers. In fact Poitiers' walls, even in the seventeenth century, were almost as extensive as those of Paris, but the town took a long time to grow into this outsize garment. Similarly, Prague took a long time to fill up the space left between the houses of the 'small town' and the new ramparts built in the middle of the fourteenth century. The same applied to Toulouse from 1400; and to Barcelona, which took two centuries (until about 1550) to reach the ramparts reconstructed around it in 1359 (the present-day Ramblas now occupy part of the site). And this was equally true of Milan with its Spanish-built fortifications.

The scene was the same in China: one town on the Yang-tse-Kiang 'has a wall ten miles in circumference, which encloses hills, mountains and plains uninhabited because the town has few houses and its inhabitants prefer to live in the very extensive suburbs'. In the same year, 1696, the upper part of the capital of Kiang-Si sheltered 'many fields and gardens, but few inhabitants'.[50]

The West had long ensured security at a low cost by a moat and a perpendicular wall. This did little to interfere with urban expansion – much less than is usually thought. When the town needed more space the walls were moved like theatre sets – in Ghent, Florence, and Strasbourg, for example – and as many times as was required. Walls were made-to-measure corsets. Towns grew and made themselves new ones.

But constructed, or reconstructed, walls continued to encircle towns and to define them. They were boundaries, frontiers, as well as protection. The towns drove the bulk of their artisanal trades, particularly their heavy industries, to the periphery, so much so that the wall was an economic and social dividing line as well. As the town grew it generally annexed some of its suburbs and transformed them, pushing activities foreign to city life a little farther away.

That is why Western towns, which grew up in such a haphazard way, little by little, have such complicated street-plans. Their winding streets and unexpected turnings are quite unlike the pattern of the Roman town, which still survives in a few cities descended from the classical period: Turin, Cologne, Coblenz, Ratisbon. But the Renaissance marked the first development of deliberate town planning, with the flowering of a series of supposedly 'ideal' geometric plans in chessboard pattern or concentric circles. This was the spirit in which the widespread urban development in the West remodelled squares and rebuilt districts acquired from the suburbs. They set down their grid-plans alongside the tortuous streets of the medieval town-centres.

This new coherence and rationalization were even better expressed in the new towns where builders had a free hand. It is curious how the few examples of grid-plan or chequerboard Western towns before the fifteenth century correspond to deliberate constructions, built *ex nihilo*. Aigues-Mortes, a small port that Saint Louis bought and reconstructed in order to have an outlet on the Mediterranean, is one example. Another is the tiny town of Mompazier (in the

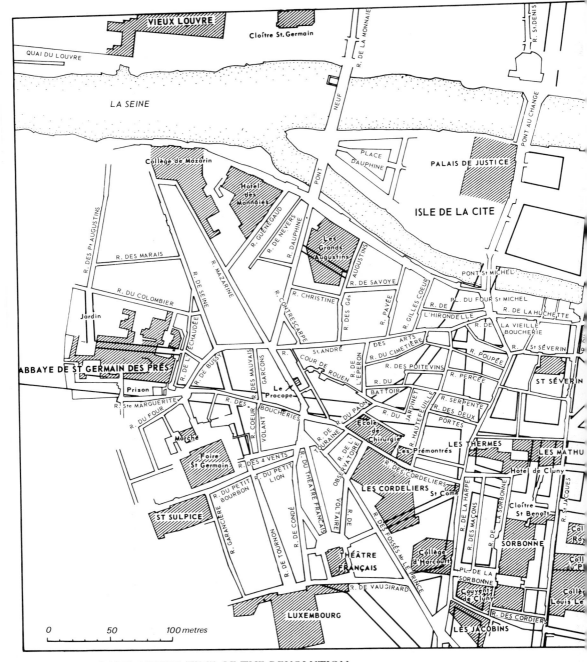

27 PARIS AT THE TIME OF THE REVOLUTION

An example of a Western town with a tangle of narrow streets. Some of the present-day axes of the city, in heavier lines (the Saint-Michel and Saint-Germain boulevards, for instance), have been drawn in to help the reader to find his way in the old Paris from the Sorbonne to the Saint-Germain market and the Abbey of Saint-Germain-des-prés, and from the Luxembourg to the Pont-Neuf. The café Procope, established in 1684, is on the rue des Fossés-Saint-Germain, opposite the place where in 1689 the Comedie-Française was opened in the same street (now called the rue de l'Ancienne-Comédie).

Dordogne), built by order of the King of England at the end of the thirteenth century. One of the squares of the chequerboard corresponds to the church, another to the market place, surrounded by arcades and with a well in the centre.[51] Other examples are to be found in the *terre nuove* of Tuscany in the fourteenth century, Scarperia, San Giovanni Valdarno, Terranuova Bracciolini and Castelfranco di Sopra.[52] But the town planning honours list gets rapidly longer from the sixteenth century. One could give a long list of the towns built on a geometric plan, like the new city of Leghorn after 1575, Nancy, which was reconstructed from 1588, or Charleville after 1608. The most extraordinary case was still St Petersburg, of which more below. Because of their late foundation, almost all the towns of the New World were similarly constructed on a pre-arranged plan. They form the largest family of grid-plan towns. Those in Spanish America were particularly characteristic, with their streets cutting the *cuadras* at right angles and the two main roads converging on the *Plaza Mayor* where stood the cathedral, the prison, and the town hall – the *Cabildo*.

The grid or chequerboard plan raises a curious problem, taking the world as a whole. All the towns in China, Korea, Japan, peninsular India and colonial America (not to mention Roman and certain Greek cities) were planned according to the chequerboard pattern. Only two civilizations produced large towns with an irregular maze of streets: Islam (including northern India) and medieval Europe. One could lose oneself in aesthetic or psychological speculations as to why such choices were made by civilizations. The West was certainly not thinking of the Roman *castrum* when it laid out its cities in sixteenth-century America. What it took to the New World was a reflection of modern Europe's interest in town planning, an urgent taste for order. It would be worth while going beyond the numerous examples of this taste to investigate its living roots.

Towns, artillery and carriages in the West

Western towns faced severe problems from the fifteenth century onwards. Their populations had increased and artillery made their ancient walls useless. They had to be replaced whatever the cost, by wide ramparts half sunk in the ground, extended by bastions, terrepleins, 'cavaliers', where loose soil reduced possible damage from bullets. These ramparts were wider horizontally and could no longer be moved without enormous expense. And an empty space in front of these fortified lines was essential to defence operations; buildings, gardens and trees were therefore forbidden there. Occasionally the empty space in the requisite spot had to be re-created by pulling down trees and houses. This was done in Gdansk (Danzig) in 1520, during the Polish-Teutonic war and in 1576 during its conflict with King Stefan Batory.

The town's expansion was thus blocked and more often than in the past it was condemned to grow vertically. Houses were very soon being built in Genoa, Paris and Edinburgh with five, six, eight and even ten storeys. Prices of plots rose incessantly and tall houses became the general rule everywhere. If London long preferred wood to brick one reason was that it made possible lighter, less thick walls at the time when four- to six-storey houses were replacing the old buildings, which generally had two. In Paris, 'it was necessary to restrain the excessive height of houses ... because a few individuals had actually built one house on top of another. Height was restricted [just before the Revolution] to seventy feet not including the roof.'[53]

Having the advantage of being without walls, Venice could expand in comfort. A few wooden piles sunk in, a few boatloads of stone, and a new district rose up on the lagoon. Heavy industry was very soon pushed back to the periphery, knackers and curriers to the island of Giudecca, the arsenal to the far end of the new district of Castello, glassworks to the island of Murano as early as 1255. It was a kind of modern 'zoning'. Meanwhile Venice spread out its public and private splendour on the Grand Canal, an old and abnormally deep river valley. Only one bridge, the Rialto, made of wood and with a drawbridge (until the construction of the present stone bridge in 1587), linked the bank on which stood the *Fondaco dei Tedeschi* (now the central post office) to the Rialto square. This marked out the vital axis of the town – from St Mark's Square to the bridge via the busy street of the Merceria. It was thus a town with plenty of room to spread itself. But in the ghetto – a narrow, walled and artificial town – space was cramped and houses shot upwards five or six storeys high.

When wheeled carriages appeared in large numbers in Europe in the sixteenth century, they posed urgent problems, and made severe town surgery necessary. Bramante, who pulled down the old quarter round St Peter's in Rome (1506–14), was one of Baron Haussmann's first predecessors in history. Towns inevitably regained a little order, more fresh air and easier circulation, at least for a time. Pietro di Toledo (1536) chose the same type of reorganization when he opened out a number of wide streets through Naples where, as King Ferdinand used to say, 'the narrow streets were a danger to the State'. The completion of the short but grand rectilinear Strada Nuova in Genoa in 1547 was of similar inspiration, as were the three new thoroughfares ordered by Pope Sixtus V, which radiated out across Rome from the Piazza del Popolo. It was no accident that one of them, the Corso, became the commercial street *par excellence* of Rome. Carriages and soon coaches, entered the towns at top speed. John Stow, who observed the first changes in London prophesied: 'The world will run on wheels.' Thomas Dekker said the same thing in the following century: 'In every street in London carts and coaches make such a thundering as if the world ran upon wheels.'[54]

Geography and urban communications

Every town grows up in a given place, becomes wedded to it and, with very few exceptions, never leaves it. The original site may or may not be a wise choice:

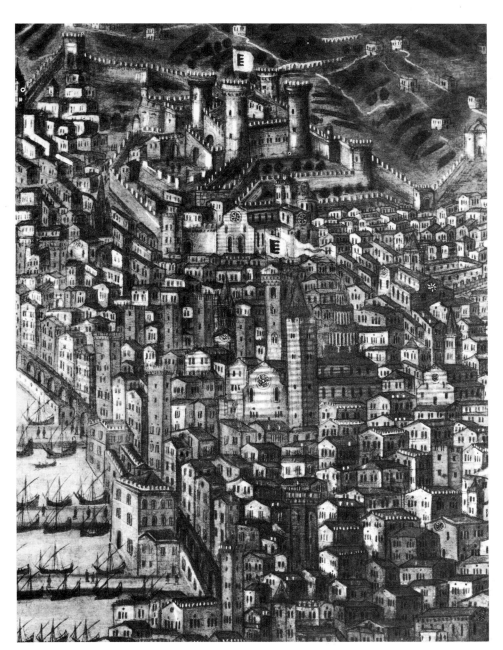

Squeezed in between the mountains and the sea, Genoa was forced to build upwards: the tightly packed houses cascade down from the fortifications to the harbour. Detail from a fifteenth-century painting. Museo Navale di Pegli. (Photo by the museum.)

its initial advantages and disadvantages stay with it for ever. A traveller who landed at Bahia (São Salvador), the then capital of Brazil, in 1684 mentions its splendours, and the number of slaves, who are 'treated', he goes on, 'with the utmost barbarity'. He also remarks on the defects of its site: 'The roads slope so steeply that if horses were harnessed to carriages they would not be able to stand upright', so there was no wheeled traffic, only beasts of burden and saddle horses. A more serious disadvantage was the sharp drop that cut off the city proper from the lower commercial district by the sea, so that it was necessary to 'use a sort of crane to bring merchandise up and down from the port to the town'.[55] Nowadays lifts have speeded up the process, but it still has to be done.

Similarly Constantinople, on the Golden Horn, the Sea of Marmara and the Bosporus, was divided by large expanses of sea water and consequently had to maintain a population of boatmen and ferrymen in perpetual employment at the crossings – which were not always without danger.

But these drawbacks were compensated by important advantages – if not, they would have been neither accepted nor tolerated. The advantages were generally those inherent in the location of the town in relation to neighbouring regions. The Golden Horn was the only sheltered port in an immense stretch of squally sea. The vast All Saints' bay facing Bahia (Salvador) was a miniature Mediterranean, well sheltered behind its islands and one of the easiest points on the Brazilian coast for a sailing ship from Europe to reach. The capital was only moved south to Rio de Janeiro in 1763 because of the development of the Minas Gerais and Goyaz gold mines.

Of course all these advantages could eventually be nullified. Malacca had century after century of monopoly; 'it controlled all the ships which passed its straits'. Then Singapore appeared from nowhere one fine day in 1819. A better example still is the replacement of Seville (which had monopolized trade with the 'Indies of Castile' since the beginning of the sixteenth century) by Cadiz in 1685. This occurred because ships with too great a draught could no longer pass the bar of San Lucar de Barremeda, at the mouth of the Guadalquivir. A technical reason was thus the pretext for a change which, though sensible in some respects, created golden opportunities for sharp-eyed international smuggling in the huge Bay of Cadiz.

In any case, whether temporary or permanent, these advantages of location were indispensable to the prosperity of the towns. Cologne was situated at the meeting point of two separate shipping routes on the Rhine – one towards the sea, the other upstream – which met at its quaysides. Ratisbon on the Danube was a reloading point for ships with too great a draught coming from Ulm, Augsburg, Austria, Hungary and even Wallachia.

Perhaps no site anywhere in the world was more privileged for short- and long-distance trade than Canton. The town was 'thirty leagues from the sea' but still felt the throb of the tide on its numerous stretches of water. Sea vessels, junks, or three-masters from Europe could therefore link up there with the small craft, the sampans, which reached all (or nearly all) of the Chinese interior using the canals. 'I have quite often contemplated the beautiful views of the Rhine and the Meuse in Europe,' wrote J-F. Michel of Brabant[56] (1753), 'but these two together are not a quarter [of what] the river of Canton alone offers for admiration.' However, Canton owed its fortune in the eighteenth century to the Manchu empire's desire to keep European trade as far to the south as possible. Left to themselves, European merchants would have preferred to get to Ning Po and the Yangtse-Kiang. They sensed the future importance of Shanghai and the advantages of reaching the middle of China.

Geography, combined with the speed, or rather the slowness, of transport at the time, also accounts for the extraordinary number of small towns. The 3000 towns of all sizes in fifteenth-century Germany acted as so many relay-points, four or five hours' journey apart in the south and west of the country, seven or eight hours apart in the north and east. Such way-stations might be located wherever means of transport changed: at ports, between *venuta terrae* and *venuta maris* as the Genoese would say, but also at points where farm-carts met river-boats or where the 'pack-saddle used on mountain paths met the wagon from the plain'. Every town was a centre of movement, giving it new impetus, constantly dispatching goods and people in all directions, and quickly replacing them with others.

It was this movement in and out of its walls that indicated the true town. 'We had a great deal of trouble that day,' complained Careri, arriving at Peking in 1697, 'because of the multitude of carts, camels, and mares which go to Peking and return from it, and which is so large that one has difficulty in moving.'[57]

The town market everywhere offered tangible evidence of this movement. A traveller remarked in 1693 that Smyrna was 'nothing but a great bazaar and fair'.[58] But every town, wherever it may be, must primarily be a market. Without a market, a town is inconceivable. A market, on the contrary, can be situated outside a village, even on a site on the open road or at a crossroads, without giving rise to a town. But a town needs to be rooted in and nourished by the people and land surrounding it.

Daily life within a small radius was provided for by weekly or daily markets in the town; I use the plural, remembering the various markets in Venice, for example, listed in Marin Sanudo's *Cronachetta*. There was the great market in the Rialto square, and near it the specially constructed *loggia* where the merchants assembled every morning. The stalls groaned under the weight of fruit, meat and game. Fish was sold a little farther on. There was another market in St Mark's Square. But every district had its own, in its main square. Supplies came from peasants from surrounding areas, gardeners from Padua, and boatmen, who even brought sheep cheese from Lombardy.

A whole book could be written on the Halles in Paris and the smaller market for game, on the Quai de la Vallée; on the regular dawn invasion of the town by bakers from Gonesse; on the five to six thousand peasants who came in the

A market in Barcelona. Anonymous painting, eighteenth century. (Photo Mas.)

middle of every night half-asleep on their carts 'bringing vegetables, fruit, flowers'; and the hawkers shouting: 'Live mackerel! Fresh herrings! Baked apples! – Oysters! Portugal, Portugal!' (i.e. oranges). The ears of the servants on the upper floors were well accustomed to interpreting the babble, so as not to go down at the wrong moment. During the Ham Fair, which took place on the Tuesday of Holy Week, 'a crowd of peasants from the areas around Paris gather in the square and in the Rue Neuve-Notre-Dame early in the morning, equipped with an immense quantity of hams, sausages and black puddings, which they decorate and crown with laurels. What a desecration of the crown of Caesar and Voltaire!' This, of course, is Sébastien Mercier speaking.[59] But a whole book could equally well be written on London and the many markets which were gradually organized there. A list of these markets fills over four pages of the guide drawn up by Daniel Defoe and his successors (*A Tour through the Island of Great Britain*), which was reissued for the eighth time in 1775.

The space nearest the town (in Leipzig it was the source of delicious apples and much-prized asparagus) was only the first of the numerous circles surrounding it.[60] Every town was a meeting-place for people and goods of all descriptions: each product linked it to a given area of the surrounding neighbourhood and sometimes to places far away. Each instance demonstrates how urban life was connected with such areas which only partly overlapped. Powerful towns were soon, certainly from the fifteenth century, drawing on regions amazingly far away. They were the instruments of long-distance relationships reaching out to the limits of a *Weltwirtschaft*, a world-economy, which they brought to life and from which they profited.

All these extensions belong to one family of interrelated issues. Depending on the period, the town affected spaces that varied according to its size. It was by turns inflated and emptied according to the rhythm of its existence. Vietnamese towns were 'little populated on ordinary days' in the seventeenth century. But twice a month on days when the great markets were held they were the scene of very great animation. At Hanoi, then Ke-cho, 'the merchants are grouped in different streets according to their specialities; silk, leather, hats, hemp, iron'. It was impossible to move for the crowd. Some of these market streets were shared by people from several villages who 'had sole privilege to set up shop there'. Such towns were 'markets rather than towns'.[61] One could equally call them fairs rather than towns, but town or market or fair, the result was the same – movements towards concentration, then dispersion, without which no economic life of any energy could have been created, either in Vietnam or in the West.

Every town in the world, beginning with the West, has its suburbs. Just as a strong tree is never without shoots at its foot, so towns are never without suburbs. They are the manifestations of its strength, even if they are wretched fringes, shanty towns. Shoddy suburbs are better than none at all.

Suburbs housed the poor, artisans, watermen, noisy malodorous trades, cheap inns, posting-houses, stables for post horses, porters' lodgings. Bremen had a face-lift in the seventeenth century: its houses were constructed in brick, roofed with tiles, its streets paved, a few wide avenues built. But in the suburbs around it the houses still had straw roofs.[62] To reach the suburbs was always to take a step downwards, in Bremen, London and elsewhere.

Triana, a suburb or rather an extension of Seville often mentioned by Cervantes, became the rendezvous for low-lifers, rogues, prostitutes and dishonest agents of the law. The suburb began on the right bank of the Guadalquivir, level with the bridge of boats which barred the way to the upper reaches of the river rather as London Bridge – on a different scale – barred the Thames. Sea shipping arriving on the tide at Seville from San Lucar de Barremeda, Puerto Santa Maria or Cadiz was unable to go beyond this point. Triana would certainly not have had its violent character nor its pleasure gardens beneath their vine arbours if it had not had Seville by its side – Seville with its foreigners, 'Flemish' or otherwise, and its *nouveaux riches*, the *peruleros* who returned there from the New World to enjoy the fortunes they had made. A census in 1561 counted 1664 houses and 2666 families in Triana with four people per family – which meant really overcrowded accommodation and over 10,000 inhabitants, the substance of a town.[63] As dishonest work did not suffice, to support itself, Triana had its artisans who produced varnished faience tiles – the blue, green and white *azulejos*, with their Islamic geometric patterns (*azulejos* were exported all over Spain and to the New World). It also had craft industries producing soap – soft soap, hard soap and lye. But it was still only a suburb. Careri, who passed through it in 1697, noted that the town of Triana 'has nothing notable except a Carthusian monastery, the Palace and the prisons of the Inquisition'.[64]

Urban hierarchies

Small towns inevitably grew up at a certain distance from large centres. The speed of transport, which moulded space, laid out a succession of regular stopping points. Stendhal was surprised at the relative tolerance large Italian cities showed towards the small and middling towns. But if they did not destroy these humbler rivals, whom they certainly persecuted (one thinks of Florence seizing half-dead Pisa in 1406, or Genoa filling in the port of Savona in 1525) it was for the excellent reason that they could not: they needed them. A great city necessarily meant a ring of secondary towns round about: one to weave and dye fabrics perhaps, one to organize haulage, a third to act as a sea port, as Leghorn was to Florence, for instance (Florence preferred Leghorn to Pisa which was too far inland and whose natives were hostile); as Alexandria and Suez were to Cairo; Tripoli and Alexandretta to Aleppo; Jedda to Mecca.

This phenomenon was particularly marked in Europe, where small towns were very numerous. Rudolph Häpke[65] was the first to use the striking expression 'an archipelago of towns', apropos of Flanders, to describe how its cities were linked to each other, and particularly to Bruges, in the fifteenth century (later to Antwerp). 'The Netherlands,' as Henri Pirenne remarked, 'are the suburb of Antwerp', a suburb full of active towns. The same was true on a smaller scale, of the market-towns around Geneva in the fifteenth century; of the local fairs

---

Opposite: The port of Seville, detail attributed to Coello, sixteenth century. (Photo Giraudon.)

round Milan at the same period; the series of ports linked to Marseilles on the Provençal coast in the sixteenth century, from Martigues on the Etang de Berre up to Fréjus; or the large urban complex that connected San Lucar de Barrameda, Puerto de Santa Maria and Cadiz to Seville; Venice's ring of urban satellites; Burgos's links with its outer harbours (notably Bilbao) over which it long exercised control, even in its decline; London and the Thames and Channel ports; or finally, the classic example of the Hanseatic ports. At the lowest level, one could point to Compiègne in 1500, with its single satellite Pierrefonds; or Senlis, which only had Crépy.[66] This detail in itself tells us a good deal about the status of Compiègne or Senlis. One could draw a series of diagrams to represent these functional ties and dependencies: some circular, some linear with intersections, some mere points.

But these patterns might have only a limited life. If traffic began to move at faster speeds without changing its favourite routes, some relay points were by-passed and went out of use. Sébastien Mercier noted in 1782 'that towns of the second and third rank are imperceptibly becoming depopulated to the benefit of the capital'.[67]

François Mauriac tells of an English visitor he welcomed in south-west France:

> He slept at the Lion d'Or hotel in Langon and walked about the small sleeping town in the night. He told me that nothing like it exists in England any more. Our provincial life is really a survival, what continues to exist of a world in the process of disappearing and which has already disappeared elsewhere. I took my Englishman to Bazas. What a constrast between this somnolent straggling village and its vast cathedral, evidence of a time when the capital of the Bazadais was a flourishing bishopric. We no longer think about that period when every province formed a world which spoke its own language and built its monuments, a refined and hierarchical society which was not aware of Paris and its fashions. Monstrous Paris which fed on this wonderful material and exhausted it.[68]

In the event Paris was obviously no more to blame than London. The general movement of economic life alone was responsible. It deprived the secondary points of the urban network to the advantage of the main ones. But these major points, in their turn, formed a network among themselves on the enlarged scale of the world. And the process began again. Even the capital of Thomas More's island of Utopia, Amaurote, was surrounded by fifty-three cities, an admirable urban network. Each city was less than twenty-four miles from its neighbours, or less than a day's travelling. The whole order would have changed if the speed of transport had been even slightly increased!

Towns and civilizations: the case of Islam

Another feature common to all towns, and yet one which was at the origin of their profound differences in appearance, was that they were all products of their civilizations. There was a prototype for each of them. Father du Halde writes in 1735: 'I have already said elsewhere that there is almost no difference between the majority of towns in China, so that it is almost enough to have seen one to get an idea of all the others.'[69] We might well apply this rapid but by no means rash judgement to the towns of Muscovy, colonial America, Islam (Turkey or Persia), and even – but with much greater hesitation – Europe.

There is no doubt that there was a specific type of Islamic town, to be found all over Islam from Gibraltar to the Sunda Isles, and this example alone may serve as a sufficient indication of the obvious relationships between towns and civilizations.[70]

Islamic towns were very large as a rule, and distant from each other. Their low houses were clustered together like pomegranate seeds. Islam prohibited high houses, deeming them a mark of odious pride (there were certain exceptions: in Mecca, Jedda, its port, and Cairo). Since the houses could not grow upwards, they encroached upon the public way which was poorly protected by Muslim law. The streets were lanes which became blocked if two asses with their pack-saddles happened to meet.

> [In Istanbul] the streets are narrow, as in our old towns [said a French traveller (1766)]; they are generally dirty and would be very inconvenient in bad weather without the pavements running along either side. When two people come face to face, they have to step off the pavement or get out of the way into a doorway. You are sheltered from the rain there. The majority of houses have only one storey which projects over the ground floor; they are almost all painted in oil. This decoration makes the walls less dark and sombre but is usually pretty grim.... All these houses, including even those belonging to nobles and the richest Turks, are built of wood and bricks and whitewashed, which is why fire can do so much damage there in so short a time.[71]

Despite the enormous difference of location, the scene was the same in Cairo, described by Volney in 1782, and in the Persian towns which another Frenchman, Raphaël du Mans, uncharitably contemplated a century earlier (1660): 'The streets of the town are ... winding,' he wrote, 'uneven, full here and there of the holes these wretches dig to piss in, according to the law, so that the urine should not make them unclean by spurting up at them.'[72] Gemelli Careri had the same impression some thirty years later (1694). The streets in Ispahan, as in all Persia, were not paved, resulting in mud in winter and dust in summer. 'This great filthiness is still further increased by the custom of throwing dead animals, together with the blood of those killed by butchers, on to the squares, and of publicly relieving oneself wherever one happens to be....' No, this was not like

View of the Grand Bazaar or principal market, Alexandria, late eighteenth century. *Description de l'Egypte*, engraving, 1812. Cabinet des Estampes, Paris. (Photo B.N.)

Palermo, as people had suggested to him; Palermo where 'the humblest house ... is better than the best in Ispahan'.[73]

Every Muslim town was an inextricable network of badly maintained lanes. Slopes were used to the utmost so that rain and streams washed down the refuse. But this apparently confused topography conformed to a fairly regular plan. The Great Mosque stood in the centre, with shopping streets (*souqs*) and warehouses (khans or caravanserai) all around; then a series of craftsmen ranged in concentric circles in a traditional order which always reflected notions concerning what was clean and what was unclean. For example, perfume and incense merchants, 'clean according to the canonists because devoted to the sacred', were next to the Great Mosque. Near them were silk weavers, goldsmiths and so on. At the outer limits of the town were to be found the curriers, blacksmiths, shoeing smiths, potters, saddlers, dyers and the men who hired out asses and went barefoot, yelling and quarrelling among their beasts. Then at the gates themselves were the country people who came to sell meat, wood, rancid butter, vegetables, 'green herbs', all products of their labour 'or their pilfering'. Another regular feature was the division of races and religions into districts. There was almost always a Christian district and a Jewish district, the latter generally under the protection of the prince's authority and sometimes as a result situated in the very centre of the town, as in Tlemcen.

Of course every town varied slightly from this pattern, if only because of its origins and its importance as a market or craft centre. The main market in Istanbul, the two stone *besistans*, was a town within a town. The Christian districts of Pera and Galata formed another town beyond the Golden Horn. The 'exchange' stood in the middle of Adrianople. 'Near the exchange [1693] is Serachi Street, a mile long and full of good shops selling all sorts of commodities; it is roofed with planks, one on top of the other, with several holes at the sides to let in daylight.' Near the mosque was 'the covered street where the goldsmiths are'.[74]

The originality of Western towns

The West quite soon became a kind of luxury of the world. The towns there had been brought to a pitch hardly found anywhere else. They had made Europe's greatness, but though this is well known, the phenomenon is not simple. Specifying that something is superior means referring either to something inferior, or to an average in relation to which that thing is superior. It means moving on sooner or later to an uncomfortable and deceptive comparison with the rest of the world. Whether one is discussing costumes, money, towns or capitalism, it is impossible, after Max Weber, to avoid comparisons, because Europe has never stopped explaining itself 'in relation to other continents'.

What were Europe's differences and original features? Its towns were marked by an unparalleled freedom. They had developed as autonomous worlds and according to their own propensities. They had outwitted the territorial state, which was established slowly and then only grew with their interested cooperation – and was moreover only an enlarged and often insipid copy of their development. They ruled their countrysides autocratically, regarding them exactly as later powers regarded their colonies, and treating them as such. They pursued an economic policy of their own via their satellites and the nervous system of urban relay points; they were capable of breaking down obstacles and creating or recreating protective privileges. Imagine what would happen if modern states were suppressed so that the Chambers of Commerce of the large towns were free to act as they pleased!

Even without resort to doubtful comparisons these long-standing realities leap to the eye. And they lead us to a key problem which can be formulated in two or three different ways: What stopped the other cities of the world from enjoying the same relative freedom? Or to take another aspect of the same problem, why was change a striking feature of the destiny of Western towns (even their physical existence was transformed) while the other cities have no history by comparison and seem to have been shut in long periods of immobility? Why were some cities like steam-engines while the others were like clocks, to parody Lévi-Strauss? Comparative history compels us to look for the reason for these differences and to attempt to establish a dynamic 'model' of the turbulent urban evolution of the West, whereas a model representing city life in the rest of the world would run in a straight and scarcely broken line across time.

Free worlds

Urban freedom in Europe is a classic and fairly well documented subject; let us start with it.

In a simplified form we can say:
(1) The West well and truly lost its urban framework with the end of the Roman Empire. Moreover the towns in the Empire had been gradually declining since before the arrival of the barbarians. The very relative animation of the Merovingian period was followed, slightly earlier in some places, slightly later in others, by a complete halt.
(2) The urban renaissance from the eleventh century was precipitated by and superimposed on a rise in rural vigour, a growth of fields, vineyards and orchards. Towns grew in harmony with villages and clearly outlined urban law often emerged from the communal privileges of village groups. The town was often simply the country revived and remodelled. The names of a number of streets in Frankfurt (which remained very rural until the sixteenth century) recall the woods, clumps of trees and marshland amid which the town grew up.[75]

This rural rearrangement naturally brought to the nascent city the representatives of political and social authority: nobles, lay princes and ecclesiastics.

(3) None of this would have been possible without a general return to health and a growing monetary economy. Money, a traveller from perhaps distant lands (from Islam, according to Maurice Lombard), was the active and decisive force. Two centuries before Saint Thomas Aquinas, Alain de Lille said: 'Money, not Caesar, is everything now.' And money meant towns.

Thousands of towns were founded at this time, but few of them went on to brilliant futures. Only certain regions, therefore, were urbanized in depth, thus distinguishing themselves from the rest and playing a vitalizing role: such was the region between the Loire and the Rhine, for instance, or northern and central Italy, and certain key points on Mediterranean coasts. Merchants, craft guilds, industries, long-distance trade and banks were quick to appear there, as well as a certain kind of bourgeoisie and even some sort of capitalism. The destinies of these very special cities were linked not only to the progress of the surrounding countryside but to international trade. Indeed, they often broke free of rural society and former political ties. The break might be achieved violently or amicably, but it was always a sign of strength, plentiful money and real power.

Soon there were no states around these privileged towns. This was the case in Italy and Germany, with the political collapses of the thirteenth century. The hare beat the tortoise for once. Elsewhere – in France, England, Castile, even in Aragon – the earlier rebirth of the territorial state restricted the development of the towns, which in addition were not situated in particularly lively economic areas. They grew less rapidly than elsewhere.

But the main, the unpredictable thing was that certain towns made themselves into autonomous worlds, city-states, buttressed with privileges (acquired or extorted) like so many juridical ramparts. Perhaps in the past historians have insisted too much on the legal factors involved, for if such considerations were indeed sometimes more important than, or of equal importance to, geographical, sociological and economic factors, the latter did count to a large extent. What is privilege without material substance?

In fact the miracle in the West was not so much that everything sprang up again from the eleventh century, after having been almost annihilated with the disaster of the fifth. History is full of examples of secular revivals, of urban expansion, of births and rebirths: Greece from the fifth to the second century BC; Rome perhaps; Islam from the ninth century; China under the Sungs. But these revivals always featured two runners, the state and the city. The state usually won and the city then remained subject and under a heavy yoke. The miracle of the first great urban centuries in Europe was that the city won hands down, at least in Italy, Flanders and Germany. It was able to try the experiment of leading a completely separate life for quite a long time. This was a colossal event. Its genesis cannot be pinpointed with certainty, but its enormous consequences are visible.

Towns as outposts of modernity

It was on the basis of this liberty that the great Western cities, and other towns they influenced and to which they served as examples, built up a distinctive civilization and spread techniques which were new, or had been revived or rediscovered after centuries – it matters little which. The important thing is that these cities had the rare privilege of following through an unusual political, social and economic experience.

In the financial sphere, the towns organized taxation, finances, public credit, customs and excise. They invented public loans: the first issues of the Monte Vecchio in Venice could be said to go back to 1167, the first formulation of the Casa di San Giorgio to 1407. One after another, they reinvented gold money, following Genoa which may have minted the *genovino* as early as the late twelfth century.[76] They organized industry and the guilds; they invented long-distance trade, bills of exchange, the first forms of trading companies and accountancy. They also quickly became the scene of class struggles. For if the towns were 'communities' as has been said, they were also 'societies' in the modern sense of the word, with their tensions and civil struggles: nobles against bourgeois; poor against rich ('thin people' *popolo magro* against 'fat people' *popolo grosso*). The struggles in Florence were already more deeply akin to those of the industrial early nineteenth century than to the faction-fights of ancient Rome, as the drama of the Ciompi (1378) demonstrates.

This society divided from within also faced enemies from without – the worlds of the noble, prince or peasant, of everybody who was not a citizen. The cities were the West's first focus for patriotism – and the patriotism they inspired was long to be more coherent and much more conscious than the territorial kind, which emerged only slowly in the first states. One can reflect upon this by looking at a curious painting representing the battle on 19 June 1502 between the citizens of Nuremberg and the Margrave Casimir of Brandenburg-Ansbach who was attacking the town. One does not have to ask who commissioned the picture. Most of the townspeople are depicted on foot, without armour, in their everyday clothes. Their leader, on horseback and dressed in a black suit, is talking to the humanist Willibald Pirckheimer, who is wearing one of the enormous ostrich-feather hats of the period and who is, significantly, leading a band of men to assist the rightful cause of the town under attack. The Brandenburg assailants are heavily armed and on horseback, their faces hidden by the visors of their helmets. One group of three men in the picture could be taken as a symbol of the freedom of the towns against the authority of princes and noblemen: two burghers with unshielded faces stand proudly one each side of an armoured horseman they are escorting away as their shamefaced prisoner.

'Bourgeois', 'burghers', in their little city strongholds: these are convenient terms but highly imprecise. Werner Sombart has placed a good deal of emphasis on this birth of a society, and more still of a new state of mind. 'It is in Florence

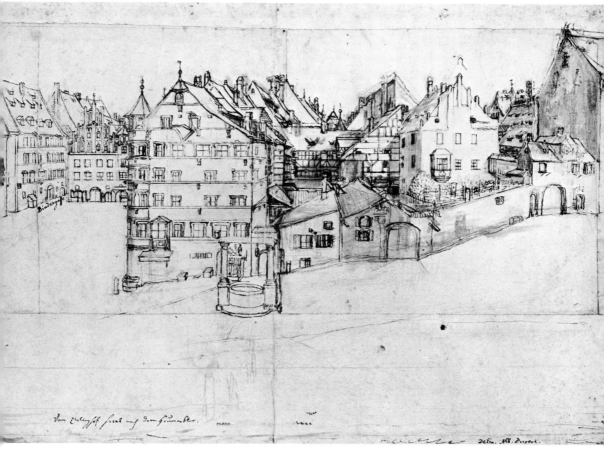

The Egidien-Theresienplatz, drawing by Dürer, Altstadtmuseum, Nuremberg. (Photo Hochbauamt.)

towards the end of the fourteenth century, if I am not mistaken,' he wrote, 'that we meet the perfect bourgeois for the first time.'[77] Perhaps. In fact the assumption of power (1293) by the *Arti Maggiori* – those of wool and of the *Arte di Calimala* – marked the victory of the old and new rich and the spirit of enterprise in Florence. Sombart, as usual, preferred to place the problem on the level of mentalities and the development of the rational spirit, rather than on the plane of societies, or even of the economy, where he was afraid of following in Marx's footsteps.

A new state of mind was established, broadly that of an early, still faltering, Western capitalism – a collection of rules, possibilities, calculations, the art both of getting rich and of living. It also included gambling and risk: the key words of commercial language, *fortuna, ventura, ragione, prudenza, sicurta,* define the risks to be guarded against. No question now of living from day to day as noblemen did, always putting up their revenues to try to meet the level of their expenditure, which invariably came first – and letting the future take care of itself. The merchant was economical with his money, calculated his expenditure according to his returns, his investments according to their yield. The hour-glass had turned back the right way. He would also be economical with his time: a merchant could already say that *chi tempo ha e tempo aspetta tempo perde*, which means much the same thing as 'time is money'.[78]

Capitalism and towns were basically the same thing in the West. Lewis Mumford humorously claimed that capitalism was the cuckoo's egg laid in the confined nests of the medieval towns. By this he meant to convey that the bird was destined to grow inordinately and burst its tight framework (which was true), and then link up with the state, the conqueror of towns but heir to their institutions and way of thinking and completely incapable of dispensing with them.[79] The important thing was that even when it had declined as a city the town continued to rule the roost all the time it was passing into the actual or apparent service of the prince. The wealth of the state would still be the wealth of the town: Portugal converged on Lisbon, the Netherlands on Amsterdam, and English primacy was London's primacy (the capital modelled England in its own image after the peaceful revolution of 1688). The latent defect in the Spanish imperial economy was that it was based on Seville – a controlled town rotten with dishonest officials and long dominated by foreign capitalists – and not on a powerful free town capable of producing and carrying through a really individual economic policy. Likewise, if Louis XIV did not succeed in founding a 'royal bank', despite various projects (1703, 1706, 1709), it was because faced with the power of the monarch, Paris did not offer the protection of a town free to do what it wanted and accountable to no one.

Urban patterns

Let us imagine we are looking at a comprehensive history of the towns of Europe covering the complete series of their forms from the Greek city-state to an eighteenth-century town – everything Europe was able to build at home and overseas, from Muscovy in the East to America in the West. How is one to classify such a wealth of material? One might begin with political, economic or social characteristics. Politically a differentiation would be made between capitals, fortresses and administrative towns in the full meaning of 'administrative'. Economically, one would distinguish between ports, caravan towns, market towns, industrial towns and money markets. Socially, a list could be drawn up of *rentier* towns, and Church, Court or craftsmen's towns. This is to adopt a series of fairly obvious categories, divisible into sub-categories and capable of absorbing all sorts of local varieties. Such a classification has advantages, not so much for the question of the town in itself as for the study of particular economies limited in time and space.

On the other hand, some more general distinctions arising out of the very process of town development offer a more useful classification for our purpose. Simplifying, one could say that the West has had three basic types of town in the course of its evolution: open towns, that is to say not differentiated from their hinterland, even blending into it (A); towns closed in on themselves in every sense, their walls marking the boundaries of an individual way of life more than a territory (B); finally towns held in subjection, by which is meant the whole range of known controls by prince or state (C).

Roughly, A preceded B, and B preceded C. But there is no suggestion of strict succession about this order. It is rather a question of directions and dimensions shaping the complicated careers of the Western towns. They did not all develop at the same time or in the same way. Later we will see if this 'grid' is valid for classifying all the towns of the world.

Type A: the ancient Greek or Roman city was open to the surrounding countryside and on terms of equality with it.[80] Athens accepted inside its walls as rightful citizens the Eupatrid horse-breeders as well as the vine-growing peasants so dear to Aristophanes. As soon as the smoke rose above the Pnyx, the peasant responded to the signal and attended the Assembly of the People, where he sat among his equals. At the beginning of the Peloponnesian war, the entire population of the Attic countryside evacuated itself to Athens where it took refuge while the Spartans ravaged the fields, olive groves and houses. When the Spartans fell back at the approach of winter, the country people returned to their homes. The Greek city was in fact the sum of the town and its surrounding countryside. And this was the case because the towns had only just come into existence (a century or two is nothing in this context), only recently emerged from the rural background. Moreover, the division of industrial activities, a source of discord in the future, did not apply here: Athens did, it is true, have the Ceramic suburb where the potters lived, but they had only small shops. It also had a port, Piraeus, swarming with foreigners, freedmen and slaves, where craft activity – one cannot call it industry or pre-industry – was becoming well established. But this activity encountered the prejudices of an agricultural society that distrusted it; it was therefore left to foreigners or slaves. Above all, Athens' prosperity did not last long enough for social and political conflicts to come to a head there and provoke quarrels of a Florentine type. Only the merest hint of such things can be detected. It might be added that the villages round about had their craftsmen and forges, where it was pleasant to warm oneself in winter. In short, industry was rudimentary, foreign and unobtrusive. Likewise, if one explores the ruins of Roman cities, one is in open country immediately outside the gates: there are no suburbs, which is as good as saying no industry or active and organized trades in their duly allotted place.

The Notre-Dame bridge in Paris, showing its tall houses which were only knocked down in 1787. On the right bank, near the site of the Place de Grève, a brisk trade is being driven, notably in wheat, wood and hay. Eighteenth-century engraving, Musée Carnavalet. (Photo Bulloz.)

Type B: the closed city: the medieval town was the classic example of a closed city, a self-sufficient unit, an exclusive, Lilliputian empire. Entering its gates was like crossing one of the serious frontiers of the world today. You were free to thumb your nose at your neighbour from the other side of the barrier. He could not touch you. The peasant who uprooted himself from his land and arrived in the town was immediately another man. He was free – or rather he had abandoned a known and hated servitude for another, not always guessing the extent of it beforehand. But this mattered little. If the town had adopted him, he could snap his fingers when his lord called for him. And though obsolete elsewhere, such calls were still frequently to be heard in Silesia in the eighteenth century and in Muscovy up to the nineteenth.

Though the towns opened their gates easily it was not enough to walk through them to be immediately and really part of them. Full citizens were a jealous minority, a small town inside the town itself. A citadel of the rich was built up in Venice in 1297 thanks to the *serrata*, the closing of the Great Council to new members. The *nobili* of Venice became a closed class for centuries. Very rarely did anyone force its gates. The category of ordinary *cittadini* – at a lower level – was probably more hospitable. But the Signoria very soon created two types of citizen, one *de intus*, the other *de intus et extra*, the latter full, the former partial. Fifteen years' residence were still required to be allowed to apply for the first, twenty-five years for the second. A decree by the Senate in 1386 even forbade new citizens (including those who were full citizens) from trading directly in Venice with German merchants at the Fondego dei Todeschi or outside it. The ordinary townspeople were no less mistrustful or hostile to newcomers. According to Marin Sanudo, in June 1520, the street people attacked the peasants who had arrived from the mainland as recruits for the galleys or the army, crying '*Poltroni ande arar!*' 'Back to the plough, shirkers!'[81]

Of course Venice was an extreme example. Moreover, it owed the preservation of its own constitution until 1797 to an aristocratic and extremely reactionary regime, as well as to the conquest at the beginning of the fifteenth century of the Terra Firma, which extended its authority as far as the Alps and Brescia. It was the last *polis* in the West. But citizenship was also parsimoniously granted in Marseilles in the sixteenth century; it was necessary to have 'ten years of domicile, to possess property, to have married a local girl'. Otherwise the man remained amongst the masses of non-citizens of the town. This limited conception of citizenship was the general rule everywhere.

The main source of contention can be glimpsed throughout this vast process: to whom did industry and craft, their privileges and profits, belong? In fact they belonged to the town, to its authorities and to its merchant entrepreneurs. They decided if it were necessary to deprive, or to try to deprive, the rural area of the city of the right to spin, weave and dye, or if on the contrary it would be advantageous to grant it these rights. Everything was possible in these interchanges, as the history of each individual town shows.

As far as work inside the walls was concerned (we can hardly call it industry without qualification), everything was arranged for the benefit of the craft guilds. They enjoyed exclusive contiguous monopolies, fiercely defended along the imprecise frontiers that so easily led to absurd conflicts. The urban authorities did not always have the situation under control. Sooner or later, with the help of money, they were to allow obvious, acknowledged, honorary superiorities, consecrated by money or power, to become apparent. The 'Six Corps' (drapers, grocers, haberdashers, furriers, hosiers, goldsmiths) were the commercial aristocracy of Paris from 1625. In Florence it was the *Arte dela lana* and the *Arte di Calimala* (engaged in dyeing fabric imported from the north, unbleached). But town museums in Germany supply the best evidence of these old situations. In Ulm, for example, each guild owned a picture hinged in triptych form. The side panels represented characteristic scenes of the craft. The centre, like a treasured family album, showed innumerable small portraits recalling the successive generations of masters of the guild over the centuries.

An even more telling example was the City of London and its annexes (running along its walls) in the eighteenth century, still the domain of fussy, obsolete and powerful guilds. If Westminster and the suburbs were growing continually, noted a well-informed economist (1754), it was for obvious reasons: 'These suburbs are free and present a clear field for every industrious citizen, while in its bosom London nourishes ninety-two of all sorts of those exclusive companies [guilds], whose numerous members can be seen adorning the Lord Mayor's Show every year with immoderate pomp.'[82] Let us come to a halt here before this colourful scene. And for the moment let us also pass over the free crafts, around London and elsewhere, which kept outside the guild-masterships and their regulations, outside their constraint and protection.

Type C: subjugated towns, of early modern times. Everywhere in Europe, as soon as the state was firmly established it disciplined the towns with instinctive relentlessness, whether or not it used violence. The Habsburgs did so just as much as the Popes, the German princes as much as the Medicis or the kings of France. Except in the Netherlands and England, obedience was imposed.

Take Florence as an example: the Medicis had slowly subjugated it, almost elegantly in Lorenzo's time. But after 1532 and the return of the Medicis to power the process accelerated. Florence in the seventeenth century was no more than the Grand Duke's court. He had seized everything – money, the right to govern and to distribute honours. From the Pitti Palace, on the left bank of the Arno, a gallery – a secret passage in fact – allowed the prince to cross the river and reach the Uffizi. This elegant gallery, still in existence today on the Ponte Vecchio, was the thread from which the spider at the extremity of his web supervised the imprisoned town.

In Spain, the *corregidor*, the urban administrator, subjected the 'free towns' to the will of the Crown. Of course the Crown left the not inconsiderable profits and the vanities of local administration to the petty local nobility. It summoned the delegates of the town *regidores* (in which office could be bought) to meetings of the Cortes – formal assemblies eager to present their grievances but unanimously voting the king his taxes. In France, the 'good towns' were just as much under orders. Though enjoying the privileges of their municipal corporations and their manifold fiscal exemptions, they did not prevent the royal government from doubling the *octrois* by its declaration of 21 December 1647 and allocating a good half of them to itself. Paris, equally under the royal thumb, helped – had to help – the royal treasury and was the centre of the large-scale fund-raising known as the *rentes sur l'Hôtel de Ville*. Even Louis XIV did not give up the capital. Versailles was not really separate from nearby Paris, and the monarchy had always been accustomed to moving round the periphery of the powerful, redoubtable city. The monarch spent some time at Fontainebleau, Saint-Germain and Saint-Cloud; at the Louvre he was on the outskirts of Paris; at the Tuileries, almost outside Paris proper. In fact it was advisable to govern these overpopulated towns from a distance, at least from time to time. Philip II spent all his time at the Escorial, and Madrid was only at its beginnings. Later the Dukes of Bavaria lived in Nymphenburg; Frederick II in Potsdam; the emperors outside Vienna in Schoenbrunn. Moreover, to return to Louis XIV, he did not forget to assert his authority in Paris itself nor to maintain his prestige there. The two great royal squares, the Place des Victoires and the Place Vendôme, were built during his reign. The 'prodigious construction' of Les Invalides was undertaken at that time. Thanks to him, wide access roads where carriages flowed and military marches were organised opened Paris to its nearby countryside on the pattern of Baroque towns. Most important from our point of view, was the creation in 1667 of a Lieutenant of Police with exorbitant powers. The second holder of this high office, the Marquis d'Argenson, nominated thirty years later (1697), 'assembled the machine – not the one that exists today', explained Sébastien Mercier, 'but he was the first to think of its main springs and mechanisms. One can even say that today this machine runs by itself.'[83]

Different types of development

But we know, of course, that urban development does not happen of its own accord: it is not an endogenous phenomenon produced under a bell-jar. It is always the expression of a society which controls it from within, but also from without, and in this respect, our classification is, I repeat, too simple. That said, how does it work when applied outside the narrow confines of Western Europe?

(1) *Towns in colonial America*. We should say 'in Latin America', because the English towns remained a separate case. They had to live by their own resources and emerge from their wilderness to find a place in the vast world; the real parallel for them is the medieval city. The towns in Iberian America had a much

Towns and Cities 521

simpler and more limited career. Built like Roman camps inside four earth walls, they were garrisons lost in the midst of vast hostile expanses, linked together by communications which were slow because they stretched across enormous empty spaces. Curiously, at a period when the privileged medieval town had spread over practically the whole of Europe, the ancient rule prevailed in all Hispano-Portuguese America, apart from the large towns of the viceroys: Mexico City, Lima, Santiago de Chile, San Salvador (Bahia) – that is to say the official, already parasitical organisms.

There were scarcely any purely commercial towns in this part of America, or if there were they were of minor importance. For example, Recife – the merchants' town – stood next to aristocratic Olinda, town of great plantation owners, *senhores de engenhos* and slave owners. It was rather like Piraeus or Phalera in relation to Pericles' Athens. Buenos Aires after its second foundation (the successful one on 1580) was still a small market village – like Megara or Aegina. It had the misfortune to have nothing but Indian *bravos* round about, and its inhabitants complained of being forced to earn 'their bread by the sweat of their brow' in this America where the whites were *rentiers*. But caravans of mules or large wooden carts arrived there from the Andes, from Lima, which was a way of acquiring Potosi silver. Sugar, and soon gold, came by sailing ship from Brazil. And contact with Portugal and Africa was maintained through the smuggling carried on by sailing ships bringing black slaves. But Buenos Aires remained an exception amidst the 'barbarism' of nascent Argentina.

The American town was generally tiny, without these gifts from abroad. It governed itself. No one was really concerned with its fate. Its masters were the landowners who had their houses in the town, with rings for tethering their

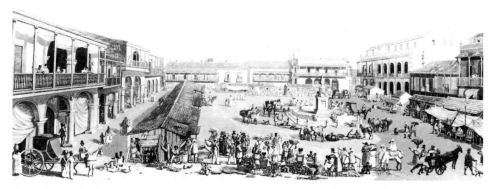

View of the Old Square, the principal market-place of Havana. From an album of pictures of America, eighteenth century. (Photo B.N.)

horses fixed on the front walls overlooking the street. These were the 'men of property', *os homens bons* of the municipalities of Brazil, or the *hacendados* of the Spanish *cabildos*. These towns were so many miniature versions of Sparta or of Thebes in the time of Epaminondas. It could safely be said that the history of the Western towns in America began again from zero. Naturally there was no separation between the towns and the hinterland and there was no industry to be shared out. Wherever industry appeared – in Mexico City, for example – it was carried on by slaves or semi-slaves. The medieval European town would not have been conceivable if its artisans had been serfs.

(2) *How should Russian towns be classified?* One can tell at a glance that the towns that survived or grew up again in Muscovy after the terrible catastrophes of the Mongol invasion no longer lived according to the Western pattern. Although there were great cities among them, like Moscow or Novgorod, they were kept in hand sometimes brutally. In the sixteenth century a proverb still asked: 'Who can set his face against God and the mighty Novgorod?' But the proverb was wrong. The town was harshly brought to heel in 1427 and again in 1477 (it had to deliver 300 cartloads of gold). Executions, deportations, confiscations followed in quick succession. Above all, these towns were caught up in the slow circulation of traffic over an immense, already Asiatic, still wild expanse. In 1650, as in the past, transport on the rivers or overland by sledge or by convoys of carts moved with an enormous loss of time. It was often dangerous even to go near villages, and a halt had to be called every evening in open country – as on the Balkan roads – deploying the carriages in a circle, with everyone on the alert to defend himself.

For all these reasons the Muscovy towns did not impose themselves on the vast surrounding countryside; quite the reverse. They were unable to dictate their wishes to a peasant world which was biologically extraordinarily strong, although poverty-stricken, restless and perpetually on the move. The important fact was that 'harvests per hectare in the European countries of the East remained constant on average, from the sixteenth to the nineteenth century' – at a low level.[84] There was no healthy rural surplus and therefore no really prosperous town. Nor did the Russian towns have serving them those secondary towns that were a characteristic of the West and its lively trade.

Consequently, there were innumerable peasant serfs practically without land, insolvent in the eyes of their lords and even the state. It was of no importance whether they went to towns or to work in the houses of rich peasants. In the town they became beggars, porters, craftsmen, poor tradesmen, or very rarely merchants who got rich quickly. They might also stay put and become craftsmen in their own villages, or seek the necessary supplement to their earnings by becoming carriers or travelling pedlars. This irresistible tide of mendicancy could not be stemmed, and indeed it often served the interests of the landlord who gave it his blessing: all such artisans and traders remained his serfs whatever

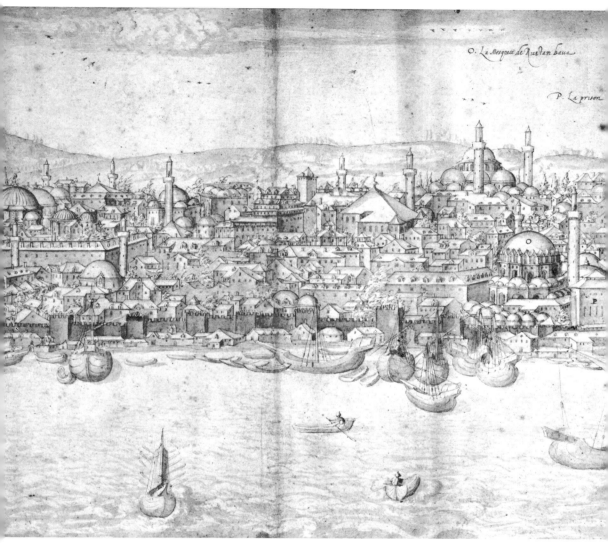

Sixteenth-century Istanbul: sea-front on the Golden Horn (fragment). Cabinet des Estampes, Paris. (Photo B.N.)

they did and however great their social success: they still owed him their dues.[85]

These examples and others indicate a fate resembling what may after all have happened at the beginning of Western urbanization. Though a clearer case, it is comparable to the caesura between the eleventh and thirteenth centuries, that interlude when almost everything was born of the villages and peasant vitality. We might call it an intermediate position between A and C, without the

B type (the independent city) ever having arisen. The prince appeared too quickly, like the ogre in a fairy tale.

(3) *Imperial towns in the East and Far East.* The same problems and ambiguities – only deeper – arise when we leave Europe and move east.

Towns similar to those in medieval Europe – masters of their fate for a brief moment – only arose in Islam when the empires collapsed. They marked some outstanding moments in Islamic civilization. But they only lasted for a time and the main beneficiaries were certain marginal towns like Cordoba, or the cities which were urban republics by the fifteenth century, like Ceuta before the Portuguese occupation in 1415, or Oran before the Spanish occupation in 1509. The usual pattern was the huge city under the rule of a prince or a Caliph: a Baghdad or a Cairo.

Towns in distant Asia were of the same type: imperial or royal cities, enormous, parasitical, soft and luxurious – Delhi and Vijnayanagar, Peking and to some extent Nanking, though this was rather different. The great prestige enjoyed by the prince comes as no surprise to us. And if one ruler was swallowed up by the city or more likely by his palace, another immediately took his place and the subjection continued. Neither will it surprise us to learn that these towns were incapable of taking over the artisanal trades from the countryside: they were both open towns and subject towns simultaneously. Besides, in India as in China, social structures already existing hampered the free movement of the towns. If the town did not win its independence, it was not only because of the bastinadoes ordered by the mandarins or the cruelty of the prince to merchants and ordinary citizens. It was because society was prematurely fixed, crystallized in a certain mould.

In India, the caste system automatically divided and broke up every urban community. In China, the cult of the *gentes* on the one hand was confronted on the other by a mixture comparable to that which created the Western town: like the latter it acted as a melting-pot, breaking old bonds and placing individuals on the same level. The arrival of immigrants created an 'American' environment, where those already settled set the tone and the way of life. In addition, there was no independent authority representing the Chinese town as a unit, in its dealings with the State or with the very powerful countryside. The rural areas were the real heart of living, active and thinking China.

The town, residence of officials and nobles, was not the property of either guilds or merchants. There was no gradual 'rise of the bourgeoisie' here. No sooner did a bourgeoisie appear than it was tempted by class betrayal, fascinated by the luxurious life of the mandarins. The towns might have lived their own lives, filled in the contours of their own destiny, if individual initiative and capitalism had had a clear field. But the tutelary State hardly lent itself to this. It did occasionally nod, intentionally or not: at the end of the sixteenth century a bourgeoisie seems to have emerged with a taste for business enterprise, and we can guess what part it played in the large iron-works near Peking, in the private porcelain workshops that developed in King-te-chen, and even more in the rise of the silk trade in Su-Chu, the capital of Kiang-tsu.[86] But this was no more than a flash in the pan. With the Manchu conquest, the Chinese crisis was resolved in the seventeenth century in a direction completely opposed to urban freedoms.

Only the West swung completely over in favour of its towns. The towns caused the West to advance. It was, let us repeat, an enormous event, but the deep-seated reasons behind it are still inadequately explained. What would the Chinese towns have become if the junks had discovered the Cape of Good Hope at the beginning of the fifteenth century, and had made full use of such a chance of world conquest?

The big cities

For a long time the only big cities in the world had been in the East and Far East. Marco Polo's amazement makes it clear that the East was the site of empires and enormous cities. With the sixteenth century, and more still during the following two centuries, large towns grew up in the West, assumed positions of prime importance and retained them brilliantly thereafter. Europe had thus made up for lost time and wiped out a deficiency (if deficiency there had been). And now here it was, tasting the luxuries, and the bitter-sweet pleasures of cities that were already becoming too big.

The states

This belated burst of growth would have been inconceivable without the steady advance of the states: they had caught up with the headlong gallop of the towns. it was now their capitals which were privileged, whether they deserved it or not. From now on they vied with each other in modernity: which would have the first pavements, the first street lamps, the first steam pumps, the first effective system for supplying and distributing drinking water, the first numbered houses. All this was taking place in London and Paris during the period just before the French Revolution.

The town that did not grasp this opportunity was inevitably left behind. The more its old shell remained intact, the greater its chance of becoming empty. In the sixteenth century, demographic growth had still favoured all the towns indiscriminately whatever their size – large or small. In the seventeenth, political success was concentrated on a few towns to the exclusion of others. Despite the depressing economic situation they grew unceasingly, and continually attracted people and privileges

London and Paris led the movement, but Naples was also in the running with its long-established privileges and with already as many as 300,000 inhabitants in the last years of the sixteenth century. Paris, which the French quarrels had reduced to perhaps 180,000 inhabitants in 1594, had probably doubled by Richelieu's time. And others fell into step behind these large towns: Madrid, Amsterdam, soon Vienna, Munich, Copenhagen and even more St Petersburg. America alone was slow to follow the movement, but its overall population was still very small. The anachronistic success of Potosi (100,000 inhabitants around 1600) was the temporary success of a mining camp. However brilliant Mexico City, Lima or Rio de Janeiro were, they were slow to collect sizeable populations. Rio had at most 100,000 inhabitants around 1800. As for the hard-working and independent towns in the United States, they fell well below these princely achievements.

This growth of large agglomerations, coinciding with the first modern states, to some extent explains the older phenomenon of the large Eastern and Far Eastern cities – their size was not a function of the density of population, which would have had to be higher in the East than in Europe (we know this is not true), but due to their role as powerful political concentrations. Istanbul probably had 700,000 inhabitants as early as the sixteenth century, but behind the enormous city stood an enormous empire. Behind Peking, which numbered three million inhabitants in 1793, there stood a single and united China. Behind Delhi there stood an almost united India.

The example of India shows how much these official towns were bound up with the prince – to the point of absurdity. Political difficulties, even the prince's whim, uprooted and transplanted the capitals several times. Apart from exceptions which confirm the rule – Benares, Allahabad, Delhi, Madura, Trichinopoly, Multar, Handnar – they wandered like nomads over quite large distances in the course of the centuries. Even Delhi was moved small distances on its own site two or three times, but its movements consisted of a kind of whirling dance around itself. The capital of Bengal was Rajinahal in 1592, Dacca in 1608, Murshihad in 1704. In each case and in the same way, as soon as the prince abandoned it the town was jeopardized, deteriorated and occasionally died. A stroke of luck was necessary for it to revive. Lahore in 1664 had houses 'much vaster than those at Delhi and Agra, but in the absence of the court, which had not made this journey for over twenty years, most of them had fallen into ruin. Only five or six sizeable streets remained, two or three of which were over a league long and contained a number of broken-down houses.'[87]

Moreover, Delhi was undoubtedly much more the Great Mogul's town than Paris was Louis XIV's. The bankers and tradesmen in the great Chandni Choke street, however rich they sometimes were, did not count in relation to the sovereign, his court and his army. When Aurangzeb embarked on the journey which brought him as far as Kashmir in 1663, the whole town followed him because they could not live without his favours and liberality. An incredible crowd formed, estimated at several hundred thousand people by a French doctor who took part in the expedition.[88] Can we imagine Paris following Louis XV during his journey to Metz in 1744?

The flowering of the Japanese towns in the same period was more similar to European growth. In 1609, when Rodrigo Vivero crossed the archipelago and marvelled at it, the largest town was no longer Kyoto, the old capital, seat of a somnolent Mikado.[89] With its 400,000 inhabitants, it was now in second place behind Yedo (500,000 inhabitants plus an enormous garrison which with the soldiers' families more than doubled the city's population: a total, then, of over a million). The third largest city was Osaka, with 300,000. But Osaka, the meeting-place of Japan's merchants, was on the eve of its great age of expansion: 400,000 inhabitants in 1749, 500,000 in 1783.[90] The seventeenth century was the 'Osaka age', a 'bourgeois' century, with what could be called Florentine aspects accompanied by a certain simplification of patrician life and the blossoming of a realistic and in some ways popular literature. This literature was written in the national language and no longer in Chinese (the language of scholars) and drew enthusiastically on the news and scandals of the Flowers district (the courtesan area).[91]

But Yedo soon moved to the fore. It was the Shogun's capital and very authoritarian with its administration and its concentration of rich landowners, the *daimyos*, who were forced to live there for half the year, under mild supervision, and who regularly came or returned to the city in long ostentatious processions. After the Shogun's reorganization at the beginning of the seventeenth century, they built their Yedo homes in a district apart from the rest of the population and reserved for the nobles, 'the only people to have their arms painted and guilded above their doors'. Some of these emblazoned doors cost more than twenty thousand ducats, according to our Spanish informant (1609),[92] From then onwards Tokyo (Yedo) did not stop growing. In the eighteenth century it was perhaps twice as large as Paris, but Japan at that period had a larger population than France and a government no doubt as dictatorial and centralized as that of Versailles.

The function of capital cities

By the laws of a simple and inevitable political arithmetic, it seems that the vaster and more centralized the state, the greater the chance its capital had of being populous. The rule is valid for imperial China, Hanoverian England, the Paris of Louis XIV and Sébastien Mercier, and even for Amsterdam, which was the real capital of the United Provinces.

These towns, as we will see, represented enormous expenditure. Their economy was only balanced by outside resources; others had to pay for their luxury. What use were they therefore, in the West, where they sprang up and asserted themselves so powerfully? The answer is that they produced the modern states, an enormous task requiring an enormous effort. They mark a turning-point in world history. They produced the national markets, without which the modern state would be a pure fiction. The 'British' market was not created solely by the political union of England with Scotland (1707), or the Act of Union with Ireland (1801); or by the abolition of so many tolls (advantageous in itself), or by the speeding-up of transport, or the 'canal fever' or the surrounding sea (a natural encouragement to free trade). It was primarily the result of the ebb and flow of merchandise to and from London, a mighty beating heart, causing everything to move at its own rhythm, capable of creating chaos or calm by turns. Added to this was the enormous cultural, intellectual and even revolutionary role of these hothouses. But the price demanded was very high.

Unbalanced worlds

The right balance had to be struck between internal and external pressures. Amsterdam was thus an admirable town. It had expanded fast: 30,000 inhabitants in 1530, 115,000 in 1630, 200,000 at the end of the eighteenth century. It aimed at comfort rather than luxury, intelligently supervising the enlargement of its districts. Its four semi-circular canals, like the concentric rings of a tree, marked the physical growth of the town between 1482 and 1658. Light and airy, with its rows of trees, quays and stretches of water, it kept its orginal character intact. Only one mistake, but a revealing one, was made: the Jordaan districts in the south-west were handed over to unscrupulous contracting companies. Foundations were badly made, canals were narrow; the whole district was situated below the level of the town. And it was of course here that there settled a mixed proletariat of Jewish immigrants, *marranos* from Portugal and Spain, Huguenot refugees fleeing France and the wretched of all nationalities.[93]

There is a risk that the retrospective traveller may be disappointed in London, the largest town in Europe (860,000 inhabitants at the end of the eighteenth century). The city had not taken full advantage of its misfortune (if one can put it that way) after the fire of 1666 to reconstruct itself in a rational manner, despite the plans put forward, in particular the very fine one submitted by Wren. It had grown up again haphazardly and only began to improve at the end of the seventeenth century when the large squares in the west were completed: Golden Square, Grosvenor Square, Berkeley Square, Red Lion Square, Kensington Square.[94]

Trade was obviously one of the driving forces behind the monstrous agglomeration. But Werner Sombart has shown that 100,000 people at the most could have lived on the profits of trade in 1700. Taken all together, profits did not add up to the civil list allocation granted to William III, £700,000. London, in fact, lived primarily off the Crown, off the high, middle-grade and minor officials it maintained (high officials were paid in a lordly fashion, with salaries of £1000, £1500 even £2000). It also lived off the nobility and gentry who settled in the town, representatives to the House of Commons who had been in the habit of staying in London with their wives and children since Queen Anne's reign (1702—14), and from the presence of holders of government bonds whose numbers grew as the years went by. An idle tertiary sector proliferated, turned its stocks, salaries and surplus to good account and unbalanced the powerful life of England to the advantage of London, making it into a unity and creating artificial needs.[95]

The same thing happened in Paris. The expanding town outgrew its walls, adapted its streets to the traffic of carriages, planned its squares and collected an enormous mass of consumers. After 1760, it was full of building sites, where high lifting wheels, 'which raised enormous stones into the air' near Sainte-Geneviève and in 'the parish of the Madeleine',[96] were visible from afar. The elder Mirabeau, the 'Friend of Man', would have liked to drive 200,000 people out of the town, starting with royal office-holders and large landowners and ending up with litigants, who perhaps would have liked nothing better than to go back home.[97] It was true that these wealthy classes and reluctant spendthrifts supported 'a multitude of merchants, craftsmen, servants, unskilled labourers' and many ecclesiastics and 'tonsured clerics'! 'In several houses,' Sébastien

St James's Square in the eighteenth century. English engraving. (Photo Roger-Viollet.)

Mercier reported, 'one finds a priest who is regarded as a friend and who is only an honest valet. ... Then come family tutors who are also priests.'[98] Not to mention bishops breaking residence requirements. Lavoisier drew up the balance sheet for the capital: under the heading of expenditure, 250 million *livres* for humans, 10 million for horses; on the credit side, 20 million in commercial profits, 140 in government bonds and salaries, 100 million from ground rents or from business activities outside Paris.[99]

None of these facts escaped the observers and economists of the time. 'The wealth of the towns attracts pleasure-seekers' said Cantillon. 'The great and the wealthy,' noted Dr Quesnay, 'have withdrawn to the capital.'[100] Sébastien Mercier listed the endless 'unproductive elements' in the enormous town.

No, [said an Italian text in 1797] Paris is not a real market place, it is too busy supplying itself; it only counts because of its books, the products of its art or fashion, the enormous quantity of money which circulates there, and the speculation on the exchanges, unequalled except by Amsterdam. All industry there is devoted exclusively to luxury: carpets from the Gobelins or

Naples in the fifteenth century: already a large city. On the left the Castel del Ovo, on its island, the great Angevin fortress of the Castel Nuovo and the breakwater dividing the double harbour, into which is sailing the squadron of galleys after the liberation of Ischia. On the Vomero hill, the charter-house of San Martino. (Photo Scala.)

the Savonnerie, rich covers from the rue Saint-Victor, hats exported to Spain and the East and West Indies, silk fabrics, taffetas, galloons and ribbons, ecclesiastical habits, mirrors (their silvering strips come from Saint-Gobain), gold work, printing.[101]

The same thing happened in Madrid, Berlin and Naples. Berlin counted 141,283 inhabitants in 1783, including a garrison of 33,088 people (soldiers and families), 13,000 bureaucrats (officials and families), and 10,074 servants; with the addition of Frederick II's court that made 56,000 state 'employees'.[102] All in all, an unhealthy situation. Naples is worth looking at in greater detail.

Naples, from the Royal Palace to the Mercato

Both sordid and beautiful, abjectly poor and very rich, certainly gay and lively, Naples counted 400,000, probably 500,000 inhabitants on the eve of the French Revolution. It was the fourth town in Europe, coming equal with Madrid after London, Paris and Istanbul. A major breakthrough after 1695 extended it in the direction of Borgo di Chiaja, facing the second bay of Naples (the first being Marinella). Only the rich benefited, as authorization to build outside the walls, granted in 1717, almost exclusively concerned them.

As for the poor, their district stretched out from the vast Largo del Castello, where the burlesque quarrels over the free distribution of victuals took place, to the Mercato, their fief, facing the Paludi plain that began outside the ramparts. They were so crowded that their life encroached and overflowed on to the streets. As today, washing was strung out to dry between the windows. 'The majority of beggars do not have houses; they find nocturnal asylum in a few caves, stables or ruined houses, or (not very different from the last) in houses run by one of their number, with a lantern and a little straw as their sole equipment, entry being obtained in exchange for a *grano* [a small Neapolitan coin] or slightly more, per night.' 'They are to be seen there,' continued the Prince of Strongoli (1783), 'lying like filthy animals, with no distinction of age or sex; all the ugliness and all the offspring which result from this can be imagined.'[103] These ragged poor numbered at the lowest estimate 100,000 people at the end of the century. 'They proliferate, without families, having no relationship with the state except through the gallows and living in such chaos that only God could get his bearings among them.'[104] During the long famine of 1763-4 people died in the streets.

The fault lay in their excessive numbers. Naples drew them but could not feed them all. They barely survived and some not even that. Next to them an undeveloped petty-bourgeoisie of half starved artisans scraped a bare living. The great Giovanni Battista Vico (1668-1741), one of the last universal minds of the West capable of speaking *de omni re scibili*, was paid a hundred ducats a year as professor at the University of Naples and only managed to live by private lessons, condemned 'to go up and down other people's staircases'.[105]

Above this totally deprived mass let us imagine a super-society of courtiers, great landed nobility, high-ranking ecclesiastics, obstructive officials, judges, advocates, and litigants. One of the foulest areas of the town, the Castel Capuaro, was situated in the legal district. It contained the *Vicaria*, a sort of Parliament of Naples where justice was bought and sold and 'where pick-pockets lie in wait for pockets and purses'. How was it, asked a rational Frenchman, that the social structure remained standing when it was 'laden with an excessive population, numerous beggars, a prodigious body of servants, considerable secular and regular clergy, a military force of over 20,000 men, a multitude of nobles, and an army of 30,000 lawyers'?[106]

'*Nobilis Neapolitana*': a noble Neapolitan lady, invisible behind the curtains of her sedan-chair (1594). (Photo B.N.)

But the system held as it always had, as it held elsewhere and at small cost. In the first place, these privileged people did not always receive rich livings. A little money was enough to move a man into the ranks of the nobles. 'Our former butcher no longer practises his trade except through his assistants since becoming a duke,'[107] meaning since he bought a title to the nobility. But we are not forced to take Président de Brosses literally. Above all, thanks to State, Church, nobility and goods, the town attracted all the surplus from the Kingdom of Naples, where there were many peasants, shepherds, sailors, miners, craftsmen and carriers inured to hardship. The town had always fed on this hardship outside its boundaries since Frederick II, the Angevins and the Spaniards. The Church – which the historian Giannone attacked in his weighty pamphlet, *Istoria civile del Regno di Napoli* in 1723 – owned at the lowest estimate two-thirds of the landed property in the kingdom, the nobility two-ninths. This was what restored the balance of Naples. It is true that only one-ninth was left to the *gente piu bassa di campagna*.[108]

When Ferdinand, King of Naples, and his wife Maria-Carolina visited Grand Duke Leopold and 'Enlightened' Tuscany in 1785, the unhappy King of Naples, more *lazzarone* than enlightened prince, grew irritated by the lessons set before him and the reforms held up for his admiration.'Really,' he said one day to his brother-in-law, Grand Duke Leopold, 'I cannot understand what use all your science is to you; you read incessantly, your people do as you do, and your towns, your capital, your court, everything here is dismal and gloomy. As for me, I know nothing, and my people are still the liveliest people of all.'[109] But then his capital city, Naples, could draw on the whole Kingdom of Naples, together with Sicily. In comparison little Tuscany could be held in the palm of the hand.

St Petersburg in 1790

St Petersburg, a new town built at the Tsar's wishes, marvellously demonstrates the anomalies, the almost monstrous structural disequilibrium of the large towns of the early modern world. And we have the advantage of possessing a good guide to the town and its neighbourhood in 1790, dedicated by its author, the German Johann Gottlieb Georgi, to the Empress Catherine II.[110]

There were certainly few more unfavourable and unpromising sites than the one where, on 16 May 1703, Peter the Great laid the first stone of what would be the famous Peter and Paul fortress. It required his unwavering will power for the town to rise up in this setting of islands and land barely above water level, on the banks of the Neva and its four branches (large and small Neva, large and small Nevska). The ground only rose slightly in the east towards the arsenal and the monastery of Alexander Nevsky, while it was so low in the west that flooding was inevitable there. When the river reached a dangerous level, a series of customary signals was set off: cannon shots, white flags in the daytime, lanterns permanently lit on the Admiralty Tower at night, bells ringing incessantly. The alarm was given but the danger was not overcome. In 1715 and again in 1775, the whole town was flooded. The threat was present every year. The town had, as it were, to rise above this mortal peril menacing it at ground level. Naturally the moment one began to dig one hit water at two feet, or at seven feet at the very most, so that it was impossible to have cellars under the houses. Despite their price, stone foundations were generally imperative even for wooden buildings, in view of the speed with which planks rotted in the damp ground. Canals also had to be dug across the whole town and edged with fascines, banks of granite blocks – as were the Moika and the Fontanka, used by boats bringing wood and food supplies.

Streets and squares in their turn had to be raised from two feet to five feet according to their location by unbelievable digging operations, and by building brick or stone masonry and arches to carry the paved roadway and at the same time allow water to flow off the road into the Neva. This prodigious task was systematically undertaken after 1770, starting with the 'fine districts' of the

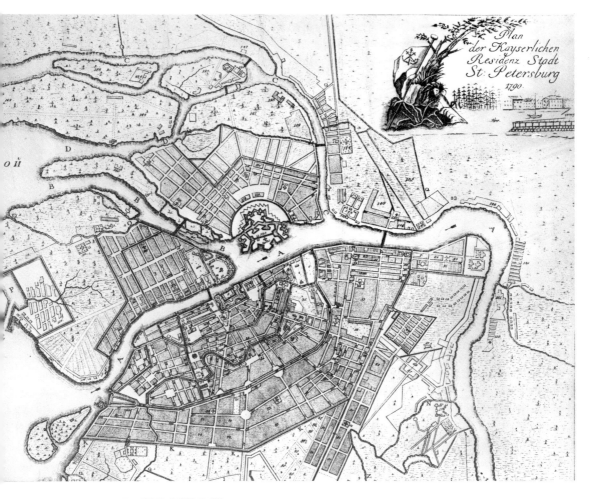

28 PLAN OF ST PETERSBURG IN 1790
A and B the two branches of the Neva; C and D those of the Nevska. In the centre, on the north bank of the Neva is the Peter and Paul fortress. To the west the large Vassili island, connected to the Admiralty by the bridge of boats. From the Admiralty on the south side of the Neva radiate the three great thoroughfares (the most eastern of which is the Nevsky Prospect). The extension of the city to the south is marked by the three semi-circular canals.

Admiralty on the banks of the larger Neva, by Lieutenant-General von Bauer, on Catherine II's orders, and at the imperial treasury's expense.

Urbanization was therefore slow and expensive. The outline of streets and squares had to be revised, inopportune proliferation of houses restricted, and public buildings and churches, even the remote monastery of Alexander Nevsky, rebuilt in stone. Many houses were also rebuilt in stone, although wood long remained the most common material. It had valuable advantages: comparative warmth inside, lack of dampness, cheapness and speed of construction. Walls were not made of squared beams as in Stockholm, but of undressed trunks. Only the façade was sometimes covered with planks: it could then be decorated with cornices and touched up in colour. A final advantage of these wooden houses was that they could be altered easily and even transported whole from one point in the town to another. The ground floor in the more expensive stone houses was often covered with granite slabs and used as a cellar, or if necessary as poor accommodation. The upper rooms were preferred, so that these houses had at least one, often two and sometimes (though rarely) three upper storeys.

St Petersburg was therefore a perpetually busy building site. Boats loaded with limestone, stone, marble, (from Ladoga or the Wiborg coast) and blocks of granite arrived via the Neva. Pine beams were floated there and in the process, it was repeatedly said, lost their intrinsic qualities. The workmen, all peasants from the northern provinces, masons or carpenters, were the most curious sight. The carpenters or *plotnidki* – which literally means wooden raft peasants (German translates the word as *Flossbauer*) – had hardly any tools except an axe. Labourers, carpenters and masons all arrived to look for work at the appropriate season. A few weeks were all that were needed for 'the foundations of a stone house to spring up' on a hitherto empty square, 'with its walls seeming to grow before one's eyes and all covered with workmen, while the mud huts where they lived stood round in the likeness of a veritable village'.

Of course the site of St Petersburg also had advantages, if only the amenities and the unparalleled beauty of its river, wider than the Seine and with livelier water movements than the Thames itself. It offered one of the most beautiful town and river views in the world between Peter and Paul, Vassiliostrov (the island of Vassili) and the Admiralty. The Neva had its boats and barges; it met the sea at Kronstadt, and after the island of Vassili, where the merchant district, stock exchange and customs were, became a very active maritime port. St Petersburg therefore really was the window opened on the West, the town Peter the Great wanted to incorporate into the violent life of his nation. In addition the Neva supplied the town with drinking water, said to be impeccable.

In winter it was icebound, transformed into a route for sledges and a meeting place for popular merrymaking. At Carnival – in 'butter' week – artificial mounds of ice were erected on the river with frameworks of planks and boards. Light sledges set off from the tops of these structures down a long clear track which the driver negotiated at a crazy speed, 'enough to knock the breath out of him'. Similar tracks were set up elsewhere, in the parks or courtyards of houses but those on the Neva, supervised by the police, brought a fabulous gathering of people. The whole town went along to watch

The river and its various branches were only crossed by bridges of boats. Two of these straddled the large Neva. The largest led to the commercial island of Vassili, from near the square next to the Admiralty (where the lifelike and grandiose statue of Peter the Great by, or rather in the style of, Falconnet still stands). It consisted of twenty-one boats, secured at both ends by loaded and firmly anchored barges. Lift-bridges between the boats let ships go through. This bridge used to be hauled in like all the others at the beginning of every autumn, but after 1779 it was left frozen in the ice. It broke up when the ice melted and the authorities waited until the water was entirely clear to reassemble it.

Its founder had envisaged the town's developing simultaneously south and north of the river, starting from Peter and Paul. But development took place asymmetrically: slowly on the right bank and fairly rapidly on the left bank of the Neva. The Admiralty quarters and Peter the Great Square on the privileged bank formed the heart of the town as far as the Moika canal, the last canal in the south to be fitted with stone quays. It was the least spacious district but the richest, the most beautiful, and the only one where stone houses (not counting the odd imperial building) were the general rule (thirty public buildings and 221 private houses, many of which were palaces). It contained the famous streets of the Great and Small Million, the magnificent road along the side of the Neva, the beginning of the Nevsky Prospect, the Admiralty, the Winter Palace and its immense square, the Hermitage Gallery, the Senate, and the marble church of St Isaac, which took such a long time to build, in the square of the same name (1819–58).[111]

Deliberate and conscious zoning separated rich from poor, pushing industries and activities that might have led to congestion – the carrying trade, for example – back towards the periphery. The carriers had a wretched town of their own beyond the Ligovich Canal, cut by empty spaces and with a livestock market. The gun foundry (a wooden building built in 1713, reconstructed in stone in 1733) was east of the Admiralty and in the vicinity of the Arsenal, erected by Prince Orlov between 1770 and 1778. The town also had its mint, its mills along the Neva, up- and downstream from the town, and its artisans, who were fed better than in Sweden or Germany, being entitled to coffee and vodka every day before their meals. It manufactured excellent cloth in the Dutch style, and a factory at Kasinka near by on the pattern of the Gobelins turned out very beautiful tapestries. The most controversial innovation was the grouping of retail shops into vast markets as in Moscow. There had been one such market on 'Petersburg-island' since 1713 (near Peter and Paul) and later another near the Admiralty. Following the fire which destroyed it in 1736 the market was moved to both sides of the 'Great Prospect' in 1784. These concentrations forced the people of St Petersburg to travel long distances. But the aim was achieved: the official and residential character of the beautiful districts was preserved

Obviously, certain unharmonious features could not be avoided. A sordid hut occasionally stood next to a palace; market gardens (to which peasants from Rostov flocked) next door to parks where military music was played on public holidays. Things could not have been otherwise in a town that was growing rapidly and favoured by high prices, high employment and high subsidies from a government that wanted to get things done. St Petersburg had 74,273 inhabitants in 1750; 192,486 in 1784; 217,948 in 1789. Sailors, soldiers and cadets (plus their families) accounted for 55,621 of the town's population in 1789, or over a quarter of the total. This artificial aspect of the agglomeration was strongly marked in the enormous difference between numbers of male and female inhabitants (148,520 males compared with 69,428 females). St Petersburg was a town of garrisons, servants and young men. If the figures for baptisms and deaths are to be believed, the town had an excess of births from time to time, but the figures are incomplete and risk being misleading. In any case the predominance of deaths between the ages of twenty and twenty-five indicate that the capital imported young people on a large scale and that they often paid their tribute to the climate, the fevers and tuberculosis.

The wave of immigrants brought all kinds of people to the city: officials and nobles hard pressed for promotion, younger sons of families, officers, sailors, soldiers, technicians, professors, artists, entertainers, cooks, foreign tutors, governesses and most of all peasants, who flocked in from the poor countryside surrounding the town. They came as hauliers and food retailers (they were even accused – and what an irony – of being responsible for the high market prices). In winter they came as ice-breakers on the Neva: the blocks were cut into pieces (this was the speciality of Finnish peasants) and used to supply the ice-houses to be found on the ground floor of every large house. Or else they were snow- and ice-shovellers at half a rouble a day: they were never done with clearing the approaches to the houses of the rich. Or they might be sledge drivers; they drove customers anywhere they wanted in the enormous city for one or two kopeks and stood at the crossroads where the drivers of the high carrioles had stood the summer before. The Finnish women were chambermaids or cooks. They adapted themselves to their tasks well and sometimes made a good match.

'These inhabitants ... composed of so many different nations ... preserved their individual ways of life,' and beliefs. Greek churches stood next to Protestant places of worship and the *raskolniki* churches. 'There is no town in the world,' continues our informant (1765), 'where more or less every inhabitant speaks such a large number of languages. Even the lowest servant speaks Russian, German and Finnish, and amongst people who have had some education one often meets some who speak eight or nine languages ... which they sometimes mix up to quite pleasing effect.'[112]

Indeed this mixture was the basis of St Petersburg's originality. In 1790 J.G. Georgi found himself wondering if the inhabitants of St Petersburg had a character of their own. He acknowledged their taste for novelty, change, titles, comfort, luxury and expenditure – in other words the tastes of men living in a capital, modelled on those of the court. The court set the tone by its requirements and its celebrations, which were as much occasions for general merrymaking, with magnificent illuminations burning at the Admiralty building, the official palaces and the houses of the rich.

'*Droshky* of a citizen of St Petersburg', an eighteenth-century engraving. Bibliothèque Nationale, Paris. (Viollet collection.)

Such an enormous town in the heart of a poor region raised endless problems of supply. Nothing could indeed have been simpler than bringing live fish from Lakes Ladoga and Onega in barges full of water. But sheep and cattle came to the slaughterhouses from the Ukraine and Astrakhan, the Don and the Volga – from 2000 versts away, even from Turkey; and there were other supplies to match. A chronic deficit had to met by the imperial treasury and the enormous incomes of the nobles. All the money of the empire flowed into the princely palaces and wealthy houses, where there were abundant tapestries, valuable furniture, carved and gilded panelling and ceilings painted in the 'classical' style. As in Paris and London, houses were divided into numerous individual rooms, with a steadily increasing domestic staff here too.

The most characteristic sight was perhaps the noisy passage of carriages and the horses in the streets of the town and the surrounding countryside. These were indispensable in a town of enormous proportions, with muddy streets and only short periods of daylight once winter had set in. On this count an imperial order had specified the rights of each person: only generals in chief or those of equivalent rank could harness six horses to their carriage plus two leading horsemen apart from the coachmen. At the lower end of the scale were lieutenants and the bourgeoisie, who had the right to two horses, and artisans or tradesmen who had to be satisfied with one. A series of prohibitions also regulated servants' liveries according to their masters' status. At imperial receptions, carriages made a small extra turn at the arrival point, which enabled everyone to see and be seen. Thus no one dared to have only a hired carriage, horses with inferior trappings or a coachman dressed in his peasant costume. A final detail: when courtiers were invited to the castle of Peterhof, situated like Versailles to the west and outside the city, it was said that not a single horse was left in St Petersburg.

Penultimate journey: Peking

We could multiply our journeys and still change none of our conclusions. The luxury of the capitals had always to be borne on the shoulders of others. Not one of them could have existed from the work of its own hands. Sixtus V (1585-90), a stubborn peasant, misunderstood contemporary Rome. He wanted to make it 'work' and plant industries there, a project which the facts rejected without the need for human intervention.[113] Sébastien Mercier and a few others dreamt of transforming Paris into a seaport in order to attract hitherto unknown activies there. Even if it had been possible to re-create Paris in the image of London, then the greatest port in the world, it would still have remained a parasitical town.

The same was true of all capitals, all the towns where the bright lights and excesses of civilization, taste and leisure glittered: Madrid or Lisbon, Rome or Venice, bent on surviving in its past greatness, or Vienna, at the peak of European elegance during the seventeenth and eighteenth centuries. And we could add to the list Mexico City and Lima, or Rio de Janeiro, capital of Brazil since 1763, which grew incessantly, becoming a handsome human creation within an already sumptous natural setting, so that travellers failed to recognize it from one year to the next. Or Delhi where the splendour of the Great Mogul survived; Batavia where precocious Dutch colonialism put forth its most beautiful and already poisonous flowers.

What finer example though than Peking, capital of the Manchu emperors: a city standing at the gates of the north and enduring the cruel Siberian cold – diabolical wind, snow and ice – for six months of the year? An enormous population (certainly two, perhaps three million) somehow or other made the best of the climate which no one could have borne without the plentiful supplies of rock coal 'which lasts and keeps the fire in five or six times longer than charcoal'.[114] Furs were absolutely essential on winter days. Father de Magaillans, whose book only appeared in 1688, once saw as many as four thousand mandarins gathered in the royal chamber of the Palace swathed 'from head to toe in extraordinarily expensive sables'. The rich literally covered themselves in furs, lining their boots, saddles, chairs and tents with them. The less wealthy made

A street in Peking, decorated for the passage of the Emperor. First quarter of eighteenth century. Bibliothèque Nationale, Estampes.

do with lambskin, the poor with sheepskin.[115] When winter came, all the women 'wear caps and coifs, whether they go out in a chair or on a horse: and they are quite right to do so', says Gemelli Careri, 'because I found the cold intolerable despite my fur-lined robe'. 'Too violent for me,' he added. 'I resolved to leave this town (November 19, 1697).'[116] 'The winter is so cold,' noted a Jesuit father a century later (1777), 'that one cannot open a window on the north side, and the ice stays a foot-and-a-half thick for over three months.'[117] The imperial canal which ensured supplies to the town was closed by ice from November to March.

In 1752, the emperor K'ien Long organized a triumphal entry into Peking to celebrate his mother's sixtieth birthday. Everything had been arranged for the arrival of sumptuous barges by river and canal, but an early cold spell interfered with the celebrations. Thousands of servants vainly beat the water to prevent it from freezing and took out the pieces of ice that formed. The emperor and his suite had to 'replace the barges by sledges.'[118]

Peking consisted of two towns, the old and the new, and many suburbs (theoretically one in front of each of its gates, the most developed being in the west where most of the imperial roads reached the town). It spread out in the middle of a vast low-lying plain, whipped by winds and, worse still, exposed to the flooding of the nearby rivers, the Pei Ho and its tributaries. When their water was running high they could break their banks, change course, and move kilometres away from their original channels.

The new town in the south was shaped like a slightly imperfect rectangle and joined to the old town on its wide northern side. The old town was a regular square, with smaller sides than the adjacent rectangle. The square was the old city of the Mings with the Imperial Palace in the centre. During the conquest of 1644 the palace suffered considerable damage which long remained visible; it was restored by the conqueror only after some time. Application had to be made to distant southern markets, particularly to replace certain enormous beams, with the inevitable delays and disappointments.

The old town had already proved inadequate to house the growing population of the capital during the Ming period, so that the rectangular town in the south was built well before the 1644 conquest. 'It had clay walls in 1524, then brick walls and gates after 1564.' But after his conquest the conqueror kept the old town for himself, making it the Tartar town, and the Chinese were pushed down to the southern town.

Both old and new towns were built on a chequerboard plan, and were of fairly late date, as is indicated by the unaccustomed width of the streets, particularly those running from south to north. In general those running east and west were narrower. Every street had a name:

> Such as the street of the King's Parents, the street of the White Tower, the Iron Lions, the Dry Fish, Spirits and so on. A book is on sale which simply gives the names and positions of the streets and this is used by the valets who accompany the mandarins on their visits and to their tribunals

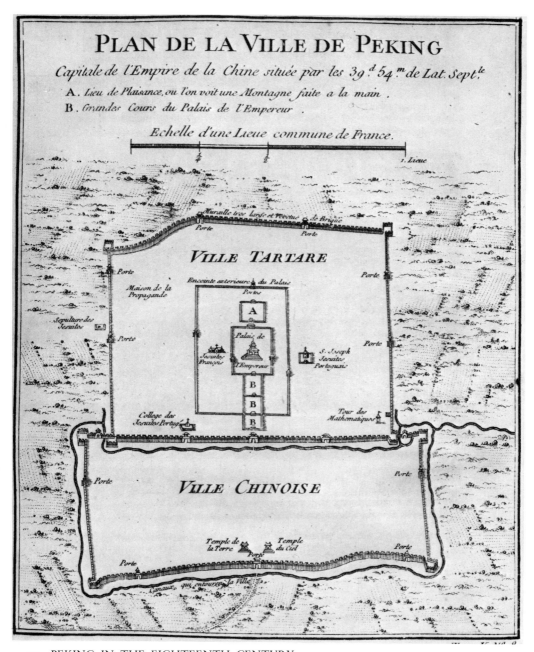

29 PEKING IN THE EIGHTEENTH CENTURY
A schematic plan showing the disposition of the three cities (the old, the new and the imperial) A: the artificial mound of the palace; B: the ceremonial courtyards. (From *L'Histoire générale des voyages*, vol. V, Paris, 1748.)

and who carry their presents, their letters and their orders to various places in the town.... The most beautiful of all these streets [although laid out from east to west] is the one called *Cham gan kiai*, that is to say the street of Perpetual Repose ... flanked on the northern side by the walls of the King's Palace and on the southern side by various tribunals and the palaces of great nobles. It is so vast that it is over thirty *toises* [almost sixty metres] wide and so famous that scholars use it to indicate the whole town in their writings, taking the part for the whole; so to say that someone is in the Street of Perpetual Repose is the same as saying that he is in Peking.[119]

These wide, airy streets were full of people. 'The multitude of people in this town is so great,' explained Father de Magaillans, 'that I cannot even attempt to give any idea of their number. All the streets of the old and new towns are full of them, the small as much as the large, and those in the centre as much as those leading to the fringes; the crowd is so large everywhere that it is only comparable to the Fairs and Processions in our Europe.'[120] In 1735 Father du Halde noted:

> [the] innumerable multitude of people who fill these streets and the congestion caused by the surprising quantity of horses, mules, asses, camels, carts, waggons and chairs, not counting various groups, one hundred or two hundred strong, who gather here and there to listen to fortune-tellers, conjurors, singers and others reading or telling some tale conducive to laughter or pleasure, or even to charlatans who distribute their remedies and demonstrate the wonderful effects thereof. People who are not of the common run would be stopped every moment if they were not preceded by a horseman who pushes back the crowd, warning them to make way.[121]

A Spaniard found no better way of conveying the congestion of the Chinese streets (1577) than to say: 'Throw a grain of corn and it will not fall to the ground.'[122] 'Tradesmen with their tools, searching for employment, pedlars offering their wares for sale were everywhere to be seen,' noted an English traveller two centuries later.[123] The multitude was obviously explained by the increased population figure in 1793. Peking at that time did not have anything like the area of London, but it was two or three times more populous.

Furthermore the houses, even those of the rich, were low. If – as they often did – they had five or six apartments, they were not 'one on top of the other as in Europe, but one after another and separated from the others by a large courtyard'.[124] Thus one should not imagine the magnificent *Cham gan Kiai* as a series of arrogant façades facing the imperial palace. In the first place it would have been unseemly to display such luxury opposite the emperor's house. And then it was customary for each of these individual palaces to have only one large gate on to the street, flanked by two fairly low buildings occupied by servants, tradesmen and workmen. The streets were thus lined with booths and shops, with tall poles, often decorated with cloth streamers, holding up their signboards. The tall houses of the nobles were away from the street, which was entirely devoted to trade and artisans' shops.

The shops of Peking: they ran in almost uninterrupted strings, concealing dwelling-houses, which were always low, without a window on the street and arranged around inner courtyards and gardens. Cabinet des Estampes. (Photo B.N.)

> This custom serves public convenience, [Father de Magaillans notes] because a good part of the streets in our towns [in Europe] are lined with the houses of wealthy people; and one is thus obliged to go a very long way to the market or the ports to obtain necessary articles, while in Peking – and it is the same in all the other towns of China – everything one could want to buy for maintenance, subsistence and even for pleasure, is to be found at one's doorstep, because these small houses are shops, taverns or stalls.[125]

The sight was the same in all Chinese towns. The same scenes appear on any eighteenth-century picture showing the line of low shops along a street in Nanking, or the houses opening on to their courtyards in Tien Tsin, or on some precious twelfth-century scroll — the same taverns with benches, the same shops, the same carriers, the same wheelbarrows with sails and the same drivers, and the same teams of oxen. Above all they show a hectic form of life where one man only grudgingly made way for another, everyone elbowing his way, subsisting by dint of work, skill and sobriety. They lived on nothing, and 'have wonderful inventions for subsisting'.

> However cheap and useless a thing may seem, it has its use, and advantage is taken of it. For example there are over a thousand families in the town of Peking alone [about 1656] who have no other trade to live by except selling matches and wicks to light fires. There are at least as many who live on nothing else but collecting from the sweepings in the streets rags of silk fabric and cotton and hempen cloth, pieces of paper and other similar things, which they wash and clean and then sell to others who use them for various purposes and profit from it.[126]

Father de Las Cortes (1626) likewise saw porters in Cantonese China who supplemented their work by cultivating a tiny garden. And sellers of herb soup were typical characters in every Chinese street. The proverb ran: 'Nothing is thrown away in the kingdom of China.' All these examples show the extent of latent omnipresent poverty. The spectacular luxury of the emperor, the great men, and the mandarins does not seem part of this lowly world.

Travellers have left us many detailed descriptions of the Imperial Palace, a city apart in the old town. It was built on the site of the Palace of the Yuans (the Mongols) and had almost inherited the sumptuousness of the Mings, although the ruins of 1644 had had to be rebuilt. Two surrounding walls, one within the other, both sizeable, very high and 'in the shape of a long square', separated it from the old town. The outside wall was 'coated inside and out with cement or red lime and covered with a small roof made of bricks glazed a golden yellow colour'. The inside wall was made 'of large bricks all of equal size and ornamented with regular battlements'; a long deep moat filled with water and 'inhabited by excellent fish' stood in front of it. Between the two walls were palaces for different purposes, a river with bridges and a rather large artificial lake to the west.[127]

The heart of the palace lay behind the second wall. This was the forbidden city, the Yellow City where the Emperor lived protected by his guards, by checkpoints at the gates, protocol, ramparts, moats and the vast corner-pavilions with twisted roofs, the *Kiao leou*. Every building, every gate and every bridge had its own name and, as it were, its own customs and practices. The forbidden city measured 1 kilometre by 780 metres. But it is easier to describe the empty, dilapidated rooms after 1900, when European curiosity could draw up inventories at its leisure, than the activity they once contained, which one suspects to have been enormous. The whole town converged on this source of power and bounty.

A measure of its extent is given by the endless detailed accounts of the emperor's income, as much in money as in kind (note the double heading). We can hardly imagine what could have been represented by the 'eighteen million six hundred thousand silver *écus*' to which the principal of the imperial income in money had risen in about 1669. Additional income (still in money) was provided by confiscations, indirect taxes and the domains of the crown or empress. Most tangible and most curious were the mass of dues in kind which filled the vast palace storehouses to bursting point – for example 43,328,134 'sacks of rice and corn', over a million loaves of salt, considerable quantities of vermilion, varnish, dried fruit, pieces of silk, light silks, raw silk, velvets, satin, damask, cotton or hempen cloth, bags of beans (for the emperor's horses), innumerable bales of straw, live animals, game, oil, butter, spices, precious wines, and fruits of all kinds.[128]

Father de Magaillans was deeply impressed by this prodigious mass of products and the piles of gold and silver platters filled with food and perched on top of each other at imperial feasts. Such a feast was held on 9 December 1669 in honour of the burial of Father Jean Adam,[129] a Jesuit father who together with Father Verbiest succeeded in raising an enormous bell to the top of one of the towers of the palace 'to the great astonishment of the court' in 1661. The bell in question was larger than the bell of Erfurt which (probably wrongly) had the reputation of being the largest and heaviest bell in Europe, even in the world. Positioning this Chinese bell necessitated the construction of a machine and the labour of thousands of arms. The bell was struck by the sentinels at regular intervals during the night to indicate the passing hours. A sentinel at the top of another tower struck an enormous copper drum in reply. The bell had no tongue and was struck with a hammer to produce 'such a pleasant and harmonious tone that it seemed to come much less from a bell than from some musical instrument'.[130] Time was measured in China in those days by burning small sticks or wicks made of a certain type of compressed sawdust with a constant rate of combustion. The westerner justifiably proud of his clocks was to have only limited admiration (unlike Father de Magaillans) for this 'invention worthy of the marvellous industry of the [Chinese] nation'.[131]

The trouble is that we know more about these great palace scenes than about the fish market, where the fish were brought live in tanks of water, or the game markets where a traveller might glimpse a prodigious quantity of roe deer, pheasants and partridges. In the sources, the unusual conceals the everyday.

London from Elizabeth I to George III

We come back from these far-off shores and return to Europe, where the example of London will enable us to conclude the chapter and, with it, the present volume.[132] Everything about this prodigious urban development is known or knowable.

In Elizabeth's reign observers already regarded London as an exceptional world. For Thomas Dekker it was 'the Queene of Cities', made incomparably more beautiful by its winding river than Venice itself judged by the marvellous view of the Grand Canal (a very paltry sight compared with what London could offer).[133] Samuel Johnson (20 September 1777) was even more lyrical: 'when a man is tired of London, he is tired of life; for there is in London all that life can afford.'[134]

The royal government shared these illusions, but it was none the less in constant fear of the enormous capital. In its eyes London was a monster whose unhealthy growth had to be limited at all costs. What alarmed the influential and propertied classes was the invasion by the poor and the proliferation of hovels and vermin that meant a threat to the whole population, including the rich. 'And so a danger to the Queen's own life and the spreading of mortality of the whole nation,' wrote Stow, who feared for the health of Queen Elizabeth and the whole population.[135] The first prohibition on new building (with exceptions in favour of the rich) appeared in 1580. Others followed in 1593, 1607 and 1625. The result was to encourage the dividing-up of existing houses and secret construction-work in poor brick in the courtyards of old houses, away from the street and even from minor alleys. What this led to was a whole clandestine proliferation of hovels and shanties on land of doubtful ownership. It was no great loss if one or other of these buildings fell victim to the law. Everybody therefore tried his luck, and networks or rather labyrinths of lanes and alleys, houses with double, triple, even quadruple entrances and exits, grew up as a result. In 1732, London was said to have 5099 streets, lanes and squares, and 95,968 houses. Consequently the rising tide of the London population was neither stemmed nor stopped. The town probably had some 93,000 inhabitants in 1563; 123,000 in 1580; 152,000 in 1593-5; 317,000 in 1632; 700,000 in 1700; and 860,000 at the end of the eighteenth century. It was then the largest town in Europe. Only Paris could compare.

London depended on its river. The town was shaped 'like a half moon' because of it. London Bridge, which joined the city to the suburb of Southwark and was the only bridge over the river (300 metres from the present bridge) was the outstanding feature of the landscape. The tide carried the ships up and down. The pool, the basin, the port of London, was therefore situated downstream from the bridge, with its quays, its wharves and the often mentioned forest of masts (not without reason: 13,444 ships in 1798). Depending on the load to be discharged, these sailing ships made their way to St Katharine's quay, frequented by coal lighters from Newcastle, or to Billingsgate quay if they carried fresh fish or were employed in the regular service from Billingsgate to Gravesend. Schooners, wherries, rowing boats with awnings, ferry boats and barges supplied transport from one bank of the river to the other and from sea-going boats to the appropriate quays – an essential service when these quays were situated upstream from the port. Vintry wharf, which received casks of wine from the Rhine, France, Spain, Portugal and the Canaries, was one such case. It was not far from the Steelyard (or Stilliard), which was the headquarters of the Hanseatic League until 1597 and 'reserved for tasting Rhine wines since the expulsion of foreign merchants'. A character in one of Thomas Dekker's plays says, 'I come to entreat you to meet him this afternoon at the Rhenish Wine house in the Stilliard.'[136]

The utilization of the river tended to extend farther and farther downstream towards the sea, particularly as the docks – basins inside the bends of the river – were not yet dug, except one belonging to the East India Company (1656), Brunswick Dock. A second, Greenland Dock, was built in 1696-1700, for the whalers. But the really big docks date from the last years of the eighteenth century. A first impression of the commercial port could be gained either at Billingsgate or at the Tower of London wharf, or better still at that essential barrier, the Customs House, burnt down in 1666 but at once reconstructed by Charles II in 1668. In fact the scene extended as far as Ratcliff, 'infamous rendezvous of prostitutes and robbers', as far as Limehouse, with its lime kilns and tanneries, down to Blackwall, where the pleasure of looking at the anchored boats was balanced by 'the very strong smell of tar'. East London – naval, artisan and slightly dishonest – was not a pleasant sight, and its stench was only too real.

A poverty-stricken population saw the riches from the moored ships dangled before their eyes, a dreadful temptation. In 1798: 'The immense depredations committed on every species of commercial Property in the River Thames, but particularly on West India produce, had long been felt as a grievance of the greatest magnitude.' The 'river pirates' who operated in organized bands, stealing an anchor or a rope when the opportunity offered, had not yet become the most dangerous of these thieves. This role was reserved for the night plunderers, the watermen and lightermen, the 'mudlarks', who combed the river ostensibly searching for old ropes, old iron, or pieces of lost coal, and finally, at the end of the line, the receivers.[137]

All these moralizing indictments taken from a *Treatise on the Police* (1797) convey very precisely the atmosphere of the dubious world of the pool – a vast kingdom of water, wood, sails, tar and menial labour on the margin of the life of the capital but linked to it by routes, of which the ordinary Londoner generally saw only one end.

Before Westminster Bridge was built (it was finished in 1750) there was, as we have seen, only one bridge across the Thames, and this (London Bridge) was lined with shops and more like a busy street than a thoroughfare. It is true that it led only to a poor suburb, Southwark, which contained a few taverns, five prisons of ominous renown, a few theatres (where Shakespeare's plays were first put on, but which did not survive the Civil War) and two or three circuses (the

The port of London, the Tower, in the background St Paul's Cathedral, end of eighteenth century. Paris, Bibliothèque Nationale. (Photo Giraudon.)

Bear Garden, the Paris Garden). The real city was on the north bank, slightly higher than the south, with its two prominent landmarks, St Paul's and the Tower of London. It extended like a 'bridgehead to the north'. For it was northwards that the whole network of roads, lanes and alleys ran that connected London to the counties and the rest of England. The major highways, all old Roman roads, ran towards Manchester, Oxford, Dunstable and Cambridge. They were the scene of a bustling throng of carts and carriages, before long stagecoaches and post-horses, by which the London traffic spilled out on to the road network.

Along the river bank (but turning its back on it) the heart of London was a concentrated area of houses, streets and squares, the City (160 hectares) marked by the old city walls. They stood on the site of the ancient Roman wall, but had disappeared by the twelfth century from the river front, where quays, wharves and floating landing-stages had breached the useless protection very early on. On the other hand they survived in a broken line, roughly forming an arc of a circle from Blackfriars Steps or Bridewell Dock up to the Tower of London. The line was cut by seven gates: Ludgate, Newgate, Aldersgate, Cripplegate, Moorgate, Bishopsgate and Aldgate. Opposite each of these gates, but far into the suburbs, there was a barrier marking the limits of the authority of London. The inner suburbs were 'liberties', districts (sometimes vast areas) outside the walls. Thus the barrier in front of Bishopsgate was situated on the edge of Smithfield, west of Holborn. Likewise, going out of Ludgate, one had to walk right down Fleet Street in order to reach Temple Bar, level with the Temple (of the knights-Templar) at the entrance to the Strand. Temple Bar was an ordinary wooden gate for a long time. This was the way in which London, or rather the City, overflowed its restricted boundaries even before Elizabeth's reign, reaching places in the countryside near by and joining itself to them by a series of roads lined with houses.

In the time of Elizabeth I and Shakespeare, the heart of the town beat inside the walls. Its centre was on the axis extending from London Bridge northwards to Bishopsgate. The east/west axis was marked out by a series of streets from Newgate in the west to Aldgate in the east. Under Elizabeth, the city crossroads was situated about 300 yards from Stocks Market, at the west end of Lombard Street.

The Royal Exchange was a couple of steps away on Cornhill. It had been founded by Thomas Gresham in 1566 and at first was called the 'Bourse' (*Byrsa Londinensis, vulgo the Royal Exchange* ran the caption on a seventeenth-century engraving) after the Antwerp Bourse. The name Royal Exchange had been granted to it by the authority of Elizabeth in 1570. According to witnesses it was a veritable Tower of Babel, especially around midday, when the merchants arrived to settle their business. However, the most elegant shops around its courtyards attracted a rich clientele. Both the Guildhall (more or less London's town hall) and the Bank of England's first home (it was housed in the Grocer's

London: Westminster in the time of the Stuarts. Engraving by Wenceslas Hollar, 1643. (Viollet collection.)

Hall, the grocers' warehouse, before occupying its sumptuous building in 1734) were not far from the Royal Exchange.

The intensity of London life also showed in its markets, West Smithfield for example, the vast area near the ramparts where horses and livestock were sold on Mondays and Fridays; or Billingsgate, the fresh fish market on the Thames; or the Leaden Hall towards the heart of the city, with its lead roof, an old corn warehouse where butchers' meat and leather were sold on a large scale. But it would be impossible to give a full account of these important centres or of the taverns, restaurants and theatres which were generally on the periphery and therefore reserved for the populace, or later, in the seventeenth century, the Coffee Houses which were so well patronized that the government was already thinking about prohibiting them. As for parts in which it was not safe to go alone, rumour, gossip and changes of fashion inclined people to suspect any street, not just the derelict monasteries where down-and-outs lurked like today's squatters. London always seems to have taken pleasure in speaking ill of herself.

But the City was never the only competitor on the banks of the Thames. By comparison Paris had a solitary fate. Westminster, upstream from London, was quite a different matter from Versailles (a late creation *ex nihilo*). It really was an old and living town. The Palace of Westminster, next to the Abbey, abandoned by Henry VIII, had become the seat of Parliament and the principal tribunals. It was the meeting place for lawyers and litigants. The monarchy had taken up its abode slightly farther away, in Whitehall, the palace beside the Thames.

Westminster was therefore a combination of Versailles and St Denis plus the Paris Parlement for good measure. I make the comparison to indicate the powerful attraction this second pole exercised in London's development. For example Fleet Street, which belonged to the City, was the district of jurists, solicitors and attorneys and law students. It looked obstinately westwards. Furthermore the Strand, which was outside the City and which ran at some distance from the Thames, to Westminster, became the district of the nobility. They established their houses there and soon another Exchange – a group of luxury shops – was opened there in 1609. Articles of fashion and wigs were the rage there from the reign of James I.

In the seventeenth and eighteenth centuries fresh expansion pushed the town in all directions at once. Appalling districts grew up on the outskirts – shanty towns with filthy huts, unsightly industries (notably innumerable brickworks), pig farms using household refuse for feed, accumulations of rubbish, and sordid streets. One such place was Whitechapel, where the wretched shoemakers worked. Elsewhere there were silk and wool weavers.

Fields disappeared from the immediate approaches to London except in the western districts where there were still stretches of green in Hyde Park and St James's Park and the gardens of wealthy houses. In Shakespeare's and Thomas Dekker's day, the town was still surrounded by green, open spaces, fields, trees and real villages where one could shoot duck and drop in at authentic country inns to drink beer and eat gingerbread (in Hogsdon) or the 'Islington White Pot', a sort of custard which earned the village of Islington a reputation. At that time 'the wind that blew in the outer districts of the capital', wrote Thomas Dekker's most recent biographer 'was not always heavy and impure: in the theatres in the south, north and north-west there was all the gaiety of Merry England, and also its subtle and vibrant imagination which penetrated the suburbs ... and the whole town'. Merry England, that is the England of the robust peasant centuries of the middle ages, was a romantic but not a false vision. But this happy relationship did not last.[138]

The ever-expanding entity of London completed its split into two parts. The movement had begun a long time before, but accelerated after the Great Fire in 1666 which practically destroyed the heart, almost the whole of the City. Before this disaster (1662) William Petty had already explained that London, where the prevailing winds blew from the west, was growing westwards to escape 'the fumes, steams, and stinks of the whole Easterly Pyle.... Now if it follow from hence that the Pallaces of the greatest men will remove Westward, it will also naturally follow that the dwellings of others who depend on them will creep after them. This we see in London where the Noblemen's ancient Houses are now become Halls for Companies, or turned into Tenements.'[139] A westward slide of the London rich thus took place. If the centre of the town was still in the vicinity of Cornhill in the seventeenth century, today it is not very far from Charing Cross, at the west end of the Strand. It has shifted a long way.

Meanwhile, the east and certain peripheral districts were becoming more and more proletarian. Poverty moved in and installed itself wherever it found room in the London world. The darkest pages of the story concern two categories of outcasts: the Irish and the Jews from central Europe.

Irish immigration began early from the most famished districts of Ireland. The exiles were peasants condemned to a bare living at home by the land system and more still by the demographic growth that shook the island until the catastrophes of 1846. They were used to living with the animals, sharing their hovels with them, and feeding on potatoes and a little milk. Inured to hardship, not jibbing at any task, they regularly found work every haymaking time as agricultural workers in the countryside around London. From there a few pushed on up to London and hung on there. They crowded into sordid slums in the parish of St Giles, their stronghold, to the north of the City, lived ten or twelve to one windowless room and accepted wages well below the general rate, as dockers, milk carriers, labourers at the brickworks, even lodging-house keepers. Brawls broke out amongst them on Sundays during drinking sessions. And they engaged in pitched battles with the competing English proletariat, who were only too glad to come to blows with the rivals they could not drive away.

The same tragedy was enacted with the Jews of central Europe, fleeing from the persecution in Bohemia in 1744 and Poland in 1772. There were as many as six thousand of them in England in 1734 and twenty thousand in London alone in 1800. Against them was unleashed the most ugly and widespread popular hostility. Attempts by the synagogues to stop this dangerous immigration, which came via Holland, proved useless. What could these wretched people do once they arrived? The Jews already settled helped them but could neither drive them away from the island nor support them. London guilds refused to admit them. They were therefore of necessity dealers in old clothes and old iron – shouting through the streets, sometimes driving an old cart – as well as rogues, filchers, counterfeiters and receivers. (Their late success as professional boxers, even as the inventors of a form of scientific boxing, did not restore their reputation, although Daniel Mendoza, a famous champion, had a following.)[140]

The London drama – its festering criminality, its underworld, its difficult biological life – can only really be comprehended from this worm's eye view of the poor. It is to be noted, however that the material situation on the whole improved, as it did in Paris, with the street paving, water supplies, building controls and advances in lighting the town.

What can we conclude? That London, alongside Paris, was a good example of what a capital of the *ancien régime* could be. A luxury that others had to pay for, a gathering of a few chosen souls, numerous servants and poor wretches, all linked however, by some collective destiny of the great agglomeration.

Did they have a measure of shared experience? There was, for example, the dreadful filth and stench of the streets, as familiar to the lord as to the common people. The generality created it, no doubt, but it rebounded on everybody.

Much of the countryside was probably relatively less dirty than the large towns until the middle of the eighteenth century; and the medieval city had been a pleasanter and cleaner place to live in, as Lewis Mumford suggests.[141] It did not sink under the weight of numbers, simultaneously bringing glory and poverty; it was wide open to the countryside and found its water locally inside its ramparts. The big city, on the other hand, could not cope with its ever-growing tasks or even ensure its elementary cleanliness. Security, the fight against fire and flood, supplies and public order took priority. And even if it had wanted to, it would have lacked the means. The worst material ignominies remained the general rule.

It was all the fault of number – huge numbers of people. But the big city drew them like a magnet. From its parasitical existence anyone could pick up a few crumbs, and find a niche. The very existence of a criminal community proved that there was always something to be gleaned from these privileged towns. Thieves inevitably gathered in the most luxurious of them. In 1798 Colquhoun was deploring that: 'The situation ... has changed materially since the dissolution of the ancient Government of France. The horde of sharpers and villains, who heretofore resorted to Paris from every part of Europe, will now consider London as their general and most productive theatre of action.' Paris was ruined and the rats were leaving the ship. 'The ignorance of the English language (a circumstance which formerly afforded us some protection) will no longer be a bar. ... At no period was it ever so generally understood by foreigners; or the French language so universally spoken, by at least the younger part of this country.'[142]

Urbanization, the sign of modern man

We need not follow in the footsteps of a sad conservative like Colquhoun. The great cities had their faults and their virtues. They created, let us repeat, the modern state, as much as they were created by it. National markets expanded under their impetus as did the nations themselves and they lay at the heart of capitalism and modern civilization which mingled its varied colours more in Europe every day. For the historian they are primarily an excellent yardstick of development in Europe and the other continents. Interpreted properly, their study leads to a general and unusually comprehensive view of the whole history of material life.

The essential problem is that of growth in the *ancien régime*. Within it, the cities were an example of deep-seated disequilibrium, asymmetrical growth, and irrational and unproductive investment on a nation-wide scale. Were the luxury and appetites of these enormous parasites responsible? This is what Jean-Jacques Rousseau says in *Emile*:

> It is the large towns that drain the state and create its weakness. The wealth they produce is an apparent and illusory wealth; a lot of money and

little effect. It is said that the town of Paris is worth a province to the king of France; I believe that it costs him several of them; that Paris is fed by the provinces in more than one respect and that most of their incomes pour into that town and stay there, without ever returning to the people or the king. It is inconceivable that in this century of calculators, not one has been able to see that France would be much more powerful if Paris were annihilated.[143]

Rousseau's comment is misconceived, but only in part. And the problem is at least stated. It is perhaps understandable that a man of the late eighteenth century who was observant of his time should ask himself whether these urban monsters did not foreshadow in the West the fate of the Roman Empire, choking on the dead weight of the city of Rome, or China weighed down by the inert mass of its great northern city, Peking. Such accumulations, he might think, would put an end to development. We now know that nothing of the sort happened. Sébastien Mercier, imagining the world in 2440,[144] made the mistake of assuming that this world of the future would not change its scale. He saw the future through the dimensions of the present he had before his eyes, France under Louis XVI, and did not suspect the immense possibilities still opening up for the monstrous agglomerations of his time.

The truth is that these densely populated cities, in part parasites, do not arise of their own volition. They are what society, the economy and politics allow or oblige them to be. They are a yardstick, a means of measurement. If they display ostentatious luxury, that is because society, the economy, and the political and cultural order are cast in this mould, and because capital and surplus wealth is poured into them, partly for want of anything better to do with them. Above all, a great city should never be judged in itself: it is located within the whole mass of urban systems, both animating them and being in turn determined by them. What was happening at the end of the eighteenth century was a progressive urbanization, which accelerated in the next century. In the changing appearance of cities like London and Paris was reflected the transition from one way of life and art of living to another. The world of the *ancien régime*, very largely a rural one, was slowly but surely collapsing and being wiped out. And great cities were not alone in bringing about the painful birth of the new order. It was often as spectators rather than participants that the capital cities watched the coming Industrial Revolution. Not London, but Manchester, Birmingham, Leeds, Glasgow and countless small mill-towns launched the new age. It was not even the capital accumulated by eighteenth-century patricians that was first invested in the new ventures. London did not take advantage of the industrial movement through her financial assets until about 1830. Paris for a moment looked as if she might welcome the new industry, but was quickly displaced by the establishment of the real industrial centres near the coalmines of the north, the water-power of Alsace, and the iron of Lorraine. This happened quite late in France. French visitors to England in the nineteenth century were horrified at the ugliness and concentration of industrialism of which they gave critical accounts: 'the last circle of hell' as Hippolyte Taine describes it. But did they realize that England in the throes of urbanization, packing the population into jerry-built towns where there was nothing to make them welcome, was a vision of the future of France and of all countries on the way to industrialization? Do visitors to the United States and Japan today always realize that they are looking at the future, near or distant, of their own countries?

Conclusion

Books, even history books, run away with their authors. This one has run on ahead of me. But what can one say about its waywardness, its whims, even its own logic, that will be serious and valid? Our children do as they please. And yet we are responsible for their actions.

Here and there I would have liked more explanation, justification and example. But books cannot be expanded to order, and to encompass all the many and varied constituents of material life would require close and systematic research, followed by much synthesis and analysis. All that is still lacking. What the text says calls for discussion, addition and extension. We have not talked about all the towns, nor all techniques, nor all the elementary facts of housing, clothing and eating.

A very old bell used to strike the hour in the little village in Lorraine where I grew up as a child: the village pond drove an old mill wheel; a stony path, as old as the world, plunged down like a torrent in front of my house; the house itself had been rebuilt in 1806, the year of Jena, and hemp used to be retted in the stream at the bottom of the meadows. I only have to think of these things and this book opens out for me afresh. Every reader, prompted by a chance memory or journey or a passage in a book, can do the same. A character in *Siegfried et le Limousin* riding out at dawn in the Germany of the 1920s feels as if he is still in the age of the Thirty Years War. A bend in a path or a street can take anyone back to the past in this way. Even in highly developed economies, the residual presence of the old material past makes itself felt. It is disappearing before our eyes, but slowly, and never in the same manner.

This book – the first of a three-volume work – does not claim to have depicted all material life throughout the whole complex world from the fifteenth to the eighteenth centuries. What it offers is an attempt to see all these scenes as a whole – from food to furniture, from techniques to towns – and inevitably to define what material life is and has been. Definition is difficult: I have sometimes consciously had to overstep the frontiers the better to identify them – in connection with the crucial phenomena of money and towns, for example. And this gives my undertaking its first purpose: if not to see everything, at least to locate everything, and on the requisite world scale.

Secondly, it was my intention, through a succession of landscapes which historians have after all only rarely depicted, and in which there is an obvious risk of descriptive incoherence, to try to classify, order and reduce this disparate material to the bold outlines and simplifications of historical explanation. This concern has informed the present volume and defined its scope, even if the programme has sometimes been sketched in rather than fully achieved – partly because a book intended for the general reader is a house from which the scaffolding should be removed. But also because we are here venturing, let me repeat, into unexplored territory: where the sources have to be individually discovered, and checked one by one.

Material life, of course, presents itself to us in the anecdotal form of thousands and thousands of assorted facts. Can we call these events? No: to do so would be to inflate their importance, to grant them a significance they never had. That the Holy Roman Emperor Maximilian ate with his fingers from the dishes at a banquet (as we can see from a drawing) is an everyday detail, not an event. So is the story about the bandit Cartouche, on the point of execution, preferring a glass of wine to the coffee he was offered. This is the dust of history, micro-history in the same sense that Georges Gurvitch talks about micro-sociology: little facts which do, it is true, by indefinite repetition, add up to form linked chains. Each of them represents the thousands of others that have crossed the silent depths of time and *endured*.

It is with such chains, such 'series', and with history in the 'long term' that I have here been concerned: they provide the horizons and the vanishing-points of all the landscapes of the past. They introduce a kind of order, indicate a balance, and reveal to our eyes the permanent features, the things that in this apparent disorder *can* be explained. 'A law', Georges Lefebvre used to say, 'is a constant.' Such constants can of course operate over the long or the intermediate term: we have devoted more attention to the former, since we have been talking of food-crops, clothing, houses and the ancient and crucial division between town and country. Material life conforms to such slow rhythms more readily than other areas of human history.

Among the constant elements, the reader will have noticed that we have placed in the foreground those arising from civilizations and from what I have called cultures. This book is not called '*Civilization* and Capitalism' without intention: it indicates a deliberate choice of language. For civilizations do indeed create bonds, that is to say an order, bringing together thousands of cultural possessions effectively different from, and at first sight even foreign to, each other – goods that range from those of the spirit and the intellect to the tools and objects of everyday life.

An Englishman who travelled in China (1793) noted that:

> In China ... [the most common] tools have something peculiar in their construction, some difference, often indeed slight, but always clearly indicating that, whether better or worse fitted for their purpose than those used in other countries, the one did not serve as a model for the other. Thus, for example, the upper surface of the anvil, elsewhere flat and somewhat inclined, is among the Chinese swelled into a convex form.[1]

He makes the same comment on the subject of forge bellows: 'The bellows are made in the form of a box, in which a movable floor is so closely fitted as when drawn back to create a vacuum in the box, into which, in consequence, the air rushes through an opening guarded by a valve and produces a blast through an opposite aperture.' This was quite different from the large leather bellows in European forges.

It is a fact that every great centre of population has worked out a set of elementary answers – and has an unfortunate tendency to stick to them out of that force of inertia which is one of the great artisans of history. What is a civilization then, if not the ancient settlement of a certain section of mankind in a certain place? It is a category of history, a necessary classification. Mankind has only shown any tendency to become united (and has certainly not yet succeeded) since the end of the fifteenth century. Until then, and the further we go back in time the more obvious it becomes, humanity was divided between different *planets*, each the home of an individual civilization or culture, with its own distinctive features and age-old choices. Even when they were close together, these solutions never combined.

I have used the expression *the long term* and *civilization*: these major categories call for a supplementary classification, based on the notion of *society* (which is present everywhere too). Everything is part of a social order – which for a historian or a sociologist is a reflection worthy of La Palisse or Monsieur Jourdain. But these commonplace and obvious truths have their importance. I have talked for pages on end of rich and poor, luxury and poverty, the two shores of human existence. These are relentless facts, in Japan as much as in Newton's England or in pre-Columbian America – where before the Spaniards arrived, very strict prohibitions regulated dress so that the people could be distinguished from their masters. When European domination reduced everyone in this society to the rank of subject 'natives', the rules and differences disappeared or very nearly. The fabrics worn – coarse wool, cotton or sisal (sackcloth) – made it virtually impossible to distinguish one from another.

But even the word society is rather vague: we really ought to talk of *socioeconomies*. Marx asked the right question: who owns the means of production, the land, the ships, the machinery, the raw materials, the finished products and, no less, the leading positions in society? It is, however, clear that the two coordinates: society and economy, are still not sufficient: the State, in all its forms, simultaneously cause and consequence, makes its presence felt, disturbs and affects relationships whether it seeks to or not, and often plays a very forceful role in those architectural structures that can be classified into a typology of world socio-economic systems: those based on slavery, those with serfs and overlords, those where there are businessmen and pre-capitalists. This is to return to the language used by Marx, and to walk some of the way with him, even if one rejects his precise words or the rigorous process by which he saw every society moving from one stage to the next. The problem remains one of classification, of a considered hierarchy of societies; no observer can escape this necessity – which imposes itself from the most elementary level of material life.

That such problems – the long term, civilization, society, economy, the state, the hierarchies of 'social' values – should present themselves at the level of the humble realities of material life, proves in itself that history is present at this level too, with its enigmas and difficulties, familiar ones which are encountered by all the human sciences when they come to grips with their subject. Man can never be reduced to one personality who fits into an acceptable simplification; though many people have pursued this false hope. No sooner has one approached even the simplest aspect of his life than one finds his customary complexity there too.

And indeed, I have certainly not devoted myself to history at this particular level for years on end because I regard it as any simpler or clearer; nor because it seemed to have numerical priority; nor because it has been neglected by the mainstream of history; nor (though this did carry some weight) because it tied me down to concrete realities at a time when, logically, philosophy, social science and mathematization are dehumanizing history. This return to mother earth was very pleasant, but it was not the deciding reason. No: I did not think it was possible to achieve an understanding of economic life as a whole if the foundations of the house were not first surveyed. These foundations the present book has tried to lay down; upon them the next two volumes which will complete the enterprise, have been built.

With *economic life*, we shall be moving outside the routine, the unconscious daily round. However, in economic life the regularities will still be with us: an ancient and progressive division of labour led to the necessary separations and encounters which nourished active and conscious everyday economic life with its small profits, its micro-capitalism (whose face was not unacceptable) barely distinguishable from ordinary work. Higher still, on the top floor, we have placed real capitalism, with its mighty networks, its operations which already seemed diabolical to common mortals. What had this sophisticated level to do with the humble lives at the foot of the ladder, the reader may ask. Everything perhaps, for they were drawn into its operations. I have tried to make this point from the first chapter of this book, by stressing the variations in level in the essentially *unequal world* of men. It was the inequalities, the injustices, the contradictions large or small, that made the world go round and endlessly transformed its upper structures, the only ones with the capacity to move. For capitalism alone had comparative freedom of movement. As the moment dictated, it could swing to one side or the other, turn simultaneously or alternately to the profits of trade or those of manufacture, perhaps to income from real estate, loans to the State or usury. In a context where other structures were inflexible (those of material life and, no less, those of ordinary economic life) capitalism could choose the areas where it wished and was able to intervene, and the areas it would leave to their fate, rebuilding as it went its own structures from these components, and gradually in the process transforming the structures of others.

That is what made pre-capitalism the source of the economic creativity of the world: it was the origin or the signal for all major material progress and for all the most oppressive exploitation of man by man. Not only because of the appropriation of the surplus value of man's labour, but also because of those disparities of strength or situation which meant that there has always been, on a national scale or on a world scale, one stronghold waiting to be captured, one sector more profitable to exploit than the others. The choice may have been a limited one sometimes, but what an immense privilege to be able to choose!

Notes

Translator's note: Wherever possible, when an English-language source is quoted in the text, the original has been traced and the page reference in the notes amended. This has not always been possible. References to works originally published in French have been left unaltered, except where there is a recent and easily available English translation.

Abbreviations used in notes:

A.d.S.   Archivio di Stato.
A.E.   Affaires Etrangères (Foreign Affairs), Paris.
A.N.   Archives Nationales, Paris. Following letter refers to series.
B.M.   British Museum (now British Library).
B.N.   Bibliothèque Nationale, Paris.
P.R.O.   Public Record Office, London.

NOTE TO INTRODUCTION

1. The first version of this book was a volume in a series which did not include footnotes. My publisher had agreed that Volumes II and III of the present work should appear with footnotes, so the revised edition of this first volume obviously required the addition of notes. Ten years ago, this would have been no problem. But now that most of my original records of references have often been reclassified, I had to hunt down hundreds, indeed thousands of references – and the hunt was not always successful. I must therefore apologize to my fellow-historians for the small number of cases where 'reference mislaid' unfortunately replaces an indication of a source which eluded my efforts.

NOTES TO CHAPTER I

1. According to Ernst WAGEMANN, *Economia mundial*, 1952, esp. vol. I, pp. 59 ff.
2. Emmanuel LE ROY LADURIE, *Les Paysans du Languedoc*, 1966, vol. I, pp. 139 ff.
3. Fernand BRAUDEL, *The Mediterranean and the Mediterranean World in the time of Philip II* (English translation 1973), vol. I, pp. 402 ff. Further references to this work will be abbreviated to *Medit.*, and all page references are to the English edition.

4. E. WAGEMANN, *op. cit.*, I, p. 51.
5. Angel ROSENBLAT, *La Población indígena y el Mestizaje en América*, I, 1954, pp. 102-3.
6. The most representative works are: S.F. COOK and L.B. SIMPSON, 'The population of Central Mexico in the 16th century', in *Ibero-Americana*, 1948; W. BORAH, 'The aboriginal population of Central Mexico on the eve of the Spanish conquest', in *Ibero-Americana*, 1963. The figures advanced by the Berkeley school have been challenged recently, in particular by Charles Verlinden at the Prato conference 1979.
7. Pierre CHAUNU, *L'Amérique et les Amériques*, 1964, p. 105; Abbé PREVOST, *Histoire générale des voyages*, vol. XV, 1759, p. 9.
8. D.A. BRADING, *Mineros y comerciantes en el México borbónico, 1763-1810*, 1975, p. 18; Nicolás SANCHEZ-ALBORNOZ, *La Población de América latina desde los tiempos precolombinos*, 1973, p. 81; B.N. CHAGNY, *Variole et chute de l'Empire aztèque*, unpublished thesis, Dijon, 1975.
9. Father A. DÁVILLA, *Historia de la fundación y discurso de la provincia de Santiago de México, 1596-1625*, pp. 100, 118, 516-17.
10. N. SANCHEZ-ALBORNOZ, *op. cit.*, p. 188.
11. *Ibid.*, pp. 121-2.
12. A. Grenfeld PRICE, *The Western Invasions of the Pacific and its Continents*, 1963, p. 167.
13. W.S. and E.S. WOYTINSKI, *World Population and Production, Trends and Outlook*, 1953; and E.R. EMBREE, *Indians of the Americas*, 1939, quoted in P.A. LADAME, *Le Rôle des migrations dans le monde libre*, 1958, p. 14.
14. P.A. LADAME, *op. cit.*, p. 16.
15. *Morphologie sociale*, 1938, p. 70.
16. Karl LAMPRECHT, *Deutsche Wirtschaftsgeschichte*, 1891, I^1, p. 163; Karl Julius BELOCH, 'Die Bevölkerung Europas im Mittelalter', in *Zeitschrift für Sozialwissenschaft*, 1900, pp. 405-7.
17. P. MOMBERT, 'Die Entwicklung des Bevölkerung Europas seit der Mitte des 17. Jahr.', in *Zeitschrift für Nationalökonomie*, 1936; J.C. RUSSELL, *Late ancient and medieval population*, 1958; M. REINHARDT, A. ARMENGAUD, J. DUPAQUIER, *Histoire générale de la population mondiale*, 1968.
18. 'The History of population and settlement in Eurasia', in *The Geographical Review*, 1930, pp. 122-7.
19. Louis DERMIGNY, *La Chine et l'Occident. Le commerce à Canton au XVIIIe siècle*, vol. II, 1964, pp. 472-5.
20. *Ibid.*
21. See the table on p. 39.
22. Leo FROBENIUS, *Histoire de la civilisation africaine*, 1936 edn., pp. 14 ff.
23. Father Jean-Baptiste LABAT, *Nouvelle relation de l'Afrique occidentale*, 1728, vol. V, pp. 331 ff.
24. This was a period of much emigration, cf. Michel DEVEZE, *L'Europe et le monde à la fin du XVIIIe siècle*, 1970, p. 331 and note 586.
25. According to the official figures for '*pasajeros a Indias*', 100,000 during the sixteenth century; G. CESPEDES DE CASTILLO (in *Historia social y económica de España y América*, general editor J. VICENS VIVES, vol. III, pp. 393-4) thinks this figure should be multiplied by two or three.
26. *Op. cit.*, p. 148.
27. *World Population, Past Growth and Present Trends*, 1937, pp. 38-41.
28. *Art. cit.*, p. 123.
29. L. DERMIGNY, *op. cit.*, vol. II, pp. 477, 478-9, 481-2.
30. *Ibid.*, table p. 475 and discussion pp. 472-5.

31. Sir George STAUNTON, *An authentic account of an Embassy ... to the Emperor of China ... taken chiefly from the papers of ... the Earl of Macartney*, 1797, vol. II, appendix.
32. W.H. MORELAND, *India at the Death of Akbar*, 1920, pp. 16-22.
33. In particular in 1540, 1596 and 1630; *ibid*., pp. 11, 22, note 1, 266.
34. See vol. III.
35. A.E. INDES Or., 18, f° 257.
36. Kingsley DAVIES, *The Population of India and Pakistan*, 1951, pp. 24-6.
37. Paul MOMBERT, *art. cit*., pp. 533-45.
38. Pierre CHAUNU, *La Civilisation de l'Europe des Lumières*, 1971, p. 42.
39. As many references from the *Gazette de France* indicate. In 1762, for example, deaths far exceeded births in London, Paris, Warsaw, Copenhagen. In the latter city there were 4512 deaths to 2289 births, whereas for the country overall, there was a balance.
40. Sir George STAUNTON, *op. cit*., vol. II, p.155.
41. P.R.O. London, 30.25.65, fol. 9, 1655. In Muscovy 'there is nobody who can exercise the trade of surgeon, apart from a few foreigners from Holland or Germany'.
42. N. SANCHEZ-ALBORNOZ, *op. cit*., p. 188.
43. Paul VIDAL DE LA BLACHE, *Principes de géographie humaine*, 1922, p. 45.
44. René GROUSSET, *Histoire de la Chine*, 1957, p. 23.
45. W. RÖPKE, *Explication économique du monde moderne*, 1940, p. 102.
46. Forthcoming book by Pierre GOUROU: *Terre de Bonne Esperance*.
47. Cf. excavations by P. NORLUND and research by T. LONGSTAFF; cf. Emmanuel LE ROY LADURIE, *Times of Feast, Times of Famine: a history of the climate since the year 1000*, tr. B. Bray, London, 1971, pp. 251-4.
48. 'Discussion: post-glacial climatic change', in *The Quarterly Journal of the Royal Meteorological Society*, April 1949, p. 175.
49. Eino JUTIKKALA, 'The great Finnish famine in 1696-1697', in *The Scandinavian History Review*, III, 1955, I, pp. 51-2.
50. B.H. SLICHER VAN BATH, 'Le climat et les récoltes au haut Moyen Age', in *Settimana ... de Spoleto*, XIII, 1965, p. 402.
51. *Ibid*., pp. 403-4.
52. Rhys CARPENTER, *Discontinuity in Greek Civilisation*, 1966, pp. 67-8. The catastrophes cited in the text support the explanation of the mystery of 'the sea peoples' (thirteenth and twelfth centuries BC).
53. Oronce FINE, *Les Canons et documents très amples touchant l'usage et pratique des communs Almanachs que l'on nomme Ephémérides*, 1551, p. 35.
54. If one accepts the figure of 350 million for 1300 and 1000 million for 1800. These are the figures on which the following calculations are based.
55. Heinrich BECHTEL, *Wirtschaftsgeschichte Deutschlands vom 16. bis 18. Jahrhundert*, II, 1952, pp. 25-6; Hermann KELLENBENZ, 'Der Aufsteig Kölns zur mittelalterlichen Handelsmetropole', in *Jahrbuch des kölnichen Geschichtsvereins*, 1967, pp. 1-30.
56. These figures are discussed in Robert MANTRAN, *Istanbul dans la seconde moitié du XVIIe siècle*, 1962, pp. 44 ff.
57. Reinhard THOM, *Die Schlacht bei Pavia (24 Februar 1525)*, 1907.
58. Peter LASLETT, *The World We Have Lost* (first edition, 1965), p. 10.
59. *Medit*., vol. II, pp. 1088 ff. It is impossible to calculate an exact figure (see HARTLAUB and QUARTI), but the Turkish fleet numbered 230 galleys, the Christian 208 plus 6 Venetian galliasses. The Turks lost 48,000 men either killed, injured or taken prisoner.
60. J.-F. MICHAUD, *Biographie universelle ancienne et moderne*, 1843, vol. 44, article 'Wallenstein'.
61. Ernest LAVISSE, *Histoire de France*, 1911, VIII (1), p. 131.

62. Louis DUPRE D'AULNAY, *Traité général des subsistances militaires*, 1744, p. 62.
63. Benedit de VASSALLIEU, alias Nicolay Lyonnais, *Recueil du règlement general de l'ordre et conduite de l'artillerie . . .*, 1613, B.N., MS Fr., 592.
64. Henri LAPEYRE, *Géographie de l'Espagne morisque*, 1960.
65. According to Robert MANDROU, *La France aux XVIIe et XVIIIe siècles*, 1970, pp. 183-4, the figure of 300,000 is usually accepted. H. LÜTHY, *La Banque protestante*, p. 26, prefers the figure of 200,000. W.G. SCOVILLE also thinks that the loss to the French economy has been over-estimated: *The Persecution of Huguenots and French Economic Development*, 1960.
66. See vol. III.
67. Andrea NAVAGERO, *Il Viaggio fatto in Spagna*, 1563.
68. Karl Julius BELOCH, *art. cit.*, pp. 783-4.
69. *Ibid.*, p. 786.
70. BRANTÔME, *Œuvres*, 1779, vol. IX, p. 249.
71. H. LÜTHY, *op. cit.*, vol. I, p. 26.
72. G. NADAL and E. GIRALT, *La Population catalane de 1553 à 1717*, 1960.
73. Barthélémy JOLY, *Voyage en Espagne, 1603-1604*, ed. L. BARREAU-DIHIGO, 1909, p. 13: all the artisans in Figueras in Catalonia 'are French, from the Haute-Auvergne'.
74. Cardinal de RETZ, *Mémoires*, 1949 edn., vol. III, p. 226.
75. Antoine de BRUNEL, *Viaje de España*, 1665, in *Viajes estranjeros por España y Portugal*, vol. II, 1959, p. 427.
76. Jean HERAULT, sire de Gourville, *Mémoires . . .*, 1724, vol. II, p. 79.
77. Louis-Sébastien MERCIER, *L'An deux mille quatre cent quarante, rêve s'il en fut jamais*, 1771, p. 335.
78. Emmanuel LE ROY LADURIE, 'Demography and the Sinful Secrets', in *The Territory of the Historian*, 1979.
79. Antoine de SAINT-EXUPERY, *Terre des hommes*.
80. P. VIDAL DE LA BLACHE, *op. cit.*, pp. 10-11.
81. G.W. HEWES, 'A conspectus of the world's cultures in 1500 A.D.', in *University of Colorado Studies*, no. 4, 1954, pp. 1-22.
82. Depending on whether one reckons the world population at 400 or 500 million inhabitants.
83. K.J. BELOCH, *art. cit.*, p. 36, note 11.
84. A.P. USHER, *art. cit.*, p. 131.
85. H. BECHTEL, *op. cit.*, pp. 25-6.
86. Jean FOURASTIE, *Machinisme et bien-être*, 1962, pp. 40-1.
87. Daniel DEFOE, *A Review of the State of the British Nation*, 1709, p. 142, quoted in Sydney POLLARD and David CROSSLEY, *The Wealth of Britain 1085-1966*, 1968, p. 160.
88. Johann Gottlieb GEORGI, *Versuch einer Beschreibung der . . . Residenzstadt St. Petersburg*, 1790, pp. 555, 561.
89. Johan BECKMANN, *Beiträge zur Oekonomie . . .*, 1781, vol. IV, p. 8. He reports apropos of the draining of the marshes in the Duchy of Bremen: 'Experience shows that the small villages [25 to 30 households] are easier to bring round to obedience than the large.'
90. Denis DIDEROT, *Supplément au voyage de Bougainville*, 1958 edn., p. 322.
91. *Ibid.*
92. Adam MAURIZIO, *Histoire de l'alimentation végétale*, 1932, pp. 15-16.
93. Affonso de ESCRAGNOLLE TAUNAY, *Historia general das bandeiras paulistas*, 1924, 5 vols.
94. Georges CONDOMINAS, *Nous avons mangé la forêt de la Pierre-Génie Gôo . . .*, 1957.
95. Ishwari PRASAD, *L'Inde du VIIe au XVIe siècle*, 1930, in *Histoire du monde*, ed. E. CAVAIGNAC, vol. VIII (1), pp. 459-60.
96. Maximilien SORRE, *Les Fondements de la géographie humaine*, vol. III, 1952, p. 439.
97. P. VIDAL DE LA BLACHE, *op. cit.*, p. 35.
98. G. CONDOMINAS, *op. cit.*, p. 19.
99. P. de LAS CORTES, *Relación del viaje, naufragio y captiverio . . .*, 1621-1626, British Museum, Sloane, 1005.
100. Rijksmuseum, Amsterdam, Asiatic department.

101. *Beschreibung des japonischen Reiches*, 1749, p. 42.
102. J.A. MANDELSLO, *Voyage aux Indes orientales*, 1659, vol. II, p. 388, and report by W. BOLTS, A.N., A.E., B III, 459, 19 Messidor, Year V.
103. Sir George STAUNTON, *op. cit.*, vol. II, p. 177.
104. G.F. GEMELLI CARERI, *Voyage du tour du monde*, 1727, vol. I, p. 548.
105. Père J.-B. LABAT, *op. cit.*, vol. V, pp. 276-8.
106. J.A. MANDELSLO, *op. cit.*, II, p. 530. Abbé PREVOST, *op. cit.*, vol. V, 1748, p. 190 (Kolben).
107. Abbé PREVOST, *op. cit.*, vol. III (1747), pp. 180-1 and 645; and vol. V, pp. 79-80.
108. *Journal d'un bourgeois de Paris, sous Charles VI et Charles VII*, 1929, pp. 150, 304, 309.
109. Gaston ROUPNEL, *La Ville et la campagne au XVIIe siècle*, 1955, p. 38, note 117.
110. Albert BABEAU, *Le Village sous l'Ancien Régime*, 1915, pp. 345, note 4 and 346, note 3; Maurice BALMELLE, 'La Bête du Gévaudan et le capitaine de dragons Duhamel', Mende Conference, 1955.
111. A.N., Maurepas, A.P., 9.
112. A.N., F 12, 721.
113. Jules BLACHE, *Les Massifs de la Grande Chartreuse et du Vercors*, 1931, vol. II, p. 29.
114. *Viaje por España y Portugal (1494-1495)*, 1951, p. 42.
115. Reference mislaid; but see Günther FRANZ, *Der deutsche Bauernkrieg*, 1972, pp. 79 ff., for several similar indications.
116. J.B. TAVERNIER, *Voyages en Perse*, Cercle du bibliophile edn., n.d., pp. 41-3.
117. H. JOSSON and L. WILLAERT, *Correspondance de Ferdinand Verbiest, de la Compagnie de Jesus (1632-1688)*, 1938, pp. 390-1.
118. J.A. MANDELSLO, *op. cit.*, vol. II, p. 253.
119. François COREAL, *Relation des voyages de François Coreal aux Indes occidentales ... depuis 1666 jusqu'en 1697*, 1736, vol. I, p. 40.
120. Reginaldo de LIZARRAGA, 'Descripción del Perú, Tucumán, Río de la Plata y Chile', in *Historiadores de Indias*, 1909, vol. II, p. 644.
121. *Voyage du capitaine Narboroug (1669)* in PREVOST, *op. cit.*, vol. XI, 1753, pp. 32-4.
122. R. de LIZARRAGA, *op. cit.*, vol. II, p. 642.
123. Walther KIRCHNER, *Eine Reise durch Sibirien* (account by Fries), 1955, p. 75.
124. Recognized by the Russians from 1696, Abbé PREVOST, *op. cit.*, vol. XVIII, p. 71.
125. A.E., M and D., Russia, 7, 1774, f°s 235-6; Joh. Gottl. GEORGI, *Bemerkungen einer Reise im Russischen Reich*, vol. I, 1775, pp. 22-4.
126. Sir George STAUNTON, *op. cit.*, vol. I, pp. 221 ff.
127. Pierre GOUBERT, unpublished research, VIe section of the Ecole des Hautes Etudes.
128. William PETTY, *Political Arithmetic*, p. 185.
129. Erich KEYSER, *Bevölkerungsgeschichte Deutschlands*, 1941, p. 302. Wilhelm SCHÖNFELDER, *Die wirtschaftliche Entwicklung Kölns von 370 bis 1513*, 1970, pp. 128-9, says 30,000 deaths.
130. Günther FRANZ, *Der Dreissigjahrige Krieg und das deutsche Volk*, 1961, p. 7.
131. L. MOSCARDO, *Historia di Verona*, 1668, p. 492.
132. G. FRANZ, *op. cit.*, pp. 52-3.
133. Bernard GUENEE, *Tribunaux et gens de justice dans le bailliage de Senlis à la fin du Moyen Age (vers 1380-vers 1550)*, 1963, p. 57.
134. Wilhelm ABEL, *Die Wüstungen des ausgehenden Mittelalters*, 1955, pp. 74-5.
135. MOHEAU, *Recherches et considérations sur la population de la France*, 1778, p. 264.
136. François DORNIC, *L'Industrie textile dans le Maine (1650-1815)*, 1955, pp. 74-5.
137. Yves-Marie BERCE, *Histoire des croquants: étude des soulèvements populaires au XVIIe siècle dans le Sud-Ouest de la France*, 1974, I, p. 16.

138. Fritz BLAICH, 'Die Wirtschaftspolitische Tätigkeit der Kommission zur Bekämpfung der Hungersnot in Böhmen und Mähren (1771-1772)', in *Vierteljahrschrift für Sozial- und Wirtschaftsgeschichte*, 56, 3, Oct. 1969, pp. 299-331.
139. *Almanacco di economia di Toscana del anno 1791*, Florence, 1791, quoted in *Medit* ... vol. I, p. 329.
140. In Venice: A.d.S. Venice, Brera, 51, f° 312 v°, 1540. Amiens: Pierre DEYON, *Amiens, capitale provinciale. Etude sur la société urbaine au XVIIe siècle*, 1967, p. 14 and note.
141. *Mémoires de Claude Haton*, in *Documents inédits de l'histoire de France*, vol. II, 1857, pp. 727-8.
142. G. ROUPNEL, *op. cit.*, p. 98.
143. A. APPADORAI, *Economic Conditions in Southern India (1000-1500 A.D.)*.
144. W. H. MORELAND, *op. cit.*, pp. 127-8.
145. Description by Van Twist, quoted in W.H. MORELAND, *From Akbar to Aurangzeb*, 1923, pp. 211-12.
146. François BERNIER, *Voyages ... contenant la description des Etats du Grand Mogol ...*, 1699, vol. I, p. 202.
147. Eino JUTIKKALA, *art. cit.*, p. 48.
148. Pierre CLEMENT, *Histoire de la Vie et de l'administration de Colbert*, 1846, p. 118.
149. G. ROUPNEL, *op. cit.*, p. 35, note 104.
150. Journal of GAUDELET, Ms. 748, Dijon Library, p. 94, quoted by G. ROUPNEL, *op. cit.*, p. 35, note 105.
151. *Journal de Clément Macheret ... curé d'Horthes (1628-1658)*, ed. E. BOUGARD, 1880, vol. II, p. 142.
152. P. de SAINT-JACOB, *op. cit.*, p. 196.
153. It was still being made only once or twice a month in the countryside near Milan, according to Paolo MANTEGAZZA, *Igiene della cucina*, 1867, p. 37.
154. This may seem a commonplace, but the closeness of the link is usefully confirmed by Enrique FLORESCANO, *Precios des maiz y crisis agricolas en Mexico, 1708-1810*, 1969; Florescano compares the dates of famines and of various epidemics in eighteenth-century Mexico (table, p. 161.)
155. Samuel TISSOT, *Avis au peuple sur sa santé*, 1775, pp. 221-2.
156. Mirko D. GRMEK, 'Préliminaires d'une ètude historique des maladies', in *Annales, E.S.C.*, 1969, no. 6, pp. 1473-83.
157. G. ROUPNEL, *op. cit.*, pp. 28-9.
158. L.S. MERCIER, *op. cit.*, III, pp. 186-7.
159. Etienne PASQUIER, *Les Recherches de la France*, 1643, p. 111.
160. Pierre de LESTOILE, *Mémoires et Journal ...*, in *Mémoires pour servir à l'histoire de France*, 2nd series, vol. I, 1837, p. 261.
161. H. HAESER, *Lehrbuch der Geschichte des Medicin*, III, 1882, pp. 325 ff.
162. A.d.S. Genova, Spagna, 11, Cesare Giustiniano to the Doge, Madrid, 21 August 1597.
163. Henri STEIN, 'Comment on luttait autrefois contre les épidémies', in *Annuaire bulletin de la société de l'Histoire de France*, 1918, p. 130.
164. M.T. JONES-DAVIES, *Un Peintre de la vie londonienne, Thomas Dekker*, 1958, pp. 334-5.
165. League of Nations, *Rapport épidémiologique de la section d'hygiène*, no. 48, Geneva, 24 April 1923, p. 3.
166. A.d.S. Florence, Medici papers, 2 September 1603.
167. A.G. PRICE, *op. cit.*, p. 162.
168. *Ibid.*, p. 172 and M.T. JONES-DAVIES, *op. cit.*, p. 335, note 229.
169. M.T. JONES-DAVIES, *op. cit.*, p. 162.
170. Malherbe, quoted by John GRAND-CARTERET, *L'Histoire, la vie, les moeurs et la curiosité par l'image ... 1450-1900*, 1927, vol. II, p. 322.
171. *Antonio Pérez*, 1948, 2nd edn., p. 50.
172. M.T. JONES-DAVIES, *op. cit*, p. 335.
173. Erich WOEHLKENS, *Pest und Ruhr im 16. und 17. Jahr.*, 1954.
174. A.E., M and D, Russia, 7, f° 298.
175. Pierre CHAUNU, *Séville et l'Atlantique*, Vol. VIII (1), 1959, p. 290 and note 1; J. and R. NICOLAS, *La Vie quotidienne en Savoie ...*, 1979, p. 119.
176. Samuel PEPYS, *Diary*, ed. WHEATLEY, 1897, vol. V, pp. 55-6.

177. Michel de MONTAIGNE, *Les Essais*, Pléiade edn., 1962, pp. 1018-19.
178. Nicolas VERSORIS, *Livre de raison*, ed. G. FAGNIEZ, 1885, pp. 23-4.
179. Etienne FERRIERES, quoted by Gilles CASTER, *Le Commerce du pastel et de l'épicerie à Toulouse, 1450-1561*, 1962, p. 247.
180. Jean-Paul SARTRE, *Les Temps modernes*, October 1957, p. 696, note 15. J. and R. NICOLAS, *op. cit.*, p. 123.
181. Henri STEIN, *art. cit.*, p. 133.
182. Comte de FORBIN, 'Un gentilhomme avignonais au XVIe siècle. François-Dragonet de Fogasses, seigneur de la Bastie (1536-1599)', in *Mémoires de l'Académie de Vaucluse*, 2nd series, IX, 1909, p. 173.
183. Daniel DEFOE, *A Journal of the Plague Year*, passim.
184. *Ibid.*, preface p. 13 citing Thomas GUMBLE, *Life of General Monk* (1672).
185. Cf. René BAEHREL's very fine article on this, 'Epidémie et terreur: histoire et sociologie', in *Annales historiques de la Révolution française*, 1951, no. 122, pp. 113-46.
186. Venice, Marciana, Italian Manuscripts, III, 4.
187. Père Maurice de TOLON, *Préservatifs et remèdes contre la peste, ou Le Capucin charitable*, 1668.
188. Cf. the preface, by Joseph AYNARD to the French edition of DEFOE's *Journal of the Plague Year* (*Journal de l'année de la peste*, 1943, p. 13).
189. M. FOSSEYEUX, 'Les épidémies de peste à Paris', in *Bulletin de la Société d'histoire de la médécine*, XII, 1913, p. 119, quoted by AYNARD in his preface, cf. note 188.
190. C. CARRIERE, M. COURDURIE, F. REBUFFAT, *Marseille, ville morte, La peste de 1720*, 1968, p. 302.
191. Letter from Monseigneur de Belsunce, bishop of Marseille, 3 September 1720, quoted by AYNARD in his preface, p. 14, cf. note 188 above.
192. Jean-Noël BIRABEN, *Les Hommes et la peste en France et dans les pays européens et méditerranéens*, 1976, vol. II, p. 185.
193. William McNeill, *Plagues and Peoples*, 1976.
194. Ping-Ti HO, 'The Introduction of American Food Plants into China', in *American Anthropologist*, April 1955, pp. 194-7.
195. E.J.F. BARBIER, *Journal historique et anecdotique du règne de Louis XV*, 1847, p. 176.
196. *Medit.*, vol. I, pp. 332-4.
197. Sir George STAUNTON, *op. cit.* vol. II, p. 374.
198. Pierre GOUBERT, *Beauvais et le Beauvaisis de 1600 à 1730. Contribution à l'histoire sociale de la France du XVIIe siècle*, 1960, p. 41.
199. Michel MOLLAT, in Edouard PERROY, *Le Moyen Age*, 1955, pp. 308-9.
200. Germain BRICE, *Nouvelle Description de la ville de Paris et de tout ce qu'elle contient de plus remarquable*, vol. III, 1725, pp. 120-3.
201. John NICKOLLS, *Remarques sur les désavantages et les avantages de la France et de la Grande Bretagne*, 1754, p. 23.
202. François COREAL, *Relation des voyages ...*, *op. cit.*, 1736, vol. I, p. 95; Carsten NIEBUHR, *Voyage en Arabie et en d'autres pays de l'Orient*, 1780, vol. II, p. 401; CHARDIN, *Voyage en Perse et aux Indes orientales*, 1686, vol. IV, p. 46: 'the great over-indulgence in meat and drink which is fatal in the Indies' for Englishmen.
203. John H. GROSE, *A voyage to the East Indies with observations of various parts there*, 1757, vol. I, p. 33.
204. T. OVINGTON, *A Voyage to Surat*, 1689, p. 87, quoted by Percival SPEAR, *The Nabobs*, 1963, p. 5.
205. Sir George STAUNTON, *op. cit.*, vol. I, pp. 242 ff. Both Cook and Bougainville, during the time they put in to Batavia, 'the land that kills', lost more crew members through death and disease than they did throughout the rest of their voyages; Abbé PREVOST, *Supplément des voyages*, vol. XX, pp. 314, 581.
206. Bernard FAY, *George Washington, gentilhomme*, 1932, p. 40.

207. Abbé Prevost, *op. cit.*, vol. IX, p. 250 (quoting from an account by Loubère).
208. Jean-Claude Flachat, *Observations sur le commerce et les arts d'une partie de l'Europe, de l'Asie de l'Afrique* ..., 1766, vol. I, p. 451.
209. Osman Aga, journal published by R. Kreutel and Otto Spies, under the title *Der Gefangene der Giauren* ..., 1962, pp. 210-11.
210. E. Keyser, *Bevölkerungsgeschichte Deutschlands*, 1941, p. 381; generally speaking the demographic expansion of the towns was not endogenous: W. Sombart, *Der moderne Kapitalismus*, vol. II, p. 1124.
211. Johann Peter Süssmilch, *Die Göttliche Ordnung in den Veränderung des menschlichen Geschlechts* ..., 1765, vol. I, p. 521.
212. Pierre de Saint-Jacob, *Les Paysans de la Bourgogne, du Nord au dernier siècle de l'Ancien Régime*, 1960, p. 545.
213. According to the publications of Carmelo Vinas and Ramon Paz, *Relaciones de los pueblos de Espana*, 1949-63.
214. *L'Invasion germanique et la fin de l'Empire*, 1891, vol. II, pp. 322 ff.
215. *Geschichte der Kriegskunst im Rahmen der politischen Geschichte*, 1900, vol. I, pp. 472 ff.
216. Rechid Saffet Atabinen, *Contribution à une histoire sincère d'Attila*, 1934.
217. Henri Pirenne, *Les Villes et les institutions urbaines*, 1939, vol. I, pp. 306-7.
218. *Gazette de France*, 1650, *passim*.
219. *Geschichte des europäischen Staatensystems von 1492-1559*, 1919, pp. 1 ff.
220. For more details and for what follows see Alexander and Eugen Kulischer, *Kriegs- und Wanderzüge. Weltgeschichte als Völkerbewegung*, 1932.
221. Otto von Kotzebue, *Reise um die Welt in den Jahren 1823, 24, 25 und 26*, 1830, vol. I, p. 47.
222. F.J. Turner, *The Frontier in American History*, 1921.
223. The voyage of the doctor Jakob Fries, published by Kirchner, *op. cit.*, 1955.
224. John Bell, *Travels from St. Petersburg to diverse parts of Asia*, 1763, vol. I, p. 216.
225. On the early stages of these excavations see W. Hensel and A. Gieysztor, *Les recherches archéologiques en Pologne*, 1958, pp. 48, 66.
226. Boris Nolde, *La Formation de l'Empire russe*, 2 vols., 1952.
227. *Medit.*, vol. I, pp. 191-2.
228. *Medit.*, vol. I, p. 110 and note 32.
229. G.F. Gemelli Careri, *op. cit.*, vol. III, p. 166.

NOTES TO CHAPTER 2

1. Montesquieu, *De l'Esprit des lois*, book XXII, chap. 14, in *Œuvres complètes*, 1964 edn., p. 690.
2. This proverb seems to have been invented by L.A. Feuerbach.
3. *Hakluyt's Voyages*, 1927 edn., vol. I, pp. 441, 448-9.
4. P. Goubert, *op. cit.*, pp. 108, 111.
5. K.C. Chang, *Food in Chinese Culture*, 1977.
6. Claude Manceron, *Les Vingt Ans du Roi*, 1972, p. 614.
7. Wilhem Abel, 'Wandlungen des Fleischverbrauchs und der Fleischversorgung in Deutschland seit dem ausgehenden Mittelalter', in *Berichte über Landwirtschaft*, XXII, 3, 1937, pp. 411-52.
8. Abbé Prevost, *op. cit.*, IX, p. 342 (Beaulieu's voyage).
9. A. Maurizio, *op. cit.*, p. 168.
10. Dr Jean Claudian, Preliminary report of International Conference of F.I.P.A.L., Paris, 1964, typescript, pp. 7-8, 19.

11. Marcel GRANET, *Danses et légendes de la Chine ancienne*, 1926, pp. 8 and 19, note.
12. J. CLAUDIAN, *art. cit.*, p. 27.
13. *An Account of the Character and Manners of the French* [by J. ANDREWS], 1770, p. 58.
14. M. SORRE, *op. cit.*, vol. I, pp. 162-3.
15. Pierre GOUROU, 'La civilisation du végétal', in *Indonésie*, n° 5, pp. 385-96, reviewed by Lucien FEBVRE, in *Annales E.S.C.*, 1949, p. 73.
16. P. de LAS CORTES, *doc. cit.*, f° 75.
17. Abbé PREVOST, *op. cit.*, vol. V, p. 486.
18. G.F. GEMELLI CARERI, *op. cit.*, vol. IV, p. 79.
19. *Ibid.*, vol. II, p. 59.
20. Memorandum on the port of Oczaskov and the trade for which it might act as an entrepot, A.E., M and D, Russia, 7, f° 229.
21. A.E., M and D, Russia, 17, f°s 78 and 194-6.
22. V. DANDOLO, *Sulle Cause dell'avvilimento delle nostre granaglie e sulle industrie agrarie ...*, 1820, XL, p. 1.
23. *Histoire du commerce de Marseille*, ed. G. RAMBERT, 1954, IV, pp. 625 ff.
24. Étienne JUILLARD, *La Vie rurale dans la plaine de Basse-Alsace*, 1953, p. 29; J. RUWET, E. HÉLIN, F. LADRIER, L. van BUYTEN, *Marché des céréales à Ruremonde, Luxembourg, Namur et Diest, XVIIe et XVIIIe siècles*, 1966, pp. 44, 57 ff., 283-4, 299 ff; Daniel FAUCHER, *Plaines et bassins du Rhône moyen*, 1926, p. 317.
25. M. SORRE, *op. cit.*, vol. I, map, p. 241: an area covering the whole Mediterranean and central and southern Europe.
26. *Medit.*, vol. I, pp. 595, 596.
27. B.N., Paris, Estampes, Oe 74.
28. *Medit.*, vol. I, p. 244.
29. Hans HAUSSHERR, *Wirtschaftsgeschichte der Neuzeit, vom des 14. bis zur Höhe des 19. J.*, 3rd edn., 1954, p. 1.
30. *Medit.*, vol. I, p. 600 and note 370.
31. Louis LEMERY, *Traité des aliments, où l'on trouve la différence et le choix qu'on doit faire de chacun d'eux en particulier ...*, 1702, p. 113.
32. Cf. J.C. TOUTAIN's table, 'Le produit de l'agriculture française de 1700 à 1958', in *Histoire quantitative de l'économie française*, ed. J. MARCZEWSKI, 1961, p. 57.
33. Jacob van KLAVEREN, *Europäische Wirtschaftsgeschichte Spaniens im 16. und 17. Jahrhundert*, 1960, p. 29, note 31.
34. *Medit.*, vol. II, p. 779.
35. In about 1740, at least 50,000 casks each weighing about 400 pounds, J. SAVARY, *Dictionnaire universel de commerce, d'histoire naturelle et des arts et métiers*, 5 vols., 1759-65, vol. IV, col. 563.
36. *Ibid.*, vol. IV, col. 565; A.N., G⁷ 1685, f° 275; A.N., G⁷ 1695, f° 29.
37. Marciana, Account by Girolamo Savina, f°s 365 ff.
38. P.J.B. LE GRAND D'AUSSY, *Histoire de la vie privée des Français*, 1782, vol. I, p. 109.
39. Abbé PREVOST, *op. cit.*, vol. V, p. 486 (Gemelli Careri's voyage); vol. VI, p. 142 (Navarrette's voyage).
40. See vol. II.
41. N.F. DUPRE DE SAINT MAUR, *Essai sur les monnoies ou Reflexions sur le rapport entre l'argent et les denrées ...*, 1746, p. 182 and note a.
42. The question still remains open, because according to all the market price-lists so far published (notably in M. BAULANT and J. MEUVRET, *Prix des céréales extraits de la mercuriale de Paris 1520-1698*, 1960) the respective variations in the price of wheat and oats have a very irregular relationship.

43. *Medit.*, vol. I, p. 43 and note 86.
44. Pierre DEFFONTAINES, *Les Hommes et leurs travaux dans les pays de la Moyenne Garonne*, 1932, p. 231.
45. L.P. GACHARD, *Retraite et mort de Charles Quint au monastère de Yuste*, I, 1854, p. 49.
46. Recorded by Lesdiguière, governor of Dauphiné, quoted by H. SÉE, *Esquisse d'une histoire économique et sociale de la France*, 1929, p. 250; L. LÉMERY, *op. cit.*, p. 110.
47. Archivo General de Simancas, Estado Castilla 139.
48. *Medit.*, vol. I, p. 571.
49. Jean GEORGELIN, *Venise au siècle des Lumières*, 1978, p. 288.
50. J. RUWET et al., *Marché des céréales ...*, *op. cit.*, pp. 57 ff.
51. P. de LAS CORTES, *doc. cit.*, f° 75.
52. Étienne JUILLARD, *Problèmes alsaciens vus par un géographie*, 1968, pp. 54 ff.
53. M. DERRUAU, *La Grande Limagne auvergnate et bourbonnaise*, 1949.
54. Jethro TULL, *The Horse Hoeing Husbandry ...*, 1733, pp. 21 ff.
55. J.-M. RICHARD, 'Thierry d'Hireçon, agriculteur artésien (13..-1328)', in *Bibliothèque de l'École des Chartes*, 1892, p. 9.
56. François VERMALE, *Les Classes rurales en Savoie au XVIIIe siècle*, 1911, p. 286.
57. Johann Gottlieb GEORGI, *op. cit.*, p. 579.
58. René BAEHREL *Une Croissance: la Basse-Provence rurale (fin du XVIe siècle-1789)*, 1961, pp. 136-7.
59. B.H. SLICHER VAN BATH, *Storia agraria ...*, *op. cit.*, pp. 353-6; Jean-François de BOURGOING, *Nouveau Voyage en Espagne ...*, 1789, III, p. 50.
60. P.G. POINSOT, *L'Ami des cultivateurs*, 1806, II, p. 40.
61. In Marc BLOCH, *Mélanges historiques*, II, 1963, p. 664.
62. Memoranda of 1796, quoted in I. IMBERCIADORI, *La Campagna toscana nel'700*, 1953, p. 173.
63. B.H. SLICHER VAN BATH, *Storia agraria dell'Europa occidentale*, 1972, pp. 245-52, 338 ff.; Wilhelm ABEL, *Crises agraires en Europe, XIIIe-XXe s.*, 1973, p. 146.
64. A.R. LE PAIGE, *Dictionnaire topographique du Maine*, 1777, II, p. 28.
65. Jacques MULLIEZ, 'Du blé, "mal nécessaire". Réflexions sur les progrès de l'agriculture, 1750-1850', in *Revue d'histoire moderne et contemporaine*, 1979, pp. 30-1.
66. *Ibidem, passim*.
67. *Ibid.*, pp. 32-4.
68. *Ibid.*, pp. 36-8.
69. *Ibid.*, pp. 30 and 47 in particular.
70. Olivier de SERRES, *Le Théâtre d'agriculture et mesnage des champs ...*, 1605, p. 89.
71. *Francois Quesnay et la physiocratie*, INED edition, 1958, vol. II, p. 470.
72. P. de SAINT-JACOB, *op. cit.*, p. 152.
73. J.-C. TOUTAIN, *art. cit.*, p. 87.
74. For these figures, cf. Hans Helmut WÄCHTER, *Ostpreussische Domänenvorwerke im 16. und 17. Jahrhundert*, 1958, p. 118.
75. J.-M. RICHARD, *art. cit.*, pp. 17-18.
76. *François Quesnay ...*, *op. cit.*, p. 461 (article 'grains', in the *Encyclopédie*).
77. 'Production et productivité de l'économie agricole en Pologne', in *Troisième Conférence internationale d'histoire économique*, 1965, p. 160.
78. Léonid ZYTKOWICZ, 'Grain yields in Poland, Bohemia, Hungary and Slovakia', in *Acta Poloniae historica*, 1971, p. 24.
79. E. LE ROY LADURIE, *Les paysans du Languedoc*, vol. II, pp. 849-52; I, p.533
80. *Essai politique sur le royaume de la Nouvelle Espagne*, 1811, II, p. 386.
81. E. LE ROY LADURIE, *op. cit.*, II, p. 851.
82. *Yield ratios, 1810-1820*, 1963, p. 16.
83. H.H. WÄCHTER, *op. cit.*, p. 143.

84. Jean GLENISSON, 'Une administration médiévale aux prises avec la disette. La question des blés dans les provinces italiennes de l'État pontifical en 1374-1375', in *Le Moyen Age*, t. 47, 1951, pp. 303-26.
85. Ruggiero ROMANO, 'A propos du commerce du blé dans la Méditerranée des XIVe et XVe siècles', in *Hommage à Lucien Febvre*, 1954, II, pp. 149-56.
86. Jean MEUVRET, *Études d'histoire économique*, 1971, p. 200.
87. *Medit.*, vol. I, p. 330.
88. Ruggiero ROMANO, *Commerce et prix du blé à Marseille au XVIIIe siècle*, 1956, pp. 76-7.
89. A.N., A.E., B^1, 529, 4 February 1710.
90. Andrea METRA, *Il Mentore perfetto de'negozianti*, 1797, V, p. 15.
91. Claude NORDMANN, *Grandeur et liberté de la Suède, 1660-1792*, 1971, p. 45 and note.
92. Werner SOMBART, *Der moderne Kapitalismus*, 1921-8, II, p. 1035; large quantities were exported from England after 1697 and from America in 1770.
93. *Bilanci generali*, 2nd series, I, 1, 1912, pp. 35-7.
94. Jean NICOT, *Correspondance inédite*, ed. E. FALGAIROLLE, 1897, p. 5.
95. J. NICKOLLS, *op. cit.*, p. 357.
96. Moscow, A.E.A., 8813-261, f° 21, Livorno, 30 March 1795.
97. Werner SOMBART, *Krieg und Kapitalismus*, 1913, pp. 137-8.
98. J. SAVARY, *Dictionnaire*, vol. V, col. 579-80.
99. W. SOMBART, *Der moderne Kapitalismus*, *op. cit.*, vol. II, pp. 1032-3.
100. Fritz WAGNER, in *Handbuch der europäischen Geschichte*, ed. Th. Schieder, 1968, IV, p. 107.
101. Yves RENOUARD, 'Une expédition de céréales des Pouilles ...' in *Mélanges d'archéologie et d'histoire de l'École française de Rome*, 1936.
102. W. SOMBART, *Der moderne Kapitalismus*, *op. cit.*, vol. II, p. 1032.
103. *Medit.*, vol. I, pp. 599-602.
104. Exact reference mislaid.
105. On the organization of the *caricatori*, cf. *Medit.*, vol. I, pp. 580-3.
106. *Medit.*, vol. I, pp. 581-2.
107. *Medit.*, vol. I, p. 640.
108. *Histoire du commerce de Marseille*, *op. cit.*, vol. IV, pp. 365 ff.
109. A.P. USHER, *The History of the Grain Trade in France, 1400-1710*, 1913, p. 125.
110. V.S. LUBLINSKY, 'Voltaire et la guerre des farines', in *Annales historiques de la Révolution française*, n° 2, 1959, pp. 127-45.
111. Abbé MABLY, 'Du commerce des grains', in *Œuvres complètes*, XIII, 1795, pp. 144-6.
112. Earl J. HAMILTON, 'Wages and Subsistence on Spanish Treasure Ships, 1503-1660', in *Journal of Political Economy*, 1929.
113. All the following figures were calculated by F.C. SPOONER, 'Régimes alimentaires d'autrefois: proportions et calculs en calories', in *Annales E.S.C.*, 1961, pp. 568-74.
114. Robert PHILIPPE, 'Une opération pilote: L'étude du ravitaillement de Paris au temps de Lavoisier', in *Annales E.S.C.*, XVI, 1961, tables between pages 572 and 573. NB an error in the last table: read 58% for 50%.
115. Armand HUSSON, *Les Consommations de Paris*, 1856, pp. 79-106.
116. Calculations based on the documents in the Museo Correr, Donà delle Rose, 218, f°s 142 ff. From calculations made for the farming years 1603-4, 1604-5 and 1608-9, and allowing for records of the stocks of cereals, average consumption in Venice would have been about 450,000 stara. Since the city's population was 150,000, per capita consumption was 3 stara (at 60 kg to the stara = 180 kg). And these are in fact the figures arrived at by an official inquiry of 1760 (3 stara of wheat or 4.5 of maize). P. GEORGELIN, *op. cit.*, p. 209.
117. Witold KULA, '*Théorie économique du système féodal ...*, XVIe-XVIIIe s., 1970.

118. Robert PHILIPPE, 'Une opération pilote: l'étude du ravitaillement de Paris au temps de Lavoisier' in *Pour une histoire de l'alimentation*, ed. Jean-Jacques HEMARDINQUER, 1970, p. 65, table 5; A. HUSSON, *op. cit.*, p. 106.
119. Louis-Sébastien MERCIER, *Tableau de Paris*, 1782, IV, p. 132.
120. E.H. PHELPS BROWN and Sheila V. HOPKINS, 'Seven Centuries of Building Wages', in *Economica*, August 1955, pp. 195-206.
121. P. de SAINT-JACOB, *op. cit.*, p. 539.
122. Giuseppe PRATO, *La Vita economica in Piemonte in mezzo a secolo XVIII*, 1908.
123. Paul RAVEAU, *Essai sur la situation économique et l'état social en Poitou au XVIe siècle*, 1931, pp. 63-5.
124. Jacques ANDRÉ, *Alimentation et cuisine à Rome*, 1961, pp. 62-3.
125. J.-M. RICHARD, *art. cit.*, p. 21.
126. Jean MEYER, *La Noblesse bretonne au XVIIIe siècle*, 1966, p. 449, note 3.
127. Reference mislaid.
128. O. AGA, *op. cit.*, pp. 64-5.
129. N.F. DUPRÉ DE SAINT-MAUR, *op. cit.*, p. 23.
130. Alfred FRANKLIN, *La Vie privée d'autrefois*, vol. III. *La cuisine*, 1888, p. 91.
131. London, P.R.O. 30, 25, 157, Giornale autografo di Francesco Contarini da Venezia a Madrid.
132. J. SAVARY, *Dictionnaire...*, *op. cit.*, IV, col. 10.
133. L.-S. MERCIER, *op. cit.*, XII, p. 242.
134. A.N., AD XI, 38, 225.
135. Denis DIDEROT, article 'bouillie', *Supplément à l'Encyclopédie*, II, 1776, p. 34.
136. L.-S. MERCIER, *op. cit.*, VIII, p. 154.
137. L.-S. MERCIER, *ibid.*, XII, p. 240.
138. According to documents I have consulted in the Cracow archives.
139. N. DELAMARE, *Traité de police*, II, 1710, p. 895.
140. *Ibid.*, 1772 edn., II, pp. 246-7; A. HUSSON, *op. cit.*, pp. 80-1.
141. A.d.S. Venice, Papadopoli, 12, f° 19 v°.
142. Museo Correr, Donà delle Rose, 218, f° 140 v°.
143. Correspondence of M. de Compans, French Consul in Genoa, A.N., A.E., B¹, 511.
144. Antoine PARMENTIER, *Le Parfait Boulanger*, 1778, pp. 591-2.
145. Jean MEYER, *La Noblesse bretonne au XVIIIe siècle*, *op. cit.*, p. 447 and note.
146. NECKER, *Législation et commerce des grains*, chapter XXIV.
147. *Diari della città di Palermo dal secolo XVI al XIX*, ed. Gioacchino di MARZO, vol. XIV, 1875, pp. 247-8.
148. N. DELAMARE, *op. cit.*, II, p. 1039.
149. *Gazette de France*, Rome, 11 August 1649, p. 749.
150. R. GROUSSET, *Histoire de la Chine*, *op. cit.*
151. FAO Yearbook, 1977.
152. Sir George STAUNTON, *op. cit.*, vol. II, p. 43.
153. M. de GUIGNES, *Voyages à Pékin, Manille et l'Ile de France ... 1784-1801*, 1808, I, p. 354.
154. Vera HSU and Francis HSU, in *Food in Chinese Culture*, ed. K.C. CHANG, *op. cit.*, pp. 300 ff.
155. Pierre GOUROU, *L'Asie*, revised edition, 1971, pp. 83-6.
156. Jules SION, *Asie des moussons*, 1st part, 1928, p. 34.
157. F.W. MOTE, in *Food in Chinese Culture*, *op. cit.*, p. 199.
158. P. GOUROU, *op. cit.*, p. 86.
159. See figures on pages 156, 157.
160. J.-B. du HALDE, *Description géographique, historique, chronologique, politique et physique de l'Empire de la Chine et de la Tartarie chinoise*, 1735, II, p. 65.
161. P. de LAS CORTES, *doc. cit.*, f° 123 v°.
162. Pierre GOUROU, *L'Asie*, 1953, p. 32.
163. *Ibid.*, pp. 30-2.
164. On Siam, E. KAMPFER, *Histoire naturelle ... de l'Empire du Japon*, 1732, I, p. 69. On Cambodia, Éveline POREE-MASPERO, *Études sur les rites agraires des*

165. P. de Las Cortes, *doc. cit.*, f° 43 v°.
166. Sir George Staunton, *op. cit.*, vol. II, pp. 381 ff. *Dictionnaire archéologique des techniques*, 1964, I, pp. 214-15; II, p. 520.
167. Michel Cartier, Pierre E. Will, 'Demographie et institutions en Chine: contributions à l'analyse des recensements de l'époque impériale' in *Annales de démographie historique*, 1971, pp. 212-18, 230-1.
168. Pierre Gourou, *Les Paysans du delta tonkinois*, 1936, pp. 382-7.
169. The details that follow are from Éveline Porée-Maspéro, *op. cit.*, I, 1942, pp. 32 ff.
170. Jean Chardin, *Voyages en Perse*, 1811, IV, pp. 102-5.
171. J. Fourastié, *Machinisme et bien-être*, *op. cit.*, p. 40.
172. Pierre Gourou, *L'Asie*, 1953, p. 55.
173. Pierre Gourou, *Les Pays tropicaux*, 4th edn. 1966, p. 95.
174. J. Spence, in *Food in Chinese Culture*, ed. K.C. Chang, 1977, p. 270.
175. Abbé Prevost, *op. cit.*, VIII, pp. 536, 537.
176. J.-B. du Halde, *op. cit.*, II, p. 72.
177. P. de Las Cortes, *doc. cit.*, f°s 54, 60.
178. *Voyages à Pékin, Manille et l'Ile de France ... 1784-1801*, *op. cit.*, I, p. 320.
179. P. Gourou, *L'Asie*, *op. cit.*, pp. 74, 262.
180. J.A. Mandelslo, *op. cit.*, II, p. 268.
181. J. Savary, *op. cit.*, IV, col. 561.
182. P. de Las Cortes, *doc. cit.* f° 55.
183. Matsuyo Takizawa, *The Penetration of the Money Economy in Japan ...*, 1927, pp. 40-1.
184. P. de Las Cortes, *doc. cit.*, f° 75.
185. Jacques Gernet, *Le Monde chinois*, 1972, pp. 281, 282, 648; Wolfram Eberhard, *A History of China*, 4th edn., 1977, p. 255.
186. F.W. Mote, in *Food in Chinese Culture*, *op. cit.*, pp. 198-200.
187. J. Spence, *ibid.*, pp. 261, 271.
188. Abbé Prévost, *op. cit.*, VI, pp. 452-3 (du Halde).
189. J. Gernet, *Le Monde chinois*, *op. cit.*, pp. 65-6; *Dictionnaire archéologique des techniques*, 1964, II, p. 520.
190. Victor Bérard, *Les Navigations d'Ulysse*, II. *Pénélope et les Barons des îles*, 1928, pp. 318, 319.
191. G.F. Gemelli Careri, *op. cit.*, IV, p. 102.
192. G.B. Samson, *The Western World and Japan*, 1950, p. 241.
193. Michel Vié, *Histoire du Japon*, 1969, p. 99; Thomas C. Smith, *The Agrarian Origins of Modern Japan*, 1959, p. 102.
194. Th. Smith, *ibid.*, pp. 82, 92.
195. *Ibid.*, pp. 68, 156, 208, 211; Matsuyo Takizawa, *The Penetration of the money economy in Japan*, 1927, pp. 34-5, 75-6, 90-2; *Recent trends in Japanese historiography: bibliographical essays*, XIIIth Moscow conference of historical sciences, 1970, I, pp. 43-4.
196. See below, vol. III.
197. G.B. Samson, *op. cit.*, p. 237.
198. Described in the *Life of Columbus by his son* under the date 5 November 1492, as 'a sort of grain called maize, which was very tasty, cooked in the oven or dried and made into flour', A. Maurizio, *op. cit.*, p. 339.
199. R.S. MacNeish, *First annual report of the Tehuacan archaeological-botanical project*, 1961, and *Second annual report*, 1962.
200. G.F. Gemelli Careri, *op. cit.*, VI, p. 30.
201. F. Coreal, *op. cit.*, I, p. 23.
202. P. Vidal de La Blache, *op. cit.*, p. 137.
203. Jean-Pierre Berthe, 'Production et productivité agricoles au Mexique, XVIe-XVIIIe siècles' in Third International Conference on Economic History, Munich, 1965.
204. F. Márquez Miranda, 'Civilisations pré-colombiennes, civilisation du maïs', in *A travers les Amériques latines*, in series edited by Lucien Febvre, *Cahiers des Annales*, n° 4, pp. 99-100.
205. Marie Helmer, 'Les Indiens des plateaux andins', in *Cahiers d'outremer*, n° 8, 1949, p. 3.
206. Marie Helmer, 'Note brève sur les Indiens Yuras', in *Journal de la société des américanistes*, 1966, pp. 244-6.

207. Alexandre de Humboldt, *Voyage aux régions équinoxiales du Nouveau Continent fait en 1799 et 1800*, 1961 edn., p. 6.
208. A. de Saint-Hilaire, *Voyages dans l'intérieur du Brésil*, part 1, I, 1830, pp. 64-8.
209. Rodrigo de Vivero, *Du Japon et du bon gouvernement de l'Espagne et des Indes*, ed. Juliette Monbeig, 1972, pp. 212-13.
210. Earl J. Hamilton, *American Treasure and Price Revolution in Spain*, 1934, p. 213, note 1, found tomatoes among the foodstuffs bought by a hospital in Andalusia in 1608.
211. Georges and Geneviève Frêche, *Le Prix des grains, des vins et des légumes à Toulouse, (1486-1868)*, 1967, pp. 20-2.
212. Carl O. Sauer, 'Maize into Europe', in *Akten des 34. Internationales Amerikanischen Kongresses*, 1960, p. 781.
213. O. de Serres, *Le Théâtre de l'agriculture . . .*, op. cit., II, p. 4.
214. A. Bourde, *Agronomie et agronomes en France au XVIIIe siècle*, 1967, I, p. 185, note 5.
215. Traian Stoianovich, 'Le maïs dans les Balkans', in *Annales, E.S.C.*, 1966, pp. 1027, note 3, 1029, note 1.
216. J. Georgelin, *op. cit.*, p. 205.
217. G. Anthony, *L'Industrie de la toile à Pau et en Béarn*, 1961, p. 17.
218. G. and G. Frêche, *op. cit.*, pp. 20-2, 34-7.
219. Memorandum on Béarn and Lower Navarre, 1700, B.N. Ms. fr. 4287, f° 6.
220. Moscow, A.E.A., 72/5, 254, f° 29.
221. P. de Saint-Jacob, *op. cit.*, p. 398.
222. Jérôme and Jean Tharaud, *La Bataille de Scutari*, 24th edn., 1927, p. 101.
223. J. Georgelin, *op. cit.*, pp. 205, 225.
224. G. and G. Frêche, *op. cit.*, p. 36,
225. Filippo Pigafetta and Duarte Lopez, *Description du royaume de Congo*, 1591, trans. by W. Bal, 1973, p. 76.
226. P. Verger, *Dieux d'Afrique*, 1954, pp. 168, 176, 180.
227. Ping-Ti Ho, 'The Introduction of American food plants into China', *art. cit.*
228. Berthold Laufer, *The American Plant Migration, the Potato*, 1938.
229. Quoted by R.M. Hartwell, *The Industrial Revolution and Economic Growth*, 1971, p. 127.
230. Cracow Archives, Czartoryski papers, 807, f° 19.
231. Johann Gottlieb Georgi, *op. cit.*, p. 585.
232. B. Laufer, *op. cit.*, pp. 102-5.
233. E. Julliard, *op. cit.*, p. 213.
234. D. Mathieu, *L'Ancien Régime dans la province de Lorraine et Barrois*, 1879, p. 323.
235. K.H. Connell, 'The Potato in Ireland', in *Past and Present*, n° 23, Nov. 1962, pp. 57-71.
236. To Dunkirk (1712): A.N., G⁷, 1698, f° 64; to Portugal (1765): A.N., F¹², f°s 143 ff.
237. Adam Smith, *The Wealth of Nations*, 1937, p. 161.
238. E. Roze, *Histoire de la pomme de terre*, 1898, p. 162.
239. J. Beckmann, *Beiträge zur Oekonomie*, *op. cit.*, V, p. 280.
240. Ch. Vanderbroeke, 'Cultivation and consumption of the potato in the 17th and 18th Centuries', in *Acta historiae neerlandica*, V, 1971, p. 35.
241. *Ibid.*, p. 21.
242. *Ibid.*, p. 35.
243. *Ibid.*, p. 28.
244. Adam Smith, The *Wealth of Nations*, 1863 edn., p. 35, quoted by Pollard and Crossley, *op. cit.*, p. 157.
245. Louis Simond, *Voyage d'un Français en Angleterre pendant les années 1810 et 1811*, vol. I, p. 160. A detail from Gabriel Sagard, *Le Grand Voyage du pays des Hurons*, 1976 edn.: the vessel that was taking him to Canada captured a small English ship on board which was found a barrel of potatoes 'which looked like big turnips, but tasted much nicer', p. 16.
246. G.F. Gemelli Careri, *op. cit.*, vol. IV, p. 80.
247. Labat, *Nouveau voyage aux isles de l'Amérique*, 1722, vol. I, p. 353.

248. G.F. Gemelli Careri, *op. cit.*, vol. VI, p. 25.
249. *Ibid.*, vol. VI, p. 89.
250. Ester Boserup, *Evolution agraire et pression démographique*, 1970, pp. 23 ff.
251. Father Jean-François de Rome, *La Fondation de la mission des Capucins au Royaume du Congo*, trans. Bontinck, 1964, p. 89.
252. Otto von Kotzebue, *Reise um die Welt ...*, *op. cit.*, vol. I, pp. 70-1.
253. Pierre Gourou, *L'Amérique tropicale et australe*, 1976, pp. 29-32.
254. *Ibid.*, p. 32.
255. J.-F. de Rome, *op. cit.*, p. 90.
256. Georges Balandier, *La Vie quotidienne au royaume de Kongo du XVIe au XVIIIe siècle*, 1965, pp. 77-8.
257. Abbé Prevost, *op. cit.*, vol. XII, p. 274.
258. Louis-Antoine de Bougainville, *Voyage autour du monde*, 1958 edn., p. 120.
259. *The Journals of Captain Cook*, ed. J.C. Beaglehole, Cambridge, 1955, vol. I, p. 75.
260. *Ibid.*, I, pp. 121-2.
261. *Ibid.*, I, p. 45.
262. Abbé Prevost, *Supplément des voyages*, vol. XX, p. 126.
263. *Op. cit.*, vol. XV, pp. 1 ff.
264. *Ibid.*, p. 87.

notes to chapter 3

1. John Nef, *War and human progress*, 1968 edn., p. 10.
2. Erasmus, *De civilitate morum puerilium*.
3. Dr Jean Claudian, F.I.P.A.L. international conference, November 1964, *Rapport préliminaire*, p. 34.
4. L.A. Caraccioli, *Dictionnaire critique, pittoresque et sententieux, propre à faire connaître les usages du siècle, ainsi que ses bizarreries*, 1768, vol. I, p. 24.
5. Gerónimo de Uztariz, *Theoría y practica de comercio y de marina*, 1724, pp. 348-9.
6. B. de Laffemas, *Reiglement général pour dresser les manufactures en ce royaume ...*, 1597, p. 17.
7. Abbé Prevost, *op. cit.*, vol. VI, p. 142 (Du Halde's voyage).
8. L.-S. Mercier, *L'An deux mille quatre cent*, *op. cit.*, p. 368, note a.
9. Werner Sombart, *Luxus und Kapitalismus*, 1922, p. 2.
10. Theodosius Dobzhansky, *Mankind evolving*, 1962, p. 325.
11. *Food in Chinese culture*, ed. K.C. Chang, *op. cit.*
12. L.-S. Mercier, *Tableau de Paris*, 1782, vol. XI, pp. 345-6
13. *Food in Chinese Culture, op. cit.*, pp. 15, 271, 280.
14. Ortensio Landi, *Commentario delle più notabili e mostruose cose d'Italia*, n.d., pp. 5-6.
15. 'Voyage de Jérôme Lippomano', in *Relations des ambassadeurs vénitiens sur les affaires de France au XVIe siècle*, vol. II, 1838, p. 605 (Collection des documents inédits sur l'Histoire de France).
16. A. Franklin, *op. cit.*, vol. III, p. 205.
17. L.-S. Mercier, *Tableau de Paris*, *op. cit.*, vol. V, p. 79
18. A. Caillot, *Mémoires pour servir à l'histoire des moeurs et usages des Français*, 1827, vol. II, p. 148.
19. L.A. Caraccioli, *Dictionnaire ... sententieux*, *op. cit.*, vol. I, p. 349; III, p. 370; I, p. 47.
20. Marquis de Paulmy, *Précis d'une histoire générale de la vie privée des Français*, 1779, p. 23.
21. A. Franklin, *op. cit.*, vol. III, pp. 47-8.

22. Le Ménagier de Paris, traité de morale et d'économie domestique composé vers 1393, 1846, vol. II, p. 93.
23. Michel de MONTAIGNE, Journal de voyage en Italie, Pléiade edn., 1967, p. 1131.
24. RABELAIS, Pantagruel, Book IV, chapters LIX and LX.
25. Philippe MANTELLIER, 'Mémoire sur la valeur des principales denrées ... qui se vendaient ... en la ville d'Orléans', in Mémoires de la société archéologique de l'Orléanais, 1862, p. 121.
26. Gazette de France, 1763, p. 385.
27. Hermann VAN DER WEE, 'Typologie des crises et changements de structures aux Pays-Bas (XVe-XVIe siècles)', in Annales, E.S.C., 1963, no. 1, p. 216.
28. W. ABEL, 'Wandlungen des Fleischverbrauchs und der Fleischversorgung in Deutschland ...', in Berichte über Landwirtschaft, p. 415.
29. Voyage de Jerôme Lippomano, op. cit., p. 575.
30. Thoinot ARBEAU, Orchésographie (1588), 1888 edn., p. 24.
31. W. ABEL, Crises agraires en Europe, XIIIe-XXe siècle, op. cit., p. 150.
32. Ugo TUCCI, 'L'Ungheria e gli approvvigionamenti veneziani di bovini nel Cinquecento', in Studia Humanitatis, 2; Rapporti veneto-ungheresi all'epoca del Rinascimento, 1975, pp. 153-71; A.d.S. Venice, Cinque Savii, 9 f° 162; Histoire du commerce de Marseille, III, 1481-1599, by R. COLLIER and J. BILLIOUDE, 1951, pp. 144-5.
33. L. DELISLE, Etudes sur la condition de la classe agricole et l'état de l'agriculture en Normandie au Moyen Age, 1851, p. 26.
34. E. LE ROY LADURIE, Les Paysans du Languedoc, 2nd edn. 1966, vol. I, pp. 177-9.
35. W. ABEL, art. cit., p. 430.
36. Noël du FAIL, propos rustiques et facétieux, 1856 edn., p. 32.
37. G. de GOUBERVILLE, Journal, 1892, p. 464.
38. C. HATON, Mémoires ..., op. cit., p. 279.
39. W. ABEL, Crises agraires en Europe, op. cit., pp. 198-200.
40. André PLAISSE, la Baronnie du Neubourg, 1961; Pierre CHAUNU, 'Le Neubourg. Quatre siècles d'histoire normande, XIVe-XVIIIe', in Annales E.S.C., 1961, pp. 1152-68.
42. R. GRANDAMY, 'La grande régression. Hypothèse sur l'évolution des prix réels de 1375 à 1876', in Prix de vente et prix de revient (13e série), 1952, p.52.
42. A. HUSSON, Les Consommations de Paris, op. cit., p. 157; Jean-Claude TOUTAIN, in Histoire quantitative de l'économie française, vol. I, Cahiers de l'I.S.E.A., 1961, pp. 164-5; LAVOISIER, 'De la richesse de la France' and 'Essai sur la population de la ville de Paris', in Mélanges d'économie politique, vol. I, 1966, pp. 597-8, 602.
43. W. ABEL, Crises agraires en Europe ..., op. cit., pp. 353-4.
44. J. MILLERET, De la réduction du droit sur le sel, 1829, pp. 6, 7.
45. Emile MIREAUX, Une Province française au temps du Grand Roi, la Brie, 1958, p. 131.
46. Michel MORINEAU, 'Rations de marine (Angleterre, Hollande, Suède et Russie)', in Annales E.S.C., 1965.
47. Paul ZUMTHOR, La Vie quotidienne en Hollande au temps de Rembrandt, 1959, pp. 88 ff.
48. L. LEMERY, op. cit., pp. 235-6.
49. P. de SAINT-JACOB, op. cit., p. 540.
50. P.J. GROSLEY, Londres, 1770, vol. I, p. 290.
51. Mémoires de Mademoiselle de Montpensier, ed. CHERUEL, 1858-9, vol. III, p. 339.
52. Abbé PREVOST, op. cit., vol. X, pp. 128-9 (Tavernier's voyage).
53. R. de VIVERO, op. cit., p. 269.
54. F. BERNIER, Voyages ..., op. cit., 1699, vol. II, p. 252.
55. Father de LAS CORTES, doc. cit., p. 54.
56. G.F. GEMELLI CARERI, op. cit., vol. IV, p. 474.

57. *Mémoires concernant l'histoire, les sciences, les arts, les moeurs des Chinois*, by the missionaries in Peking, vol. IV, 1779, pp. 321-2.
58. Ho SHIN-CHUN, *Le Roman des lettrés*, 1933, pp. 74, 162, 178.
59. G.F. GEMELLI CARERI, *op. cit.*, vol. IV, p. 107; P. de MAGAILLANS, *Nouvelle Relation de la Chine*, 1688 (written in 1668), pp. 177-8.
60. R. MANTRAN, *Istanbul dans la seconde moitié du XVIIe siècle, op. cit.*, p. 196.
61. G.F. GEMELLI CARERI, *op. cit.*, vol. I, pp. 63-4.
62. *Ibid.*, vol. V, p. 305.
63. R. BAEHREL, *Une Croissance: la Basse-Provence rurale* ..., *op. cit.*, p. 173.
64. L. SIMOND, *Voyage d'un Français en Angleterre* ..., *op. cit.*, vol. II, p. 332.
65. L.S. MERCIER, *op. cit.*, 1783, vol. V, p. 77.
66. *Ibid.*, p. 79.
67. A. FRANKLIN, *op. cit.*, vol. III, p. 139.
68. *Medit.*, vol. I, p. 152 ('buntings').
69. L.-S. MERCIER, vol. V, p. 252.
70. *Ibid.*, p. 85.
71. *Voyage de Jérôme Lippomano, op. cit.*, vol. II, p. 609.
72. MONTAIGNE, *Journal de voyage en Italie, op. cit.*, p. 1118.
73. *Ibid.*, p. 1131.
74. Alfred FRANKLIN, *La Vie privée d'autrefois*, vol. IX, *Variétés gastronomiques*, 1891, p. 60.
75. MONTAIGNE, *Journal de voyage* ..., p. 1136.
76. MONTAIGNE, *Essais*, Pléiade edn., 1962, pp. 1054, 1077.
77. *Les Voyages du Seigneur de Villamont*, 1609, p. 473; *Coryate's Crudities* (1611), 1776 edn., I, p. 107.
78. A: FRANKLIN, *op. cit.*, vol. I, *La civilité, l'étiquette et le bon ton*, 1908, pp. 289-91.
79. Alfred GOTTSCHALK, *Histoire de l'alimentation et de la gastronomie* ..., 1948, vol. II, pp. 168, 184.
80. MONTAIGNE, *Essais, op. cit.*, p. 1054.
81. C. DUCLOS, *Mémoires sur sa vie*, in *Œuvres*, 1820, vo. I, p. LXI.
82. G.F. GEMELLI CARERI, *op. cit.*, vol. II, p. 61.
83. J.B. LABAT, *Nouvelle Relation de l'Afrique occidentale, op. cit.*, vol. I, p. 282.
84. Baron de TOTT, *Mémoires*, vol. I, 1784, p. 111.
85. Ch. GERARD, *L'Ancienne Alsace à table*, 1877, p. 299.
86. According to the archives of Stockhalpen and Alain DUBOIS, *Die Salzversorgung des Wallis 1500-1610, Wirtschaft und Politik*, 1965, pp. 41-6.
87. Dr CLAUDIAN, First international conference of F.I.P.A.L., 1964, preliminary report, p. 39.
88. A. FRANKLIN, *La Vie privée d'autrefois, La cuisine, op. cit.*, pp. 32, 33, 90.
89. *Medit.*, vol. I, p. 151 and note 183.
90. Archives of Bouches-du-Rhône, Amirauté de Marseille, B. IX, 14.
91. J. SAVARY, *op. cit.*, vol. II, col. 778.
92. L. LEMERY, *op. cit.*, p. 301.
93. A.N., 315, AP 2, 47, London, 14 March 1718.
94. G.F. GEMELLI CARERI, *op. cit.*, vol. II, p. 77.
95. *Voyage ... de M. de Guignes, op. cit.*, vol. I, p. 378.
96. Patrick COLQUHOUN, *The Police of the Metropolis*, 6th edn., 1800, p. 92.
97. Bartolomé PINHEIRO DA VEIGA, 'La Corte de Felipe III', in *Viajes de extranjeros por España y Portugal*, vol. II, 1959, pp. 136-7.
98. L. LEMERY, *op. cit.*, p. 295.
99. Antonio de BEATIS, *Voyage du cardinal d'Aragon ... (1517-1518)*, ed. Madeleine HAVARD DE LA MONTAGNE, 1913, p. 119.
100. J. SAVARY, *op. cit.*, vol. V, col. 182; and vol. I, col. 465.
101. CARACCIOLI, *Dictionnaire, op. cit.*, vol. I, p. 24.

102. Giuseppe PARENTI, *Prime Ricerche sulla rivoluzione dei prezzi in Firenze*, 1939, p. 120.
103. G.F. GEMELLI CARERI, *op. cit.*, vol. VI, p. 21.
104. *Journal de voyage en Italie*, *op. cit.*, p. 1152.
105. MONTESQUIEU, *Voyages en Europe*, p. 282.
106. G.F. GEMELLI CARERI, *op. cit.*, vol. II, p. 475.
107. A. FRANKLIN, *op. cit.*, vol. IX, *Variétés gastronomiques*, 1891, p. 135.
108. Jacques ACCARIAS DE SERIONNE, *La Richesse de la Hollande*, 1778, vol. I, pp. 14, 192.
109. P. BOISSONNADE, 'Le Mouvement commercial entre la France et les îles Britanniques au XVIe siècle', in *Revue historique*, 1920, p. 8; H. BECHTEL, *op. cit.*, vol. II, p. 53. The Schonen fisheries were abandoned in 1473.
110. Bartolomé PINHEIRO DA VEIGA, *op. cit.*, pp. 137-8.
111. J. SAVARY, *op. cit.*, vol. III, col. 1002 ff.; Ch. de LA MORANDIERE, *Histoire de la pêche française de la morue dans l'Amérique septentrionale*, 1962, 3 vols., vol. I, pp. 145 ff. on green cod; pp. 161 ff. on dry cod.
112. A.N., K series (now returned to Spain), full reference mislaid.
113. E. TROCME and M. DELAFOSSE, *Le Commerce rochelais de la fin du XVe siècle au début du XVIIe*, 1952, pp. 17-18, 120-3; J. SAVARY, *op. cit.*, vol. III, col. 1000.
114. J. SAVARY, *op. cit.*, vol. III, col. 997.
115. B.N., new acquisitions, 9389, chevalier de Razilly to Richelieu, 26 November 1626.
116. A.N., A.E., B III, 442.
117. Paul DECHARME, *Le Comptoir d'un marchand au XVIIe siècle d'après une correspondance inédite*, 1910, pp. 99-110; N. DELAMARE, *Traité de police, op. cit.*, vol. I, p. 607; Ch. de LA MORANDIERE, *op. cit.*, vol. I, p. 1: Fishermen 'are in the habit of saying "I caught some 25-to-the-thousand cod" which means that 1000 of such cod after salting would weigh 25 quintals (1 quintal = 50 kilograms). The best size yielded 60 quintals for a thousand, medium-sized 25 and small 10.'
118. N. DELAMARE, *op. cit.*, vol. III, 1722, p. 65.
119. Moscow, A.E.A., 7215-295, f° 28, Lisbon, 15 March 1791.
120. G. de UZTARIZ, *op. cit.*, vol. II, p. 44.
121. N. DELAMARE, *op. cit.*, vol. I, 1705, p. 574 (1603).
122. *Variétés, op. cit.*, vol. I, p. 316.
123. A. FRANKLIN, *La Vie privée d'autrefois*, vol. III, *La Cuisine, op. cit.*, p. 19 and note. Ambroise PARE, *Œuvres*, 1607, p. 1065.
124. N. DELAMARE, *op. cit.*, vol. III, 1719, p. 65.
125. J. ACCARIAS DE SERIONNE, *La Richesse de la Hollande, op. cit.*, vol. I, pp. 14, 192.
126. Wanda OESAU, *Hamburgs Grönlandsfahrt auf Walfischfang und Robbenschlag vom 17-19 Jahrhundert*, 1955.
127. P. J.-B. LE GRAND D'AUSSY, *Histoire de la vie privée des Français, op. cit.*, II, p. 168.
128. Kamala MARKANIAGA, *Le Riz et la mousson*, 1956.
129. J. ANDRE, *Alimentation et cuisine à Rome, op. cit.*, pp. 207-11.
130. J. SAVARY, *op. cit.*, 1761, vol. III, col. 704. It was also called *maniguette* and *maniquette*. A.N., F 12, 70, f° 150.
131. SEMPERE Y GALINDO, *Historia del luxo y de las leyes suntuarias*, 1788, vol. II, p. 2, note 1.
132. *Le Ménagier de Paris, op. cit.*, vol. II, p. 125.
133. Gomez de BRITO, *Historia tragico-maritima*, 1598, vol. II, p. 416. Abbé PREVOST, *op. cit.*, vol. XIV, p. 314.
134. Dr CLAUDIAN, *Rapport préliminaire*, art. cit., p. 37.
135. A.N., Marine, B⁷ 463, f°s 65 ff.
136. MABLY, *De la situation politique de la Pologne*, 1776, pp. 68-9.

137. BOILEAU, *Satires*, Garnier-Flammarion edn., 1969, Satire III, pp. 62 ff.
138. K. GLAMANN, *Dutch-Asiatic Trade, 1620-1740*, 1958, table 2, p. 14.
139. Ernst Ludwig CARL, *Traité de la richesse des princes et de leurs Etats et des moyens simples et naturels pour y parvenir, 1722-1723*, p. 236. John NICKOLLS, *op. cit.*, p. 253.
140. K. GLAMANN, *op. cit.*, pp. 153-9. Chinese sugar disappeared from the European market after 1661.
141. Sir George STAUNTON, *op. cit.*
142. A. ORTELIUS, *Théâtre de l'univers*, 1572, p. 2.
143. Alice Piffer CANABRAVA, *A industria do açucar nas ilhas inglesas e francesas do mar das Antilhas (1697-1755)*, 1946 (typescript), pp. 12 ff.
144. I am relying here on information from the Cyprus end: what is referred to as a large sale in 1464 concerned some 800 quintals: L. de MAS-LATRIE, *Histoire de l'île de Chypre*, vol. III, 1854, pp. 88-90. On 12 March 1463, the *trafego* galleon from Venice found there was no sugar to load, evidence that production was low, A.d.S. Venice, Senato mar, 7, f° 107 v°.
145. Lord SHEFFIELD, *Observations on the commerce of the American States*, 1783, p. 89.
146. These figures for Paris are taken from Lavoisier, quoted in R. PHILIPPE, *art. cit.*, table I, p. 569 and Armand HUSSON, *Les Consommations de Paris, op. cit.*, p. 330.
147. Pierre BELON, *Les Observations de plusieurs singularitez et choses mémorables trouvées en Grèce, Asie, Judée, Egypte, Arabie et autres pays étranges*, 1553, pp. 106, 191.
148. Abbé RAYNAL, *Histoire philosophique et politique des établissements et du commerce des Européens dans les deux Indes*, 1775, vol. III, p. 86.
149. W. SOMBART, *Der Moderne Kapitalismus, op. cit.*, vol. II 2, p. 1031.
150. J.-F. de ROME, *op. cit.*, p. 62.
151. John PRINGLE, *Observations on the Diseases of the Army in camp and garrison ...*, London, 1752.
152. J.A. FRANÇA, *Une Ville des Lumières: La Lisbonne de Pombal*, 1965, p. 48; Suzanne CHANTAL, *La Vie quotidienne au Portugal après le tremblement de terre de Lisbonne de 1755*, 1962, p. 232.
153. Jean DELUMEAU, *Vie économique et sociale de Rome dans la seconde moitié du XVIe siècle*, 1957, pp. 331-9; on Genoa, cf. J. de LALANDE, *Voyage en Italie*, vol. VIII, pp. 494-5.
154. *Variétiés*, vol. II, p. 223, note 1.
155. J. GROSLEY, *Londres, op. cit.*, vol. I, p. 138.
156. L.S. MERCIER, *L'An deux mille quatre cent quarante, op. cit.*, p. 41, note a.
157. L.S. MERCIER, *op. cit.*, vol. VIII, 1783, p. 340.
158. B. PINHEIRO DA VEIGA, *op. cit.*, p. 138.
159. *Food in Chinese Culture, op. cit.*, pp. 229-30.
160. *Ibid.*, p. 291.
161. B. PINHEIRO, *op. cit.*, p. 138.
162. A.N., A.E. B 1, 890, 22 June 1754.
163. Jean BODIN, *La Réponse ... au Paradoxe de M. de Malestroit sur le faict des monnoyes*, 1568, f° 1 r°.
164. Comte de ROCHECHOUART, *Souvenirs sur la Révolution, L'Empire et la Restauration*, 1889, p. 110.
165. Francis DRAKE, *The Second circumnavigation of Earth or the renowned Voyage of Sir Francis Drake*, 1625.
166. G.F. GEMELLI CARERI, *op. cit.*, vol. II, p. 103.
167. R. HAKLUYT, *The Principal Navigations, Voyages, Traffiques and Discoveries of the English Nation*, 1599-1600, vol. II, p. 98.
168. Jean d'AUTON, *Histoire de Louys XII, roy de France*, 1620, p. 12.
169. *Felix et Thomas Platter à Montpellier, 1552-1559 et 1595-1599, notes de voyage de deux étudiants bâlois*, 1892, pp. 48, 126.
170. *Medit.*, vol. I, pp. 198, 209.
171. Le Loyal Serviteur, *La Très Joyeuse et très Plaisante Histoire composée par le Loyal Serviteur des faits, gestes, triomphes du bon chevalier Bayard*, ed. J.C. BUCHON, 1872, p. 106.

172. J. BECKMANN, *op. cit.*, vol. V, p. 2. According to a document of 1723, 'for some time now, since the custom has been adopted of putting wine in bottles of thick glass, all sorts of people have begun making and selling stoppers made of cork', A.N., G⁷, 1706, f° 177.
173. *Histoire de Bordeaux*, ed. Ch. HIGOUNET, vol. III, 1966, pp. 102-3.
174. Archivo General de Simancas, Guerra antigua, XVI, Mondejar to Charles v, 2 December 1539.
175. J. SAVARY, *op. cit.*, vol. V, col. 1215-16; the *Encyclopédie*, 1756, vol. XVII, p. 290, article 'Vin'.
176. Gui PATIN, *Lettres, op. cit.*, vol. I, p. 211 (2 December 1650).
177. L.-S. MERCIER, *op. cit.*, vol. VIII, 1783, p. 225.
178. J. SAVARY, *op. cit.*, vol. IV, col. 1222-3.
179. L.A. CARACCIOLI, *op. cit.*, vol. III, p. 112.
180. Bartolomé BENNASSAR, 'L'alimentation d'une capitale espagnole au XVIᵉ siècle: Valladolid', in *Pour une histoire de l'alimentation*, ed. J.-J. HEMARDINQUER, *op. cit.*, p. 57.
181. Roger DION, *Histoire de la vigne et du vin en France*, 1959, pp. 505-11.
182. L.-S. MERCIER, *Tableau de Paris, op. cit.*, vol. I, pp. 271-2.
183. G.F. GEMELLI CARERI, *op. cit.*, vol. VI, p. 387.
184. A. HUSSON, *op. cit.*, p. 214.
185. K.C. CHANG, in *Food in Chinese Culture, op. cit.*, p. 30.
186. P.J.-B. LE GRAND D'AUSSY, *op. cit.*, vol. II, p. 304.
187. *Ibid.*
188. *Storia della tecnologia*, ed. Ch. SINGER *et al.*, 1962, vol. II, p. 144.
189. *Ibid.*, pp. 144-5 and J. BECKMANN, *Beiträge zur Oekonomie*, 1781, vol. V, p. 280.
190. G. Macaulay TREVELYAN, *History of England*, 1943, p. 287, note 1.
191. René PASSET, *L'Industrie dans la généralité de Bordeaux ...*, 1954, pp. 24 ff.
192. *Histoire de Bordeaux*, ed. C. HIGOUNET, *op. cit.*, vol. IV, pp. 500, 520.
193. P.J.-B. LE GRAND D'AUSSY, *op. cit.*, vol. II, pp. 307-8.
194. *Ibid.*, vol. II, p. 315.
195. A. HUSSON, *op. cit.*, pp. 212, 218.
196. A.N., A.E., B¹, 757, 17 July 1687. Letter from Bonrepaus to Seignelay.
197. A.N., Marine, B⁷, 463, f° 75.
198. Cf., for example, N. DELAMARE, *op. cit.*, vol. II, pp. 975, 976, or the decision of the court of the Parlement in September 1740, for prohibition in time of famine.
199. *Vom Bierbrauen*, Erffurth, 1575.
200. Reference mislaid.
201. ESTEBANILLO-GONZALEZ, 'Vida y hechos', in *La Novela picaresca española*, 1966, pp. 1796, 1799.
202. M. GACHARD, *Retraite et mort de Charles Quint, op. cit.*, vol. II, p. 114 (1 February 1557).
203. André PLASSE, *La Baronnie du Neubourg. Essai d'histoire agraire, économique et sociale*, 1961, p. 202; Jules SION, *Les Paysans de la Normandie orientale: étude géographique sur les populations rurales du Caux et du Bray, du Vexin normand et de la vallée de la Seine*, 1909, p. 154.
204. J. SION, *op. cit.*
205. René MUSSET, *Le Bas-Maine, étude géographique*, 1917, pp. 304-5.
206. A. HUSSON, *op. cit.*, pp. 214, 219, 221.
207. *Storia della tecnologia, op. cit.*, p. 145.
208. *Chroniques de Froissart*, 1868 edn., vol. XII, pp. 43-4.
209. M. MALOUIN, *Traité de chimie*, 1735, p. 260.
210. *Storia della tecnologia, op. cit.*, vol. II, p. 147 and Hans FOLG, *Wem der geprant Wein nutz sey oder schad ...*, 1493, quoted *ibid.*, p. 147 and note 73.
211. Lucien SITTLER, *La Viticulture et le vin de Colmar à travers les siècles*, 1956.
212. R. PASSET, *op. cit.*, pp. 20-1.
213. *Bilanci generali*, 1912, I¹, p. LXXXVIII.
214. J. SAVARY, *op. cit.*, vol. V, col. 147-8.

215. Papers concerning the Intendance of the three bishoprics of Metz, Toul and Verdun, 1698. B.N., Ms. fr. 4285, f°s 41 v° 42.
216. Guillaume GERAUD-PARRACHA, *Le Commerce des vins et des eaux de vie en Languedoc sous l'Ancien Régime*, 1958, pp. 298, 306-7.
217. *Ibid.*, p. 72.
218. *Storia della tecnologia, op. cit.*, vol. III, p. 12.
219. Jean GIRARDIN, *Notice biographique sur Edouard Adam*, 1856.
220. L. LEMERY, *op. cit.*, p. 509.
221. J. PRINGLE, *op. cit.*
222. L.-S. MERCIER, *Tableau de Paris, op. cit.*, vol. II, pp. 19 ff.
223. L. LEMERY, *op. cit.*, p. 512.
224. Gui PATIN, *Lettres, op. cit.*, vol. I, p. 305.
225. AUDIGER, *La Maison réglée*, 1692.
226. J. SAVARY, *op. cit.*, vol. II, col. 216-17.
227. In 1710, the *syndics du commerce* in Normandy protested against a ruling forbidding any spirits not made from wine. A.N., G⁷, 1695, f° 192.
228. According to N. DELAMARE, *op. cit.*, 1710, p. 975 and Le POTTIER DE LA HESTROY, A.N., G⁷, 1687, f° 18 (1704), the 'invention' dates from the sixteenth century.
229. J. SAVARY, *op. cit.*, vol. II, col. 208 (article 'eau-de-vie').
230. J. de LERY, *Histoire d'un voyage faict en la terre du Brésil*, 1580, p. 124.
231. P. Diego de HAEDO, *Topographía e historia general de Argel*, 1612, f° 38.
232. J.A. de MANDELSLO, *op. cit.*, vol. II, p. 122.
233. E. KAMPFER, *op. cit.*, vol. III, pp. 7-8 and vol. I, p. 72.
234. *Mémoires concernant l'histoire, les sciences, les moeurs, les usages, etc. des Chinois*, by the French missionaries in Peking, vol. V, 1780, pp. 467-74, 478.
235. Sir George STAUNTON, *op. cit.*, vol. II, p. 7.
236. Abbé PREVOST, *Histoire générale des voyages*, vol. XVIII, 1768, pp. 334-5.
237. According to information from my friend and colleague Ali MAZAHERI.
238. *Food in Chinese Culture*, ed. K.C. CHANG, *op. cit.*, pp. 122, 156, 202.
239. According to a manuscript note by Alvaro Jara.
240. Reference mislaid.
241. Mademoiselle de Montpensier's memoirs, quoted by A. FRANKLIN, *La Vie privée d'autrefois, le café, le thé, le chocolat*, 1893, pp. 166-7.
242. Bonaventure d'ARGONNE, *Mélanges d'histoire et de littérature*, 1725, vol. I, p. 4.
243. Letters of 11 February, 15 April, 13 May, 25 October 1671, and 15 January 1672.
244. A. FRANKLIN, *op. cit.*, p. 171.
245. Amsterdam Archives, Koopmansarchief, Aron Colace the Elder.
246. G.F. GEMELLI CARERI, *op. cit.*, vol. I, p. 140.
247. L. DERMIGNY, *op. cit.*, vol. I, p. 379.
248. Gui PATIN, *Lettres*, vol. I, p. 383 and vol. II, p. 360.
249. *The Diary of Samuel Pepys*, ed. LATHAN and MATTHEWS, 1970, vol. I, entry for 25 September 1660, 'a cupp of Tee (a China drink) of which I had never drank before'.
250. L. DERMIGNY, *op. cit.*, vol. I, p. 381.
251. A. FRANKLIN, *op. cit.*, p. 122-4.
252. L. DERMIGNY, *La Chine et l'Occident. Le commerce à Canton, op. cit.*, accompanying volume, tables 4 and 5.
253. Sir George STAUNTON, *op. cit.*, vol. I, p. 22.
254. S. POLLARD and D. CROSSLEY, *The Wealth of Britain, op. cit.*, p. 166.
255. Sir George STAUNTON, *op. cit.*, vol. II, p. 528.
256. Leningrad Archives, exact reference mislaid.
257. *Food in Chinese Culture, op. cit.*, pp. 70, 122.
258. Pierre GOUROU, *L'Asie, op. cit.*, p. 133.
259. Quoted by J. SAVARY, *op. cit.*, vol. IV, col. 992.
260. Sir George STAUNTON, *op. cit.*, vol. II, p. 70.
261. J. SAVARY, *op. cit.*, vol. IV, col. 993.
262. Exact reference mislaid.

263. P. de Las Cortes, doc. cit.
264. J. Savary, op. cit., vol. IV, col. 993.
265. G. de Ustariz, op. cit. (French trans. of 1753, vol. II, p. 90.)
266. The following details are taken from Antoine Galland, De l'origine et du progrez du café. Sur un manuscrit/arabe/ de la Bibliothèque du Roy, 1699; Abbé Prevost, op. cit., vol. X, pp. 304 ff.
267. J.B. Tavernier, op. cit., vol. II, p. 249.
268. De plantis Aegypti liber, 1592, chap. XVI.
269. Pietro della Valle, Les Fameux Voyages ..., 1670, vol. I, p. 78.
270. According to his son, Jean de La Roque, Le Voyage de l'Arabie heureuse, 1716, p. 364.
271. A. Franklin, La Vie privée d'autrefois, le café, le thé, le chocolat, op. cit., p. 33.
272. Ibid., p. 22.
273. Ibid., p. 36.
274. De l'usage du caphé, du thé et du chocolate, anon., 1671, p. 23.
275. A. Franklin, op. cit., pp. 45, 248.
276. For the following paragraph, cf. Jean Leclant, 'Le café et les cafés à Paris (1644-1693)', in Annales, E.S.C., 1951, pp. 1-14.
277. A. Franklin, op. cit., p. 255.
278. Suzanne Chantal, La Vie quotidienne au Portugal ..., op. cit., p. 256.
279. Fr. J.-B. Le Grand D'Aussy, op. cit., vol. III, pp. 125-6.
280. L.-S. Mercier, Tableau de Paris, op. cit., vol. IV, p. 154.
281. Gaston Martin, Nantes au XVIIIe siècle. L'ère des négriers, 1714-1774, 1931, p. 138.
282. Pierre-François-Xavier de Charlevoix, Histoire de l'Isle Espagnole ou de S. Domingue, 1731, vol. II, p. 490.
283. Dictionnaire du commerce et des marchandises, ed. M. Guillaumin, 1841, vol. I, p. 409.
284. On the various qualities of coffee, see the Correspondence of Aron Colace, Gemeemte Archief Amsterdam, passim, years 1751-1752.
285. M. Morineau, 'Trois contributions au colloque de Göttingen', in De l'Ancien Régime à la Révolution française, ed. A. Cremer, 1978, pp. 408-9.
286. R. Paris, in Histoire du commerce de Marseille, ed. G. Rambert, vol. V, 1957, pp. 559—61.
287. L.-S. Mercier, Tableau de Paris, vol. I, pp. 228-9.
288. Journal de Barbier, ed. A. de La Vigeville, 29 November 1721.
289. Quoted by Isaac de Pinto, Traité de la circulation et du crédit, 1771, p. 5.
290. L.-S. Mercier, L'An deux mille quatre cent quarante, op. cit., p. 359.
291. A.d.S. Venice, Cinque Savii, 9, 257 (1693).
292. Jules Michelet, Histoire de France, 1877, XVII, pp. 171-4.
293. L. Lemery, op. cit., pp. 476, 479.
294. André Thevet, Les Singularitez de la France antarctique, 1558, ed. P. Gaffarel, 1878, pp. 157-9.
295. Storia della tecnologia, op. cit., vol. III, p. 9.
296. L. Dermigny, op. cit., vol. III, 1964, p. 1252.
297. According to Joan Thirsk, unpublished paper, Prato Conference, 1979.
298. A. Thevet, op. cit., p. 158.
299. J. Savary, op. cit., vol. V, col. 1363.
300. Mémoire, by M. de Montsegur (1708), B.N., Ms. Fr. 24 228, f° 206; Luigi Bulferetti and Claudio Costantini, Industria e commercio in Liguria nell'età del Risorgimento (1700-1861), 1966, pp. 418-19. Jérôme de La Lande, Voyage en Italie ..., 1786, IX, p. 367.
301. George Sand, Lettres d'un voyageur, Garnier-Flammarion edn., p. 76; Petite Anthologie de la cigarette, 1949, pp. 20-1.
302. L. Dermigny, op. cit., vol. III, p. 1253.
303. Quoted by L. Dermigny, ibid., vol. III, p. 1253.
304. Ibid., note 6.
305. Abbé Prevost, op. cit., vol. VI, p. 536 (Hamel's voyage, 1668).
306. Suzanne Chantal, La Vie quotidienne au Portugal ... op. cit., p. 256.
307. P. de Saint-Jacob, op. cit., p. 547.
308. Abbé Prevost, op. cit., vol. XIV, p. 482.
309. Cf. vol. III.

NOTES TO CHAPTER 4

1. P. GOUBERT, *Beauvais et le Beauvaisis de 1600 à 1730 ...*, *op. cit.*, p. 230.
2. Bartolomé BENNASSAR, *Valladolid au Siècle d'or. Une ville de Castille et sa campagne au XVIe siècle*, 1967, pp. 147-51.
3. Jean-Baptiste TAVERNIER, *Les Six Voyages ...*, 1682. I, p. 350.
4. Personal memories and photographs.
5. G.F. GEMELLI CARERI, *op. cit.*, II, p. 15.
6. S. MERCIER, *Tableau de Paris*, *op. cit.*, I, p. 21, and II, p. 281.
7. *Ibid.*, IV, p. 149.
8. E.J.F. BARBIER, *Journal historique et anecdotique du règne de Louis XV*, *op. cit.*, I, p. 4.
9. Gaston ROUPNEL, *La ville et la campagne au XVIIe siècle*, 1955, p. 115.
10. X. de PLANHOL, 'Excursion de géographie agraire. IIIe partie: la Lorraine méridionale', in *Géographie et histoire agraires, actes du colloque international de l'Université de Nancy, Mémoire n° 21*, 1959, pp. 35-6.
11. F. VERMALE, *op. cit.*, pp. 287-8 and notes.
12. P. de SAINT-JACOB, *op. cit.*, p. 159.
13. René TRESSE, 'La fabrication des faux en France', in *Annales E.S.C.*, 1955, p. 356.
14. A. de MAYERBERG, *Relation d'un voyage en Moscovie*, 1688, p. 105.
15. M. de GUIGNES, *op. cit.*, II, pp. 174-5.
16. Abbé PRÉVOST, *op. cit.*, VI, p. 24.
17. *Ibid.*, p. 26.
18. *Ibid.*, pp. 69-70.
19. A. de MAYERBERG, *op. cit.*, pp. 105-6.
20. *La Pologne au XVIIIe siècle par un précepteur français, Hubert Vautrin*, ed. Maria CHOLEWO-FLANDIN, 1966, pp. 80-1.
21. J.A. de MANDELSLO, 1659, *op. cit.*, II, p. 270.
22. STAUNTON, *op cit.*, vol. II; M. de GUIGNES, *Voyage à Pékin ...*, 1808, II, pp. 11, 180 and *passim*.
23. L.S. YANG, *Les Aspects économiques des travaux publics dans la Chine impériale*, 1964, p. 38.
24. Pierre CLÉMENT, Sophie CHARPENTIER, *L'Habitation Lao, dans les régions de Vientiane et de Louang-Prabang*, 1975.
25. *Voyage du Chevalier Chardin en Perse*, 1811, IV, pp. 111 ff.
26. Noël du FAIL, *op. cit.*, pp. 116-18.
27. Johann Gottlieb GEORGI, *Versuch einer Beschreibung der Russisch Kayserlichen Residenzstadt St Petersburg ...*, 1790, pp. 555-6.
28. Hermann KOLESCH, *Deutsches Bauerntum im Elsass. Erbe und Verpflichtung*, 1941, p. 18. 'When a tenant wants to build his house, he collects 5 *Hölzer* (tree-trunks), for the lintel, cross-beam, ridge-pole and two roof-beams.'
29. F. VERMALE, *op. cit.*, p. 253.
30. Romain BARON, 'La bourgeoisie de Varzy au XVIIIe siècle', in *Annales de Bourgogne*, July-September, 1964, p. 191.
31. *Archéologie du village déserté*, 2 vols., Cahiers des annales n° 27, 1970.
32. X. de PLANHOL and J. SCHNEIDER, 'Excursion en Lorraine septentrionale, villages et terroirs lorrains', in *Géographie et histoire agraires, actes du colloque international de l'Université de Nancy, Mémoire n° 21*, 1959, p. 39.
33. Docteur Louis MERLE, *La Métairie et l'évolution agraire de la Gâtine poitevine*, 1958, chap. III, pp. 75 ff.
34. *Ricerche sulle dimore rurali in Italia*, ed. Centro di Studi per la geographia etnologica, Florence University, from 1938.
35. Henry RAULIN, *La Savoie* (1977), the first volume in the collection *L'Architecture rurale française. Corpus des genres, des types et des variantes*, which will use previously unpublished data from a survey made between 1942 and 1945 under the direction of P.L. DUCHARTRE and G.H. RIVIÈRE.

36. O. BALDACCI, *La Casa rurale in Sardegna*, 1952, n° 9 in *Ricerche sulle dimore rurali,* collection quoted above, note 34.
37. C. SAIBENE, *la Casa rurale nella pianura e nella collina lombarda,* 1955; P. VILAR, *La Catalogne et l'Espagne ..., op. cit.,* II.
38. Jacques HILAIRET, *Dictionnaire historique des rues de Paris,* 6th edn., 1963, I, pp. 453-4, 553-4, 131.
39. Madeleine JURGENS and Pierre COUPERIE, 'Le logement à Paris aux XVIe et XVIIe siècles', in *Annales E.S.C.,* 1962.
40. On the foregoing, see S. MERCIER, *op. cit.,* I, pp. 11, 270.
41. P. GOUBERT, *op. cit.,* p. 230, note 34.
42. G. ROUPNEL, *op. cit.,* pp. 114-15.
43. P. ZUMTHOR, *la Vie quotidienne en Hollande ..., op. cit.,* pp. 55-6.
44. Lewis MUMFORD, *The City in history,* 1961, p. 383.
45. Peter LASLETT, *The World we have lost,* 1971 edn., p. 5.
46. Louis DERMIGNY, *Les Mémoires de Charles de Constant sur le commerce à la Chine,* 1964, p. 145, and M. de GUIGNES, *op. cit.,* III, p. 51.
47. S. POLLARD and D. CROSSLEY, *The Wealth of Britain,* pp. 97 ff.; M.W. BARLEY, in *The Agrarian History of England and Wales,* ed. Joan THIRSK, IV, 1967, pp. 745 ff.
48. Marc VENARD, *Bourgeois et paysans au XVIIe siècle. Recherches sur le rôle des bourgeois parisiens dans la vie agricole au sud de Paris,* 1957.
49. William WATTS, *The Seats of the Nobility and Gentry in a collection of the most interesting and picturesque views ...,* 1779
50. Fynes MORYSON, *An Itinerary,* 1617, I, p. 265.
51. Bernardo Gomes de BRITO, *Historia tragicomaritima,* VIII, 1905, p. 74.
52. Bernardino de ESCALANTE, *Primeira Historia de China* (1577), 1958, p. 37.
53. Abbé PREVOST, *op. cit.,* V, pp. 507-8 (voyage by Isbrand Ides, 1693).
53. *Mémoires ...* by the missionnairies to Peking, *op. cit.,* II, 1777, pp. 648-9.
55. M. GONON, *La Vie quotidienne en Lyonnais d'après les testaments, XIVe-XVIe siècles,* 1968, p. 68.
56. P. de SAINT-JACOB, *op. cit.,* pp. 553, 159.
57. *Le Guide du pèlerin de Saint-Jacques de Compostelle,* ed. Jeanne VIELLIARD, 1963, p. 29.
58. *Ordonnance de Louis XIV ... sur le fait des eaux et forests, 13 août 1669,* 1703, p. 146.
59. Daniel DEFOE, *A Journal of the Plague Year,* Penguin edn. 1966, pp. 155 ff.
60. *Medit ...* vol. I, p. 455.
61. *Ibid.,* I, pp. 255-6.
62. Quoted in Louis CARDAILLAC, *Morisques et chrétiens. Un affrontement polémioque,* 1977, p. 388.
63. My source for this information is Branislava TENENTI, director of research at the École des Hautes-Études.
64. Pierre Daniel HUET, *Mémoire touchant le négoce et la navigation des Hollandais ... en 1699,* ed. P.J. BLOCK, 1903, p.243.
65. Osman AGA, *Journal,* edited by R. KREUTEL and Otto SPIES, under the title *Der Gefangene der Giaueren,* 1962, p. 150.
66. Rodrigo de VIVERO, *Du Japon et du bon gouvernement de l'Espagne et des Indes,* ed. Juliette MONBEIG, *op. cit.,* p. 180.
67. G.F. GEMELLI CARERI, *op. cit.,* II, p. 17.
68. *Le Japon du XVIIIe siècle vu par un botaniste suédois,* ed. Claude GAUDON, 1966, pp. 241-2.
69. M. de GUIGNES, *op. cit.,* II, p. 178.
70. CHARDIN, *op. cit.,* IV, p. 120.
71. *Ibid.,* IV, pp. 19-20.
72. Armémag SAKISIAN, 'Abdal Khan, seigneur kurde de Bitlis au XVIIe siècle et ses trésors', in *Journal asiatique,* April-June 1937, pp. 255-67.
73. Some of my critics have regarded the word 'biology' as an exaggeration: I did not, of course, mean it literally. But it is certainly true that no European *adult* is capable, without long years of practice, of sitting cross-legged on the floor for hours on end. (Chardin, who lived in Persia for ten years, got used to it in the end and even found it comfortable.) The

reverse is also true: Indian and Japanese friends have told me how in Paris cinemas they secretly bring their legs up on to the seats into the only position they find really comfortable.
74. G.F. GEMELLI CARERI, *op. cit.*, I, p. 257.
75. Sir John BARROW, *Travels in China*, 1804, p. 90.
76. M. de GUIGNES, *op. cit.*, 1795, I, p. 377.
77. Marie-Loup SOUGEZ, *Styles d'Europe: Espagne*, 1961, pp. 5-7.
78. I use this word throughout to signify a level lower than that of a 'civilization'.
79. J.-B. LABAT, *op. cit.*, II, pp. 327-8.
80. Gilberto FREYRE, *Casa Grande e Senzala*, 1933; *Sobrados e Mucambos*, 1936.
81. J.B. LABAT, *op. cit.*, IV, p. 380.
82. C. OULMONT, *La Maison*, 1929, p. 10.
83. Henri HAVARD, *Dictionnaire de l'ameublement et de la décoration...*, 1890, IV, p. 345; J. WILHELM, *La Vie quotidienne au Marais, au XVIIᵉ siècle*, 1966, pp. 65-6.
84. A. FRANKLIN, *op. cit.*, IX: *Variétés gastronomiques*, p. 16.
85. *Ibid.*, p. 19.
86. N.-A. de LA FRAMBOISIÈRE, *Œuvres...*, 1613, I, p. 115.
87. J. SAVARY, *op. cit.*, IV (1762), col. 903.
88. *ibid.*, II (1760), col. 114.
89. William HARRISON, 'An historical Description of the Iland of Britaine', in R. HOLINSHED, *Chronicles of England, Scotland and Ireland*, 1901, I, p. 357.
90. M. de MONTAIGNE, *Journal de voyage en Italie, op. cit.*, p. 1154.
91. S. POLLARD and D. CROSSLEY, *Wealth of Britain..., op. cit.*, pp. 98, 112.
92. M. GACHARD, *Retraite et mort de Charles Quint*, *op.cit.*, II, p.11.
93. M. de MONTAIGNE, *Journal de voyage en Italie, op. cit.*, p. 1129.
94. Éli BRACKENHOFFER, *Voyage en France 1643-1644*, 1927, p. 143.
95. British Museum, Sloane Ms. 42.
96. E. BRACKENHOFFER, *op. cit.*, p. 10.
97. Marquis de PAULMY, *op. cit.*, p. 132.
98. *Encyclopédie populaire serbo-croato-slovène*, 1925-9, III, p. 447. I am indebted for this and other information to Madame Branislava Tenenti.
99. M. de MONTAIGNE, *Journal de voyage en Italie, op. cit.*, p. 1130.
100. Edmond MAFFEI, *Le Mobilier civil en Belgique au Moyen Agen*, n.d., pp. 45-6.
101. For the preceding paragraph, *ibid.*, pp. 48, 49.
102. Charles MORAZÉ, in *Éventail de l'histoire vivante*, 1953, (Studies in honour of Lucien Febvre), I, p. 90.
103. The Princess Palatine, quoted in Docteur CABANÈS, *Mœurs intimes du passé*, 1st series, 1958, pp. 44, 46.
104. Ch. MORAZÉ, *art. cit.*, pp. 90-2.
105. L.-S. MERCIER, *Tableau de Paris, op. cit.*, XII, p. 336.
106. Reference mislaid.
107. Quoted in CABANÈS, *op. cit.*, p.32.
108. MONTAIGNE, *Journal de voyage en Italie, op. cit.*, pp. 1130-2.
109. E. BRACKENHOFFER, *op. cit.*, p. 53.
110. Quoted in CABANÈS, *op. cit.*, p. 32.
111. *Ibid.*, p. 35.
112. B.N., French Mss., new acquisitions, 6277, fº 222 (1585).
113. CABANÈS, *op. cit.*, p. 37 and note.
114. L.-S. MERCIER, *Tableau de Paris, op. cit.*, XII, p. 335.
115. *Ibid.*, X, p. 303.
116. Comtesse d'AULNOY, *La Cour et la ville de Madrid; relation du voyage d'Espagne*, ed. Plon, 1874-6, p. 487.
117. A. WOLF, *A History of Science, Technology and Philosophy in the 18th Century*, 1952, pp. 547-9.
118. *Storia della tecnologia*, ed. C. SINGER et al., *op. cit.*, II, p. 653.
119. E. MAFFEI, *op. cit.*, p. 5; J. SAVARY, *op. cit.*, III, col. 840 and II, col. 224.
120. E. MAFFEI, *ibid.*, p. 4.
121. André G. HAUDRICOURT, 'Contribution à l'étude du moteur humain', in *Annales d'histoire sociale*, April 1940, p.131.
122. E. MAFFEI, *op. cit.*, pp. 14 ff.
123. *Ibid.*, pp. 27-8.

124. Quoted in A. FRANKLIN, *op. cit.*, IX: *Variétés gastronomiques*, pp. 8, 9.
125. E. MAFFEI, *op. cit.*, p. 36.
126. Ch. OULMONT, *La Maison*, *op. cit.*, p. 68.
127. As Mario PRAZ argues in his splendid book (*La Filosofia dell'arredemonto*, 1964) on which I have drawn considerably for the next two pages.
128. Princesse PALATINE, *Lettres*, 1964 edn., p. 353, letter dated 14 April 1719.
129. A house in the Place Vendôme cost 104,000 *livres* in 1751; one in the Rue du Temple 432,000. (That is for the main building only.) Ch. OULMONT, *La Maison*, *op. cit.*, p. 5.
130. *Ibid.*, p. 30.
131. *Ibid.*, p. 31.
132. L. MUMFORD, *The City in history*, *op. cit.*, p. 384.
133. GUDIN, *Aux mânes de Louis XV*, quoted by Ch. OULMONT, *op. cit.*, p. 8.
134. *Ibid.*, p. 9.
135. L.-S. MERCIER, *Tableau de Paris*, *op. cit.*, II, p. 185.
136. Anon., *Dialogues sur la peinture*, quoted by Ch. OULMONT, *op. cit.*, p. 9.
137. M. PRAZ, *La Filosofia dell'arredamento*, *op. cit.*, pp. 62-3, 148.
138. Quoted by M. PRAZ, *ibid.*, p. 146.
139. L. MUMFORD, *op. cit.*, p. 385.
140. L.-S. MERCIER, *Tableau de Paris*, *op. cit.*, V, p. 22 and VII, p. 225.
141. Eugène VIOLLET-LE-DUC, *Dictionnaire raisonné d'archéologie française du XIe au XVIe siècle*, 1854-1868, VI, p. 163.
142. G. CASTER, *Le Commerce du pastel et de l'épicerie à Toulouse 1450-1561*, *op. cit.*, p. 309.
143. *Journal d'un curé de campagne au XVIIe siècle*, ed. H. PLATELLE, 1965, p. 114.
144. Marquise de SÉVIGNÉ, *Lettres*, 1818 edn., VII, p. 386.
145. STAUNTON, *op. cit.*, vol. II, p. 440.
146. J. SION, *Asie des moussons*, *op. cit.*, p. 215.
147. K.M. PANIKKAR, *Histoire de l'Inde*, 1958, p. 257.
148. Mouradj d'OHSSON, *Tableau général de l'Empire ottoman*, quoted in Georges MARÇAIS, *Le Costume musulman d'Alger*, 1930, p. 91.
149. G. MARÇAIS, *ibid.*, p. 91.
150. P. de MAGAILLANS, *Nouvelle Relation de la Chine*, *op. cit.*, p. 175.
151. R. de VIVERO, *op. cit.*, p. 235.
152. VOLNEY, *Voyage en Syrie et en Égypte pendant les années 1683, 1784 et 1785*, 1787, I, p. 3.
153. J.-B. LABAT, *op. cit.*, I, p. 268.
154. Jean-Baptiste SAY, *Cours complet d'économie politique pratique*, V, 1829, p. 108.
155. Abbé Marc BERTHET, 'Études historiques, économiques, sociales des Rousses', in *A travers les villages du Jura*, 1963, p. 263.
156. MOHEAU, *op. cit.*, p. 262.
157. *Ibid.*, pp. 261-2.
158. P. de SAINT-JACOB, *op. cit.*, p. 542.
159. Luigi dal PANE, *Storia de lavoro in Italia*, 1958, p. 490.
160. *Voyage de Jérôme Lippomano*, *op. cit.*, II, p. 557.
161. Orderic VITAL, *Historiae ecclesiasticae libri tredecim*, 1845, III, p. 324.
162. Ary RENAN, *Le Costume en France*, n.d. pp. 107-8.
163. François BOUCHER, *Histoire du costume en Occident*, 1965, p. 192.
164. Jacob van KLAVEREN, *Europäische Wirtschaftsgeschichte Spaniens im 16 und 17 Jahrhundert*, 1960, cf. 'mode' in index and p. 160, note 142; *Viajes de extranjeros por España*, *op. cit.*, II, p. 427.
165. Amédée FRÉZIER, *Relation du voyage de la mer du Sud*, 1716, p. 237.
166. ESTEBANILLO-GONZÁLEZ, *Vida y hechos ...*, in *La Novela picaresca española*, *op. cit.*, p. 1812.
167. *Zocoli* were shoes with very high wooden soles, cut away in the centre, to protect ladies' feet from the wet ground in Venice.

168. London P.R.O. 30-25-157, Giornale autografo di Francesco Contarini da Venezia a Madrid.
169. S. LOCATELLI, *Voyage de France, mœurs et coutumes française, 1664-1665 ...*, 1905, p. 45.
170. M.T. JONES-DAVIES, *Une Peintre de la vie londonienne, Thomas Dekker*, 1958, I, p. 280.
171. L.-S. MERCIER, *Tableau de Paris, op. cit.*, I, pp. 166-7.
172. R. de VIVERO, *op. cit.*, p. 226.
173. *Voyage du chevalier Chardin ..., op. cit.*, IV, p. 1.
174. *Ibid.*, IV, p. 89.
175. Jean-Paul MARANA, *Lettre d'un Sicilien à un de ses amis*, ed. V. DUFOUR, 1883, p. 27.
176. Marquis de PAULMY, *op. cit.*, p. 211.
177. Ernst SCHULIN, *op. cit.*, p. 220.
178. CARLO PONI, 'Compétition monopoliste, mode et capital: le marché international des tissus de soie au XVIIIe siècle', typescript, paper given to Bellagio Conference.
179. J.-P. MARANA, *op. cit.*, p. 25.
180. L.-S. MERCIER, *Tableau de Paris, op. cit.*, VII, p. 160.
181. J. SAVARY, *op. cit.*, V, col. 1262; Abbé PREVOST, *op. cit.*, VI, p. 225.
182. Father. de MAGAILLANS, *op. cit.*, p. 175.
183. *Ibid.*
184. L.-S. MERCIER, quoted in A. GOTTSCHALK, *Histoire de l'alimentation ..., op. cit.*, II, p. 266.
185. ANDREWS, *op. cit.*
186. Dr CABANÈS, *Mœurs intimes du passé*, 2e série, *La vie aux bains*, 1954, p. 159.
187. *Ibid.*, pp. 238-9.
188. *Ibid.*, pp. 284 ff.
189. *Ibid.*, pp. 332 ff.
190. Jacques PINSET and Yvonne DESLANDRES, *Histoire des soins de beauté*, 1960, p. 64.
191. Dr CABANÈS, *op. cit.*, p. 368, note.
192. L. MUMFORD, *op. cit.*, p. 468.
193. L.A. CARACCIOLI, *op. cit.*, III, p. 126.
194. A. FRANKLIN, *Les Magasins de nouveautés*, II, pp. 82-90.
195. ANDREWS, *op. cit.*, vol. II, p. 35.
196. L. A. CARACCIOLI, *op. cit.*, III, pp. 217-18.
197. For the next two paragraphs, cf. A. FANGÉ, *Mémoires pour servir à l'histoire de la barbe de l'homme*, 1774, pp. 99, 269, 103.
198. Marquis de PAULMY, *op. cit.*, p. 193.
199. M. PRAZ, *la Filosofia dell'arredamento, op. cit.*

NOTES TO CHAPTER 5

1. M. MAUSS, *Sociologie et anthropologie*, 1973, p. 371.
2. Marc BLOCH, 'Problèmes d'histoire des techniques'. Review of: Commandant Richard LEFEBVRE DES NOËTTES, 'L'Attelage, le cheval de selle à travers les âges. Contribution à l'histoire de l'esclavage', in *Annales d'histoire économique et sociale*, 1932, pp. 483-4.
3. G. LA ROËRIE, 'Les transformations du gouvernail', in *Annales d'histoire économique et sociale*, 1935, pp. 564-83.
4. Lynn WHITE, 'Cultural climates and technological advances in the Middle Ages', in *Viator*, vol. II, 1971, p. 174.
5. Between 1730 and 1787, a series of decrees by the Paris Parlement forbade the replacement of sickles by scythes: Robert BESNIER, *Cours de droit*, 1963-4, p. 55. See also René TRESSE in *Annales, E.S.C.*, 1955, pp. 341-58.
6. Reference mislaid, possibly a lecture by Pirenne.
7. See below, vol. III.
8. Abbot P. USHER, *A History of mechanical inventions*, 1954 edn., p. 335.
9. Quoted by M. SORRE, *op. cit.*, II, p. 220.
10. Reference mislaid.
11. E. LE ROY LADURIE, *Les Paysans de Languedoc, op. cit.*, I, p. 468.

12. L.-S. MERCIER, *Tableau de Paris, op. cit.*, IV, p. 30.
13. P.G. POINSOT, *L'Ami des cultivateurs, op. cit.*, II, pp. 349-41.
14. Note by Paris Duverney, A.N., F¹², 647-8 (a proposal in 1750 to exempt lands 'tilled by hand' from *taille*.
15. STAUNTON, *op. cit.*, and Abbé PREVOST, *op. cit.*, VI, p. 126.
16. Father de MAGAILLANS, *op. cit.*, pp. 141, 148.
17. G.F. GEMELLI CARERI, *op. cit.*, IV, p. 487.
18. *Ibid.*, p. 460.
19. Jacob BAXA, Guntwin BRUHNS, *Zucker im Leben der Völker*, 1967, p. 35. SONNERAT gives fairly precise sketches of these elementary machines in *Voyage aux Indes orientales et à la Chine*, 1782, I, p. 108 – Engraving 25, the oil-mill.
20. *Mémoires ...*, by the missionaries of Peking, *op. cit.*, 1977, II, p. 431.
21. Voyage of François BERNIER, *op. cit.*, 1699, II, p. 267.
22. L.-S. MERCIER, *Tableau de Paris, op. cit.*, VIII, p. 4.
23. A. de HUMBOLDT, *Essai politique sur le royaume de la Nouvelle Espagne, op. cit.*, II, p. 683.
24. A. de SAINT-HILAIRE, *op. cit.*, I, pp. 64 ff.
25. Nicolás SÁNCHEZ ALBORNOZ, *La Saca de mulas de Salta al Peru, 1778-1808*, published by the Universidad Nacional del Litoral, Santa Fe, Argentina, 1965, p. 261-312.
26. CONCOLORCORVO, *Itinéraire de Buenos Aires à Lima*, 1962, introd. by Marcel Bataillon, p. 11.
27. *La Economia española según el censo de frutos y manufacturas de 1799*, 1960, pp. VIII and XVII.
28. N. Sánchez ALBORNOZ, *op. cit.*, p. 296.
29. G.F. GEMELLI CARERI, *op. cit.*, IV, p. 251.
30. Émilienne DEMOUGEOT, 'Le chameau et l'Afrique du Nord romaine', in *Annales, E.S.C.*, 1960, n° 2, p. 244.
31. Xavier de PLANHOL, 'Nomades et Pasteurs. I. Genèse et diffusion du nomadisme pastoral dans l'Ancien Monde', in *Revue géographique de l'Est*, n° 3, 1961, p. 295.
32. M. de GUIGNES, *op. cit.*, I, 1808, p. 355.
33. Henri PÉRÈS, 'Relations entre le Tafilalet et le Soudan à travers le Sahara', in *Mélanges ... offerts à E.F. Gautier*, 1937, pp. 409-14.
34. Exact reference mislaid: probably A.N., A.E., B III. But these estimates are confirmed by J.B. TAVERNIER, *op. cit.*, I, p. 108.
35. Abbé PREVOST, *op. cit.*, XI, p. 686.
36. *Libro de agricultura*, 1598, pp. 368 ff.
37. C. ESTIENNE and J. LIÉBAUT, *L'Agriculture et maison rustique*, 1564, f° 21.
38. *François Quesnay et la physiocratie, op. cit.*, II, pp. 431 ff.
39. B.N. Estampes, 1576 – maps and plans, Ge D 16926 and 16937.
40. P. de LAS CORTES, document quoted, British Museum, London.
41. J. de GUIGNES, *op. cit.*, III, p. 14.
42. Abbé PRÉVOST, *op. cit.*, VI, pp. 212-13; J.-B. DU HALDE, *op. cit.*, II, p. 57.
43. Father de MAGAILLANS, *op. cit.*, pp. 53-54.
44. Abbé PRÉVOST, *Voyages ..., op. cit.*, VII, p. 525 (Gerbillon).
45. See below, vol., II.
46. *Medit.*, I, p. 469.
47. Abbé PRÉVOST, *op. cit.*, VIII, pp. 263-4 (voyage of Pyrard, 1608).
48. *Les Six Voyages de Jean-Baptiste Tavernier, op. cit.*, II, p. 59.
49. Giovanni BOTERO, *Relationi universali*, Brescia, 1599, II, p. 31.
50. G. F. GEMELLI CARERI, *op. cit.*, II, p. 72.
51. *Relazione di Gian Francesco Morosini, bailo a Costantinopoli, 1585*, in *Le Relazioni degli ambasciatori veneti al Senato*, ed. E. ALBÉRI, series III, vol. III, 1855, p. 305.
52. *Médit.* I, 348.
53. Théophile GAUTIER, *Constantinople*, 1853, p. 166.
54. J. LECLERCQ, *De Mogador à Biskra, Maroc et Algérie*, 1881, p. 123.
55. A. BABEAU, *Le Village ..., op. cit.*, pp. 308, 343-4.
56. On the purchase of horses from England, Ireland, Spain, Algeria, Tunisia,

Morocco, Arabia, Naples, Sardinia, Denmark and Norway, see A.N., O1, boxes 896-900.
57. A.d.S., Mantua, A° Gonzaga, Genova, 757.
58. Mediceo Papers, A.d.S., Florence.
59. J.-B.-H. LE COUTEULX DE CANTELEU, *Étude sur l'histoire du cheval arabe*, 1885, especially pp. 33-4.
60. *Médit*, I, p. 283.
61. Jules MICHELET, *Histoire de France*, ed. Rencontre, V, 1966, p. 114.
62. VASSELIEU, dit Nicolay, *Règlement général de l'artillerie* ... 1613.
63. LAVOISIER, 'De la richesse territoriale du royaume de France', in *Collection des principaux économistes*, XIV, 1966, p. 595.
64. P. QUIQUERAN DE BEAUJEU, *La Provence louée*, 1614. The price difference became even greater later on, when hillsides came into cultivation. In 1718, a mule was worth twice as much as a horse. R. BAEHREL, *Une Croissance; la Basse-Provence rurale*, *op. cit.*, p. 173.
65. R. BAEHREL, *ibid.*, pp. 65-7.
66. LAVOISIER, *op. cit.*, p. 595; *Réflexions d'un citoyen-propriétaire*, 1792, B.N., Rp 8577.
67. L.-S. MERCIER, *Tableau de Paris*, *op. cit.*, I, p. 151; IV, p. 148.
68. L.-S. MERCIER, *Tableau de Paris*, *op. cit.*, III, pp. 300-1, 307-8.
69. L.-S. MERCIER, *Tableau de Paris*, *op. cit.*, IX, pp. 1-2.
70. *Ibid.*, X, p. 72.
71. E.J.F. BARBIER, *op. cit.*, I, pp. 1-2.
72. L. MAKKAI, 'Productivité et exploitation des sources d'énergie, XIIe-XVIIe', unpublished paper, Prato conference, 1971.
73. Greffin AFFAGART, *Relation de Terre Sainte (1533-1534)*, ed. J. CHAVANON, 1902, p. 20.
74. F. BRAUDEL, 'Genève en 1603', in *Mélanges d'histoire ... en hommage au professeur Anthony Babel*, 1963, p. 322.
75. Robert PHILIPPE, *Histoire et technologie*, typescript, 1978, p. 189.
76. E. KÄMPFER, *op. cit.*, I, p. 10.
77. *Storia della tecnologia*, ed. C. SINGER, *op. cit.*, II, p. 621. Source of Polish statistics mislaid. Some incomplete figures in T. RUTKOWSKI, *The mill industry in Galicia* (in Polish), 1886.
78. And indeed this corresponds to the estimate made by Vauban in *Projet d'une dîme royale*, 1707, pp. 76—7
79. L. MAKKAI, *art. cit.*
80. *Storia della tecnologia*, II, *op. cit.*, pp. 625-7, Jacques PAYEN, *Histoire des sources d'énergie*, 1966, p. 14.
81. Lynn WHITE, *Medieval Technology and Social Change*, 1962, p. 8.
82. CERVANTES, *Don Quixote*, quoted by WHITE, *ibid.*, p. 88, *Divine Comedy, Inferno*, XXXIV, *ibid.*, p. 88; *Divine Comedy, Inferno*, XXXIV, 6.
83. *Storia della tecnologia*, *op. cit.*, p. 630.
84. On the next two paragraphs, see *ibid.*, vol. III, pp. 94 ff.
85. Models on show in the Deutches Brotmuseum in Ulm.
86. Ruggiero ROMANO, Per una valutazione della flotta mercantile europea alla fine del secola XVIII', in *Studi in onore di Amintore Fanfani*, 1962, V, pp. 573-91.
87. All the preceding calculations were based on information provided to me by J.J. HEMARDINQUER.
88. Maurice LOMBARD, *L'Islam dans sa première grandeur*, 1971, pp. 172 ff.
89. Bartolomeo CRESCENTIO, *Nautica mediterranea*, 1607, p. 7.
90. *Annuaire statistique de la Meuse pour l'An XII*.
91. Paul W. BAMFORD, *Forests and French Sea Power, 1660-1789*, 1956, pp. 69, 207-8 and *passim* for the data in the two preceding paragraphs.
92. François LEMAIRE, *Histoire et antiquites de la ville et duché d'Orléans*, 1645, p. 44; Michel DEVÈZE, *La Vie de la forêt française au XVIe siècle*, 2 vols, 1961.
93. J. SION, *Les Paysans de la Normandie orientale ...*, *op. cit.*, 1909, p. 191.
94. R. PHILIPPE, typescript, *op. cit.*, *p. 17.*
95. F. LÜTGE, *Deutsche Sozial- und Wirtschaftsgeschichte*, 1966, p. 335.

96. Bertrand GILLE, *Les Origines de la grande métallurgie en France*, 1947, pp. 69, 74.
97. A. KECK, *A short history of mines in Polish territories* (in Polish), 1960, p. 105. Antonina KECKOWA, *Saltmines in the Cracow region, XVI-XVIIIth centuries* (in Polish, with German summary), 1969.
98. For preceding paragraph, see data provided by Micheline BAULANT based on deliberations of the Bureau of the City of Paris.
99. Michel DEVEZE, unpublished communication. Prato Conference, 1972.
100. Father de MAGAILLANS, *op. cit.*, p. 163.
101. *Médit ...*, I, pp. 122, 387, 174.
102. Thomas PLATTER, *op. cit.*, p. 204.
103. Antonio de GUEVARA, *Épistres dorées, morales et familières*, in: *Biblioteca de autores españoles*, 1850, XIII, p. 93.
104. B.L.C. JOHNSON, 'L'influence des bassins houillers sur l'emplacement des usines à feu en Angleterre avant circa 1717', in *Annales de l'Est*, 1956, p. 220.
105. Reference mislaid.
106. Quoted by S. MERCIER, *op. cit.*, VII, p. 147.
107. P. de SAINT-JACOB, *op. cit.*, p. 488.
108. *Dictionnaire du commerce et des marchandises*, ed. M. GUILLAUMIN, 1841, I, p. 295.
109. J.-C. TOUTAIN, 'Le produit de l'agriculture française de 1700 à 1958: I, Estimation du produit au XVIIIe s.', in: *Cahiers de l'I.S.E.A.*, July 1961, p. 134; LAVOISIER *op. cit.*, p. 603.
110. Father de MAGAILLANS, *op. cit.*, pp. 12-13.
111. *Médit ...*, I, p. 219.
112. Guy THUILLIER, *Georges Dufaud et les débuts du grand capitalisme dans la métallurgie, en Nivernais au XIXe siècle*, 1959, p. 122 and references. Other examples in Louis TRENARD, *Charbon et Sciences humaines*, 1966, pp. 53 ff.
113. Max PRINET, 'L'industrie du sel en Franche-Comté avant la conquête française', in: *Mémoires de la société d'émulation du Doubs*, 1897, pp. 199-200.
114. M. ROUFF, *Les Mines de charbon en France au XVIIIe siècle*, 1922, pp. 368-86, 418.
115. Jean LEJEUNE, *La Formation du capitalisme moderne dans la principauté de Liège au XVIe siècle*, 1939, pp. 172-6.
116. *Médit*, I, p. 623.
117. J. NICKOLLS, *Remarques sur les avantages et les désavantages de la France et de la Grande-Bretagne, op. cit.*, p. 137.
118. *Ibid.*, p. 136.
119. See vol. III.
120. John U. NEF, 'Technology and civilization', in *Studi in onore di Amintore Fanfani*, 1962, V, especially pp. 487-91.
121. These are hazardous calculations and therefore open to discussion. The whole question should be re-opened, according to suggestions by Jacques LACOSTE, 'Rétrospective énergétique mondiale sur longue période (mythes et réalités)', in: *Informations et réflexions*, April 1978, n° 1, who bases himself on PUTNAM's book, *Energy in the future*. He does not contest the energy hierarchy presented here, but
(1) thinks that the energy available to men in the pre-industrial period was more plentiful than is often thought – but that it was often wasted;
(2) that the wood crisis which first appeared in the sixteenth-century had effects comparable to the present oil crisis.
122. *Histoire générale des techniques*, ed. M. DAUMAS, 1965, II, p. 251.
123. Abbé PREVOST, *op. cit.*, VI, p. 223.
124. Cf. vol. III.
125. Lewis MORGAN, *Ancient Society*, 1877, p. 43.
126. Stefan KUROWSKI, *Historyczny proces wyrostu gospodarczego*, 1963.
127. E. WAGEMANN, *Economia mundial, op. cit.*, I, p. 127.
128. P. DEYON, *Amiens, capitale provinciale ..., op. cit.*, p. 137.
129. Ferdinand TREMEL, *Das Handelsbuch des Judenburger Kaufmannes Clemens Körber, 1526-1548*, 1960.

130. A.-G. HAUDRICOURT, 'La fonte en Chine: Comment la connaissance de la fonte de fer a pu venir de la Chine antique à l'Europe médiévale', in *Métaux et civilisations*, II, 1946, pp. 37-41.
131. *Voyage du chevalier Chardin, op. cit.*, IV, p. 137.
132. N.T. BELAIEW, 'Sur le "damas" oriental et les lames damassées', in *Métaux et civilisations*, I, 1945, pp. 10-16.
133. A. MAZAHERI, 'Le sabre contre l'épée ou l'origine chinoise de "l'acier au creuset"', in *Annales, E.S.C.*, 1958.
134. J.W. GILLES, 'Les fouilles aux emplacements des anciennes forges dans la région de la Sieg, de la Lahn et de la Dill', in *Le Fer à travers les âges*, 1956; Augusta Hure, 'Le fer et ses antiques exploitations dans le Senonais et le Jovinien', in *Bulletin de la société des sciences historiques ... de l'Yonne*, 1933, p. 3; 'Origine et formation du fer dans le Sénonais', *ibid.*, 1919, pp. 33 ff; A. GOUDARD, 'Note sur l'exploitation des gisements de scories de fer dans le département de l'Yonne', in *Bul. de la Société d'archéologie de Sens*, 1936, pp. 151-88.
135. J.W. GILLES, *art. cit.*
136. J.-B. LABAT, *op. cit.*, II, p. 305.
137. *Histoire générale des techniques, op. cit.*, ed. M. DAUMAS, II, pp. 56-7.
138. Ferdinand TREMEL, *Der Frühkapitalismus in Innerösterreich*, 1954, pp. 52 ff.
139. *Ibid.*, p. 53, fig. 87.
140. Auguste BOUCHAYER, *Les Chartreux, maîtres de forges*, 1927.
141. B. GUENÉE. *Tribunaux et gens de justice dans le bailliage de Senlis à la fin du Moyen Age (vers 1380-vers 1550), op. cit.*, p. 33, note 22.
142. *Storia della tecnologia*, ed. C. SINGER, *op. cit.*, III, p. 34; M. FRANÇOIS, 'Note sur l'industrie sidérurgique ...', in *Mémoires de la société nationale des antiquaires de France*, 1945, p. 18.
143. I have not been able to locate the document consulted in Venice (A.d.S. or Museo Correr) giving numbers of iron workers. There are good descriptions of this activity in 1527, 1562 and 1572 in *Relazioni di rettori veneti in Terraferma*, XI, 1978, pp. 16-17, 78-80, 117.
144. Richard GASCON, *Grand commerce et vie urbaine au XVIe siècle; Lyon et ses marchands*, 1971, pp. 133-4.
145. Eli HECKSCHER, 'Un grand chapitre de l'histoire du fer: le monopole suédois', in *Annales d'histoire économique et sociale*, 1932, pp. 131-3.
146. *Op. cit.*, table in appendix.
147. Arturo UCCELLI, *Storia della tecnica*, 1945, p. 87.

NOTES TO CHAPTER 6

1. Aldo MIELI, *Panorama general de historia de la ciencia*, II, 1946, p. 238, note 16.
2. Carlo M. CIPOLLA, *Guns and sails in the early phase of European expansion 1400-1700*, 1965, p. 104.
3. *Storia della tecnologia*, ed. C. SINGER, *op. cit.*, II, p. 739.
4. Friedrich LÜTGE, *Deutsche Sozial- und Wirtschaftsgeschichte*, 1966, p. 209.
5. *Storia della tecnologia*, ed. C. SINGER, *op. cit.*, p. 739.
6. Lynn WHITE, *Medieval Technology and Social Change*, 1962, p. 101.
7. Jorge de EHINGEN, *Viage ...*, in *Viajes estranjeros por España y Portugal*, ed. J. GARCÍA MENDOZA, 1952, p. 245.
8. C.M. CIPOLLA, *Guns and sails in the early phase of European expansion ..., op. cit.*, pp. 106-7.
9. C. de RENNEVILLE, *Voyages ..., op. cit.*, V, p. 43.
10. SANUDO, *op. cit.*, III, pp. 170 ff.
11. Michel MOLLAT, in *Histoire du Moyen Age*, ed. E. PERROY, *op. cit.*, p. 463.
12 and 13. Karl BRANDI, *Kaiser Karl V*, 1937, p. 132.

14. W. Sombart, *Krieg und Kapitalismus*, op. cit., pp. 84-5.
15. *Chroniques de Froissart*, 1888 edn., VIII, pp. 37 ff.
16. Sanudo, *Diarii*, I, 1879, col. 1071-2.
17. Ralph Davis, 'Influences de l'Angleterre sur le déclin de Venise au XVIIe siècle', in *Decadenza economica Veneziana nel secolo XVIII*, 1957, pp. 214-15.
18. Memorandum from the Chevalier de Razilly to Cardinal Richelieu, 26 November 1626, B.N. Ms. n.a., 9389, f° 66 v°.
19. Le Loyal Serviteur, *La Très Joyeuse et Très Plaisante Histoire ... de Bayard*, op. cit., 1872 edn., p. 280.
20. Blaise de Monluc, *Commentaires*, Pléiade edition, 1965, pp. 34, 46.
21. For the two preceding paragraphs, see W. Sombart, *Krieg und Kapitalismus*, op. cit., pp. 78 ff.
22. Miguel de Castro, *Vida del soldado español Miguel de Castro*, 1949, p. 511.
23. M. de Montaigne, *Journal de voyage en Italie*, op. cit., p. 1155.
24. *Medit.*, vol. II, p. 839.
25. Reports from Savorgnan de Brazza, last years of sixteenth century, either in Archivio di Stato, or the Museo Correr in Venice.
26. W. Sombart, op. cit., p. 88.
27. *Ibid.*, p. 93.
28. F. Breedvelt Van Veen, *Louis de Geer 1587-1655 (in Dutch)*, 1935, pp. 40, 84.
29. In about 1555 (?). Former K series in Archives Nationales, Paris, now transferred to Simancas.
30. *Medit.*, vol. II, p. 841.
31. *Medit.*, vol. II, p. 801.
32. P. de Las Cortes, document quoted.
33. G.F. Gemelli Careri, op. cit., IV, p. 374
34. A. Blum, *Les Origines du papier, de l'imprimerie et de la gravure*, 1935.
35. Lucien Febvre, H.J. Martin, *L'Apparition du livre*, 1971, pp. 41-2.
36. *Ibid.*, pp. 42, 47.
37. *Ibid.*, p. 47.
38. *Ibid.*, p. 20.
39. *Ibid.*, p. 36.
40. T.F. Carter, *The Invention of Printing in China and its spread westward*, 1925, passim, esp. pp. 211-18.
41. Loys Le Roy, *De la Vicissitude ou Variété des choses en l'Univers*, 1576, p. 100, quoted in René Étiemble, *Connaissons-nous la Chine?*, 1964, p. 40.
42. L. Febvre, H.J. Martin, op. cit., pp. 60 ff., 72-93.
43. *Ibid.*, p. 134.
44. *Ibid.*, p. 15.
45. *Ibid.*, pp. 262 ff.
46. *Ibid.*, p. 368.
47. *Ibid.*, p. 301.
48. *Ibid.*, pp. 176-88.
49. Jean Poujade, *La Route des Indes et ses navires*, 1946.
50. *Medit.*, I, p. 550
51. The question remains debatable, at least in the view of an expert like Paul Adam. But on an Egyptian fresco representing the journey of Queen Hatchepsut to the Red Sea, I was interested to note, alongside the Egyptian ships with square sails, a small local boat with a triangular sail – a detail about which I have in vain looked for comment from Egyptologists.
52. See vol. III.
53. Richard Hennig, *Terrae incognitae*, III, 1953, p. 122.
54. There has been published a considerable literature on the subject, since P. Pelliot, 'Les grands voyages maritimes chinois au début du XVe siècle', in *T'oung Pao*, XXX, 1933, pp. 237-452.
55. Alexander von Humboldt, *Examen critique de l'histoire de la géographie du nouveau continent et des progrès de l'astronomie nautique aux quinzième et seizième siècles*, 1836, I, p. 337.
56. Jean Bodin, *La République*, 1576, p. 630.
57. Thomé Cano, *Arte para fabricar ... naos de guerra y merchante*, 1611, p. 5 v°.
58. Laurent Vital, *Premier Voyage de Charles Quint en Espagne*, 1881, pp. 279-83.

59. Czartoryski Museum, Cracow, 35, f°s 35 and 55.
60. G. de MENDOZA, *Histoire du grand royaume de la Chine ...*, 1606, p. 238.
61. R. de VIVERO, *op. cit.*, p. 194.
62. J.-B. du HALDE, *op. cit.*, II, p. 160.
63. Sir John BARROW, *op. cit.*, p. 39.
64. STAUNTON, *op cit.*, vol. I, pp. 499-501, 441.
65. Jacques HEERS, in 'Les grandes voies maritimes dans le monde, XVe-XIXe siècles', *XIIe Congrès ... d'histoire maritime*, 1965, p. 22.
66. R. de VIVERO, *op. cit.*, p. 22.
67. J. HEERS, in 'Les grandes voies maritimes ...', *art. cit.*, p. 22.
68. P. VIDAL DE LA BLACHE, *Principes de géographie humaine, op. cit.*, p. 266.
69. Joseph NEEDHAM, lecture at the Sorbonne.
70. M. de GUIGNES, *Voyage à Peking ..., op. cit.*, I, pp. 353-4.
71. Abbé PREVOST, *op. cit.*, VI, p. 170
72. *Voyage du médecin J. Fries*, ed. W. KIRCHNER, *op. cit.*, pp. 73-4.
72. CONCOLORCORVO, *op. cit.*, pp. 56-7.
74. *Ibid.*, p. 56.
75. *Voyage faict par moy Pierre Lescalopier*, published in part by E. CLÉRAY, in *Revue d'histoire diplomatique*, 1921, pp. 27-8.
76. G.F. GEMELLI CARERI, *op. cit.*, I, p. 256.
77. Father de MAGAILLANS, *op. cit.*, pp. 47 ff.
78. G.F. GEMELLI CARERI, *op. cit.*, III, pp. 22-3.
79. Georg FRIEDERICI, *El Carácter del descubrimiento y de la conquista de América* (Spanish translation), 1973, p. 12.
80. G.F. GEMELLI CARERI, *op. cit.*, VI, p. 335.
81. J. HEERS, 'Les grandes voies maritimes ...', *art. cit.*, pp. 16-17; W.L. SCHURZ, *The Manila Galleon*, 1959.
82. Jean-François BERGIER, *Les Foires de Genève et l'économie internationale de la Renaissance*, 1963, pp. 218 ff.
83. M. POSTAN, in *The Cambridge Economic History of Europe*, II, pp. 140, 147.
84. Otto STOLZ, 'Zur Entwicklungsgeschichte des Zollwesens innerhalb des alten Deutschen Reichs', in *Vierteljahrschrift für Sozial- und Wirtschaftsgeschichte*, 1954, p. 18 and note.
85. Gerónimo de UZTARIZ, *Théorie et pratique du commerce et de la marine*, 1753, p. 255.
86. M. POSTAN, in *The Cambridge Economic History of Europe*, II, pp. 149-50.
87. P. du HALDE, *op. cit.*, II, pp. 158-9.
88. Father de MAGAILLANS, *op. cit.*, pp. 158-9, 162, 164.
89. G.F. GEMELLI CARERI, *op. cit.*, IV, p. 319.
90. STAUNTON, *op. cit.*, vol. II, p. 451.
91. G.F. GEMELLI CARERI, *op. cit.*, III, p. 29.
92. Jacques HEERS, *Gênes au XVe siècle*, 1961, pp. 274 ff; *Medit.*, I, p. 581.
93. *Ibid.*, p. 302.
94. A report of the capture by Sir John BURROUGH, in R. HAKLUYT, *The Principal Navigations ...*, ed. 1927, V, pp. 66 ff.; Alfred de STERNBECK, *Histoire des flibustiers*, 1931, pp. 158 ff.
95. *Medit ...*, I, p. 277.
96. H. CAVAILLES, *La Route française, son histoire, sa fonction*, 1946, pp. 86-94.
97. Henri SÉE, *Histoire économique de la France*, I, 1939, p. 294.
98. L.-S. MERCIER, *Tableau de Paris, op. cit.*, V, p. 331.
99. MACAULAY, quoted by J.M. KULISCHER, *Storia economica ..., op. cit.*, II, p. 552; Sir Walter BESANT, *London in the time of the Stuarts*, 1903, pp. 338-44.
100. Arthur YOUNG, *Voyage en France*, 1793, I, p. 82.
101. Adam SMITH, *The Wealth of Nations*, Everyman edition, vol. II, p. 217.
102. L. DERMIGNY, *La Chine et l'Occident. Le commerce à Canton au XVIIIe siècle, 1719-1833, op. cit.*, III, pp. 1131 ff.
103. See vol. II.

104. H. Bechtel, *Wirtschaftsgeschichte Deutschlands, op. cit.*, I, p. 328.
105. Armando Sapori, *Una Compagnia di Calimala ai primi del Trecento*, 1932, p. 99.
106. P. de Saint-Jacob, *op. cit.*, II, p. 164.
107. *Storia della tecnologia*, ed. C. Singer, *op. cit.*, II, p. 534.
108. J.-B. Say, *Cours complet d'économie politique pratique*, 1966, II, p. 497, note 2.
109. *Der moderne Kapitalismus, op. cit.*, II, pp. 231–420.
110. See vol. II.
111. See vol. II.
112. Marcel Rouff, *Les Mines de charbon en France au XVIIIe siècle (1744–1791)*, 1922, pp. 368 ff.
113. *Voyage du Chevalier Chardin..., op. cit.*, IV, pp. 24, 167–9.
114. Thierry Gaudin, *L'Écoute des silences*, 1978.
115. *Storia della tecnologia*, ed. C. Singer, *op. cit.*, III, p. 121.
116. A.d.S. Venise, Senato terra.
117. Marc Bloch, *Mélanges historiques*, 1963, II, p. 836.
118. Arch. Simancas, E° Flandes, 559.
119. A. Wolf, *A History of Science, technology and philosophy in the 16th and 17th centuries*, pp. 332 ff.
120. D. Schwenter, *Deliciae physico-mathematical oder mathematische und philosophische Ezquick stunden*, 1636.
121. A.N., A.E., B^{III}, 423, The Hague, 7 Sept. 1754.
122. Gerhard Mensch, *Das technologische Patt*, 1977.

NOTES TO CHAPTER 7

1. N. du Fail, *Propos rustiques et facétieux, op. cit.*, pp. 32, 33, 34.
2. Madame de Sévigné, *op. cit.*, VII, p. 386.
3. A.N., H 2933, f° 3.
4. G.F. Gemelli Careri, *op. cit.*, I, pp. 6, 10 ff and *passim*.
5. Harvey's discovery of the circulation of the blood: 1628.
6. William Petty, 'Verbum Sapienti', 1691.
7. L.F. de Tollenare, *Essai sur les entraves que le commerce éprouve en Europe*, 1820, pp. 193, 210.
8. I am thinking of *Some Considerations on the Consequences of the Lowering of Interest and Raising the Value of Money*, 1691. Cf. Eli Heckscher, *La Época mercantilista*, 1943, pp. 648 ff.
9. Jacob van Klaveren, 'Rue de Quincampoix und Exchange Alley, die Spekulationsjahre 1719 und 1720 in Frankreich und England', in *Vierteljahreschrift für Sozial-und Wirtschaftsgeschichte*, Oct. 1963, pp. 329–59.
10. Princesse Palatine, *Lettres ... de 1672 à 1722*, 1964, p. 419, letter of 11 June 1720.
11. See below, vol. II.
12. Scipion de Grammont, *Le Denier royal*, 1620, p. 20. Several authors mention the use of salt as currency – in the form of small blocks, they usually say, varying in size from place to place.
13. J.-B. Labat, *op. cit.*, III, p. 235.
14. *Ibid.*, p. 307.
15. *Monumenta missionaria africana, Africa ocidental*, VI, *1611–1621*, ed. Antonio Brasio, 1955, p. 405.
16. Li Chia-Jui, article in Chinese mentioned (n°54) *Revue bibliographique de sinologie*, 1955.
17. Italian press report.
18. Paul Einzig *Primitive money in its ethnological, historical and economical aspects*, 1948, pp. 271–2.
19. *Ibid.*, pp. 47 ff; E. Ingersoll, 'Wampum and its history', in *American Naturalist*, 1883.

20. W.G.L. RANDLES, *L'Ancien Royaume du Congo des Origines à la fin du XIXe siècle*, 1968, pp. 71-2.
21. G. BALANDIER, *La Vie quotidienne au royaume de Kongo ..., op. cit.*, p. 124.
22. Vitorino MAGALHÃES-GODINHO, *L'Économie de l'Empire portugais au XVe et XVIe siècles*, 1969, pp. 390 ff.
23. G. BALANDIER, *op. cit.*, pp. 122-4.
24. Adam SMITH, *Wealth of nations*, Everyman edition, vol. I, p. 20-1.
25. Pierre VILAR, *Or et monnaie dans l'histoire*, 1974, p.321.
26. ISAAC CHIVA, typescript on Corsica; and Germaine TILLION, 'Dans l'Aurès: le drame des civilisations archaïques', in *Annales, E.S.C.*, 1957, pp. 393-402.
27. François LA BOULLAYE, *Les Voyages et observations du Sieur de la Boullaye ...*, 1653, pp. 73-4.
28. C.L. LESUR, *Des progrès de la puissance russe*, 1812, p. 96, note 4.
29. W. LEXIS, 'Beiträge zur Statistik der Edelmetalle', in *Jahrbücher für Nationalökonomie und Statistik*, 1879, p. 365.
30. Ruggiero ROMANO, 'Une économie coloniale: le Chili au XVIIIe siècle', in *Annales, E.S.C.*, 1960, pp. 259-85.
31. Manuel ROMERO DE TERRERO, *Los Tlacos coloniales. Ensayo numismático*, 1935, pp. 4, 5.
32. *Ibid.*, pp. 13-17. There was no copper coin in Mexico before 1814.
33. Reference mislaid.
34. E. CLAVIÈRE and J.-P. BRISSOT, *De la France et des Étas-Unis*, 1787, p. 24 and note 1.
35. Alfons DOPSCH, *Naturalwirtschaft und Geldwirtschaft in der Weltgeschichte*, 1930.
36. In Corsica for instance, *Medit.*, vol. I, p. 383, note 129.
37. Museo Correr, Dona delle Rose, 181, f° 62.
38. M. TAKIZAWA, *The Penetration of Money economy in Japan ... op. cit.*, pp. 33 ff.
39. *Ibid.*, pp. 38-9.
40. Andrea METRA, *Il Mentore perfetto de'negozianti, op. cit.*, III, p. 125.
41. Venice, Marciana, *Scritture ... oro et argento*, VII-MCCXVIII, 1671; Ugu TUCCI, 'Les émissions monétaires de Venise et les mouvements internationaux de l'or', in *Revue historique*, 1978.
42. A.N., A.E., B III, 265 (1686), Mémoires généraux.
43. V. MAGALHÃES-GODINHO, *L'Économie de l'Empire portugais au XVe et XVIe siècles, op. cit.*, pp. 512-31.
44. *Ibid.*, pp. 353-8.
45. *Ibid.*, pp. 358 ff.
46. G.F. GEMELLI CARERI, *op. cit.*, III, p. 278.
47. *Ibid.*, III, p. 2.
48. *Ibid.*, III, p. 226.
49. V. MAGALHÃES-GODINHO, *op. cit.*, pp. 357, 444 ff.
50. *Ibid.*, pp. 323, 407 ff.
51. *Ibid.*, pp. 356-8.
52. F. BALDUCCI PEGOLOTTI, *Practica della mercatura*, 1766, pp. 3-4.
53. For the preceding paragraphs, see V. MAGALHÃES-GODINHO, *op. cit.*, pp. 399-400.
54. P. de MAGAILLANS, *Nouvelle Relation de la Chine, op. cit.*, p. 169.
55. V. MAGALHÃES-GODINHO, *op.cit.*, p. 518.
56. Maestre MANRIQUE, *Itinerario de las Misiones que hizo el Padre F. Sebastián Manrique*, 1649, p. 285.
57. B.N., Ms. fr. n. a. 7503, f° 46.
58. P. de LAS CORTES, *doc. cit.*, f° 85 and 85 v°.
59. *Doc. cit.*, note 57.
60. G.F. GEMELLI CARERI, *op. cit.*, IV, p. 43.
61. 'Mémoire sur l'intérêt de l'argent en Chine', in *Mémoires concernant l'histoire, les sciences, etc.* by the Missionaries of Peking, IV, 1779, pp. 309-11.
62. L. DERMIGNY, *La Chine et l'Occident. Le commerce à Canton ..., op. cit.*, I, pp. 431-3.
63. Abbé F. GALIANI, *Della Moneta*, 1750, p. 214.

64. G. de Uztáriz, *op. cit.*, p. 171.
65. G.F. Gemelli Careri, *op. cit.*, VI, pp. 353-4, 1719 edition.
66. See vol. III.
67. On the *Kipper-und Wipperzeit*, F. Lütge, *Deutsche Sozial- und Wirtschaftsgeschichte, op. cit.*, pp. 289 ff.
68. Earl J. Hamilton, 'American Treasure and Andalusian Prices, 1503-1660', in *Journal of Economic and Business History*, I, 1928, pp. 17, 35.
69. Raphaël du Mans, *Estat de la Perse en 1660*, ed. Ch. Schefer, *op. cit.*, p. 193.
70. Karl Marx, *Capital* (1938 reprint of 1889 edn.), Vol. I, p. 68, note 2.
71. Frank Spooner, *L'Economie mondiale et les frappes monétaires en France, 1493-1680*, 1956, p. 254.
72. *Ibid.*, p. 21.
73. Josef Kulischer, *Allgemeine Wirtschaftsgeschichte des Mittelalters und der Neuzeit*, 1965, II, p. 330.
74. P. de Saint-Jacob, *op. cit.*, p. 306.
75. Antonio della Rovere, *La Crisi monetaria siciliano (1531-1802)*, ed. Carmelo Trasselli, 1964, pp. 30 ff.
76. E.J.F. Barbier, *op. cit.*, I, p. 185.
77. See below, Vol. II.
78. For details on this paragraph, see below, Vol. III.
79. 'Maximes générales' in *François Quesnay et la physiocratie*, I.N.E.D., edition, *op. cit.*, II, p. 954 and note 7.
80. Werner Sombart, *Le Bourgeois*, 1926, pp. 38-9.
81. F. Galiani, *Della Moneta, op. cit.*, p. 56.
82. L.-S. Mercier, *Tableau de Paris, op. cit.*, I, p. 46.
83. W. Lexis, 'Beiträge zur Statistik der Edelmetalle', *art. cit.*
84. *Ibid.*
85. Geminiano Montanari, *La Zecca*, 1683, in *Economisti del Cinque e Seicento*, A. Graziani, 1913, p.264.
86. I. de Pinto, *Traité de la circulation et du crédit, op.cit.*, p.14.
87. B.N., Ms. fr., 5581, f° 83; cf. *Il Mentore perfetto de'negozianti, op. cit.*, V, article 'Surate', p. 309.
88. F. Spooner, *op. cit.*, pp. 170 ff.
89. Josef Kulischer, *Allgemeine Wirtschaftsgeschichte des Mittelalters und der Neuzeit*, 1965, II, pp. 344-5.
90. *Ibid.*
91. Luigi Einaudi, preface to edition of the *Paradoxes inédits du seigneur de Malestroit*, 1937, p. 23.
92. E. Pasquier, *Les Recherches de la France, op. cit.*, p. 719.
93. F. Braudel and F. Spooner, 'Prices in Europe from 1450 to 1750', in *Cambridge Economic History of Europe*, IV, p. 445; the figures for American gold and silver are of course from Earl J. Hamilton.
94. I. de Pinto, *Traité de la circulation ..., op. cit.*, p. 33.
95. Joseph A. Schumpeter, *History of Economic Analysis*, 1954, p. 317.
96. F. Galiani, *Della Moneta, op. cit.*, p. 278.
97. I. de Pinto, *Traité de la circulation ..., op. cit.*, p. 34.
98. *Ibid.*, p. 34, note.
99. A.N., F^{12}, 2175, III. Documents of 1810 and 1811 on non-payment of debts contracted during the siege.
100. F.W. von Schrötter, *Fürstliche Schatz und Rent-Cammer*, 1686, quoted by Eli Heckscher, *op. cit.*, pp. 652-3.
101. P. de Saint-Jacob, *op. cit.*, p. 212.
102. See below, II chap. II.
103. M. de Malestroit, 'Mémoires sur le faict des monnoyes ...', in *Paradoxes inédits du seigneur de Malestroit*, ed. Luigi Einaudi, 1937, p. 105.
104. David Hume, 'On the balance of trade', *Essays Moral, Political and Literary*, 1752.
105. L.S. Mercier, *op. cit.*, IX, pp. 319-20.
106. S.D. Gotein, 'The Cairo Geniza as a source for the history of Muslim civilization', in *Studia islamica*, III, pp. 75-91.
107. H. Laurent, *La Loi de Gresham au Moyen Age*, 1932, pp. 104-5.

Notes 601

108. John LAW, 'Premier mémoire sur les banques', in Œuvres ... contenant les principes sur le Numéraire, le Commerce, le Crédit et les Banques, 1790, p. 197.
109. B. SCHNAPPER, Les rentes au XVIe siècle. Histoire d'un instrument de crédit, 1957, p. 163.
110. See below, vol. II.
111. Medit., I, p. 581-20.
112. Ibid., p. 582.
113. Reference mislaid.
114. J.A. SCHUMPETER, History of Economic Analysis, p. 321.
115. Ibid.
116. Recherches sur le commerce, 1778, p. VI.
117. S. de GRAMONT, Le Denier Royal, 1620, p. 9.

NOTES TO CHAPTER 8

1. From 'The German Ideology' (1846), in Karl MARX, Pre-capitalist Economic Formations, ed. Eric HOBSBAWM, 1964, p. 127.
2. In the first edition of this book.
3. In Towns and societies, ed. Philip ABRAMS and E.A. WRIGLEY, 1978, pp. 9, 17, 24-5.
4. Voyages d'Ibn Battûta, ed. Vincent MONTEIL, 1969, I, pp. 67-9.
5. R. BARON, 'La bourgeoisie de Varzy au XVIIe siècle', in Annales de Bourgogne, art. cit., pp. 161-208, esp. pp. 163-81, 208.
6. P. DEANE, W.A. COLE, British Economic Growth, 1964, pp. 7-8.
7. R. GASCON, in Histoire économique et sociale de la France, ed. BRAUDEL and LABROUSSE, I¹, p. 403.
8. H. BECHTEL, Wirtschaftsstil des deutsches Spätmittelalters. 1350-1500, 1930, pp. 34 ff.
9. Cahiers de doléances des paroisses du bailliage de Troyes pour les états généraux de 1614, ed. YVES DURAND, 1966, p. 7.
10. O. SPENGLER, The Decline of the West.
11. J.B. du HALDE, Description geographique, historique, chronologique, politique et physique de l'Empire de la Chine et de la Tartarie chinoise, 1785, I, p. 3.
12. E. KÄMPFER, op. cit., III, p. 72.
13. J. KULISCHER, op. cit., Italian edn., vol. II, pp. 15-16.
14. R. CANTILLON, op. cit., p. 26; M. REINHARDT, 'La population des villes ...', in Population, April 1954, 9, p. 287.
15. J. KULISCHER, op.cit.; for Russia, B.T. URLANIS (in Russian, Moscow, 1966) gives a figure of 3·6% (urban population over 500,000 ha.) quoted by V.I. PAVLOV in Historical premises for India's transition to capitalism, 1978, p. 68.
16. C. BRIDENBAUCH, Cities in the Wilderness, 1955, pp. 6, 11; on Japan, Prof. FURUSHIMA, quoted by T.C. SMITH, The Agrarian origins of modern Japan, 1959, p. 68.
17. Jan de VRIES, The Dutch rural economy in the golden age, 1500-1700, 1974, table, p. 86.
18. M. CLOUSCARD, L'Être et le code, 1972, p. 165.
19. Jane JACOBS, The Economy of cities, 1970.
20. Morris BIRKBECK, Notes on a Journey in America (1818), facsimile edn., 1966, pp. 98-9.
21. F. LÜTGE, op. cit., p. 349.
22. R. GASCON, in Histoire économique et sociale de la France, ed. BRAUDEL et LABROUSSE, ¹I, p. 360.
23. According to W. ABEL, reference and discussion in vol. III.
24. Georg STEINHAUSEN, Geschichte der deutschen Kultur, 1904, p. 187.
25. La Civiltà veneziana del Settecento, ed. the Giorgio Cini Foundation, 1960, p. 257.

26. Reference mislaid.
27. Archivo General de Simancas, *Expedientes de hacienda*, 157.
28. 'Saco de Gibraltar', in *Tres Relaciones históricas*, '*Colección de libros raros o curiosos*', 1889.
29. *Medit* . . ., vol. I, p. 267.
30. Jean PUSSOT, *Journalier ou mémoires*, 1857, p. 16,.
31. Ernst Ludwig CARL, *Traité de la richesse des princes et de leurs états*, 1723, II, pp. 193, 195.
32. A. de MAYERBERG, *op. cit.*, pp. 220-1.
33. See vol. III.
34. STAUNTON, *op. cit.*, vol. II, p. 108.
35. L.-S. MERCIER, *Tableau de Paris, op. cit.*, IX, pp. 167-8; VI, pp. 82-3; V, p. 282.
36. *Medit.*, vol. I, pp. 341-2.
37. C.-E. PERRIN, 'Le droit de bourgeoisie et l'immigration rurale à Metz au XIIIe siècle', in *Annuaire de la Société d'histoire et d'archéologie de la Lorraine*, XXX, 1921, p. 569.
38. H.J. BRUGMANS, *Geschiedenis van Amsterdam*, 8 vol., 1930-3.
39. See above, chapter 1, note 39.
40. Quoted by Hugues de MONTBAS, *La Police parisienne sous Louis XVI*, 1949, p. 183.
41. L.-S. MERCIER, *Tableau de Paris, op. cit.*, III, pp. 226-7, 232, 239.
42. *Ibid.*, p. 239.
43. G.F. GEMELLI CARERI, *op. cit.*, I, p. 370.
44. *Voyage . . . de Pierre Lescalopier, op. cit.*, p. 32.
45. Hans MAUERSBERG, *Wirtschafts-und Sozialegeschichte Zentraleuropaïscher Städte in neueren Zeit*, 1960, p. 82.
46. *Voyage de M. de Guignes, op. cit.*, I, p. 360.
47. J.A. de MANDELSLO, *op. cit.*, II, p. 470.
48. P. de MAGAILLANS, *op. cit.*, pp. 17-18.
49. Léopold TORRES BALBAS, *Algunos Aspectos del mudejarismo urbano medieval*, 1954, p. 17.
50. G.F. GEMELLI CARERI, *op. cit.*, IV, p. 105.
51. P. LAVEDAN and J. HUGUENEY, *L'Urbanisme au Moyen Age*, 1974, pp. 84-5, and fig. 279.
52. Charles HIGOUNET, 'Les "terre nuove" florentines du XIVe siècle', in *Studi in onore di Amintore Fanfani*, III, 1962, pp. 2-17.
53. L.-S. MERCIER, *op. cit.*, XI, p. 4.
54. M.T. JONES-DAVIES, *op. cit.*, I, p. 190.
55. F. COREAL, *Relation des voyages aux Indes occidentales, op. cit.*, I, pp. 152, 155.
56. H. CORDIER, 'La Compagnie prussienne d'Embden au XVIIIe siècle', in *T'oung Pao*, XIX, 1920, p. 241.
57. G.F. GEMELLI CARERI, *op. cit.*, IV, p. 120.
58. G.F. GEMELLI CARERI, *op. cit.*, I, p. 230.
59. L.-S. MERCIER, *Tableau de Paris, op. cit.*, VI, p. 221; V, p. 67; IX, p. 275.
60. J. SAVARY, *Dictionnaire . . ., op. cit.*, V, col. 381.
61. Vu QUOC THUC, in *Les Villes . . .*, ed. Société Jean Bodin, 1954-1957, II, p. 206.
62. Reference mislaid.
63. According to the *Padrón* de 1561, Archivo General de Simancas, *Expedientes de hacienda*, 170.
64. G.F. GEMELLI CARERI, *op. cit.*, VI, pp. 366-7.
65. Rudolf HÄPKE, *Brügges Entwicklung zum mitteralterlichen Weltmarkt . . .*, 1908.
66. B. GUENÉE, *Tribunaux et gens de justice dans le bailliage de Senlis . . ., op. cit.*, p. 48.
67. L.-S. MERCIER, *op. cit.*, III, 1782, p. 124. moitié du XVIIe siècle, *op. cit.*, p. 27.
69. Perè du HALDE, *op. cit.*, I, p. 109.
70. In what follows, I have drawn on the unpublished papers of the colloquium *Les Villes* at the Ecole Pratique des Hautes Etudes, VIe section, 1958.
71. R. MANTRAN, *Istanbul dans le seconde moitié du XVIIe siècle, op. cit.*, p. 27.
72. Raphaël du MANS, *Estat de la Perse en 1660 . . .*, ed. Ch. SCHEFER, 1890, p. 33.
73. G.F. GEMELLI CARERI, *op. cit.*, II, p. 98.
74. G.F. GEMELLI CARERI, *op. cit.*, I, p. 262.

75. W. ABEL, *Geschichte der deutschen Landwirtschaft*, 1962, pp. 48, 49.
76. Giovanni PECLE et Giuseppe FELLONI, *Le Monete genovesi*, 1975, pp. 27-30.
77. W. SOMBART, *Le Bourgeois*, op. cit., p. 129.
78. C. BEC, *Les Marchands écrivains à Florence, 1375-1434*, 1967, p. 319.
79. L. MUMFORD, op. cit., pp. 353-4.
80. The following two paragraphs were inspired by Max Weber.
81. M. SANUDO, *Diarii*, XXVIII, 1890, col. 625.
82. J. NICKOLLS, *Remarques sur les avantages de la France ...*, op. cit., p. 215.
83. L.-S. MERCIER, *Tableau de Paris*, op. cit., VIII, p. 163.
84. B.H. SLICHER VAN BATH, *Yield Ratios, 810-1820*, op. cit., p. 16.
85. See vol. III.
86. J. GERNET, *Le Monde chinois*, op. cit., p. 371.
87. Abbé PREVOST, *Voyages*, op. cit., X, p. 104, according to Bernier.
88. *Ibid.*, p. 103.
89. Rodrigo de VIVERO, *Du Japon et du bon gouvernement de l'Espagne et des Indes*, ed. Juliette MONBEIG, 1972, pp. 66-7.
90. YASAKI, *Social Change and the City in Japan*, 1968, pp. 133, 134, 137, 138, 139.
91. R. SIEFFERT, *La Littérature japonaise*, 1961, pp. 110 ff.
92. R. de VIVERO, op. cit., pp. 58, 181.
93. L. MUMFORD, op. cit., p. 443-4.
94. P. LAVEDAN and J. HUGUENEY, *Histoire de l'Urbanisme*, op. cit., p. 383.
95. W. SOMBART, *Luxus und Kapitalismus*, op. cit., pp. 37 ff.
96. L.-S. MERCIER, *Tableau de Paris*, op. cit., VIII, p. 192.
97. MIRABEAU père, *L' Ami des Hommes ou Traité de la population*, 1756, part II, p. 154.
98. L.-S. MERCIER, *Tableau de Paris*, op. cit., I, p. 286.
99. LAVOISIER, *De la richesse territoriale du royaume de France*, 1966 edition, pp. 605-6.
100. F. QUESNAY, 'Questions intéressantes sur la population, l'agriculture et le commerce ...', in *F. Quesnay et la physiocratie*, op. cit., II, p. 664.
101. A. METRA, *Il Mentore perfetto ...*, op. cit., V, pp. 1, 2.
102. W. SOMBART, *Luxus und Kapitalismus*, op. cit., p. 30.
103. Prince de STRONGOLI, *Ragionamenti economici, politici e militari*, 1783, I, p. 51, quoted by L. dal PANE, in *Storia del lavoro in Italia*, op. cit., pp. 192-3.
104. *Ibid.*
105. René BOUVIER and André LAFFARGUE, *La Vie napolitaine au XVIIIe siècle*, 1956, pp. 84-5.
106. *Ibid.*, p. 273.
107. C. de BROSSES, *Lettres historiques et critiques sur l'Italie*, An VII, II, p. 145.
108. R. BOUVIER and A. LAFFARGUE, op. cit., p. 273.
109. *Ibid.*, p. 237.
110. Johann Gottlieb GEORGI, *Versuch einer Beschreibung der ... Residenzstadt St. Petersburg*, op. cit., passim, for the following paragraphs.
111. *Guide Baedeker Russie*, 1902, p. 88.
112. J. SAVARY, *Dictionnaire ...*, op. cit., V, col. 639.
113. J. DELUMEAU, op. cit., pp. 501 ff.
114. P. de MAGAILLANS, op. cit., p. 12.
115. *Ibid.*, pp. 176-77.
116. G.F. GEMELLI CARERI, op. cit., IV, pp. 142, 459.
117. The missionaries in Peking, *Mémoires concernant l'histoire, les sciences, les mœurs ...*, op.cit., III, 1778, p. 424.
118. Letter from Père Amiot, Peking, 20 October 1752, in *Lettres édifiantes et curieuses écrites des missions étrangères*, XXIII, 1811, pp. 133-4.
119. Father de MAGAILLANS, op. cit., pp. 176-7.
120. *Ibid.*, p. 278.
121. J.-B. du HALDE, op. cit., I, p. 114.
122. G. de MENDOZA, *Histoire du grand royaume de la Chine ...*, op. cit., p. 195.
123. STAUNTON, op. cit., vol. II, p. 124.
124. P. SONNERAT, op. cit., II, p. 13.

125. Father de MAGAILLANS, *op. cit.*, pp. 277-8.
126. Abbé PRÉVOST, *op. cit.*, VI, p. 126.
127. Father de MAGAILLANS, *op. cit.*, pp. 278 ff.
128. Father de MAGAILLANS, *op. cit.*, pp. 268-71.
129. *Ibid.*, pp. 272-3.
130. *Ibid.*, pp. 150-1.
131. *Ibid.*, pp. 153-4.
132. For the following pages, I have consulted: William BESANT, *London in the Eighteenth Century*, 1902; André PARREAUX, *La Vie quotidienne en Angleterre au temps de George III*; Léonce PEILLARD, *La Vie quotidienne à Londres au temps de Nelson et de Wellington, 1774-1852*, 1968; LEMONNIER, *La Vie quotidienne en Angleterre sous Elizabeth*; T.F. REDDAWAY, *The Rebuilding of London after the Great Fire*, 1940; *The Ambulator, or the stranger's Companion in a tour of London*, 1782; George RUDE, *Hanoverian London*, 1971; M. Dorothy GEORGE, *London Life in the Eighteenth Century*, 1964,.
133. M.T. JONES-DAVIES, *op. cit.*, I, p. 193.
134. M.T. JONES-DAVIES, *op. cit.*, I, p. 149.
135. John STOW, *A Survey of London* (1603), 1720, II, p. 34.
136. M.T. JONES-DAVIES, *op. cit.*, I, p. 177.
137. P. COLQUHOUN, *A Treatise on the Police of the Metropolis*, 1801 edn., pp. 53-71.
138. M.T. JONES-DAVIES, *op. cit.*, I, p. 166.
139. W. PETTY, *A Discourse of Taxes and Contributions*, 1689, p. 22.
140. P. COLQUHOUN, *op. cit.*, pp. 158 ff., 176.
141. Lewis MUMFORD, *The City in History*, *op. cit.*, pp. 296 ff.
142. P. COLQUHOUN, *op. cit.*, pp. 358-9.
143. Jean-Jacques ROUSSEAU, *Emile, Œuvres Complètes*, Pléiade edition, IV, 1960, p. 851.
144. S. MERCIER, *L'An deux mille quatre cent quarante*, *op. cit.*

NOTE TO CONCLUSION

1. STAUNTON, *op. cit.*, Vol. II, p. 289.

Index

Abel, Wilhelm, 133
Abrams, Philip, 481
Academy of Sciences, Paris, 310
acorns (as food), 112
Adam, Edouard, 244
Adam, Father Jean, 547
Adam, Robert, 310
Aertsen, Pieter, 314
Africa: population, 34, 39, 42-4, 46, 53; and population of America, 34, 43, 53-4; exploration of, 62; colonization of, 101; diet in, 104; maize in, 158, 166-7; manioc in, 173; hoe-culture in, 174-6; tobacco in, 265; lack of furniture in, 285; poverty in, 292-3; dress in, 314; textiles in, 325; human labour in, 339; horses in, 346; currency in, 437, 442-4
agave (plant), 248
Agricola (i.e. George Bauer), 355, 431
agriculture: and diet, 107; methods, 114-18, 345; hoe-cultivation, 174-5; and stock-raising, 196-7; and development of technology, 335, 338-9, 345, 385, 430-1; animal power in, 344-5, 350; and development of towns, 486-9; *see also* individual crops and animals
Aigues-Mortes, 495
Alain de Lille, 511
Alaminos, Antón de, 418
Alaska, 100
alcohol, 133, 183, 222, 227, 241-9
Alessandro della Purificazione, Father, 470
Algeria, 312
Algiers, 282, 312
Al Kindi, 248
Alpini, Prospero, 256
Alsace, 170, 275
Alva, Fernando Alvarez de Toledo, Duke of, 349, 392, 463
Amboise, Jacques d', 277
America (New World): population, 35-6, 38-9, 43, 46, 48, 53, 526; conquest of, 36-7, 56; disease in, 37-8, 89; exploration of, 62; wild animals in, 67; mortality in, 91; and European expansion, 98, 100; pre-Columbian diet, 104; wheat in, 109; potatoes in, 167, 172; hoe-culture in, 174, 176; prehistoric settlement of, 176; fur trade in, 181-2; stock-raising in, 197; meat-eating in, 201; fish and fishing, 214; sugar cultivation in, 226; wine in, 231-2; drink in, 247-9; tea in, 252; tobacco in, 261; animal power in, 341-2; forests and timber in, 363-4; navigation to, 409, 420; seamen, 425; money and barter in, 445-7; precious metals from, 454, 457-8, 460, 463, 466; towns in, 483-6, 497, 520-2; big cities in, 526; *see also* individual countries

Amerindians, 37, 176, 341
Amiens, 75, 374
Amman, Jost, 432
Amsterdam: plague in, 88; and spice trade, 222-3; and spirits, 247; and tea trade, 251-2; and tobacco, 262; brick buildings in, 268; housing, 278; and copper, 384; Bank of, 464; exchange, 474, 530; size and dominance, 527-8
Angkor Wat, 149
animals, 65-9; for power, 339, 341-52, 371
Anne of Austria, Queen of Louis XIII, 206
Anne, Queen of England, 528
antimony, 383, 399, 454
Antwerp, 222, 303, 504
Apollonius of Perga, 402
apples, 241
aqueducts, 228
Arabs, 407, 412; *see also* Islam
arak, 233, 247
Araucanians (people), 98
Arbeau, Thoinot, 192
Archimedes, 401-2
Argenson, Marc René Voyer d', Marquis, 520
Argentina, 98, 124, 129, 201, 232, 341, 416-17, 446, 522
Armada, Spanish (1588), 395
Armagnac, 244
Armagnac, Georges d', Cardinal, 85
armies, 51-3; *see also* war
arms and armour, 380, 382, 393-5; *see also* individual weapons
arquebuses, 392, 395-6

605

arsenals *see* arms and armour
artillery, 385–8; shipboard, 288–92, 395; manufacture and cost, 395–6; use of, 396–7; inventions for, 434; and towns, 497
Asia (and Far East): population, 42, 44, 46; famines in, 76–7; diet in, 104, 146; rice in, 147–50; maize in, 158–9, 167; hoe-culture in, 174; and early settlement of America, 176–7; alcohol in, 247; houses in, 274; towns in, 524; *see also* individual countries
Astrakhan, 97, 101
Atlantic Ocean, 407–10; *see also* America
Attila the Hun, 94
Atabinen, Rachid Saffet *see* Saffet Atabinen, Rachid
Athens, 515
Augsburg, 139, 140–1
Aulnoy, Comtesse d', 302
Aurangzeb, Emperor, 77, 199, 339, 396, 526
Australia, 98, 180, 326
Austria, 428
Auton, Jean d', 233, 388
Azores, 232
Aztecs, 158–9, 161, 178; *see also* Mexico

Baber, Emperor, 97, 397
Bach, Johann Sebastian, 92
Bachelard, Gaston, 186
Bacon, Roger, 386
Bahia (São Salvador, Brazil), 265, 500, 521
bakers, 137, 139; *see also* bread
Balkans, 194
bananas, banana trees, 174, 176–7
Bank of England, 464, 472–3, 553
Bank of France, 474
Bank of Stockholm, 472
banks and banking, 464, 470–6
barbarians, 93–4
Barbier, Edmond Jean François, 461
Barbon, Nicholas, 324
Barcelona, 495
Bardi (of Florence), 127
barley, 109–10, 114, 121–2, 134, 156, 239
Barrow, Sir John, 188
barter, 444–8, 457, 469–70, 476; *see also* money
Basques, 181, 214, 216
Bassano, Jacopo, 209
Bataillon, Marcel, 341
Batavia, 38, 91, 251, 540
Bath, B.H. Slicher von, 122
baths, bathrooms, 285–6, 310, 329–30

Bauer, Lt.-Gen. von, 535
Bavaria, 74, 84, 520
Bayard, Pierre du Terrail, Seigneur de, 234, 392
bayonets, 393
beans, 112–13, 431
beards, 330–2
Beaujeu, P. Quigueran de, 350
Beauvais, 71, 73, 266, 278, 285
beef, 197–9
beer, 238–40, 241
beggars, 75–6, 196; *see also* poor
Behanzin, 443
Belgrade, 199
Belidor, B. Forest de, 337
Bell, John, 100
Beloch, Karl Julius, 39, 46, 47, 54, 60
Belon, Pierre, 422
Benedict XII, Pope, 127
Bering, Vitus Jonassen, 100
Berlin, 486, 531
Bernard, Samuel, 277
'Besançon fairs', 448
Beukelszoon, William, 215
Bicker, 318
Bilbao, 506
bills of exchange, 472–4, 477
Birbeck, Morris, 485
birth rates, 55, 71–3, 92
Black Death, 33, 36, 47, 71, 83–4, 88–9, 193; *see also* plague
Black Sea, 101
Bloch, Marc, 334
Blois, 78
boars (wild), 67–8
Boccaccio, Giovanni, 85
Bodin, Jean, 232, 409
Bohemia, 122, 239
Bologna, 300
Bonnac, Marquis de, 434
Bonnefons, Nicolas de, 203
books *see* incunabula; printing
Bordeaux, 234, 238, 243
Boserup, Ester, 174
Boston, Mass., 483
Botelho, Diego, 412
Botero, Giovanni, 347
Bougainville, Louis Antoine de, Comte, 34, 178–9
Bouguer, Pierre, 431
Bourbon island *see* Réunion
bourgeoisie, 314, 482, 512–13, 524
Brabant, 420
Brackenhoffer, Éli, 297

Index   607

Bramante, Donato Lazzari, 498
Brandenburg-Ansbach, Casimir, Margrave of, 512
Brandt, Isabella, 320
brandy, 241-4, 246-9
Brantôme, Pierre de Bourdeilles, Seigneur de, 54
braziers, 300-302
Brazil: disease in, 37-8; exploration of, 62-3; Portuguese expansion in, 98; meat-eating in, 201; sugar cane in, 224-7, 521; tobacco exports, 265; slave labour in, 339; animal power in, 341-2; money in, 445; gold from, 460, 521; towns in, 521-2
bread: deficient, 78; grains for, 108, 110-12, 126; in diet, 130, 132-3; grades of, 135-8, 194; weight of, 139, 142, 145; home-baking of, 139, 142; prices, 142-3, 145; riots, 144-5; Europeans demand, 171-2
bread-fruit, 174
Bremen, 503
Brescia, 379-80, 395
Breughel, Jan, 314, 415
brick, 267-8, 270-1, 273, 498, 503
brigandage, 424, 428
Brindsharis (people), 64
Brosses, Président Charles de, 533
Brouwer, Adrien, 283
Brown, E.H. Phelps, 133
Bruges, 403, 419, 504
Brunel, Antoine de, 54
buckwheat, 112, 114, 134, 136, 156
Buedkalaer, Joachim, 189
Buenos Aires, 37, 484, 521
Buffon, Georges Louis Le Clerc, Comte de, 349, 373
bugs, 310
Bureau brothers, 387
Burgos, 506
Burgundy: famines in, 78; mortality in, 92; wheat consumption in, 134; maize in, 166; meat consumption in, 198; distilling in, 246; tobacco in, 264; houses in, 275; personal possessions in, 283; peasant dress in, 315; fashion in, 318
Burma, 159, 167
Burrough, Sir John, 423
Bushnell, David, 434
Bussy-Castelnau, Charles Joseph Pâtissier, Marquis de, 102
butter, 210-12
Buyer, Barthélemy, 401
Byzantium, 326

cabbages, 170
cabs, 340, 352
Cadiz, 500, 506
Caillé, René, 422
Cairo, 481
California, 232
Cambodia, 149-50, 273
camels, 342, 347
camphor, 248
Camus, Albert, 84
Canada, 37, 63
canals, 422-3
Canaries (islands), 232, 409
cannon see artillery
Cano, Tomé, 409
Cantillon, R., 467, 476, 483, 530
Canton, 500-1
Cape Horn, 180
capital (financial), 475; see also credit; money
capitalism, 28, 475-6, 513-14, 562
Capuchin Order, 232
Caracas, 249
caravans, 422
carbohydrates, 130
Careri, G.F. Gemelli see Gemelli-Careri, Giovanni F.
Carletti, Francesco, 439
Carr-Saunders, Sir Alexander Morris, 42-4
carriages, 291, 350-2, 415-17, 423-5, 498, 539-40, 552
carrots, 171
Cartouche, Louis Bourguignon, called, 260, 560
cassava, 172-3; see also manioc
Cassy-les-Vitteaux, 92
Castille, 92, 511
Catherine Cornaro, Queen of Cyprus, 224
Catherine II (the Great), Tsarina of Russia, 101, 108, 534-5
cattle, 158, 176, 192-3
Cayenne (island), 259
censuses, 39-40
cereals see grain
Cervantes Saavedra, Miguel de, 503
Ceylon, 253
chairs, 287-90, 304
champagne, 235-6
Champagne, 419-20, 477
Champlain, Samuel de, 180
Chang, K.C., 187-8
Chappe brothers, 434
charcoal, 362, 365-7, 370, 376, 393-4
Chardin, Jean, 91, 150, 273, 323, 376, 430

608 Structures of Everyday Life

Charlemagne, Emperor, 238
Charles the Bad, 242
Charles the Bold, Duke of Burgundy, 329, 348
Charles I, King of England, 473
Charles II, King of England, 549
Charles V, Emperor, 90, 112, 234, 240, 292, 297, 331, 388, 410, 460
Charles VI, King of France, 90, 129
Charles VII, King of France, 386-7
Charles VIII, King of France, 223, 328, 331, 349, 385, 388, 460
Charles IX, King of France, 81
Charlestown (U.S.A.), 483
Charlevoix, Father Pierre François Xavier de, 180, 259
Chatal Yüyük, 484
Chauliac, Guy de, 80
Chaunu, Pierre, 29
cheese, 210-11
Che Kiang, 264
Cheng Huo, 407
cheques (bank), 476
chestnuts, 112, 134, 143-4
Chichimec Indians (Mexico), 178
chick-peas, 112-13
children, 491
Chile, 98, 201, 232, 445
chimneys, 298-300
China: population, 33-4, 39-41, 44-7; new crops in, 44; internal migrations, 45; marriage age in, 47; living space in, 48; natural disasters in, 49; population density, 61, 64; harvests in, 74; famines, 76; and barbarian conquests, 94, 96-7; and colonial markets, 102; decolonization of, 102; diet in, 105-6; wheat in, 108, 146; poor in, 111, 285; rejects livestock, 120; rice in, 145-9, 151-5; expansion, 152; mountains unexploited, 153-5; maize in, 167; luxuries in, 184; food and cookery in, 187-8, 200-1; meat-eating in, 199-201; table manners in, 207; ignores dairy products, 211; lacks eggs, 213; fish and fishing in, 214; sugar cane in, 224, 226; water supply in, 230; beer in, 238, 248; alcohol in, 248; tea from, 249-55; hot drinks in, 254-5; and opium, 261; tobacco in, 262, 264; building materials in, 270-3; houses in, 280, 282, 285; domestic heating in, 286, 290; furniture in, 288-91; dress in, 312-14; textiles in, 325-7; lack of soap in, 330; coal in, 336, 368, 370; labour and tools in, 338-9; camels in, 343; few horses in, 345-6, 348; windmills in, 358; timber in, 366; technology in, 372; iron manufacture in, 375-7; gunpowder and arms in, 385-7, 396-7; printing in, 397, 399, 401; paper in, 399; ships and navigation, 403, 406-7, 410-12; 415; roads in, 415-16, 418; travel to, 419-20; inland water transport, 422, 429; money and currency in, 440, 442-3, 448, 451-7, 472; and European trade deficit, 462; towns in, 483, 486, 497, 500-1, 524-5, 540-7; craftsmen in, 489; urban fortifications in, 492, 494-5
chocolate, 222, 249, 257, 262
cholera, 81, 88-90
Chou-King-fu, 271
Chukchi (people), 65
Church, the, 332
cider, 239, 240-1
cigarettes, 262
Cipolla, Carlo, 387
cities *see* towns and cities
citizenship, 518
civilizations, 56-63
Claviere, E. *and* J.P. Brissot, 446
clay, 2
cleanliness, 328-30
climate, 49-51
clocks, clockmaking, 431
clothing, 183, 311-28; *see also* fashion; textiles
Clusius, Carolus, 169
coaches *see* carriages
coal, 302, 336, 367-71, 375-6, 454, 540
coca leaves, 261
Cochinchina, 224
coconut palms, 174
cod, 214-15, 216-20
Coeur, Jacques, 28, 384
coffee, 163, 223, 249, 256-62
Cognac, 244
coins *see* currency; money
coke, 336, 368-70, 375-7, 434-5
Colace, Aaron, 249
Colbert, Jean-Baptiste, 363-4, 395
Collegio Borromeo, Pavia, 130
Colmar, 243
colocasia *see* taro
Cologne, 51-2, 71, 500
colonization, 98, 100-2
Colquhoun, P., 556
Columbus, Christopher, 81, 261, 409, 418
colza, 156

Index   609

communication, 416; *see also* navigation; roads; transport
compasses, 403, 407
Compiègne, 506
Condé, Louis II, Prince of, 317
Congo, 166, 175, 177, 227
Constantinople *see* Istanbul
Contarini, Francesco, 320
contraception, 55
convicts, 339
Cook, Capt. James, 34, 178-80
cookery, 187-9, 202-5, 212, 220-4; *see also* diet; food; stoves
copper, 383-4, 395; in coin, 446, 450-3, 455, 457-9, 477
coral, 443, 452
Cordoba, 524
Coreal, Francisco, 91, 161
Cortez, Hernando, 37
Coryate, Thomas, 206, 304
cosmetics, 330-1
Cossacks, 101
Coster, Lourens Janszoon, 397
costume (dress), 311-28
cotton, 156, 325-7, 373, 435, 442
Coubert, Jacques-Samuel, Comte de, 277
country, countryside, 281-2; *see also* villages
Courteline, 130
Couteau, Procope (Francesco Procopio Coltelli), 257
cowries, 441-4, 451
Cracow, 278
crafts, 488-9
credit, 439-40, 457, 470-5; *see also* banks; money
Crépy (near Senlis), 72
Crimea, 477
Cromwell, Oliver, 473
crop rotation, 114-20
Cuba, 38, 226, 261-2
currency, 441-4, 446, 451, 458-60; *see also* money
cutlery and silver, 203, 205-9
Cuzco, 267
Cyprus, 224-5, 232

dairy produce, 210-12
damask steel, 376-7
Danzig, 127-9
Dauphiné, 379, 395
Davanzati, Bernardo, 467
Davis, Kingsley, 46
death rates, 47, 71-3, 91-2, 330
Defoe, Daniel, 61, 86, 503

Dekker, Thomas, 82, 321, 548-9, 554
Delamare, Nicolas, 250
de Las Cortes, P. *see* Las Cortes, Father
Delbrück, Hans, 93
Delhi, 524, 526, 540
Denain, Battle of (1712), 53
Denmark, 202, 216, 265
Deschamps, Hubert, 175
Dias, Bartolomeo, 408
Dictionnaire sentencieux, 328, 330
Diderot, Denis, 137, 432
Didot, François Ambroise, 400
Dieppe, 218
diet: and disease, 78; nature of, 104; and grain, 129-33; calory level, 129-33; rice in, 151-2; and new foodstuffs, 171; peasant, 187-8; and luxuries or stimulants, 261
digging stick *see* hoe
Dijon, 76, 80, 268, 278
disease and diseases, 36-8, 43, 78-80, 88-90, 315; *see also* epidemics; plague; and individual diseases
distilling, 241-7, 248
Dobzhansky, Theodosius, 186
Domesday Book, 357
doors, 296-7
Dopsch, Alfons, 447
Douet d'Arcq, Louis C., 221
Dragonet, François, 86
Drake, Sir Francis, 232
dress, 311-28, 561; *see also* fashion; textiles
drink, drinks, 130, 227-30
dromedaries, 342
drought, 51
drugs, 261, 462
drunkenness, 236
Dubois, Guillaume, Cardinal, 211
Duclos, Charles Pinot, 206, 257
Duperron, 434
Dupleix, Joseph François, 102
Dupré d'Aulnoy, Louis, 53
Dupré de Saint-Maur, N.F., 111-12, 137
Dzungaria, 97

Easter Island, 178-9
East India Company, 251, 261
East Indies, 184
eating habits, 205-7
Ecole des Mines, Paris, 432
Ecole des Ponts et Chaussées, Paris, 432
Edward III, King of England, 386
Eekloo (Flanders), 72-3
eggs, 210, 212-13, 224
Egypt, 43, 108, 224, 226, 314

Einaudi, Luigi, 466
Elizabeth I, Queen of England, 548, 552
Embree, E.R., 38
Encyclopédie, 170, 234-5, 432
energy *see* power
engineering, 431-2; *see also* technology
England: census, 40; population, 54; wolves eliminated in, 66-7; poor in, 75; epidemics in, 80-1; grain yields in, 122-4; grain exports, 126; potatoes in, 168-70; glass in, 183; meat eating in, 197-8; table manners in, 206; cod fishing, 216, 218-19; sugar consumption, 225, 227; water supply, 228; wine drinking in, 233; beer in, 238-9; gin in, 246, 252; chocolate in, 249; tea in, 251-3; tobacco in, 262, 265; country houses in, 282; glass windows, 297; fireplaces in, 302; interiors, 307; peasant dress in, 315; wool in, 326; horses in, 350; shipbuilding, 363; industrial revolution in, 369-70, 372-3, 558; iron manufacture in, 381-2; naval guns, 388, 391-2, 395; metal money in, 458, 466; trade with Russia, 463; paper money and credit in, 471-3, 476; towns in, 482-3, 487, 491, 511; dominance of London, 514, 528; *see also* Bank of England; London
English Channel, 410
Epernay, 487-8
epidemics, 33, 38, 72, 78-82, 89-90; *see also* disease; plague
Erasmus, Desiderius, 184, 295, 300
Eric the Red, 406
Escalante, Bernardino de, 282
Este, Duke of, 299
Estienne, Charles, 344
Estoile, Pierre de l', 80
Ethiopia, 108
Euclid, 402
Eugène, Prince of Savoy, 349
Europe: population, 39-43, 46-7, 54, 64; wild animals in, 66; famines in, 74-8; maize in, 74, 89, 120, 167; diet in, 105, 171-2, 190; grain in, 108-10, 122-3, 127; agricultural patterns in, 155; potatoes in, 74, 167-70; meat eating in, 197-9; fish and fishing, 214-15, 219; pepper and spices in, 222-4; alcoholism in, 227; wine in, 231-7; beer in, 238-40; tea in, 251, 253; houses in, 274; furniture and interiors in, 293-4; dress of poor in, 314; fashion in, 315-25; textiles, 325; horses in, 347-50; watermills in, 358; shipping, 362; use of wood in, 362; energy and machines in, 371; iron manufacture in, 376-9, 381-2; energy and machines in, 371; iron manufacture in, 376-9, 381-2; artillery in, 396; navigational supremacy, 402, 406-7, 409-10, 412, 415; inland water transport in, 421; money in, 440, 457-67; towns in, 509-20; large cities in, 525-6; *see also* individual countries and towns
exchange rates, 464-6; *see also* barter; credit; currency; money
exploration, 62, 406, 415; *see also* navigation
Eyragues (Provence), 72

Fail, Nöel du, 274, 436
fairs, 419-20, 477
Famine Pact, 129
famines, 33, 51, 73-8, 111, 158
fashion, 25, 311-33
fasts and fasting, 214-15
feasts *see* cookery; food
Ferdinand I, Archduke of Austria, 410
fertilizers (agricultural), 116-17, 155-6, 158
financiers, 437-8; *see also* banks; money
Finé, Oronce, 51
Finland, 60-1, 77, 274
firearms, 392-3, 395-6
fireplaces, 298-302
fires, 268
fish, 130, 214-20
Fisher, Irving, 468
Flanders, 170, 487, 489, 504
flax, 326-7, 399
fleas, 310
floors, 294-6
Florence: famines in, 74; plagues in, 85, 87; grain trade, 127, 129; urbanized countryside, 282; and *Arte della Lana*, 487, 490, 519; fortifications, 495; and Pisa, 504; communal struggles in, 512, 515; bourgeoisie in, 512-13; subjugated by Medici, 519
'Flour War' (France), 129
fodder (animal), 196-7
food, foodstuffs: introduction and distribution of, 163-4; luxury, 184, 187-8, 202-5; and table setting, 203, 205, 207-9; everyday, 210-12; *see also* cooking; diet; and individual commodities
Forest, Bernard, 431
forests, 363-5, 367
forks (eating), 183, 203, 205-9
fortifications (urban), 491-5, 497
Fourastié, Jean, 61, 133
Fragonard, Jean Honoré, 278

Index 611

France: population, 33-4, 54, 350; emigrations to Spain, 54-5; density of population, 60-1; wolves in, 66-7; famines in, 74, 78; epidemics in, 80-1; syphilis in, 82; plague in, 84-6; grain in, 110-11, 129; agricultural methods in, 117-18, 121; grades of bread in, 136-8; maize in, 164-6; potatoes in, 169-70; luxuries in, 183; food and cookery in, 187-9, 223; meat eating in, 196, 198; table manners in, 206; butter in, 212; cod fishing, 216, 218; sugar consumption, 226; snow water in, 231; chocolate in, 249; tea in, 250-1; coffee in, 259-60; tobacco in, 261-2; rural houses in, 276; stoves in, 301-2; interiors in, 307-10; fashion in, 312, 318; peasant dress in, 315; horses in, 348-50; oxen in, 350; watermills in, 358; shipbuilding, 363; iron manufacture in, 379-81; and naval guns, 389, 395; arms manufacture in, 393; roads in, 424; metal money in, 458, 464; money of account in, 464-6; towns in, 482, 511, 520; *see also* individual towns
Francis I, King of France, 66, 183, 243, 331, 388, 393, 460, 482
Francis II, King of France, 81
François, Father Jean, 175
Frankfurt, 510
Frederick II, King of Prussia, 129, 520, 531
Frederick William I, King of Prussia, 464
Freeman, M., 248
Fries, Jacob, 416
Friuli, 379, 489
Froissart, Jean, 386
Fuchs, Leonhart, 164
fuel, 158, 365-7
Fueter, Edward, 96
Fugger family, 28, 296, 384, 461, 472
Furetière, Antoine, 492
furniture: distribution and use of, 275, 283-94, 296; manufacture and design of, 303-6; arrangement of, 306-11; *see also* houses; interiors; and individual items
furs, fur trade, 68-9, 181-2, 443
Fustel de Coulanges, N.D., 93
fustian, 326

Gabriel, 299
Galiani, F., 464, 467
Galvez, Bernardo de, 248
Gama, Vasco da, 222, 402, 408, 412
game (wild), 67
gardens, 282
Garonne, river, 354, 356

gas lighting, 434
Gascon, Richard, 482, 486
Gattinara, Mercurio, 388
Gautier, Théophile, 347
Gdansk (Danzig), 497
Geer enterprises (Sweden), 395
Gemelli-Careri, Giovanni F.: and wild animals, 65; and crop rotation, 159; and bread, 172; and vegetables in China, 199; and Persian table manners, 206; and chocolate, 249; on seating, 291; on labour in China, 339; on Arab boats, 422; carries money, 439; on minting coins, 450; and servant payment in China, 455; and Portuguese imported silver, 458; on Peking traffic, 501; on Triana, 504; on Persian streets, 507; on Peking, 542
Geneva, 419, 504
Genghis Khan, 94
Genoa: plague in, 87; grain trade, 129; bread in, 139, 142; aqueducts, 228; poor in, 285; shipping, 403, 419; and barter, 448; money and finance in, 464, 472, 512; houses and planning in, 497, 498-9; and Savona, 504
George II, King of England, 252
Georgi, Johann Gottlieb, 534, 538
Germania, 39, 100
Germany: population, 60, 71; famines, 74; plague in, 84-5; mortality in, 92; potatoes in, 170; meat eating in, 190, 192, 196-9; fish eating in, 216; cookery, 223; drinking habits in, 233-4; beer in, 238-9; cider in, 241; spirits in, 247; tobacco in, 265; houses in, 275; windows in, 297-8; domestic heating in, 300; and interiors, 307; peasant dress in, 315; arms manufacture in, 395; barter in, 447-8; metal money in, 459-60; cities and towns in, 482-3, 501, 511
Ghent, 420
Giannone, Pietro, 533
gin, 246, 252
Giunta family, 401
glass, 183, 296-7
Gmelin, Johann Georg, 248
Goa, 91, 93, 152, 272
Gohory, Jacques, 262
gold, 383-4, 445, 521; in coin, 458-63; value, 459-61, 463, 465-6; world production, 461; stocks, 466-7; *see also* money
gourds, 177, 180
Gournay (Normandy), 212
Gourou, Pierre, 152, 154, 176, 254
Gozler (*later* Eupatoria), 109

grain (cereals): in diet, 105-7, 129-33; cultivation, 108-11; prices, 111-12, 133-43, 196; and crop rotation, 114-20; yields, 121-4; trade, 124-9, 166; alcohol from, 133, 241, 246-7; and potato consumption, 170; *see also* individual grains
Gramont, Scipion de, 478
Grandamy, René, 133-5
Granson, Battle of (1476), 329
Greece (ancient), 515
'Greek fire', 403
Greenland, 49
Gresham, Thomas, 552
Gresham's law, 460
Greuze, Jean Baptiste, 278
Gribeauval, Jean Baptiste Vaquette de, 388
Grosley, P.J., 198
groundnuts, 167, 177, 431
Grousset, René, 48
gruel (porridge), 135-7, 146
Guadeloupe, 259
Guevara, Antonio de, 366
Guignes, Chrétien Louis Joseph de, 151, 211, 272
guilds (town), 519
Guinea, Gulf of, 101
guingettes, 236-7
Guise family, 277
Gujerat, 450-1
gunpowder, 385-7, 393-6
guns *see* artillery; firearms
Gurvitch, Georges, 479, 560
Gustavus Adolphus, King of Sweden, 129, 392
Gutenberg, Johann, 397, 399-400

Haedo, Father Diego de, 313
hair, 330-2
Halbwachs, Maurice, 38
Halde, J.B. du, 148, 151, 410, 507, 544
Hamburg, 196
Hamilton, Earl J., 130
Hanoi, 503
Hanseatic League, 506, 549
Häpke, Rudolph, 504
haricot beans, 163-4, 223
Harington, Sir John, 310
harness, 334, 344-6
harvests, 49-51; *see also* grain
Haudricourt, A.G., 337, 376
Haussmann, Georges Eugène, Baron, 498
Hawaii, 178-9
heating (domestic), 286, 290, 298-301, 434
hemp, 327, 399

hemp, Indian, 261
Henry VIII, King of England, 393, 553
Henry II, King of France, 388
Henry III, King of France, 465
Henry IV, King of France, 80, 311
Hérauld, Jean, Lord of Gourville, 64
herbs, 295
Herrera, Alonso de, 344
herring, 215, 218
Hewes, Gordon W., 56, 62, 178
Hireçon, Thierry d', 121
hoe and hoe-cultivation, 174-82
Hogarth, William, 252
Hokusai, 339
Honfleur, 218
Hopkins, Sheila V., 133
hops (brewing), 238
horses: wild in Tierra del Fuego, 177; as meat, 202; working, 339, 344-7, 349-50, 352, 371; in America, 342; origins and distribution of, 344-8; in China, 345-6, 348; feeding, 347, 352; in war, 347-9; breeding and trading of, 349-51; and transport, 429; in St Petersburg, 539-40
hospices, 418
Houghton (Norfolk, England), 282
houses, housing: types and building materials, 266-74; rural, 274-7; urban, 277-80; as work-places, 280; interiors, 283-311; fashion and design of, 308-9; height of in towns, 497-8
Humbolt, Alexander von, 122, 163, 341, 407
Hume, David, 471, 474
Hungary, 48, 122, 197, 201, 358
hunting, hunters, 66-70, 176, 178
Huygens, Christiaan, 431
hygiene, 47, 328-30

Iberia, 60; *see also* Spain; Portugal
Ibn Batuta, 422, 481
Incas, 158-60, 169, 267; *see also* Peru
incunabula, 400
India: population, 33-4, 36, 46, 48, 61, 64, 157; famines in, 74, 76, 158; English mortality in, 91; and nomad conquests, 96-7; decolonization, 102; wheat in, 108, 157; rice in, 146-7, 155, 157; agricultural development, 157; maize in, 167; and hoe-cultivation, 174; non-meat eating, 199; lacks eggs, 213; spices from, 220-1; sugar cane in, 224; alcohol in, 233, 248; and opium trade, 261; tobacco in, 264; building materials in, 267, 272; houses in, 280; furniture in, 285, 289; fireplaces in,

286; dress in, 312, 314, 318; textiles in, 325, 327, 451; animal power in, 339, 344; human labour in, 339; few horses in, 346; technology in, 372; iron and steel manufacture in, 376-7; gunnery in, 396-7; travel routes to, 419-20; money in, 448-51, 457; village crafts in, 489; towns in, 497, 524, 526
Indian Archipelago, 64, 261, 286
Indian Ocean, 402
Indians (American), 98, 180-1, 247-9, 313-14, 443; *see also* Amerindians
Indochina, 64, 174, 180
Indonesia, 38
infant mortality, 90
inflation, 452, 459, 466; *see also* money
influenza (*grippe*), 89-90
inns, 417-18
interiors, 283-311
inventions, 334-5, 371, 432-5; *see also* technology
Iran *see* Persia
Ireland, 43, 169-70, 197, 555
Irish, 42
Irkutsk, 68-9, 100, 486
iron, 373-82, 395; *see also* steel
iron-works, 366-8, 370, 373
irrigation, 149, 154; *see also* water
Isfahan, 507, 509
Islam, Muslims: population concentrations, 64; and colonization, 102; and dairy produce, 211; and wine, 232-3; tea in, 255; coffee consumption, 260; house design in, 266, 273, 280, 285; nomads in, 274; public baths, 285; furniture in, 286, 291; textiles, 325; and camel, 343; horses in, 347-8; use of artillery, 396-7; expansion, 403; ships and navigation, 412, 415; travel in, 418; money in, 440, 448-9; town and country in, 486; towns and civilization, 507-9, 524
Istanbul (Constantinople): size, 51, 526; water supply, 228, 230-1; country houses near, 282; horses in, 347; site difficulty, 500; houses and streets in, 507; market in, 509; as town, 523
Italy: population, 33, 60-1; land improvement in, 124; potatoes in, 168; distilling in, 246; tobacco in, 262; house interiors, 307; dress in, 317; silk industry in, 324, 326; windmills in, 359; money in, 464; towns in, 504, 511
Ivan the Terrible, Tsar of Muscovy, 396

Jacobs, Jane, 484
Jacobsz, Dirk Bas, 318, 331
Jahangir, Emperor, 451
Jamaica, 227, 259
Janequin, Clément, 215
Japan: population, 34, 64, 155-6, 527; rice in, 147, 152, 155-7; agricultural production, 156-7; maize in, 167; meat eating in, 199; and dairy products, 211; lacks eggs, 213; fish and fishing, 214; sugar in, 226; alcohol in, 248; tea in, 254-5; tobacco in, 264; house interiors, 285-6; furniture in, 289-91; dress in, 312, 314; horses in, 347; copper in, 384; arms in, 396-7; printing in, 397; ships and navigation, 410, 412; economic crisis in, 437; money in, 448-9, 452; towns and cities in, 483-4, 497, 527
Java, 224, 253, 259-60, 452
Jenkinson, Anthony, 104
Jericho, 484
Jews, 555
John II of Austria, Don, 318
John II (the Good), King of France, 446
John II, King of Portugal, 412
Johnson, Samuel, 548
Joly, Barthélemy, 356
Judenberg (Austria), 374
Julian (the Apostate), Emperor, 238
Julius II, Pope, 331
Justinian, Emperor, 326

Kamchatka, 68-9, 100
Kämpfer, E., 65, 247-8, 357, 419
Karakorum, 97
Kazan, 97, 101
Kherson, 84, 477
Kiakhta, 68
K'ien Long, Emperor of China, 542
King, Gregory, 43
Knaust, Heinrich, 239
Koberger, Anton, 401
kola trees, 177
Korea, 64, 264, 497
Kublai Khan, 94
Kuczynscki, Robert René, 42
Kula, Witold, 237
Kulischer, Alexandre and Eugène, 97
Kulischer, Josef, 27, 483
Kurowski, Stefan, 373, 381
Kurumbas (people), 64
kvass (Russian drink), 245
Kyoto, 527

Labat, Father J.B., 207, 293, 314, 442
La Bicoque, Battle of (1522), 52
La Boullaye, François, 445
labour: agricultural, 117; human, 337-9; and mechanization, 434-5; division of, and towns, 479, 481, 484
La Chapelle-Fougerets (Rennes), 71
Ladame, Paul A., 38
Laffemas, B. de, 184, 236
La Hontan, Jean d', Baron, 180
Lambadis (people), 64
Lamprecht, Karl, 39
land, 431
Lande, Ortensio, 188
Languedoc, 33, 54, 122
Laos, 273
La Rochelle, 216
La Roque, Sieur de, 256
Las Casas, Father Bartolomé de, 36
Las Cortes, Father: and wild animals, 65; on Chinese harvests, 108, 114, 148-9, 152; on rice-eating, 151; on Chinese meat eating, 199; drinks cold water, 254; on Chinese furniture, 290; on Chinese silk clothing, 312; on lack of horses in China, 345; on Chinese arms, 396; and travellers' chairs, 422; on Chinese payment in silver, 454; on gardens in China, 546
Laslett, Peter, 52
Lautrec, Odet de Foix, Vicomte de, 392
La Vallière, Louise de La Baume Le Blanc, Duchesse de, 308
Lavoisier, Antoine Laurent, 196, 350, 434, 530
Law, John, 440, 471, 473-5
lead, 228, 383, 399
Lefebvre, Georges, 560
Lefebvre des Noëttes, Richard, 334
Leghorn (Livorno), 127, 497, 504
Le Grand d'Aussy, P.J.B., 132, 239, 258
Le Mans, 284
Lemery, Louis, 110, 112, 197, 210-12, 245, 261
Lent (fast), 214, 220
lentils, 112
Léon, Pierre, 372
Lepanto, Battle of (1571), 53, 393
leprosy, 88
Le Roy, Loys, 399
Léry, Jean de, 247
Lescalopier, Pierre, 417
Lescarbot, Mars, 180
Levant, 220-1
Lévi-Strauss, Claude, 510

Lexis, W., 463-4
lice, 310
Liebaut, Jean, 344
Liège, 368-9
life expectancy, 90
lighting, 310-11
Lima, 521, 526, 540
Lippomano, Girolamo, 188
liqueurs, 245-6
Lisbon, 166, 228, 262, 403, 540
livestock, 116-18, 120, 155, 192, 196
living standards, 33, 133-43, 193-4
Lizarraga, Reginaldo de, Bishop of Santiago, 67
llamas, 341
Locatelli, Abbé S., 320
Locke, John, 439
Lombard, Maurice, 511
London: population, 47, 548; ice fairs, 50; epidemics, 80; plague in, 85-6, 88; bread in, 139; milk consumption, 211; water supply, 228-30; coffee in, 256; brick buildings in, 268; 1666 fire, 268, 554; housing, 280; lack of baths, 330; metal money in, 458; city walls, 491; wheeled traffic in, 498, 552; Bridge, 504, 548; satellite ports, 506; and national economy, 514, 528; guilds, 519; development as big city, 525, 528-9, 540, 548-56; shipping and docks, 548-9; Irish and Jews in, 555; and industrial revolution, 557
Londonnière, R. de, 36
looms, 337, 371
Lorraine, 239, 246
Lot, Ferdinand, 117
Louis IX, St, King of France, 465, 495
Louis X, King of France, 419
Luois XII, King of France, 243, 277, 331
Louis XIII, King of France, 49, 81, 332
Louis XIV, King of France: table manners, 25, 206; and 'little ice age', 49; grain purchases, 129; and fast days, 214; and interior design, 307-8; and baths, 330; and beards, 332; and horses, 348; and inventions, 434; and financiers, 475, 514; and Paris, 514, 520, 526
Lübeck, 100, 247
Lull, Raymond, 241
Luther, Martin, 222
luxury, luxuries, 183-7, 202-4, 306-11, 333
Lyons, 381, 472

Mably, Abbé Gabriel Bonnot de, 48, 84, 222
Macartney, George, 1st Earl, 69, 272

machine-gun, 434
machines, machinery, 334-9, 353-61, 371-2; see also technology
mackerel, 215
MacNeil, William H., 88-9
Madagascar, 147, 175
Madeira, 232
Madrid, 80, 531, 540
Magaillans (Magalhães), Father Gabriel de, 338, 346, 368, 421, 453-4, 540, 544-7
Magalhães-Godinho, V., 451, 457
Magdeburg law, 100
Magellan, Ferdinando, 178, 385
Magellan Straits, 180
Maintenon, Françoise d' Aubigny, Marquise de, 434
maize; distribution of, 74, 89, 120, 163-7, 177, 431; consumption of, 134, 161, 172; for gruel, 136; in Asia, 146, 155, 158-9; origins, 158-9; cultivation, 159-63; characteristics, 161; yields, 161, 166; accessibility, 163; names for, 164; varieties, 172; in American hoe-cultivation, 177, 181; drinks from, 238, 247
make-up see cosmetics
Makkai, Lazlo, 358
Malacca, 500
malaria, 38, 117, 149
Malherbe, François de, 82
Malta, Knights of St John of, 231
man: as work machine, 337-9, 371
Manchuria, 67
Manchus, 44, 94, 97, 105
Mandelslo, J.A., 152, 247
manioc, 146, 163, 173-4, 177, 247; see also cassava
manners (table), 205-7, 560
Manrique, Sebastien, 454
Mans, Raphaël de, 507
Mansard, François, 299
Mantua, Marquis of, 349
manure see fertilizer
Manutio, Aldo, 401
Maoris, 176
Marañon y Espinosa, Alonso, 82
maraschino, 246
marble, 271
Maria Theresa, Queen of Louis XIV, 249
markets, 459, 481, 501-3, 509, 537
Markgraff, 226
Márquez Miranda, Fernando, 161
marriage, 47, 71
Marseilles, 84, 88, 109, 125, 127, 129, 192, 477, 506, 518

Marston Moor, Battle of (1644), 52
Martin V, Pope, 228
Martinique, 259-60
Marx, Karl, 459, 479, 513, 561
Mary of France, Queen of Louis XII, 277
Maryland, 265
maslin, 134
mathematics, 401-2
Mauriac, François, 506
Mauritius, 67, 224
Maurizio, A., 105
Mauro, Fra, 407
Mauss, Marcel, 186, 334
Maximilian, Emperor, 25, 387, 560
Mayas, 158, 161, 267
Mayence, Siege of (1793), 468
Mazaheri, Ali, 377
Mazarin, Cardinal, 183, 277
mead, 247
meat: in diet, 104-7, 130, 133; and superfluity, 183; cooking, 189; consumption of, 190, 192, 194-202, 223; prices, 196; salted, 197-8; dried, 201-2; and spices, 221, 223
Medici family, 519
Medici, Catherine de, 183, 261, 295
Medici, Cosimo de, 348
Medici, Maria de, 137, 228
Mediterranean, 155, 403, 409, 419-20
Melanesia, 179
Melville, Herman, 311
Ménagier de Paris, 190, 221
Mendoza, Daniel, 555
Menon, 189
Mensch, Gerhard, 435
Mercier, Louis-Sebástien: on birth control, 55; on bread, 133, 138; on porcelain, 186; on wines, 235; on stimulants, 260; and stone buildings, 268; on tapestries, 296; on stoves, 302; on house design, 309; on fashion, 321, 325; on convict labour, 339; on congested Paris, 352; on wealth in Paris, 463; on money system, 471; on servants in Paris, 490; on Paris markets, 503; on small towns, 506; on Paris police, 520; on Paris priests, 530; on proposed development of Paris, 540; on future world, 557
mercury, 383
Mesopotamia, 174
metallurgy, metals, 369-70, 382-4; see also individual metals
Methuen, John, 232
Mexico: population, 35-6, 39; epidemics in,

Mexico—contd.
    36-7; maize in, 158-61, 177; bread in, 172; meat eating in, 201; vines in, 232; alcoholic drink in, 247-9; chocolate from, 249; silver, 454
Mexico City, 37, 521, 526, 540
Meyer, Jean, 142
mezcal, 248
Michel, J.F., of Brabant, 501
Michelet, Jules, 261
Milan, 318, 420-1, 493, 495, 506
milk and milk-products, 210-12
millet, 109-11, 113, 136, 146, 164, 177, 238, 247-8
mills, milling: of grain, 142-4; water-driven, 353-9, 371; numbers of, 358-9; wind-driven, 353, 358-61; design of, 359-61
mines, mining, 355
Mirabeau, Victor Riquetti, Marquis de, 529
Mocha, 258-9
Mombert, Paul, 39, 46-7
Mompazier, 495
Mondejar, Duke of, 234
money: and economy, 436-40, 444-7; in China, 440, 442-3, 448, 451-7; forms of currency, 441-4; outside Europe, 448-9; paper, 452-3, 470-6; of account, 454, 464-6; metal, 458-64, 475; hoarding and circulation, 461-4, 467-70; stocks, 466-8, 476; and credit, 474-8; technique and function of, 476-8
Mongols, 94-7, 105, 419, 452
Monluc, Blaise de, 392
Montagu, Lady Mary Wortley, 330
Montaigne, Michel de: and plague, 85, 86; on meat dishes, 190; on luxury dining, 203, 205-6, 213; curiosity, 280; on glass windows, 297; on German houses, 297, 300-1; on Augsburg armoury, 393
Montausier, Charles de Sainte-Maure, Duke of, 206
Montecuccoli, Alonso, 81
Montenegro, 166
Montespan, Françoise Athenaïs Mortemart, Marquise de, 308
Montesquieu, Charles de Secondat, Baron de, 104, 213, 434
Montmorency, Anne de, Connétable, 90
Montpellier, 246, 266
Montpensier, Anne Mary Louise (d'Orléans), Duchesse de, 199
Montpezat (Bas-Quercy), 196
More, Sir Thomas, 506
Morgan, Lewis, 373

Moriscoes, 53
Moro, Lodovico, 387
Morocco, 255, 346-7
mortality rate *see* death rate
Moscow, 84, 101, 270, 489, 522
Mote, F.W., 187, 248
Mozambique, 101
mules, 341-2, 346, 350
Mulliez, Jacques, 118, 120
Müller, Heinrich, 194
Mumford, Lewis, 308, 514, 556
Münzer, Thomas, 67
Muscovy, 74, 97, 239, 272; *see also* Russia
Musée de Cluny (Paris), 277
muskets, 392, 395

Nagays (people), 104
Nangis, Guillaume de, 317
Nanking, 546
Nates, Edict of: repealed, 53
Naples: famine and grain exports, 143; supplies snow water, 231; horse-breeding in, 349; money and exchange in, 464, 466-70, 474; town plan, 498; development as big city, 525, 531-4
Naples, Battle of (1528), 52
Naples, Ferdinand, King of (and Queen Maria-Carolinea), 533
National School of Bakery (France), 137
Navagero, Andrea, 54
Navarre, 421
navies, 51, 53
navigation (ocean), 385, 402-15, 418-19
Necker, Jacques, 143
Nef, John, 381
Nertchinsk, Treaty of (1689), 97
Netherlands (Holland): population, 60-1, 484; potatoes in, 170; meat eating in, 192, 197; butter in, 212; and fishing, 216, 218; whaling, 220; and spices, 222, 224; water supply in, 228; spirits in, 233, 244, 246-7; beer in, 238-9; chocolate in, 249; and tea trade, 251-3; tobacco in, 265; interiors in, 307; dress in, 318; windmills in, 259; naval successes, 392; artillery, 395; ships, 425; trade with Russia, 463; towns in, 484, 504
Neva river, 534-8
Newcastle-upon-Tyne, 369
Newcomen, Thomas, 434
Newfoundland, 214, 216-17, 219
Newport (America), 483
New Spain, 226, 248, 262, 313, 341, 460
New World *see* America
New York, 483

New Zealand, 98, 176, 178-80
Nicot, Jean, 261
Niebuhr, Carsten, 91
Nogais (people), 97, 101
nomads, 94-8, 273-4
Normandy, 240-1
Norway, 60, 216
Novgorod, 522
Numantia, 238
nuns, 324
Nuremberg, 239, 242-3, 300, 512

oats, 110-12, 114, 116, 121-2, 134, 136
Oceania, 34, 38-9, 42, 46, 174
Octavian, Sieur, 301
Odessa, 84
Ohsson, Mouradj d', 312
oil palms, 174
Okhotsk, 100
Olinda, 521
olive oil, 212
Oliver, François, 331-2
Olonne (near La Rochelle), 216
Oost Indische Companie, 222, 224, 250, 264
opium, 261
Opium War (1840-2), 102
Oran, 84
Orderic Vitalis, 317
Orford, Robert Walpole, 1st Earl of, 282
Orléans, 424
Orlov, Prince, 537
Ortelius, Abraham, 225
ortolans, 202
Osaka, 527
Osman Aga, 91, 136, 286
Ottoman Empire, 54; *see also* Turkey
oxen, 342-4, 347, 350-1, 441-2
oysters, 215

paddy-fields, 147-51, 153, 156-7; *see also* rice
Pallavicini, 145
palm-trees, 177, 247
Panama, 172
paper, 397, 399-400, 452-3, 470-2
Paré, Ambroise, 220
Paris: wolves in, 66; poor in, 75-6, 284; epidemics in, 80; plague in, 85, 88; bread in, 138-9, 144; mills in, 143, 356; meat eating in, 196, 258; butter in, 212; cod in, 218; sugar consumption in, 225, 227; water supply, 228-30; wine consumption in, 235, 239; *guingettes*, 236-7; beer in, 239; cider in, 241; variety of drinks in, 246; coffee in, 256-60; houses in, 267-8, 277-8, 308; urbanized countryside, 282; fashion in, 318; horses and carriages in, 350, 352; traffic congestion in, 352; and road travel, 424; money circulation in, 468, 471, 474-5; poor newcomers to, 490-1; deaths in, 490-1; town plan, 496; height of houses in, 498, 516-17; markets in, 501-3; and provinces, 506; and Louis XIV, 514, 520, 526; craft guilds ('Six Corps'), 519; and Crown, 520, 526; development as big city, 525-6, 529; Rousseau on, 557
Parmentier, Antoine, 142, 170
Pascal, Blaise, 189
Pascal (Hatarioun), 257
Pasquier, Etienne, 466
Patin, Gui, 235, 245, 250
Pavia: diet, 130; Battle of (1525), 52-3, 388, 392, 396
Pavia, Francis of, 301
pearls, 462
peas, 112-14
peasants: risings, 49, 210; and village size, 62; and land improvement, 124; diet, 132, 187-8, 192, 194-5; and salt tax, 210; furniture and possessions, 283-4; dress, 311, 314-15; clean-shaven, 332; and iron manufacture, 373, 378; use of money, 448-9, 460, 467, 470; and towns, 489; in Russia, 522
Pegolotti, F. Balducci, 452
Peking: population of, 47, 526, 540; Manchus conquer, 97; city wall, 492, 494; traffic in, 501; development as city, 524-5, 540-7; town plan, 542-3
pepper, 183, 220-4, 262, 462
Pepys, Samuel, 85, 215, 251, 352
Perez de Chinchón, Bernardo, 285, 291
perfumes, 224, 330
Périer brothers, 230
Persia (Iran): wild animals in, 67, 70; wheat in, 108; rice cultivation in, 150; table manners in, 206; diet in, 211; wine in, 232; distilling in, 248; house design in, 266-7, 273; fireplaces in, 286; furniture in, 288-9; dress in, 323; horses in, 347, 429-30; windmills in, 358; steel in, 376; artillery in, 397; travel in, 418, 429; money in, 499-50, 459; town streets in, 507
Peru: smallpox in, 37; maize in, 159-61; potatoes in, 168; sea fishing, 214; sugar cultivation in, 226; vines in, 232; Indian costume in, 314; fashion in, 318; mules in, 341; silver, 463

Pescara, 285
Peter I (the Great), Tsar of Russia, 63, 97, 101, 445, 534, 536-7
Petit, Jean, 401
Petty, William, 71, 439, 467, 475, 554
Pfister, Albrecht, 400
Philadelphia, 483
Philip II, King of Spain, 82, 90, 474, 520
Philip III, King of Spain, 212, 230
Philip IV, King of Spain, 317
Philip VI (de Valois), King of France, 386
Philippe, Robert, 356
physiocrats, 463
Piacenza, 448
Pie Cheng, 397
Pigafetta, Filippo, 166
Pinheiro da Veiga, Bartolomé, 231
Pirckheimer, Willibald, 512
Pirenne, Henri, 335, 504
Pisa, 504
plague: spread of, 37, 81, 83-8; and population, 71; frequency of, 78, 87-8; described, 80, 83; brandy as medicine for, 242
Plantin, Christophe, 401
Plassey, Battle of (1757), 102
Platter, Félix, 234
Platter, Thomas, 366
Pliny, 220-1
Poinsot, P.G., 337
Poitiers, 135, 495; Battle of (AD 732), 347
Poivre, Pierre, 224
Poland: population, 60, 168; and Tartar threat, 95; grain yields in, 122, 124; grain trade, 125-6, 128-9; potatoes in, 167; meat eating in, 197; spices in, 222; cookery in, 223; beer in, 238-9; spirits in, 247; wooden houses in, 272; stoves in, 301; dress in, 312, 318; animal power in, 344; watermills in, 358; forests and timber, 364, 366; money values in, 466
Polo, Marco, 419-20
Polynesia, 176-9
Poma de Ayala, Felipe Guaman, 160
Pomerania, 365
Poni, Carlo, 324
poor, the: and famines, 75-6; and disease, 81, 85; life expectancy, 90-1; feeding of, 111; calory intake, 130, 132; and grain prices, 133-4; and new crops, 164; maize eating by, 166; and luxuries, 186-7; meat eating by, 192, 197; beer drinking, 239, 241; housing for, 278, 280; lack of possessions, 283-4; dress, 311, 314-15, 318; as town immigrants, 489-91

Popelinière, 299
population: changes in, 31-4, 46-9, 51-5, 71-3; statistics of, 34-41; estimates of world, 40-4, 46, 51; and living space, 48-9; and climatic changes, 49; and emigration, 54-5; density of, and levels of civilization, 56-64; and diet, 105; and new crops, 163-4; urban, 482-3
porcelain, 186
pork, 198
porridge *see* gruel
Porto Belo, 38
Portugal: and spice trade, 222; aqueducts in, 228; and naval guns, 390; sailing ships and navigation, 403, 405, 409, 412, 423; land clearance in, 431; mints coins, 450-1; metal money in, 458-9
potatoes, 74, 163, 167-72, 177, 181, 223, 431
Potherie, Claude Charles Le Roy, Sieur de, 180
Potosi (Peru), 163, 168, 232, 460, 526
Poujade, Jean, 402
poultry, 212-13
power: sources of, 336-72
Prague, 266, 278, 495
Praz, Mario, 333
Prévost d'Exiles, Abbé Antoine François, 180
prices, 436, 455, 457, 468; *see also* individual commodities
priests, 324, 332
primitive people, 64-5, 180-2
printing, 385, 397-402, 432
Procope (café), 257, 259, 496
Protestants, 54
Prussia, 60, 124, 170
pulque (drink), 248
pulses, 112, 144
Pussot, Jean, 487

Quesnay, François, 117, 121-2, 344, 463, 530
quinine, 261

Rabelais, François, 189-90
Raca, Suleiman Mustapha, 256
Raleigh, Sir Walter, 169
Ramelli, Agostino, 431
ramparts (urban), 491-5, 497
Ramponeau, Jean, 236
Raphael, Sanzio, 299
Ratisbon, 500
rats, 83-4
Ratzel, Frédéric, 65
Raynal, Abbé Guillaume Thomas F., 226
Razilly, Isaac de, Chevalier, 392

Réaumur, René Antoine, 376
Recife, 521
reindeer, 343-4
Reinhardt, Marcel, 39, 483
Reiss, A.J., 223
Rembrandt van Rijn, 280
Restif de La Bretonne, Nicolas Edme, 330
Retz, Cardinal de (Jean François de Gondi), 54
Réunion (island), 224, 259
Rey, Jean, 434
Rheims, 487-8
rice: cultivation and distribution, 110-11, 145-50, 161; continuous growing, 114, 150-2; characteristics, 145; yield, 151; consumption of, 151-3; wine, 152, 247; price, 152, 457; trade, 156-7; varieties of, 172; spirit (arak), 233, 247; as money, 448, 452
Richelieu, Alphonse Louis Du Plessis, Cardinal, Bishop of Lyons, 249
Richelieu, Armand Jean Du Plessis, Cardinal, 111, 392
rifles, 392-3
Rio de Janeiro, 48, 500, 526, 540
Rios, Baltasar de, 434
rivers, 356-7, 365-6, 371, 421-2, 424, 428-9
roads, 415-21, 424-30
rococo style, 310
Rocroi, Battle of (1643), 396
Rome: barbarian conquest of, 93; bread in, 145; pepper and spices in, 220-1; aqueducts in, 228; beer in, 238; firewood in, 300; town plan, 498; ancient towns, 515; Sixtus V and, 540
Roscher, Wilhelm, 167
Rosenblat, Angel, 35, 38
Roupnel, Gaston, 80
Rousseau, Jean-Jacques, 557
rudders (ships'), 403, 405, 410, 412
Rudolph I (of Habsburg), King of Germany, 420
Rueff, Jacques, 186
Ruel, Jean, 164
Ruhr, 369
rum, 246, 248-9
Rumford, Sir Benjamin Thompson, Count von, 302
runners (foot-messengers), 430
Russell, J.C., 39, 43
Russia: population increases in, 47, 168; fur-trapping in, 68-9; expansion of, 97, 100-1; wheat in, 108-9; spices in, 222; drinking habits in, 234, 245; tea in, 252-3, 255; houses in, 274-5; lack of furniture in, 285; iron production in, 381; road travel in, 416, 522; money in, 445, 463; towns in, 483, 489, 522; village crafts in, 489
rye, 109-11, 114-15, 121-2, 125, 134, 136-7, 139

Sachau, Ernst, 422
Saffet Atabinen, Rachid, 94
sails, 362, 371, 403-5, 410-12
Saint-Antoine (ship), 413
Saint-Exupéry, Antoine de, 56
Saint-Hilaire, Auguste de, 163, 341
St Petersburg, 61, 92, 264, 497, 526, 534-40
Saint-Simon, Louis de Rouvroy, Duc de, 206
Saint-Stephen, Order of, 349
Salerno, 241
salmon, 214-15
salt, 197-9, 209-10, 216, 437, 442
Salviati, Mgr, 203
Salzewedel (Brandenburg), 71
Samoyeds (people), 65
Sand, George, 262
Santiago de Chile, 521
Santillana (near Santander), 266
Santo Domingo, 37, 225, 259-60
Sanudo, Marin, 188, 424, 427, 501, 518
Sanvoort, D. van, 318
São Paolo (Brazil), 62-3
São Salvador *see* Bahia
Saragossa, 54
Sardinia, 276
Sartre, Jean-Paul, 85
Savary, J., 216, 236, 247, 262, 296
Savona, 504
Say, Jean-Baptiste, 314, 428
Schafer, E.H., 248
Schöngauer, 297
Schrotter, F.W. von, 469
Schumpeter, J.A., 475-6
Schweinfurth, Georg, 422
Schwenteer, Daniel, 434
Scipio, 239
scythe (implement), 335
sea *see* navigation; ships and shipping
seafoods, 214-20
seals, 66, 69
sea-otters, 68-9
'secular crises', 435
Segovia, 228
Séguier, Pierre, Duc de Villemar, 250
Seignelay, Jean-Baptiste Colbert, Marquis de, 239

Seine river, 350, 352, 354, 356
Selim (son of Suleiman the Magnificent), 232
Senegal, 207
Senlis, 506
Serres, Olivier de, 121, 164, 168
servants (domestic), 280
Sète, 244
Sévigné, Marie (de Rabutin-Chantal), Marquise de, 249, 311, 437
Seville, 43, 54, 262, 500, 503-6, 514
Shakespeare, William, 552, 554
Sheffield, John B. Holroyd, 1st Earl of, 225
shells: as currency, 441-3
ships and shipping: volume of, 362; timber requirements, 363; guns on, 388-92, 395; design and rig, 403-7, 410, 412, 422-3; travel by, 418-19; building, 423, 431; crews, 425; costs, 428
shoes, 320
Shove, D.J., 49
Siam, 91, 248, 273, 419
Siberia, 67-8, 97-8, 100, 486
Sicily, 124, 125, 127-8, 461
silk, 311, 317-18, 324-6, 450, 452, 462
silver, 383-4; as money, 445-6, 449-55, 457-61, 463, 477; in China, 454-5; value, 459-61, 463, 465-6; in trade, 462-3; stocks, 466-7
Singapore, 500
Sixtus V, Pope, 464, 498, 540
slave trade, 34, 43, 53, 265
slaves, 339, 346-7, 442
Slovakia, 122
'small-corn' (maslin), 109
smallpox, 37-8, 47, 79, 88
Smith, Adam, 170-1, 425, 428, 441, 445
Smyrna, 501
snuff, 262
soap, 330
Sombart, Werner, 27, 127, 186, 197, 428, 512-13, 528
sorghum, 146
South Africa, 98
soya beans, 111, 146
Spain: population changes in, 33, 54; French immigrants, 54-5; population density, 61; fish eating in, 215-16, 219; chocolate in, 249; iced drinks in, 255; tobacco in, 261-2; seating in, 291-2; braziers in, 302; dress in, 317-20, 323; mules in, 341; horses in, 348-9; windmills in, 358-9; iron manufacture in, 381; arms, 393, 395; metal money in, 458-9, 463; subjugated towns in, 519-20

Spekle, Daniel, 344
spelt (grain), 109, 114
Spencer, J., 187-8
Spengler, Oswald, 401, 482
spices, 220-2, 440, 462
Spinolas (of Genoa), 130
spirits (drink), 233, 241-8; see also individual drinks
Spon, Jacob, 257
Staunton, Sir George, 44, 248, 251, 410, 422
steam, 371-2, 434
steel, 374-8; see also iron
Steen, J., 283
Stefan Batory, King, 497
Stendhal (Marie-Henri Beyle), 228, 504
stimulants, 260-65
stone: as building material, 267-71, 273, 534-6
Storaci, Giovanni Vicenzo, 144
stoves, 300-2, 366
Stow, John, 498, 548
straw, 272-3, 275, 295
Strongoli, Ferdinando, Prince of, 532
Styria, 378-9, 395
submarines, 434
Suez isthmus and canal, 402, 412
sugar: cane, 163, 180, 224, 521; as luxury, 183; distribution and popularity, 224-7; rum and spirits from, 246, 248
Sully, Maximilien de Béthune, Duc de, 332, 367, 464
sumptuary laws, 311; see also luxury
Süssmilch, J.P., 92
Sweden: population of, 60; as grain exporter, 126; potatoes in, 170; alcohol in, 247; tobacco in, 265; metal manufacture in, 373-4, 381, 384; arms manufacture in, 395
sweet potatoes, 89, 146, 155, 167, 176-7, 180, 431
Switzerland, 170
swords, 376-7
syphilis, 48, 81-2, 88-9, 329

table: laying of, and manners, 203-9
Tahiti, 176, 179-80
Taine, Hippolyte, 558
Taiwan, 224
Talikota (India), 64
Tamberlaine, 323
tapestry, 296, 306, 308
Tardin, Jean, 434
taro (colocasia), 146
Tartars, 95, 101-2

Tasman, Abel Janszoon, 34, 178
Tavernier, Jean Baptiste, 199, 347, 376, 449
tea, 249-57, 262
technology: defined, 334, 431; and invention, 334-5, 371, 432-4; spread of, 385-435; uneven progress of, 430; development and training, 431-2; effect on labour, 434; application, 435
telegraph, 434
Telemachus, 155
tents, 273-4
textiles, 323, 325-8, 433, 451; see also individual textiles
thatch, 273, 275
Thevet, Jean, 261
Tibet, 358, 452
Tierra del Fuego, 177
tiles, 268, 275, 294
Tilly, Joan Tserclaes, Graf von, 395
tin, 383, 399
tobacco, 163, 222, 260-5
Tobolsk, 100
Tokyo (Yedo), 483, 527
Toledo, 278
Toledo, Pietro di, 498
Tolon, Father Maurice de, 87
tomatoes, 163, 223
Tonkin, 403
tools, 335, 337-8
Tott, François de, Baron, 207
Toulon, 88
Toulouse, 495
Tournay, Siege of (1745), 468
Toutain, J.C., 121
towns and cities: size and population, 51, 62, 481-4; and famines, 74-5; provisioning of, 124-5, 486-7, 539; and rice-growing, 155; water supply of, 228; housing in, 277-8; nearby country houses, 281-2; poverty in, 284-5; and mills, 356-7; development of, 479, 484-7, 510-11; markets in, 479, 481, 501-3; defined, 479, 481; and division of labour, 479, 484-5; and bourgeoisie, 482, 512-13, 524; and countryside, 486-9; newcomers to, 489-91, 518; security and fortification of, 491-5, 497; street plans, 495-7; height of houses in, 497-9; carriage traffic in, 498; locations and communications, 498, 499-504; suburbs, 503-4; and satellites, 504, 506; culture and political status of, 507-25, 556-8; and state, 511, 514, 526-7, 556; and development of capitalism, 512-14; categories of, 514-15, 518-20; citizenship, 518; guilds in, 519; big cities, 525-58
trade routes, 419-21; see also navigation
transport: and animal power, 341-6, 349-50, 352; in China, 346; regional forms, 422-3; speed of, 424, 426-7; cost of, 425, 427; effect on trade, 424-9; currency payment for, 469
Trèves, 39, 238
Triana (Seville), 503-4
Troyes, 75, 268
'truck system', 448
tuberculosis, 81, 88, 90
Tull, Jethro, 115
Tupinambas (S. American Indians), 247
Turgot, Anne Robert Jacques, 125, 127, 129, 424
Turkey: mortality in, 91; and nomads, 94-5; meat eating in, 201; eating habits in, 206-7; dairy produce in, 211; dress in, 312, 318; horses in, 347-8; naval guns, 389; arms, 393, 396-7; economic crisis in, 437; money in, 440, 448-9, 459; tribute in, 445
turkeys, 189
turnips, 157, 171
turtles, 202
Tuscany, 315, 334
Tuscany, Cosimo I de Medici, Grand Duke of, 349
Tuscany, Leopold, Grand Duke of, 533-4

Uelzen, 84
Ukraine, 108-9
Ulm, 74, 230, 519
underwear, 314, 329-30
United States of America, 61, 218, 428, 526; see also America
Urals, 381
Urdaneta, Andrés de, 418
Usher, A.P., 40, 44, 61
Ustariz, Gerónimo de, 184, 189, 256

Valais (Switzerland), 209
Valéry, Paul, 48, 424, 429
Valladolid, 211-12, 215, 230-1, 236, 266
Valle, Pietro della, 256
Vallière, General Florent de, 388
Vandenbroeke, C., 170
Van Ouder Meulen, 478
Varzy (Nièvre, France), 482
vegetables, 104-7, 170-1, 177, 223; see also individual vegetables
Velasquez, Diego Rodriguez de Silva y, 2
Venice: immigrants in, 71; famines in, 75; influenza in, 89; women in, 92; grain in,

622 Structures of Everyday Life

Venice—*contd.*
109, 127-9; 'minor foods' in, 113; bread consumption in, 132; bread weight in, 139, 142; maize in, 165-6; banquets in, 185, 188; meat eating in, 192; and spice trade, 222; water supply, 228-9; wine consumption in, 236; fashion in, 318; and cotton trade, 326; naval guns, 388-9; arsenal, 393; gunpowder in, 394-5; and trade routes, 421; travel times to, 424, 426-7; inventions in, 433; metal money in, 461; banks in, 473; and countryside, 486; incomers from Friuli, 489; expansion, 498, 540; markets in, 501; satellite towns, 506; citizenship, 518
Vérard, Antoine, 401
Verbiest, Father Ferdinand, 67, 547
Vernet, Joseph, 278
Verona, 71
Versailles, Palace of, 299, 308
Versoris, Maître Nicolas, 85
Vico, Giovanni Battista, 532
Vidal de La Blache, Paul, 56, 412
Vienna, 540
Vietnam, 273, 503
Vijayanagar, 64
villages, 61-2, 274-7, 281-2, 481, 489; *see also* peasants
Villard de Honnecourt, 355
Villars, Claude Louis Hector, Duc de, 53
Villeneuve, Arnaud de, 220, 241
Vinci, Leonardo da, 401-2
vines, 231-3, 236, 240, 253, 487; *see also* wine
Virginia, 264
Vivaldi brothers (navigators), 406
Vivero, Rodrigo, 163, 286, 323, 396, 410, 412, 527
vodka, 246
Volney, Constantin François Chasseboeuf, Comte de, 314, 507
Voltaire, François Arouet de, 89, 278, 294

Wächter, Hans-Helmut, 121, 124
Wagemann, Ernst, 34, 416, 484
wages: and grain prices, 133-5; after Black Death, 193; decline in, 196; and price of horses, 337; in textile industry, 433, 468; in money economy, 468-9
Waldfogel, Procope, 397
Wallenstein, Albrecht W.E. von, Duke of Friedland, 53
Wallis, Samuel, 179-80
walls, wall-coverings, 296

Walpole, Horace, 282
wampum, 443-4
war, 92-3, 102, 170, 219
Warsaw, 32
Washington, Augustine, 91
water: drinking, 227-31; power, 351-6, 371, 379; and paper manufacture, 399; transport, 421-2
water closets, 310
Watt, James, 433
Weber, Max, 509
Weigert, 244
wells, 228-9
Welser (firm), 28
Werth, E., 175
West Indies, 38, 225-7, 246-7, 409; *see also* individual islands
Westminster, 553-4
whales, 181, 214, 220; oil, 311
wheat: cultivation and consumption of, 108-14; and crop rotation, 114-20; yields, 120-4, 151; trade in, 125, 166; prices, 134-5, 196; for bread, 136-9, 172; compared with rice, 145-6, 151; distribution of, 161; and spread of potatoes, 170; varieties of, 172
whisky, 246
White, Lynn, 334-5
wigs, 332
Wilcox, W.F., 41, 44, 46
wild men, 64-5
William III, King of England, 528
wind power, 353-4, 358-9, 371
windows, 296-7
wine, 130, 133, 195, 231-7, 239-44, 487
wolves, 66-7
women, 92, 314, 317, 321-3, 330
Won San-Kwei, 40
wood: for buildings, 266, 268, 270, 272-4, 498; for flooring, 294; for heating, 300, 366-7; for furniture, 303; in construction, 356, 362-4; as source of energy and fuel, 362-7, 371; transport and supply of, 365-7; and printing, 400
wool, 315, 325-6
Woytinski, W.S. and E.S., 38
Wren, Sir Christopher, 528
Wurttemberg, 61

Ximenes family, 129

Yamal peninsula, 65
yams, 146, 176, 180
Yedo *see* Tokyo

yellow fever, 38, 48
Yersin, Alexandre, 84
Young, Arthur, 118, 120, 425
Yucatan, 267
Yugoslavia, 285, 286
Yun Leang Ho, 108
Yura Indians, 163

Zanzibar, 64
Zara, 246
zimbos, 442-4
zinc, 383
zocoli (shoes), 320
Zonca, Vittorio, 431
Zytkowicz, Leonid, 122